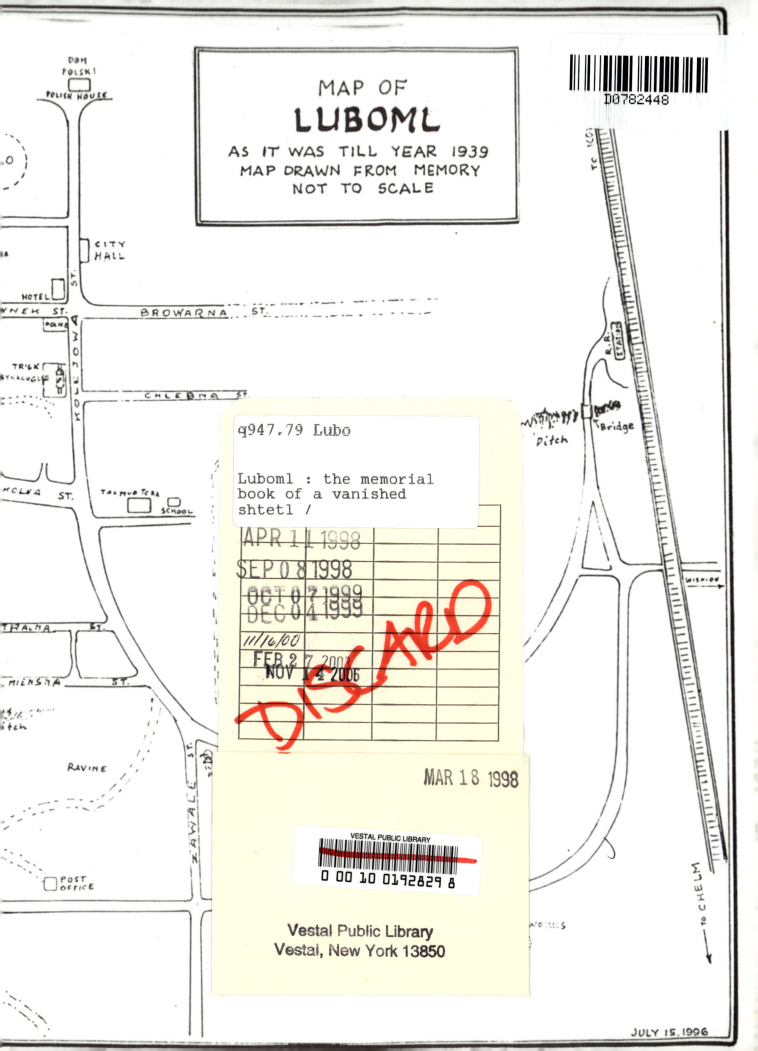

D0782448

q947.79 Lubo

Luboml : the memorial
book of a vanished
shtetl /

APR 1 1 1998
SEP 0 8 1998
OCT 0 ? 1999
DEC 0 4 1999
11/16/00
FEB 2 7 2001
NOV 1 4 2006

DISCARD

MAR 18 1998

VESTAL PUBLIC LIBRARY
0 00 10 0192829 8

Vestal Public Library
Vestal, New York 13850

SECOND POLISH REPUBLIC, 1921–1939

Baltic Sea

LITHUANIA

EAST PRUSSIA
(GERMANY)

GDANSK

VILNA

BIALYSTOK

Vistula

POLAND

Bug

BRZESC
NAD BUGIEM

PINSK

Prypec

WARSAW

LODZ

KOWEL

CHELM **LUBOML**

RADOM

LUBLIN

LUCK

ERMANY

ROWNE

KRAKOW

USSR

LWOW (LEMBERG)

TARNOPOL

CZECHOSLOVAKIA

STANISLAWOW

ROMANIA

Previous pages: The Great Synagogue of Luboml looking from the northwest. Stepenyer Shtibl, Thilim Shtibl, and Schnayder (Tailors') Shtibl at right, ca. 1930. Photo by Szymon Zajczyk. (Courtesy of Polska Akademia Nauk, Instytut Sztuki)

LUBOML

THE MEMORIAL BOOK
OF A
VANISHED SHTETL

KTAV PUBLISHING HOUSE, INC.

Copyright © 1997
Libovner-Voliner Benevolent Society
Library of Congress Cataloging-in-Publication Data

Sefer yizkor li-kehilat Luboml. English.
    Luboml : the memorial book of a vanished shtetl / edited by Berl
Kagan.
        p.   cm.
    ISBN 0-88125-580-7 (alk. paper)
    1. Jews--Ukraine--Līuboml'. 2. Holocaust, Jewish (1939-1945)–
-Ukraine--Līuboml'. 3. Līuboml' (Ukraine)--Ethnic relations.
I. Kagan, Berl.   II. Title.
DS135.U42L497   1997
947.7'9--DC2   197-6197
                                                                              CIP
                                                                              r97

This English translation of the *Yizkor Book of Luboml* was jointly underwritten by the Libovner-Voliner Benevolent Society and the Aaron Ziegelman Foundation.

CONTENTS

APPENDIXES

Entrance to the Great Synagogue from the *poolish*, ca. 1930. Photo by Szymon Zajczyk. (Courtesy of Polska Akademia Nauk, Instytut Sztuki)

Interior of the Great Synagogue showing the Holy Ark and the *bima*, ca. 1930. Photo by Szymon Zajczyk. (Courtesy of Polska Akademia Nauk, Instytut Sztuki)

FOREWORD TO THE ENGLISH TRANSLATION

The original *Yizkor Book of Luboml* was a very personal and cathartic undertaking that started in 1967 and was published in Israel in 1975, in Hebrew and Yiddish. Later, members of the Libovner-Voliner Benevolent Society in New York, specifically Victor Gershengorn and Nathan Eiger, decided to produce an English translation of the *Pinkas Libivne* as the book was popularly called by the landsleit (Libivne was the Yiddish name for Luboml). Other society members wanted the same, so that their offspring and the English speaking world could read about and experience the legacy. The book would provide invaluable testimony on the culturally rich Jewish life in the shtetl before the Shoah.

Current scholarship speaks of the yizkor book as a new genre of writing. In the Luboml book, vignettes of daily life, descriptions of community institutions and testimony of the Holocaust are presented in a humble, matter-of-fact style. They are synopses of life and death imprinted on the psyches of survivors, thoughtfully laid out almost as a bearing of witness to truth under God's eyes.

The English edition is a complete translation of the original yizkor book. Additionally, we have included two new pieces and an appendix of recent articles about Luboml and the efforts to create an exhibition about the shtetl. A few of the illustrations have been replaced because the photographs used in the original could not be located. The list of martyrs which appeared in the *Yizkor Book of Luboml* has also been expanded to include additional names of those killed by the Nazis in October 1942.

The nine-year project was beset by many problems that could only have been resolved because this was a labor of love. It required special skills and knowledge of Luboml, concerns for accuracy in translation and authenticity, faithfulness to the authors' characters and integrity of language, while enhancing clarity and readability.

There were seemingly endless roadblocks, both emotional and financial, that had to be overcome. Only the persistent demands and total devotion of committee members and landsmen, such as Victor Gershengorn, who would call and say, "Nathan, nu?" could have led to the completion of this book. Benjamin Rosenzweig provided invaluable assistance, remembering names of martyrs and their children. Toby Axelrod, a journalist whose roots are from Luboml, lent her editing and organizational skills, as did Eleanor Sobel, my wife.

Ultimately, Aaron Ziegelman, who had left Luboml in 1938 at the age of 9, brought his special vision and financial support to the project. Believing only the highest quality was worthy for a memorial of his birth town, and in remembrance of all the martyrs, Aaron Ziegelman guided the project through its last years of refinement, and ultimately to its printing.

Many others contributed to the birth of the English translation. Special thanks to all the landsmen from Luboml: Abraham Getman for continuous moral support, Victor and Rubin Lichtmacher, Benjamin Rosenzweig, Bernard Meller, Moshe Samet, z"l, Hershel Bergerbest, Chanah Gitalis, Yosef Karpus, Yitzhak Sheyntop (Sheyn), Max Fisher, Yankel and Matl Rayz, Avraham Raz, z"l, Malka (Sobel) Gitelis, Rivke Milshteyn, Khane Nemetz, Shmuel Goldberg, Chaim and Nieshl Dorenboy, Menachem Erlich,

Shneyer Vishnits, Nathan Blumen, Moshe Blumen, Esther (Ziegelman) Kessler, Malka Sfard, z"l, Murray Getman, Hershl Krupodelnik. and all the others.

We also thank Fred Wasserman, Director of the Luboml Exhibition Project, who took a special interest in our work and coordinated the final production of this volume. Roberta Newman and Daniel Soyer also assisted in numerous ways. Bernard Scharfstein, Richard White, and Dorcas Gelabert of KTAV were enormously helpful.

Special thanks to all family members who gave moral support, provided information as needed and gave editors the time to work. We feel the translation of the yizkor book will be worthy of our lost families and communities so tragically destroyed.

Last but not least, I thank my dear wife Eleanor, who gave me so much courage, moral support and strength, and never failed to assist me.

Nathan Sobel, Editor

ACKNOWLEDGMENTS TO THE ORIGINAL
YIZKOR BOOK OF LUBOML

It is our pleasure to thank all the members of our town and the vicinity, both here and abroad, who contributed their part, each according to his ability, to bring this book out into the light of day.

May a blessing come upon the chief editor, Mr. B. Kagan of New York, who, in addition to his excellent professional editing of the Yiddish material, contributed the fruits of his extensive research and expertise in the original and comprehensive chapter on the history of the Jewish community of Luboml, "*Di geshichte fun yidn in Luboml.*"

We extend our honor and respect to the memory of our late friend, Yakov Hetman (z"l), who edited the Hebrew part of this volume, determined the format of its various chapters and encouraged many of us to lend a hand to make this book a success.

The Editorial Committee

EDITOR:
B. Kagan

EDITOR OF THE HEBREW PART
Y. Hetman

EDITORIAL COMMITTEE IN U.S.A.
N. Eiger; Dr. E. Aimes; V. Gershengorn; F. Lerner; N. Sobel;
M. Samet; B. Rosenzweig; R. Shnaider; W. Roseman;
Z. Faigen (Argentina)

EDITORIAL COMMITTEE IN ISRAEL
Y. Hetman; N. Tchelet; I. Garmi; M. Lipshitz; M. Ehrlich

FOREWORD TO THE ORIGINAL
YIZKOR BOOK OF LUBOML

After much hesitation, we decided six years ago (1968), together with a number of former citizens of our town now in New York and Argentina (to an extent under their influence and even pressure), to publish a Luboml Memorial Book dedicated to the victims of the Shoah.

We feared we would not find the emotional strength to contribute to the book and that we would not find individuals ready to encourage others to participate in this important undertaking.

It would require much hard work: collecting literary material, pictures, and historical sources (documents, records, and more) to tell the history of Luboml's Jewish community—an ancient community, an important Jewish city.

Finally, we worried about finances; the undertaking would require a considerable investment.

And what was more, we feared difficulties when we asked Holocaust survivors to relate memories of terror and suffering in the Luboml ghetto, of personal acts of courage, of escaping the claws of the German beast in the moments before total destruction, of several last-minute escapes to the forest from the well of death, of the participation of one such survivor in a rebellion in the Sobibor death camp, and of many who fought in the heroic war of the Red Army against the vicious Nazi enemy.

More than once we doubted whether our friends would have enough emotional strength to raise bitter recollections from the depths of their consciousness—recollections about the terrible days of destruction, about horrors and tribulations from beginning to end, from which they were saved at the last moment.

With a sense of sacred duty to erect a monument of remembrance to the deceased of our town and the surrounding area, we finally approach the realization of our objective: The long-awaited book of Luboml is published. It will serve as a Yizkor [memorial] light for the dead.

Yisroel Garmi (Grimatlicht)
Luboml Memorial Book Committee
Tel Aviv, Israel, 1974

HISTORY OF THE JEWISH COMMUNITY IN LUBOML
By Nathan Sobel

The town of Luboml* and its Jewish Community have been known to exist since the 2nd half of the 14th century, according to recorded historical sources. Luboml was already mentioned in the year 1366 in an official agreement between Algerad the Great, Prince of Lithuania, and Kazimierz (Casimir) the Great, King of Poland, whereby Luboml was rendered as a tenancy to Jerzy Narimontowicz the Prince of Bielsk. We therefore can assume that Luboml had served as a community prior to that time.

In 1392, the Polish King Wladyslaw (Ladislas) Jagiello visited Luboml and he liked it so much, that he built a fortress and a church. In the chronicles of the King's visit to Luboml, it is mentioned that a Jew named Shmuel appeared before him. Some people claim that the name Luboml stems directly from the visit of King Jagiello when he allegedly, said *Lubo Mil* (pleasant, delightful, lovely) or *Lubo mi tu* (I am delighted here). The remnants of the fortress still remain on the artificial hill called "Gorka Jagiellonska" (Jagiello's Hill). Next to the hill is the church. In 1569, Luboml, which was part of the royal properties owned by King Zygmunt (Sigismund) III, was given as part of the dowry to his daughter when she married Wojewoda Wiechowski from Kiev, who was the Hetman of the Cossacks. Towards the end of the 18th century, Luboml was inherited by the Baron Branitzki. In 1782, the Branitzkis built their castle in Luboml

*Although Luboml is the official name in Polish and Russian, as well as in Ukrainian, the Jews called it "Libivne." Another name for Luboml used about 80–90 years ago was "Zavalie."

and they surrounded it with a huge garden and orchard. In the same year, the Branitzkis' income from the town is recorded to have reached 26,470 guilders, which in those days was considered as a huge fortune.

At the end of the 18th century, the District of Wolyn—including Luboml—was severed from Poland and annexed by Russia. Towards the end of the 18th century, in 1793, when Russia, Austria and Germany completed their second conquest of Poland they divided the bounty—Poland—among them. As long as the town belonged to the Branitzkis, it served as the center of the entire region and enjoyed prosperity and benefited from the economic boom and natural growth. But in 1820 all the land and domains in and around Luboml became Russian Government property. The Russians, in turn, apportioned the land and domain among the entrusted clerks of the territory. This sub-dividing of land had such an adverse influence on the local economy, that even the construction of the Radzivishlianski railroad through the town did not help and the town never again was as prosperous. Another very important factor in the economic decline was the frequent fires that often used to completely destroy the wooden structures with their straw roofs. Our parents and grandparents still remembered the great fire that had occurred in the year 1881. The last great fire that virtually gutted the entire town occurred on the 25 of June, 1941, when the retreating Soviet army and the advancing Nazi army fought the battle of Luboml.

In any event, Luboml was under Russian rule from the end of the 18th century until Poland was recreated in 1918.

With the outbreak of World war II in September, 1939 Poland was conquered by the Nazi hordes. Eastern Poland including Luboml fell as bounty to Soviet Russia. It remained a Soviet border town until 1941 when Nazi Germany attacked the Soviet Union. Since the end of World War II, Luboml has again been a Soviet border town.

★

It is difficult to determine the exact time, when Jewish settlement in Luboml occurred. But most researchers, including Dr. Philip Friedman, Prof. Ber Mark, and Dr. Raphael Mahler determined that by the 11th century there were established Jewish communities in the Volhynia region and that Luboml was one of them. It is a fact that in 1370, a Jewish community already existed in Luboml, and that official documents of that period contain the names of Jews from Luboml. Were it not for the Holocaust, Luboml Jewry could have celebrated the 600th anniversary of its existence, as one of the oldest Jewish communities in Poland.

We have neither records nor details of the development of the Jewish settlement in Luboml. However, there is a general consensus that at least a century passed till an organized Jewish community was formed. According to the available statistics of the Jewish census in Poland in 1550, there were 39 full households in Luboml, consisting of about 390 people. In towns such as Chelm, Ludmir and Belz, which were considered at that time to be major communities, there were less Jews than in Luboml. The City of Lublin, considered then among the most important, had only 3 households more than Luboml. It is therefore clear that the beginning of the second half of the 16th century, marked the beginning of the blossoming and growth in prosperity of the Luboml Jewish community. It is not a coincidence that precisely then the Luboml Jews received the authority to appoint a rabbi, who according to the law of the land at that time, had very broad administrative powers and authority in the field of religion. From that period on for a period of several centuries, there were many famous Rab-

bis that reigned in Luboml. Among the gaonim and Torah giants of that period are Rabbi Shimon Wolf Orbach, Rabbi Avraham Pollak, Rabbi Moshe Mess, Rabbi Yoel Sirkis (1620), Rabbi Shmuel Ish Horowitz, Rabbi Moshe Katzenelbogen and Rabbi Gedalyahu (Maharam) from Lublin. Some of these Rabbis also conducted Yeshivoth in Luboml that were very famous and drew Torah scholars from near and far. The town suffered very difficult times during the years of 1648–1649 when the Chmielnicki hordes and the Cossack murderers overran the Ukraine like a horrible tempest, wiping out hundreds upon hundreds of Jewish communities and settlements. An estimated half a million Jewish men, women and children were slaughtered in the most horrifying manner. The historical source books describing these horrible pogroms and destructions mention among others Luboml. In one of the books, *Tit HaYavan*, it is told that "600 houseowners lived then in this town, and just about all of them were killed."

After the suppression of the Chmielnicki revolt in 1652, the Jewish community in Luboml resumed its growth in spite of the fact that it had been almost destroyed completely physically and economically. In the protocols of the "Vaad Arba Aratzoth" (the Committee of the Four Lands) from the year 1667 on the subject of head taxes, it is recorded that for that year the head tax that was imposed on the Luboml Jewish community was estimated to be 8,100 guilders, while the tax of the Posen (Poznan) community was only 1,600 guilders, that of Przemysl 7,810 guilders, and of Tiktin 1,520 guilders. These figures are evidence of the relatively rapid rehabilitation and reestablishment of the Luboml Jewish community after the "Ta'ch and Ta't" (1648 and 1649) pogroms. During the latter years of the 16th century, or during the first half of the 17th century (the exact date has never been determined), the great old synagogue was built in Luboml. Since this was the period of constant wars with the Tartars and the Cossacks, the architectural style reflected that of a fortress.

The Luboml synagogue was one of the finest and most important of the synagogues of this period. It is always mentioned as such in the annals of the old East European Synagogues. The main structure was approximately four stories high, and adjacent to it was a lower structure for women worshippers. Each of the two connected buildings had a unique Moorish battlement rising above the roof line, surrounding it like a ribbon. Unique carvings and corbelling (outward projection of tile structure) around the main building added a magnificence that served as an inspiration for other such synagogues of this period.

The interior of the synagogue was no less important or elaborate. It was decorated with an abundance of Jewish symbols and motifs on graceful wall frescos and paintings which portrayed implements of biblical sanctuary, animals, plants, and musical instruments. The holy ark too was unique from an artistic point of view. It embodied a special blending of graceful carved and sculptured Jewish religious motifs with native style, creating a design of high artistic value.

The majority of the Luboml population were Jews, and the town bore the typical Jewish "Shtetl" character for many generations. In the beginning of the 18th century, Luboml was the best established Jewish community in the entire Chelm-Belz region.

During the period of World War I, when the town was under Austrian rule, Luboml even had a Jewish mayor. When that war ended, Luboml created a world "first," by printing and putting into use 6 postage stamps (including 2 views of the famous synagogue). The inscriptions were in four languages including one in Yiddish—"Shtot Post Luboml" (only the United Nations exceeds Luboml by imprinting in five languages).

In the two decades between the two World Wars, there was a great Jewish cultural and social renaissance in the town. Many cultural organizations, youth and sports clubs, and a multiplicity of Zionist, national and religious movements; theatre groups, libraries, Jewish and Hebrew schools and Yeshivoth; charitable (Gemiluth Chasadim) organizations; and kitchens for the orphans and poor were established. Banks, merchants associations, artisan and craftsmen organizations, and many other kinds of organizations also thrived.

The town was sizzling and prospering. Many youths as well as families left their homes and discovered the outside world with its opportunities. Large numbers emigrated, mostly to the U.S.A., Palestine, Canada and Argentina.

World War II put an end to all that. In 1939 when the war broke out, the town was for lengthy periods in chaos. The Poles ran, leaving a vacuum. Armed Ukrainian bands took over, robbing Jewish stores and homes. Then Polish bands of "Andekes" overran the town, slaughtering about a dozen Jews in cold blood. The Germans marched in for a short period and left. Subsequently, a civic group including Jews took into their own hands the responsibility for maintaining order in the chaotic interim period. Shortly thereafter, the Russian Army marched in. They wasted no time, changing things, and among them the Jewish character of the town. Luboml was transformed into a security border town with more Russian soldiers than the local population, since the border with German occupied Poland was established at the Bug River, only about 10 miles away.

When the Nazi hordes overran the Soviet Union on June 22, 1941, Luboml was the first community to be hit, since it was on the main route of the Nazi march eastward. The oppression and persecution of the Jews started at the very beginning. Since most of the Jewish residential quarters of the town were burned out, all the Jews were herded into three Jewish sections: Kusnishtcher, Koleyova and Chelm Streets. Gradually all their remaining possessions were confiscated by the German and Ukrainian Nazis. The movement of Jews was restricted and tightened almost daily, and thousands of Jews, starting with the age of 10, were driven to work daily to perform various menial jobs. Jews and Jewish residences were marked with the yellow shame marks, and the Jews themselves were slowly starved to death. Periodically the Nazis would conduct a so-called "Chapun"—grabbing of Jews, trucking them away and killing them off secretly. The Security Guard over the three ghetto quarters was tightened. The Jews from all the surrounding villages were herded into the already dense ghetto. Although deprived of all communication media, some news reached us of the various Nazi atrocities: A holocaust, we just could not conceive, and would not believe could happen in the 20th century. All over Europe the Nazis succeeded in dehumanizing the Jewish population, during this two year period. Then, on Hoshana Raba of 1942, the final chapter of the 12,000 Luboml Jews began. The German Nazis, with the help of their Ukrainian puppets and Polish "freedom fighters," grabbed all the remaining Jews, herded them first in the synagogue, and from there marched them out of town under tight guard to where the brick works (Cegelnia) was located, where five huge graves were ready to swallow them all. Without concentration camps, or crematoria, they succeeded 100% in their task of eliminating the Jews from Luboml. Only a handful actually survived the Holocaust.

And so ended a 600 year old Jewish chapter called Luboml-Libivne in a most horrifying way.

We shall never forget, we shall never forgive, and the innocent blood must be avenged.

Southeast view of the Great Synagogue in Luboml (Photo taken before synagogue was plastered).
(Courtesy of the Central Archives for the History of the Jewish People)

THE EARLY DAYS

THE HISTORY OF LUBOML'S JEWS
By Berl Kagan

The General Community

The town of Luboml, called Libivne [in Yiddish], in the last few centuries a little-known Jewish community of Russia-Poland, is one of the oldest such settlements in Eastern Europe.

What befell Luboml's Jewish community is no different from the fate of other such communities in Russia-Poland: After occupying a recognized place on the Jewish map, the settlement suffered a steep decline.

It was by no means unusual for Jewish communities in Eastern Europe—great Jewish urban areas for many years—to decline and, conversely, for small, unimportant Jewish communities to become in time centers of Jewish culture.

The truth is that Luboml never was a Jewish metropolis, for it lacked two important criteria: (1) Its location meant it had no prospects of becoming an important center that would attract masses of Jewish settlers. (2) It had no great yeshiva to make it attractive as a Torah center. But during Luboml's heyday—evident from its rabbis and their role in the Council of the Four Lands—the town held a noteworthy position among the Jewish communities of Volhynia.

Not only was Luboml an old Jewish community in Russia-Poland, it was an early urban settlement in general.

In the middle of the 14th century, Luboml is mentioned in an agreement between the Lithuanian Prince Algerad and Casimir the Great. As a result of that agreement, Luboml was handed over in 1366 as a leased estate to the prince of Bielsk, Jerzy Nachimontowicz. It is clear that if the town already served as an object of commercial trade or as a gift, its origins must be even earlier.

Luboml did not long remain in the possession of Prince Nachimontowicz. In 1377, during the reign of Ludwig of Hungary, the town and entire district of Chelm reverted to the Polish kingdom.

In 1392, King Wladislaw Jagiello spent some time in Luboml. He reportedly liked it so much that he had a cloister built there, which still stands today. There is even conjecture that the very name of the town came from Jagiello. While visiting the locale, he is said to have remarked either *Lubo mil* (sweet and lovely), or *Lubo mi tu* (it's very pleasant for me here)—and that remained the official name of the town.

There was also a small hill in town called Jagiello's hill and, close by, a church. A legend circulated among local Christians that the church was connected with the hill, which was Jagiello's fortress.

In 1569, Luboml was part of the royal domain and Zygmunt III gave it as a wedding present to his daughter when she married the *wojewoda* [administrator] Wiechowski of Kiev, hetman of the Cossacks.

In the closing decades of the 18th century, Luboml became the property of the descendants of Baron Branitzki. The new owners brought order to the affairs of the town and surrounding area. In 1782, the Branitzkis took in 26,470 zlotys from Luboml—a considerable sum for those days.[1]

In the second half of the 19th century, the town experienced another economic slump. Around 1820, all the estates around Luboml—which had gone back to the Russian domain—

1

were parceled out to government functionaries who had distinguished themselves in administering the territories. This had a negative effect on Luboml's economy.

The later construction in Luboml of a railroad station on the Nadvishliansky line gave a bit of an economic boost to the town, but Luboml never regained its former prosperity.

Frequent fires played a considerable role in Luboml's economic downfall. Almost all the houses in those early days were made of wood, and many of them also had straw roofs, so a small fire often would turn into a major inferno and cause nearly total destruction.

Just as Luboml shared the economic fortunes of all Volhynia, so did it share the political sphere. Having as its neighbors Lithuania, then a Eastern European great power, to the north, Russia to the east and south, and Poland to the west, the province of Volhynia often was pressured by three powers. More than once, it found itself handed from one to the other.

This political instability and the changes in Volhynia's political-territorial status had a strong influence on local economic life—sometimes favorable, sometimes not. The worse a town's geographic position, the more it suffered from such changes. Such was the case with Luboml.

Lithuania, which from the 14th through the early 16th century was a dominant power, ruled over all Volhynia for long periods. A considerable number of clashes occurred over Volhynia between Lithuania and Poland or the Russian nobility. Lithuania stretched to the Black Sea, and for many years the entire Kiev region found itself under Lithuania's domain.

After lengthy battles between Lithuania and Poland, a peace treaty was signed in 1366 between the Lithuanian Prince Lubart and the Polish King Casimir the Great. Through that treaty Casimir acquired Belz, Chelm, and Ludmir, along with a section of territory west of the Turia River: Horodle, Trisk, Ratne, Kamien-Koshirsk, and Volochin. Within this area was Luboml.

Lubart was the Volhynian, or Wladimir, prince, and ruler of the Chelm principality.

But peace treaties are not forever. When, in time, one side feels stronger and has hopes of taking back that which it was forced to give up, it goes off to war again. This most certainly was the case centuries ago.

Despite the 1366 Lubart-Casimir peace agreement, many wars ensued between Lithuania and Poland over Volhynia, especially over those places that bordered the two lands. And Luboml was situated not far from the Lithuanian-Polish border.

We do not know about all those wars and broken peace agreements. But the peace treaty of Zygmunt, the son of Kestutys, grand duke of Lithuania is well known. On October 15, 1432, he gave Poland part of the border areas belonging to Volhynia, including Luboml.

And it was not long before war once again broke out between these two neighboring states. Already in 1440, just a few years after the Kestutys treaty, war was ignited between Lithuania and Poland. The Lithuanian Prince Sangushka in that year tried forcibly to take back a number of towns. Among them was Luboml. However, Sangushka was not successful.[2]

Military actions between Lithuania and Poland in and around Volhynia stopped in the middle of the 16th century. The Lithuanian grand duchy was already in decline and found itself in the process of disintegration.

In 1569, a federation was established between Poland and Lithuania, known as the Lublin Alliance. Formally, this was a voluntary agreement between two equal parties. In reality, the union took the form of a Polish *diktat*, which exploited the extreme weakness of the Lithuanian grand duchy and forced upon Lithuania a series of strict conditions. One was that Volhynia be transferred to the Polish kingdom. In an official decree of May 25, 1569, it was announced that Volhynia would be annexed to Poland.[3]

However, if the bloody conflict between Poland and Lithuania was settled on the battlefields of Volhynia, these same regions saw troubles approach from other directions—primarily from their southeastern neighbor.

The rich, black fields of Volhynia aroused the appetite of the Russians quite a bit. And on many occasions they attacked the region.

The tragic climax of these attacks came in 1648–49, when bands of Cossacks overran the region, robbing, plundering, and murdering mercilessly. These events will be recounted when we come to the chapter on the Jews of those areas.

In 1802–1803, tens of thousands of Cossacks loosed themselves once again on Volhynia and caused new destruction.

In 1806, a few years after the Cossack attacks, Swedish armies marched through Volhynia. They forced a heavy tribute on the local populace and plundered everything in their path. Needless to say, in all these bloody attacks Jews suffered terribly.

For 224 years Volhynia lay within the borders of the Polish kingdom. But at the end of the 18th century, Volhynia was torn from Poland and attached to the Russian state. This took place in 1793, when Russia, Germany, and Austria partitioned Polish territory for a second time.

From that time until the First World War, Volhynia belonged to Russia. With the establishment of the newly independent Poland in 1918, a large portion of Volhynia once again reverted to Polish control.

In 1939, a portion of Volhynia (and with it Luboml) was annexed to Russia. After several years of Nazi occupation in 1941–44, Luboml again belonged to the Soviet Ukraine.

How Old Is the Jewish Settlement in Luboml?

An overview of Volhynia's history, with its economic and political changes, will help illustrate the development of the Jewish settlement in Luboml.

It is difficult to determine exactly when Jews began to settle in Luboml. Such documents as could help determine the first signs of Jews in the town are not extant. In any case, we have not been able to find such documents. Thus there are differences of opinion as to the beginnings of Luboml's Jewish settlement.

N. B. Gelber, an authority on the history of Jews in Russia-Poland, writes that "in general, no Jewish settlement existed before the 15th century." Exceptions are the towns of Kremenitz and Lutsk.[4]

If Gelber's thesis is correct, then we have to look for the beginnings of Jewish settlement in Luboml in the 15th century. But not all Jewish historians agree with Gelber.

One who differs is Philip Friedman, also an authority on the history of Polish-Russian Jewry. In his article "The Jews of Chelm," whose history is closely knit with that of the Jews of nearby Luboml, Friedman writes that "regarding Luboml we have documentary evidence of Jewish settlement in the years 1370–1382." He says that the names of various Jews of Luboml are noted in contemporary official documents.[5]

Of the same opinion is another Jewish historian, Ber Mark. In his book on the history of Polish Jews, he writes that in the 14th century many new Jewish settlements were established, and that among the earliest of these was Luboml. He says that facts are available regarding a small group of Jews there around 1370, the result of a large official colonization scheme and the building of new towns in Volhynia and the surrounding Polish areas.[6]

Raphael Mahler, one of our younger historians, writes in his major work *Jews in Early Poland* that in the 14th century there was already a small number of Jewish communities in Greater Poland, Lesser Poland, Belorussia, and the Chelm district—for which he gives only one example, Luboml in 1370–1382.[7]

Gelber's thesis is to be discounted because of the historical evidence brought by Friedman, Mark, and Mahler. All point to the same date—1370—as the genesis of Jews in Luboml. If not for Hitler's horrible destruction, the Jews of Luboml could have celebrated their 600th anniversary—one of the few Jewish communities in Poland with such a long heritage.

Evidently, it is impossible to rely on information from even the most important encyclopedias when it comes to the beginnings of Jewish settlement in Luboml.

According to the [evidently mistaken] *Jewish Encyclopedia*, the *Encyclopaedia Judaica,* and the *Yevreyska Entziklopedia*, Jews first began settling in Luboml in the first quarter of the 16th century—150 years later than was actually the case.

Development and Heyday of Jewish Luboml

No settlement came about in one day, and no Jewish community appeared overnight. The period during which a new Jewish settlement evolved into a community with all the requisite characteristics clearly took a number of decades, especially as the tempo of life was much slower then than it is today, and Jewish life slower yet.

We have no chronological data to give us a picture of the gradual development of Luboml's Jewish community. However, we can establish that at least 100 years passed before it came into being and began to take its place on Volhynia's Jewish map.

The growth of the Luboml community was helped by two processes characteristic of Polish Jewry in the 16th century, and on which historian Mahler takes the following positions: (1) there was continuous movement of Polish Jews from the big cities to the small towns; (2) even more characteristic was the migration of many Jews from western Poland toward the southeastern provinces.[8]

Here we can add that Jewish emigration tended to go from areas of greater economic development to those of lesser development, where Jews hoped for support from the ruling classes, who were generally willing to encourage pioneering enterprises.

At that time vast territories in Volhynia and the Ukraine lay empty, or only sparsely populated, and it was to those areas that Jews moved in the 16th and 17th centuries. From that migration a series of settlements sprang up in Volhynia, both small and large, and Luboml was most likely one of them.

In the late 16th century and early 17th, the Jews of Luboml began establishing their community. Nearby towns began to view Luboml as an important community.

This is evident from a royal decree in 1520 regarding tax collection from Jews of the Chelm-Belz district. It mentions the Jews appointed to collect Jewish taxes in those places: Yoske Zussmanovitch from Belz, Yisroel of Bosk, Asher of Luboml, and Yudka from Chelm.[9] It is obvious that in this case people were chosen not from distant or unimportant places but rather from communities important because of their position or number of inhabitants—and Luboml was at that time one of the significant communities in the district.

In that period Luboml was most likely under the jurisdiction of Rabbi Yehuda Aron, the Chelmer Rav, who in 1522 was appointed by Zygmunt I (1506–1548) to be grand rabbi of the then-unified districts of Lublin, Chelm, and Belz. In 1520 he was appointed by the same king to collect taxes from the Jews of those three districts, which included Luboml.

In 1541, after the death of R. Yehuda Aron, Zygmunt I appointed grand rabbis for Lesser Poland and for Belorussia and Podolia—the esteemed rabbi of Lublin, R. Shalom Shachne, the father-in-law and teacher of the Rema and an outstanding student of R. Yakov Pollack, and the rabbi of Cracow, R. Moyshe Fishel.

Since Chelm fell under the jurisdiction of R. Shalom Shachne, Luboml also found itself under his judicial jurisdiction.

The administrative-legal jurisdiction of these two grand rabbis was actually very broad, and the outlying communities were greatly dependent upon them. This can be seen from the three major functions with which they were entrusted: (1) the right to punish or excommunicate anyone who transgressed religious law or disobeyed the community; (2) confirmation in office of newly appointed rabbis and others; and (3) the right to live anywhere within the territory under their jurisdiction.[10]

That Luboml was an important Jewish town not only in the northwestern section of Volhynia and region (for several years within the territory of the "nine communities") but also in a section of the Lubliner district, is seen from a statistic of 1550.

That was the year of the first census of Poland's Jews. In the census there numbered 39 households in Luboml (about 390 souls).[11] To understand the importance of this figure in those times, we must compare it to other local Jewish communities. Clearly, communities that later outgrew Luboml were originally much smaller. Chelm, Ludmir, and Belz, which during the period of the Council of the Four Lands became major cities, had fewer Jews in 1550 than Luboml. Jewish Belz had 22 households—about one half the number in Luboml; Ludmir, 30 households; and even Chelm had less than 39 households.

More striking is the comparison with Lublin, which even then was among the most important Jewish communities: It had about the same number of Jewish households as Luboml (only three more).

Indeed, from that point on—that is, from the 1550s—we can determine the beginnings of the blossoming of Luboml's Jewish community.

However, it is necessary to add the following comments:

Establishing periods in human history is generally artificial. Historical processes are so intertwined, they grow in and out of one another to such an extent, that it is almost impossible to say that one period ends and another begins in such and such a year. If history must be divided into periods, these are only approximate and designed to make it easier to understand the complicated course of world history.

This is as true for local history as it is for general history on a broader scale. Certainly this was so for the development and prime of Luboml.

If we want to tie the beginnings of Jewish life in Luboml to a major event in general history, we would identify the Lublin Confederation (Union or Alliance) of 1569, as a turning point in the history of Poland that could not but have a deep effect on Volhynia and on its Jewish settlements in particular. It is true that Luboml 's development occurred a bit later, but historical processes cannot be measured exactly.

It is no accident that in the 1560s, the Jews of Luboml were given permission to appoint a rabbi, to whom the proclamation gave quite broad religious-administrative authority. This was probably their very first rabbi.

And it is no mere coincidence that, starting after the initiation of the Lublin Confederation, the office of Luboml's rabbi was filled by a series of distinguished rabbis who graced the town for centuries thereafter and about whom much more will be told.

The first rabbi of Luboml, we believe, arrived in 1556, and only one year later the Jews of Luboml obtained the privilege from King Zygmunt Augustus. That is, the various local magistrates, apart from district magistrates, no longer had the power to try Jews, and Jews received the right to appeal verdicts of the district court directly to the king.[12] This privilege freed Jews from having to deal with local, lower officials and strengthened their security and sense of stability.

In that same year, the Luboml kehila [community] issued a very interesting decree (takhana) that has been preserved in a Jewish book. It is interesting first of all because it is the opposite of other decrees with which we are familiar.

Generally, diaspora Jews lived in more crowded quarters separated from their Christian neighbors. This happened not only during the Middle Ages but also in the modern era, and to a marked extent Jews maintain that tradition even up to the present day.

This segregation occurred not only for religious reasons, though within a community it is easier to observe Yiddishkeit and keep Christian influences to a minimum. Here, it was no less an expression of group interest in times of danger, and since Jews in the extraordinary condition of diaspora found themselves under siege and subject to attacks and pogroms, they wanted to be among Jews in order to better defend themselves in times of trouble.

But the decree of Luboml's Jewish community seemed to oppose such segregation. In it, the community forbade the town's Jews even to dare buy a house or property from a non-Jew if it was within the area where Jews lived. And the community warned that anyone who did not adhere to this decree would be severely punished.

We learn about this interesting and important decree from Rabbi Yoel Sirkis, himself a rabbi in Luboml, known as the Bach (named after his book *Bayit Chadash*—"The New House").[13]

In a shortened, nonliteral Yiddish translation, the decree reads as follows:

In 1558, the Luboml community forbade any local householder from purchasing a house or land from a non-Jew in a town or neighborhood where Jews lived. The Kahal [community] came to the conclusion that if non-Jews did not want to live among the Jews, there was a danger that non-Jews might set fire to Jewish houses or demand that the Jews be driven out.

Those Jews who did not obey the decree were forced to return the purchased houses or property to the Christians. In 1577, this decree was renewed by the Kahal, with the consent of the local rabbi, R. Avrom Pollack.

Finally, the renowned R. Sirkis tells about one Jew, Reuven, who was allowed to buy a piece of property from a non-Jewish neighbor in order to build something for himself. But since Reuven bought more than he was allowed, the Kahal forced him to follow the decree. After Reuven's death, his heirs sold the whole house and the surrounding property to Moyshe First, who wanted to expand the house and build on the property. The gaon (rabbi) was asked about this.

The scholar's answer was written in 1601. From it we learn, first, that 50 years after its initiation the decree of the Luboml Kahal was still in force; that one of Luboml's householders was called Moyshe First; and that R. Yoel Sirkis was still serving as the av beth din (head of the rabbinical court) in Luboml.

In 1559, after the death of the (gaon) scholar Shalom Shachne, the unification of the Lublin-Chelm-Belz districts was completed. Belz and Chelm, which almost consistently record their history together, formed a state of their own and had a separate Va'ad (committee). Their rabbi was the scholar and mystic R. Eliyohu, the R. of Chelm, son of the aforementioned R. Yehuda Aron.

The capital of the state was Chelm. Only three other major communities could send a representative to the Va'ad: Belz, Hrubyeshov, and Luboml. At the time of the 1569 unification of Lithuania and Poland, Luboml was still considered one of the major communities in that district.[14]

Christian-Jewish economic relations outside the boundaries of the town were quite lively, especially when it came to leasing estates. A revision of revenues from 1569 shows that Luboml's Jews held eight parcels of land, leased a flour mill and three lakes, and paid for the lease of the estate with money, pepper, saffron, and fish, for a total of 400 gold ducats. The Jews who leased a mill around Luboml were called Laska and Michel.[15]

Until 1569, Volhynia belonged to the Lithuanian grand duchy. Its Jewish inhabitants were, naturally, subject to Lithuanian law in reference to privileges, taxes, etc.

After the Lublin unification, when Volhynia was torn from Lithuania and returned to the Polish crown, the Polish legal code understandably replaced the Lithuanian one.

In the beginning, this caused some confusion. It caused disputes between Jews in Volhynia and the ruling officials, who often exploited the unclear situation to the detriment of the Jews.

The Jews of Volhynia, however, did not remain silent. They attempted through various means to intercede with highly placed officials in the newly acquired territories, and influence them to take more into account the interests of the Jews there and not cheat them by falsely interpreting the new decrees.

However, this did not have good results. Therefore, the Jews of Lutsk tried their luck in attaining the intervention of the king himself. In 1576 they sent a memorandum to the Polish king, Stefan Batory, in which they listed the grievances inflicted upon the Jews in the newly acquired Volhynian territories, and requested that the king grant them the same rights accorded Jews in the rest of Poland.

On December 1, 1576, a royal decree was promulgated granting the Jews of Volhynia the same rights that Jews had in all of Poland.

This had a positive effect on the development of Jewish settlements in Volhynia. The increased internal Jewish immigration in Poland in the

From *She'elot Uteshuvot* ("Questions and Answers"), by Grand Rabbi Yoel Sirkis. Printed in Frankfurt am Main by Jan Wust Press, 1697. (This illustration continues on pages 7 and 8)

ולא גורם בו לא הנא ענינו ולא שום אדם בעולם ולאחריה
לו שום הנאה בעולם מאותו קרקע עד כאן תורף ההסכמה
והנה אחר זה התירו הקהל לראובן לקנות מקנת קרקע מן
הגוים סמוך לביתו כי היה קרקע שלו קנר לבנות עליו
וראובן עבר וקנה יותר ממה שהתירו לו או אז נזרו עליו
הקהל שלא לבנות על קרקע זו כי אם על אותו שיעור
שהתירו לו ועל היותר בנום תשום אפילו
להעמיד שם בהמתיו וראובן קיים נזירת הקהל ובנינים
ועשה היקף מחיצה מקנים סביב כל הקרקע שקנה מן הגוי
אחר כך מת ראובן ויורשיו מכרו לכהר משה פירמסט כל
הבית וכל הקרקע וחזקה נפת כהר ר משה להרחיב את
ביתו ולבנות על אותה קרקע ועתה ירינו רבינו אם יש
היתר בזה אם לאו ·

תשובה

לפע"ד דברי ההמסקנא בפרק מי
שהחשיך כמי שבין מלאכתו במועד
ומת לדלדיה קנבו רבנן לגריה לא קנסו רבנן ומת וכתב
הרי"ף והרא"ש שם · וכן הגורס און נכור ומת
והמוכר עבדו לגוים ומת לא קנסו רבנן בנו אחריו
והכין אסקהו לכל חדא וחדא בדוכתיה וכן הלכה
וא"כ נדון דידן נמי אעפ"י שקנסו רבנן הקהל לראובן
שלא ישחמש על היתר לפי שעבר כזה על גזורתם בעונם
נ"ם מכל מקום לבניו לא קנסינן והם היו מתירין
לבנות על אותה קרקע וא"כ גם להר"ר משה דקתא
מחמתיהו לבנות עליה שהרי כלון ההסכמה לא
נזכר שלא לבנות על הקרקע שביתה של גוים כ"א
שלא ילך כ"ה ויקנה בית או קרקע מום להסכמה הקרקע
וכו' ופשיטא דאפילו ראובן בעצמו שקנה הקרקע
ועבר על התרם לא בשביל זה נאסרו עליו הקרקע
בהנאה כיון שלא נזכר זה בחרם דנדמיה קנינהו אלא
שהקהל קנסו אותו כנך על שעבר על ההסכמתם
ונזירתם בעונם נתם וזה וזה יש בידם להפקיר ממון שים
לו בעולם ולאבד וכוכח כפי מה שיראה לנדור פרבת
הדור ולחזק ולהוק בדק כו' כמו שכתב הרמב"ם בפרק כ"ד
מהלכת סנהדרין והטור נח"מ בתחלתו וכסופו אבל
מדינא אין הקרקע נאסרה בשביל שעבר על התרם וזה
דבר פשוט הוא והארין כו הריב"ם סימן קע"ו להוגיא
מלב הטועה לומר שאם נזרו חרם על דבר שלא לעשות
ועשה כמויד והרוים שנב המצות נאסרים עין עליו
כי אותו נדון דומה לשאלותחינו וכין שאין הקרקע
נאסרה לראובן בעצמו אם כן בניו אחריו ולאתא
מחמתיהו אין לאטיל עליהם שום קנם ושום עונש
דאינהו לא קא ענבי מידי · וכן פסק בירדכי פרק
החונל כבם ריב"א אמטור שלא הספיר הנוזכר להעמיד
נדין עד שעת התשובר דפטורין בניו אבל אם קם המטור
נדין ונתחיב נתחייבו הנבכס והו לא ירשו להו
הנבכס ונפרק הגונל בחרא כתב שם נבם הלכות
גדולות ביאור לדברים אלו דהיינו שנתחייב ממון עבור
מלשינות ומת דאפילו למ"ד מלוה על פה אינה נבנית מן
היורשים הכא גובה כשרבור בדן דקלא אית ליה אבל
חייבוהו בית דין דין קנם כשרברו בנו אחריו ע"כ הרי
מבואר דכל שחייבוהו בית דין דין קנם אין קונסין בנו
אחריו :   ואין לומר דהולכין אחר כוונת ההסכמה
שהיא היתה מחמאה פן ירפרו בתי יהודים אם וזלום
וכו' ואם כן אף בבניו אחרין עומדא תשמא זו במקומה
אם יבנו בית חדא על הקרקע של גוים הא לאו מלתא הוא
דפשיטא דהקהל לא חששו כי אם על מתי דשביחא
כנון אם לא יהא שום איסור לקנות מן הגוי שכל אחד
ואחד יבא ויקנה וכיון ויהיה כל היהודים בעיר אבל
אמלתא דלא שכיחא חששא אים על התרם ויחזיק
הקרקע

שאלה

הקרקע בידו ויהיה כעובר על החרם כל ימיו וירשו בניו
אחריו וינגנו על אותה קרקע הא וודאי לא אסיק
אדעתייהו בשעת החרם וכלאסיק ברים כתובות דאונם
דלא שכיחא לא אסיק אדעתיהו והכי איתא בפרק
השלח והכי איתא נמי בפרק הזהב לר' יוחנן דאמר
מעות קונות ומפני מה אמרו משיחה קונה גזרה
שמא יאמר לו נשרפו חטיך בעלייה דכותיה במילתא
דשכיחא גזרו ביה רבנן אבל רבנן דלא שכיחא
כגון שהחליף דמי שור בפרה או דמי חמור בשור
ודאי מעות קונות וכן מכר לו כאלו
דקנה לרב הונא קאמר התם דם"ל כר' יוחנן דמעות קונה
דבר תורה ומילחא דלא שכיחא כי הא לא גזרו רבנן
והכא איתא כדוכתי' טובא ·   ועוד דאין הולכין
אחר כוונת ההסכמה אלא א"כ שהוא נ"כ בכלל לשון
ההסכמה כמו שנראה מכואר ממ"ש הרב"א הביאו כ"י
כ"י סימן רי"ח (נהב"ה רמ"א ס"ס הנוכר)וז"ל שאלה
הקהל החרימו שלא ירוד אים פלוני בעצרב פ' על
זמן ידוע ונתוך הזמן שכר שם חנות לעשות שם מלאכתו
ויטוע שלא החרימו אלא שלא ידוד שם וזהינו נקרת דירה
אלא במקום שאוכל ושותה · תשובה לשון דירה נופל
על ענינים רבים יש שהוא כעין ישיבה במקום וכו' ויש
שהוא כמו עיכוב במקום וכו' ונופל גם כן למי שהוא דר
במקום אחד ביום אחד וכו' ולפיכך הכל מה שהוא ענין
אם מה שהחרימו על ענין שחתו שלא יהא עמהם
וכו' אפילו עמהם בחנות כלל אבו' ואם מחמת שלא יקבע
דירה עמהם הדין עמו וכו' וכל אנדרים והחרמות נדונין
לפי מה שהוא ענין כו' הנה מבואר דהולכים לפי מה
שהוא הענין וכלבד שיהא כמשמע הלשון שהוניאו כפי זה
דאם כן לא נרין לומר לשון דירה נופל על ענינים
רבים וכו' אלא דאם הוא היה נופל על עיכוב
במקום אפילו אם היה הענין שחשוהו שלא יהא שייך
עמהם מ"מ מאחר שלא הוניאו כן כפירהם לא היה כ
איסור חרם כיון שלא החרימו עליו כפירהם
·

ומזה הטעם פסק גם האשר"י כהיה חבירו מפני כו
שיאכל עמו ואמר קונם ביתך שאני נכנם · טיפת נונן
שאני טועם עמך דמותר לכנות לביתו ולשתות עמו טיפת
נונן שלא נתכוין אלא לשם אכילה ומותר לו לריש
באכילה ושתיי' כיון שלא הוניאו כפיו ולא דמי לרישא
כהיו מפנירין בו ליקח בת אחותו ואמר קונם שנהנית לי
שלא נתכוין אלא לשם אישות דאישות בכלל הנאה היא
ואע"ג דהרמב"ם (י"ד סי' רי"ח סעיף ד') פסק דנם
באמר טיפת נונן כוון אסור בכאילה ושתיה וכן איתא
בחוספתא וכן פסק הר"ר ירוחם וראוי להחמיר כאיסור
דאוריתא כוותי' הם וודאי איכא למימר דבכלל טיפת
נונן שאני טועם הוא דהלשון משמע כאלו אמר אינ
אוכל ואיני שותה עמך לא הרבה ולא מעט אפילו טיפה
אינני טועם ולישנא קטיעא הוא למימר לשתות לו
כוון דלא נתכוין אלא לשם שתי' ואכילה · אבל כ"ד
וכלשון החרם לא הוכר כי אם שלא יקנה בית או קרקע
כתוך חומה אף הרמב"ם מודה דאין בכלל לשון זה שלא
ונהנה בית על הקרקע של גוי אם לא קנה מגוי ותדע
שהרי כמרדכי פרק התקבל פסק אכיונא דגנון דיין שנורו
הקהל שלא לקנות ביתחנו גוי דאם בא להחליף ביתבבית עם
הגוי דאסור דחילוף בית נמי מיקרא וכיני כו' דאלמא דאי
לאו דמיקרי וכיני לא היה כזה שום איסור אעפ"י דלפי
הענין היה שייך נם הטעם שהחרימו על קניות בית גוי
בחלוף כמו כובנא דאם לא היה שייך כאלופין
למה פסק לחיסור אלא הולכים אחר כוונת החרמים
בלחן בטיפת נונן למוחר לשתות נונן שלא נתכוין אלא
לשם אכילה
·

ונמשך לפי זה דאפילו אם יבא
איזה גוי ויערער על אותו קרקע לומר שהוא שלו דמוחר
לו להר"ר מה לשכר לפבר את הגוי כדי שיחזיק הגני הקרקע

1560s, particularly after the Lublin Confederation, became even more intensive. Jewish communities became larger, Jewish towns sprang up around the big cities, and later on there was an increase in the number of outlying Jewish village communities.[16]

This was a direct result of a comprehensive colonization program undertaken by the great landowners of Volhynia, Podolia, and the Ukraine in the second half of the 16th century.

In that same period, a number of new towns were built in which many Jews settled. These Jews came from a number of places in Poland, particularly from towns where they had waged an unceasing struggle with Christian citizens (*mieshtchanes* —city dwellers) who were against giving Jews the right to live among them. Many Jews, weak and worn out from the struggle, gave up their positions and emigrated to the eastern portions of the country, where, according to law, the towns were the private possessions of the new landowners who had built them.

These newly landed nobles were interested in the rapid growth and development of their towns and therefore were willing to give Jews

who settled there considerable rights. Hence there were no limitations on trade or handicrafts nor on the conditions of colonization and establishing residency.

All commerce was concentrated in the hands of Jews, including the artisan trades and a number of industries connected with agriculture.

The Jews enjoyed the right to vote for district councils and were free from paying taxes and payments to the royal coffers.

This was all done to provide favorable terms for development. In those towns the Jews aligned themselves with the middle class, an alliance that every owner of a town was interested in promoting. The above description of the situation was given by B. Gelber.[17]

A similar picture of the Jewish situation in Volhynia at that time is presented by another well-known Jewish historian, Raphael Mahler. He specifically emphasizes the economic side of development and the Jewish professions. He writes:

> The strongly developed commercialization of the Polish estates was connected with the growth of agricultural exports and was tied to the rise of a significant liquor industry that had already in the 16th and especially in the 17th century brought a large number of Jews significant wealth.[18]

This sort of estate was widespread throughout the southeastern part of Poland and in Volhynia.

In Volhynia as in other southeastern regions, Polish-Russian magnates often gave their Jewish lessees, along with a lease, income in cash and the power of administration over their entire province, including the shtetls. These lessees would rule over the territory of the landowner and the accompanying farmers.

It is important to keep this in mind, for Luboml found itself among the places where these processes were taking place, and it could not remain untouched by them. We saw earlier that Luboml Jews had become lessors, and later we find them again as lessees—on quite a large scale.

We know of a Jew from Luboml who was a lessee on a large scale in the first half of the 17th century. His name was Shmuel Aronovitch and he was a whisky wholesaler who held the lease for other local revenue. In 1611, a royal decree extended his license for 20 years.[19]

But it was not just a question of leases—local or district-wide—for mills or liquor breweries located beyond the borders of the towns. During that time there was a great increase in Jewish village settlement on the outskirts of town, but most Jews still lived in the town, and for those who could not start a business the major problem was getting a job.

And precisely in this area, Jews met with great difficulties. As in Poland in general, in the eastern provinces Jewish artisans suffered attacks and persecution on the part of both the law and Christian artisans.

But this occurred mainly in larger cities. In the small towns of Volhynia—and Luboml could be considered such—Jews generally had the right to take up various crafts and in many instances were allowed to join the craft guilds.[20]

A number of Luboml's Jews were then engaged in business in or outside of town, and many of them dealt in leather, grain, cattle, and textiles—as was the case with many Jews in the Chelm-Belz district.

When we speak of trade in those areas, it is pertinent to recall the opinion of historians regarding fundamental differences between the economic structure of Jewish life in Poland (Greater and Lesser Poland, as well as Mazowie) and of Jewish life in Volhynia, Belorussia, and Lithuania.

From court proceeding we see that while Jews in the first group were generally mentioned in connection with lending activities, Jews in the second group primarily were associated with business transactions. In fact, the bankers of those areas often were known as significant merchants.

The heyday of Jewish life in Luboml was also the shining era of the local rabbinate. For 50 to 60 years—from the last quarter of the 16th century to the middle of the second quarter of the 17th century—the seat of the Luboml rabbinate was graced by rabbis considered to be among the most brilliant in their generation. A number of them also operated yeshivas in Luboml. Students from afar would come to learn Torah from them; more will be said about them later.

The Chmielnicki Massacre

Over several generations, the Jewish community continued to grow, expand, and establish solid roots. The Jews of Luboml looked forward, with trust, to the continued development of their small community.

However, the skies over the Jews in all Volhynia suddenly became overcast. The Jewish settlements of Volhynia, Ukraine, Podolia, and Poland were set on fire. A murderous sword was lowered on their heads—Chmielnicki and his Cossack bands brought on the Jews bloody massacres. This was the worst period yet in the history of the Jewish diaspora. The mass murders and destruction of 1648 and 1649 had begun.

The Chmielnicki bands passed like a storm through the Jewish towns and settlements, burning, raping, and murdering. In countless Jewish settlements not a single soul remained alive. The few Jewish communities not destroyed by the Ukrainian murderers could thank only pure chance, because it was only a lucky accident that their communities remained intact. The Jews of Luboml did not have such luck.

The terrible disaster happened in a year for which the Jewish masses had great hopes—the year 1648.

The religious Jewish masses—and who among the Jews was not religious?—believed that in 1648 salvation would come to them. For years, the Jews had discussed among themselves the prophecy in the holy book, the Zohar, that in this year, calculated from the numerical equivalent of the [Hebrew] letters representing 1648, the Jews would be liberated from their afflictions and "each man will dwell on his land."

The fact that the year believed to be the year of salvation was instead the year of disaster caused even more confusion and despair in Jewish hearts.

There is a difference of opinion as to how many Jews perished in the Chmielnicki slaughters—not only among historians but also among eyewitnesses.

In one lamentation about the "fateful year of 1648," there is talk of the destruction of 300 Jewish communities. In *Yaven Metzula*—one of the basic books about this period—it is stated that 700 Jewish communities were destroyed. The writer of *Tza'ar Bat Rabim* states the number as 744. Reb Mordche of Krezmir estimates the number of dead at 120,000 souls, *Megillat Eifa* puts the number at "a few thousands," and *Tit HaYavan* [by Shmuel Faibisz, son of R. Natan Faitl] gives yet another number of dead.

In reference to the destruction of the Jews from Volhynia, the Russian writer Wladimirek Badanow states that from 1649 to 1652, during the period of the Chmielnicki uprising, about 90 percent of the local Jewry was killed, among them the residents of Luboml.

In almost all sources where the events of 1648 and 1649 are discussed, Luboml is referred to as one of the Jewish communities that perished. In other contemporary writings, the town of Luboml is not mentioned by name, but from writings describing the unfortunate period it is clear that Luboml, too, was a victim of the Chmielnicki murders.

In *Tzuk Ha-Itim* by Meyer Szeberszin, Luboml is not specifically mentioned. The author talks about Kremenitz, Lutsk, Ludmir, Dubno, and Belz. Yet, at the same time, he mentions that "in northern Chelm and the entire region Jews were killed."

It is clear that "northern Chelm and the entire region" includes Luboml, which throughout its

Text from *Questions and Answers* by Gershoni, vol. I, compiled by R. Gershon Ashkenazi, and printed in Frankfurt am Main, 1699.

history was connected with the region of Chelm.[21]

In Nathan Hanover's *Yaven Metzula*, it is clearly stated that "in the land of Volhynia, in the community of Ludmir, Lubemla (Luboml), Lutsk, Kremenitz, and surrounding communities, the [Cossacks] mass-murdered thousands of Jews."[22]

And in *Tit HaYavan* [by Faibisz, son of Rabbi Faitl], Luboml is specifically mentioned and the number of dead in the town is stated: ". . . and from there he went to Lubemila (Luboml), and there, out of 600 homeowners, almost all were murdered."[23]

Shmuel Faibisz was the son of a contemporary of the fatal events in 1648 and 1649; yet it can be accepted that his accounting of 600 dead is based on assumption rather than actual statistics. However, the figure can provide us with an approximate number of Jews in Luboml in this period. Here another difficulty presents itself: the author uses in his "statistics" an abbreviation that has to be deciphered.

The usual and accepted translation of *B"B* is *ba'ale batim*—homeowners. We noted that the historians who touch upon this specific portion of Jewish history interpret the aforementioned abbreviation in the same way. However, we are having difficulties accepting this as fact.

If we accept the preceding presentation, then we have an exaggerated number of Jews living in Luboml in that period. The word "homeowner" refers to a head of a family, and considering that a Jewish family in that period consisted, on average, of four-five members, including families without children, the Jewish community of Luboml during the period of 1648–49 would have had about 2,400–3,000 Jews in total—a highly exaggerated figure.

Our translation of the above-mentioned abbreviation *B"B* is not "homeowners" but benei berit—"Sons-of-the-covenant," or souls, and this is more likely the real number of Jewish inhabitants of Luboml in those years.

The names of those killed in 1648 and 1649 in Luboml—and of those killed in the next few dozen years—are not known. There is one exception, but he was killed in Tolchin, not Luboml. His name was Moyshe Ber Shmuel, and he was the sexton [shamos] in Luboml. He was called Ber Mirwar.

The two witnesses were also from Luboml: Yehuda Leyb and Temerl, daughter of Aron. This was reported in the book *Avodat HaGershoni* by R. Gershon Ashkenazi (Frankfurt am Main, 1699).

From various descriptions of the fatal years of 1648 and 1649, reported by second-generation survivors, we learn indirectly about the position occupied by Luboml's Jewish community in the broad spectrum of the surrounding Jewish life.

In the previous citation from *Yaven Metzula*, Luboml is mentioned together with the large communities of Ludmir, Lutsk, and Kremenitz, and is encompassed in "the surrounding communities."

From this, as well as from other materials, we can deduce that before the Chmielnicki massacre, at the end of the first half of the 17th century, Luboml had an important Jewish community, and occupied a visible position in the inner Jewish life of the surrounding region.

★

Such total destruction as the Chmielnicki murderers executed in Luboml must have contributed to the complete cessation of development of the Jewish community. There remained no Jewish settlement to speak of—and who would begin to rebuild a Jewish life?

If, by a miracle, some Jewish families did remain in Luboml, they were not capable of executing the task.

Maybe the Jews from the surrounding area? But they too were victims of the Chmielnicki murderers. However, Jewish history proceeds without logic.

Immediately following the Chmielnicki pogroms, Jews began to rebuild the settlement. Jews came from the vast, surrounding forests where they had been hiding from the massacres. It is possible that many refugees who—as is usual in such terrible times—ran where their eyes took them, remained in their newfound homes after the pogroms ceased.

One thing is sure: the old Jewish inhabitants of Luboml were annihilated and the new Jewish settlement began with completely new elements.

It is obvious the Jewish community in the town did not form in one or two years, but the rate of revival was much faster than one might expect.

This is not only attributable to the almost mystical vitality of the Jewish people in times of great danger. A major role was played in this case by the specific, objective conditions.

During this period, Jewish economic interests were bound to the landowners and dukes, as well as to other neighboring nobility. But the economic interests of the latter were also dependent on the dynamic middleman position of the Jew, on his trade and leasing of land.

The noblemen were vitally interested in having others rent their forests, haul their wood, fish in their lakes, use their mills, distill their liquor, manage their estates, and collect their debts for them; and the Jews were best suited for these tasks. Because of this, the nobility and magnates did everything within their power to attract the Jews to come back to the destroyed settlements and rebuild them.

This is how we can explain the quick rebuilding of the Jewish settlement in Luboml. We can see that this is how it happened, because already in 1671, King Michal Wishnovietzky renewed all previous privileges of the Luboml Jews. Had the Jewish community in Luboml been half destroyed and empty, and had it represented a small village-type settlement, then the Polish king would not have issued new statutes for city privileges that the Jews previously had.[24]

And so, less than 20 years after the suppression of the Chmielnicki uprising in 1652, a Jewish community in Luboml was functioning again, and, it appears, was active and reasonably well off.

That the Jewish community in Luboml quickly rebuilt itself to the status it had held until 1648–49, and that the community was not composed of poor Jews, can be seen clearly from a document four years older than the 1671 decree of King Wishnovietzky.

In the protocols of the Council of the Four Lands for 1667, there is a listing of the per capita taxes for that year. The listing is by district, but larger towns are mentioned separately—and among them is Luboml, only 15 years after the suppression of the Chmielnicki uprising.

To get a clear picture of the inter-Jewish position of Luboml, it is necessary to compare some of the per capita figures in the previously mentioned protocols.

The tax for Luboml was set at the sum of 8,100 gulden; for the town of Posen (Poznan) 1,600; for Przemysl 7,220; for Tiktin 1,520; and for the whole Zusmir district, 8,460. Belz had a similar tax to Luboml's—8,460 gulden.[25]

This indicates a quick economic recovery for the Jews of Luboml as well as Luboml's renewed status in the district soon after the Chmielnicki destruction.

At approximately the same time there is further evidence of Luboml's speedy recovery: The construction of the famous Great Synagogue.

This synagogue was one of the oldest in Poland. It was famous for its architectural design and its artistic interior, especially the Holy Ark. It belonged to the category of "fortified synagogues," which served also for defensive purposes.

There were many such fortress synagogues, especially in eastern areas of the Polish kingdom.

The building of synagogues of this type—fortified against enemy attack—was ordered by the government. During times when the government was not sufficiently developed to protect all its citizens, a number of cities, states, and settlements in strategic areas became fortified defense positions.

If a synagogue was built in an already fortified city, it did not have to double as a fortress in times of trouble. These synagogues were protected by the whole defensive system of the town, in which Jews also played a part.

But the law to build fortified synagogues did apply to areas outside the city's system of defenses.

It cost much more to build this sort of fortified synagogue than to build a regular one. For that reason, small, poor communities built their prayer-houses near the border of a fortified city. But wealthier and more populous communities were more likely to choose the option of building fortress synagogues. In many places the walls were set into strong escarpments and the outside was surrounded with a protective gallery in which there were holes for shooting.

When King Zygmunt III gave the community in Lutsk permission to build a new synagogue

(May 5, 1626), he set the following conditions: "that the Jews . . . the Rabbanites . . . should set aside on the roof certain prepared positions on which to place weapons [in order] to participate in defense."

The greatest number of such fortified synagogues were built in the second half of the 17th century. Among these was the synagogue in Luboml.[26]

★

And so the heyday of the Luboml community, interrupted during the Chmielnicki massacres, resumed relatively quickly and lasted through the 17th century and most of the 18th.

As has already been pointed out, Luboml was always a part of the Chelm-Belz district. A series of documents shows that for about 100 years, 1664–1754, this area was often called the Nine Towns. Included in the district were Chelm, Belz, the Zamoiski holdings, and a number of settlements in the Lublin vicinity. For tax purposes, the Zamoiski holdings were generally not included.

The larger communities of the Chelm-Belz district in 1717 were Luboml, Chelm, Belz, Oleshitz, Shiniave, Varsh (Sokol), and Tishvitz. When we add Zamosc, a chapter unto itself, the total is nine, which is why the area was called the Nine Towns.

The Jews of Luboml were, for most of their history, more connected with Jews of the west than the east, more with Lublin than with Kovel, Lutsk, or Ludmir. In the ledger of the Lublin Hevra Kadisha (Burial Society) from 1685, there is an entry for expenses for "guests from Luboml."[27] Also, rabbinical contacts and family relationships were greater with Lublin than with neighboring communities east of Luboml.

In 1721, the per capita tax for Luboml was 833 gulden. In 1729 it was reduced to 544 gulden, for in that year Luboml was struck by a terrible fire that destroyed a large part of the town. Here we note the strange fact that among the few remaining buildings were the Great Synagogue, the Catholic church, and the Greek Orthodox church.

From the list of the victims of the fire we see that in addition to shopkeepers, the city's Jews included tailors, glaziers, watchmakers, and barbers.

In 1762, a dispute broke out between a Jew from Luboml and the Chelm-Belz council, revealing that the city then boasted some quite well-off householders.

The Jew's name was Reb Dovid son of Efrayim (Fraimovitch), and he, together with Berk, son of Isaac from Chelm, and Reb Isaac, son of Yosef from Belz, were seeking 6,024 gulden from the council.[28] If Reb Dovid son of Efrayim received only a third for his portion, that was considered a fine sum for those times.

By the way, this fellow was a great entrepreneur, associating with nobles with whom he had various dealings. As previously mentioned, in 1765 he was the representative from Luboml to the Chelm-Belz council.

Though the Luboml community quickly recovered from the massacres of 1648–49 and regained its economic and Jewish position, the Chmielnicki massacres certainly had a negative effect on the growth of Jewish population. In 1765, almost 120 years after 1648–49, 850 people lived in the town, somewhat fewer than before. In the surrounding villages there were 476 Jews.[29]

The Ledger (Pinkas)

At the beginning of the 1720s, an association in Luboml began to keep a ledger (pinkas) in which events in the life of the association were recorded. Understandably, these events were connected with the general Jewish life and no less with events in the Christian environment. For this reason, such ledgers are primary source material for Jewish history.

This ledger encompassed more than 200 years of Jewish life in Luboml (1720–1927), with several interruptions, either because during those years records were not kept, or because they were lost. These intervals were 1801–1802 and 1861–1896.

In the inventory of Hebrew documents found in the National Library of Hebrew University in Jerusalem, archivist Yisoschor Yoel mentioned the Luboml Ledger [which had been borrowed and brought to Israel for study in the 1930s]. He called it the "Registry of the Tailor's Association," but historian Israel Halperin later correctly pointed out Yoel's mistake—the ledger belonged not only to tailors, but also to other craftsmen: butchers, furriers, goldsmiths, felshers (barber-cum-apothecary), jewelers, and porgers [of meat, to make it kosher].[30]

Later, to our great sorrow, the ledger was returned to Luboml without the library in Israel having made a photocopy. Just a few pages were copied by Halperin and we present the Hebrew text separately [in translation here].

This ledger was very carefully guarded by the association. Proof comes from a regulation of 1780:

> The association agrees that the book be cared for under the protection of an appointed trustee, and he is forbidden to transfer it or other documents to anyone else other than the head of the Rabbinical Council, or to the association as a whole, when it meets in full session.

To our great regret and our even greater amazement, the library of the Hebrew University had less understanding of the historical value of this document than did the simple workmen of 200 years ago.

We do not know when or how the Luboml Ledger came to the Jerusalem library. From the aforementioned inventory we know it was there in 1934. In response to this editor's question, the management of the library said that at the request of the Luboml community, the library had sent back the ledger in 1936. In that year, Hitlerism already was rising rapidly and times were already dangerous—and our National Library in Jerusalem did not have the simple thought that before sending the pinkas back to Europe they ought to make a copy. The ledger was destroyed along with the entire community of Luboml.

It is good that Israel Halperin managed to save at least a few pages by publishing a few of its regulations, which we present here in a free translation into Yiddish [here in English]. With our added punctuation and explanations in parentheses, they read as follows:

A. (approximately 1720)

It is strictly forbidden to encroach on a fellow member's work. When one person has started a job for a Jewish ba'al-bait [householder]—or for a non-Jew—it is forbidden for someone else to take it over.

Also, if a servant of one of the tailors leaves a job in the middle, it is forbidden for another to hire the servant. It is also forbidden for an apprentice to engage in tailoring before he has been accepted into the association.

If someone from the association goes to buy a cow from a non-Jew, a second person cannot buy that cow. And, also, if someone is standing near the cow (with the intention of buying it), it is forbidden for there to be a group of more than two. Also, if someone wants to take meat to a non-Jew, a second person cannot follow him with meat.

Someone accepted to the association does not have voting rights for three years. However, he must pay initiation fees of not less than 12 gulden.

B. (Undated)

When someone whose father or father-in-law is already a member of the association becomes a member, he will pay not less than 12, but no more than 15 gulden. Anyone coming into the association from the outside will be charged as the association sees fit, in coordination with the opinion of the rabbis.

Page from Luboml Workers' Ledger (Pinkas).

A craftsman may not keep an apprentice for more than three years after his marriage, at which time he becomes a full-fledged member of the guild.

Apprentices to tailors, butchers, furriers, goldsmiths, doctors, porgers, and jewelers must pay two gulden per year.

Tailors shall not do the work of furriers, but they can share the work together. The tailor and the furrier, instead of that garment, which the tailor shall sew at a distance of two viorsts from our communities and vice versa . . . [sic].[31-32]

C. (1757)

[These are supplements to the rules and are found on page 28 of the ledger:]

1. Those who work for Poles may not work for Jews. And one shall not keep a worker to work for Poles and shall even send him two viorsts away from the town.

2. A worker may not work independently (for Jews or Poles) until he gets married and comes before the association and it makes its decision about him, as it sees fit. Then he can work wherever he wants.

3. The first year after becoming a member, he may not have a helper. After that, he may be just like all the other members.

4. Tailors shall not do the furriers' work, and vice versa, even accidentally and not even in towns two viorsts from one another.

5. Also, a furrier's worker may not do independent work until he marries, comes before the association and has the decision made about him, as previously mentioned.

Whoever disobeys these rules shall be fined in the amount of three yashni [a certain coin] at the synagogue, besides the shame and disgrace before the entire community.

Page from the Luboml Workers' Ledger.

These are the declarations of the prominent and wealthy men, with the concurrence of the head of the rabbinical court, on this fifth day of Chol Hamoed Pesach, 1757.

D. (1766)

The entire burial society of the tailors' guild has adopted a rule forbidding any member from enrolling his son, son-in-law, or any other craftsman, from the year 1766 until 1790.

E. (1791)

With God's help, and may He make his journey pleasant and allow him to support himself by the work of his own hands—R. Asher Zelig, son of Eliezer, who is a goldsmith and whose father is a member of our guild, has petitioned us, the tailors and butcher's guild, to accept him into our guild so he can be one of us. And when we saw merit in his request, we agreed unanimously to accept him into our guild and requested that he pay 30 gulden as an initiation fee.

F. (1792)

May this be recorded for posterity and be a reminder as something to observe and never to violate: It once happened that a householder troubled a craftsman to sew fine garments for his son to wear as the groom, and another craftsman bid for the chance to sew the clothes, and that is already trespassing, which the holy Torah has warned us against.

And so we all got together to forge a compromise between the two craftsmen and the house-

holder—and the workmen and the householder were fined. That is, the householder must pay a 10 gulden fine, for he caused him to lose a day's wages, and the craftsman must pay a 10 gulden fine, for he caused him to lose a day's wages, and [both] the craftsmen must pay a 10 gulden fine because this took place between them.

And from now on if something like this happens, we will punish him even more than this, as the association will decide. And we pass this with all gravity and severity, not jokingly at all, today, the first day of the week, 22 days in the month of Shvat, 1791.

G. (1797)

We also have decided that none of us shall take another man's worker until the master and the worker shall come before the association and present their cases to the association, and as the association decides, so shall they act. And if one party does not

Page from the Luboml Workers' Ledger.

Page from the Luboml Workers' Ledger.

agree, he shall be punished as the association shall decide, and the complaints shall be brought before the association's elders.

The Period of Decline

The heyday of the Luboml community, a period that began during the second half of the 16th century, lasted about 200–225 years. Keeping in mind that the periodization of history is generally artificial, we reckon the beginning of the decline of Jewish life in Luboml from the 1760s or 1770s.

If we want to connect the period of decline with an important event in the general history of Polish Jewry, we must mention the dissolution of the Council of the Four Lands.

That great administrative institution, which played a fundamental role in the lives of the Jews in Poland and Lithuania, was liquidated by the Polish Sejm in 1767. At approximately that time there are signs of decline in the Luboml community, both in internal affairs and in its position relative to surrounding communities.

An undisputed sign of the importance of a Jewish community in those times was the status of its rabbinate—but in the second half of the 18th century (and even a bit earlier) there were no longer any rabbinical luminaries shining in the heavens above Luboml as in previous times. The days when world-renowned geniuses occupied the rabbinical authority in Luboml were over.

The decline of Luboml's Jewish community is connected with one of the most decisive events in Polish history—the division of the Kingdom of Poland among Russia, Prussia, and Austria, especially the last two partitions in 1793 and 1795, when Volhynia was torn away from Poland and annexed to the kingdom of the tsar.

It is no coincidence that Luboml's prime was connected with the Polish-Lithuanian unification of 1569, the Lublin Union, and that Luboml's decline was connected with the partition of Poland. The Chelm-Belz district in which Luboml was found was connected, both Jewishly and economically, more to areas to the west of it in Poland than to places to the east in Volhynia.

The detachment of Volhynia from the Polish kingdom at first brought economic hardships to the Russian-annexed territories. It took a while for Volhynia to adapt to the new administrative directives and the new economic structure. The negative economic effects were felt longer and more severely in the district which was on the border of Poland and Volhynia—and Luboml shared this fate.

Another important event connected primarily with the history of Jews in Volhynia must be taken into account in order to understand the decline of the Luboml community.

The effects of this event can be seen in the following statistics:

In 1790 there were 31,027 Jews living in 422 communities in Volhynia. In 1849 the number of Jews was 174,457 in 141 communities. In 1897 there were 397,722 Jews in 133 places.

When those dry numbers are analyzed, the following becomes apparent:

From 1790 to 1849—a period of about 60 years—the number of Jews in Volhynia increased approximately sixfold, but there were only one-third as many Jewish communities. If the proportion of people to settlements in 1849 had been the same as in 1790, there would have been 2,500 communities.

The same trend is evident in 1897. From 1849 to 1897—a mere 50 years—the number of Jews in Volhynia increased two and one-half times, while the number of communities not only did not grow, but actually decreased.

This trend is most impressive when we consider the statistics for the entire century, 1790 to 1897.

In that period, the number of Jews in Volhynia rose from 31,027 to 397,722—a thirteenfold increase. At the same time, the number of settlements decreased from 422 to 133, a drop of more than two-thirds.

These figures point to a tremendously important event in the history of the Jews in Volhynia:

From the end of the 18th century, with the partition of Poland, a great consolidation of Jewish communities in Poland began. Due to these conditions, an internal migration took place, reducing the diffusion and increasing the concentration of Jewish communities in Volhynia. On account of this consolidation, some communities gained population and others lost. Luboml was one of the losers.

בית ישראל דד' ארצות
ה'תכ"ז – ה'תקכ"ד
(1764 - 1667)

Map of Jewish communities in the Four Lands. Luboml is located between Kovel and Chelm.

Luboml, once referred to as a large city, was reduced in the second half of the 19th century to the point where great rabbis and learned men had not even heard of it.

The growth of Luboml's Jewish population in the 18th century was very slow.

In 1847, there were 2,130 Jews in Luboml. In 1881, a fire broke out and many of the town's 450 houses were destroyed.

Luboml did not suffer from the pogroms of the 1880s, as most of Volhynia was untouched by them. From a list of pogroms in those years we see that while there were five in all of Volhynia, the Kiev district had 63, Poltava 22, and Kherson 52.[33]

In addition, Volhynia was spared for the most part from the 1905 pogroms, as can be seen from another table: While there were 700 victims of pogroms in Volhynia, in Podolia there were

19,000, in Kiev 32,000, in Poltava 14,000, and so on.[34]

The 1897 census shows the number of Jews in town as 3,297 out of a total population of 4,470.[35]

Though the heyday was long gone, Jewish life in Luboml was intense. Of central importance was the study of Torah. In 1897 there were not fewer than 17 cheders teaching 370 children.

In 1898, a Talmud Torah was established with 60 students.

We learn from Luboml resident D. Finkelshteyn, in a report to the Hebrew newspaper *HaMelitz* in 1897, that, with the permission of the government, a Talmud Torah was established. He tells how money was collected for the cause and the institution established.[36]

A year later, the same correspondent writes to the same newspaper that the school is doing well. This time he tells how the Talmud Torah was set up through the intervention of Moyshe Afeldman, a wealthy man of Luboml who also saw to it that children had clothes and shoes.

The same letter reveals that the town's official government rabbi at that time was Hillel Boguslovksy and that in the Talmud Torah he taught "language and literature," meaning Russian and other studies.[37]

Luboml, like most towns in Volhynia, was Chasidic through and through. Chasidic shtiblach [small houses of worship] dominated Jewish life. The winds of Enlightenment were almost nonexistent until the First World War.

If anyone in town was a bit of a maskil [enlightened person], he had to hide from the light of day. If he wanted to read a Hebrew newspaper, he had to hide it. It was not even evident that nearby, in Kremenitz, the "rebbe" and guiding light of the enlightenment in Russia, Yitshak Ber Levinson, lived and disseminated his teachings. The Stepenyer, Kotsker, and Rizhiner (Chasidim) completely obscured his light.

This may be why Luboml is hardly mentioned in the Hebrew press, which began activity in the 1850s.

We have located only five reports from Luboml—four in *HaMelitz* and one in *HaTsefirah*. Two from *HaMelitz* already have been mentioned. Two other entries were from H.

Maidansky[38] and Ben-Tsiyon Datil.[39]

The first tells a story of someone with one eye being taken into the army, thereby warning the Jews not to mutilate themselves in order to get out of military service. The other is about a convert to Judaism, a stranger in town, who was arrested and gave the name Michal ben Shimon Topolye, born in Opalin.

It is perhaps worthwhile mentioning here that the writer of the other two letters in *Ha-Melitz*, D. Finkelshteyn, at some point ran away from our town on account of the strict observance of his grandfather, R. Arye Leyb Finkelshteyn.

But it is important to bring out the fact that, notwithstanding the strict fanaticism of the town's leaders, a positive attitude developed regarding activities on behalf of Palestine. This cannot be said of hundreds of towns in Poland where, under the impact of the rebbes and rabbis who said that one must not "hurry the End" (bring the Messiah), every effort for Eretz Yisroel was made much more difficult.

In Luboml, not only was there no hindrance to work on behalf of Palestine but every shtibl and bet midrash contributed money to the cause. We can see from this that it was not just the work of a few but of the majority in town. This would not have been possible without the consent of the local rabbis and rebbes.

In a 1909 financial report of the society to help Jews settle in Syria and Eretz Yisroel, contributions from Luboml are mentioned and there is a list of people who helped the effort and made contributions:[40] M. Afeldman, Yosef Afeldman, Kolk, Yitshak Rozenblit, Zev Afeldman, M. Fein, M. Baretzki, H. Baran, M. Eizenberg, Yakov Yeshayan Ehrlich, Leybl Rozin, Yosef-Chaim Zin, Shmuel Gelbardt, Shloyme Samet, Pinchas Kroyt, Chayim Kroyt, Fishel Listhoys, Chayim-Tsvi Veytinfeld, Moyshe Gelman, Yisroel Rotenshteyn, Zev Shteynberg, Hersh Gelbord, Yosef Bialer, Moyshe-Nuta Gortenshteyn, Abba Klig, Moyshe Kroyt.

This activity took place in the Rizhiner synagogue, the Talmud Torah minyan, the Trisker Shul, the Great Synagogue, the Bet Midrash, and the Kotsker Shtibl.

That list has more "activists" than contribu-

tors. But there are other lists—and those are much longer—of contributors.

From 1911, the list is as follows:[40a]

In the synagogue of the Trisker Chasidim through M. Afeldman, contributions were made by: Leyb Rosin, Chayim-Tsvi Veytinfeld, Dovid Veyner, Shloyme Samet, Shmuel Gelbardt, Yosef-Chaim Zin, Pinchas Kroyt, Chayim Kroyt, Zalman Rotenstreich, Yudel Zwick, Eliyohu Rozensweig, Dovid Kramer, Shmuel Baran, Yisroel Rotenstreich, Fishel Listhoys, Moyshe Gelman, Kalman Kopelzon, Netanel Roinstreich, Mordche Schwartzburg, Tsvi Ehrlich, Shmeul-Leib Haberman, Zev Shteynberg, Yudel Patrushke, Shloyme Rayz, Motl Zechshteyn, Chayim-Meyer Shvarts, Yosef Green, Chayim Tsvi Blumen (SH"B), Chayim Sokolovsky, Henech Varshniter, Avrom Yitshak Hornshteyn, Mordche Dubetski, Chayim Tsvi Hoyrental, Hersh Gelbord, Ben-Tsiyon Hirschenhorn, Shmuel Ginzburg, Yakov Perlmuter.

In the minyan of the Talmud Torah, Mendl Frechter got contributions from: Moyshe Kroyt, Levi Gelbord, Mendl Eizenberg, Chayim Baran, Kalman Kramer, Boruch Verber, Moyshe-Yitshak Kahan (Kagan?), Yisroel Eisenberg, Yakov Lakritz, Yeshayahu Haberman, Litman Berger, Yehoshua Lis, Yeshayahu Dovid Zilberblach.

Yitshak Rozenblit was the active one in the synagogue of the Kotsker Chasidim. The contributors were: Yitshak Blushteyn, Chayim Feigeles, Leyzer Kandelshteyn.

In the Rizhiner Shtibl the contributors were: Moyshe Sfard, Avrom and Gedalia Grimatlicht, Abba Klig.

In the Minyan Mitaskim the contributors were: Avrom Feiferman, Mendl Feldmus, Chayim Zimmerboim.

In the Great Synagogue: Yosef Afeldman, Yisroel Monik.

In the list for 1912, many of the same names appear. Additional names were: Moyshe Melamed, Yoel-Ber Bronshteyn, Berl Shlechter, Leybish Blumenzweig, Yudel Stanzaritzer, Yisroel Leiblau, Yisroel Natanson, Moyshe-Fishel Zapiler, Wold Konchitzky, Yakov Haksman, Moyshe-Notl Gortenshteyn, Avrom Veynshteyn, Yitshak Sheyner, Dovid Sanison, Yisroel Koltracht, Meyer Sandlshteyn, Leyb Kandelshteyn, Yakov-Dovid

Feiferman, Tsvi Lipshitz, Miriam Honiszon.

In 1913 the contributors are:[41]

In the synagogue of the Chasidim of [erased]: Leyb Rosen, Shmuel Gelbardt, M. Afeldman, Dovid Veyner, Yakov Hadsman, Chayim Kroyt, Pinchas Kroyt, Dovid Kramer, Zalman Rotenshteyn, Shloyme Samet, Fishel Listhoys, Yosef-Chaim Zin, Shmuel Baran, Moyshe Gelman, Kalman Kopelzon, Yosef-Leib Zechshtein, Moyshe Melamed, Leybish Blumenzweig, Yoel-Ber Bronshteyn, Chayim Tsvi Hoivental, Henech Varshniter, Hersh Gelbord, Chayim-Meyer Shvarts, Yakov Volk, Yakov Rosensweig, Kirsch Bleichman, Yisroel Leyb Levi, Eliezer Shofman, Shmuel-Leyb Guberman, Natanel Rosenstrach, Zev Shteynberg, Binyomen Krein, Yudel Stanzaritzer, Avrom Horenshteyn, Yosef Ginsburg, Shloyme Rayz, Chayim Sokolovsky, Moyshe Yudel Dunitz, Motl Dubetzky, Avrom Hirschenberg, Shmuel Ginzburg, Chayim Hersh Zeilingold, Tsvi Ehrlich, Motl Kailis.

In the Great Synagogue: Yudel Zweick, Wolf Kontshitzki, Yisroel Monik.

In the synagogue of the Kotsker Chasidim: Yitshak Blushteyn, Motl Blushteyn, Shimshon Shlive, Berish Shternboim, Yisroel Kaltract, Meyer Sandlshteyn, Kleiber, Yitshak Rozenblit.

In the Minyan Mitaskim: Yakov-Dovid Feiferman, Mendl Feldmus, Miriam Chinenzon.

The minyan of the Rizhiner Chasidim, through Abba Klig: Moyshe Sfard, Avrom Grimatlicht, Gedalia Grimatlicht, Eliyohu Vidra, M. N. Gortenshteyn, Asher Sfard, Yosef Notz [Gotz?], Monish Vidra, Mordche Shamash, Mordche Ehrlich, Motl Shneider, Asher Shamash, Yitshak Dovid Gelibter, Hersh Vidra, Aron Trachtenberg, Abba Grimatlicht.

In the Talmud Torah minyan, through Chayim Baran: Moyshe Draut, Mendl Eizenberg, Avrom Veynshtock, Litman Berger, Mordche Luxemburg, Moyshe Dovid Fulmer, Hersh Kornfeld, Yakov Vishnits, Yehoshua Lis, Moyshe Fishel Zapiler, Dovid Dobrovitzki, Leyzer Kaufman, Yeshayahu Huberman, Noach Terner, Netanel Weysman, Yonah Zinter, W.D. Zilberblach.

These were the contributors. But there was only one actual member registered with the society in Odessa for the years 1899–1901, Eliezer Afeldman. And in 1903 there was also only one registered member from Libivne.

In 1908, the organization listed as a member M. Kroyt; in 1909, Afeldman; and in 1909, M. Feiferman and Afeldman.[42]

Luboml–Libivne: The Town's Jewish Name

As in many towns in Poland, the Jews of this Volhynian settlement gave a Yiddish name to their home.

The official name of the town was Luboml. In olden times the town was called Lubomle, and in a document from 1562 it is called Libomla.[43] In rabbinic literature, especially in the older works, the town was mainly known as Lubomla (very often reversed as Lubelma or Lubleme). But in the language of the people it was entirely Yiddishized to Libivne.

The name Libivne was used not only during the last three or four decades of the community's existence, but for a long time before. Some 200 years ago, the name Libivne (or Libavne, Libivna) is found in a rabbinic text. In his endorsements of the books *Margaliyot HaTorah* and *Damesek Eliezer,* Aron-Yoel ben Dovid identifies himself as "head of the Rabbinical Court of Libavna." If a local rabbi already used the name Libivne in 1782, then it is clear that the local Jews used that name even before that, perhaps 250–300 years ago.

A second rabbinic text—a much later one— the *Likutei Tsvi* of Tsvi Hersh from Yanova (Pietrokov, 1909), includes an endorsement by the "Dayyan [Judge] and Moreh Tzedek [Righteous Teacher] of the Community of Libivne."

There has been at times great confusion around the name Libivne-Luboml, and at other times it is just a curiosity.

The renowned rabbi of Lemberg, R. Yosef-Shaul Natanson, in his notes on the book *Tiv Gitin,* which discusses the names of towns, wrote about Luboml that "it seems that it is today called Lublin, and I remember [!] that many old books call the city of Lublin Lubomla [Luboml]." Even a rabbi from Lemberg, which, after all, was located not all that far from Luboml, confused it with Lublin.[44]

Rabbi H. N. Dembitzer, a great expert on rabbinic genealogy, pokes fun of R. Yosef-Shaul

Natanson "for making a mistake and combining two distant places" like Lubomla [Luboml] and Lublin into one town.[45]

Yakov-Mendl Shteif, author of the *Matzevat Kodesh*, also confused Lublin with Luboml.

The confusion around Lublin-Luboml was so great that many times it was said the Bach was not the rabbi of Luboml but rather of Lublin. This had echoes even as far as Germany, and the great historian Graetz found it necessary to clarify that the Bach was never head of the rabbinical court in Lublin but rather in Luboml.

Even M. Steinschneider, the great Jewish bibliographer, who was exacting in every way, became confused about the name Luboml and in brackets put a question mark as to whether it is the same as Lublin.[46]

And even YIVO, especially careful with Jewish geographical names, in one of its publications knew nothing of the Yiddish name Libivne. There the Yiddish name is also listed as Luboml and in brackets, Lubevne.

RABBIS OF LUBOML

Who Was the First Rabbi?

If we were to divide the history of the rabbis of Luboml into periods, we would be able to connect them with only two of the three previously determined periods in the general history of the Jews of Luboml—heyday or decline. We have no information on the rabbis of the first period—at least this writer did not come across any such material.

We first come across the name of a rabbi in Luboml in the early 1550s, just as the prime of the Jewish community in Luboml began.

And what about the years before?

We know of Jews in Luboml as early as 1370, and it may be that they already were there a decade or two earlier. Is it possible that from 1370 until 1550—nearly two centuries—Luboml was without a rabbi?

As we have seen, Luboml began to develop long before its peak. We know that in its early days Luboml was considered one of the four major cities of the Chelm-Belz district. So how is it possible that Luboml's Jews would have gone for so long without a "local authority"—a rabbi?

True, we know from Jewish history that many Jewish communities for many years did not have their own rabbis, but shared one with surrounding communities. Smaller communities, which for many reasons, mostly financial, could not afford their own rabbi or the kind of rabbi they wanted, got together with other communities and engaged a common rabbi. We know of such cases from the history of the Jews in Poland, Lithuania, Germany, and other lands.

We do not know of a case where a well-developed, important Jewish community went for 200 years without having its own rabbi and instead shared with other communities one rabbinical authority.

That is what logic would dictate, but we have no evidence from history. So the names of previous rabbis of Luboml remain under the dark curtain of the last century of the Middle Ages and the beginnings of the modern era. We may write only of those Luboml rabbis for whom we have concrete sources.

Rabbi Hersh Yellen

In the well-known book *Tzemach Tzedek*, whose author, R. Menachem Mendl Krochmal, lived in the 17th century close to the time of which we speak, mention was made of the scholar R. Hersh as rabbi of Luboml. The same term is used in a later work, the *Seder HaDorot* of Yechiel Heilperin.

Using that source, bibliographer and Jewish-Polish cultural historian Chayim Doberish Friedberg writes that R. Hersh was the first rabbi in Luboml.[47] A Rabbi Hersh from Luboml is also mentioned in an official Polish document. The document is dated 1556, precisely the same period about which we speak; thus he is clearly the same Rabbi Hersh.

In that document, promulgated by King Zygmunt Augustus II, mention is made of the "Jew Hersh, known as Yellen." He is called a "doctor of the Mosaic law," as rabbis were then often known. He was given authority to deal with all religious matters for the Jews of Luboml.

This interesting and historically important document of the history of the Luboml Jews reads as follows (from a photostat of the Latin original, with a Polish introduction):[48] "In the chronology of the Luboml rabbis, R. Hersh Yellen is the first official rabbi in that town, and perhaps it is more correct to say that he is the first rabbi of whom we know."

R. Hersh was rabbi in Luboml from 1556 until approximately the beginning of the 1570s.

No books remain from the first rabbi of Luboml. Neither were his new interpretations mentioned in the books of other rabbis of the day. Nevertheless, it appears that he was one of the most prominent rabbis of his time. For example:

When the author of the *Tzemach Tzedek* writes about one of the great luminaries of his time the Maharsha (R. Shloyme Luria), and he wants to mention other great rabbis of the time, he says: "And in his day great men and men of renown disseminated Torah in Poland and Russia," and among them he puts in second place "R. Hersh, of Lubomla [Luboml]."

The Great Rabbi Avrom Pollack

From the great luminary R. Hersh begins a chain of "world-renowned men" who for 100 years graced the rabbinate in Luboml. Among them was one who was among the greatest commentators in his generation, one whose words are still adhered to today, the great genius, "the Bach," who will be dealt with in a later chapter.

The second person to assume the rabbinate in Luboml was R. Avrom Pollack. This must have been in the early 1570s. We have from the year 1577 an endorsement by him with his signature as "head of the yeshiva and the rabbinical court in Lubomla [Luboml]."

In that year he renewed the previously mentioned regulation of the Luboml kehilla, whereby Jews were not permitted to purchase houses from non-Jews in sections where Jews lived.

Here it is perhaps pertinent to point out that R. Avrom Pollack signed himself as R"M—the "Rosh Metivta" or "Head of the Yeshiva." Whether he himself established the yeshiva in the town or whether it already existed, it is important to underline the fact that a yeshiva existed in Luboml and that students undoubtedly came from other places, considering that the head of the yeshiva was recognized as one of the great rabbis of his day.

Here, moreover, mention should be made that the yeshiva existed after R. Pollack, and in the times of the Bach it drew many students. One was the future gaon [great rabbi], the Taz (Dovid Segal).

R. Avrom was a gaon, and son of a gaon. His father was R. Yakov Pollack, one of the greatest rabbis of his time, the author of *HaHilukim*, who with his acumen in the study of Torah left his stamp on all yeshivas to this day.

R. Avrom's father-in-law was also a well-known authority in his day, the Gaon R. Yitshak Bezalelsh, head of the rabbinical court of Ludmir, often cited in the Meforshim and in the Rishonim and Acharonim. (R. Yitshak was the grandfather of the Taz.)[49]

R. Avrom's first wife was probably herself a native of Luboml. After her death, when he was rabbi in Apt, R. Avrom remarried, this time to one of the daughters of the Maharshal, Sarah.[50]

This second rabbi of Luboml also left no scholarly works. R. Chaim-Natan Dembitzer nevertheless includes him among the "ten luminaries, among the noblest of all of Poland," who collectively gave their endorsement to the *Matanot Kehuna*, the well-known principal commentary on Midrash Rabbah.[51] He is also mentioned in number four of the responsa of the Bach.

R. Avrom Pollack held the post of rabbi for about eight years. After leaving Luboml, he became rabbi in Apt, where he died in 1589.[52]

A descendent of R. Avrom Pollack was the gaon and mystic Yehuda Leyb, son of Yosef of Pinsk, head of the rabbinical court in a number of communities, who at the end of his life went to Palestine and died in Jerusalem.

Pollack's name is known through his works *Kaneh Chochmah* (Frankfurt am Main, 1683) and *Da'at Chochmah Mekor Chochman Kavod Chachamin*. His works were widely disseminated during his lifetime. He is lauded in the book *Vayakhel Moshe* by the great kabbalist Moyshe ben Menachem of Prague (p. 12). In his youth he was the rabbi in Buchov, in Belorussia. In 1660, there was a terrible pogrom there, in which close to 300 Jews were killed. R. Yehuda Leyb saved himself, his wife, and his daughter. He then moved to Pinsk, where he taught much

Torah. At the end of his life, he moved to Palestine and died in Jerusalem.[53]

The Great Gaon R. Yehuda Leyb Son of Eliezer

It is not entirely clear to us what happened to the rabbinate in Luboml after R. Avrom Pollack. In the Ledger of the Council of the Four Lands there is a signature from 1597 reading "signed by Yuda, known as Leyb, son of Eliezer of Lubomla." A signature from the previous year reads "Leyb of Lubala." Yisroel Halperin conjectures that this Leyb is the Yehuda Leyb, son of Eliezer and "of Lubala" could be "of Lubomla."

It is not easy, however, to conclude from this that R. Yehuda Leyb was rabbi in Luboml. His signature lacks the usual rabbinical [title] *Hune*, *HuP'eK* or "head of the rabbinical court," although the traditional phrase "signed by" is present. "Of Lubomla" could refer to his place of origin as well as to the place where he served as rabbi.

Nevertheless, since we do not know of a rabbi in Luboml from the 1580s to the 1590s, we can perhaps accept that R. Yehuda Leyb was the local authority during that time, or for a part of it. R. Yehuda Leyb died in 1598.[53a]

The Gaon R. Moyshe Mess

Around 1596, one of the greatest commentators of his generation became the rabbi of Luboml. He is more often known by the name of his book, *Mateh* [staff of] Moshe, than by his own strange name, R. Moyshe Mess, which means "corpse."

The author of the *Mateh Moshe* was born in 1550 in Przemysl, where his father, R. Avrom, was martyred. He was one of the best-known students of the Maharshal.

At a rather early age he became the head of the rabbinical court in Belz. There was a yeshiva there, and R. Moyshe taught a great deal and raised a great number of disciples.

As can be seen in the foreword to his *Mateh Moshe*, his serene days in Belz did not last long. He moved to Ludmir [Vladimir-Volinsk], to his father-in-law, the philanthropist R. Shmuel, where he began writing. But things did not go well for him. His great aim was to have students and teach them the Torah, but he could not attain this in Ludmir. In Ludmir he also lost his only son.

He writes candidly about these things in the forward to his book *Mateh Moshe*:

I was carefree in my youth and unconcerned, peaceful at home and tranquil in my abode. I sat in God's house in the city of Belz, surrounded by many students eager to hear my voice, to hear the words of the Lord. And they were many, these sons of the Lord, learning at my side, those before me around the table, around this table before the Lord. Until trouble and suffering pursued me and drove me away from this inheritance of the Lord. And so the storms of time have tossed me and brought me to this place, Ludmir, a metropolis in Israel, the home of my father-in-law, Shmuel, a generous counsellor and benefactor, may God protect him. Here, too, I had no peace nor tranquility, for I could not fulfill my desire to disseminate Torah and glorify it... and so I decided that since I could not derive Torah from my mouth to my students, though that would be better, I would write books... and hope that those words would be as satisfying as the ones from worthy students... even though I knew that there would be those who would rise against me saying: "Moyshe, who has appointed you a judge and leader to point the way for us?" "And I would answer every one You have spoken well... Who am I, in fact, and what is there in my life that points me in the direction of this task?"

And I will be troubled and not quite sure, but my inner feelings and ideas will goad and prompt me, saying: "Wake up, sleepy one! Even if they don't listen to you, they will hear the words of your rabbi, for I have been the disciple, especially of the great rabbi, luminary of the exile, Gaon of Israel our teacher and master Shloyme Luria, who raised thousands of disciples. I dined regularly at his table, I saw and carefully watched all of his customs and his laws, and that should suffice and reassure you and be for a blessing."

R. Moyshe survived great personal tragedy. While he was writing his *Mateh Moshe* his only son died, and he ends the book with the following heart-rending words:

Blessed be my Living Refuge... who has helped me to complete this work, titled after my name but created and fashioned in honor of His Name, let my name be remembered thus, for this is my memorial and my namesake, which shall comfort me in the tragedy of having lost my son whom God took from me, and I ask of the Lord, my Refuge and Redeemer, that He comfort me and honor me with a living posterity."

From Ludmir, R. Moyshe moved to Przemysl,

where he became the local rabbinical authority. But he was not there long and in 1596 we already find him as a teacher in Luboml, as can be seen from the end of his book *Ohel Moshe*, where he writes: "And it is hereby completed in the holy community of Lubomla, this second day of Tammuz, may these words of Torah never cease."

The uneasy and unlucky rabbi continued in his post for another few years in Luboml. From there he moved to Apt, and there he served as rabbi and head of the rabbinical court for the whole Cracow district.

In the ledger of the Council of the Four Lands his signature appears three times: in 1590 on a declaration signed by "thirty pious rabbis, upholders of the world" that no rabbi should try to obtain a position by giving presents or loans; in 1597, when the previous regulation was repeated and strengthened; and in 1603, when he signs himself "Moyshe, son of the holy R. Avrom, of blessed memory."[54]

Moyshe Mess died in Apt in 1606.

Both in his own time and in later years people wondered how it was that he had acquired such an unlucky and strange same as Mess (Yiddish and Hebrew for "dead"). One theory is that he came from a long line of "Teachers of Torah" or "Upholders of the Torah" (the acronyms of which spell out "Mess"). In time the indication that this acronym was an abbreviation was dropped altogether. In encyclopedias he is listed as "Matt." And perhaps this is a reference to the closing words of his book, *Mateh Moshe*, as we saw above: "Blessed is my living rock [God] . . . who has sustained me to complete this book, which is entitled by my name."

Other rabbis did not want to refer to this frightful name. So we find that a friend of his, the well-known gaon and scholar R. Binyomen Aron Selnick, calls him "Our master and teacher Moyshe, the man who lives" [in his book *Masa'ot Binyomen*, number 46 and elsewhere], and R. Moyshe Mess's pupil, Menachem Mann, head of the rabbinical court in Vienna, also calls him "Our great teacher, Moyshe, the man who lives [in his *New Responsa of the Bach*]."

The most important book of R. Moyshe Mess was his *Mateh Moshe*, which is now a treasure. The title page says: "Little in quantity and great in quality, dealing with all necessary laws, with the study of Torah, prayer and the doing of worthy deeds, etc." First published in Cracow in 1591, it was reprinted in 1720 in Frankfurt am Main, and other editions followed. In recent years, two new editions were printed: in London, 1958, and in Brooklyn, 1964.

The author of *Klilat Yofi* says that the author of the *Mateh Moshe* was considered one of the greatest authorities on halakhic matters and many decisions dealing with practical matters rely on his work.

It is interesting to bring up at this point the following strange case:

A ruling of R. Moyshe Mess, whose father was a martyr, was used in our own times in an issue dealing with martyrs.

The *Mateh Moshe* said: "Whoever does not know for sure the day on which his father or mother died shall choose a certain day, fast, and say the mourner's prayer—this I was taught by my teacher the Maharshal of blessed memory."

The Israeli minister Dr. Yosef Burg mentioned this in one of his speeches, and many Jews orphaned during the Holocaust adopted it.

Another great book of R. Moyshe Mess is the *Ohel Moshe* on the Bible and the commentary of Rashi. His son, R. Avrom, had it printed in 1616 in Prague. A new edition was recently published in Israel.

His book *Six Hundred and Thirteen Commandments* (*Taryag Mitzvot*) was published in Cracow in 1581.

The author of *Seder HaDorot* says (on p. 237) that R. Moyshe Mess wrote two more books: *B'er HaTiv* and *B'er HaTorah*. It seems that these remained in manuscript form.

His responsa were referred to in *Mish'at Binyomen* and also in the responsa of the "Maharam of Lublin." His endorsement is also found in the *Machzik Bedek*, a portion of *Tikunei Zevach* of R. Moyshe, son of Mordche Bronschvik.[55-56]

In responsa of the Bach he is referred to as R. Moyshe of Premiszla (Przemysl).

The Great Gaon R. Shimon-Wolf Auerbach

When did this rabbi assume the post in Luboml?

We pose this question at the outset, for the

answer is more complicated than for any other rabbi in Luboml.

According to encyclopedias and rabbinical anthologies, R. Shimon-Wolf was the fourth rabbi in Luboml, following R. Moyshe Mess. We would use the same order, except that according to our calculations it has no basis, as it conflicts with other facts and data. Why?

It is clear from all available sources, among them his tombstone, that the first three rabbinical posts of R. Shimon-Wolf were Turbin, Luboml, and Lublin. The time he spent in the first two communities is unknown to us, but we do know that he was head of the rabbinical court (and head of the yeshiva?) in Lublin from 1579 until 1585.

By all accounts, since R. Shimon-Wolf was head of the rabbinical court in Luboml before he went to Lublin, his tenure in Luboml must have been prior to 1579. But if we assume the accuracy of all encyclopedias and rabbinical genealogies, it appears that R. Shimon-Wolf was rabbi in Luboml after R. Moyshe Mess.

But we are certain (from one of his own books) that R. Moyshe Mess was rabbi in Luboml from 1596 to 1597, thus R. Shimon-Wolf would have been head of the rabbinical court at the end of the 1590s, a full 20 years after he came to Lublin. But this is impossible for another reason: The rabbinate in Luboml at that time was occupied.

In short, the issue is very confused, and it seems to us that R. Shimon-Wolf was not rabbi in Luboml after R. Moyshe Mess but after R. Avrom Pollack—and he was there only for a very short time.

The rabbi and sage R. Shimon-Wolf, son of Dovid Tevli Auerbach, was one of the most esteemed rabbis of his time, as can be seen from all the important posts he later held. In one place he is referred to as nothing less than "one of the seven pillars of the world, a light to the Exile"—and this was no exaggeration, as sometimes happens when rabbinic titles are given, for among the other seven pillars we find such geniuses and Torah luminaries as the Maharshe," the Bach, and the author of *Ollelot Ephraim*, R. Shloyme Ephraim Lunshitz.[57]

Before coming to Luboml, R. Shimon-Wolf was head of the rabbinical court in Turbin, but there, too, he remained only a short while.

That R. Shimon-Wolf was one of the greats of his time can be deduced from the fact that he ran a great yeshiva in Lublin at the same time as the Maharam, who already was considered one of the greatest gaonim; he was at the same time a rosh metivta in another yeshiva, while serving as av bet din [head of the rabbinical court] in the town.

In all the talk of the Maharam being the competitor of R. Shimon-Wolf, there is no little exaggeration. True, the Maharam was not one of the easiest to be around and did not particularly suffer from modesty. He thought highly of his own genius and had sharp words even for the greatest scholars of his day and of previous eras. There are biting comments in his books directed at scholars such as the Bet Yosef, the Ramah, the Maharsha, Rashal baal HaLevushim, and the Samah. For example, in his responsa (sec. 194) the Maharam of Lublin says about the Bet Yosef, "I have not only caught him on this viewpoint, but I have stacks and stacks of opinions contrary to his and to the erroneous words he has said."

But in the beginning the Maharam did get along with R. Shimon-Wolf. They even coordinated the studies in the yeshivas so that they were both teaching the same tractate. The two sages had apparently agreed that on the basis of their simultaneous innovations a grand intellectual talmudic structure would later be built, the details of which are not known.

But this idyll did not last. The dispute—a dispute for the sake of Heaven—broke out precisely because of their simultaneous new interpretations of the same talmudic tractate.

We learn of this from the well-known Serotzker Rav, R. Yosef Levinshteyn, who was related, through his father and mother, to both the Maharam and R. Shimon-Wolf.[58]

After every session, especially when it was a difficult one and each rosh yeshiva had to resolve difficult issues, students from both yeshivas later asked one another, "How did your rabbi decide the issue?" When the answer was not identical, the students began to quarrel, each saying their rabbi had given the correct answer.

The quarrels among students obviously had to reach their rabbis. When the communal leaders saw that a simple compromise could not prevent the conflict from continually flaring up anew, they decreed that the students could not tell one another of the new interpretations of their respective rabbis. Anyone who violated the ban would be expelled from the yeshiva.

It was quiet for a short while, but not for long. The Maharam and R. Shimon-Wolf, each in his own yeshiva, had difficulty with a Tosefot (a commentary from the generation following Rashi). After a long and sharp extrapolation the Maharam cleared up the difficult issue. But R. Shimon-Wolf explained it in a completely different way: He said that there was simply a typographical error, that the letter vav had been dropped from the Tosefot, and that this explained the entire problem.

The Maharam wanted to know how R. Shimon-Wolf had interpreted the Tosefot. So he asked his students to find out from the students of R. Shimon-Wolf. But the latter said nothing, due to the ban. So once the students of the Maharam grabbed one of R. Shimon-Wolf's students, beat him up, and forced him to give his rabbi's interpretation of that difficult Tosefot.

Then the Maharam openly declared to his students that only his interpretation was the correct one. And from that a great controversy flared up between the Maharam and R. Shimon-Wolf. The community had to intervene, and when there was no longer any alternative, the community decreed as follows:

The whole controversy would be written in a letter to be sent to R. Shloyme Aboav in Amsterdam and he would decide the matter. If his decision was in favor of one of the Lublin rosh yeshivas, the other would lose the right to remain as head of the (other) yeshiva (rosh metivta.) If they both lose, then they both must leave Lublin.

Both the Maharam and R. Shimon-Wolf agreed to this and the entire city waited with great expectation for the answer from the rabbi of Amsterdam.

When the answer came from Amsterdam, the community gathered for a meeting in which both adversaries also participated. There they opened the sealed letter from R. Shloyme Aboav, on which nothing at all was written, except for the large letter vav.

It was clear that the decision was in favor of R. Shimon-Wolf.

The community decided that R. Shimon-Wolf should take the place of the Maharam and become the av bet din and the master and teacher in Lublin.

But R. Shimon-Wolf refused to accept the offer. He declared that because of such a minor issue they should not reject as great a gaon as the Maharam.

The community was not satisfied and invited the Maharsha to assume the rabbinate in Lublin; he had previously been the av bet din in Ostreve (Ostrow).

The great Maharsha accepted the offer of the Lublin community. Both the Maharam and R. Shimon-Wolf were astounded as to why the Maharsha acted the way he did. Firstly, he knew they had both been rejected by Lublin; and secondly, the importance of Ostrow as a Torah center was in those days greater than Lublin. So why did he agree to accept the rabbinical authority in a smaller place, since one should "go to a higher level of holiness and not a lower one"?

The Maharsha's action became clear the very first Saturday when he gave his first sermon.

Among other things the Maharsha said:

> I have a question for you, the leaders of Lublin, and one for myself. The question for you is: Everyone knows that the rabbinate of Ostrow is higher than that of Lublin, so why did it occur to you to ask me here to become your rabbi?
>
> This is also the question for myself, but for myself I have an answer: Even if Ostrow were many times greater than it is now, I would not have there two such outstanding masters [baale batim] as the Gaon, the Maharam and the Gaon, R. Shimon-Wolf. Your question I cannot answer.

And then he ended as follows:

> Since I have seen your desire that I should become your rabbi, I hereby exercise that authority and declare that both the Maharam and R. Shimon-Wolf should remain in Lublin and continue teaching Torah among you.

And so it was, but soon R. Shimon-Wolf received a proposal to become rabbi in another community, and the Maharam remained as av bet din in Lublin, but they did not engage a second rosh yeshiva.

After leaving Lublin, R. Shimon-Wolf became the av bet din and master and teacher in Przemysl. He remained there a long time, longer than in any of his previous or later positions.

Around 1620, he went to Posen (Poznan) and became av bet din and grand rabbi for Great Poland.[59]

Here it is interesting to mention the important entries in the Posen ledger that have a bearing on R. Shimon-Wolf and his forebears.

We find here some of the important details of R. Shimon-Wolf's life in Posen.

As we can infer from the entries in the Posen community ledger, R. Shimon-Wolf was a native of Posen. His mother, the Rebbetzin Rivke, and his brother, R. Yitshak, lived there, and it seems that his father, R. Dovid Tevli, filled a number of functions there until 1620.

At the beginning of 1628 R. Shimon-Wolf received a written invitation from the community in Vienna to assume the rabbinate there. The Posen community then improved his material conditions, and both sides signed an agreement that R. Shimon-Wolf would not leave Posen unless he was going to move to Palestine, as he had planned.

This contract, however, did not last. In the summer of 1629 R. Shimon-Wolf got another invitation for the rabbinate of Vienna, and this time he accepted.

But he was there only a short time. From there he went to Prague, where he became the master and teacher and av bet din for the whole state of Bohemia. There he came into conflict with the commentator Yom Tov about prohibitions and permissions in rabbinical law.

And he did not remain long in Prague, for he died in November 1631.

In the Posen ledger we learn that R. Shimon-Wolf, whose first wife was one of the four daughters of the Rashal, later married someone named Roza, the daughter of R. Yosef.

It is a great tragedy that such a great rabbi left no written works.

The practical effect of this is that he was virtually forgotten and his influence on the development of later rabbinic literature is almost nil. We know there were a few handwritten manuscripts left, but in time they were lost.

He is only mentioned in the books of others, or they present some of his talmudic innovations: in the *Ohr Zadikim* of Meyer Poppers; the

Responsa of the Maharam of Lublin; *Kav HaYashar*, of Tsvi Hersh Koydenover; *Ateret Z'kenim* of Menachem Mendl Auerbach, in *Lev Arye* and *Sha'ar Nefilat Ephraim*.

His concurring opinions are present in *Si'ach Yitshak*, by Yitshak son of Shmuel Halevi (Basel, 5387) *Zichron Moshe*, by Moyshe son of Zevulun Eliezer, published in Lublin (5371).

B'er Mayim Chayim, by Yakov son of Yitshak (Cracow, 5376).

Slichot Vepizmonim (Penitential Prayers and Hymns), by Eliezer Ashkenazi, Cracow (5343).

R. Shimon-Wolf was one of the "seven pillars of the world" who, in the Council of the Four Lands, gave their endorsement to the publication of the well-known book, *Yesh Nochlin*, by Avrom, son of R. Shabtai Horowitz, the father of *Shalah*.

His signature appears in 1606 on a proclamation of the Council of Four Lands for the Gromnitzer Fair.[60]

The first rabbi of Chelm, the Gaon R. Shimon Auerbach, was his uncle, a brother of his father, R. Dovid Tevli.[61]

His tombstone in the Prague cemetery reads:

A wolf was snatched away on Wednesday the 17th of Mar Heshvan, Our Master and Teacher and Head of the Rabbinical Court for all of the Bohemia District, the Pious Gaon, our great master and teacher R. Shimon-Wolf Auerbach, son of our teacher Dovid Tevel, of blessed memory.

> O cursed, barren, bitter day!
> Day when we were bereft of lights
> And the heavens covered by dark clouds.
> There will be weeping for generations
> Over our Father of the Court who has been buried in
>   the ground
> On the 17th day of a month when the moon is occluded
> They were to us like a fortress.
>
> He was Av bet din and our Master and Teacher in
>   Turbin, Lubomla, Lublin, Przemysl, Poznan, Vienna,
>   Prague, and all the surrounding areas.
> All these communities will, alas, cry with one voice
> Woe, that the crown has fallen from our brow
> A giant fish has been hooked and taken from us
> Summoned to the Yeshiva-on-High.
> A candle has gone out, the entire golden menorah of
>   Israel darkened
> And we are left with a terrifying, dark fear
> A dark, cloudy, overcast day
> Who will now show us the way

Who will give proof to the many and remove the
    barriers in the way
Who will publish his books and bring them to the light
    of day?
Put on sackcloth, mourn and eulogize him with tears
Cry long and bitterly, it will shriek in our ears.
Our weeping will be as rivers for years and years.[62]

This inscription takes up all four sides of the
tombstone. The end is not given here, and one
part in the middle has been scratched off.

The Gaon R. Yoel Sirkis-Yaffe (Bach)

The greatest rabbi Luboml ever had was R. Yoel
Sirkis, one of the most esteemed scholars and
pillars of Torah learning to grace the rabbinic
world during the last few hundred years, and
whose books still live today wherever there still
exist places where a true word of Torah can be
found.

The Gaon R. Yoel Sirkis, usually known by
the acronym of his most important work, *Bayit
Chadash*, the Bach, was born in Lublin in 1561.

His first post was in Pruszany and the second
in Lukov (Likeve).

He was already rabbi in Luboml in 1600.
From that year we already have two of his responsa
that he wrote to the Maharal of Prague about a
deserted wife.[63]

After Luboml the Bach was av bet din in
Mezhbiezh, Belz, and Shidlov. Since he already
was serving in Mezhbiezh in 1605, we can assume
that he occupied Luboml's rabbinical chair for
four to five years.[64]

The Bach was not exclusively wrapped up in
the world of Torah. He showed great interest in
Jewish life in general, and he showed great organizational ability. As soon as he came to Luboml,
he renewed the old regulation about not purchasing houses from non-Jews within the Jewish areas
of settlement, a regulation that had been strengthened previously (in 1577) by R. Avrom Pollack.[65]

The reason Bach left Luboml is related in the
following anecdote:

There was a Jewish scholar who lived in the
town who was very modest. He sat day and night
studying Torah. No one knew the extent of his
learning, as he studied only for himself.

Once he came to the Bach, handed him a
manuscript, and said with great respect: "My
teacher, these are some of my explications of the
Talmud that I jotted down from time to time
while I studied. I would very much appreciate it
if the Rebbe could please look at them and give
his opinion about them."

The Bach took the manuscript. That evening
he looked at them for a few hours and was
astounded. He saw that this modest Jew, who had
never studied formally, was really a great scholar
and expert in the "sea of the Talmud," and that
his opinions were deep and had great authority.

The Bach did not sleep at all that night. "Such
a great Jew is right here in my town and I didn't
even know it." The next morning he called a
meeting of the leaders of Luboml and said:[66]

"Let it be known that you have here in Luboml
a great scholar who surpasses me in Talmud and
halacha, and therefore I see it as my duty to
relinquish my position as rabbi, since he is more
fit to serve in that position."

And that is how the Bach left Luboml and
became rabbi in Mezhbiezh.

From 1615 until 1618 he was the av bet din in
Brisk d'Lita (Brest-Litovsk). Why did he leave
such a metropolis so quickly?

We find the answer in a story that today
sounds very strange to us, but which is characteristic for those times.

It is told that the day the Bach left Brisk, the
city notables accompanied him a considerable
distance from town. A number of times he said to
them, "Turn back," but they did not listen to him.
Then the Bach said to them, "There is a great deal
of difference between us. You are stubborn; I tell
you to turn back and you do not listen to me. Were
you to say to me, 'Please turn back' I would do so
right away."

This gives us a hint as to the reason why the
Bach had to leave Brisk: A few zealous baalebatim
came out against his staying in Brisk because of
his failure to continue studying late at night (they
saw no candle in his window after midnight).[67]
Incidentally, many rabbis were fired by their
communities for this reason.

These stories about one of the great scholars
sound very strange to us, but even if they are
legends they are characteristic of the demands

placed by the Jews of those times upon their spiritual leaders.

After leaving Brisk in Lithuania, the Bach was av bet din and teacher in the great community of Cracow, where he lived from 1618 until his death in 1641.[68]

Students streamed to his yeshiva in Cracow from all over Poland and Lithuania, and many later became great rabbis and scholars.

The Bach not only led the yeshiva in Cracow. In other places where he served, he either established yeshivas or enlarged those already existing, among them Luboml's.

The following story is connected with the Bach's yeshiva in Luboml—and some say it was Myazovitz—and even if it is not entirely true, it is a nice story to relate in any event.

One of the Bach's best pupils was R. Dovid Segal, one of the greatest of the more recent scholars, known primarily as the Taz after his commentary *Turei Zahav*. The Bach very early on saw the scholarly tendencies of his pupil and greatly encouraged him, bringing him into his circle.

Once, when the Bach and a few of his best students sat at the Sabbath table and were talking Torah off-handedly, the young Dovid brought up the Rambam, who in his *Hilchos Sefer Torah* (Bk. 7, halacha 6) wrote, "The scribe came across a word which had ten letters, more or less."

And Dovid asked:

"Where in the Torah do we find a word that has ten letters or more?" He knew of words with a maximum of nine letters such as *lemishpachoteyhem* (Genesis 8:19) or *leyishma'elim* (Genesis 37:27).

So the Bach answered:

"Let us call Rivke and hear what she has to say."

Rivke was the Bach's daughter, very pretty and very learned in the Bible. She was 12 at the time, and when they repeated the question to her, she said:

"In the Torah itself, there are no words with ten letters. But in Prophets [Isaiah 18:21], the word *lemishpachoteyhem* is written out, fully spelled out, with the vav"—i.e., ten letters—"but this has nothing to do with the Rambam's laws

regarding the writing of a Torah scroll."

And after thinking a while, she said:

"I think I have found an answer. This law of the Rambam also applies to writing the Scroll of Esther and there (9:3) is a word with 11 letters: veha'achshedarpanim."

The Bach then stood up and said:

"My daughter, you are clever, in addition to being as beautiful as the moon."

And following this, the young Dovid said: "Perhaps it is time to 'sanctify the moon.'" (A play on words, as the same word *mekadesh* is used in reference to the wedding ceremony.)

Later that night, after the Sabbath, Rivke became engaged to Dovid and the Taz in fact later became the son-in-law of the Bach.[69]

While in Cracow, the great Bach had a dispute with a small, local cantor. How is it that a world-famous rabbi has a dispute with a minor local cantor? It happened like this.

In the bet midrash where the Bach prayed, there was a cantor who said he knew Talmud better than the rabbi. He would think up stupid questions and come to the Bach in front of everybody to try to show off or catch the rabbi.

It happened that once, while chanting from the Torah, the cantor found an error in the scroll. There was a word containing an extra letter, a yod; instead of "Yehoshua," the word was written as "Yehoshia."

The cantor said that the Torah scroll was defective, but the Bach disagreed. The cantor laughed and said they should take out another Torah scroll.

The Bach, a modest man who was very careful regarding relations among his fellow men, at that point lost control and said to the cantor:

"Fool, boor! I tell you, you don't have to take out another Torah."

The cantor answered cheekily: "You yourself are the boor!"

In response the Bach said:

"You are excommunicated, for you do not follow what your rabbi has told you. You are altogether a heretic and a scoffer at the words of our scholars."

The cantor did not give in and continued to speak insultingly to the rabbi. The rabbi then brought the issue to the Gaon R. Levi, the av bet din and teacher in Lublin, who responded, to his dismay, that the cantor was correct, even without consulting the Bach.

Then the Bach wrote a lengthy response about the entire issue showing the Lublin rabbi that he was not correct. And at the end he writes: "And from the moment your decision reached me, all of my senses have been disoriented. Alas, this mockery of Torah."[70]

The strange decision of the Lublin rabbi had a profound effect on the health of the Bach and perhaps shortened his life.

The Bach, distinguished by extraordinary sharpness and unusual expertise, was nevertheless not very strict. He would base his decisions only on a proof-text from the Mishnah or Talmud and the Rishonim. He complained against those who relied only on the *Shulchan Aruch*, and even said that a rosh yeshiva and local rabbinic authority was permitted to accept presents, something that goes against the Rambam.

The Bach gave permission for cantors to use church tunes in synagogue, as long as they were not 100 percent Christian melodies.

The Bach was not one to impose stricture upon stricture only to cover any doubt. He said that if anyone had doubts that he was doing the right thing, he might become more strict himself but not demand it of others. He wrote as follows:

> For we do not go by anything unless we find it in the Talmud and if someone in all modesty does not want to depend only upon himself, let him act exclusively for himself but not impose it upon the generations after him who will be more strict than he—but if not, let him bring clear proofs from the Talmud.

It is interesting that even then the Bach was in favor of teaching the *Neviyim U'Ketuvim* (Prophets and Writings) to small children. This was against the opinion of Rashi, who said: "Torah, but not the rest."

In his book the Bach says: "Every pious man should see to it that even if he must hire someone, he should teach his child the Prophets and Writings, even though it may be difficult." And no wonder. He also said: "Teach them grammar so that they will know the roots of the holy language, past, present, future, singular and plural."

The well-known gaon R. Shabtai HaCohen, the Shach, came out against the Bach sharply. The Gaon of Vilna later supported the Bach, saying that "Mikra" meant the whole of Torah, the Prophets, and Writings.

The Bach was not only lenient in this regard. In the Cracow Talmud Torah he passed a ruling that they must teach the students the entire Tanach.

When it came to accepted customs, he could, in fact, be strict in applying the letter of law if he did not see the necessity or find a valid source for them. He did not hold with the saying that "a custom overrules a law." And so he came out against the widespread customs of breaking a glass under the marriage canopy and of men dressing up on Purim in women's clothes.

On account of his original and independent approach to a number of issues he acquired many opponents and their number increased when he came out sharply against pilpul, which was already then widespread among many scholars.

This is what he wrote about those who used the pilpul method: "Do not seek after boastful words and falsehoods . . . for they are a flirtation, merely academic language, a mere representation of things—a vanity and misfortune, they are a mistake."

In a softer vein, he writes about pilpul in the introduction to his *Bayit Chadash* (Yoreh Deah):

> I come to awaken and remind my students and children that they should not hurry to report to those who wave the sieve over the sources of halacha, and also know that even if anyone has an answer or sweet response he should not present it here, for it is not correct in its interpretation coming out of the Talmud. Our only prayer and request is that in our hearts we will know how to understand, discern, learn, and teach the true Torah so that we may keep and observe all the words of Torah with love. And if permission is granted to the head of a yeshiva to sharpen his students [their understanding] in this manner, then this way of approaching the truth should remain in that yeshiva and should be oral and never reach the printed page.

The Bach was a disciple of Kabbalah (Jewish mysticism) and spent a lot of time studying it. He said this was the "source of the halacha."

He came out against philosophy in the sharpest terms, calling it heresy. It is no accident that three rabbis from Amsterdam turned to him with the question of what they should do about a doctor who scoffed at the Talmud and considered only philosophy an important field of knowledge.[71]

Although the Bach was so anti-philosophy, he nevertheless read the *Moreh Nevuchim* (of the Rambam) and even cited it a number of times in his books. Perhaps the great name of the "Great Eagle" (that is, Rambam), influenced him in this regard.

It is interesting that the Bach, the proponent of clear thought and cold rationalization, later became involved deeply in the Chasidic world, where legends were even woven around his name. Perhaps the reason for this interesting occurrence is that the Bach had a deep interest in the Kabbalah, and even more important, for a considerable time he was the rabbinic authority in Mezhbiezh, a sanctified town to Chasidim.

With that town is connected one of the Chasidic legends about the Bach.

The legend says that once the Baal Shem Tov was in Mezhbiezh, studying with his disciples. There was a question regarding a certain prohibition. His greatest pupils, among them R. Yakov Yosef, author of *Toldot Yakov Yosef*, and R. Meyer Margaliyot, author of *Meir Netivim*, began arguing about it. They brought up the conjecture of the Bach, who had determined that at the time the prohibition was established, the rule was not followed. They also discussed the opinions of the Taz and other great commentators who sought the decision of the Bach regarding this matter.

After hearing all this the Baal Shem Tov said:

"Here, in the city of Mezhbiezh, the Bach was the rabbinic authority, and so the law is as he states, especially since we clearly know that not only was he a great scholar but also a truly pious man."

In the responsa of the Bach we find a treasure trove of material regarding the history of the Jews of his time. Since we have learned that rabbinical literature contains a wealth of historical material on Jewish life, researchers continue to draw from its bounty. Among the richest are the works of the Bach, which became sources for Ben-Tsiyon Katz, Zalman Rubshov-Shazar, Shimon Dubnow, S. A.

Horodetzki, Mordche Kossover, and others.[72]

As we say that "the apple does not fall far from the tree," so can we say that a brilliant student does not fall far from his outstanding rabbi. And his teachers and rabbis were R. Shloyme, R. Leibishes, a great and well-esteemed rabbi—the av bet din in Lublin and the author of the holy *Sheleh* was also one of his disciples; the Gaon R. Tsvi Hersh Shur (R. Hersh Alsacer), one of the best students of the Ramah; and the Gaon R. Meshulam Feibush, av bet din and teacher in Cracow before the Bach.[73]

The Bach's greatest pupils were his son-in-law R. Dovid Segal, the Taz; the Gaon R. Menachem Mendl Krochmal, the Tzemach Tzedek; the Gaon R. Gershon Ashkenazi, author of *Avodat HaGershoni*; the Gaon R. Menachem Mendl Auerbach, author of *Ateret Z'kenim*; the Gaon R. Tsvi Hersh Klausner, Av bet din in Lvov and Lublin; the Gaon R. Mendl Baas, the av bet din in Frankfurt am Main.

The Bach almost always is called R. Yoel Sirkis, though his real last name was Yaffe, since his father was R. Shmuel Yaffe and his grandfather was the well-known gaon R. Moyshe Yaffe of Cracow. Sirkis was his mother's maiden name, and it is with her name that the Bach has gone into history. The name Sirkis was spelled many ways.

His wife was named Beyle. She was R. Avrom Hertske's daugher and Hertske was the son of R. Naftali Hertz, the av bet din in Lvov. She died in 1638.[74]

The Bach had two sons and two daughters. One son, R. Yehuda Leyb, was av bet din in Chentchin and then judge in Cracow. The second son, the Gaon R. Shmuel Tsvi Hersh, was av bet din in Pinchew.[75]

The Taz, as was previously mentioned, was the husband of his eldest daughter Rivke. His second son-in-law, husband of his younger daughter Esther, was the Gaon R. Yehuda-Zelik, son of Yitshak from the well-known Frankfurt family Mazia-Ashkenazi, who was for a long time judge in Lvov and was called R. Yehuda Zeilikl. He was a great scholar, a member of the rabbinic council in Cracow, together with the Tosefot Yom Tov and the Gaon R. Yishai, son of Yosef, the Meginei Shlomo. His name often is mentioned by those other scholars and his signature also appears in the Cracow ledger. Esther died in 1648.[76]

The most well-known grandchild of the Bach was the Gaon R. Arye Yehuda Leyb, av bet din of Cracow and Brisk, author of the *Sh'agat Arye*, whose father was the Bach's son R. Shmuel, who published a number of his father's books.[77]

One of the Bach's grandchildren lived in Luboml. We know nothing about him except that his same was R. Yitshak and that he was a wealthy, pious man. The well-known R. Avrom HaMagid, author of *Magen Avraham*, was R. Yitzchak's son-in-law.[78] Another grandchild of the Bach was the Gaon R. Betsalel, author of *B'Shem Bezalel*. Soreh, mother of R. Simcha Bunem, the disciple of the "Holy Jew," was R. Betsalel's daughter.[79]

A great-grandchild of the Bach was the Gaon R. Yoel of Brisk, the av bet din in Buchov. He was the son of the Sh'agat Arye.[80]

One of the descendents of the Bach was the rabbi Gaon R. Boruch Mandelboim (R. Boruch Turover). He was born in 1835; his father was R. Mordche Leyb, a judge.

R. Boruch was rabbi in Turov, Stolin, and Masheve. He was a well-known preacher and the right hand of the great master and teacher R. Aron of Karlin. In 1874 he moved to Jerusalem, where he led the Ohr Hadash yeshiva, a Chasidic Torah center.

In 1891, he went to Europe as an emissary. For a week he was a guest of R. Shimon-Wolf Rothschild in Frankfurt and influenced the Jewish millionaire to support various religious and philanthropic institutions in Palestine.[81] R. Boruch is author of *Noda B'She'arim* (Jerusalem, 1904) and the *Ketz Ha-Yamim*.

The most important of R. Yoel Sirkis' books was the *Bayit Chadash*, whose abbreviation was the name by which he was best known to Jews. The first edition of the book was published in Cracow, 1631.

His responsa for prohibitions and lenient judgments and his rulings on monetary matters were published first in 1697 in Frankfurt am Main; his new rulings, in Koretz in 1819. They were published again later.

His *Mashiv Nefesh*, a commentary on the Book of Ruth, came out in Lublin in 1616. He also brought out a galley proof for an edition of the

Talmud, Tosefot, and the Rosh, Warsaw, 1824.

Still in manuscript form remain the following:

A commentary on the prayerbook according to the Kabbalah; a commentary on the *Pardes Rimmonim* of R. Moyshe Cordovero; and new rulings on the Talmud and *Shulchan Aruch*.

He intended to move to Eretz Yisroel but could not carry out this plan.

The inscription on his tombstone in the cemetery in Cracow reads:

Here lies buried:

A crown of Torah. Author of the book *Bayit Chadash*.

The beginnings of his wisdom revealed themselves in the holy community Prozna

And increased in the holy community of Lukov.

The light of his learning shone on all in the holy community Lubomla.

He gave of his sweet wealth in the holy community of Mezhbiezh.

Preferred over the fountain of wisdom in the holy community in Belz,

Followed God faithfully as a pet dog in the holy community of Shidlow,

Pronounced the laws of Torah and justice in the holy city of Brisk in Lithuania,

His well-springs were widespread from the holy town of Cracow.

Shout to the very heavens, this pious and modest man, who enlightened us and

All the House of Israel is no more

And now he gives to the world of his honor, his radiance, and his brilliance

A Torah more precious than gold, than all jewels.

This treasure-house of Torah is forever closed to us . . .[82]

The Gaon Rav Moyshe

Around 1605–1606 there was a teacher in Luboml named R. Moyshe. We have neither his family name nor his father's first name. There were two rabbis in Luboml with the first name Moyshe, but we have more details about them and also know their fathers' names. We can more or less orient ourselves as to when they assumed their posts in Luboml, and about that more will be said later.

About the "plain" Moyshe we have only one source—a well-known book, *Eitan HaEzrachi*, by the Gaon R. Avrom Shrenzel Rapoport (Ostrow, 1796). There, in the portion Naso, it mentions that the author eulogized the gaon, great teacher and rabbi, Moyshe, great scholar and av bet din in

Lubomla (1617). As usual, there follow words of Torah, but not a single word about the deceased. That is all.

Since the Bach left Luboml around 1604–1605, and later a rabbi of Luboml, R. Gedalia, assumed his post in 1618, and since we know of no other rabbis between them, we can surmise that the "plain" R. Moyshe was rabbi in Luboml from approximately 1605 until his passing in 1617.

The Gaon R. Gedalia Son of R. Meyer

In 1618, the rabbinic authority was assumed by R. Gedalia. His father was the Maharam of Lublin, and though the son was not as illustrious as the father, in his time he held a rather important place in the world of Torah learning.

That this was the case, not only on account of his having an illustrious father but based on his own merit, can be seen from a book to which he gave his approval and for which the other approving party was no less than the Tosefot Yom Tov. The book was the *Nachalat Tsvi* of Tsvi Hersh Toch Firer, and his approbation is dated "Lubomla, 1618."

His approbation also appears on:

Etz Shatul of Gedalia the son of Shloyme Lifshitz, which is a commentary on the book *HaIkkarim* of R. Yosef Albo.

K'toret HaSamim of Mordche, son of Naftoli Hersh of Karmzir, and on the *Shulchan Aruch* of 1634.

The last two are not dated from Luboml.

R. Gedalia was the son-in-law of the Gaon R. Aron HaLevi, teacher and scholar in Lvov. R. Gedalia is mentioned a number of times in the responsa of the Maharam of Lublin, in the *Eitan HaEzrachi*, and in the responsa of the Bach.

R. Gedalia was a rabbi in Luboml until 1630.[83]

The Gaon R. Shmuel Ish-Hurvitz

After R. Gedalia, the rabbinical post in Luboml was occupied by the Gaon R. Shmuel Ish-Hurvitz.

His father, the Rabbi and Gaon R. Aron Meshulam-Zalman Ish-Hurvitz, was a cousin of the holy Shalah.

According to *Ateret HaLevi'im*, R. Shmuel was son of the holy Rabbi Aron Meshulam Zalman and the grandson of R. Yeshayahu Hurvitz, brother of the Shelah's grandfather, R. Shabtai. According to the genealogical book by Chayim Dov-Berish Friedberg, *Toldot Mishpachat Hurvitz*, R. Shmuel was a great-grandson of R. Aron Meshulam Zalman and a contemporary of R. Shabtai Sheftel, son of the holy Sheleh.

The Gaon R. Yehoshua, son of Yosef, author of *Meginei Shlomo*, was R. Shmuel's brother-in-law.

From 1625 until 1630, R. Shmuel was rabbi in Bubno. From 1630 on he was rabbi in Luboml until his death in 1635. His grave is located there.[84]

The Gaon R. Moyshe Katzenellenbogen

After R. Shmuel, the next rabbi in Luboml was the Gaon R. Moyshe Katzenellenbogen. His father, Rabbi Meyer, was av bet din in Brisk and son of R. Shaul Wohl. R. Moyshe's father-in-law was R. Binyomen Beinish, the parnas in Pozen, one of the leaders of the Council of the Four Lands and a son-in-law of the Maharam of Lublin. R. Binyomen Beinish's father, R. Zecharia Mendel the Elder, was brother-in-law of the Maharal of Prague.

R. Moyshe assumed the position in Luboml around 1635–1636. This was his first position, and later he became rabbi in Chelm and Mohilev.

The ledger of the Council of Four Lands for 1643 lists R. Moyshe Katzenellenbogen as one of the participants on the council.[85]

His rabbinical approbation is found in the following works: *Damesek Eliezer* of Eliezer, son of Shmuel, Lublin, 1646; *Ahavat Zion*, Lublin, 1639.

He must have been the rabbi in Luboml for a number of years.[86]

The Gaon R. Yonah Te'omim

The new av bet din of Luboml, the Gaon R. Yonah, son of Yeshayahu Te'omim, was one of the great sages of his generation. Over a period of 50 years he served as rabbi in seven or eight communities, indicating that he did not have a great deal of tranquility in his life. He found his way to Eastern Europe from Prague, and when a wave of troubles washed over the Jews he left Poland for Western Europe.

His first position was in Nemirov. From there he went to Luboml.

When did R. Yonah become rabbi in Luboml, and how long did he remain there?

From his approbation to the work of Alexander Bendet, son of R. Yosef Segal, *Avodat HaLevi* (Cracow, 1639), we see that in that year he was already in Luboml. There he signs himself "Yonah, son of Yeshayahu Te'omim of Prague, av bet din of Lubomla."

Since we know he did not remain rabbi for long in any one place, we can assume he was rabbi in Luboml for only a few years.

After Luboml he took positions in Belz, Grodno, Pinsk, Vienna, and Metz, where he became rabbi in 1660. He received an invitation while in Metz to take over the position in Posen, but declined.

The Gaon R. Yonah Te'omim, better known as the author of *Kikayon D'Yonah* ("Yonah's Gourd"), his most important book, was born in Prague in 1596.

His son, R. Yechezkel Yehoshua Feivel Te'omim-Frankel, served as rabbi in Ziltz and the Przemysl district. He is the author of *T'ka' B'Shofar* (Breslau, 1719). In that book he carries on a sharp discussion with the community of Przemysl for having dismissed him from his post. He was the son-in-law of R. Arye Leyb, av bet din in Cracow—the Grand Rabbi, R. Leyb.

His second son, the Gaon R. Yitshak Meyer Te'omim, was rabbi in Trebitch, Hamburg, Amsterdam, Zholkiev, Slutzk, Pinsk, and Przemysl.[87] He brought out an edition of the *Ein Yakov* with all the commentaries, known as the *Kutonet Ohr*.

R. Yonah's wife, Beyle, was the daughter of the Gaon R. Meyer Wohl, av bet din in Brisk of Lithuania.[88]

The signature of that rabbi of Luboml appears on: *Bet HaLevi* of R. Yeshayahu Hurvitz (Venice, 1666); *Shach, Yoreh Deah* (Cracow, 1646); and *Magid Mesharim* of Yosef Karo (Lublin, 1648).

R. Yonah Te'omim died in 1669. This is part of the inscription on his headstone:

> May God remember the soul of the pious Gaon,
> Widely known and famous
> Prolific teacher who wrote
> About the specifics of many different things,
> A godly man, Av bet din, Our Master and Teacher
> Yonah, son of our Master and Teacher Yeshayahu
>   Te'omim of Prague
> Who served more than 50 years
> In many great communities
> Such as Nemirov, Lubomla, Belz, Horodno,
> Pinsk . . .
> And when God sorely tried the people of Poland
> With catastrophes one after another
> And their world was overturned
> With confusion and harsh decrees,
> The "dove" [Yonah] flew away to Vienna,
> Where he excelled over others,
> And from there came to the community of Metz
> Where the "dove found a resting place for the sole
>   of her foot,"
> A place to find comfort after the sadness
> And tribulation he had known in Poland . . .
> From there to Posen
> From which he longed not to depart
> And there he left a legacy, his book,
> *Kikayon D'Yonah*.
> He passed away and was buried on the first day of
>   Pesach in the year 1669.[89]

The Gaon R. Moyshe Son of Yitshak

The rabbi after Yonah Te'omim was R. Moyshe son of Yitshak. His father was the parnas and a leader in Pinsk.

R. Moyshe was one of the most esteemed rabbis of his time. He was better known by the name of his book, *Mehadura Batra*, or as R. Moyshe R. Yitshak R. Bunemsh.

He also came from a distinguished family: He was son-in-law of the Maharsha, a grandson of the Rama and a disciple of the Maharam of Lublin.

In the introduction to *Mehadura Batra*, he complains that on account of "wanderings and meanderings" brought about by the terrible pogroms of 1648–49 many of his writings and innovations were lost.

His brother-in-law was the Gaon R. Yitshak Segal, av bet din in Lvov,[90] and his son-in-law was the Gaon R. Moyshe Margaliyot, av bet din in Tarnigrod.[91]

The *Mehadura Batra* was cited a number of times in the responsa of the Maharam of Lublin, in the *Masa'ot Binyomen*, in *Birkat Tov* and *Nechamot Zion*.

The approbation of R. Moyshe son of Yitshak is found in: *Siftei Cohen* on *Yoreh Deah* of Shabtai Cohen (Cracow, 1646); *Amudehah Shiv'ah,*

Betsalel son of R. Shloyme of Kobrin (Lublin, 1666); *Nechamat Zion* (Frankfurt am Main, 1652); *Nofet Zufim*, Betsalel son of R. Shloyme of Kobrin; and the siddur of the Shelah.

It is difficult to know exactly when the author of the *Mehadura Batra* became av bet din in Luboml. But it is clear that in 1646 he already was there, since the foregoing approbation to the *Siftei Cohen* is dated 1646 and Luboml is mentioned. He held the position in Luboml from the mid-1640s until 1653. After leaving Luboml he became av bet din in Lublin.

He died in Lublin in 1669.[92]

The Gaon R. Eliezer Margaliyot

In the 1660s, the position of rabbi in Luboml was held by R. Eliezer Margaliyot. In 1667 he participated in the Council of the Four Lands during the fair at Gromnitz, and from that year we have his approbation to the well-known *Safra D'Tzni'uta D'Ya'akov* (Amsterdam, 1669), where he signs himself "declared to be living and working in this place, Lubomla."[93]

R. Eliezer was the son of the Gaon R. Menachem Mendl Margaliyot, who is mentioned in the *Klilat Yofi* as "Me'or HaGolah." He is mentioned in the *Tzemach Tzedek* and regarding a deserted wife in the Tach. He was av bet din and teacher and master in Przemysl and Pinsk.

One of his sons-in-law was the gaon and mystic R. Moyshe Zev, son of the gaon and mystic R. Yehuda Yudl, av bet din of Kovel. R. Moyshe Zev was av bet din and teacher and master in Minsk and the district of Smilovitz. Later he became rabbi in Furth.[94]

R. Eliezer had seven brothers, six of whom were rabbis in various communities in Poland.

R. Eliezer's son, Rav HaGaon R. Yehuda Margaliyot, was av bet din in Potik.

A descendant of R. Eliezer's, six generations later, was the Gaon R. Moyshe Zev, av bet din in Bialystok, Tiktin and Horodno, the well-known author of *Mar'ot HaTsovaot* and *Agudat Ezov*; from the seventh generation, Rabbi Alexander Margaliyot, av bet din in Satanov; and in the eighth generation the brothers—recent commentators, authors of the *Responsa Bet Ephraim*, *Tiv Gitin*, and *Sha'are Teshuva*.[95]

The above-mentioned *Sifra D'Tzni'uta D'Ya'akov* is the work of the mystic gaon Yakov Ashkenazi, known as R. Yakov Temerelsh of Vienna.

The following is written therein about those who give their approbation: "Ornaments of their generation, all outstanding and knowledgeable in the realm of the mysteries, who lit up the earth with the glory of their wisdom."

This is evidence that R. Eliezer also dealt in Kabbalah.

The *Shem HaGedolim Hechadash* calls R. Eliezer "the great Gaon of his generation."

R. Eliezer remained rabbi in Luboml until about 1667.

Two Rabbi Yakovs

From the end of the 1660s until the mid-1680s we find two persons with the same first name, Yakov, who were rabbis in Luboml at the same time. Since their fathers' names are not always mentioned, it is difficult to say exactly which one is being discussed, therefore we have put them both into one chapter.

One is R. Yakov son of Yonah Katz. That he was the first of the two can be seen from the dating of his signatures. In paragraph 272 of the Ledger of the Council of the Four Lands for 1669, he is listed among the signatories.[96]

A few years later, in 1672, in paragraphs 325, 326, and 327, we find the signature "Yakov, son of my master and father, rabbi and teacher R. Yonah Katz of blessed memory, from Lubomle."

The doubt about his having held that position stems from the fact that his signature is not accompanied by the usual rabbinic appellations, "declared to be living and working in such-and-such a place," etc.

In any case, by the first half of the 1670s we no longer find the name of R. Yakov son of Yonah Katz, but that of R. Yakov son of Mordche. In 1674 we find one of his approbations, given in Luboml, for the book *Migdal David* by R. Eliezer Lipman of Brod.

In 1680, in the Ledger of the Council of the Four Lands, we find him listed as being in Luboml.

From the same year we have another of his consents, also from Luboml, for *Kaneh Chochmah*

V'Derech Chochmah of Yehuda Leyb, son of Yosef (Frankfurt am Oder, 1681).

In 1683 the ledger "declares Yakov Kahana of Luboml"—and this is, it seems, R. Yakov son of Mordche.[97]

Endorsements by R. Gaon Yakov son of Mordche are found on *Kaneh Chochmah V'Derech Chochmah*, Yehuda Leyb son of Yosef Pochovitzer (Hamburg, 1692); *B'er Ashak*, Yehuda Leyb son of Yosef Pochovitzer (Frankfurt am Oder, 1681); *Tikunei HaZoar*, *Divrei Chachamim*, *Kriyat Vatikin*, and *Ein Yisroel*.

R. Yakov son of Mordche was rabbi in Luboml until 1684.

The Gaon R. Yonah Halevi

After the Gaon R. Yakov son of Mordche, the rabbinical post in Luboml was occupied by Gaon R. Yonah, son of Hillel Halevi, author of the *Bet Hillel*. He also is known as the "Gaon HeHarif" ("incisive" or "sharp").

His father, Gaon R. Hillel, was av bet din in Chelm and Vilna.

R. Yonah was father-in-law of the Gaon R. Tsvi Hersh, av bet din in Shotland and the surrounding area.[98]

It is difficult to determine the exact term of his stay in Luboml.

The Gaon R. Yisroel Isser

A son of the Gaon R. Moyshe son of Yitshak, author of the *Mehadura Batra* (who himself was av bet din in Luboml)—namely, Rabbi Gaon R. Yisroel Isser—followed his father as rabbi in the town.

He considered himself one of the greatest rabbis of his generation, and it is not surprising that after leaving Luboml he became av bet din in two of the largest communities of the day, Brisk and Lublin. According to some sources, he was also rabbi in Pinsk.

R. Yisroel Isser has his approbations in the *Divrei HaBrit* of 1720 and on the *Gaon Tsvi* by Moyshe Tsvi-Hersh Heller of 1730.

R. Mordche R. Leibishes of Zholkieve, a prominent and wealthy man who was parnas of the Council of the Four Lands, worthy of both heav-

enly and earthly rewards, was his son. R. Mordche is father-in-law of the Rav Gaon R. Yitshak Katz Rapoport, av bet din, master and teacher in the Great Kloiz of Ostrow.[99]

R. Gaon R. Yisroel Isser died in Lublin.

The Gaon R. Eliezer Laizer

At the beginning of the 18th century the rabbinate in Luboml was filled by Rav Gaon R. Eliezer Laizer, who was also known as Leyzer Mendl's.

He was married to the daughter of R. Pinchas Moyshe Harif, av bet din and teacher and master in Lvov, a very wealthy man.

There are no details of his tenure in Luboml, but it is almost certain that in 1710 R. Eliezer Laizer was already the local rabbinic authority. His son, the Gaon R. Moyshe Chayim, was rabbi in Komorno, Zlochev, and Lvov.

In 1728, a terrible tragedy befell the Jews of Lvov. An apostate by the name of Philipovitch came to the town, repented, and resumed his life as a Jew. He was arrested. During the investigation he said that a few Jews had told him to convert; those Jews were condemned to death by burning. There was also a decree to arrest and burn R. Moyshe Hayim. But he escaped to Chatin in Bessarabia, where he died in 1761. His three remaining sons took on the name Gelernter or Hochgelernter.

The author of *Metzudat David* (Altona, 1706), R. Dovid son of Moyshe, was a grandson of the Gaon R. Eliezer Laizer, and he brings the latter's commentaries in his book.

For a short time, R. Dovid was rabbinical judge in Vilna.

The Gaon R. Yisoschor Ber

At the beginning of the 1720s—perhaps even earlier—R. Yisoschor became rabbi in Luboml.

His approbation from the year 1722 is found in the book of R. Yisroel son of Binyomen, *Zera Yisrael*, where he signs "Scholar of the community Lubomla."

In 1724, his approbation from Luboml appears again in *Bet Lechem Yehuda* by Tsvi Hersh, av bet din in Olik. In the same year his signature appears in a rabbinic decision in the Ledger of the Council of the Four Lands concerning a suit brought by a beadle (shamash) from Breslau against a rival. He signs: "Declared by the young Yisoschor Ber of Lublin scholar from Lubomla."[100]

That R. Yisoschor Ber was not in Luboml before 1716 can be determined from his approbation on *M'samche Lev* by Mordche Gimpel, where he does not sign himself as the av bet din in Luboml.

R. Yisoschor left no written works, but his words of Torah are quoted in the *Adnei Paz* of Meyer, son of R. Levi (Novidvor, 1789).

R. Yisoschor Ber's father was the Rav Gaon R. Meyer son of Binyomen Wolff, Heilperin, who was rabbi in Chelm, Apt, and Lublin, a son-in-law of the Gaon R. Dovid Segal, the Taz.[101]

The Gaon R. Yosef, Son of Yisroel

The next rabbinic authority in Luboml after R. Yisoschor Ber was Rav Gaon R. Yosef, son of Yisroel. We do not know the exact years of his service, only that it began in the 1720s or 1730s.

There is an approbation of his on the *B'chinat Olam* from the year 1741 in Luboml and on the *Lev Simcha* from 1757.

In the Ledger of the Council of the Four Lands from 1755, his signature appears with the addition "residing in the holy community of Luboml."

We deduce that R. Yosef son of Yisroel was rabbi in Luboml until the end of the 1750s or beginning of the 1760s.

The Gaon R. Yitshak Isaac

In 1760–65, the Luboml rabbinate was occupied by Rav Gaon R. Yitshak Isaac, son of Nachman. He must have remained rabbi there until the mid-1780s.

R. Yitshak was one of the most well-known of the Scholars of the Kloiz of Brody, considered by their contemporaries as "princes of men, outstanding rabbis, scholars of wisdom of the Great Kloiz [synagogue] of the holy community of Brody." In this kloiz many outstanding scholars, rabbis, and Torah luminaries would meet and study Torah all week, including the nights, going home only for the Sabbath.

We understand that most, if not all, of those who frequented this well-known kloiz in Brody did not hold permanent rabbinic posts. A rabbi cannot leave his flock for such long stretches of time, especially from a town like Luboml, which, considering the modes of transportation available in those days, was quite a long trip from Brody.

Usually those who came to the kloiz were great scholars who had left their rabbinic positions and preferred to spend all their time in the study of Torah in the company of other great scholars.[102]

In the year 1786, we find an approbation of R. Yitshak Isaac in the *Nefesh David* (Lemberg, 1790), though we know someone else was there a year earlier. It could be that both were rabbis together for a short period in Luboml, a case of "two kings utilizing a single crown."

Two Rabbis

From around 1785 until the end of the 18th century, the Luboml rabbinate was considerably confused.

Besides the previously mentioned approbation in Luboml of Rav Gaon R. Yitshak Isaac son of Nachman in the year 1786, there is another (for the *Torat Moshe*) dated Luboml, 1785, by a Yonah, son of Yosef Halevi.

Ten or 15 years later, there actually was a rabbi in Luboml with approximately the same name, with one difference: his first name had the addition "Yisroel." Even if this was, as we suggest, one person, we do know that between 1787 and 1791 there was another rabbinic authority in town.

Therefore we have no choice but to surmise that, from 1785 until 1786, perhaps coterminously with Yitshak Isaac son of Nachman, Gaon R. Yonah ben Yosef Halevi was rabbi in Luboml and his approbation appears on the *Torat Moshe*.

From 1787 to 1791 the position was held by Gaon R. Aron Yoel ben Dovid. His Luboml-dated approbations appear in the *Margaliyot HaTorah* (Poritzk, 1787) by R. Tsvi, son of Shmuel Zeynvel and in the *Damesek Eliezer* (Poritzk, 1790).

R. Aron Yoel died in 1791.[103]

The Gaon R. Yisroel Yona Landau

In the mid-1790s, the Luboml rabbinate was occupied by Rav Gaon R. Yisroel Yonah Segal Landau. He was the Luboml rabbinic authority until 1820. In that year, he became rabbi in

Kampen, Posen, where he died in 1824.

R. Yisroel Yonah is the author of the great work *Ma'on HaBrachot*, a commentary on Tractate Brachot, printed in Dierenfurt in 1806. He is also author of *Knesset Yisroel*, on the tractates Beitza and Nezikin; the *Ein HaB'dolach*, on the legends in the Talmud; and *Zmirot Yisrael*, commentaries on the Bible.

R. Yisroel Yonah's wife was Gitel, and their daughters were Feigel, Elke and Hana.

His father was the Gaon R. Yosef Segal Landau, av bet din in Chmelnik.

His brother, R. Yakov Simche Landau, was av bet din in Apt, and a second brother, Rav Gaon R. Arye Lieber Landau, was av bet din in Koretz.

Rav Gaon R. Yosef Shmuel Landau, R. Yisroel Yonah's son, became av bet din in Kampen after his father's death. The son died at the age of 37, on the 13th of Kislev, 1837. His place was taken by R. Yisroel Yonah's son-in-law, Rav Gaon R. Mordche Zev Ashkenazi.

R. Yosef Shmuel Landau is author of *Koor HaBechina*, which has the approbations of the sages Hatam Sofer and R. Akiva Eiger. The *Koor HaBechina* was published with corrections a bit later in Warsaw, in 1929.

In the *Goren Atad* (Warsaw, 1837) R. Yosef eulogized his relative R. Gaon R. Yechiel Ettinger.

From the frontispiece of the *Koor HaBechina* we see that R. Yisroel Yonah Landau was a descendant of R. Leibish, av bet din and teacher and master in Lvov, of the *Noda B'Yehuda* Maharam Padua, the Maharal of Prague, and the *Maale BaKodesh*.[104]

R. Moyshe Chayim

From 1820 until the end of the 1850s, we know almost nothing about the Luboml rabbinate. It is strange that as we approach our own time we know less about the rabbis of Luboml than we do about those of 100 years before. It is known only that during this time—or for a portion of that time—someone by the name of R. Moyshe Chayim served as rabbi of Luboml. Since R. Yisroel Isser had a son named Moyshe Chayim who was a rabbi, we surmise it was he who was rabbi in Luboml for a few years.

The Gaon R. Yehuda Arye Finkelshteyn

In 1858, the Rav Gaon Yehuda Arye Finkelshteyn became rabbi in Luboml. In 1912, he wrote that he was serving as av bet din in Luboml, and he presumably remained there as rabbi until the outbreak of the First World War in 1914.[105]

His approbation from the year 1901 is found in the book *Likutei Tsvi* by Tsvi Hersh of Janow (Pietrokov, 1909). He signs: "Yehuda Arye, son of Eliezer Domitz, of the holy community of Libivne."

In town he was simply known as R. Leibe. He was the grandfather of the wife of the later dayyan (judge), R. Leybl Melamed. An enthusiastic Chasid of Trisk, he once went off barefoot to see the Magid of Trisk. He did a pretty good job of tearing up the skin of his feet and suffered from it a long time. R. Leibe died in 1915.

Three Rabbis

After R. Leibe's death, little Luboml had three rabbis—or two rabbis and a judge—at the same time. The various Chasidic factions in town could not agree on one rabbi.

One of the three, R. Arye Leybish HaCohen London, was recognized officially by the government as the religious leader of the local Jews and from about 1927 to 1936 he was the chief rabbi.

R. Leybish was the son of the Voislovitser Rav, R. Yoshe London, and brother of R. Dovid Veytsfrucht (London), who was mayor of the town during the Austrian occupation.

The second rabbi, or "the dayyan," as he was called, was R. Leybl Melamed. He was rabbi until the Holocaust and perished with the entire community. He undertook much philanthropic work (tzedaka) and everyone respected and supported him.

The third rabbi, Rav Pinchas Oselka, was brought to Libivne in 1918–19 through the initiative of a group of householders who could not and would not make peace with the idea that either of the two rabbis, removed as they were from worldly matters and not even speaking Polish, should serve as rabbi of the town. Rabbi Oselka came from the Warsaw district, spoke Polish well—he was a good orator altogether—

and had a pleasant, modern appearance. In addition, he was a nationalist and a great scholar.

The youngest rabbi in town, who was chosen in 1936 and perished with the rest of the Jews of Luboml, was R. Alter, son of Ben-Tsiyon London, a grandchild of the elder R. Leybish HaCohen London.

A Table of the Rabbis of Luboml (1556–1914)

On the basis of the foregoing material we present a chronological table of Luboml's rabbis for a period of more than 350 years. The order here differs from that which appears in a number of other sources. We believe our order to be correct, though many dates are approximate.

R. Hersh Yellin, 1556–1569/70

R. Avrom Pollack, 1570–1577

R. Shimon Auerbach, 1578–1579

R. Yehuda Leyb son of Eliezer, 1580(?)–1597

R. Moyshe Mess (Mat), 1597–1598

R. Yoel Sirkis, 1599–1604

R. Moyshe, 1605–1617

R. Gedalia son of R. Meyer, 1618–1630

R. Shmuel Ish Hurvitz, 1630–1635

R. Moyshe Katzenellenbogen, 1636–1638

R. Yonah Te'omim, 1639–1641/42

R. Moyshe son of R. Yitshak, 1643–1653

R. Eliezer Margaliyot, 1658/59–1667

R. Yakov son of R. Yonah Katz, 1668–1684

R. Yakov son of Mordche, also 1668–1684

R. Yonah Halevi, 1685(?)–1690(?)

R. Yisroel Isser son of R. Meyer, 1691–1707(?)

R. Eliezer Laizer Mendeles, 1708–1719

R. Issaschar Ber, 1720–1728

R. Yosef son of R. Yisroel 1730–1762/63

R. Yitshak Isaac, 1765–1781/82

R. Yonah son of Yosef, 1782–1791

R. Aron Yoel son of Dovid, also 1782–1791

R. Yisroel Yonah Landau, 1821–1857

R. Moyshe Chayim, also 1821–1857

R. Yehuda Arye Finkelshteyn, 1858–1915

R. Arye Leybish HaCohen London, 1918–1936

R. Pinchas Oselka, 1918–1938

R. Leybl Melamed the Dayyan, 1916–1942

R. Alter Ben Tsiyon London, 1936–1942[106]

★

To this chapter it is appropriate to add the name of a few people who, while not rabbis, identified very strongly with matters of Torah.

Around the 1720s there was a dayyan in Luboml by the name of R. Yakov. He helped publish *Massechet Hulin* in Amsterdam in 1728.

The name of another Luboml resident is connected with the publication of a book 140 years earlier. His name was Menashe Yakov, son of Yehuda Levi, and the book is *Derech Tov* by Shimon, son of Yitshak Halevi Ishenburg, published in Cracow, 1590.

And the third Lubomler, Yehuda, son of

Cover of R. Yisroel Yonah Landau's *Ma'on HaBrachot*. He was Luboml's rabbi, 1794–1820.

Eliezer, was also instrumental in bringing out his book, the sixth edition of *Ein Yakov* , which at that time still went under the name *Ein Yisrael*. The book came out in Prostitz in 1603.

In the introduction to *Divrei Dor*, Dovid son of R. Shmuel (Svoliva, 1912) says that the "compiler and proofreader" for the book is Aron, son of R. Yakov Halevi. R. Aron also provided comments. In his "apology," R. Aron calls himself "a grandson of the great leader, master and teacher R. Shmuel Shachor, of the holy community Luboml, *y'z'v*."

The last Lubomler who undertook to publish other people's works now lives in New York. This is R. Shloyme Baruch Rubin. The *Bet Yisrael*, with its second section, *Kerem Yisrael*, of Reuven Zak, which came out in Lublin in 1913, was again published in New York through R. Shloyme Baruch Rubin's efforts. He published a new edition of *The Genealogy of Chernobyl and Rozin* by Aron Tverski (Lublin, 1938).

Advance Subscribers in Libivne

Authors, particularly rabbinic authors, used to travel around the various Jewish communities to get subscribers, who paid for a book in advance of publication.

These subscribers called themselves "prenumeranten." In many books there were lists of the early subscribers and their towns. These lists have important historical significance.

Advance subscribers from Luboml appear in books by the following authors:

Menorah HaTehorah, by Uziel Meizlish, Lemberg, 1884:
R. Chayim Tsvi, ritual slaughterer and examiner of the Trisker Shtibl
R. Yakov, of the Kotsker Shtibl
R. Eliezer Badeinski
R. Chayim

The same names are found in a similar list in the *Etz Ha Da'at Tov* by Uziel Meizlish (Lemberg, 1886), *Kol Yehuda*, by Yehuda Leyb Segal Berenson (Berdichev, 1907), and *Pri HaRamzal*, by Yitshak Noah Tcherkis (Bilgorai, 1909).

More than 50 advance subscribers are in the *Kol Ya'akov* by R. Meyer son of R. Yitshak (Bilgorai, 1929) and they are: HaRav R. Pinchas (Oselka), Moyshe Babad, Moyshe Nutl Gortenshteyn, Zev Lifshitz, Mechl Vidra, Yitshak Sanison, Yitshak Meyer Grimatlicht, Dovid Zayd, Shloyme Samet, Aron Shub, Meyer Shub, Mendl Meshkis, Abba Klig, Hersh Ber Shamis, Avrom Sheyner, Lipe Grimatlicht, Moyshe Sher, Yonah Shek, Mendl Sobel, Akiva Freidman, Shmuel Leyb Haberman, Shmuel Laks, Leybl Englander, Yakov Sfard, Heschel Lipshitz, Ben-Tsiyon Papier, Moyshe Reyzman, Nachum Shoster, Henech Varshniter, Moyshe Povroznik, Yitshak Honik, Yitshak Emmerbaum, Manes Greenberg, Kalman Kopelzon, Avrom Gershenberg, Asher Shenbaum, Mordche Frechter, Yakov Leyzer Tchesner, Tsvi Lifshitz, Mendl Frechter, Yosef Schneider, Eliyohu Lerner, Avrom Lichtmacher, Yisroel Leyb Lichtenshteyn, Yitshak Shtilerman, Fishel Wein, Eliyohu Shterenbaum, Avrom Shneier, Shimon Danziger, Chayim Reyzman.

NOTES

[1] *Slovnik Geografitshny Polsky.*

[2] Dr. Philip Friedman in *Sefer Ratne*, Buenos Aires, 1954f.

[3] Dr. N. B. Gelber in *Sefer Koretz*, Tel Aviv, 1959, p. 18.

[4] Ibid., p. 18.

[5] *Yizkor Buch Chelm*, Johannesburg, 1954, p. 13.

Mr. Yakov Hetman of Tel Aviv testifies that he saw a document in the Chelmer Museum, a chronological notice of King Jagiello, in which it is said: "When I was in Luboml the Jew Samuel came to me. . . ."

[6] Ber Mark, *Geshichte Yidn in Poiln*, Warsaw, 1955, p. 24.

[7] *Di Yidn in Poiln*, II-1, New York, 1946.

[8] Ibid., p. 44.

[9] Dr. Meir Balaban in *Yevrezkiya Starina*, Petrograd, 1910, II-1, p. 189.

[10] *HaTzofeh LeHokhmat Yisrael*, Budapest, 5691, number 2, p. 87, the article by Tsvi Ish Hurwitz; Dr. M. Balaban, *Die Yidn Shtot Lublin*, Buenos Aires, 1947, p. 36; Y. Trunk in *Dos Buch fun Lublin*, ed. N. Shemen, Paris, 1957, p. 47.

[11] Dr. Friedman's article in *Yizkor Buch Chelm*, Johannesburg, 1954, p. 16.

[12] Mathias Bersohn, *Dyplomatarjusz dotyczacy Zydow w dawnej Plsce*, Warsaw, 1919, Nr. 67.

In the same document, this privilege was given to the Jews of Chelm and Ratne as well.

[13] *She'elot U'Teshuvot Bach HaYeshanot* 4; regarding Rabbi Pollak and the Bach (R. Yoel Sirkes), see further in the chapter on "Rabbis."

[14] Dr. N. B. Gelber in *Pinkas Hurvishov*, Tel Aviv, 1962, p. 31.

HaTzofeh LeHokhmat Yisrael, Budapest 5691, year 15, nr. 2, p. 87, the article of Tsvi Halevi Ish Hurwitz, "LeKorot HaKehillot BeYisrael." Reb Eliyahu was known by the name Eliyahu Baal Shem, and as one of the greatest rabbis of his generation. He is cited in *She'elot U'Teshuvot Bach* 77, and in *She'elot U'Teshuvot HaRashal* 42. His grandson was the author of the noted work *Sefer Chakham Zvi*, R. Tsvi Ashkenazi.

[15] "Regesti i nadpisi" I, 1899, p. 241, nr. 537.

[16] Dr. Yakov Shatzky in his introduction to Natan Neta Hanover's *Yeven Metzulah*, Vilna, 1938, p. 28.

[17] *Sefer Butchatch*, Tel Aviv, 5716, p. 45.

[18] *Di Yidn fun Poiln*, New York, 1946, II-6, p. 66.

[19] Ibid., p. 63.

[20] Ibid., p. 69, 81.

[21] *Otzar HaSafrut*, Cracow, 5649–5650, p. 123.

[22] *Yeven Metzulah* (reprint edition), Jerusalem, 5728, "Sippurei HaGezerot BiShnot Tah ve Tat," p. 37, New York, 1938, p. 58.

[23] H.Y. Gurland, *LeKorot HaGezerot BeYisrael*, Cracow, 1898, p. 16.

[24] M. Bersohn, *Dyplomatarjusz dotyczacy Zydów w dawnej Plsce*, Warsaw, 1910, nr. 291.

[25] *Pinkas Vaad Arba Aratzot*, ed. Israel Halperin, Jerusalem, 5705, p. 495.

[26] Meir Balaban, *Di Yidn in Poiln*, Vilna, 1930, p. 260.

Reb Shlomo Baruch Rubin, an old inhabitant of Luboml, who now resides in New York, tells that he remembers an inscription, which was hung in the highest place in the synagogue, and which read as follows: "Greater will be the honor of this LAST Temple than the First." The word "LAST" was the year number 5279–1510. Other former Lubomlites, especially those now in Israel, do not recall such an inscription, and it is not noted in the works of the many Polish Jewish historians and researchers of Jewish art. In any case, if there was such an inscription, there could have been a mistake in the calculation of the year if Reb Shlomo Baruch had not noticed that yet another word or additional letters, has been capitalized.

[27] Shlomo Baruch Nissenboim, *LeKorot HaYehudim BeLublin*, Lublin, 5660, p. 14.

[28] In *Pinkas Vaad Arba Aratzot* for the year 5522.

[29] The Polish historian Kletzinksky-Klutzitzky in Dr. Gelber's *Pinkas Harubishov*, p. 34.

[30] All of the following regarding the Libivner Pinkas is built on Israel Halperin's work, *Pinkas HaHaburah shel Baalei Melakhah BeLuboml*, Tel Aviv, 5695, II. This is an exception to our remarks regarding the Jerusalem Library's usual care in these matters.

[31-32] Whether it was badly copied from the pinkas, or whether it was written thus in the pinkas itself, this part of the decree is unclear.

[33] *Die Judenpogrome in Russland*, Köln-Leipzig, 1919, p. 189.

[34] Ibid., p. 218.

[35] The given numbers regarding Jews in the statistical sources are not always the same, but the differences are generally small, and do not change the general picture.

[36] *HaMelitz*, 1897.

[37] Ibid., 1898.

[38] *HaMelitz* 1882, nr. 44.

[39] Ibid., 1888—this issue could not be found.

[40] *Heshbon HaNedavot shel HaVaad Le'Ovat HaHevrah LiTemikhat Bnei Yisrael Ovedei Adamah U'Vaalei Melakhah BeSuriya Uve'Eretz HaKedoshah LiKniyat Adamah Be'Eretz Yisrael*, Odessa, 1909, pp. 54, 79.

[40a] Ibid., Odessa, 1912, p. 201.

[41] Ibid., Odessa, 1914.

42 Ibid., Odessa, 5663.

43 *Reshumot* 5, Sidra Hadashah, Tel Aviv, 5713. Dr. Refael Mahler's article, "Shemot Yehudiyim shel Mekomot BePolin HaYeshanah, p. 154.

44 Yechiel Michel Zunz, *Ir HaTzedek*, Lemberg, 1874, p. 62, note.

45 H.N. Dembitzer, *Kelilat Yofi*, Cracow, 5648, p. 38.

46 In the geographical index of his *Catalogus Librorum Hebraeorum*, Hildesheim, 1964.

47 *Luhot Zikaron*, Frankfurt am Main, 5664.

48 Mathias Bersohn, *Dyplomatarjusz dotyczacy Zydow w dawnej Plsce*, pp. 71–72.

49 Yisroel Tuviah Eisenstadt, *Daat Kedoshim*, Petrograd, 1897–1898, p. 6; H.D. Friedberg, *Luhot Zikaron*, Frankfurt am Main, 5664, p. 9; Arye Yehudah Leib Lifshitz, *Avot Atarah Levanim*, Warsaw, 5687, p. 213.

50 *Hagoren*, Sefer I, Berdichev, 5658, article, "Dor Yesharim," by Yosef Kohen Zedek, p. 7; Shmuel Zeynvel Kahana, *Anaf Etz Avot*, Cracow, p. 24.

51 H. N. Dembitzer, *Mikhevei Bikoret*, Cracow, 5652, 8. The author however erred in his note that Reb Avraham Pollak was Rabbi in Luboml in the year 5318 (1558). According to this, Reb Avrom was Rabbi in Luboml *before* Reb Hirsch—in contradiction to all the sources.

52 Yosef Levinstein, *Dor Dor VeDoreshav*, Warsaw, 5660, p. 12.

53 H.N. Dembitzer, *Kelilat Yofi*, Cracow, 5648, pp. 48–49.

53a *Dor Dor VeDoreshav*, p. 80. A year or two of his Libivner rabbinate overlaps that of R. Moyshe Mess.

54 *Pinkas Vaad Arba Aratzot*, Jerusalem, 5705, pp. 15, 62, 63.

55-56 S. Y. Finn, *Kiryah Ne'emanah*, Vilna, 5620, p. 56. See also: Yosef Levinstein, *Dor Dor VeDoreshav*, Warsaw, 5660, p. 89; H.D. Friedberg, *Luhot Zikaron*, Frankfurt am Main, 5664, p. 9; S. A. Horodetzki, *Kerem Shlomo*, Drahabitsh, 5657, p. 39. There was another great scholar who was also called "Moyshe ben Hakadosh Reb Avraham." True, he lived a good deal later (died in 1681); nevertheless, the *Daat Kedoshim* (Petersburg, 1897–1898) does well to prove this and provide a distinction between them. That scholar, who was av bet din in Horodno and the author of *Tiferet Lishlomo*, signs himself "*migeza Zevi*," and in that way we may distinguish him from Reb Moyshe Mess.

57 *Kelilat Yofi*, Cracow, 5648, p. 87b.

58 In his article "Toldot Maharam MiLublin in *HaGoren* I, Berdichev, 5658, pp. 40–44.

There is a good account of the dispute in Eliezer Steinman, *Tzintzenet Haman*, Tel Aviv, 1964, volume I, p. 21.

59 The Berlin *Eshkol Encyclopedia* reports that Reb Shimon Wolff was av bet din of Pozen in 1625. Israel Halperin makes the same mistake in his *Pinkas Vaad Aratzot*. That this is a mistake can be seen from *Pinkas Pozen*. Regarding Reb Shimon Wolff's stay in Pozen, see Dr. Philip Bloch in his article, "Über S. Wolff Auerbach Oberrabiner von Grosspolen," *Gedenkbuch zur Erinnerung an David Kaufman*, Breslau, 1900.

60 *Kelilat Yofi*, p. 27; *Pinkas Vaad Arba Aratzot*, pp. 24, 456; S. A. Horodetzki, *Kerem Shlomo*, Drahabitsh, 5657, p. 32; Aharon Walden, *Shem HaGedolim HeHadash*, Warsaw, 5630, p. 18; Yosef Levinstein, *Dor Dor Vedoreshav*, Warsaw, 5660, p. 119; Avraham Epstein, *Mishpahat Luria*, Vienna, 5661, p. 20; H.D. Friedberg, *Luhot Zikaron*, Frankfurt am Main, 5664, p. 9; S. B. Nissenboim, *LeKorot HaYehudim*

61 *HaMeasef*, Peterburg, 1902, article of Dr. Shimon Milner, "LeKorot HaYehudim BeChelem."

62 Shlomo Rapaport, *Gal Ed*, Prague, 5616, p. 75.

63 *She'elot U'Teshuvot HaBach HaYeshanot*, 77, and *She'elot Uteshuvot HaBach HaChadashot*, 59.

64 Shimon Moyshe Chanes, *Toldot HaPoskim*, Warsaw, 5689, p. 185; Meir Balaban, *Shalshelet HaYuhasin shel Mishpachat Orenstein-Brode*, Warsaw, 5691, p. 8.

65 See at length in the chapter on R. Avrom Pollak. Regarding a series of his *takkanot* in Cracow, new and renewed, see: P.H. Wetstein, *Kadmoniyot MiPinkasaot Yeshanim*, Cracow, 5652, p. 5.

66 Y.L. Maimon, *Sarei HaMeah*, III, pp. 16–17, and in A. Steinman's *Tzinztenet Haman*.

67 A. L. Feinstein, *Ir Tehillah*, Warsaw, 1886, p. 24.

68 The *Tzemah David* (Frankfurt, 5452, p. 47) and *Ir HaTzedek*. Others say: 1640.

69 Y. L. Maimon, *Sarei HaMeah*, III, pp. 16–17.

70 *She'elot U'Teshuvot HaBach HaChadashot*, 42; *Ir HaTzedek*, p. 69; G. Bader, *Dreisig Doros Yidn in Poiln*, New York, 1927, p. 52.

71 Meir Balaban, *Shalshelet HaYuhasin shel Mishpahat Orenstein-Brode*, Warsaw, 5691, p. 8.

72 See, for example, J. Unna, "Historisches aus den Responsen des R. Joel Serkes," *Jahrbuch der jüdisch-historisch-literarischen Gesellschaft in Frankfurt a/M*, 1904.

73 Shimon Moyshe Chanes, *Toldot HaPoskim*, Warsaw, 5689, p. 185; *Entzyklopediya LeToldot Gedolei Yisrael*, Jerusalem, 5708, III, p. 716; Shlomo Baruch Nissenboim, *LeKorot HaYehudim BeLublin*, Lublin, 5660, p. 27.

74 S. Z. Kahana, *Anaf Etz Avot*, Cracow, 5663, p. 34; *Pinkas Vaad Arba Aratzot*, p. 27.

75 Meir Balaban, *Shalshelet HaYuhasin shel Mishpahat Orenstein-Brode*, Warsaw, 5691, p. 8; Shimon Moyshe Chanes, *Toldot Haposkim*, Warsaw, 5689, p. 185; *Kelilat Yofi*, p. 27.

76 P. H. Wetstein, "MiPinkasei HaKahal BeKrakow," in *Tehillah LeDavid . . . LeZikhron . . . David Kaufman*, Breslau, 5660, p. 75; Meir Balaban, *Shalshelet HaYuhasin shel Mishpahat Orenstein-Brode*, Warsaw, 5691, p. 8; *Kelilat Yofi*, p. 51; Shlomo Buber, *Anshei Shem*, Cracow, 5658, p. 175.

77 *Ir Tehillah*, p. 199; *Toldot HaPoskim*, p. 185.

78 Aharon David Twersky, *Sefer HaYahas Tchernobil VeRuzhin*, Lublin, 5698, p. 145.

79 Meir Schwarzman, *Ve'Eleh Toldot HaRebbi HaRishon MiGur*, Jerusalem, 5718, p. 76.

80 Moyshe Menahem Walden, *Ben Yekhabbed Av*, Pietrokov, 5683, p. 16.

81 David Tihdar, *Entzyklopediya LaHalutzei HaYishuv U'Vanav*, I, Tel Aviv, 1947, p. 59.

82 There is a great deal of secondary literature on the Bach, aside from the citations noted above. See also: *Ir HaTzedek*, p. 177; S. Buber, *Anshei Shem*, Cracow, 5655, p. 56; S. Z. Kahana, *Anaf Etz Avot*, Cracow, 5663, p. 19; *Luhot Zikaron*, p. 9 and later work of Prof. K. Mirsky. Simhah Asaf, when he calculates the rabbinic positions held by the Bach in his *Be'Oholei Shem* (Jerusalem, 5703, p. 57), left out the Bach's time in the Libivner rabbinate. Incidentally, not all books which record the wording of the Bach's headstone (*matzevah*) have the same wording.

83 In Yosef Levinstein's *Dor Dor VeDorshav* (p. 29) is

written that Reb Gedaliah died in 5391 (1621), but this is altogether impossible. The *Encyclopedia Judaica* notes that Reb Gedaliah was Rabbi in Luboml from 1618–1647, but this too cannot be correct, because there were other rabbis there in the meantime.

[84] Pinchas Pesis, *Ir Dubno VeRabbaneha*, Cracow, 5662, p. 14; Pinchas Pesis, *Ateret HaLeviyim*, Warsaw, 5662, p. 19; *Sefer Dubno*, Tel Aviv, 5626, p. 89; *Dor Dor Vedorshav*, p. 120. The author of *Dor Dor Vedorshav* says that Reb Shmuel died in 1653. This is presumably a printer's error; the correct year is 1635.

[85] Moyshe Gelernter, *Uriyan Telita'ei*, Ramat Gan, 5724; Arye Yehudah Leib Lifshitz, *Avot Atarah Levanim*, Warsaw, 5687, p. 211; *Pinkas Vaad Aratzot*, p. 70; *Daat Kedoshim*, p. 89. The last cited confuses the rabbinical approbation of another Luboml Rabbi, also named Reb Moyshe, but with the patronym "b'Reb Yitshak," on the *Shakh*, *Yoreh De'ah* 406, with the name of one Reb Moyshe b'Reb Meir.

[86] According to Friedberg's *Luhot Zikaron* (p. 70), Reb Moyshe b'Reb Meir Katzenelboigen was Rabbi in Luboml after Reb Moyshe Mess. This does not conform with the chronology of Luboml Rabbis, and is a contradiction to the dates of other rabbinic posts in Luboml in that time.

[87] Yosef Kohen Zedek in *HaGoren*, I, Berdichev, 5658, p. 7.

[88] Tsvi Ish Hurwitz, *LeKorot HaKehillot BePolonia*, New York, 5729, p. 40; Yitshak Meir Katzenelbogen, *Hevel HaKesef*, Brooklyn, 5697, pp. 42, 50; Mordechai Rubenstein, *Nit'ei Ne'emanah*, Jerusalem, 567, par. 40.

[89] M. Finer, *Matzevot Kivrot HaRabbanim Ve'anshei Shem. . .* (Berlin, 1961). Reuven Margalit, the author of *Hillula DeTzadika* (p. 15), writes that Reb Yonah died in 1665, but the headstone, understandably, is more reliable.

It is hard to understand why the name of Reb Yonah Teomim is missing from all the lists of Luboml Rabbis which we could consult: the *Eshkol Encyclopedia*, *Encyclopedia Judaica*, Friedberg's *Luhot HaZikaron*, and others. From the rabbinic approbation from Luboml, and even more from his headstone, it is clear that he served as Rabbi in Luboml.

[90] S. B. Nissenboim, *LeKorot HaYehudim BeLublin*, Lublin, 5660, p. 61; Reuven Margaliyot, *Toldot Adam*, Lemberg, 5672; *Anaf Etz Avot*, p. 58; M.M. Bieber, *Mazkeret LiGedolei Ostraha*, Berdichev, 1907, p. 46; *Avot—Ateret Levanim*, p. 163; *Luhot Zikaron*, p. 9.

[91] Kadish Rakatz, *Nifla'ot HaYehudi*, in a section of *Bet Tzadikim*, p. 98.

[92] *Arba Aratzot* that Reb Moyshe b'Reb Yitshak died around 1672/73.

[93] *Pinkas Vaad Arba Aratzot*, p. 105, par. 261; *Mafte'ah*

Haskamot of Dr. Leopold Löwenstein, Frankfurt a/M, 1923, nr. 2216.

[94] *Daat Kedoshim*, p. 78; *Shem HaGedolim HeHadash*, pp. 8, 18, 51; *Kelilat Yofi*, p. 68.

[95] *Otzar HaSafrut*, article "Shem U'She'erit," by Yosef Kohen Tzedek; *Anaf Etz Avot*, p. 20; *Avot Ateret Levanim*, p. 170; *Ir HaTzedek*, p. 43.

[96] The signature is "Yakov Frie of Luboml." Since such a name as "Frie" does not occur earlier, and not later in those parts, Israel Halperin, the editor of the *Pinkas*, concludes that could be a scribal error for "BRI"KH"—"b'Reb Yonah Katz." This assumption makes good sense, because we find this name just a few years later on.

[97] Israel Halperin remarks here that we must add the patronym "b'Reb Yonah Katz" to "Yakov Kahana." In our view, he is mistaken. He has overlooked the signature of Yakov b'Reb Mordche in 1680, and has forgotten that the name Yakov b'Reb Yonah Katz does not occur after 1672.

It is stated in *Dor Dor VeDorshav* (p. 67) that the Gaon Reb Yakov Mordche of Luboml died in 1705. More likely, this should be "Yakov ben Mordche."

[98] S.Y. Finn, *Kiryah Ne'emanah*, p. 171; *Luhot Zikaron*, pp. 9, 82.

[99] Reuven Zak, *Kerem Yisrael*, New York, 5719, p. 78; Moyshe Markowitz, *Shem HaGedolim HaShelishi*, Vilna, 5670, p. 28; *Yekhabbed Av*, p. 17; *Mazkeret LiGedolei Ostraha*, p. 77; *LeKorot HaYehudim BeLublin*, p 61. In *Dor Dor VeDorshav* it states here that Reb Yisroel Iser died in 1669. It is clear that this is not correct.

[100] Moyshe Gelernter, *Uriyah Telita'ei*, Ramat Gan, 5724.

[101] David Magid, *Toldot Mishpehot Ginzberg*, Peterburg, 5659, p. 29; Tsvi Horowitz, *LeKorot HaKehillot BePolonia*, New York, 5729, pp. 59–60; *LeKorot HaYehudim BeLublin*, pp. 68, 170; *Hagoren*, I, p. 49; *Pinkas Vaad Arba Aratzot*, pp. xlviii, 297, 299; *Mafte'ah HaHaskamot*, nr. 1532.

[102] *Arim Ve'Imhaot BeYisrael*, VI, Jerusalem, 5715, p. 64.

[103] *Dor Dor VeDorshav*, p. 19; *Mafte'ah HaHaskamot*, nr. 255, 294.

[104] *Yekhabbed Av*, pp. 17, 21; *Luhot Zikaron*, p. 9. A. Heppner and J. Herzberg, *Aus Vergangenheit und Gegenwart der Juden und jüdischen Gemeinden in den Posener Landen*, Koschmin-Bromberg, 1909, pp. 518–519.

[105] S. Z. Gottlieb, *Ohel Shem*, Pinsk, 1912, p. 102.

[106] In *Yizkor Buch Chelm*, Johannesburg, 1954, p. 209, is stated that the "Tosefot Yom Tov" was av bet din in Luboml. No one had remarked on this until then, and it is certainly without foundation.

REMEMBRANCES
By Yisroel Garmi

The official name of the town was Luboml. But the Jews of the town and the surrounding areas used to call it Libivne. Until the end of the First World War, the town belonged to the Ludmir region, which was included in the district of Zhitomir, the capital of Volhynia. The regular formulation in documents and the official address for mail was: Miasteczko Luboml, Wladimir Wolinski Uyazd, Zhitomirskaya Gubernia.

The estimated number of residents until World War I was 6,000, half of them Jews. Most non-Jewish residents were Ukrainians (more than 90 percent) and the rest Poles.

Most of the Jews lived in the center of town by the marketplace, on the main streets that led from it and in the alleys close to the synagogue. A few Jewish families lived apart, near the railroad tracks, and a few others on the non-Jewish streets on the outskirts of town and in the surrounding areas.

On the "Polish Street," or Garden Street, as it was then called, most of the community institutions were located: the Russian school, community hospital (which burned down even before the First World War), army enlistment office, jail, firehouse, etc. That is where the officials and the clergy lived: the Orthodox priest (the *galach*) and his assistant, the *dyak*, the Catholic priest (the *ksiondz*), and most of the Russian intelligentsia.

That is where the three churches were located: the Catholic one, the *kosciol*, which covered a large area, and two Orthodox ones. On the eastern side of this street, almost for its entire length, stretched a garden of fruit trees, hence its name "Street of the Garden"—property of the landowner Kampyoni, and next to it the grove

(*dos veldl*)—both of which were used for strolling during the summer months.

The Heart of the City: The Marketplace

The marketplace (*der mark*), which was located, as mentioned, in the center of town, was the "center" in a number of ways. Most of the stores and shops were located there. On this rather large tract (which was about 400 x 400 yards, i.e., 40 acres), great fairs were held once a month or once every three weeks (on Thursdays), and regular market days on Mondays; and this is where general events and official celebrations took place.

From the marketplace, which was the highest point in the city, four main streets branched out and descended, as did a number of alleyways. On the western side, the street that was called in those days Rimatcher Street (after the village of Rimatch); to the north, Kusnishtcher Street; to the south-southwest, Golden Street; and to the east-northeast, Polish street. The names of the streets and alleys changed with the ruling powers.

It appears that the marketplace was the oldest part of the city. Attesting to this fact were the large houses, the brick buildings, and many of the stores, which were built in a particular antiquated style and were the property of the landowner Kampyoni—and, of course, the "mound" (*dos bergl*) on the southeastern side. This mound covered a huge cellar, with many, many rooms branching off in all directions, a kind of large labyrinth, the walls of which were built of very thick bricks, and with domed ceilings through which airways reached upward and out. This huge cellar was in the form of a large circle, covered with layers of

44

Partial northeasterly view of the marketplace in 1917.

earth to a great thickness on all sides, and on the topmost layer stretched out over the entire area were chestnut trees, widespread and lovely to behold, in whose shade many young people rested and spent time during the summer months.

This basement-mound formerly served as storage space for fruit, potatoes, and more. During the Austro-German occupation, part of it served as a prison and after that as a storage place for potatoes (when the Austrians evacuated the city in the fall of 1918 and the Poles took over, many Jews were killed and wounded by the Polish police when hungry masses burst into the cellar to get potatoes).

A number of stories and legends were woven around this basement-mound: stories of spirits and ghosts that lived there, of its rooms and countless hiding places that twisted around and made their way to the center of the marketplace. All efforts to penetrate it were unsuccessful, and anyone who tried did not come out the same as he went in.

The Jews lived on the seven major streets of the city and its many alleyways—about 14 in number. The non-Jewish residents also lived on seven streets and a number of alleyways, some of which were the continuation of the streets where Jews lived. Most of the houses were single-story wooden structures, and a few were brick, called "walls." Most of the roofs on Jewish houses were shingles (*shindlen*), and of the non-Jews, straw. Fires were a frequent occurrence, and the biggest became a kind of historical landmark by which to date birthdays and various other events. Often we heard from our grandparents: "This happened in such and such a year, after the big fire."

The elders of the city and recorders of its history figure the beginnings to have been in the 15th century, and perhaps even before, if one relies on oral history passed from generation to generation.

To support their words they would bring proof from the old cemetery. There were two cemeteries in town, both quite large; the first, the old cemetery, spread out within the confines of the city near the road leading to the railroad station, was estimated to be hundreds of years old. Its southern portion had almost no remaining headstones, for most had sunk into the ground over the years or had disintegrated because of rain and wind.

In this section there were a few great oak trees whose crowns spread wide and that were thought to be hundreds of years old; in the northern section, where thick trees grew very close together, many tombstones still remained, as did a number of crypts (small stone or wooden structures on top of the graves) on the graves of some saints and great scholars of Israel. This is where people came to visit the graves of their ancestors on Tisha B'Av and during the month of Elul (a tradition before the High Holy Days). Those in the know would point to the common grave of two martyrs—a bride and groom murdered under their bridal canopy by the Haidamakes (Cossacks) during the years of the murderous pogroms in 1648–49.

די אַלטע שול אין ליובאָמל (וואָלין)

פון ש. אַנ—סקי'ס קאָלעקציע אין מוזיי פון דער

ווילנער היסטאָריש-עטנאָגראַפישער געזעלשאַפט.

Związek Towarzystw Opieki nad Sierot. Żyd. Rzeczypos- politej Polskiej, Warszawa.	פֿאַ־באַנד פֿון צענטראַלעס פֿאַר יתומים-פֿאַרזאָרגונג אין פוילן, וואַרשע.

Calendar page from 1926. (Copied from collection of S. An-ski, Vilna Museum.)

In this connection I recall the visit of the famous writer and author of *The Dybbuk*, S. An-ski, of blessed memory, and his companion the journalist Alter Kacyzne, who visited the city around 1911. The esteemed guests gathered a number of the elders of the town in the shtibl of the Radziner Chasidim and over a glass of whiskey, a glass of hot tea, and toasted cookies made of spelt (*retchene kichelach*), they lingered at the table for many hours and wrote down their many stories and legends of events that had taken place in the distant past.

It is no wonder that a number of motifs in *The Dybbuk* were from notes the writer took with him from his visit to our town of Luboml. An example comes in the words of the Idler in the play:

> When the wicked one Chmiel, may his name be blotted out forever, fell upon the city and slaughtered many hundreds of souls, among those who died were a bride and groom, at the very moment they were making their marriage vows.

More evidence for the venerable age of our town was derived from the Great Synagogue, which was beautifully built in the style typical of the 16th or 17th century. In those days many synagogues in Poland and the Ukraine were built like fortresses, with positions for gun emplacements on the roof. Most fortified synagogues were built in the second half of the 16th century, which saw "the war against the Tatars and the Cossacks; the most important of these, from an architectural standpoint, were the ones in Luboml, Lutsk, Srigod, Brody, and Leshniov" (in the words of researcher Y. Finkerfeld in the *Hebrew Encyclopedia*, vol. 8, s.v. "Synagogue".

The Great Synagogue

Our synagogue really was quite beautiful, a high-storied, broad structure that stood out among the town's other buildings in its splendor and could be seen for miles. The top of its architectural parapet surrounding the roof gave the appearance of an ancient, fortified wall. As children, we were mesmerized by the drawings of the powerful lions on the eastern face, covered with gold paint, and especially by the paintings inside the synagogue on the four walls; pictures of the Leviathan and the Primeval Ox, the tambourine, harp, cymbals and the rest of the musical instruments from the Temple [in Jerusalem]. And more beautiful than all the rest—the doors to the Holy Ark, whose decorations reached all the way to the ceiling.

We were also proud and boasted about the beautiful lectern (*balemer*) in the center of the synagogue. Its four carved hexagonal pillars reached upwards to the domed ceiling, and from it copper chains descended, with huge crystal chandeliers that flickered in a rainbow of colors. It was an impressive sight when a procession of Torahs ascended the stairs to the high lectern as the entire congregation stood by.

The walls and high arching windows on three sides also made a special impression. We were amazed by the force of the acoustics in the synagogue, and when we had a chance to remain there alone we would shout and wait excitedly for the echo that came to us from all directions.

On the other hand, we were afraid to pass close to the synagogue alone at night—the "time when the souls of the departed came to the synagogue for prayer and the reading of the Torah."

The Surroundings

The city was located on a broad flat plain, which spread out for miles and was covered by thick forests of pine and fir trees in the areas where the ground was lighter and sandier, and birch trees, beeches, ashes, poplars, and oaks in heavier, damper ground. Brooks and lakes filled with various sorts of fish, among them the famous Lake Shvitazh, were spread out along the northern and northwestern segments of the area, bordering on the swamps and forests of Polesia (southwestern Belorussia). About 7 to 9 miles from the city, the river Bug meandered, forming the border between western Ukraine and Poland.

Most of the soil in the area was thin and light, which mainly supported the growth of rye, barley, spelt, millet, and potatoes, and of course, there was abundant pasture land. There was very little heavier, richer soil on which wheat, flax, oats, and other crops grew. In a few places there were orchards of fruit trees, especially apples, plums, and pears. The city itself excelled in a great number of gardens with fruit trees, a few belonging to Jews, most of them to the residents of the

suburbs, non-Jews. Especially worthy of praise was the large garden owned by Kampyoni, which stretched out over a considerable area of the eastern part of town.

On the southern edge of town ran the railroad tracks that were a direct connection between east and west, from Kiev through Zdolbunov, Rovno, Kovel, and other towns in the east, and to Chelm, Lublin, and Warsaw in the west.

On that same side, south of the city, an old dirt road led south to Vladimir Volinsk (Ludmir), a distance of 60–65 *versts* (about 40–43 miles); on the western edge ran the strategic road that was paved, it appears, at the end of the previous century, leading to Brisk of Lithuania (Brest-Litovsk), 85 miles to the north. Roads wound from all entrances to the city—all of them wide, dirt roads, with acacias, plane trees, and willows growing alongside—and led to the adjacent small towns and villages.

Streets and Ditches

Though the city itself sits on high ground, during the rainy season it would drown in sinking mud, which made travel difficult both for pedestrians and vehicular traffic—the wagon, of course.

Crossing from house to house and street to street was accomplished by walking over thin wooden planks (*briklach*) stretched out the entire length of the main streets on both sides. Underneath were the trenches, for sewage and rainfall, connected with the main, large drainage ditches that drew off water to the outskirts of the city.

Those who lived in the low-lying areas had it particularly hard—the area around the bath-house and alleyway of the butcher shops. During the rainy season the connection with villages—the major source of livelihood—was greatly weakened or cut off altogether and the townspeople, who walked around with nothing to do, prayed and anxiously awaited an improvement in the weather.

During the First World War an attempt was made to pave the road with wooden planks by the Austro-German conquerors, employing refugees from other occupied territories. This attempt was halted immediately at the end of the war. In 1919–20, the first roads were paved with crushed stone in the main thoroughfares of the town.

Black basalt stones for the purpose were brought by railroad from the vicinity of Kremenitz.

At the beginning of the 1920s there was still no lighting on the streets of the town. Only the fuzzy bit of light that here and there seeped through from the windows of the houses lit the way for passersby. Walking through town at night, on unlit streets, during the rainy season, was therefore sufficiently hard. Illumination of the streets with electric light began in 1925–26, with the construction of the first power station by the Grimatlicht family and their partners.

Economic Sources

The sources of the town's economy, trade, and craftsmanship were derived mainly from the villages. Small-time farmers came to town, especially on Fair Day, to sell their produce: cattle, horses, chickens, eggs, pig bristles, wool, skins, mushrooms, flax, potatoes, etc. The merchants and craftsmen of the city, for their part, supplied the visiting villagers with all that was not made on the farm: shoes and clothing, leather and soles for shoes, fabrics and textiles, kerosene, tar and pitch; pruning knives, sickles, and other metal tools; oil, sugar, salts, white flour, medicine and liquor; harnesses, reins and wagons; and sometimes even grain for sowing in the field after a year of drought.

While they were in the city, the villagers took the opportunity to frequent the inns and taverns, to enjoy good food and drink. Many fell into a drunken stupor, or became rowdy and returned

View of the Luboml railroad station.

to their villages singing hoarsely and with their faces banged up from having gotten into fistfights with their drinking companions.

The Village Population

In this area it must be pointed out that, except for agriculture as practiced by the local landowners and a few German and Czech settlers, the state of farming was backward and primitive compared with other areas of the country.

Many villagers, with holdings too small and poor from which to make a living, were forced to look for work outside the village and went to work during the harvest for the large landowners gathering potatoes, sugar beets, and other produce, and during the winter they worked for the lessees of the forests (mostly Jews), chopping down trees and bringing them to the sawmill or to the train.

I remember well how the villagers wandered around at the end of summer and the beginning of fall, as great numbers of them went through the city to the railway station, on their way to their tasks and then on their way back home. Sometimes they would stay over and become "guests" of the train station for a day or two, in order to continue enjoying the sight of the trains coming and going.

Most of the village population was illiterate; they were slow moving, apathetic, and lazy, and their comprehension very slow. Ignorance was deeply rooted, as if it were destined. The elders were very pious in their Orthodox religion and went to church quite often. There was a lot of superstition among the village population, steeped in obscurantism. They tended to believe any sort of fabulous tale.

It's no wonder then that the city-folk, both Jewish and non-Jewish, saw the muzhiks as inferior and took a superior attitude to them. For our parents the word "goy" meant someone oafish and silly, such as the village muzhiks, and for every sin we committed regarding religious matters we got rebuked with, "A goy like you!"

The term *oorl* (uncircumcised) also was part of everyday speech when two Jews were having it out in front of the non-Jew while haggling over prices. When a muzhik and a Jew exchanged insults and rebukes in the heat of the moment, while buying or selling, it was really viewed as "nothing" and soon the injury was redressed and the bargaining continued to a satisfactory conclusion. The Jews had specific terms when referring to gentiles, and these were evidence of the spiritual and emotional distance between the two worlds.

In normal times the relationship between Jews and gentiles was more or less stable, without anything out of the ordinary occurring. Jewish families scattered in the surrounding villages had nothing to fear. They even visited and stayed over in non-Jewish homes (though they did not eat anything because it was not kosher), and there were many Jews who sought out the villagers for business.

Jewish Occupations

Most of the Jews in the town either engaged in various crafts or were small businessmen, while a minority were in industry and wholesale merchandising. The main craftsmen were shoemakers and various types of tailors, stitchers (who cut and sewed the uppers and were known as *zagatovtschiks*), masons and builders, hatmakers and furriers, tinsmiths and blacksmiths, wagon makers, carpenters, painters, barbers, butchers, and bakers.

The bakers worked mostly the nights before market days and fairs, selling to the villagers, as during the rest of the week Jews baked their own challas and bread. The wagon-drivers had a semiskilled profession, both those who had well-cared-for horses and handsome buggies or nice wagons for carrying passengers and packages to the train and to neighboring towns, and the *drikers,* who carried lighter freight within town in their rickety wagons hitched to a single, lame, undernourished horse.

Some merchants exported agricultural produce, such as eggs, cattle, horses, grain, skins, furs, bristles, fish, fresh and dried fruits, lumber, mushrooms, etc. The export reached the large cities of Poland, especially Warsaw, and also Danzig and Germany, through Silesia.

There also were some businessmen who leased forests and fruit orchards. Workmen, cattle merchants, and horse sellers also went with their merchandise to fairs in nearby towns; in large part the business was wholesale; many stores, most of them small, were centered around the marketplace. On fair days additional stands were set up in various corners of the marketplace by craftsmen to sell their wares: hats, shoes, clothes etc.

First Inklings of Industry

Industry was very limited in those days and played a minor role in the economy of the town. Its beginnings hark back to a textile factory on Golden Street, which burned down and was not rebuilt. Its remaining brick walls stood for a long time, marked by fire and smoke, until they were removed by someone who bought the property and put up a nice house.

There also were the beginnings of a beer industry, whose building on Brovarnia Street became a ruin. We even know of an attempt to make canes on the Polish street. There were two brickworks, a furnace for burning bones, a mill for carding wool, a number of windmills, and three oil presses actually operated by horse-power.

In the adjoining village of Horodno there was a distillery owned by the Russian Defense Minister, Suchomlinov. During World War I, when the Russian army was retreating and the front was approaching our area, the machines and copper tanks were disassembled and sent east into Russia. The supply of alcohol was poured into a local lake and killed all the fish. It took a good many years until the supply of fish replenished itself.

With time the motorized engine arrived in our town; in 1905, the first machine was brought in for the oil press by the Grimatlicht family. After a few years they put in a larger engine to operate a flour mill, which they had built right beside the oil press. In that same period, the Kroyt family put up a sawmill near the railroad station, run by a motorized engine. Two additional up-to-date flour mills were installed near the main road, one by a partnership between Yonah Landinier and Sirtshok on the west side of town, and the second by the Gelman-Roizman-Wollwushes partnership on the southwest side.

With the end of World War I, partners Moyshe Reyzman and Kalman Kopelzon put up the first distillery (*goralna* in Yiddish), whose products, alcohol and spirits, were sent all over Poland. In 1925–26, the Grimatlicht family and their partners put up a power station, and in 1928 the first movie theater in town was opened by the partnership of M. Tzechshteyn, Abba Grimatlicht, Moyshe Fux, and Y. Roisman.

Contact With the World at Large

Until the outbreak of the First World War in 1914, life in the town continued as it had for years, with set patterns and without noticeable changes. It seemed as if life would continue like this forever, that the town and its environs formed a small world unto itself, for itself, separate and closed to influences from the outside.

The few people who did leave the town and traveled to distant places were those who were unemployed and went to America, and virtually none of them returned. Those few who, after many years of hard work, returned to settle, or those who came on short visits to their families, had almost no influence whatsoever on the town.

Generally, one left the city to travel only a short distance, usually for business matters, to buy goods and in certain seasons to accompany agricultural produce to the big cities.

Sometimes Chasidim made a long journey to see their rebbe. I remember just such a trip that my father, of blessed memory, took to Austria, to see the Rizhiner Rebbe, who lived in Sadigura in Galicia.

Such a journey involved great difficulty and was not inexpensive: acquiring a passport stamped by the district governor who lived in the distant capital, getting a visa from the Austrian consulate, etc.

Making a Living

Making a living was not easy, and for some in the town it was even hard. The energy of most people (including youth) was devoted to efforts to support themselves.

During the week, everyone worked from early morning until late at night, like a busy colony of ants, this one in a workshop or factory, someone else in a store or at a trade. Many families helped themselves with a bit of farming they undertook close to home: a milk cow, a few laying hens, and a vegetable garden.

Even so, there were not a few families in such dire straits that they ate coarse bread and meager gruel. Yes, many, many people knew how to make do with very little and yet still be "contented with their lot."

Mutual help in the form of *g'milas chesed* — giving loans without charging interest and without collateral—and the anonymous giving of charity were widespread and provided support and encouragement in hard times.

There were very few people in town who were well-off. Rich people, or *gvirim* as they were called in everyday language, were really just a handful. Some lent money (charging interest) and were really not looked upon favorably by the townspeople, who saw them as exploiting a difficult situation—*protzentnikes* whose fists were tight and whose hearts were of stone.

There is a story about one of them, "rich as Korach" and "stingy as a Scot," who, upon his death, was refused burial ceremonies by the Chevra Kadisha [burial society] until the family contributed the sum of 300 rubles from the inheritance to pay for a new fence around the new cemetery. The talks lasted three days until the request was fulfilled and the deceased was brought to his final rest.

The Jews of the town were naive, innocent, upstanding, and truthful. Simplicity, earnestness, readiness to help their fellow man in his day of distress were their good qualities. They were religious and had a conscience, and almost none broke the law.

They knew how to stand firm in times of trouble against various assailants and to frustrate their evil designs, and with courage found a way to escape attacks.

Spiritual Life

But man does not live by bread alone. In the evenings, when they turned away from work and making a living, and especially during the long autumn and winter nights, they went to the bet midrash and the shtiblach [little prayer houses]

to learn a page of Talmud, or Mishnah, and the simple folk went to listen to a talk on the *Ein Yakov* or the *Chayye Adam*.

Sometimes crowds flocked to the bet midrash to listen to a preacher or teacher who had come to town. I still remember those nights when the shtiblach were full of people, full of light, and Jews of all ages sat around the long tables, crowding both sides, learning Gemara to a pleasant singsong tune.

I remember the simple folk, standing around the tables near the door, or near the stoves, telling stories or reviewing the words they had heard from scholars and tzadikim [righteous people] before.

The desire of every Jew in town, for which he was willing to sacrifice all his worldly goods, was that his sons become scholars, and that at least one of them be thought of as a learned man.

Sabbath in Our Town

On the eves of the Sabbath and holidays, people tried to finish work early and add time to the holy day, as pious Jews were wont to do. With the approach of the Sabbath or holiday, everyone tried to forget the worries of making a living, to divest himself of the materialism of the work week, and to infuse the environment with the Sabbath or holiday spirit, a spirit of happiness and tranquility.

All those Jews who throughout the week had been out in the villages seeking their livelihood—or who had to be in other far-off places—tried hard to return home even on Thursdays. Any Jew who came back late and came into town on the Sabbath eve at nightfall saw himself as a sinner and tried to sneak in through the alleyways and courtyards in order to make his way home.

In the afternoon, the men started to make their way to the bathhouse to cleanse themselves with steam, with hot and cold water and immersion in the ritual bath (*mikve*). At the same time, the women were making other preparations for the Sabbath—cooking, cleaning, and washing their children's hair.

With the setting of the sun, the mothers received the Sabbath with the lighting of candles on tables set with the best, as their eyes filled with tears and their lips whispered the prayer *Elohei Avraham*. They did not forget, of course, to drop a few coins into the tzedaka box on behalf of R. Meyer Baal HaNes, or other charity boxes that hung in a corner of the room.

With evening there was the impressive sight of hundreds of men, in their Sabbath best, walking with their children to the synagogues and shtiblach of all kinds. And only on the nastiest days, when the rain poured without let-up and the streets were filled with muddy puddles, did the residents of the outlying streets stay home and make their minyans [prayer groups of the required ten men] there.

During the early morning hours, many rose and came to the bet midrash to say psalms or went to the mikve for ablutions there. At about 8:00 or 9:00 in the morning, after reading and studying the Torah and a page of Gemara at home, they flocked to the synagogues for prayers, even the women.

The simple folk, who prayed quickly in the bet midrash or their own little shuls, would finish before the Chasidim in their shtiblach. Especially well known in our town were the Radziner Chasidim, who, in addition to identifying themselves by the blue thread in their *tzizit* (fringes), were known to begin their Sabbath prayers late, not until after 10 o'clock.

Sabbath Zmiros [songs] were heard in the courtyards and in the streets in front of many homes on Sabbath afternoons, and it was especially pleasant to hear the melodies of certain families who had particularly nice voices.

After an afternoon nap, students and Torah scholars made their way to the bet midrash to study a page of Gemara and the simple folk studied Mishnayos and *Ein Yakov*. The children went to their teachers to study *Pirkei Avot* in the summer, and *Borchi Nafshi* in winter. Women stayed at home and read *Kahal Chasidim*, *Tz'ena U'rena*, and others.

In summer many workers and young people took a walk on the Polish Street and in the nearby grove to get a breath of fresh air. Very pious Jews refrained from taking walks, for they were afraid of overstepping the limit of the distance they were allowed to walk on the Sabbath.

More than once the townspeople suffered the misfortune of having the eruv [boundary within which observant Jews may carry items on the Sabbath] break. In these instances Avrom the Lame, of blessed memory, who was one of the most observant people in the town and was in charge of putting up the eruv and seeing to it that it remained without a break, would make the rounds of the synagogues and announce an emergency situation, where it was forbidden to carry anything outside of one's house.

On these Sabbaths, children under 13 would carry their parents' prayerbooks and shawls to the synagogues and back. This also applied, of course, to the Sabbath cholent [a stew that cooks throughout the Sabbath, on a stove that remains lit], which they put into their neighbors' stoves, and which they were usually allowed to carry on the Sabbath.

From the beginning of the Sabbath until early Sunday morning, no non-Jew was seen in the main streets of the town, and the marketplace was still. A non-Jew who forgot what day it was, and came into town by mistake, turned around and left in shame.

When a Child Is Born . . .

It is worthwhile mentioning a typical custom of our townspeople, in the days when children were brought into the world "in a good and fortuitous hour" in their parents' homes, with the help of grandmothers and aunts who drew their knowledge from the births of their own children or of others in the family, or with the help of the midwife (sans diploma) of the town, known as *di bobe* (Granny).

When a woman was ready to give birth, a curtain was drawn about her bed that would divide her from the rest of the house for reasons of modesty and against the "evil eye." The women would paste up on the door lintels printed copies of the *Shir Hama'alot* psalms. Some also put under the woman's head a copy of the holy book *The Angel Raziel*, as a talisman protecting mother and child against bad spirits, devils, and all sorts of evil forces.

If a son was born, the beadle would announce this festive event to the congregation at

the end of Friday evening services in the synagogue and the congregation was invited to come
to the home, after they had their dinners, for a
Shalom Zachar. At tables set with baked goods
and liquor, and particularly with cooked
chickpeas seasoned with pepper and salt (*arbes,*in
Yiddish) and with various kinds of drinks—soft
and hard—the assembled guests would sing and
discuss Torah on the happy occasion.

On all eight days leading up to the circumcision, the little children whose schoolroom was
closest to the home where the baby was born,
accompanied by the rebbe's helper (the *behelfer*—
or sometimes *belfer*) would come to the bedside
and read prayers, including the *Sh'ma* and
HaMalach HaGoel Mikol Ra, and as payment for
their pains they were given a handful of candies
and nuts.

The circumcision, naturally, was performed
at home, and the skin was wrapped in a cloth and
put in a box of sand in the Great Synagogue. It
was customary to nurse the child for a long time,
and if the mother did not have enough milk, or it
stopped too soon, a wetnurse would be hired.

Until the child learned to stand up and walk,
he was kept mostly in his crib, a boat-shaped
little basket woven of shoots and strung to the
ceiling. The child slept in it and spent most of the
day there, and in order to quiet him when he cried
or to get him to go to sleep, the cradle was rocked
like a swing.

The birthrate was generally high, but the
mortality rate was also high.

The Cheder

When a boy reached the age of three, he was
already sent to the cheder [school], to the nearest
teacher for small children. I remember very well
my first day in cheder with the rebbe R. Yisroel,
who lived across the street; I was brought there
wearing my father's talis [prayer shawl], carried
by the young behelfer, while my mother and grandmother shed tears of joy and happiness.

The first things we learned were the letters of
the Hebrew alphabet—*kometz alef, aw*—in order
to become familiar with letters and vowels. Then
they taught us all the particulars necessary to be
able to read the Siddur easily. This was our only

textbook until gradually we progressed to the
Chumash [Pentateuch].

The occasion marking the beginning of the
study of the Chumash usually took place at home
among family members on a Sabbath, when the
rebbe would come to talk about the pupil's
progress. A diligent student would give a small
talk on a timely topic, which had set formulations.

One began as follows: "I have auspiciously
begun to study Chumash: Chumash means 'five'—
the five books of the Torah"—and here the candidate would begin reciting the names of the books
in order, with the help of the five fingers on his
hand, explaining their contents.

Another formulation was: "Rav Ashi said:
'Why do the children begin with study of Leviticus,
telling of the sacrifices [in the Temple] and not
with the book of Genesis [the beginning of the
Torah]?' It is because we, the small children, are
like a pure sacrifice," etc.

Studying the commentary of Rashi, with its
characteristic script, was a middle stage and a
transition to the start of studying Gemara with
another rebbe. At age eight or nine children
started to study Gemara—one lesson per week, a
page or page and a half. Thursday was quiz day.
The student had to read in front of the rebbe his
lesson in Talmud and in the weekly Torah portion, which the rebbe had taught in the previous
four days. The students always were tested in a
set order, starting with the best and ending with
the least capable, the one who had a "hard time
understanding" and was the last in line. Any
student who did not know the lesson as he was
supposed to had to remain beside the rebbe's
table until everyone finished—sometimes until
8:00 or 9:00 in the evening.

There was quite a large number of teachers
for the little children—perhaps three to five on
every street—and they were especially concentrated in the alleys near the synagogue. They
made a meager living—and their work was backbreaking, from morning until late at night, often
including an hour or two on Sabbath afternoon.

The pedagogy of those days did not forbid
corporal punishment, and it was often employed
in many cheders, depending on the disposition
and mood of the teacher. We must give praise to

one melamed of delicate nature and good heart, who, rather than beat a student who did not do well, banged himself several times on the head.

Many parents also sent their daughters for a few hours of study—separate from the boys, of course—learning how to read prayers and a little bit of Chumash.

Cheders were generally in a rebbe's private home—usually a small narrow room where the students barely fit in and were always crowded. Until the age of five or six the youngsters still enjoyed a bit of freedom of movement and a few games: pitching buttons at a hole, hide-and-seek, horses, chasing pigs and throwing stones at their non-kosher hides, and others.

When the rainy autumn and snowy winter came, however, we were stuck in the narrow house of the rebbe for many long hours, except for short breaks in the afternoon to eat, and toward evening to go to the synagogue for the afternoon and evening prayers. On those days the cheder became a kind of prison, and our only wish was to escape from its yoke and its oppressive atmosphere.

It is no wonder that we could hardly wait for the approach of the month of Nisan—when we had a long break—a week before the Pesach [Passover] holiday. We were always praying for the intervention of blind fate so that something out of the ordinary would happen that would give us a bit of free time. If the rebbe got sick or someone in his family died, and as a result we were free for a day or two from studies and being cooped up in the cheder, there were no bounds to our happiness. We were always grateful to the non-Jewish government inspector of schools, who caused trembling among the melamdim who were teaching without a license, and that is how we unwittingly enjoyed a brief respite.

Talmud Torah

The Talmud Torah was the official educational institution of the community, and it is where primarily poor children and orphans learned, since they had no way of paying for a rebbe.

The building of the Talmud Torah was large—three large classrooms and a teachers' room. In the largest front room, enlightened folks prayed on Sabbaths. There was a large field around the building where students played at recess and enjoyed a bit of fresh air.

In addition to religious subjects, prayers, and Chumash, they were taught some arithmetic and Russian. The Talmud Torah was overseen by the official government-appointed rabbi, who saw to it that the education provided was in the spirit of the times.

The name of the rabbi in my day was Bogoslavsky, an elderly Jew with a trimmed beard, a large, broad nose, and a square-shaped yarmulke on his head, who had a serious and strict look to his face. The permanent teacher for the students in the lower grades was Moyshe Yitshak Kagan, of blessed memory, who lived in a small house next to the Talmud Torah, in the middle of a fenced-off fruit orchard and lovely garden into which we longed to enter.

The standing of the Talmud Torah and its importance grew in time, with the arrival of the licensed teacher Shammai Frankfurt from Kovel, who was well-loved by all and was, it seems, a Zionist supporter. He was elegantly dressed, had nice manners, a felt top hat on his head and a shiny walking stick in his hand, and he bowed to all in greeting. (It is worth mentioning that Shammai Frankfurt was the founder and director of the Hebrew high school in Kovel [near Luboml] in the 1920s.) Even today I can hear the lovely melodies of the songs "Zion Tamati, Zion Hemdati" and of "Sham Bamakom Arazim Menashkim Avei Rom" and others, which came through the windows of the Talmud Torah and could be heard from afar. We students in the nearby cheder would sneak up and stand under the windows and listen to those lovely songs, which touched us deeply and moved us to longing for our land.

At about the age of Bar Mitzvah, many students left the cheder or Talmud Torah and slowly were initiated into the adult world, either to learn a trade or to help their parents in business. A small number did continue to study—Gemara and Tosefot and even the Posekim—with the few truly learned teachers or on their own in the shtibl, helped by those who devoted all their time to Torah study for its own sake.

Forward-looking and enlightened parents saw to it that their sons learned secular subjects as well. For this purpose, children would go weekly for an hour or two to a private tutor or to the Talmud Torah. They paid particular attention to writing and nice-looking penmanship.

I remember the first Hebrew teacher in town, Mr. Lisyuk of blessed memory, who was quite handsome and had a nice disposition. He came from Rozhishch. One of the books he used was *Spoken Hebrew* by Krinsky, and also the *Bikkurim* of Pinchas Shifman, afterward known as Ben Sira.

The Problem of Military Conscription

When the boys grew and were approaching the age of 18, everyone began worrying about how to get them out of army service. The period of service, or military work, as it was called in those days, lasted three full years, sometimes more, and the conscript was often sent to the farthest reaches of Russia; soldiers received few leaves, and given the state of transportation at that time, it was almost impossible for them to visit home.

The estrangement from family, in a foreign and often hostile environment, was therefore lengthy, and on top of that the Jewish soldier was likely to have to violate the Sabbath and holidays and eat non-kosher food. It is no wonder then that parents looked for all sorts of ways and excuses to get their sons out of conscription, or at least to shorten their terms of service as much as possible.

At the beginning of the 20th century, there was still a very vivid memory of the decree of Nicolai I in 1827, following which 12-year-old boys were snatched from their parent's homes and were sent to special military institutions—usually in Siberia and the easternmost regions—to prepare and train them from a young age to become faithful soldiers to the tsar and his empire.

These conscripts, called "cantonists," served over 25 years, tortured with all sorts of punishments that their "educators" invented for them to convince them to convert. There were many stories about how they courageously withstood, with unusual devotion, all these terrible trials

without giving in.

I remember a house on our street, across from that of Yakov Meyer Osnat (Pietrushka) to which people used to point and say that in this house the cruel "snatcher" Moyshe Helis lived. And I also remember the cantonist Avromche, who was a guest in our synagogue (the shtibl of the Rizhiner Chasidim) for many months. I, at the request of my departed mother, would bring him food. When he felt like it, Avromche would tell us young children stories of the life of the cantonists, and he would finish with a Russian song about their days of trial and tribulation that they sang to keep up their spirits. All these stories and reminiscences created an atmosphere of revulsion at serving in the army.

Mortifications of the Flesh and Fistfights

One way to get out of the army was to lose so much weight as to be under the minimum requirement. This was achieved by many fast days and little sleep. For this purpose those who had been called up were organized into squads and together they would organize "night shifts." They passed the time in various games in the bet midrash chosen for the purpose—usually the Kotsker shtibl. They also wandered around town and through the marketplace at night and pulled all sorts of pranks. For nourishment they munched on sunflower seeds, and their basic food was a few buckwheat rusks.

Through these mortifications they managed to lose a lot of weight, became very weak, pale, and their eyes bulged out of their heads. There were also some who had themselves mutilated by persons especially given to that task. The most common blemish was a hernia, and the second was pulling teeth. Some cut off their right forefingers or mutilated themselves in other ways—a very dangerous practice that often led to permanent disability. In addition to these methods, they sought other, more sure ways—bribing members of the draft board.

The time for appearing at the draft board was usually September–October, after the harvest. The number from all the surrounding villages reached the hundreds and the call-up lasted several weeks. Village boys would stay in town in Jewish homes, for a small fee, mostly in the Tea Inn, and every morning they gathered around the draft board—the Prisudstva on Polish Street, and waited their turn.

Out of boredom the recruits from the villages—big, brawny fellows—would get drunk, in spite of the ban against selling liquor during these few weeks, and they would start some mischief in the marketplace. They started harassing the passing Jews and often fistfights broke out in which the villagers actually received most of the blows from the hardy city fellows, who gave it back to them many times over.

The best of our lads were Yehosua Shayndl Ranes, Avromele Moyshe Avrams (called "Mazik"), and Itzik "the devil" Komtches.

Our victories were even greater when among the recruits there were Jewish boys from Odessa, who for some reason were listed as having been born in our town and therefore had to come here to register. These fellows were really agile at striking blows, and the non-Jewish recruits left the arena pretty battered.

A Purpose: "Tachlis"

With a boy's release from conscription or at the end of military service, the parents started to worry again, and this time about "a purpose"—meaning marriage and a job. Almost all matches were the work of a professional matchmaker or members of the family. Sometimes matches were made within the courts of the rebbes, where many Chasidim met, and there acquaintances were arranged under the tutelage and with the blessing of the rebbe.

Before a prospective bride was brought to meet the prospective groom, the mother of the groom would go, or would travel accompanied by an experienced aunt, to see what the bride was like. And, in turn, the father of the bride would go to meet the groom, see what he was like, and how proficient he was in the Talmud and commentary. Whoever wanted to have a Torah scholar for a son-in-law had to promise, in addition to the dowry, a stipend for his livelihood (*kest*), including food and other expenses, for a number of years and perhaps also a partnership in business.

As was the custom in those days, it took some time until a match was concluded. From that point on, preparation began for the wedding, which also often took many months. Most weddings in our town took place in the summer, and the preparations were vast: sewing new clothes, preparing a place for the newlyweds to live, sending personal invitations to family members and many friends, hiring the musicians (klezmer), the wedding entertainer (badchan), etc.

Almost without exception, the *chuppah* [wedding canopy] was put next to the Great Synagogue on the southern side, the side with the entry to the *polish* [anteroom]. There was a famous musical group in the city at that time made up of the head of the family and its musical leader (on violin) R. Yakov Hersh Klezmer and his three sons: Arele, who played the flute; Sender, the trumpet; and Yossele, the drums; and also Nyusi (a member of the family), who played the flute.

Menashe "Badchan," the entertainer, was like a fountain pouring forth folk sayings. He was great at rhyming. At will he could bring the audience to tears or he could raise them to a level of ongoing laughter.

The matter of a place to live was solved fairly easily: Inside [the home of the groom's parents] there was a little alcove (*alker*), or they would build a small room onto the father-in-law's house and everyone tried to manage as best they could. They were under the same roof with the parents and were in business together, too—one big family commune.

The Marketplace and the Fair

Most important occasions in the life of the town centered on the marketplace. All news went out from it and all information came back to it.

In many ways the marketplace was also the place for entertainment and enjoyment. Official celebrations and meetings took place there, the mounted police held their exercises there, waving their bayonets and swords while riding their horses; the army, passing through on the way to summer maneuvers, would bivouac there; and a visiting circus would also set up its tent there.

On fair days, the marketplace was so crowded that passage was almost impossible, even for pedestrians. It was filled with the villagers' wagons and with animals they brought for sale, which were tied to the wagons. The villagers and their families spent most of their time sitting on or standing around the wagons until they finished their sales and then they rushed around to the stores to buy what they needed, and then spent a bit of time at the taverns before returning to the village.

During successful fairs the marketplace was so crowded that many who came had to find places to park their wagons on the streets nearby and in the alleyways. The area of the marketplace was divided into various definite sections: the southeastern corner for the horse auction and the section nearby for cows; on its northern section, pigs and stands for selling pork and other products; and the northwestern section for shoes, clothing, furs, hats, and other furnishings.

The noise was deafening; voices of vendors and buyers, mooing of cows, whinnying of horses, snorting of pigs—all these filled the area of the marketplace, which bustled and hummed without let-up until the late afternoon.

The town looked forward with great expectations to regular market days every Monday, and especially to the big fair, which took place once every three weeks on Thursday. Everyone prayed for good weather, which would enable the villagers to turn out in great numbers. After a successful fair, everyone was in a good mood for a number of days.

Events and Experiences

Life in the town continued on its regular course and flowed as a quiet stream. There were few memorable events. One that is etched in our memory is the flight of a hot-air balloon, with its two pilots, over the city.

There was tremendous excitement. Everyone went out into the street to look at this marvel and didn't take their eyes off it until it slowly disappeared over the horizon to the north of the city.

The excitement increased the following day when a caravan of wagons entered the city, bearing the deflated balloon, the net and basket—the pilot's compartment—and the two engineer-

pilots, dressed in rubber suits. Many people followed the wagons and gazed at these impressive things had come to us from the outside world, and this was a topic of conversation for quite some time.

I also remember the arrival of the Rebbe of Sadigura in our town. His Chasidim put up a series of triumphal arches on the street of the railway station (known as the Golden Street in those days), and the main arch at the entrance to the Talmud Torah was attractively decorated. When the carriage approached the gate, the Chasidim unhitched the horses and they themselves pulled the carriage up to the door.

The Rebbe of Sadigura was considered an especially honored guest and was lodged with great ceremony in the building of the Talmud Torah, not in the private house of one of his Chasidim, as was usual with other rebbes.

Another memorable occasion was the death of the rav, R. Leibe (Arye) Finkelshteyn, our beloved rabbi, who was a great scholar and outstanding teacher. R. Leibe held the rabbinic post for many years and was esteemed and beloved by many people in the town and the entire surrounding area. He died at a ripe old age, but even so his death made an unforgettable impression on the hearts of the Jews of the city. It was a public funeral and he was accompanied on his last journey by everyone in the town.

Superstitions

There is no need to emphasize that most people in the town were religious. From the very beginning our lives were bound by religious strictures—on weekdays and even more so on the Sabbaths and holidays. At every turn we had to remember and observe the positive and negative commandments, beginning with the moment we first opened our eyes in the morning until we went to sleep at night.

The belief in the world-to-come, in the paradise reserved for the righteous and all who feared Heaven and, to differentiate, Hell—reserved for the wicked and sinners of all sorts as punishment for what they had done in this world—all this was deeply rooted in us.

As a result there was a constant spiritual

struggle within us between the good inclination and the bad inclination, which tempted and lured us to desire all sorts of forbidden things. Remorse and pangs of conscience of the penitent visited us after every transgression.

In addition, the belief in ghosts and spirits was widespread, and also in the souls of the departed, who would come in the dark of night to pray at the Great Synagogue. On cloudy days and the long nights of autumn, when outside the howling of dogs and the shooshing of the wind were heard, we thirstily and fearfully listened to our grandparents tell horror stories about the ghosts. These made a long-lasting impression and it took quite a while until we were free of them.

First Sprigs of Enlightenment

Books of the Enlightenment or irreligeous books (which our parents called "unkosher, defiled") were rare, and reading them was done in private, away from prying eyes. I still remember the excitement I felt when I found the treasure-trove of books belonging to my brother Gedalia and my father, of blessed memory, which was buried deep in one of the drawers.

This collection included *Those Who Err in Life* by Peretz Smolenskin, the first volume of *At the Parting of the Ways* by Ahad Ha-Am, *Di Klatshe* (The Nag) and *Dos Vintshfingerl* by Mendele Mocher Sforim, and the Hebrew primer *Bikkurim* by Pinchas Shifman. This and a Chumash with Russian translation were plucked out of my hands by my grandfather, of blessed memory, who contended that they were heretical books, and the proof of it was that pictures of the authors in the books showed them to be clean-shaven, and some even had mustaches like non-Jews.

It is worth mentioning that even examining the *Moreh Nevuchim* (*Guide for the Perplexed*) of the Rambam was forbidden. My rabbi and teacher R. Yankl Moyshe Feiveles, of blessed memory, who actually helped me read this book, would nevertheless come with me into a corner, usually in the evenings, in order to avoid the evil eye.

Newspapers were also rare. The number of issues of *Haynt* and *Moment*, distributed and supplied by Shmuel Leyb Guberman, was very small. Only during the time of the Beilis trial (1911–13) did readership increase.

The little bit of the spirit of the Enlightenment and progress that began to penetrate our town at that time must be credited first and foremost to a small group from our town who had gone off to other Torah centers—these were the few fellows who went to study in yeshivas. In some of them the spirit of Enlightenment had taken hold and turned them—and those few women studying in Gymnasia in the big city—to worldly matters.

To them we must add the brave young people who went off to faraway cities, mostly Warsaw and Odessa, to study a trade, and in great measure the young enlightened men from the outside who married wealthy girls from our town and came here to live. Because of them, secular books in Hebrew, Russian, and Yiddish became more available, and the number of people in town who read them grew. Under their influence some people in town began to trim their beards and earlocks, and to wear shirts with ironed collars.

These new customs often gave rise to heated discussions at home, and especially to impassioned responses from the extremely Orthodox during worship on Sabbaths and holidays. In the shtiblach of the Chasidim of Rizhin, Kotsk, and Radzin, many times the service was interrupted as a protest against the looseness and audacity of these renegades. I remember well the interruptions in our shtibl (Rhyzhin), and following them the arguments and scuffles, and the exchanges of sharp words between the pious extremists and the "free" youths trying to defend one of their friends and prevent him from being expelled from the synagogue.

Things got to the point sometimes that the fanatics and hot-heads even called in the authorities, the *ryatniks* and their accompanying *strazhniks*. They would come into the synagogue hesitantly, confused, and stand among all those people wrapped in prayershawls and not quite understand the nature of the argument.

Neither could the muttered explanations clear things up. In the end the police would leave the

synagogue, perplexed as to why they had been
called in the first place and what had been expected of them.

From this point of view, things were no better
for us from 1918–1921 when the various youth
groups, HaShomer HaTsair and HeChalutz, began their Zionist activities: lecture series and
meetings, founding a Hebrew and Yiddish library, collecting funds for the Keren HaKayemet
and Keren HaYesod, amateur plays, pioneering
activity in preparation for emigration to Palestine, etc.

All these were viewed by the fanatics as a
deviation from the right path, irresponsibility,
and turning to evil ways, and many times sharp
words were exchanged. Shouts against the "little
Zionists" and their supporters were even heard
in our shtibl, and I was given the name "Yerav'am
ben Navat," as if to say that I was a sinner and was
encouraging others to do the same, on account of
my participation in the youth organizations.

Members of Histadrut HaOved in Luboml.

BETWEEN THE TWO WARS
By Yechezkiel Kahn

To envision more clearly the life of the Jews in Luboml-Libivne during the early days of Poland's independence, we must describe briefly the events occurring in the town and its environs prior to World War I. We can well imagine what a panic the outbreak of World War I had created in the shtetl, especially among its Jewish population. For the Jews have learned from their tragic history that, during a war, they always suffer more than everyone else, even more than the participants in the struggle.

The first call for mobilization came on Shabbat Chazon (the Sabbath before Tisha b'Av) in 1914. The whole community was in an uproar. Every place through which the mobilized reservists passed suffered damage, and the Jews were the chief sufferers. Whoever attempted to travel by train took his life in his hands.

The frontline, poised for a while at Luboml, did not stay there too long. By the 9th day of Elul, 1915, the Austrian army had taken the town. The soldiers requisitioned everything: flour, salt, kerosene, gold, metal, even the bedding.

A famine spread quickly through the shtetl. In its aftermath came all kinds of diseases, and medication was difficult to obtain. The tragic situation in Libivne was evident from the fact that, during the first year of the Austrian occupation, there were many deaths among the town's inhabitants. Moreover, during that year, there were no weddings among the Jewish people.

Several Jewish families, especially those of the upper class, decided not to stay. They packed their bags and ran deeper into Russia. They continued wandering back and forth along their paths of exile, only to return later to the shtetl to rebuild their lives.

Jews living in the villages and towns around Libivne suffered, too. However, they fared slightly better. They at least had enough to eat.

The Austrians left Libivne in the fall of 1918, and the Polish army occupied the town (the Poles were then in control of most of Volhynia) until, in the summer of 1920, a struggle broke out between the Poles and the Bolsheviks. Finally, the town went under Bolshevik control. The front line was not far from town—on the Bug River, about 11 miles away.

With the signing of an agreement between the Bolshevik and Polish governments that divided Volhynia, the town of Libivne returned to Polish control. And life in the shtetl slowly returned to normal. During that time, many homeless refugees began to return from the surrounding areas. Some settled in the town and began to make a living.

As if the war and the Polish-Bolshevik struggle had not been enough of a burden, there was the additional woe of pogroms in the smaller villages near Libivne.[1] The pogroms were perpetrated by various bands coming from many different areas.

In 1919, a wave of pogroms descended upon the Ukraine, Podolia, and Volhynia. The Jews of Libivne suffered particularly at the hands of the Balechtovtze murderers, for during the postwar turmoil, the Balechtovtze murderers had occupied 19 areas around Libivne. During the pogroms, 131 Jews were killed, and about 600 Jews ran to Libivne and settled there.[2]

Between 1918 and 1921, 90 places in Volhynia were subjected to 122 pogroms and 80 other attacks.[3]

The environs of Libivne were terrorized by

60

these bands, though the town itself did not suffer so much violence. By the end of 1918, there had been only a couple of victims attacked by the temporary police and Ukrainian hooligans. Five Jews were killed; many were wounded, and many homes and businesses were looted and vandalized. This was the sum total of the damage done by the pogroms at that time in the shtetl.[4]

In September of 1920, the Jews from Libivne suffered another series of excesses, carried out by the Polish soldiers during their evacuation and reevacuation.[5]

Relief Efforts

Pogroms continued to rampage. Traveling over roads became dangerous. But the Jewish people immediately undertook to carry out their old tradition of charity and relief. Yet the Libivner Jews, having suffered from pogroms and war, and having had their population increased by the influx of refugees—both their own people and strangers—were in no position to form any effective system of relief by their own efforts.

The main relief, therefore, came from outside Jewish organizations, the chief among them being the Joint [American Jewish Joint Distribution Committee]. From the very onset, beginning in 1917, the Joint initiated and operated a public kitchen, which provided daily free lunches to the needy. And later, in 1919, on the initiative of representatives of Vladimir-Volinsk (Ludmir), Libivne organized a relief committee called Ezra (Hebrew for "help").

In 1920, the occupying Bolshevik government put a stop to this relief work. But when the Poles returned to Libivne, they permitted the Ezra Committee to reorganize, and it became part of the regional committee of Kovel [a neighboring town].

The Libivne Ezra Committee and the Jewish relief committees of the surrounding towns were strongly dependent upon the relief provided by the Joint.

Letters written in October 6, 1919, by Joint emissary Isidor Hershfeld, to the New York Central Bureau are valid proof that this Jewish-American relief organization had somehow managed even in that early period to bring relief to the smaller shtetls of Volhynia. At that time, when nothing was as yet functioning normally, Libivne did not receive relief directly from the Joint but got it through the Vladimir-Volinsk District Committee.

This arrangement did not function too well. Because of postal delays and lack of railroads, moneys had to be sent by special messengers. This method was fraught with enormous risk, both to the messengers and the moneys. But there was no other way out at that time.

A letter written on December 11, 1920, sent by the Rovno Joint to the Warsaw Joint Bureau, reported on a regional conference that took place on November 24, 1920, in Vladimir-Volinsk. The representative from Luboml was Dovid Veyner, who reported that the town then had a population of 8,000 and that 5,000 of them were Jews.[6]

The monthly relief expense-budget amounted to 34,000 marks. Relief money for the Jews of Shatsk was also included in this amount. There were 300 students in the school, of whom 180 were from poor families. He further stated that the school alone was in need of 70,000 marks, and that 83,000 marks were needed for other urgent matters.

At the request of the Ezra Committee, at the beginning of 1921, the Joint opened (and supported) an infirmary in Libivne, where 1,530 Jewish children were examined weekly. Some were provided with cod-liver oil, as appeared in the records of the Joint for April 10, 1921.

The Joint engaged Dr. Sh. Rosenshteyn for the infirmary, as well as nurse Lisa Pomerants, who later married Moyshe Chasid. Joint funds also supported 135 poor families in the town. Pogrom victims and refugees received monthly subsidies.

One of the Joint's monthly reports on funds distributed to the town from December, 1920, to June, 1921, states that Luboml received the following: socks, winter undergarments, pillows, blankets, razor blades, overcoats, soap, rice, milk, cocoa, sugar.

The town's relief committee consisted of Kalman Kopelzon, chairman and Joint representative; A. Budman, vice-chairman for the Tze'ire Tzion; Dovid Veyner, Zionist representative; Ch.

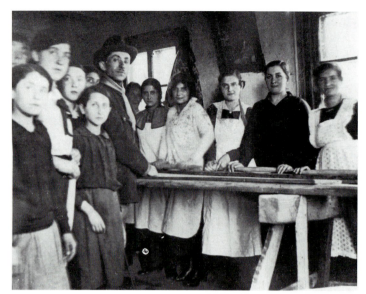

Volunteers baking matzo for the
needy, ca. 1919–20.

Greenberg, representative of the Orthodox Jews;
Chayim Tsin, and Abba Klig.

The Joint played a very big role in helping to
rebuild Jewish Libivne from its economic disaster. In addition, during the first postwar years, the
Jews of Libivne received help from other sources.

One was the Libivne Relief Committee of
New York, which at the first opportunity had sent
$300, a significant sum of money at that time of
inflation. This committee, consisting of Libivner
compatriots in America, also sent help later to
their half-ruined hometown.

Not a small role in improving the economic
situation of Libivner Jews was played by the
direct relief their American compatriots sent to
relatives in the shtetl. From March to April 1920,
the Jews of Libivne received from relatives in
America the sum of 61,000 marks—quite a siz-
able sum!

Right after the war, town communal activists
tried to provide help to those who wanted to start
a small store or a workshop but who lacked the
money for such an enterprise. These men had the
idea to start a fund for this purpose. The result was
the formation of the Gmilat Chessed Kase [a fund
for loans without interest]. A chief initiator of this
fund was Shloyme Samet, and all the members of
the Ezra Committee became his coworkers.

At first, funds came from the Libivner Jews
themselves. The largest part, however, came from
the Joint.

The first Gmilat Chessed after the war did not
last long in Libivne. Only in 1926 was a new
Gmilat Chessed organized, on a much better
foundation; and again the moneys for the fund
came from the Joint. According to a 1929 report,
the Gmilat Chessed distributed that year loans
amounting to 10,076 zlotys.

In 1937, the Libivne Gmilat Chessed had 337
members. The Joint provided credit that year to
the tune of 8,725 zlotys, while the Tsekabe gave
2,173 zlotys. The capital of the Gmilat Chessed
was 4,653 zlotys. The Gmilat Chessed distributed
loans amounting to 14,000 zlotys.[7]

Shloyme Friedman was the secretary of the
Gmilat Chessed for many years. He writes in one
of his letters that it was thanks to the initiative of
HaRav HaGaon Reb Pinchas Oselka (the chief
rabbi of the town), that the following rule was
made: for every kilogram of meat for the Sabbath,
a stamp of 10 groshen was to go to the Gmilat
Chessed. The same letter spoke of a fund-raising
campaign inaugurated by the Gmilat Chessed, in
which the local HeChalutz participated by pro-
claiming a flag-day for the benefit of the Gmilat
Chessed.[8]

The economic life of the Jews of Libivne had
very strong ties with Bank Ludowy (the People's
Bank), which was organized later and was con-
trolled by Motl Privner and Leyzer Finkelshteyn.
It was also closely related to the Bank Kupiecky
(the Merchants' Bank), headed at first by Shmuel

Epshteyn, who later was replaced by Meyer Yitshak Veytsfrucht.

During the first few years after World War I, the Jews of Libivne had, in addition to their other worries, the difficult problem of war orphans—Jewish children who had lost a father, mother, or both parents in the war or pogroms.

In general, Volhynia had suffered a great deal from the war. The number of orphans in its communities came almost to 12,000, of whom 7,000 were direct victims of the war, and the great majority of them roamed in the forests and fields or hid in cellars.

In Libivne proper there were more than 300 orphans. At first, the local Jews were not able to help these orphans. And so the Joint took over the task.

In the early 1920s, societies for aiding the orphans sprang up throughout the territory. In June, 1926, a conference of such societies met in Rovno, where a central committee was selected. Motl Privner was elected as the local representative.[9]

Work on behalf of the orphans proceeded at a high level in Libivne for several years. Public assemblies were held; meetings were called often; and well-formulated plans were carried out. We read a report in a local magazine that a large youth assembly was called, at which Motl Privner lectured on the subject of orphan relief. It was at that assembly, held April 10, 1926, that the League of Friends of the Jewish Orphan was formed. Twenty-five youths immediately signed up as members.[10]

The same month another gathering was held to discuss the orphan situation. Chairman Avrom Sheyntop later reported on it. The meeting elected an executive committee consisting of Avrom Sheyntop, chairman; Motl Privner and Moyshe Esterzon, vice-chairmen; Zalman Barnboym, manager; Shmuel Bokser and Melech Oselka, secretaries; Avrom Reznick, treasurer; and Motl Grimatlicht, Gedalia Zilberblech, Yakov Blumen, and Leybish Pregal, members-at-large.[11]

During the Jewish Orphan Week observance, at which the executive committee was selected, the following people participated as well: Yitshak Samet, Yisarel Kramer, and Moyshe Volvushes.[12]

The list of items distributed to orphans in 1927 included material for 14 coats, 20 suits, and 43 boots.[13]

During one fund-raising campaign of the Orphan Committee, a policeman arrested two fund collectors. These people had to appear before the justice of peace. However, instead of them, the chairman of the Libivner Committee, Avrom Sheyntop, reported to the judge. After he explained the purpose of the fund-raising, the judge dismissed the charge and the confiscated money was returned to the committee.[14]

Another report indicated that, from January to October, 1927, the income of the town's Orphan Committee was close to 4,500 zlotys; the major part of that expense went for food—2,943 zlotys; while the rest of the expenditures were used for education, 278; medical help, 80.35; clothing, 404 zlotys. This report was made by Leybish Pregal at a meeting of the Orphan Committee.[15]

Some funds for relief were appropriated for the Libivner Jewish Orphan Committee by the municipality, which allotted to it an annual subsidy. In 1927 this subsidy amounted to 600 zlotys.[16]

Statistics

As noted earlier, there were many conflicting rumors regarding the population of Jews in Libivne after World War I. Most of these rumors were false. The only valid statistic in regard to the Libivner Jews is found in the official census taken in 1921 by the government of independent Poland. The census covered Libivne as well as the surrounding communities. We quote the figures from that census:

Luboml, which was both a *powiat* [district] and a *gmina* [municipality], numbered 3,141 Jews out of a population of 6,000. The Luboml powiat had the following gminas:

Gmina Berezce (Berzhets) had 29 villages, some of which had Jews:

Berezce ---------------------- 100 Jews (Berzhets)
Czmykos ---------------------- 11 Jews (Shmikets)
Jagodzin ---------------------- 30 Jews (Yadene)
Jankowice -------------------- 30 Jews (Yankovets)

Rymacze ----------------------- 70 Jews (Rimatch)
Sztun ------------------------- 11 Jews   (Shtin)
Zamlynie --------------------- 22 Jews (Zamlinie)

Gmina Holevne had 35 villages, some of which had Jews:

Byk ------------------------------ 3 Jews   (Bik)
Czeremoszna Wola ----------- 8 Jews   (Volie)
Halinowola ------------------- 29 Jews
                                     (Halinovolie)
Holovno --------------------- 23 Jews (Holevne)
Horodno --------------------- 24 Jews (Horodne)
Kuczany --------------------- 26 Jews(Kutshane)
Maslowice ------------------- 10 Jews(Maslovits)
Stara Huta -------------------- 29 Jews   (Hute)
Sukacze ----------------------- 29 Jews (Sikatsh)

Gmina Hoyshtsh had 32 villages, some of which had Jews:

Budniki ------------------------ 7 Jews   (Budnik)
Grochowiska ------------------- 4 Jews
                                     (Grochovisk)
Huszcza ----------------------- 43 Jews(Hoyshtsh)
Opalin ---------------------516 Jews (Opalin)
Wola Ostrowiecka ----------- 17 Jews
                                     (Ostrovolie)
Rowne ----------------------- 52 Jews   (Rovno)
Przekurki -------------------- 14 Jews (Prikurke)
Smolary Rogowe -------------- 6 Jews   (Smolari
                                       Rogove)
Smolary Stolenskie ----------- 8 Jews   (Smolari
                                       Stolenski)
Wilczy Przewoz -------------- 18 Jews   (Pervis)
Wolka Uhruska --------------- 3 Jews   (Ugrusk)
Zaluze ------------------------ 11 Jews(Zaluzshe)

Gmina Luboml had 21 villages, some of which had Jews:

Boremszczyna ---------------- 5 Jews
                                 (Boremshtshine)
Luboml----------------------255 Jews   (Luboml,
                                       village)
Maszow ---------------------- 48 Jews (Masheve)
Podhorodno ----------------- 42 Jews
                                    (Podorodne)
Radziechow ------------------ 37 Jews(Radechov)
Ruda ------------------------- 31 Jews   (Ride)

Wiszniow -------------------- 50 Jews   (Vishnyev)
Zapole ----------------------- 15 Jews   (Zapilie)
Zastawie ----------------------- 9 Jews (Zastavke)
Zawale ----------------------129 Jews   (Zavalie)

Gmina Pulme had 24 villages, some of which had Jews:

Kamionka -------------------- 5 Jews (Kaminke)
Ostrowie -------------------- 18 Jews (Ostreve)
Piszcze ---------------------- 34 Jews (Pishtsh)
Pulemiec ------------------- 30 Jews (Pulemits)
Pulmo ---------------------- 64 Jews   (Pilme)
Wolka Chrypska ----------- 13 Jews   (Volke)
Zalesie ---------------------- 11 Jews   (Zaleshe)

Gmina Shatsk had 26 villages, some of which had Jews:

Butmer ----------------------- 8 Jews   (Butmer)
Holadyn --------------------- 5 Jews   (Holodne)
Switeskie Smolary --------- 17 Jews   (Smolary
                                     Sviteskie)
Switez ----------------------- 42 Jews   (Svitets)
Szack ----------------------238 Jews   (Shatsk)
Wilica ----------------------- 10 Jews   (Vilitse)

Gmina Zgoran had 15 villages, some of which had Jews:

Humilnice ------------------ 17 Jews (Humnets)
Kusniszcze ------------------ 19 Jews
                                    (Kusnishtch)
Nudyze---------------------- 21 Jews (Nudizsh)
Palap------------------------ 56 Jews   (Polapy)
Sokol ------------------------ 7 Jews   (Sokol)
Zhorany---------------------- 5 Jews   (Zgoran)

   —*Skorowidz Miejscowosci Rzeczypospolitej Polskiej*, Vol. IX (Warsaw, 1923).

   In 1931, Poland carried out a second population census. The figures of that census have not been open to the public—in any case, we have not seen them. It is known, however, that in 1931 Libivne had 4,111 residents. We can assume that this is very near the truth, and we can therefore accept that the number of Jews in Libivne at that time must have been more than 3,500.

   —*Columbia-Lippincott Gazetteer* (New York, 1956).

The whole district of Libivne had, in 1921, 56,264 residents. In 1931, the same area had a population of 85,396 souls.

—*The Polish and Non-Polish Populations of Poland,* Census of 1931.

During the Nazi occupation, however, as reported in the section on the Holocaust, the Jewish population of Libivne increased sharply due to the influx of refugees from the surrounding small villages and other places.

Chinuch (Jewish Education)

Prior to World War I, when Jewish life in the small towns of Russia–Poland had not as yet been shaken from its spiritual foundations, it had been dominated by religious elements and by the generations-old traditional Torah institutions. Life in Libivne was no exception in this regard.

After World War I, new winds began to blow in the small towns of the new Poland and former Russia. Significant events in the world and among Jewry had a great influence on the small-town way of life, as well as on the citadel of Judaism— the sanctified educational institutions.

As it was everywhere else, so it was in Libivne.

The old *chinuch mosdot* [educational institutions]—the cheder [the traditional one-room, one-teacher school for children], the Talmud Torah (a more structured, traditional elementary school), the yeshiva (an Orthodox Jewish all-day institution of talmudic learning)—did not, however, give up their positions too easily. They tried to modernize somewhat, but refused to cede the field entirely.

The chief struggle in this respect was directed against the Tarbut schools. Orthodox Jews not only interfered with the establishment of

היושיבה הקדושה בלואבמל

Students and melamdim (teachers) from the Luboml Yeshiva, 1934.

these schools, but, once the schools were established, some Libivner Jews fought against them
with all their might.

As a weapon in this struggle, some Libivner
Jews contemplated establishing a modern Jewish
religious school for children, conducted in the
Orthodox spirit. They therefore founded in
Libivne a Yavneh school, though that came much
later. The Tarbut school was founded in the early
1920s, while the Yavneh school began to function
in the mid-thirties. It was only in a report of 1937
that first mention was made of the Libivne
Tachkmoni (meaning "wisdom" or "academy")
school, which affiliated with the Mizrachi-spon-
sored Yavneh schools in Poland.[17]

Some Orthodox Jews of the shtetl were not
satisfied with the struggle against Tarbut or with
their efforts to support the old chinuch-mosdot in
town. Instead, they wanted to expand even further local Torah education.

After much effort, they succeeded in setting
up in Libivne a yeshiva k'tana [small yeshiva],
fashioned on the Novorodka type. They engaged
Rabbi Noach Katzman as head of the yeshiva. In
a letter dated the 18th day of Nisan, 1933, sent by
the Libivne Va'ad HaYeshivot (Yeshiva Committee) to the Lutsk Regional Yeshiva Committee, it
was written that the town needed funds to bring
the head of the yeshiva and his family to Libivne.
The letter was signed by the members of the
Libivner Yeshiva Committee: R. Arye Leybish
HaCohen London, Avrom Sheyner, Moyshe Wein,
Henech Friedman (the rest of the names are
illegible).

Another letter asking for help for the yeshiva
ktana was sent to the regional committee of Va'ad
HaYeshivot, headquartered in Vilna. The letter
was penned by Libivne's other rabbi, R. Pinchas
Oselka.

In 1935, other members were co-opted to the
Libivne Va'ad HaYeshivot: Reuven Tuzman (head
of the Noach Katzman Yeshiva), Matityahu
Melnitser, Meyer Shoychet, Beynish Melamed.

In 1936, the Libivne Va'ad HaYeshivot was
reorganized. New names were added to the mem-
bership: the newly elected young rabbi, Alter
London, Kalman Meyler, Emanuel Yarin-
Kesboym, Meyer Sandlshteyn, Dovid Katz,
Liptsye Gleizer, Pinchas Granatshteyn, Avrom

Tzvi Tzukerman.

In a letter sent by the Libivne Va'ad
HaYeshivot, local Jews kept complaining that the
yeshiva ktana was in financial trouble because
the Metzudat Yeshiva Lublin kept pushkes [char-
ity collection boxes] in every home![18]

Out-of-town students of the yeshiva ktana
used to esn teg ("eat days" [have meals at various
Jewish homes in the shtetl]. One rabbi of the
yeshiva was Reb Zalman, who married the daughter of Chayim Fisher, Rivke Tzimmerboym. The
yeshiva ktana existed until the Holocaust.

We must mention here that the religious
institutions of the shtetl, besides receiving regular support from outside Jewish organizations,
also received help from the Jewish-American
Ezrat-Torah, which supported many religious
organizations in Eastern Europe in the postwar
period.

During the first few years after the war, funds
were sent to the dayan [judge] R. Yehuda Leyb
(Leybl) Melamed for distribution.[19]

Political Parties

During the time of the independent Polish
state (1918–39), political parties were a most
dynamic force within Jewish social life in
Luboml. There were many Jewish parties, but
the majority of them—the most active and the
most influential—were those which belonged
to the Zionist movements or that were concen-
trating their efforts on preparing to rebuild
Eretz Yisroel [the Land of Israel].

Of all these Zionist parties, the most lively and
most active were the Zionist youth organizations:
HaShomer HaTsair, HeChalutz, and Beitar.

The first such party created in Libivne was
Poale Tsion, with Hershl Chasid at its head.

The first Zionist youth organization in Libivne
was the HaShomer HaTsair. Its founders were
Yisroel Grimatlicht (Garmi), Berl (Bebi) Veyner,
Nathan Blumen, Zalman Fisher, Leibele Melamed,
Eliyohu Frechter, Shmuel Barg, Yitshak Shneider,
Moyshe Volvushes, Dobrovodke, and Yakov
Blumen.

In the beginning (1919–20), the majority of
the HaShomer HaTsair members were girls—60
of them. They were organized in kvutzot. The
leaders of the kvutzot were Nechome Veyner,

Lyuba Shames-Vishnits, Yehudit Tsurif, and Zelde Listhoyz.

HaShomer HaTsair was a great force in the shtetl, but later its influence waned somewhat, for two reasons. First of all, it was purely a scouting organization, without any particular political stamp, except, obviously, for its general Zionist inclination. Moreover, the Polish powers-that-be put all kinds of obstacles in the way of the efforts of Jewish youth.

Later, when HaShomer HaTsair evolved into a party, its program came under the suspicion of the Polish authorities. By that time the honeymoon of the Polish democracy was over. The regime, especially after the Pilsudski revolution, had become more and more reactionary, more chauvinistic, and more antagonistic toward the Jews—therefore HaShomer HaTsair, with its declared sympathy for the Soviet Union, began to be looked upon by the Polish authorities as a disloyal element.

Police began to spy more diligently upon the activities of HaShomer HaTsair. They made a raid once on a meeting held by HaShomer HaTsair in a little forest near the shtetl. They beat up some of the young people and arrested the others. Such acts by the police had a negative effect upon the growth of this organization.

The second cause was an internal Zionist one.

As a Zionist scouting organization, HaShomer HaTsair had the warmest sympathies of all Zionist parties. At the beginning, it was the sole darling of Zionist parties everywhere, and they supported its educational and cultural activities as well as financially. But when HaShomer HaTsair became a party, the relationship of other Zionist parties toward it changed all over the world, obviously also in Libivne.

And when in 1920–21 the older members of HaShomer HaTsair formed HeChalutz in Libivne, almost all the Zionists who had formerly sup-

HaShomer HaTsair members on a Lag BaOmer outing, 1929.

Active members of Keren Kayemet LeYisrael (JNF), 1925–26. *Standing right to left*: A. Sandlshteyn, Y. Bargrum, Sh. Weingarten, M. Shapiro, M. Asolka, Y. Teytelboym. *Second row, right to left*: M. Privner, Sh. Shliva, A. Zagagi, Gelibter, A. Klig, M. Lederson, M. Kreizer. *Third row, right to left*: M. Grimatlicht, Sh. Russman, Y. Samet, Z. Fisher, M. Volvushes, L. Pregal, and Sh. Bokser.

ported HaShomer HaTsair transferred their sympathies and their support to the new organization. One can well understand that this did not do HaShomer HaTsair any good.

HeChalutz, which operated under General Zionist slogans, though in its ideals it leaned toward Labor Zionism, attracted a great many Jewish youth of the town. Among the first of those who made aliyah [went to settle in Israel], even before the founding of the HeChalutz in 1920–21, were Motl Grimatlicht and Hershl Fuks (may his soul rest in peace).

When HeChalutz was established in 1921, some of its members began to work at hachsharah (preparatory training for prospective agricultural immigrants to Palestine); the first training they received was in carpentry, which took place in the home of the Soloveytshik family. Their teacher was Efrayim Fantuch (the son-in-law of Tana Stolyar). This

teacher made aliyah together with his entire family (he died a year ago in Tel Aviv).

At the beginning of 1923, the following made aliyah to Israel: Note Blumen [changed his name to Nathan Tcheleth]; just after him, Yisroel Grimatlicht [changed his name to Yisroel Garmi]; after them (1924–25), Elye Frechter, Bebik Veyner [changed to Gafni, may he rest in peace], Sheyndl Yafe, Malke Krayzer, Leybish Gleizer, Henech Kornfracht, Moyshe Lederson, Yisrolke Yeruchems, Yakov Mayzels, and others.

It is important to note that, before all the others—I believe in 1920—Motek "Royfe" (paramedic or folkhealer) and his family went to Israel to settle. They had left the shtetl when World War I broke out and went to Odessa, and from there they made aliyah to Israel; at the same time, during the aliyah campaign of the Yesomey Belkind, Ch. Shildergemeyn also left for Israel.

Among others, it is worthwhile mentioning

Members of HeChalutz, 1931.

the aliyah of the bobe (midwife), whose name was Rochl-Leye. She had been a midwife in the shtetl for many years. She was quite successful in her work and was respected by everybody. She spent her last years in Jerusalem with her daughter, who was married to the famous Rabbi Kosovsky, the author of a concordance to the Talmud.

In 1934, a hachsharah-kibbutz arrived at the shtetl from the Kloszovo HeChalutz. It consisted of 20 young men and 10 young women, most from Volhynia. In 1935, this kibbutz sent its first agricultural pioneers on aliyah to Israel.

The HeChalutz leaders later organized

Beitar parade celebrating the unveiling of the flag in 1933. (Courtesy of the Jabotinsky Institute)

HeChalutz Hatsair, which developed very nicely. Arye Shtern, the first Israeli representative to Rome, was one of the first members of HeChalutz Hatsair in Libivne.

In the mid-thirties, a branch of Ha'Oved was organized. It was an artisans' organization of the Labor Zionist movement. It had about 50 members, 10 of whom had made aliyah. The local HeChalutz helped with organizing Ha'Oved and leading it. At the regional conference of Ha'Oved held in Lutsk, the Libivner chapter sent two

formed its own hachsharah-kibbutz in the shtetl. Two such hachsharah groups were one too many for such a small shtetl; they led to frequent unbridled rivalry and competition for the very few jobs in and about Libivne.

The Beitar hachsharah-kibbutz took in members only from other towns, while the Beitar groups in Libivne sent their own members to complete their hachsharah elsewhere.

There existed also a Brit Hachayal group, with the following men active in it: Yisroel Kramer,

Members of the Beitar sports organization, HaKoach, 1930: *From right to left*: Sh. Kroyt, V. Reyzman, Sh. Gershenberg, M. Eizenberg, F. Goldborten, A. Brikman, L. Tzimerboym, Y. Reif. *Second row*: B. Eizenberg, Sh. Zilberberg, M. Lifschitz. *Third row*: A. Fuks, M. Zilberblech, M. Kosover.

representatives, Mendl Varshniter and Berl Volvushes.

Beitar, organized in 1929, also developed rapidly and soon became an important force in the shtetl. Its founder and first mefaked [commander] was Yitshak Shapiro, and after him Shmuel Zilberberg. The commanders at different times of its existence were Yakov Getman, Chayim Huberman, and Chayim Honig.

Beitar had its own soccer team. It used to play in matches both with local and outside teams.

This Revisionist youth organization also

Shmuel Fuks, Berke Sfard, Moyshe Sfard, Moyshe Klerer.

Many clashes took place between the organizations of the Revisionists and the Labor Zionists, especially during party meetings.

Moyshe Lifshitz was the secretary of the Revisionist Organization for many years.

But despite all the disputes and clashes among the parties, and despite the tricks they played on each other, the time between the two world wars was the best and most interesting for the Jewish youth of Libivne. It was a time when the national

Jewish youth were living with a great dream of individual and national redemption—a dream that was burned together with its dreamers in the Hitler crematoria.

A Dramatic Group

Regarding the pious Jews it is not appropriate to speak of cultural work. Naturally, among them Torah is everything; and whatever is connected with the Torah is automatically considered the highest and best. All other things are *dvorim b'teylim* [idle words]. The spiritual center is the bet midrash, the cheder, the yeshiva—these are the places where the pious Jew carries out what the secular Jew calls "cultural work."

The secular Jews think differently. Their cultural work is not so monolithic; it reaches out into many domains. But inasmuch as it has been connected with the activities of Jewish political parties since World War I, it is represented in the party work. An exception is local Jewish theater work, which has not always been tied to a particular party.

Immediately after World War I, a Jewish dramatic group was organized in Libivne. Its founder and leader, from its very inception, was Hershl Chasid. At times he was also its dramatic director.

The group put on a series of performances, including *Bar Kochba*, *Hertsele Meyuches* ("The Heart of an Aristocrat," by Yisroel Helfant of Rakovits), *Yeshiva Bocher* ("The Torah Student"), *Tzezeyt un Tseshpreyt* ("The Dispersed"), directed by Avrom Blushteyn, *Mirele Efros*, *The Kreutzer Sonata*, etc.

Later the troupe was reorganized, especially through the efforts of HaShomer HaTsair, and it put on such plays as *Kol Nidre*, *A Mentsch Zol Men Zayn* ("You Must Be a Man"), *Chasye di Yesoyme* ("The Orphan Girl"), *Der Dorfs Yung*

("The Peasant Boy"), etc., directed by Yakov Dreksler, and later by Fayvele Dreksler from neighboring Chelm.

Participants at that time were Hershl Chasid, Avrom Blushteyn, and Chasye Pomerantz, who was the main singer in the play *Bar Kochba*, Rivke Rayz, Tobe Rayz, Chaymke Kagan, Elke Eizenberg, Niemetz, Moyshe Chosid, Rivke Dubetsky, Chome Friedman, Avrom Ziegelman and Abba Grimatlicht, who was the official prompter for the troupe. Later participants were Nechome Veyner, Gitele Veyner, B. Veyner, Y. Grimatlicht, Yehudith Tzurif, Z. Listhoyz, Yisroel Kramer, and Zalman Fisher.

Profits from the performances were used for various Jewish causes in the shtetl—social and cultural.

In later years, other local Jewish amateur theater groups put on performances in the shtetl. These performances would inject a holiday atmosphere into the monotonous life of the shtetl, and Jewish youths and Jews in general would fill the theater halls.

And though what follows has nothing to do with the Jewish theater, it is somewhat related to Libivne's amateur actors: An all-Ukrainian dramatic group was founded in Libivne. After the Austrians evacuated the town, the leader of this troupe came to Hershl Chasid and suggested that Jews, together with Ukrainians, take over the town and hand it over to the Ukrainian army, which was about to enter.

After this conversation, Hershl Chasid went to Mordche Natanzon to consult with him on what to do. Natanzon advised him to have nothing to do with the Ukrainians if he wanted to avoid bringing trouble upon himself and upon all the Jews in the shtetl. And Hershl followed his advice.

NOTES

¹ From a table in *Recueil de Matériaux sur la Situation Economique des Israëlites de Russie*, Paris, 1906, p. 32, it is apparent that the number of Jews residing in towns and small shtetlach in Volhynia was greater than in the provinces of Vitebsk, Kiev, Poltava, Kherson, Bessarabia.

² This information, as with the previous data, are based on documents to be found in the Central Archive of the "Joint" in New York. I wish to thank Mrs. Ruzha Klepfisch, the director of that archive, for her friendly help.

³ G. Gergel in *Shriftn far Ekonomik un Statistik*, II-1, ed. Yakov Leshtshinski, Berlin, 1926, p. 107.

⁴ L. Chasanowitsch, *Die Polnischen Judenpogromme in November und Dezember 1918*, Stockholm, 1919, p. 29.

⁵ *Der Tzeitv. Yid. Natzional-Rat un der Siyem-Klub bei im*, ed. Y. Grinboim, Warsaw, 1923, pp. 85–86.

⁶ It is stated in a report from Volhynia "Joint" for the period October 1919–June 1920 that Libivne has 10,500 inhabitants, of which 6,500 were Jews. These numbers, and similar ones, cannot be relied on. Reliable statistics are only those which come from a reliable source.

⁷ Nearly all this information comes from "Joint" reports. See also: *The Gemilath Chessed Kasses in Poland*, New York, 1937, p. 37.

⁸ *Folkshilf*, January, 1933.

⁹ *Fun Yohr tzu Yohr*, calendar for 1929, Warsaw, pp. 81–82.

¹⁰ *Unzer Hilf*, nr. 3, Rovno, 1926.

¹¹ Ibid.

¹² Ibid., nr. 7, 10 November.

¹³ Ibid., February, 1927.

¹⁴ Ibid., January, 1927.

¹⁵ Ibid., November, 1927.

¹⁶ Ibid., August, 1927.

¹⁷ *Mif'alot HaHistadrut 'Yavne' she'al yad Ha'Mizrahi' BePolin*, Warsaw, 5693. Here we must note that though Libivne had a "Tarbut" school in 1919, no delegate from there was sent to the first national conference of the "Tarbut" schools in Poland while the small town of Masheve was represented by a delegate (Tartarovski). See: *Tarbut*, Warsaw, 5682, III.

¹⁸ The attached letters are to be found in the archive of YIVO-New York. I wish to thank Yechezkiel Lifshitz, the YIVO archivist, for allowing me access to these letters.

¹⁹ *Zikaron Besefer*, New York, 5681.

WORLD WAR I AND ITS AFTERMATH
By Yisroel Garmi

The First World War broke the framework of shtetl life and shattered its very foundations. The Jewish community was crushed by continuous trials and tribulations that swept over it wave after wave. The constant pain and terror overpowered it from the time of the Austro-German occupation through the Russian Revolution and all the resulting upheavals. And then came the wars between the Soviet Union and Poland. These events left scars in the hearts and minds of everyone. They shattered traditional lifestyles, dreams, and illusions, and thus prepared the groundwork for vital changes in the strivings and hopes of the youth.

★

Until 1915, life in the shtetl remained unchanged because the front was far away—in Galicia near the Carpathian Mountains, and in East Prussia. Gradually, however, news began to reach us about the destruction in Galicia and about the troubles that befell the Jewish communities with the arrival of the Russian Army.

The call for conscription was a source of great worry for many families. The actions of the Russian army passing through the villages on its way to the front, and the looting and pillaging by the Cossacks—who broke into Jewish stores and homes—filled the population with horror. They also began to grab people off the street in order to force them to dig ditches and erect barbed-wire fences south of our town, near the village of Vishnyeve. My friend Yitshak Schneider (z"l) and I snuck in among the grown-ups who were caught in the square, and we were sent to dig trenches and put up barbed-wire fences. We got half a ruble a day for our work, while adults got one ruble.

When the job was finished in our town, the Russians conscripted many people to dig ditches and put up wire-fences near the forests and swamps near the village of Kurpivnik, 15–18 miles north of our town. The housing and the food provided for the forced laborers was unbearable.

How well I remember my ride there with the wagoner Boruch Tsiziz (z"l). The purpose of these trips was to bring food, taleysim [prayer shawls], and prayerbooks to the Jewish laborers. My father (z"l) and my rebbe, Reb Hersh of Kritnitse, were among the conscripts. On the way back we met many refugees from villages near the approaching front. And the Cossacks, who roamed the roads on their horses, honored us with whip-lashes every time they passed us.

The Great Russian Retreat

The great retreat of the Russian army from Galicia and western Poland began at the end of June, 1915, as the front moved eastward. Field hospitals for the wounded were set up in our town. Day and night, reinforcements streamed to the front by railroad and over dusty roads. Heavy artillery, cannons hitched to three pairs of horses, moved on the highway toward Brest-Litovsk [Brisk]. Numerous army camps were set up around our town for last-minute training of newly drafted soldiers.

Jewish refugee families began to arrive in our shtetl. Thunderous sounds of cannons pierced the stillness of the night, and the flaming red skies were a clear sign that the war was nearing our town.

The local Russian government officials started to leave, taking their families eastward. The local peasantry began a virtual flight in their wake, and so did the town's Ukrainians. Some Jewish families, who were connected to the Russian officials and imbued with patriotism toward Russia, packed their belongings and likewise headed eastward.

The atmosphere in the shtetl became increasingly depressing. Military ambulances began to bring in victims, mostly from poison gas used by the Germans. Others were mortally wounded by dum-dum bullets. The fields around the town were rapidly filled with graves. Several leading Jews of the shtetl were summoned to the town's commandant, who threatened them with heavy fines or other penalties if any townspeople were caught spying.

After several days, however, the armies

Dovid Prussman, son of Gitl Prussman, of 86 Brisk Street, as a soldier in the Russian army. He is shown here as a German prisoner of war (#3997) in the Diratz camp, 1918.

stopped their movements and the cannons were silenced. A dead stillness engulfed our town as anticipation of what was about to happen filled the people with fear. The last divisions of soldiers, with their weapons and field-kitchens, passed through our streets as they made their way northeast, walking in disorderly fashion toward the Polesian woods. The Cossack horsemen formed the rearguard, being the last to leave.

For the next few days, the shtetl became a virtual ghost town. The people shut themselves in their houses and hardly a soul ventured into the street. Here and there a hardy soul peeped out into the street or even stepped out for a moment. No lights were visible in the evening, and silence enveloped the shtetl.

Tension grew by the hour as we waited impatiently for the Austrian vanguard to fill the void created by the retreating Russians. Three days after the retreat, and a few hours before the Austrians' arrival, the Cossacks, together with Ukrainian peasants from Horodno—a village known to be a nest of murderers—spread through our town to rob and pillage Jewish property.

As they busied themselves grabbing booty from Jewish stores in the town square, and tried to set fire to the house of Yakov Feller, a rain of bullets was showered upon them by Austrian soldiers in blue uniforms who had reached the western side of the town.

The memory of these events is well ingrained in my mind, perhaps because of the tragicomic occurrence involving my uncle, Lipe Grimatlicht. This is how it happened: While the Cossacks were fleeing, and the sound of the bullets was heard, my uncle peeked out through the door of his house to see what was going on.

A Cossack, passing by on his horse, aimed at my uncle and his bullet just missed my uncle's house, to be embedded in the wall of the house next door—that of the Samets family a house that shared a roof with my uncle's house.

Horrified, my uncle began to yell that he was shot and was about to die. Not satisfied with his announcement to his own family, he ran to our house, which was not far from his, and broke into the house, shouting, "They shot me and I'm dying!" It took us a while to convince him that the bullet hadn't even touched him.

Under Austrian Occupation

The Austrian army entered the town toward evening. Our people received them with joy, and as evening descended they stood in their doorways holding lamps to light their way.

The front had moved further east and we all felt greatly relieved. Danger seemed to have passed us by. For the time being, there was enough food, and we dared hope that the war, with all its horrors, would soon be over and life would return to normal.

Not much time had passed, however, when our hopes and illusions were shattered. First, the conquering Austrians confiscated all our wheat, flour, produce, and other food products from the stores and warehouses. Then they took our animals—horses and cows. They even took away the only cows from families with many children. I shall never forget the night of terror when dozens of gendarmes and soldiers suddenly surrounded the streets, going from one courtyard to another confiscating the cows. They beat our people with gun-barrels, not even sparing women or children who tried to stop them from stealing their cows.

The conquerors became increasingly cruel. They grabbed men in the street for all kinds of forced labor. They caught women, too, forcing them to pick nettle, apparently for use as cloth. Women also had to wash the floors and clean the living quarters of officers.

To travel by train or commute by wagon to other towns was forbidden, unless one obtained a special permit. Food became scarcer day by day. Hunger was widespread. The food that some were able to get from villages did not last long. Even the villages suffered from hunger. By the summer of 1916, the whole population suffered from hunger.

The Typhoid Plague

The typhoid epidemic broke out that summer, and with it also came cholera and dysentery, playing havoc in our shtetl. There was hardly a house without a death. The mortality rate was very high, and the Chevra Kadisha (burial society) worked day and night to lay the dead to rest. Some of the bodies were brought to the cemetery

The house of Yakov Feller, at the southernmost corner of the marketplace. Next to it is the Hotel Tseylingold.

and buried at once, without any funeral.

The plague ran wild during the summer months, reaching its peak in October and November, 1916. The authorities offered no help. Our town had no doctors then. Instead there was a feldsher [paramedic], Motek Royfe, who took the place of a doctor in the shtetl. But he left together with the retreating Russians, going east. The only thing the authorities did was to mark every house hit by the epidemic with a cross, to mark it for future disinfection.

In those awful days of suffering, townspeople organized into self-help groups to aid the sufferers. Each street had its group, the members of which were on duty day and night, on call to any house struck by the disease. They washed the patient with alcohol, put cold compresses on his head, and stayed at his bedside during the night, without consideration to the danger of infection.

The Black Chupa
(The Black Wedding Canopy)

It is interesting to mention the black wedding canopy that the shtetl elders arranged in the month of Elul that year, as a remedy against the plague. An orphan girl, who was paralyzed and who lived near Shmuel Velvl the gravedigger's house, agreed to marry an orphan, a poor, unknown boy who had come to town as a visitor.

Our townspeople looked like shadows, with their slow, hesitant walk and heads bent low by the burdens of sorrow and bereavement that had touched almost every house. Women ran to the cemetery, where they fell upon the graves of their relatives or some righteous person to pour out their hearts, to tell of their sorrow and pray that the lives of their loved ones be spared and that the plague end.

From the cemetery they next ran to the synagogue and with heart-breaking cries prayed before the holy ark, imploring God to stop the cholera so that the children would not be left orphans.

How shocking and frightening was the sight of these women bursting into the synagogue during the Sabbath or holiday service, making their way through the praying men to stand before the ark! All prayer stopped as the wailing women opened the ark and with heartrending, terrifying

voices, cried out the following:

"O holy Torahs, ask God to send us mercy. He should grant full recovery to the sick mother who is wrestling with the Angel of Death. Pray that the babes not be left orphaned."

Before leaving, the women again turned to the men and pleaded softly: "Oh, you pure Jews! Pray for the life of this sick patient, that she not be taken from her family, *cholile* [God forbid]!"

The Problems of Cleanliness

The authorities issued strict orders and warnings about cleanliness. People were to be punished for the slightest infraction of the rules. Sanitation men were recruited from among older reservists, who roamed the streets together with policemen. They examined the courtyards, alleys, and side-streets to make sure orders were enforced.

If someone was caught throwing slop-water into the street, or if the feces of humans or animals was found near a house, the owner of the house was whipped several times and locked up for several days in the local prison. They used the front part of Barnboym's house as a prison.

In those days the people did not know of (or did not need) the institution called a toilet. Hence cleanliness was rarely observed outside the home. Things somehow took care of themselves without much trouble. If someone had to do a "small one," he would turn to the wall of a building wherever he happened to be, mostly in an alleyway or between two buildings, do "his thing," and then go about his business.

To do a "big one," his problem was just as easily solved, either in the yard behind the house or on special lots for this purpose located between the Talmud Torah and the cemetery, or behind the Kotsker shtibl. There was a kind of "gentlemen's agreement" between the sexes— one would not trespass on the other: each knew the limits of the other's area of "sustenance"!

Neither was garbage disposal too difficult. Every home had a vessel for waste disposal that contained waste and bath-water. Assorted garbage would go into it as well.

When the vessel was full, someone emptied it into the small sewage canals that ran on both sides of the street, or into the [vacant] lots, or, to a certain extent, even into areas around the house.

Water was naturally absorbed by the earth, and solid matter in no time found its way into the stomachs of pigs, these natural "sanitation workers" that crawled about in packs in every corner and every alleyway, enjoying this bounty.

During the war, however, when these beneficial animals disappeared, the problem of cleanliness and sanitiation grew ever worse. The person who was doing "number one" was fined a silver Russian ruble, and "number two," five rubles in gold. Twice a day we would sweep the front of the house and the whole area around it. The people would tremble when they caught sight of the sanitation crew approaching. They would quickly take out brooms and rakes and scrape up any bits of dirt they might have missed earlier.

Because of typhoid fever, another plague accompanying cholera, the sanitation group would detain people from time to time and examine their hair and clothing for lice. If they found any, they would take them instantly to the public bathhouse, where they would force them to undress, disinfected them with hot steam, and shaved their heads—even the heads of girls.

Quite often they would shave men's beards, in spite of the protests and pleading of the victims. I remember well the tragicomic event that happened to our neighbor Elye Moyshe Feygeles: After his beard was shaved off, he covered his head with a red kerchief to cover the nakedness of his face and made his way home in shame, his clothing wet and wrinkled from the steam.

When he opened the door, his wife Finya, taking him for a beggar, offered him alms; but, shortly, both burst into tears.

The Young Men from Out-of-Town

At the beginning of the summer of 1916, groups of young men came to the shtetl from surrounding areas—Lutsk, Rovno, Rozhishch, and elsewhere. They were of mobilization age and some were deserters from the Russian army. Fearing their own towns would be retaken by the Russians, they settled temporarily in our town.

Most had had a high school education, and their influence on the youth of the shtetl soon became evident. We admired them and absorbed every word they uttered. Most spoke a perfect Russian, and some also knew German. One was a photographer who opened a studio in our town—something new to us. These young men tried any kind of work that came their way, especially in agriculture, in which many Jewish families from town were engaged, potatoes being the main crop, because of the wartime lack of food. There was a great deal of abandoned land available, and anyone had only to ask for it to get free land to cultivate. Some of these men, headed by Binyomen Farshtey, joined the civilian militia for the government. To this day I cannot understand how such educated and aristocratic young men could allow themselves to serve as "whips" whom the government used against the Jewish community!

The founders of the Hilfs Fareyn in Luboml. *Right to left*: Y. Tseylingold, Y. Samet, A. Blushteyn, A. Grimatlicht.

Volunteers in the public kitchen, 1917–18.

Conditions Improve

In the summer of 1917, conditions improved a little. Oppression lessened and persecution ceased. Some of our people settled down and found ways of making a living by cultivating land to produce vegetables, such as carrots or beets. Unlike many others, they stopped suffering from hunger or malnutrition.

Veteran Austrian soldiers benefited from this produce, too. Russian war prisoners helped by caring for old or wounded horses. They also helped themselves by sneaking out at night to raid the fields, filling their bags with potatoes and other vegetables. Some came to the Jews on Sabbath eves to beg for bread or potatoes.

Self-Help and Cultural Activities

The Hilfs Fareyn [self-help group] was organized that summer—an institution to help the needy (I do not remember who supported it—the Red Cross or the Joint). It formed a public kitchen (Folks Kich) that served hot meals to all comers, who also could take meals home. The kitchen, which operated from 1918 to 1919, no doubt saved many a family from dying of hunger.

The first such kitchen was located in the home of Motl Yisroel Sonyes son in the market-place, but later moved to the home of Asher Hursh on Chelm Street. The self-help group and kitchen were run by volunteers, both young men and women.

Binyomen Farshtey from Lutsk, together with other young people, formed a cultural group. Its members used to gather on Sabbath afternoons in the hall of the kitchen and sit for hours in rapt attention, listening to readings of Gratz's *History of the Jews*, followed by fascinating discussion and explanations.

I often snuck over with my friend Veyner to listen to these readings while standing under a window. The group became a nucleus for widespread cultural activities that lasted in the shtetl from 1918 to 1919, the year when Poland annexed our area.

Austrians Leave; Russians Arrive

Only vague echoes of the Russian Revolution, reached our town, or of the possibility of peace, the Balfour Declaration—and about what generally was going on in the world. It was no wonder, then, that the sudden departure of the Austrian-German authorities came as a complete surprise to us. More surprising was the entry of the Polish cavalry after a week of complete chaos, with no government except for local militia formed after the Austrians had left.

How well I remember the early morning hours, when rumors spread through town that the government administration, police, and quartermaster corps in charge of supplies all had left town in

Hershl Chasid, a Chalutz (pioneer) from the enlightened town youth.

a great hurry, abandoning town in the middle of the night and heading west.

Those who were quick-witted among us ran to the homes and the offices of the Austrian

Needy townspeople wait near the public kitchen (Folks Kich) for a warm meal. The kitchen was located in the house of Motl Yisroel Sonyes in 1917.

officials, to be quickly convinced that it had indeed happened; that the conquering regime had really collapsed and left for good; so the mob ransacked the empty homes and took everything they could. Soon afterwards, crowds formed around the warehouses, breaking into cattle corrals—and a fight started over the division of the spoils. People loaded sacks of provisions on their backs: potatoes, sugar, salt, flour, etc. Everyone was grabbing—in no time at all, the warehouses were empty and abandoned.

Small units of soldiers stationed in nearby villages, not being aware of the situation, had come in for supplies as usual. They were stunned when the crowd ordered them to leave their horses and wagons behind, and leave quickly on foot to the railroad to join other troops leaving the front to go home to their families.

The following day the townspeople were surprised to see another contingent of soldiers, hundreds of them, loaded down with equipment; they stopped in town for several hours before leaving on their way west. They were Czech soldiers who had deserted from the army, taking with them their ammunition. The soldiers were organized into special units, returning to Czechoslovakia in an orderly manner.

Some of the soldiers, being drunk, tried to attack passersby or break into homes to rob them. The town militia opened fire, and the fighting lasted several hours, but luckily there were no casualties. They left in the afternoon and order was restored.

When the Poles arrived, a civilian administration was established. But it took the townspeople some time to get used to the new regime. The relationship of the administration to the Jews was a difficult one; all public activities and functions of the youth organizations were viewed with suspicion and obstructed by the new regime. This was before the area was officially annexed to the newly created Polish state.

Zionist Organizations

Life slowly returned to normal. Peasants returned from their wanderings to their farms, resuming daily tasks. Contact with the Jews of Poland proper was strengthened, and business and financial activities increased. Along with this, the desire grew among the youth to organize and take part in the variegated social and Zionist activities on the upswing among Polish, Galician, and Lithuanian Jewry, and in the bigger towns of Volhynia. This came as a result of the Balfour Declaration, as well as of the Chalutz Aliyah movement looming on the horizon.

The first signs of youth organizing into parties appeared at the end of the summer of 1918, with the Austrians' departure and the Poles' entry. The first to be founded was the Poale Tsion party. One of its organizers and most ardent members was Hershl Chasid (the oldest son of Leyzer Isaacs, z"l), whose image impressed the youth in our town—for he was a brave and fearless fighter for progress and against religious rigidity, which had hemmed in our daily life with all sorts of prohibitions, preventing us from receiving an education and leaving the shtetl for the wide open outside world.

He, more than anyone else, dared to rebel against accepted customs; to raise the flag of revolt. He wore a hat, a tie, and a white starched collar; he shortened his coat and shaved his beard; and above all, he spread "forbidden books" among us. He was the first to organize an amateur theatrical group, staging plays and playing the lead parts. The income from the plays went to cover party expenses.

The performances brought a breath of fresh life into the hearts of young people, for they broke somewhat the boredom and emptiness of shtetl life and served as a source of inspiration and encouragement for our cultural activities.

The Local Theater

The first play produced (in great secrecy and with self-sacrifice) was *Hertsele Meyuches* ("Hertsele the Aristocrat"). It was performed in the "great hall" of Motl Yisroel Sonyes, which was changed into a theater by taking apart the walls in some rooms and the stable to form one large hall.

On rainy days the roof leaked, but the understanding audience took the dripping from the ceiling and the puddles underfoot with great equanimity.

The next play was Goldfaden's operetta *Bar*

Kochba, which ran for quite some time. Its success was beyond our expectations, and its influence was felt for a long time. Everyone was impressed by the strong and beautiful voice of the actress, Feyge Pomerantz, the daughter of Sholem Yitshe, the town water-carrier. She played the role of Dina, Bar Kochba's sweetheart. Her songs continued to be sung by everybody in town for many years to come.

This, too, was a brave deed of Hershl Chasid's—encouraging a poor girl, a seamstress by trade, by teaching her to act, preparing her for a leading part that she filled so successfully. Hershl played Bar Kochba himself; he wore a black cape, a sort of pelerine from the Napoleonic era, and a wide-brimmed toreador's hat, making a tremendous impression on the public.

The townspeople waited impatiently for the big day when the curtain would rise on the charming play, the content of which and the cast names they knew long beforehand—from those lucky enough to attend rehearsals (held mostly on Saturdays). The putting on of plays involved great effort not only for the actors, who had to overcome the opposition of their parents, memorize their parts, prepare the appropriate costumes, etc., but also for the devoted helpers, the "technical corps," who had difficult tasks: to get censorship permits from officials, which required traveling to the big city (Lublin or Warsaw); finding somebody to use his "pull" to get that permit; to prepare the hall and stage; to bring in benches from the synagogue (mostly by stealing) and chairs from private homes; finding large lamps to light the hall (also taken from the synagogue); borrowing stage props, such as furniture; bringing a make-up specialist from the big city; engaging musicians (klezmer) to play before and during

Members of Tarbut committee with author Rachel Feigenberg, 1929. *Sitting, right to left*: Y. Garmi (Grimatlicht), N. Veyner (Blau), the author Feigenberg (Emory), Y. Samet, M. Volvushes. *Standing, right to left*: Kahn, M. Varshniter (Henech), Dov Ivri (Volvushes), M. Grimatlicht.

Cast of *The Jewish King Lear*, August 1919.

the intermissions, as well as for the dances that followed the performances and lasted well after midnight.

The buffet, a source of income almost equal to that of the play, was staffed by volunteers of the technical corps. All participants in the play—actors and all the others—regarded their tasks as holy and performed their jobs with devotion and great enthusiasm, despite their parents' opposition.

I shall always remember the unusual devotion of my friends Nathan Blumen, Eliyohu Frechter, and Yitshak Schneider (z"l), who constituted the technical corps of our amateur troupe in HaShomer HaTsair. They did their work with great efficiency, in spite of, and perhaps because of, the fact that everything had to be done in secret, so that their parents, who were strictly Orthodox, would not find out.

The opening of the play always took place on Saturday night. If the play was a success, it was repeated Sunday evening. The names of the cast were kept secret so that their parents would not find out. This was especially important for the

women, since their parents regarded their appearance on any stage as entirely unacceptable.

I well remember the opposition of my parents when they found out for the first time that I was playing a role in *Tzuzeyt un Tzushpreyt* ("The Dispersed"), by Sholem Aleichem. I played the role of Sashke, a boy who loved to play with cats. They were also opposed to my brother Abba, who was the prompter, a very important task, without which no play could go on.

We would prepare posters announcing the play in a beautiful handwriting, coloring the name of the play and surrounding it with an attractive border. We would paste the posters on walls of houses just before the advent of the Sabbath, so that religious members of the shtetl would not be able to remove them.

Choirs and a Library, Thanks to the Theater

It is hard to exaggerate the value and impact this theatrical activity had on the lives of the youth. In addition to injecting a lively spirit into people's hearts and creating a cultural atmosphere, this activity led to the creation of choirs. And the money the performances brought in became the endowment for the first library in Yiddish and Hebrew, established by the HaShomer HaTsair movement; it paid for reading rooms affiliated with other movements and for inviting speakers from the Union of Writers and Journalists from Warsaw.

The fact that there was already a hall suitable for performances made possible the visits of other theater troupes, among them the Azazel satirical company, a group of the finest actors from the Moscow Theater, who had left Bolshevik Russia, as well as the singer Broche Tzefira and Nachum Nardi from Palestine.

I believe the first performance by a visiting troupe was in 1927, and movies began in 1928. The first performance took place in the Dom

HaShomer HaTsair membership card.

HaShomer HaTsair library rules, which the borrower of a book had to obey, 1920.

Members of HaShomer HaTsair in Luboml, 1922.

Polski, the palace of the landowner Kampyoni, and only after the opening of the Radio movie theater did performances move there.

In the wake of successful first performances by the local troupe (*Hertsele Meyuches, Bar Kochba,* and *Tzuzeyt un Tzushpreyt*), theatrical activity broadened, and in time many other plays were presented, such as: *God, Man and the Devil, The Yeshiva Boy, Be a Mensch, Kol Nidre, The Farm Boy, Hassia the Orphan, The Slaughter,* etc.

New directorial talent also was added: Israel Elfant from the village of Rakovitz, Avrom Blushteyn of Pervis, and the cousins from Chelm, Yankle and Fayvel Dreksler.

Among the most outstanding actors were Feyge Pomerantz, Chome Friedman, Chamka Kagan-Schneider, Avrom Ziegelman, Niemetz, Yitshak Chiniuk, Yisroel Kremer, Zalman Fisher, and Bebik Veyner, all of blessed memory—and may they be granted long life, Rivtse Reiz-Rozenfeld, Nechome Weiner-Blau, Yehudit Tzurif-Halperin and Zelda Listhaus.

The Youth Movement

Contributing to the achievements of local youth in the beginning of Polish sovereignty [late 1918] was a group of intellectual youths from the nearby town of Chelm, who had political experience and who often stayed over in our town. These young people, mostly members of Poale Tsion or the Bund, awakened our youth to political activities and lively debates on relevant topics. Among them was a young poet, Mechele Ribayzen, who elicited both our curiosity and a sense of awe. Under the influence of these fellows we began reading socialist literature; we lustily sang the songs "Hulyet, Hulyet Beize Vinten" ("Whirl, Whirl You Angry Winds") by Avrom Reisen, "Hemerl, Hemerl Klap" ("Pound Away, Little Hammer") by Y. L. Peretz, etc. We also often sang the romantic song:

Black eyes radiate fire
And your eyes are so dark!
You've thrown a red-hot spark into
My own true boyfriend's heart.

Among these youths was a student—still wearing his cap from the University of Warsaw—named Motek Ivri (z"l), who evidently was an active member of the HaShomer HaTsair movement in Congress Poland, and thanks to him we can be proud of the HaShomer HaTsair movement in our town. In a short time this movement included most of the young people from the ages of 13 to 17. Out of this group came the nucleus for a local branch of HeChalutz and the impetus to found the first Hebrew school, through which some youngsters were inspired to learn Hebrew (mostly on their own) even before the school was opened.

The writer of these lines, together with his friends Bebik Veyner (later on in Palestine he called himself Dov Gafni), Leibele Melamed, (who was murdered, with other victims in Russia, by the cruel tyrant Stalin and his cohorts), Zalman Fisher, Yitshak Schneider (Itche the Scribe's son), may they know a long and good life, Nathan Blumen-Tchelet (Nute the Schochet's son), Eliyohu Frechter, and others, was among the first to meet in secret with the older comrade Motek Ivri to discuss the nature of the movement. These discussions soon became lessons on the aims of the movement and the means of realizing them, as well as marching drills and actual prac-

Jewish National Fund committee and Zionist Youth organization, 1930. *First row, right to left*: M. Volvushes, Y. Samet, M. Reyzman, Sertchuk, Y. Kramer, Dov Ivri (Volvushes), M. Estherton. *Second row, right to left*: M. Grimatlicht, N. Weiner-Blau, M. Shapiro, S. Fisher, N. T'chelet (Blumen), R. Reiz-Rosenfeld, M. Kreizer, L. Afeldman. *Third row left to right*: Reyzman, Tzukerman, Tz. Kroyt (Ferst), M. Varshniter, S. Gershenberg, Sh. Kornfracht.

tical activity: organizing youth into groups and having frequent conclaves and discussions—in the summer in fields and forest groves and in winter months in the party meeting-place—during which we explained to our members the theory of the movement, its goals and aspirations and ways to bring them about in our daily life here as well as in future aliyah to Palestine.

While our activities increased, the involvement of older youth broadened to include more segments of the population. In addition to the Poale Tsion party, the Tze'irei Zion party was established, after that the Hit'achdut, and after that the General Zionists and the Mizrachi.

One of the important activities around which all party activities could gather was collecting for the Keren HaKayemet Le'Yisroel, and after that also for the Keren HaYesod. The outstanding volunteers who took on these worthy causes with great diligence and fervor were Beni Rozenfeld (z"l) and his wife Rivtse (née Reiz), may she have long life, who then emigrated to America.

In time, cultural activity expanded, finding expression in the new reading rooms and new library (in addition to the one that had been established by HaShomer HaTsair), the banquets and lectures, the new choir and "mock trials" on various topical issues. These activities were accomplished by local talent as well as artists and lecturers from the outside, generally invited by the Union of Writers and Journalists in Warsaw.

Add to these, of course, the visiting lecturers from the Keren HaKayemet and the Keren HaYesod and from the various political parties.

Special mention ought to be made of the Keren HaYesod emissary Moyshe Rozenberg (nicknamed "Moysey"), who passed away a few years ago in Haifa, and the representative of the cultural center in Rovno, S. Rozenhak, who also died in Haifa, in 1969.

Limiting Our Progress

The local authorities did not look favorably on these activities and began in numerous ways to halt our progress. For instance, they forbade members of our movement, HaShomer HaTsair, to engage in scouting, and especially to parade through the streets of the city on Lag BaOmer, the 20th of Tammuz, and other days. We had to get special permits, obtained with great difficulty through the intervention of the prominent citizens of the town.

The authorities also decreed that we must have a permit for any meeting or assembly, even for having books or maintaining a reading room, not to mention for a performance. Getting a permit depended on bringing certification from the government censor (in Lublin) that the play contained no propaganda or anything derogatory against the authorities and government.

Many times we engaged in our activities in secret; we often were taken to jail, from which we were freed after a day or two through the intervention of community leaders who assured the authorities we did not belong to the Communist party and that our only purpose was to organize youth to emigrate to Palestine.

In this context I recall an incident that occurred in our town when a memorial was convened on the anniversary of the death of Dr. Max Nordau, of blessed memory. The hall was packed, and on a table two memorial candles flickered. Just then the Police commandant came by and began grilling us on the meaning of this meeting being held without a permit.

One participant answered, in not very fluent Polish: "Sir, Max Nordau has died"—but using the feminine form. The policeman, thinking we were holding a memorial service for a woman who had just passed away, was satisfied and went on his way.

In fact, these persecutions never really let up. Government representatives always found another excuse to forbid our activities and put a stop to them, and each time they brought up their suspicions and fears that we were engaging in underground activity directed against the authorities.

Persecutions and Pogroms

In spite of oppression and persecution by the authorities, we continued our activities without let-up until war broke out between Poland and Soviet Russia in the summer of 1920.

The attitude of the authorities toward Jewish residents in captured territories of Volhynia and Lithuania (the Kressy) became more strict. Persecutions against those even slightly suspected of supporting Bolshevism grew daily. Organizational and cultural activity was restricted, and all activity centered on worries about day-to-day existence—and fear of the day after.

Troops making their way to the front often attacked Jews; riding a train became a life-threatening event because of outbursts by troops and their harassment of Jewish travelers with all sorts of insults and even physical assaults—spitting in their faces, pulling off their earlocks and cutting their beards, delivering blows, chasing and throwing them off the cars.

Particularly notorious were the soldiers of General Haller—the "Hallerchikes"—known for perverted attacks. On their way to the front, they would get off the train at intermediate stops and bully the Jews waiting there. And more than once, when a train had to remain for a while in a station, they went into town and broke into Jewish homes and shops to pillage and steal.

The Jewish populace feared the future, particularly the retreat of the Polish army and approach of the front to the outskirts of our city. They had had the experience of the previous war, of attacks and murder they suffered when the conquering Polish army came through in the fall of 1918.

The demoralizing fear grew when they learned that with the retreating Polish army were remnants of Petlura's Ukrainian army, Denikin's army, and the murderous bands of Bulak Balechovitz, who had joined the Poles against the Bolsheviks.

Intimations of destruction quickly turned into bitter reality. Word came of the slaughter of Jews in towns to the north—Kremne, Shatsk, Iflis, and others—by Bulak Balechovitz's murderers and local bullies, began reaching our town.

For more than a week, wild bands wreaked havoc without let-up: They harassed, raped, and killed in all sorts of horrible ways a great number of Jews in the villages. The dead, and even parts of bodies, lay strewn about for days, until they were gathered for proper Jewish burial at the cemetery in town.

I remember how a group of young people volunteered for this final act of charity, among them my father's brother, of blessed memory, and also Nute Blumen, may he know long life. Immediately after the Bolsheviks captured the town, they went out with carts, armed with rifles given them by the authorities—to the surrounding villages, gathered the corpses, and brought them to their final rest.

Only through a miracle were the Jews of our town saved from the fate of their brothers in surrounding areas. And this is how:

When it was learned that another regiment including remnants of Petlura's, Denikin's, and Balechovitz's forces was due to pass through town in its retreat to the other side of the Bug River, the community leaders immediately called an advisory session to decide how to fend off the danger likely to befall the Jews and their property from these bands.

It was clear to all that there was only one way to save the situation, and that was to intercede with the city authorities and the military commander to reroute the retreat at a distance from the city.

After their consultation, the community leaders immediately set about raising funds, and a delegation was organized—at the head of which was the new rabbi, Rabbi Pinchas Oselka, of blessed memory, who spoke Polish very well. The community delegation turned to the Catholic priest, and with his help and intervention—and, of course, with the presentation of considerable sums—the military commander agreed to arrange the retreat far from the city limits.

The Barefoot Army

On the heels of the retreating Polish army that took up positions on the other side of the Bug River about 10 miles from town, the Red Army advanced into the city in the early morning hours without opposition and without incident.

The entry of the Red Army was not particularly festive or impressive—not what one would expect of a conquering army. The opposite was true: The first troops, in torn clothes and with meager equipment, aroused both disappointment and surprise. Ragged and worn, they made their way through the city to the front—tired, some walking, some riding the train, but most on farmers' small carts hitched up to skinny, sorry-looking horses—and accompanying them, a few pieces of artillery. They were called "the barefoot ones."

After a few days the Soviet government began to organize, setting up headquarters in a few houses in the center of town. The civilian authorities set up shop in the Afeldman house, and the "Cheka" in Shmuel Ochs' house. Here, one room was put aside to serve as a jail.

The RevCom, or revolutionary committee, was established. Some local residents participated, fulfilling various tasks. Among the participants were members of the Chinyuk family, who had long believed in the Communist idea.

Life in the city did not return to normal. All business was curtailed; most stores remained closed; villagers virtually stopped coming into town to sell produce and buy needed supplies. Confidence in Soviet currency faltered. For fear of requisitioning [by the army], stores were totally emptied of their goods and everyone worried about keeping a supply.

Adults wandered idle, worried about what tomorrow would bring. In contrast, the youth, many workmen, and the less well-off received the Soviet regime with reserved happiness, with hope and expectation that some recognizable change would take place in their lives.

In spite of our doubts, we saw the entry of the Red Army and Soviet authorities as a highly significant event, which was going to redeem us and free us from the narrow, stifling confines in which we had had to live until that time. Within us, hopes were aroused for a breakthrough to a new way of life, with increased and promising possibilities.

We spent part of our time reading newspapers and propaganda literature in the reading room, which opened a few days after the Red Army moved into the Shmuel Hetman house, and the rest of the time we spent near the concert stage set up in the market square near the Natanson house. Many young people came here to listen to a violin recital (the violinist was a Jewish fellow from Kiev) and to the songs and recitations of an army entertainment troupe that

had arrived by special train. The performances almost always were a prelude to propaganda speeches on the new order to be built by the Soviets on the ruins of the capitalist world.

In the Company of the Red Soldiers

Part of our time was spent playing dominoes and chess with the soldiers, talking with them, etc., and in the evenings we joined them for performances in the theater set up for them in Kampyoni's large house (for repairs they hired the local "bourgeois" elements, Moyshe Reyzman and Kalman Kopelzon). These soldiers were from various units of shock troops quartered in town and they lived in Jewish houses together with the families.

They were often intelligent people, with a clearly Communist consciousness. Their relations to local inhabitants were polite and correct and the term *tovarishch* ["comrade"], which they even used when speaking to us, had an element of familiarity (it removed the barriers between us).

We also used to walk among the wounded who arrived from the front and offer them cups of milk. At first the wounded were concentrated in the small square in front of the Catholic church. There, the severely wounded were laid on ragged blankets spread on the ground, and before many of them could be moved to hospitals in the rear, they died.

I remember one evening, the day before the retreat, when one after another cart filled with wounded came through. We discovered many Jews among them, and I remember one from Tomashov, wounded very badly, who begged us to try and notify his family somehow so they would remember to say Kaddish after he died.

Help for the Soviet Army

Our support for the new regime grew in stages, as did the desire to cooperate; youth began to respond to requests by the authorities for volunteers for all sorts of jobs. Some older ones, among them my two older brothers, volunteered to load coal onto the armored trains that had come to bombard the enemy entrenched on the banks of the Bug.

Also, my father—who refused to give up the

pair of horses we'd had since the German occupation (and with which we cultivated our fields), responded "willingly," so to speak, transporting in his wagon a number of soldiers and their artillery to the front; and he remained there in the trenches a number of weeks until his younger brother came to replace him

A Sobotnik Operation
That Was Not Carried Out

My friend Bebik Veyner and I were called to the offices of the authorities in the Afeldman house, where we were received nicely by an elderly man named Kolashnikov. He admonished us to bring the young people we led into the Komsomol, in return for which we would gain access to high school and university, so that we could get a higher education and integrate into the life of the Soviet regime, which would solve the Jewish problem.

As a first step, he told us to parade the very next Sabbath, with red flags flying, to the railroad station, where we would engage in some loading work for the army. This would be called Sobotnik work and would symbolize the beginning of the new path for our youth as we integrated into the Komsomol.

We hesitated to give him a clear commitment on observing this Sobotnik commandment, and explained that first we had to call a general meeting of all the youth groups to organize from scratch, to find the way into their hearts—a task that would take some time.

The Poles Return

In the meantime, the Poles began a counterattack, and the Soviets began to retreat eastward, so the front came close to home once again. On a Friday, at the end of the month of Elul (August–September), Polish planes began bombing our city and one bomb fell beside the flour mill owned by Volvushes, Gelman, and Royzman, near Mendl Eizenberg's home and Hershl Lifshitz's house, along the main road.

As a result, Mendl Eizenberg's eldest son, Yisroel, was wounded and died, as did Mendl's brother, also named Yisroel; Moyshe Lifshitz,

may he live a long life, was severely wounded in the legs.

The next day, early Sabbath morning, the Polish vanguard entered after an exchange of fire with Soviet troops. With the Soviet retreat, bloody

Hersh Fuks, an early immigrant to Eretz Yisroel.

massacres again raged in surrounding villages, committed by the murderous bands of Bulak Balechovitz with the help of village bullies. The Polish occupiers resumed these attacks, and once again we realized we had to leave that bloody place as soon as possible, and that our future lay in Eretz Yisroel.

A Vain Appeal That Did Not Cause a Stir

With the reestablishment of Polish authority in the areas of the Kressy, and the return of normalcy, Zionist activity was vigorously revived. As in other towns and villages, a few activists, from the movement began to think about establishing a Hebrew school in our town. We discussed it with a few adult Zionist activists and with their agreement we called a meeting of progressive-thinking parents in the Talmud Torah on a Sabbath afternoon.

At this meeting it was almost unanimously decided to start this activity and from that point on we began to publicize the project, verbally and in writing. I remember how I met with two members of HaShomer HaTsair, B. Veyner (Gafni) and Leybl Melamed, and we renewed publishing our appeal to the parents, spiced with talmudic sayings.

One Friday afternoon we met in the Rizhiner shtibl, where my parents davened [prayed], and we made a number of posters which we then pasted on the doors of most synagogues in advance of the Friday evening service, as was customary in those days. The posters were handwritten, in the beautiful penmanship of Leibele Melamed, who was known to have artistic talent (after a while, he went to Soviet Russia, completed studies at the academy in Kiev, and exhibited in many shows. During the Stalinist bloodbaths Leibele Melamed was killed, too).

We hoped that the appeal would make a big impression on its readers—our parents—and that

Mordche Grimatlicht, the first halutz to emigrate to Eretz Yisroel.

they would unanimously and immediately decide to establish the Hebrew school.

But only a few hours passed before our enthusiasm began to wane. Our parents read the poster, some superficially, some intently, but they called no meetings and did not even speak about it—as if it did not concern them.

Despite our disappointment, we were not discouraged, and we continued to bother the more active parents about it. We also used the fact that in the neighboring town of Masheve there already was a Tarbut school and we told our parents it would make them look poor in comparison if they did not achieve what a small town like Masheve had managed to accomplish.

Rachel Leah, the bobe (midwife).

Motek Royfe and family, the first Jews from Luboml to emigrate to Eretz Yisroel, 1921.

Hebrew Teachers Come to Our Town

As a result of our unending requests, several parents finally took the initiative in bringing a Hebrew teacher from Novgorod Volinsk, named Budman—at the recommendation of Hershl Ehrlich, who knew Budman as an outstanding pupil from their student days.

I remember well when he first came to town. My uncle, Abba Klig, an active General Zionist who had worked a lot toward establishing the school, hosted the teacher in his home until he was completely settled and accompanied him to our synagogue that first Sabbath. We all kept looking at him.

He wore a dark coat, which did not seem especially to warm his thin body, and on his bald head he wore a student cap with a shiny brim. He had an intelligent, thin face and spoke Hebrew with a pure Ashkenazi accent. Before long, the organized parents brought another teacher from Warsaw, the capital city—Palevski by name—who was a follower of the German educator Friedrich Froebel, and spoke an elegant, fluent Hebrew with a Sephardic accent. He was the one from whom the children learned proper Hebrew pronunciation and how to sing the latest Hebrew songs.

With an increase in the number of students, additional teachers were brought, among them Dubelman, who came from a nearby town across the Bug River and was known for his Hebrew poetry being published in the journals; and Yakov Blumen, son of R. Aaron the Shochet [ritual slaughterer] and the grandson of the Kiresher Shochet, who was self-taught and had reached the level of a teacher with broad knowledge in Hebrew, which he successfully introduced as the spoken language in his home—a daring act at that time.

This is a good opportunity to mention that even before the Hebrew school was established and the teachers arrived, the sounds of spoken Hebrew often were heard among members of the HaShomer HaTsair movement, who bought Hebrew books and on their own reached a level where they could speak fairly easily among themselves.

The Hebrew school continued for only a few years, but its influence was felt for a long time after it closed. Many children continued to learn Hebrew from private tutors, especially from Yakov Blumen, and they spoke it well.

Pioneering and Aliyah

At the beginning of 1921, a group of young men from HaShomer HaTsair formed HeChalutz HaTsair, the framework within which they began preparing for emigration to Palestine. With the help of ORT [Organization for Rehabilitation and Training, a charitable Jewish organization founded in 1894], a carpentry shop opened in the Soloveyshik home, and several fellows (including Nute Blumen) learned the carpentry trade there under the dedicated direction of Efrayim Fantuch, the son-in-law of Tane the carpenter, who himself later went to Palestine and passed away in Tel Aviv.

Elye Frechter learned to be a blacksmith at Yitshak the Blacksmith's. Bebik Veyner (Gafni) went to the ORT school in Vilna. Some parents could not come to terms with the fact that their sons wanted to become artisans and workers, for this marred their middle-class status. But their children prevailed and the training continued until their aliyah to Palestine.

The aliyah to Palestine from our town started with the emigration of Mordche Grimatlicht and Tsvi Fuchs (from the village of Volie), who went in 1921. Then Nute Blumen (Nathan Tchelet) followed, and also Israel Grimatlicht (Garmi) at the beginning of 1923.

Along with the emigration of the Belkind orphans, a member of the Shildergemein family also went and was for many years a member of Kibbutz Heftziba.

In 1924–25 many more left, among them Bebik Veyner (Dov Gafni) of blessed memory, who studied engineering at the Technion in Haifa; Eliyohu Frechter, Arye Zagagi, Henech Kornfracht, Moyshe Lederson, Malke Dreizer (of blessed memory), and Yakov Mayzels, from the nearby village of Visotzk. From that point on, emigration to Palestine was sporadic; it increased in the 1930s.

At this point it is worthwhile mentioning the aliyah of the Lederman family, that is, Motek Royfe and his family, at the beginning of the 1920s. Motek Royfe actually was the first from our city to go. He left from Odessa, where he had lived since he left Luboml during the first World War, on the eve of the occupation by Austro-German forces. The prettiest of his daughters was once chosen as beauty queen of Tel Aviv in those days, and she married the nephew of Prof. [Chayim] Weizmann, Israel's first president.

We also note the aliyah of an outstanding older woman, who is perhaps unknown to our younger folks—Rachel Leah, the midwife (known as Bubbe), who had a wonderful reputation and whom everyone admired. She took with her a Torah that had been written in memory of her beloved son, who died at an early age; she lived in Jerusalem near her daughter, who had emigrated as a young girl and was married to a famous rabbi, author of a concordance to the Talmud, Rabbi Kosovsky, of blessed memory.

AFTER WORLD WAR I
By Meyer Natanzon

In my day there were three rabbis in town. Why three, you ask? Because the town had a variety of Chasidim who could not come to an agreement about having one rabbi for the entire community.

The rabbi of the Trisker Chasidim in town was the rabbinical judge [dayan]. Rabbi Leybl Melamed. The Rizhiner, Radziner, and others had as their rabbi Pinchas Oselka, and the Kotsker had Rabbi Leybish Landau. Before this period, the town's rabbi was Leyb Finkelshteyn.

Rabbi Finkelshteyn's son, Dovid, wrote anonymously in the journal *HaTsefirah* at an early age. At home, of course, he was afraid to read a newspaper or write for one. For these purposes, he used, quietly, the Kotsker prayer room.

With regard to the Zionist movement, local youth were not far behind other shtetls in Volhynia. In the early 1920s, we organized the Keren HaYesod in Luboml. The most important members were myelf, Elke Eizenberg, Mendl Eizenberg's daughter, Gedalia Grimatlicht, and Leybish Gleizer. Elke was the treasurer.

In light of the fact that the times were uncertain and robberies were a regular occurrence, Elke's brother Srulik buried the money collected for Keren HaYesod. Later he was killed and we could not find the buried money.

Occasionally we were visited by party leaders from Warsaw or other towns. One, I. Mereminski, participated in a public trial we held of Dostoyevski's *Crime and Punishment*.

In the home of Shmuel Bershtat, a kind of club was organized where Jewish youth gathered and participated in heated and interesting debates about Jewish problems that seemed at the time the most important issues in the world.

A year or two after the war, a Tze'ire Tzion party was organized in town. At the beginning, its chairman was Asher Budman, founder of our Tarbut school; Natanzon was vice-chairman and Elke Eizenberg was secretary. Active members in the organization were L. Gleizer and M. Grimatlicht. The various Zionist parties took control of the entire town. The Bund was very weak. Among the locally active Bundists was Yeshaye Sheyntop.

The Jewish Communists, though few, were quite active in certain circles. The three brothers from the Chiniuk family were all Communists. During the time of the Polish-Bolshevik war, just after World War I, when the Bolsheviks occupied Luboml for a few weeks, the few Jewish Communists in town played an important role.

After the Poles took back Luboml, they arrested some of the Communists and sent them to Kartez Bereze (an exile camp). The father of Chiniuk and his son Chayim-Hersh died in that Polish camp. Ben-Tsiyon came back a sick man. He later escaped to Soviet Russia with his brother Itzik.

A Ukrainian leader in town once said to Hershl Chasid: "Let us go help the Russians against the Poles." Hershl told me about it, and I reminded him: "Have you forgotten what Chmielnicki and his cohorts did to the Jews? We will be the first victims." He listened to me. It so happened that this time the Poles guarded us from the Ukrainian pogroms.

Hershl Chasid was the leader of a drama group in town. The group especially performed plays by Jacob Gordin. The plays were presented in Motl Yisroel Sonyes' brick building, in front of which was a tavern. At night everything in the tavern was rearranged into a theater hall.

During the German-Austrian occupation of the First World War, the town suffered greatly from lack of food. The forced labor tormented everyone. Every second day, people received 4 $^1/_2$ pounds of bread mixed with sawdust. The pieces of wood were removed from the bread, and it was eaten as if it were the best cake.

During the later period, the headman in town was a German or Austrian colonel. He was a liberal man. He overlooked the illegal trade across the Bug River and, as a result, the town's situation with food became much easier. Before his departure from the town, this colonel appointed a committee that consisted of six Christians and six Jews, among them Meyer Natanzon, Kalman Kopelzon, Leybish Gleizer, and Gedalia Grimatlicht. He also provided arms for self-defense against bandits from surrounding areas.

Until the middle of the 1920s, there were two Jewish pharmacies, owned by Kalman Kopelzon and Israel Natanzon. In reality, the two were only "drug stores," but they dispensed all kinds of prescriptions. The real pharmacy belonged to a Pole.

Until about 1920, Luboml had no Jewish doctor. We only had two feldshers (paramedics): Motl Royfe and Hersh Royfe.

A JEWISH POSTAGE STAMP

Luboml-Libivne is the only town in Poland, and perhaps the entire world, where a stamp was issued with a Yiddish inscription. This was not done by Jews but by the local authorities for the whole population.

At the end of World War I, Europe was going through terrible confusion. Once-powerful Germany and Austria-Hungary lay defeated and partitioned. Russia was in the throes of a civil war. The formerly enslaved peoples in those nations began to show nationalistic tendencies, demanding independence for the territories in which they resided. And they did get self-determination through the victorious Allies, the Western powers.

One of the newly risen nations in Europe was Poland. The formation of a new government apparatus could not be accomplished rapidly. Neither could the postal system between different areas of Poland be put in order too quickly.

Therefore local Polish authorities organized their own temporary postal system, at least for neighboring areas, and issued temporary postal stamps. In the majority of areas, the authorities used the former stamps of Germany or Austria-Hungary, overprinting Polish words on them.

Some towns, however, issued their own stamps. Their names were printed on the stamps in several languages, according to the minorities in the towns. One of the towns was Luboml, where a series of six stamps was issued in 1918. They had pictures of important town buildings and the words "City Post Luboml" appeared in four languages—Polish, Ukrainian, German, and Yiddish.

We are including photographs of the stamps issued for Libivne. On these stamps we see the old Libivner synagogue, the marketplace with its brick stores, the Catholic church, and the Greek Orthodox church.

יהדות ובולאות

בין ההופעות השונות בחו"ל, שיש להן תוכן או כתובת עברית או קשר אחר לעבריות, נזכיר ראשית את בולי העיר ליובומיל, שהופיעו בשנת 1918. בולים אלה הופיעו מטעם דואר העיר, מאחר שהנהלת המדינה אז לא היתה מרוכזת בידי שלטון כללי עבור המדינה כולה. במצב כזה היו נוהגות ערים להוציא בולים מיוחדים משלהן, שהיו בשימוש באותה העיר ובסביבתה. אנו מציינים את הבולים הללו כטיוחד, הואיל והם נדפסו, בניגוד לבולים אחרים מאותו מין, גם באידיש. הבולים הללו הופיעו ב-4 שפות : אידיש, אוקראינית, פולנית וגרמנית.

Stamp and excerpt from article, *left*, taken from Isidor Zeiman, *Olam HaBulim* ("World of Stamps"), Masada Publications, Tel Aviv, 1947. The article notes that this series of stamps is unique in including Yiddish along with the other languages.

Postage stamps in Yiddish, Polish, German, and Ukrainian were issued by the local authorities in 1918. 5 (groshen)—light green, with an easterly view of the Great Synagogue. 10—red, view of the marketplace and stores. 20—dark green, with a view of the Catholic church. 25—dark blue, another view of the Catholic church. 50—gray-green, a view of the Greek Orthodox (Pravoslav) church.

THE ANCIENT LEDGER THAT WENT ASTRAY
By Moyshe Lifshitz

In the 1930s, the well-known historian and noted Zionist personality Dr. Yitshak Shipper came to lecture in our city. He stayed for two or three days, met with many elders of the town, many of them quite up in years, and heard them tell of interesting local events; he visited various synagogues and paged through numerous books; but he spent most of his time in the Great Synagogue.

There, in a large wooden box that stood in the corner near the entrance, were the tattered remains of old holy books, including prayerbooks and volumes of the Talmud no longer fit to be used, and all sorts of torn manuscripts and old notes to which no one had paid any attention.

In this very box Dr. Shipper found, among other things, a large well-organized pinkas [ledger] written in Hebrew and mostly in good condition.

This was a ledger kept, it seems, by the rabbis and administrators of the community and their assistants, containing a history of the city for hundreds of years in the form of a listing of all sorts of events, disasters, decrees, and proclamations against the Jews of the city and the surrounding area.

After a cursory, on-the-spot check, Dr. Shipper determined that the ledger had historical significance, for it shed light on Jewish life over a very long period of time—not only of the Luboml community, but also of the surrounding vicinity in Poland and Russia.

Among other things, he discovered in the ledger minutes of the professional association that included all the Jewish artisans in the city and vicinity. There were also regulations of the guild of tailors and other artisans that included

clear, progressive sections on the rights and responsibilities of members. From these it was learned that hundreds of years ago, a professional association had existed in Luboml whose members enjoyed social benefits that workers in the rest of the world achieved only after generations of struggle—such as minimum wage, days off, holidays, and the rights of trainees and apprentices. There were prohibitions and ground rules regarding professional competition relating to both employer and employee.

The ledger also had minutes of community meetings and various communal organizations.

Dr. Shipper decided to take the ledger with him to Warsaw for further study and, based on his personal integrity, signed for it and promised to return it as soon as possible, though no one asked him to do that. It actually belonged to no one; in fact, no one had really known it existed.

When Dr. Shipper examined the material carefully, he found a treasure-trove of historical material on that period in Jewish life. And again, out of communal responsibility, he wrote to a number of people in the city, telling them with great delight of the historic importance of the ledger. He also said he had transferred the book to the Hebrew University in Jerusalem for additional study and examination by other historians, and added that in his opinion, the natural place for the book to be kept would be the historical archives of the university in Jerusalem.

When Dr. Shipper's letter reached us, it suddenly awakened a wave of local patriotism in some of our people. Most active were Yosef Bornshteyn and Yitshak Handlsman, leaders of the craftsmen in the city (incidentally, Y.

Bornshteyn was not from Luboml, but had married a woman from the town). They were a small but vocal minority, and they insisted that the ledger be returned. The correspondence stretched out over a number of years and this writer, as secretary of the community (Va'ad HaKehilla) was charged with the task.

Dr. Shipper suggested all sorts of solutions: a monetary reimbursement or valuable museum piece for the ledger; he also suggested supplying a handwritten or photocopy so that the original could stay in Jerusalem.

All these solutions were rejected by those who saw themselves as caretakers of a ledger that, inter alia, dealt with matters relating to crafts-men, and they demanded the return of the original book. In the end, under the threat of police action or resort to judicial procedure against him personally by exploiting the written receipt and guarantee that he had given of his own volition at the time, Dr. Shipper was forced to request that the Hebrew University Library return the ledger to the Va'ad HaKehilla.

The ledger was returned in or around 1938 [or 1935; see letter below], and, of course, you know the end. Its fate was that of the Jews of the city, of whom only a few remained, a shadow of the life that had been. From the ledger, too, only a few fragments (barely a shadow) remain.

12.8.60

Dear Mr. Tchelet,

In answer to your undated letter, we hereby reply.

We once had the ledger of the tailors guild in Luboml or the years 1720–1780. It was sent to Luboml in 1935, upon request, but to our regret, it was not returned, and we therefore determine that it has been lost.

We have some printed archival material, and it may yet be possible to find other literature on the history of the community in the bibliography of the Encyclopedia Judaica, *Eshkol Publications, Berlin, vol. 10, p. 1171. Some of that material is in our library. You can visit us any day. We suggest the first visit be during our working hours, i.e., before 2:30 p.m. Our reading room is open until 10 p.m.*

Yours truly,
Dr. Y. Yoel
Assistant Director

Translation of letter to Nathan Tchelet from Jewish National and University Library.

Original letter to Nathan Tchelet.

LIFE, RECONSTRUCTION, AND CREATIVITY

ORGANIZATION OF THE JEWISH COMMUNITY [KEHILA]

The Last Chapter of the History of the Jews of Luboml, 1918–1942
By Moyshe Lifshitz

Just as World War I ended in 1918, fighting broke out between Poland and Soviet Russia. Again, most of the victims were Jews, mainly those in small towns and villages in Russia, the Ukraine, Galicia, and Poland. There were pogroms against them, their property was looted, their money stolen, and their houses burned. Jewish blood was again spilled by Ukrainian, Russian, and Polish "patriots," who supposedly performed these deeds for ideological and nationalistic reasons—"for nation and fatherland."

When the war ended, our town, like others, saw destruction in every aspect of Jewish life. Poverty and ruin touched every level of society. There was not a single communal organization—either appointed or organized—to represent Jewish interests to the new government. There was no institution that could offer help to those in need.

There were a few shtadlanim [intercessors]—honorable Jews who, out of the goodness of their hearts, tried to help those who were suffering, primarily by supplying daily material needs. But this effort had no legal basis, no organizational framework, no public oversight, and, worst of all, no funds. Understandably, in this sort of situation, the results of their activities were practically nil.

Our town, Luboml, like the entire Volhynian district, was annexed to Poland, which was again politically independent. The new government was chauvinistic, reactionary, nationalistic, antagonistic to Jewish interests, and did not even want to give Jews full rights as the rest of the citizens had, including the minorities—Ukrainians, Germans, and others.

But under the influence of the winds of liberalism and humanitarianism blowing across the world in those days, especially in Europe and America, and in consideration of the aspirations of various peoples for political independence and of individuals for freedom and equality, it was necessary even for Poland—willingly or unwillingly—to give Jews some autonomy.

The Jews demanded full rights as a national minority equal to those of all other citizens. They sought the right to organize and conduct cultural, educational, and religious life according to their wishes, practice, and traditions. Poland had no choice but to grant a certain autonomy to its Jewish citizens, which only on the surface seemed like real autonomy.

Officially, it seemed as if Jews were enjoying full civil rights, but this was a superficial victory, since in reality the situation became worse, especially in the years preceding World War II, when Nazi influence was particularly strong in Poland. In a turn for the worse, more restrictions were placed upon the Jews, such as a ban on the kosher slaughter of meat, a *numerus nullus* [nonadmission of Jews] in the universities, heavy taxes, restrictions on acquisition of land for agriculture, etc.

As said, the autonomy given the Jews was limited and insufficient from the very beginning, but in spite of that, from a certain standpoint both sides were satisfied. The Polish government was satisfied with the propaganda effect on the outside world and on world Jewry, and, in fact, autonomy provided a kind of economic relief to the government, since freedom of religious observance and national education was granted on the clear condition that the Jewish community itself bear the cost, without any participation from the government.

On the other side, it gave the Jews a chance to organize life more or less based on their traditions, customs, and religious laws, although the financial burden was heavy. The Jewish community continued to press for financial participation by the government, but with no substantial results.

The only concrete expression of autonomy for the Jews of Poland was the publication of the laws and regulations authorizing the establishment of separate community councils for Jews in all parts of the country. This was approximately in 1923–24. That is when organizing for elections to the Jewish community councils began.

The First Elections to the Community Council

In our town of Luboml, the first elections for the Jewish community took place in 1926. Only men had the right to vote from age 21, after having lived in a given place for at least a year. Those over 24 years of age had the right to be elected.

Since regulations limited communal activity to the religious sphere, worship and social welfare, a struggle for control took place in the community, as in other small towns outside the large cities, where political in-fighting was more sophisticated. Pressure to gain influence came from various Chasidic synagogues in town. It is interesting that in 1926 no local political party contested the elections, despite the fact that most of the town's inhabitants were supporters of the Zionist or other parties.

The feeling among citizens toward the council was that it was an institution for local matters only, and that it was wrong to allow politicians to get a toehold. Even if a politician was religious and well-respected in his synagogue, simply being a "party man" disqualified him in the eyes of voters from becoming a council member. And so all the members of the first council were elected according to shtiblach [small synagogues or shuls] and by the tradesmen's organizations, which also represented two shuls, one near the Great Synagogue, and the Tailors' Bet Midrash on Chelm Street.

In 1926, eight members were elected to the first council to represent the Chasidim as follows: Moyshe Reyzman—Stepenyer Chasidim; Yitshak Shloyme Sirchook—Kotsk; Moyshe Sfard—Rizhin; Hershl Lifshitz—Radzin; Manes Greenberg—the "operators" [misaskim]; Meyer Landgeyer—Bet HaMidrash HaGadol; Rabinovitz—the Tailors' Bet Midrash. [Manes Greenberg, a mason, and Rabinovich, a tailor, represented the tradesmen in town.]

The eighth councilor was Kalman Kopelzon, who appeared on a separate list and received only 28 votes, not enough for a mandate. But since he had aligned himself before the elections in a technical bloc with other lists, and the number of votes he received happened to make up the largest bloc of remaining votes, he managed to slip into the elected council.

It is paradoxical that the Trisker Chasidim, the largest group as well as the richest, had no one on the council. This can be explained by the fact that their candidates were known as active Zionists and though most of [the followers] were themselves Zionists, or Zionist supporters, they preferred recognizably religious candidates rather than party candidates. They therefore voted for religious people other than Trisker Chasidim, or boycotted the election altogether.

The elections were approved by the authorities, according to the law, and R. Moyshe Reyzman was elected head of the council. He was then in his fifties, respected, clever, with a nice appearance. At that time he was very wealthy and on good terms with the authorities. He had good ideas and good intentions, and was ready to devote a lot of time and energy to community affairs—and at that time Jewish matters required a lot of activity.

But fate was cruel to him. His star declined, he had business troubles and became a victim of fraud perpetrated by one of his "friends"—losing all his money and property. He hoped to get out of the mess and devote himself to communal affairs and offer the benefit of his experience and energy, and so remained head of the community for a long time and did not resign. On top of all these troubles, and perhaps because of them, he suddenly took sick with the flu in the middle of the summer. And after a few days he died in the hospital in Lublin and was buried in that city. He left a wife and one son, Mendl, penniless. They lived in our town and met their deaths with the rest of our martyrs in October 1942, during the final elimination of the ghetto by the Nazis.

After R. Moyshe Reyzman died, his place was taken by the eldest member of the council, R. Yitshak Shloyme Sirchook. He was old and frail, had no experience in communal affairs, and knew not a word of Polish, and it can be said that he was strictly a ceremonial leader. Community affairs actually were handled effectively by the secretary, R. Shimon Shor, who until then served as rabbiner [government-appointed rabbi]. Mr. Shor was secretary of the council until 1930.

The Elections of 1931

In 1931, elections were held for a new community council. In these elections, too, political parties did not participate as such, but this time there were candidates from the synagogues who were known to be Zionists or supporters of the Zionist movement. Elected were:

From the Trisker Chasidim, Aron Rusman, Nathum Shtern; from the Rizhiner Chasidim, Motl Kreizer; from the Radziner Chasidim, Hershl Lifshitz; from Kotsk, M. Y. Veytsfrucht; from the Bet Midrash HaGadol, Yehoshua Grimatlicht. From the Tailors' Bet Midrash and as representatives of the craftsmen's organization, Pinchas Krupodelnik (plasterer) and Yakov Ferdzon (shoemaker). M. Y. Veytsfrucht was chosen to head the council.

The first thing the community council did was to organize the ritual slaughter [for kosher meat] in an orderly and convenient manner for the public. Until then [sites were] scattered, in the homes of the shochetim [slaughterers], in unsanitary conditions, with no price supervision and uniformity.

There were four shochetim in the town, and they became employees of the community, working under its supervision and according to its instructions. Their wages were fixed at a certain percentage determined by a contract between the shochetim and the community. A convenient building was constructed in the center of town,

next to the home of the town rabbi, R. Leybish London; sanitary equipment was installed, and this was the only place for the slaughter of fowl brought from all parts of the city, mostly on Thursdays and on the days before holidays.

It was forbidden for a shochet to slaughter in his own home or any other place. The slaughterhouse was open from early morning to late at night. A community appointee was always there [in the beginning it was R. Mordche Schlein]. He collected money in exchange for "shechita cards" according to a price list established by the community, and every day he gave the money to the community.

Slaughter of cattle took place in the city abattoir, where the cattle were brought by Jewish butchers. There, too, the city appointee sat and collected the fee according to prices fixed for every type of animal. According to the contract between the community and the shochetim, the gross fees were divided at 55 percent for the community, 45 percent for the slaughterers. This was then divided according to a previously-agreed-upon index. The charges, payment of fees, and bookkeeping all were done by the community.

Active shochetim were R. Aron Shochet [Blumen], his son Itche, Leyb Blumen, the latter's son-in-law R. Immanuel, and R. Meyerl Shochet [that was really his last name]. In addition, there was R. Avromche Horobes, who, because of his age, no longer worked but received a small weekly pension that the others gave him from their earnings [15 zlotys a week].

Elections for a Rabbi

According to the legislation, the community was entitled to only one rabbi, and had to pay his salary from its budget. Prior to this, the authorities had appointed the elderly R. Leybish London, rabbi of the Kotsker Chasidim. R. London, being the official rabbi of the community, was authorized to conduct weddings and divorces, and register and provide certificates of marriage and divorce, birth and death.

Besides him, there were two other rabbis in town: the judge [dayan] R. Leybl Melamed, rabbi of the Trisker Chasidim, and R. Pinchas Oselka, rabbi for the Chasidim of Rizhin, Radzin, and others. In order not to show favoritism, these two rabbis were put on the community books in official capacities, though not as rabbis: one in charge of the cemetery [R. Oselka] and the other in charge of Jewish education and the synagogue [R. Melamed]. In these capacities the government authorized their receiving salaries from the community budget, though much lower than that of the official rabbi, R. Leybish London.

R. London, being an extreme conservative, was strongly antagonistic toward Zionism, but not actively. The other two, R. Leybl Melamed and R. Oselka, were much younger, more modern, liberal in their outlook and they supported Zionism.

R. Oselka himself was an active Zionist and in 1935 participated as a delegate in the founding of the New Zionist Organization in Vienna. He often gave public sermons, speaking in favor of traditional, nationalistic education in the spirit of religious Zionism.

The judge, R. Leybl Melamed, a modest, humble person, was very concerned with elementary education for poor children and orphans, and was very active in social work and philanthropy. He was accepted and liked by all. Almost every disagreement between Jews of the city, every case to be judged, came before him. He judged impartially and both sides accepted his decrees.

In the summer of 1934, R. Leybish London, of blessed memory, was nearly 80 when he died of a heart attack. His death was a source of great sorrow for the Jews. Mourning was decreed until the end of the funeral, held [according to Jewish law] the day after his death.

All businesses in the city were closed. The funeral was organized by the community, and those who participated were the leaders of the community, the district commissioner [starosta], the mayor and representatives of the town council, representatives of various institutions, the rabbis of Lutsk, Brisk, Kovel, and the vicinity, all the Jewish pupils from government schools, led by their teachers and counselors, and practically all the Jewish residents of the city, as well as many non-Jewish ones.

During the funeral, the deceased was brought to the Great Synagogue, which was filled to capacity, and there the rabbis of Lutsk and Brisk gave their eulogies. The various ceremonies and the procession lasted several hours.

With the passing of R. London, the question arose as to who would be his successor. This was a central problem for the Jews for quite some time. It was constantly being discussed in all the synagogues and community institutions, and among all the public personalities. There were three applicants: R. Pinchas Oselka, of the Rizhiner and Radziner Chasidim; R. Leybl Melamed of the Trisker Chasidim; and the grandson of R. Leybish, the deceased, R. Alter London, of the Chasidim of Kotsk.

R. Leybish had prepared his grandson, Alter, to take his place when the time came and had seen him as his natural successor. For years, he instructed him in rabbinical matters and gave him responsibility for marriages, birth and death certification, etc.

R. Alter was a young man of about 20, quiet and modest, whose father, Rabbi Leybish's son, had been killed by the Petlura gang in the Ukraine. R. Alter was ordained at a very young age by the heads of the yeshivas in accordance with [Jewish] law.

Of course, all the followers of Kotsk and all the members of the London family, which was one of the largest in town, gave their time and energy and worked enthusiastically and with great dedication to have R. Alter appointed to the rabbinical position as successor to his grandfather, who had been the town rabbi since the beginning of the century.

R. Leybish's oldest son and R. Alter's uncle, R. Meyer London, worked particularly hard for this, contributing much from his own pocket to the campaign expenses.

As opposed to previous practice, whereby the city's rabbi was appointed by the authorities, usually through favoritism and on the basis of recommendations by people close to the seat of power, the new law now in effect mandated that the rabbi be elected by all Jewish men over the age of 21, by individual, secret ballot. The voter list contained more than 1,000 names.

The Jews of the city immersed themselves in the excitement of the elections for rabbi. This commotion lasted more than two years. The elections took place on November 5, 1936. In addition to three local rabbis—R. Pinchas Oselka, R. Leybl Melamed, and R. Alter London—a number of other rabbis from central Poland and Galicia also submitted their candidacy, responding to an advertisement in the newspapers, published in accordance with the law. But the "outsiders" had little chance of being elected, for no one locally really knew them, and no one was interested in bringing a fourth rabbi to town.

The main competition was between R. Alter London and R. Leybl Melamed, both of whom had enthusiastic supporters. But R. London's people were livelier and more clever, and saw to it that the election of R. Alter would be assured.

The community council elections of 1931 were conducted in an expectant atmosphere, affected by the upcoming rabbinic elections. R. Leybl's relatives knew, because of the rabbi's age and failing health, that they had to be prepared for any sudden "eventuality" and therefore saw to it that many members of their family and supporters of Rabbi London would be sitting on the council.

In these elections, all lines between the Chasidim and the various shtiblach were blurred, as were all public and ideological boundaries, and the candidates for the council—though they officially appeared to be representing the synagogues—were really friends or relatives of the London family.

Also, the electorate voted for the most part based on its relationship with the rabbi. For instance, it was known that a segment of the Trisker Chasidim, the bastion of R. Melamed, voted for the Kotsker list of candidates headed by R. London's nephew, because they were friends or relatives of the London family. Using this tactic, they assured themselves of a majority on the council and the chairmanships. Later on, in 1934, the community council chose the committee for election of the communal rabbi, whose absolute majority—and particularly its chairman and vice-chairmanwere supporters of R. London. This spoiled all hopes for R. Melamed and on

election day was a deciding factor in the results.

As said, rabbinic elections took place on November 5, 1936, from 7 a.m. to 9 p.m. Almost 1,000 people voted, and the majority were for R. Leybl Melamed. But due to a technical trick, the majority was turned into a minority and it was decided that R. Alter had received about 20 votes more than R. Melamed.

R. Alter London was declared the rabbi of the city, and he served in that position until he was killed by the Nazis in July 1941. He was one of the first martyrs in our city.

The Community Council of 1936

On November 3, 1936, two days before the elections for rabbi, there were elections for the community council. This time, too, the rabbi's supporters made sure their people got onto the council, so there would be a strong faction to support him.

In these elections there were already candidates on the lists from the shtiblach, known to be Zionists, who also were elected. In 1936, those elected were R. Meyer Sandlshteyn, from the Kotsker Chasidim; R. Avrom Grimatlicht of the Rizhiner Chasidim; R. Aron-Leybish Lichtmacher from the Radziner Chasidim; R. Asher Tannenbaum and R. Nathum Stern from Trisk; for the synagogue of the Misaskim and the Chasidim of Stepen: R. Velvl Sheinwald; and two from the craftsman's guild.

The council continued to carry on its duties along much the same lines as before. They added to their agenda a major task, that of creating a Yavneh Hebrew school for national, religious education. And with the cooperation of other public figures, organizing for this school began. The community gave the refurbished building of the Talmud Torah for the new school and the council offices were transferred from this building to a private house on Teatralna Street, which was rented bi-annually.

A segment of the extremist religious Jews caused a furor and objected strenuously to the Yavneh school. They even brought the Radziner Rebbe, R. Shloymele Leiner, of blessed memory, who stayed about two weeks, giving speeches against the school. He also organized a big demonstration at the community building. It is important to note that this was the first time the rabbi of Radzin came to our town. This was just prior to the destruction that came to the Jewish people as a result of the war and the cruel Hitlerite plague that caused the terrible tragedy of European Jewry. The destruction of its spiritual and cultural glory erased all struggles, antagonisms, and misunderstandings among different sectors of Jews, among these the struggle over the Hebrew school for the Jews of Luboml.

Ways the Community Operated

The primary tasks of the community, as set out in the legislation, were: administering matters pertaining to ritual slaughter [shechita] and kashrut in general; traditional and religious education; administering and maintaining the synagogues and houses of worship [shtiblach]; the ritual bath [mikvah]; the cemetery and burial matters; providing for rabbis, shochetim, and other personnel; administration and registration of marriages, divorces, births, and deaths; and social welfare activities to provide for the poor and sick.

The community also owned several public buildings, such as the Talmud Torah and the large grounds surrounding it; a public bath—the only one in town for the entire population [also the non-Jews]; the Linat Hatsedek [public hostel]; and acres and acres of pasture land near the city, which the municipality wanted to take from the Jews and over which there was a struggle for many years. It was the responsibility of the council to administer, maintain, and preserve all this Jewish communal property.

The administrators [parnassim] held meetings every two weeks and, if necessary, more often. At these meetings they dealt with the ongoing affairs of the community and made decisions. Once a year they prepared the annual budget, which gave evidence of all the activities and requirements of the community. After the budget was accepted by the committee, it was presented to the district authorities in Lutsk [a nearby city] for approval. In most cases they would change the proposed budget, and that is how they limited even more the operations of the

Distribution of clothing to poor children in 1929, with the participation of guests from the United States and the trustees and board of the Talmud Torah.

community. The community had to report in writing to the authorities on the implementation of its budget and on its activities. Representatives of the district [*starosta*] of Luboml audited the financial books every year.

The community council was made up of eight councilors, elected for a four-year period. They received no salary, no financial remuneration or benefits of any sort. This was an honorary position, filled by volunteers.

The official rabbi of the community, R. Leybish London—who was not elected but appointed by the authorities—had the right to participate in the council meeting and vote. Only rarely, in crucial, fundamental matters, did R. London utilize that option, and in general he was neutral and did not vote on either side.

The implementation of council decisions, all related technicalities, and reporting to the council and the authorities on this implementation was in the hands of the community secretary. This was a paid position.

All funding came from the Jews themselves.

Sources of funds were kosher slaughter fees, burial fees, and charges for tombstones, and a direct tax on the Jews for community purposes [called *etat*].

The government never contributed to the community expenses and never supported its requirements. Nor was there financial assistance from any other outside source, with two notable exceptions: one—in 1936, the district governor in Lutsk appropriated 1,000 zlotys for refurbishing the Great Synagogue, thought to be an historical site; and the other—in 1938, when the Joint [Jewish Joint Distribution Committee] in London sent $20 for distribution among the poor.

The Cemeteries

For matters concerning the cemetery there was a special committee made up of three councilors. This committee determined the charges for burial or for a license to put up a monument, in accordance with the ability of the family of the deceased to pay. Because in the eyes of the family burial fees sometimes seemed excessive, shout-

Holy Ark donated to the Lines Hatsedek synagogue by the Gershengorn family in memory of their mother, Devorah.

Sewing course held in the Katz family's Victoria Hotel in the early 1930's.

ing matches often broke out, which might even lead to violence. In general, the permit for burial or putting up a monument was given free, or a symbolic fee was charged.

One of the most important tasks for which the community council deserves great credit was the maintenance and security provided for the cemetery.

In Luboml there were two cemeteries for Jews. The older one, in the center of the town, had been closed for many years; the one then being utilized was about three miles from town.

There used to be a nice Jewish custom that from the first half of the month of Nissan until Passover eve, and during the entire month of Elul—in addition to personal memorial days— people went to the cemetery to spend private moments with the souls of the departed. It was a kind of personal religious observance full of emotion, mysticism, and holiness.

One revered grave in the old cemetery was that of a tzadik [righteous person] of previous generations, R. Moyshe Maneles, a forebear of our family, and the Bargrum and Getman families, on the side of the three sisters who were the grandmothers of the families. There was a small struc-

ture over the grave called the "tabernacle" [ohel], and next to it we used to gather, pray, and ask for heavenly mercy.

Non-Jews lived in the vicinity of the cemeteries. They made fun of the sentiments of the Jews and desecrated the honor of the dead. They always were trying to turn the area into a no-man's land and to use it for pasture. No security arrangements helped because it was a very large area, unfenced and open on all sides. A lack of funds made it impossible to engage a full-time guard. So the community council's good efforts to guard and supervise the cemetery are worthy of praise.

In 1930, both cemeteries were fenced off with heavy wire fencing, nearly eight feet high, on strong wooden bases. The length of the fence was several thousand yards, and because the expense of erecting the fences was very high, it took several years to complete the task. It was done in stages. When the fence was finally up, the situation was rectified, since the place was now closed off and more dignified,

Note that the authorities considered the old cemetery an historical site. The reason was that within its boundaries stood a number of huge trees that experts believed to be more than 1,000 years old. Those trees were cared for by the nature conservation corps, and it was against the law to tamper with them. In general, the government respected all these places and sites holy to the Jews.

The Maintenance of the Public Bath

Another indispensable function on behalf of the Jewish population was the administration and maintenance of the public bath—the only one in town—and of the ritual bath [mikvah]. Maintaining the public bath was a heavy burden on the community. The building was old; the pumps, pipes, and other operational equipment were old and worn out, and required great expense for repair and maintenance.

It was not normally the community's responsibility to cover the costs of a sanitary, hygienic operation such as a city bathhouse, which operated for non-Jews as well. But it seems that on account of the mikvah, which shared some equipment with the city bathhouse, the community preferred to bear the heavy financial burden rather than give non-Jews a say in running the ritual bath.

Educational Functions

The Jewish community's educational activities were concentrated in the management of the "Talmud Torah," a school in which orphans and poor children studied, receiving a free elementary Torah and religious education. Most of this school's expenses were covered by the Kehila's budget. Aside from this, the Kehila distributed small sums to the "yeshiva" in the town, in which about thirty young men from the town and surrounding areas continued their religious education.

The principal of the Talmud Torah was a good Jew, R. Moyshe Yitshak Kagan. He was the vital spirit behind this institution: teacher, counselor, spiritual advisor, guardian, a father to the children studying there—he filled all these functions. This man was devoted to the children and was concerned for their Torah education to the point of self-sacrifice. Even under the Soviet regime, and with great danger to himself, he continued to teach his poor children the ele-

ments of religion and Judaism, though such education was illegal.

The supporters and the primary activists of the Talmud Torah were: the religious court judge, R. Leybl Melamed (R. Leybl Dayan), R. Avrom Scheiner, and R. Shlomo Samet. They devoted themselves to this educational institution heart and soul, were concerned with providing its financial support, the upkeep and refurbishment of its building, for the provision of water, wood for heating in winter, lighting at night—in short, all its needs.

The "yeshiva"—Yeshivat Bet Yosef (Nevarhadok), an institution devoted to Torah education, in which older religious students studied, was founded around 1931. The yeshiva was founded and managed by R. Noah Katzman, who was not originally from Luboml but settled there with his family in 1930. He was born and bred in Davidgorodok (Grodno province). He was about 35 years of age, clever, a lamdan and knowledgeable besides, and of pleasing appearance. He was involved not only with the educational life of the school, but also its material and financial side. In the course of time the yeshiva developed into an institution which had great educational influence on the young men of the town, many of whom sought to study in it.

Social and Medical Aid

The Kehila supported a hostel named Lines Hatsedek, or, as it was known popularly, "the hekdesh." This was a building of several rooms, some of which were available for the poor or for transient beggars to stay for a short period of time. Another part of the building was devoted to the yeshiva.

The community's social aid efforts were hampered by lack of funds. The little money available was primarily devoted to a small pension for the childless aged, who were without other means of support, a system of one-time grants for urgent cases, and the provision of medical aid and free medicine for poor patients.

It should be noted that the provision of medical aid to the poor was facilitated by the volunteer efforts on the part of the Jewish physicians in town. At one time this role was filled by Dr.

Greenberg of the town of Proskorov, and in later years it was Dr. Amsttzivovski, who moved to Luboml from Volkovisk; they were always ready to visit a poor patient, to examine him and provide medical assistance at the request of the Kehila, in return for a nominal payment from the Kehila treasury.

It should also be noted that another "good Jew," the owner of a pharmacy, Muttel Nathausen, used to distribute various medicines to poor patients either free of charge or for a nominal fee.

The Synagogue

Another important communal function was the upkeep of the main synagogue and various other houses of prayer. In our town there were a number of houses of prayer, each affiliated to one or another chasidic movement. These were the shtiblach of the Trisker Chasidim, those of Kotsk, Rizhin, Radzin, and the small synagogue of the Stepenyer Chasidim. Aside from these there were other houses of worship, whose members were not affiliated with any particular chasidic group, but were ordinary Orthodox Jews, workers, artisans, wagon-drivers, porters, peddlers—what are usually called "amkha." These prayed in the synagogue of the Misaskim, most of whom were Stepenyer Chasidim, or in the Bet Midrash HaGadol, the small Tailors' Bet Midrash in Chelm Street, in the Talmud Torah, and in two small synagogues: one of the "Tehillim sayers," and the other the Tailors' Synagogue. Aside from all these, there were minyanim on Sabbaths and festivals in the houses of the Rebbe of Stepen and in the private house of R. Meir Feigeles, a Radziner hasid.

The Great Synagogue was located in the center of town. It had been erected in the sixteenth century, apparently by one of the last Polish kings of the Jagiello dynasty, that is, with his permission and financial aid, and, according to tradition, by Count Branitzki. The stories handed down from generation to generation gave varied and even strange reasons for this. It is clear beyond doubt that the Jews of that time were unable to erect such a splendid structure, whose architectonic design and architectural style was one of the most beautiful and interesting in all of Poland. It was a giant building, the largest in town, built of special stone, and resembled a fortress.

The structures of the other houses of worship (shtiblach) were built of wood, and were of small or moderate size, with one large hall and a small room. In some of them there was a women's section as well. Each of them had many large windows. Furniture was scarce, generally made up of long, narrow, primitive tables and benches, some put together out of unfinished pieces of lumber. On Sabbaths and festivals the tables were covered with tablecloths, but even then not all tables were covered. Once in every few years the walls and ceilings would be whitewashed in simple fashion. These synagogues had no architectural embellishments or interior decorations. In contrast to the primitiveness and simplicity of the buildings and furniture, the ritual objects and appurtenances were beautiful and expensive. The Torah crowns, pointers, chains, tablets, lamps, goblets for wine were of pure silver. The Torah mantels and the curtain for the ark (parokhet), which existed in great profusion, were made of fine silk or from velvet in magnificent colors. Most of these appurtenances were donated by women, in honor of some family event, or to fulfill a personal vow, or for the memory of a deceased family member. Generally speaking, the work was artistically done, invested with careful thought and considerable imagination.

The ark in the Great Synagogue was of astounding beauty, a combination of artistry and real religious feeling, with figures and designs of biblical inspiration.

In each house of prayer, and in particular in the Great Synagogue, there were a large number of Torah scrolls, sets of Talmud, prayer books, and other religious works. These were the gifts and donations of individuals or families, or donated by the inhabitants of surrounding hamlets, which themselves did not have a minyan, or which were bought with synagogue funds.

Confiscation of Prayer Shawls As a Tax Measure

Those who prayed regularly at each of the houses

of worship took upon themselves the responsibility for providing the funds to cover the expenses of keeping them clean, providing water, light, heat during the winter, security, etc. They did this by means of donations, vows, and selling *aliyot* on Sabbaths and festivals—all voluntarily and usually generously. If it happened on occasion that there was a deficit, the *gabbai* would announce the "confiscation of prayer shawls" at the Torah reading on a Sabbath, and would permit them to be redeemed after the Sabbath with a cash payment. With the end of services that morning, each worshipper would place his prayer shawl on the table and go home without it, as a sign of solidarity and agreement with the "confiscation." Even those who had actually fulfilled all their obligations toward the synagogue would do the same. This "confiscation" was the only involuntary means of fund raising available to the *gabbai*, but it was stronger than any other means, for the worshippers could not pray without a prayer shawl. Immediately after the conclusion of the Sabbath the "debtors" would hurry to pay their debts and redeem their prayer shawls.

Each day, most of the town's Jews would come to their houses of worship in the early hours of the morning for the Shacharit prayer, and for Minhah and Maariv towards evening. On Sabbaths and festivals the houses of worship were completely full. Many young peope would come, and many women would come to pray in the women's section.

Old people would remain in synagogue all day, every day of the week. They would study Torah in small groups or as individuals, discussing *hiddushei Torah* (new interpretations) or Talmud passages. Less learned people would study *Ein Yakov*, a popular collection of talmudic legends and non-legal statements.

Earning a Living and Governmental Decrees

The yoke of sustaining and supporting one's family fell primarily on the men; a woman's obligation was to be the housewife and raise the children. However, storekeepers' wives helped their husbands run the store: there were also women who sold vegetables and fruits, or fish, in the market, or worked as seamstresses.

Half of the town's Jews were artisans of all sorts (there were almost no artisans among the non-Jews of the town, aside from shoemakers). They worked hard to earn their poor living: their work days extended from dawn to the late hours of the night (as in the case of tailors and shoemakers), and they ate their meals hurriedly while working. They interrupted their work only for prayers in the morning and evening.

On Fridays and on the eve of festivals the work day would end at between noon and 1 PM. On Friday nights and on Sabbaths and festivals these Jews would feel like princes—free of work, clean and wearing festive clothes, until the end of the Sabbath or festival. Then the work would begin anew, for the entire week.

Work was carried out by hand, without the aid of machinery, or any mechanical contrivance, aside from the usual sewing machines. Despite this, or perhaps thanks to this, they produced work which was clean and expert.

A segment of the town was made up of storekeepers or small businessmen, whose income and profit was dependent on the weekly fair, which occured every Monday. On that day the peasants of the neighborhood, near and far, would gather in the town, bring with them their products or produce for sale, and purchase their own necessities from the Jews. Another good day for the storekeepers was Thursday, when the Jews would purchase their necessities for the Sabbath. The major worry of each was to earn a living, and the Sabbath was the central worry: for Sabbaths and festivals it was necessary to prepare fine, tasty dishes and many courses, while during the week small amounts of simple food was sufficient.

There were also peddlers, who made a circuit of the small hamlets on foot, or with a horse-drawn wagon, or they moved from one fair to another, buying and selling whatever came to hand. Most of them would leave their houses and families at the start of the week, immediately after the end of the Sabbath, returning home on Friday.

Note should be taken of a significant number of unemployed Jews without the means of earning a livelihood, whose economic situation was very poor, and who were in need of communal support, charity and help.

In particular, the situation of the up and coming generation was hard, actually unbearable; they had no future in the town. There was no need for more artisans, the storekeepers already there made their living with great difficulty as it was; there were no other places of employment in town or in the neighborhood, for there were almost no industrial enterprises or large places providing work. A few isolated enterprises did exist, such as a sawyer's plant, and three flour mills, two small and one medium size, which primarily provided employment for the owners and their families. Many young people therefore left town and emigrated to Argentina, Brazil, the United States and other places. A significant number of young people were successful, thanks to their Zionist vision and their kibbutz preparations (*hakhsharah*), in getting visas to emigrate to Eretz Israel.

In the last years before the second World War, the political and economic situation of the Jews of the town worsened, as in all the cities of Poland. Under the influence of the Hitlerian poison, Polish and Ukrainian chauvinism increased, antisemitic behavior became sharper, more insulting, more provocative and forceful than ever.

Competition by Polish and Ukrainian cooperatives was more intense in business and in the workforce, even improper, in that they were founded and supported by [Polish] communal funds and by the governments concerned. In these years heavy taxes and additional charges were levied against Jews. Among other things, a fourteen-year moratorium on payment of peasant debt was decreed, and all documents of indebtedness were cancelled for this period of time. The Jews who had loaned the peasants money were required to repay the interest they had levied, and other Jews were imprisoned for daring to attempt to collect their debts from the peasants. Overnight many Jews became desperately poor, and themselves became indebted.

Aside from these economic decrees, which made the lives of the Jews more difficult, there were also administrative rulings which embittered their lot still more. Among these were the ruling on urbanization (civic improvement); these rulings primarily concerned the center of town and its immediate neighborhood, that is, the parts of town in which the Jews alone lived. They were required to improve the appearance of their houses, and to make all kinds of changes, such as lowering balconies, etc. Because of lack of financial and technical means, it was impossible to carry out these improvements, and the result was that old buildings were torn down, and many families were left homeless.

In that era every day brought a new decree, and the Jews were left in fear for the future. They looked ahead with heavy hearts, hoped for better and more tranquil times—and then the war broke out.

LUBOML'S ECONOMIC SITUATION UP TO 1939
By Moyshe Bialer

There was a densely populated, organized, thriving community in town whose main occupations were business and the trades. The Jewish community constituted 60 percent of the total population. In the whole Luboml district there were more than 100,000 Ukrainians and a small number of Polish residents [usadniks] whose main occupation was farming. In spite of the differences in religion, race, nationality and occupations, the Jews and non-Jews complemented each other in the economic sphere and formed a single economic unit.

What was the economic structure of each of these components?

More than half of the city's population made a living from business, as was said before, which was basically retail and based on the labor of family members without outside help. It was centered around the market place [rynek]. This was a town square that measured 400 x 400 yards, where farmers parked their wagons when they came every Monday to the "big fair" [yarid] and every Thursday to the "little fair." Those who had shops on the square were the business elite of Luboml. Following them were those whose shops were on the adjacent streets, but no further than 350 feet from the square.

Another group consisted of those with small stores on other streets, and at the crossroads near the entrance to the city. A large number of peddlers who had no stores spread out their wares along these roads and in the square itself on market days, and would buy and sell anything that came to hand. Another sort of peddler went out to the villages on Sunday mornings to visit the village homes with a wagon full of merchandise to barter or sell for cash, returning home just before the Sabbath with either a bag full of money or with farm produce and poultry.

Another type of merchant [exporters] bought agricultural produce and sold it in the big cities. There were also several wealthy merchants who dealt in the export of cattle, grain, and lumber through Silesia to Germany, and to Danzig. Business also provided service jobs, such as agents, wagondrivers, porters, etc.

Until the last years before the war, business was exclusively in the hands of the Jews and while there was stiff internal competition, it was still possible to live respectably, though frugally.

But around 1934, alongside increasing animosity on the part of the authorities, new factors appeared in the business sector: agricultural marketing cooperatives [spoldzielna rolnicza] run by non-Jews. They competed successfully with the Jews—both because of official support from the government, which did not tax them and lent them money interest-free, and because of propaganda among farmers not to buy from Jews. And as if that were not enough, the Polish Treasury authorities finished the job by slapping various heavy taxes precisely on the Jews, thereby damaging the Jewish businessmen even more. This policy of dispossession put Luboml's economic viability in grave doubt. It was the main reason for the depression, bitterness, and lack of self-assurance that most of the community felt at this time.

The next most important sector was that of craftsmen. It is noteworthy that the Jews of Luboml were outstanding craftsmen in all areas, especially in building. The primary occupations were sewing, tailoring, shoemaking, carpentry, blacksmithing, metal work, locksmithing, hair-

Luboml's printing press, Express.

dressing, and the manufacture of ropes and cables. In most cases people put in much more than an eight-hour day.

Then came light and medium manufacturing, including the three flour mills, the lumber mill, the tannery and leather bag and pouch factory, and the printshop. Outside of the flour and lumber mills, which employed people as porters and in other tasks, the light manufacturing sector was also generally a family affair, and very few people were hired outside the owner's immediate family.

There was no real heavy industry. There was a distillery [Gorzelnia-Gralnia] owned by Jews, which did not operate during the last period because it was very hard to get the necessary permits. This operation, which at one time was the pride of the Jews, closed down except for the making of Passover liquor [pesachovka] because of official hostile policy toward the Jews.

In the employment sector, mention should be made of the independent professions—teachers, clerks [in the Jewish institution only], rabbis, and other religious functionaries. To round out the picture, mention should be made of the People's Bank [Bank Ludowy], run by Motl Privner, which was a financial stimulus and supported Jews in times of trouble, as well as the free loan fund, which, because of the increase in those dependent upon it, became an important institution.

The Surrounding Area

In the term "surrounding area" we include all 111 villages and communities in the Luboml district. The main portion of this group lived by agriculture. There were rich farmers who owned larger tracts of land and farmers of the middle and lower classes who had smaller areas, but nevertheless all made a living from farming. The poorest group also engaged in secondary jobs, such as logging in the forest, bringing the wood to the city and chopping it for firewood for the Jews in the city.

To give an idea of the poverty of some farmers, it is worthwhile to relate several facts: a poor farmer would split a match into two or four sections in order to be thrifty; many lit cigarettes by striking metal against a stone; many wore shoes made of bark [postoly], and those who had real shoes walked barefoot until they reached the city and then put on their shoes.

In spite of the high percentage of poor farmers, there were many who were wealthy and had purchasing power. They were the ones who brought their produce to town, and with the money they received they bought all sorts of necessities. Therefore, they were the primary factors in the Luboml economy.

And so the planting and harvesting seasons were low points in the Luboml economic year, and after the harvest, just before the [New Year] holidays, was the high point of activity.

In summary, note that though Luboml was not on a major highway or near an industrial area or a port, and though it had no natural resources, the Jewish community, which was lively, organized and had a lot of initiative, managed to support itself—meagerly, yet honorably.

A major factor was the friendship and brotherhood that existed among them.

Members of the committee and players of Jewish soccer club (Zydowski Klub Sportowy). *Standing first row, right to left*: D. Lerner, S. Milshteyn, M. Tzukerman, Y. Teytelboym, M. Dubetzki; *second row*: M. Dubetzki, C. Oyvental, A. Brikman, Y. Gitelis, M. Oyvental, M. Fisher, L. Melnik, B. Kagan; *third row*: Y. Krupodelnik, M. Fisher, F. Goldburten.

OUR SHTETL
By Dr. Ben-Zion Bokser

I came to America in 1920, and my memories of my shtetl, Libivne, are scant and not at all clear. Perhaps it is worthwhile to tell what I do remember.

I used to study in Moyshe Yitzhok's cheder. He had a fiery temperament. When he was teaching us Psalms, he would chant the chapters beautifully. I was so thrilled by his singing that instead of looking into the Psalms, I would look at him. The *rebbe* [teacher] noticed this and let me have it right on the spot.

During World War I, when Austria was occupying Libivne, Austrian officers were quartered in our house. Things were terrible at home. My father was in America during the war and so we could not get any financial support from him as we had before the war. My mother, therefore, took to baking all kinds of *kichlech* [cookies], and I would sell them at the station.

The Austrians opened a school and hired two female teachers, who were brought from Galicia. I studied in that school. I remember that they taught us German patriotic songs, such as "Ich Habe Einen Kameraden" [I have a friend] and "Gott Behalte, Gott Beschutze Unser Kaiser, Unser Land" [God keep, God protect our kaiser, our land].

During the occupation, the Austrians introduced forced labor. All men had to report to them on specified days. The rich men escaped forced labor by paying a sum of money.

The Jews of Libivne led a strict Orthodox life. But soon new ideas began to influence them. It was not long before such movements as Zionism and socialism found many supporters there. I remember a confrontation between the pious Jews and the more modern ones, not because of differences in ideology but on the question of how one was to dress: one young man had been brave enough to put on a tie. To pious Jews this act was a symbol of doing away with old traditions of the shtetl, and they called him an *apikoyres* [heretic].

Every Sabbath, before dawn, the shames [sexton] of the synagogue would stand in the middle of the street and call the Jews to the synagogue to say the Psalms. He would knock on the shutters of each house to make sure the Jews did not oversleep. I still remember his chant. The shames had a beautiful voice and he would sing out his call: "Kumu na, hit'orru na, hit'yatzvu na—Shteit oyf tzu avoydas HaBoyrey"—"Get up, wake up, stand up, to do the holy work of the Creator."

During the time of transition from Austrian occupation to Polish independence, when there was no stable government structure, there were many pogroms [against Jews]. We were afraid the gentiles also would attack the Jews in Libivne. A few young people organized a self-defense group; and when a group of hooligans did show up to attack some houses, the Jews of the self-defense group successfully chased the attackers away.

MY HOMETOWN
By Velvl Royzman

My hometown Libivne [Luboml], is located 8 miles from the Bug River, halfway between Kovel and Chelm. Out of 9,000 inhabitants, 6,000 were Jews.

A large part of the land on which the town stood was owned by a Polish *poritz* [rich land-owner] named Kampyoni. His land contained the big square marketplace with its brick stores; a historic hill nearby, and a big orchard that was open to everyone. The "palace" where Kampyoni had lived was used as the office of the magistrate,

A group of youths from our town.

and the "hall" served as a cinema where films were screened until a real movie house was built. The movie house was owned by partners Yisroel Royzman [my brother], Abba Grimatlicht, and Moyshe Fuks. Kampyoni also owned the entire Polish Street and the small forest that lay below it.

Libivne also had several Chasidic shtiblach [little houses of prayer].

The town's rabbi, R. Leybish London, used to pray in the Kotsker shtibl [its Chasidim were the followers of the Rebbe of Kotsk]. Among those who prayed in that shtibl were members of the Shliver family, who were known for their beautiful voices. Their praying before the congregation was famous all over.

The honor of conducting prayers during the High Holy Days belonged to R. Zeynvel Shliver— he had a claim to this "job" for all time. When he would begin to pray Musaf [morning prayer for Sabbath and holidays], the shtibl would become dead silent. His *Hineni* ["Here I am"—another prayer of the High Holy Days] could move a stone; I will never forget.

In general, the Kotsker Chasidim were known for the marches and melodies they composed. The Sabbath night *m'lave malke* [meal to bid farewell to Sabbath], with its heartfelt songs and pious dances, has remained with me as if etched forever on my mind.

There was an old man in the Kotsk shtibl whose name was R. Koone. People said he was 100 years old, and maybe even more. He used to live in the Kotsker shtibl, sleeping on a bench near the stove. During the interval between the [evening] prayers of Mincha and Ma'ariv, he would tell stories and events of long ago. He would begin each story with, "It happened once that . . ." If someone asked him how long ago was "once," he would scratch his head and say, "About 50 or 60 years!"

The young people of Libivne were fine youths. The majority belonged to Zionist parties. The town had organized a Tarbut school, which educated the young people in a Zionist spirit. The town also had a big library that offered a choice of Hebrew and Yiddish books. Meetings, discussions, and recreational gatherings brought in an income for the Jewish National Fund. The majority of the Jewish youth had one goal—to *oyle zayn* [emigrate] to Palestine, the Land of Israel. Unfortunately, only a small number were lucky enough to do so.

The young people of Libivne also were active in sports. There was a Jewish Sports Club: Zydowski Klub Sportowy. The Libivne football [soccer] team was well organized. There were football matches between Jews and Poles or Ukrainians that attracted people from the whole town. There were also fights among players, especially if the Jewish team won and the Polish or the Ukrainian team could not stand having lost. This was a common occurrence in almost every small town in Poland.

Libivne was a small shtetl. The only big industries were the three mills that produced flour and oil. Other goods were imported from Warsaw or other Polish cities.

The biggest of the three big mills, which was electrified, belonged to the Grimatlicht brothers; the second, to partners, Efrayim *der Geler* [the yellow one] Royzman, Moyshe Gelman, Volvushes and Binyomen Melamed [Koltun]; the third mill belonged to Yone Mel and Sertchuk. The mills also had presses producing oil for the peasants in the surrounding villages.

There was also a well-developed egg distribution business. The eggs were candled, sorted by size, packed in cartons, stored in a big warehouse, and then exported to big cities in Poland.

Then there were the *shmateleynikes*—Jews who traveled from Sunday to Friday by horsedrawn wagon, selling their wares to peasants in the surrounding villages. They were really peddlers who sold cheap toys and housewares, exchanging them for old rags. They also bought from the peasants chickens, eggs, butter—whatever they could get.

A group of students from our town home for summer vacation: *from right*, A. Frumerman, Ch. Feller, A. Zatz, M. Ginzburg, Bat-Sheva Mekler, A. Shtern, A. Reyzman, Ch. Kroyt, Y. Shtern and Y. Hetman.

There was a Jew, Shamele *Protsentnik* [money lender for interest]. He was very tiny, with short legs. All day long he would run around in the streets, practicing *geben* and *nemen* [give-and-take] with whoever needed a hundred or two, for a day, week or month. He used to carry in his pockets a long, narrow roll of paper with numbers on it, as well as symbols that only he could interpret. He never owned a measly groshen himself—he only "gave and took."

There were women in Libivne called beterkes. They kept track of the anniversaries of everybody's death and made a living out of the few groshen they begged from the bereaved to go to the cemetery in their stead to ask the dead to intercede on their behalf.

I remember once hearing one such beterke talking to a dead person after knocking three times on the tombstone: "*Tsadeykes Tzadeykes Zlate Bas Chave* [Righteous righteous Zlate, daughter of Chave]! Do you know who is standing before you? I, Rashke Bas Memke beseech you on behalf of your daughter . . . "

MY LIBIVNE
By Chane Achtman (Kroyt)

Luboml-Libivne lay on the Kovel-Lublin railroad, a shtetl in old Poland. But to me, Libivne was not only a shtetl distinguished on the map of Poland for its Ukrainian population and its Polish settlers, all known anti-Semites. To me, Luboml was and will forever remain—Libivne!

Libivne, with its spirited Jews and its kosher Jewishness; Jews in their *kapotes* [long caftans], *kasketn* [caps], *furazhkes* [fur hats]; as well as short-coated Jews of all political affiliations, from the "right" to the "left"; Jews who were proud in their poverty—exhausted, oppressed, weary at their weekday workbenches and in the stores where they worked.

On Sabbaths and on holidays you could not recognize them. All of them yiras-shomayim'dik [filled with the fear of Heaven], shining, rejuvenated; the evyonim [poor people] and beggars, all looked then like the richest of men.

Libivne also had its women: Jews with *kupkes* [night hats] and kerchiefs on their heads: wigs were worn only by those who had money; Jews saddled with children. Many lived and suffered in hunger and in poverty, in crowded houses, in alkers [cubicles], in airless rooms or in cellars, without hygienic accommodations; busy all Sabbath long with their Korban-Minches [women's prayer books in Yiddish] and their Tsene-U'renes [Bible text and commentary for women, in Yiddish].

The pages were soaked with bitter tears, and though at times the reader did not know what was written there, she nonetheless read everything with a real Jewish heart, with emotion for Jewish troubles and worries.

Libivne and its youth—the dear Libivner youth; a youth without a tomorrow and without a future; a dreaming youth; a thinking youth. "What will the future bring us?" Youth, some of whom had faith in the Messiah son of Dovid, and some who had faith in Marx and Engels; others yet in Herzl and a return to Zion; a youth that, when in the long cold winter nights the windows were coated with frost and snow, would study by themselves, reading either a small prayerbook or a treyfe [taboo, non-kosher] book about socialism or Zionism, under the threat of excommunication by their parents.

To me, Libivne was not a town of gentile streets, settled by Poles and Ukrainians, all Jew-haters, but a town of Jewish streets and narrow alleys, with their little houses that were barely able to stand.

In this gray, tragic landscape of poverty, a more happy picture emerged at times, a picture of comfort and wealth of one or another rich man in town.

For example, take the names of some of the rich men: Reyzman, Kopelzon, Kroyt, and other rich men in Libivne, literally millionaires [by old standards]. I should mention the Natanzon drugstore: It was not a regular drugstore where you could get castor oil for the stomach, or love potions for lovesick gentile girls. This druggist, being an honorable and virtuous man, also did healing. Many times he himself diagnosed a case and then wrote and prepared a prescription for the sick person.

Another interesting woman was Kroyt's daughter-in-law—my mother, Serl Kroyt! She operated a sawmill all by herself for a long time. She climbed over boards and beams; measured, calculated and sold lumber; competed with her business rivals and usually came out on top.

There were only a few places of learning, culture and art. And so the Libivne youth organized its own theater, producing Yiddish plays such as *Bar Kochba* and *Shulamith.*

The organizers were my mother Serl, Chamkele Veyner, and Zelde Listhoyz [she later was saved from the Nazi liquidation of the town in 1942 by hiding in a German bunker]. They were the "stars," the actresses and singers in the Libivne performances.

At times the youth gathered for a literary discussion: They would read a book and then discuss it, expressing their opinions.

Their lives were permeated with a deep sense of Jewish pride, and they would not allow any hooligans to "shpayen in di kashe" [insult them] by "toying" with Jewish stores or institutions. People still remember the "sixty strong men" who protected Jews against attacks. Efrayim Gelbord was stabbed to death by a hooligan while protecting a Jew in the marketplace during a market day.

O Libivne! My hometown that lies in ruins! You shall live in my heart forever!

IN PEACEFUL TIMES
By Wolf Sheynwald

There had never been many peaceful times for the Jews of Libivne. Troubles, epidemics, and attacks often plagued us. But if we compare them to the days of the Nazi occupation, then they were very calm days—we could even say idyllic.

Several thousand Jews worked hard to make a living, educated their children in Torah and to do good deeds, and carried the burden of their Jewishness, more beloved than heavy. They married off their children, and these continued to lead proper Jewish lives, which had been planted in Libivne hundreds of years ago. The weekdays were hard, but the Sabbath and holidays enhanced the grayness and softened their worries.

We lived through World War I with affliction and pain, but still survived. At that time, in 1915, Libivne was occupied by the Austrians—and though they were different Austrians [from the later occupiers], the Jews nonetheless suffered from them a great deal.

When the Austrians and Germans entered Libivne in 1915, they received a friendly welcome. People came out to greet them, carrying bread and salt. The majority of the city's representatives were Jews.

After several weeks in Libivne, the Germans moved 15 miles away from the shtetl. There they put up an artificial boundary line between themselves and the Austrians, the latter remaining in Libivne until Germany's defeat.

A few months after the German-Austrian occupation, we began to feel the war. The small supply of food the Jews had prepared was used up. A new war began for the majority—a war against hunger, which began to plague Jewish families more and more severely. People began to try to remedy the situation by smuggling, but that was fraught with danger.

Then there was the added trouble of *chapenish* [capture]. The Austrian authorities instituted a system of forced labor. When they did not have enough laborers, they simply began to kidnap people from the streets and even from their homes.

The kidnappings especially harassed the refugees who had come in large numbers into Libivne from the surrounding areas.

In the third year of the war, a typhoid epidemic broke out in Libivne. It was followed by a cholera epidemic. Many people fell victim to these two epidemics, and the population was helpless against the plagues. Here I must tell a story of what many considered to have been a miracle.

The rabbi of the shtetl proposed that the Jews marry off a poor couple in the cemetery and that they read psalms during the ceremony. He said this would stop the epidemic. There was a poor widow in the shtetl who was a cripple. She had a daughter, fast reaching the age of being called an old maid. The good people found a groom for her daughter, the son of Pinchas-Yosye Binyomen's. They brought the couple to the cemetery and married them off.

All the Jews of the shtetl read psalms during the ceremony. In a short time, the epidemic lost its fury; fewer people got sick and the pious Jews attributed this to a miracle sent down from heaven.

During the Austrian rule in Libivne, the mayor of the town was R. Dovid Veytsfrucht. He was a great scholar and an ordained rabbi. He did everything he possibly could to make the lot of the Jews easier during the war. Naturally, the possibilities for reducing suffering were very limited because of the war situation. But he did manage to help quite a few families; because of him they had enough bread to feed their families.

At the end of the war, the Austrians retreated from the shtetl, leaving behind food, clothing, and even guns. The Jewish youths took the guns and organized their own watch to protect against attacks and robberies during that confused and lawless time of transition.

At that time of confusion, we had a taste of the rule of the Bolsheviks, whom we called the "barefooted ones" because they wore seedy uniforms and worn-out shoes. They lasted about four or five weeks in our town. But in this short time they did us much harm. They robbed us, mostly of food and clothing.

After the Poles chased out the Bolsheviks, order in the shtetl gradually was restored. The *starosta* [regional governor] owned an estate in Stavke. He was a good man who raised the people's spirits after their terrible war experience.

From 1920 on, the Jews of Libivne again began to get financial help from relatives and compatriots in America; and their economic situation was much improved. Moreover, emigration to the United States became evident.

The new Polish government gave Jews permission to organize a kehila [Jewish communal self-government] to deal with social and religious matters of the Libivner Jews. The first chairman of the kehila was Moyshe Reyzman, of blessed memory. The members were Manes Greenberg, Hershl Lifshitz, Meyer Landgeyer, Moyshe Sfard, Shloyme Yitshak Sirtchuk, Rabinowitch, Kalman Kopelzon. In the 1930s, which I remember more clearly, each shul proposed its own candidate for the kehila council.

In 1936, just before the new kehila elections, I was nominated to run for the council as a representative of the small Stepenyer Shul, where I used to pray. The members elected then were Asher Tenenboym and Nachum Shtern from the Trisker shtibl [small Chasidic shul], Avrom Grimatlicht from the Rizhiner shtibl, Pinchas Krupodelnik and Yankl Peretzson from the artisans' shul, Aron Leyb Lichtmacher from the Radziner, Sandlshteyn from the Kotsker shtibl.

The kehila's executive council lasted until

Pupils and teachers of the Yavneh school celebrating Chanukah, 1930.

the outbreak of World War II. Its secretary was Moyshe Lifshitz, who held that position from 1929 on. The new members elected Asher Tenenboym as their chairman. He was a Zionist; in fact, most members were Zionists.

★

Three rabbis served the religious needs of the community: R. Leybish London [nicknamed "Henshl's," for his mother Henshl], R. Pinchas Oselka, and R. Leybl Melamed, the dayan [judge]. The starosta demanded that the Jews elect one of the three as the official rabbi for the town. This led to a great many quarrels. The congregation of the Kotsker shtibl wanted to appoint the grandson of R. Leybish to the rabbinate chair one Reb Alter [London]. All those who attended the *bet midrash* wanted to see R. Oselka occupy the chair of honor as official town rabbi. And the congregation of the Trisker shtibl wanted R. Leybl Dayan elected.

Elections took place and R. Alter was chosen as town rabbi, with the help of the town's artisans. We, as the executive council of the kehila, did not want to discriminate among the three rabbis and gave the two unelected rabbis both salaries and positions—one as head of the Chevra Kadisha [burial society], and the other as head of the Great Synagogue.

Famous Chasidic rebbes used to come to the shtetl once a year to visit the Libivner followers of their particular sects. The exception was the Rizhiner rebbe, who visited us only once. The town received him with great honor. The Stepenyer Chasidim bought a house for the Stepenyer rebbe and he came to live in the shtetl together with his whole family.

Libivne was a Zionist town. Zionists occupied important positions in almost every town organization and accomplished a great deal of work. Important proprietors and most of the young people did a great deal for the Keren HaKayemet and for Keren HaYesod [Jewish National Fund]. The agricultural training camp of the HeChalutz, the Labor Zionist youth movement was supported by the town's Zionist organization. The day of aliyah [when trained pioneers left for Palestine to work its land] was a big holiday for the town's youth.

The youth organized such clubs as Hechalutz, Beitar and Hashomer HaTsair, which conducted cultural and educational activities.

There was a Yavneh school in Libivne, under the auspices of the Mizrachi [Orthodox Zionists]. There were also about 20 melamdim [teachers] who taught in the cheders.

In 1939, the Zionists planned to erect a Tarbut school. The Radziner rebbe came to town at that time and called all the Jews together for a meeting in the big shul, where he spoke out severely against the Tarbut and Yavneh schools. He said they bred apikorsim [heretics] and Jews must not permit this.

The rebbe, who was staying at the home of my friend, Avrom Lichtmacher, called together all the members of the kehila's executive council and tried to convince us that we must not allow the Yavneh school to be built. But we did not accept his advice. The kehila office was transferred from the Talmud Torah [Orthodox school] to another place, and we decided to build the Yavneh school. This was in 1939, and you can well understand that all our plans were destroyed by the coming war.

FOUR YEARS IN LIBIVNE
By Dr. Edward Amshchibovsky

I came originally from Volkovisk. Several years before World War II, I came to Libivne as a doctor to practice medicine. During the few years I was there, I became acclimated to the town and made friends with some of its leading Jews.

My best friends were Rabbi Tversky, as well as his son Moyshele and his family. Though I was a misnaged [opponent of Chasidism], we became very friendly. We would discuss *meinyeney deyoma* [current events] in a very calm manner, though, as can well be understood, each of us had a different point of view.

Libivne had a rosh yeshiva [head of a ye-shiva] who was a very wise man. He did not believe in doctors and he would say, *"Im HaShem lo yishmor ir shav shok'du shomreya!"* [If God does not protect a city, all its guards are in vain!]. One Friday eve he called me in to treat his child for diphtheria: It was a case of pikuach nefesh [her life was in danger and one is required to violate most religious restrictions in order to save a life]. On that Sabbath evidently the head of the yeshiva did have faith in doctors!

As a doctor, I became friendly with both pharmacy proprietors, Kopelzon and Nathanzon. I also spent a lot of time with the lawyers Katz and

Members of HeChalutz HaTsair at a Zionist gathering in 1929.

123

Shpayzman, with the veterinary doctor Lacks, and others.

The few years in the shtetl passed very quickly. War clouds were gathering over Libivne. But even before the war came to Libivne, the Soviets occupied the entire region. I was ordered to organize a polyclinic. We had 15 doctors working in it, as well as two dentists, one of whom was my brother-in-law, Martin Glasman.

The Soviet authorities also gave me the task of organizing a women's hospital and I carried out the assignment. I worked in that hospital almost two years, until the Germans occupied us.

In 1939–40, Luboml had many Jewish refugees from Poland: the Dunyets family from Chelm, Dr. Lipnovsky from Lodz, Dr. Rozentzvayg Tanenboym from the glass factory in Chelm, etc. All settled in temporarily. They were waiting for the war to end so as to be able to return home.

Under the Soviet regime, people could not make a living. They worked but hardly earned enough for bread, and they lived in poverty, without a future. Their only hope was that the war would end and the Russians would leave. We thought often about the Land of Israel as an independent state. We talked about it only in secret, for such talk smacked of counter-revolution.

The following will illustrate how the Russians enslaved the population: The NKVD [Soviet secret police] would summon people to its chambers, instill tremendous fear in them, and force them to spy on their neighbors.

I do not wish to reveal any names, but honorable people have told me that they were forced to do so or be deported to Siberia.

When the German-Soviet war broke out, and Libivne was in danger of being occupied by the Nazis, I, Dr. Glasman, Dr. Lipnovsky, and some others went on foot to [the nearby town of] Kovel, because trains had stopped running. There we went to the *Voyenkom* [war committee], wishing to enlist. They told us, "Go home. We will send for you when we need you."

After spending some time under the Nazis in Kovel and later in Trisk, where Dr. Lipnovsky helped me, I returned to Libivne. I again began to organize the Jewish hospital. I bought medicines wherever I could, desiring mainly to prevent an epidemic. When I discovered a patient had developed typhoid, I isolated him in the hospital. There were no more cases of typhoid in Libivne!

I often spoke with Kopelzon, head of the Judenrat, about organizing defense groups in the woods, but he really believed that if we obeyed the Nazis, we would survive.

I talked about running into the woods with the lawyer Zatz, who was appointed by the Germans to head the Jewish militia in the Ghetto. He proposed that we hide out for one or two days during the slaughter, then go into the woods with guns and there organize a group.

I disagreed. But when I saw there was no way out, I forged some Aryan documents for myself and my brother-in-law and we fled Libivne.

MEMORIES
By Yakov Elfant

Of all the holidays observed in our shtetl, the most visible was Simchat Torah. All the other holidays were celebrated in the homes or synagogues, but Simchat Torah was celebrated in the streets, before the eyes of the gentile neighbors.

On the day when the Jewish people rejoiced with the several-thousand-year-old festival of the Torah, Luboml's Jews would bring the Torah scrolls out of the synagogue into the street and later return them with song. The cantors and the others leading the prayers would sing during the ceremony, and the rest of the Jews would help them.

Another occasion when Jews celebrated their holiday in the streets was Rosh Hashana [Jewish New Year], when they went to Tashlich [ceremony of throwing bread or stones, symbolizing sins, into a body of running water]. There was noise during this celebration too, but it came from another source—from the obnoxious gentile boys who would throw stones at the Jews going to Tashlich. But many times the Jews returned the beatings in kind, giving blow for blow to the attacking gentiles.

This would happen especially during Christian festivals—Easter, Christmas, and New Year's Eve. Peasants would come to the shtetl to attend services, and from time to time they would get in the mood to have some fun at the expense of the Jewish inhabitants of the town. Drunken youths would start up with Jews who were passing by and would beat them up.

When the Jews began to scream, Jewish youths would come running to their aid. Among them were the so-called "three hundred" [a group of young men who organized themselves to act as protectors of Jews against the gentile hooligans of the town].

The following were members of the group: Yitsikl Shed [devil] and his brother, Shaye Grimatlicht, Shloyme-Meyer Yoynes, and others. They would grab the long wooden poles from the peasants' wagons and beat the wild drunken peasants ferociously and chase them out of town.

BYGONE DAYS
By Menachem Rubinshteyn

In my childhood memories, the cheder occupies a central place; my father brought me to the cheder when I was only a boy of five years. My first rebbe [cheder teacher] was R. Natan Hamunetzer, who lived near the Big Shul. From him I passed on to R. Moyshe Shneyers [Povroznik]; and then to R. Moyshe Yoseles [Melamed]. All these melamdim [cheder teachers] lived on one narrow alley, and it seems to me that all Luboml children passed through this alley.

After this, as we progressed, all of us began to study at the cheder of Avrom der Poylisher [Avrom the Pole], whose real name was R. Avrom Goldhacker. He was a respected Jew who also had a good disposition. But in his capacity as a rebbe, he was pleasant to us only until Thursday. For on Thursdays we had to review what we had learned in the Gemara [commentaries on the Mishnah] that we had studied all week. Then he examined us very strictly. Incidentally, three of his sons ran away during the war to Russia and reside now in Leningrad. Prior to the war, the oldest son, Leybl Goldhacker, was a teacher in the town's public school.

To write about Luboml, it is impossible not to mention its strong Zionist movement. I remember when an emissary from Eretz Yisroel came to our town to organize a chapter of the Hechalutz movement: This was in the 1930s. He was Aaron Berdichevsky from Kibbutz Yagur.

I was a member of HeChalutz Hatsair, whose leaders were Yitsik Samet and Berl Volvushes [later known as Dov Ivri]. They were our guides, teaching us to converse in Hebrew in Kampyonis's

Members of Kibbutz Klosova resting after their work as wood cutters.

orchard. We often became involved in heated debates. Leybish Perl was a kind of political commissar to us. Our patrons on behalf of the party were Motl Privner, Leyzer Finkelshteyn, and Shmuel Royter.

Of special inspiration to our town's kibbutz hachshara [preparation camp for agriculture] were the chalutzim who came from out-of-town. This kibbutz was located near the flour mill owned by Grimatlicht and his partners. The kibbutz members had to support themselves by working, and Luboml was not an industrial town. Conditions for providing employment were poor.

Some of our kibbutz members found work at Chayim Kroyt's lumber mill. They were less productive than the other workers. But Chayim used to say: "That's O.K. The Zionist movement has already cost me so much money. Let it cost me a little more."

With the help of local Zionists, kibbutz members got work chopping wood for heating. And so they helped us, and we helped them by cutting down trees and making boards and lumber.

I remember also a black Friday in Luboml, the day that Efrayim Gelbord was murdered. It happened between eight and nine in the morning, when bands of drunken hooligans attacked some Jewish storekeepers selling fruits and vegetables.

The hooligans began to break up the stalls and scatter the produce. And when Efrayim ran out to chase them away, one of them drew a switchblade knife and killed him on the spot. A dramatic chase after the rioters began at once, with all the other young people of the town participating; but the murderer hid in the attic of one of the houses. The people kept a watch on him until the police came and took him away. The arrangements for Efrayim's funeral were made the very same day, and the whole town fell into deep mourning.

THE EXPLOSION IN THE DISTILLERY

The explosion of a steam-boiler [in the distillery] was a terrible tragedy. It happened on the 22nd day of Av, 1919. The first victim was Boruch Chesner, one of the workers in the distillery who was a close relative of Moyshe Reyzman's family.

The explosion tore him into little bits. The second victim was Yisroel "Urke" [his nickname], who suffered for several days before he died. Large parts of Avrom Lichtmacher's body were scalded. He was brought to the hospital in Lublin, where he spent several months and finally recovered.

The funeral of Boruch Chesner was attended by the whole town. The leftist youth—then under the leadership of leftist activists from Chelm, who were agitating for the Bund—used the occasion of the mass funeral to propagandize for the "class struggle." They carried placards and made protest speeches against the exploiters of the working class, etc.

"Honor the fallen worker Chesner" was written on the placards at the funeral. But in reality, it was the funeral of one of our own Jews who had been killed in an accident, and the whole town came to pay respect to him on his last journey.

The funeral of Boruch Chesner, first victim of the distillery explosion in 1919.

128

THE JEWS OF THE VILLAGE OF STAVKE
By Efrayim Lerner

When Efrayim Stavker decided to marry off his daughter Chaye-Tove, he came to Libivne, talked it over with the melamed [Hebrew teacher] Avrom-Moyshe Meshcheches, and they decided on a shiddach [match]. They did not have to ask the children themselves, because in those days, over 100 years ago, the decision lay with the parents. Nor were the bride and groom capable of making decisions, since the boy and the girl were 13 and 14 years old!

The bride later became my grandmother on my mother's side. She told me that though they were not supposed to see each other until the wedding ceremony, she stealthily peeked from behind her veil to look at her groom. And she felt dejected, for he was a small skinny boy from his constant sitting and learning Torah, while she was a village beauty, healthy and full of life.

After the wedding, they came to live in the village. My grandfather was employed in a mill and used to visit the city quite often.

Stavke had 12–15 Jewish families. Among them was our family and Hershele Shamays, with his four families. Some families had settled in Stavke during World War I. They even had a melamed whom we nicknamed Itsye Stavke. After he died, the village brought a teacher from the outside.

I remember my grandfather when he was a lessee. He had leased the estate of the village landlord, including the orchard and the fields, paying an annual fee. The landlord would stay in St. Petersburg, seldom coming to the village.

I remember the wedding of grandfather's youngest daughter, Rayntse, which was celebrated in the landlord's manor. My father had hired the band of Libivne musicians led by Yakov Hersh Klezmer. With them was old Pesach with the white beard, which was in harmony with his black clarinet.

During World War I, all my grandfather's children lived in the village.

By then I was already a grown-up fellow. My cousins and I used to go to the neighboring village, Ovlotchim, to buy fish. I remember some of the names of the Jews of that village: R. Ovadye *der Krumer* [the lame], who was head of the kehila; Moyshe der royber [the robber], who used to tell jokes, being somewhat of a wedding entertainer.

R. Ovadye der Krumer would arrange a minyan [quorum of ten Jews needed for certain prayer services] at his house on the Sabbath and conduct services. Lending his home for holiday services too, he acted both as cantor and reader of the Torah.

The village of Ladin was about a mile from Stavke. Moyshe Ladiner lived there with his family and made a living from his mill, which pressed oil from seeds. On the High Holy Days and during Sukkot, his family used to pray with my grandfather's minyan.

A kosher slaughterer would come to us on Thursdays from the neighboring town of Masheve, walking from village to village. I always wondered how he had the strength to walk so far on foot while carrying a heavy sack with his slaughterer's knives, as well as several cuts of meat he had received as a supplement to his payment for slaughtering.

During World War I, the Jewish people would hire a young man to teach village children to read and write Yiddish. It happened that my grandfather, passing by, heard the teacher explain to the children that z"l meant *zol lebn* ["may he live"], instead of *zichrono livracha* ["may his memory be blessed"]. It stands to reason that the next morning the young man had to leave the village.

When people traveled from Libivne to Stavke, they had to pass the villages of Vishnyeve, Rodochov, Shmikets, Olesk, and Stavochar. Each of these villages had several Jewish families. Most were known to us, and we would stop in to have a chat with them, as, for example, with Asher Radochover and his beloved wife (may she rest in peace). They were great believers in the tradition of *hachnosas orchim* [hospitality].

The young people of the neighboring villages used to spend their leisure time together. I and a couple of my friends organized a small library. Only a couple of the original organizers are still alive.

The following helped establish the library: Boruch Fingerhut, who is now in Argentina, and Kalman Roytenshteyn, both from Ovlotchim.

Sometimes we stopped over in Stavotchik, at the home of the observant Jew Dovid Mamit, who lived there with his wife Chane and their children. Two dear people, they too would receive us well, with expressions of good will. Luckily, their two children were able to escape to America. They told me with tears in their eyes how they were forced to dig graves for their parents, whom the murderers had shot in front of their home.

The Jews in the villages led hard lives. And Stavke was no exception. First of all—making a living; there was no stable means of support. In general, people lived from their orchards, from selling cattle, chickens, etc., and the profit was very small. Winters were especially hard, and many suffered hunger.

Despite everything, Jewish life flourished in the villages around Libivne. Hard-working village Jews led traditional Orthodox lives, carried out God's commandments, cherished the Sabbath, and knew how to rejoice on their holidays.

AUTOBIOGRAPHY OF A JEWISH DAUGHTER
By Rochl Leichter (Weysman), z"l

It is an accepted opinion that memoirs are written only by famous people, who, together with their personal memories, also write about the life of their generation, about encounters with prominent political and social activists, etc. Above all, they write their memoirs when they have already reached advanced age.

I, however, am quite young as compared to other writers of memoirs. I have no accomplishments that would make it worthwhile to put down my life on paper for the public to read. And yet I have an urge to relive my personal experiences once more; to penetrate the labyrinth of my not too distant past and to try to discover the strengths that carried me through and helped me overcome everything I had to carry on my weak shoulders.

And maybe, maybe my writing will interest all those who have only heard of the hell, where a Jewish daughter was roasted and yet was not entirely consumed by the fire.

I was born in 1918 in Volhynia. Just as our shtetl had an official name, Luboml, and a Jewish name, Libivne,so did each street have an official name given it by the authorities and a name the Jews gave it. The street where we lived also had two names; The Poles called it Koleyova, for it led to the railroad station, but the Jews called it simply the Ban-Gas—Railroad Street.

Others called it Golden Street. Why Golden? Many years ago, before the street was paved, it was full of potholes and mud, especially in autumn. And a joke was born about the street: When a stranger complained, asking why such a muddy street was called Golden Street, the people would answer: "When you go to the other streets, you will see that our street is indeed a Golden Street

in comparison with the others."

People told me that across the street from my house was a big residence with a long stable. A fine proprietor lived there (I do not remember his name), who was in charge of the post office. The government paid him a monthly salary and he also took care of the horses, giving them food. The horses were used especially to pull out from the mud all those landowners who used to sink into it with their beautiful coaches. Naturally, besides his monthly wages, he was tipped quite handsomely each time he pulled a coach out of the mud!

But we did have a beautiful market square, which any other town would have been glad to have. The market was built around a huge square area. Part of it had stores—beautiful, tall brick

Rochl Leichter (Weysman) z"l

131

buildings, with round ledges in front; they were built in a beautiful style and were painted white. The stores occupied only one corner of the square.

Brisk Street bordered it on the north and Chelm Street on the west (Chelm Street was also called Rimatch Street). This street was long and densely built. The street began at the market-place and was full of stores selling shoes, haber-dashery, dishes, food, etc. There was also a fish store near Chelm Street.

Where the street ended, outside the town, it intersected another street that both Gentiles and Jews called Biselovska. It was at this intersection that the Jews who lived in the vicinity would wait to buy from peasants everything they were bring-ing to town: from grain and eggs to tobacco. Be-yond that point were some of the smaller gentile houses, with small gardens and fruit trees. At the very end of the long streets were the fields that surrounded the shtetl.

To the right of Brisk Street was another large row of old-fashioned stores. Each house had a little store in the front, and a deep, large residence in back. This neighborhood also had taverns, as well as state-licensed stores for cigarettes and tobacco. These small stores lined both sides of the street till the intersection with Polish Street, occu-pied mostly by Poles. Polish Street was about a mile long.

An orchard stretched over the entire length of the right side of the street. The gardens belonged to the town's landowner, Kampyoni, who lived nearby. He owned all the stores on that street and the storekeepers paid him an annual rent. Actu-ally, the storekeepers had those stores for genera-tions, having either inherited them or received them as dowry for their children. They even had the right to sell the stores, but they had to pay rent to the rich landowner.

Of all the streets, the one that has been etched in my memory was Polish Street, for it had the school I attended as a child. In general, this street was different from the others; it had fewer houses, which therefore did not crowd each other as much as in other streets. In the city park, one side was occupied by the garden with its deli-cious pears and winter-apples. On the other side was a row of government buildings, spaced far apart. They housed the offices of the municipal-ity, the Department of Finance, the Catholic church and the Greek Orthodox church. Trees and greenery surrounded the buildings, unlike the other streets of the town.

On the Sabbath or on leisure days, the towns-people promenaded on this street; it was their favorite spot for a stroll. This whole area, with its fragrant air, enticed young people out of their dwellings. The older ones, as well, would come out for a stroll here, after they had eaten their Sabbath cholent and had a nap. The younger ones were not too lazy to go beyond the town, to the nearby Boris Woods.

Oh, if only that little wood could reveal the secrets of the loving young couples who used to sneak into the thickets, to lose themselves in their fantasy of a better future when they were married and would not have to hide their feelings; and meanwhile they would steal a kiss or two as a deposit!

I was born just in the "right" time. World War I was almost over. It was in fact over, but other troubles soon began—epidemics. Typhoid fever was rampant in our area, leaving few Jewish homes untouched. I was then nine months old. We lived near the Talmud Torah, in a tiny room, rented from Yitshak the Wagoner.

As my father told me later, my mother had just finished kneading dough in a small trough half the size of a small keg, which had a cover, when suddenly someone ran into the house, shout-ing loudly to my mother that she should go and help my uncle because he was very ill.

Not thinking of the danger, she quickly ran to him in order to sponge him down with alcohol—the only cure known at that time. My mother caught the disease right then and there, and died after one day's sickness.

After this terrible tragedy, my father decided to leave the little Talmud Torah street and even the shtetl itself, where the epidemic was raging because of overcrowded conditions. His sister Sosye lived in the village of Vishnyeve, somewhat less than two miles away. The village had plenty fresh air as well as a garden in front of every house. And his sister was also able to help him to take care of the little orphaned children.

We did not have to think long. My father was so spent, so frightened, like after a big fire, at the sudden catastrophe, that he was ready to leave the town at once. He was afraid that if he stayed one more day after mother died he would lose his children too. The question was—how could he pack up the children and the few possessions, and leave the city?

We could get neither horse nor wagon; and even if we could have gotten them, we had no money to pay for them. And so my father came up with a plan. Every married couple owned a chest about seven feet long, made of strong wood, and bound with iron hoops. The bottom had iron bars, screwed on with stout, heavy screws. The bars varied in length and thickness, and could serve as an axle, for they had iron wheels attached at each end. It was a primitive contraption, but it was strong. The upper part of the chest was a cover, and it had iron bars attached to it, for use either to open the chest or to keep it from closing. The cover was a bit rounded, and the chest was painted green.

On either side of the chest, at the head and at the foot, were two iron handles for moving the chest from one place to another. Why do I call them the "foot" and the "head"? Because the chest was sometimes used as an extra bed. When a guest came, and we had no place to put him up, the chest became a temporary bed. During the summer, the chest held the winter clothes, for it was big enough to hold almost all of the household's goods. Some families would store their Sabbath candlesticks in the chest, or silver goblets and silver flatware, or a copper pestle and mortar, or a silver tray. The chest swallowed everything.

This was done for two reasons; firstly, it had a strong lock as protection against theft; and secondly, if the copper vessels were not put away, the children used them a toys and would bang on them, making noise.

My father therefore planned to use the chest as a wagon, to move our things to the village. He took off the heavy belt from his pants, attached it to one of the two handles, and put all our bags and baggage and the children into the four corners of the chest, and off we went. He yoked himself to his belt, and the chest was on its way.

The village was not too far from the town— we could see the village of Vishnyeve from the railroad station. It stretched as one long street, about a mile or so long. On one side it bordered the village of Masheve, and on the other end it bordered Kotseres. It didn't take us too long to reach the village.

My aunt Sosye and my uncle Getsl Chinenzon had a big house with three large rooms. We arrived there at twilight and found a fine, large dwelling, an exception to the little low huts of the neighboring peasants. My aunt Sosye received us with heartfelt kindness.

Next morning, my father found a small house near my aunt's. It was empty because many peasants had run away to Russia during the war. The house was whitewashed and cleaned; panes of glass were put into the windows and the house became spic and span.

We all enjoyed the fresh air. The older children were running around, free as larks, in the gardens and the fields. Everything in the village was freer—even the gardens of strangers were open to us. When I came to the village I was a weak child, for in the postwar time there was no proper food to nourish a child. We thanked God for a piece of dry bread to fill our stomachs. And so I became ill as soon as we got there, and I was sick for a long time. They fed me genilkelech (small pears), which grew not far from our new home. These small pears ripened in late autumn. Each peasant had such a pear tree on his lot. The pears or were soft, a little rotted, and sour in taste.

The pear trees grew wild and abundantly in our area. No one forbade people to pick the fallen ripe pears, which were piled up even in the fields. Every peasant owned such a pear tree, which also served as a benchmark, separating his property from another's. The trees would grow tall and scatter their fruit far and wide.

The term genilkelech was also the nickname of the village youth. It was a custom that village Jews of Volhynia would come to town during the holidays. Those living in distant villages brought their freezing children bundled up in bedding. The town's children would run after them yelling, "Here come the genilkes!" and throwing genilkelech at them, and the village Jews felt very insulted. Very often the visiting villagers would manage to enter the town at night so as not to be noticed. But when the town's children noticed a village child, they would surround him with cat-calls of "genilye."

I do not remember how long I was sick. My father once told me it lasted half a year. No one expected me to be well again. But a "miracle" occurred: I somehow managed to get over my sickness and to improve, until I became well enough to be like the other children.

Meanwhile, war broke out between the Russians and the Poles, with the Russians eyeing Poland and Warsaw. How odd the Russian "army" appeared to us then: ragged, barefoot, and naked. The little they did have on was made up of all sorts of mismatched garments.

The first thing the Bolsheviks did was call together the entire population in the market-place, put up a table, and set an agitator upon it, who began to propagandize about all the "good things" that the "comrades" of the Bolshevik government could expect. They turned the heads of the mob to such an extent that they expected paradise to be just around the corner. But when after awhile they found that instead of paradise things were going from bad to worse, they began to sober up.

The Jews in our region suffered a great deal from roving bands, especially from the Ukrainian Balechovtzes, who murdered, robbed Jewish possessions, and violated the women. Even after the Poles returned and took over the government there were pogroms against Jewish businesses. It was touch and go as to whether the bands would also come to our town. But a couple of Jewish proprietors, headed by R. Pinchas Oselka, brought a petition to the Catholic priest Yostschembsky, who helped prevent an attack.

My oldest sister began her training as a seamstress. It was customary to teach every girl how to sew, as well as how to read and write. Naturally, she had to know how to pray and how to write a Yiddish letter, while a little knowledge of Russian did not hurt either. My oldest sister showed a great talent for learning. And since she was busy all day with studying and preparing her lessons and with practicing on the sewing ma-

chine, the family began to look upon me, a four-year-old, as a grown-up and began to teach me how to take care of the house.

With time, I took over the housework. I even painted the chimney with white lime with a home-made brush. Such a brush was braided from special soft, long grass, bound in the middle, and turned over a few times at the binding to create an edge for brushing. All the loose grass was cut off with an axe—a good brush came out of it. Whoever wanted to invest more time in finishing the brush would put it in hot water to soften it and by doing this make it a better brush.

In time I noted that I became more and more involved in domestic chores. While children of my age were involved in games in the street, or in class, I was bound to the home, peeling potatoes, cooking, cleaning, and doing other chores. Every time I ran out to play my sister called me back home. More than once I used to ask my older sister why all the other children could play and no one interrupted them and called them back home. So what do you think my sister answered me? "They have mothers, so they do the work for them."

So I began to ask my father to take in a mother, so I would have one too. Then, like other children, I would have time to play and study. My father's sister approved of the idea.

One bright day my father did bring a mother into our home and said: "So Rachel, here, I brought you a mother!" I ceased to do all the work in the house. I ran around with children all day long to make up for all the time passed. I felt like a bird who had escaped the cage. Who was my equal? But the older children immediately said that father had brought home a stepmother.

The fact that she was really a stepmother became quickly apparent. She began to rule the house with a strong hand, began to beat the children for the smallest infraction. My father could not stand it and one day my "new" mother disappeared from our home. My career as a child quickly ended, and once again I became bound to the house.

Time moved on. I grew and developed, and with luck began to attend school. I did not have enough time because the household with all its chores were on my head and in my small hands. I had to prepare food for the whole family and keep the house clean, so it was not easy to study.

I did not have books and had to borrow from friends. Writing paper was also limited. On cold days I caught a cold because it was some way from home to the school. Only with great effort could I succeed in finishing my housework and prepare my homework.

I was a good student. My teacher, Chikowolski, was a good teacher, and his lessons were interesting to the students. My younger brother was the best student. There wasn't anything he did not know. He especially excelled in drawing.

At one point the teacher called on my father and asked him to send my brother Yitshak to an art school in a larger town. In his opinion my brother had a great talent for art. The teacher even said that in such a case the government would provide a stipend, and that he would even request it.

However, he could not persuade my father. One, he could not imagine his child so far away from him. Two, who knows, maybe he would fall in, God forbid, among Christians, and be so confused as to forget his Jewish roots?

Time continued to move forward. The situation slowly began to improve. On a request from my sister, my father rented a sewing machine because my sister had mastered the tailoring profession. All our Christian neighbors began to bring in orders for dresses, blouses, and children's items. My sister cut and finished everything on her own. Everybody praised Shmuel Dovid's "capable children."

In the towns, a child who showed some talent or willingness to learn, could achieve something. But children who had no desire wasted their best years. In most cases they remained uneducated. They had neither a Jewish education nor general education; few of these children even finished the public school, so when they came together socially with others they felt very bad. A girl who did not finish the public or, later, the Tarbut school felt the effects later on.

In our village there were only four grades in the public school. I asked my father to arrange so that I could study in Luboml. To my surprise my father easily agreed. In a few years, I finished public school in Luboml and returned to the village, where I worked and made a living.

The outbreak of the Russian-German war suddenly brought an end to everything. We were all forced into the Luboml Ghetto, where my entire family was annihilated, along with all the other Jewish inhabitants. For two years I hid in the surrounding forests. After the war I went to Russia, where I located my childhood friend and bridegroom, Israel Leichter. We were married in 1948 and went to Israel.

FOND MEMORIES OF MY SHTETL
By Menachem Erlich

Luboml, my hometown, has a good place in my memories. It was a relatively small town. It was not surrounded by large mountains, nor was there a clear stream of water running through it. Luboml was just a small, plain town, situated in widespread, low-lying land in Greater Volhynia.

This was where I was born. In this town lived my kindhearted grandmother and my strict grandfather. In Luboml I first felt the love of my mother and the admiration of my father. I also felt the strict hand of my father. In Luboml, I felt the heartbreak of first love and, as I matured, the pangs of growing pains. In Luboml, that small town of my childhood, everything that I felt, everything that happened to me, was for the first time. It is for this reason that Luboml has such a pleasant place in my memories.

Nevertheless, I did not live my life in Luboml. I did not build my family there with the love of my life. My children did not call my mother "grandma" or my father "grandpa" there.

Toward the end of my adolescence, cruel fate was to erase this small quiet corner off the face of the earth. To erase the vibrant life within it, its citizens, its children, its hopes and its dreams.

I remember the town as being clean. It had paved roads, wooden sidewalks, and later concrete sidewalks as well. The roadway was paved with square basalt stones, and it was slanted so that the rainwater would not flood it. I remember the men who paved the road. They crouched on their knees, doing their work in the clean sand. In their hands they held special hammers. They used a shovel to remove the sand and a spade to flatten the surface where the stones were to be placed. Then they would take the stone and put it in, trying every which way until it fit perfectly.

The stone would remain in the road for generations to come.

The paving of the road, not unlike the building of a two- or three-story home, was a major event in our town. On such an occasion we children would spend all our free time at the site. We would watch and inspect what was going on. With wonder and admiration we looked up to the strong and capable builders and road pavers.

In the southeastern corner of the town square stood the only cinema of our town. Its lights shone from a square frame that hung from the front of the building, and penetrated arrogantly through the darkness of the marketplace at night. This light was the kind that blinds you and irritates the eye; it was exciting, not quieting.

To that theater we were drawn like moths to light, in the hopes of sneaking in for the treat of seeing the latest detective movie. Nevertheless, after an hour or so of false hope that we might get inside, we'd leave quietly, disappointed by the light that had betrayed us. All of us walked toward our homes, each one of us choosing one of the four main roads that led us away from the town square.

To my mind, it was a very organized man who planned the town. It seems that first of all he built the town square, including all the stores. The town square was closed in on three sides, and the fourth side, the northern side, was left open and one could see Jagiello Hill and the Orthodox church, as well as the home of the Polish pharmacist.

From the center of the town square this "organized" man determined four points using a ruler. These four points represent the four major roads in our town: Railroad Street, Chelm Street,

Kusnishtcher Street, and Polish Street. The Jews first settled at the center of the town square and alongside those four main streets. They built their homes, brought children into the world, and generation after generation contributed their share to the character of our small town, Luboml.

No one determined a border to the streets where the Jews lived. Nevertheless, it is a fact that there was a certain spot on the line drawn by the designer, where Jewish life stopped and the life of Luboml's gentile citizens began. It just happened that the Jews lived in the center of town and gentiles' homes and fields surrounded the Jewish part of town like a belt.

I remember the residents of our town being divided into different classes. There were scholars and those who were thirsty for knowledge, merchants and craftsmen, rich and poor, widows and orphans, lucky men and those who had run out of luck, fishermen and owners of carriages, water carriers and beggars.

The life of our town was conducted in surprising harmony. There was acceptance of the laws and judgment from "above" without criticism concerning unfairness, that some were better off economically, or that property was not distributed equally.

We children conducted our lives differently from the adults, according to our own set of rules. These rules were made by those boys who were physically superior.

Our parents, however, did not divide themselves into groups as we did. They did not fight. They accepted their lot without thinking or protesting, at least not out loud. They argued about important world issues, about large wars. Nevertheless, they never spoke about their own wars, their struggle to survive from day to day. They accepted their economic standing as a decree from heaven or they blamed it on their personal failures.

In their favor, it could be said that they were fair, proper, and decent. A man's economic standing did not affect his social standing. One's honesty and intelligence were his ticket to a favorable social standing. It is for this reason that I think highly of our town's citizens.

I also remember our town's places of worship, many of which were shtiblach [small syna-

gogues] belonging to Chasidim. There was also a bet midrash and the central synagogue.

These places of worship were like a haven of refuge to most Jews of Luboml. Toward evening, after a long hard day of standing in the store, the Jew would come to the bet midrash to shake off the day's hardships. He would delve into a problem posed in the Talmud or listen to a lesson on *Ein Yakov.*

In this manner he would lessen the worries on his mind, such as the fact that he had not paid for certain school lessons or that he did not have a proper dowry for his daughter who had come of age.

Here in the shtibl and the bet midrash the ways of mutual aid, secret alms-giving, and sincere charity were permanently set. Those who were poor and forced to wander from town to town came to these places to request shelter when they passed through Luboml. There each person compared his life to the sorrow and hardships of others, and as a result his life seemed brighter. In the bet midrash and the shtibl men revealed the details of their worries and added them to all the worries of the community. Men were encouraged to let go of some of their problems and look forward to a new tomorrow.

In the shtibel and Bet-Midrash, men tried to determine the future course of events in world politics, such as the time at which the next war would break out, etc. There was always one question that kept repeating itself: "Is this or that for the good of the Jewish people?"

Our community was connected to the outside world through the post office, the railroad, and horse-drawn carriages. Letters and packages came in the mail, mostly from America, from relatives who had gone to try their luck across the Atlantic Ocean. In our imagination, all of them across the ocean were millionaires, eating like kings and dressing like princes.

The receiving of packages was a major event, and in order to distribute the different presents among family members one needed the wisdom of Solomon. The packages also caused jealousy among neighbors who were not lucky enough to have relatives overseas. A telegram would, in most cases, bear bad news of a family disaster or tragedy. It was only on rare occasions that a telegram bore important information directed at the entire community.

The train would slowly enter the station at the edge of the town. Then it would apply its brakes with a deafening, shrieking noise and eventually stop at the entrance of a wooden building, painted green, on which it said "Luboml" in Polish.

Most of the time, cargo from the trains was distributed among the town's merchants. Then the train would return, carrying few passengers. During certain seasons the merchants would send out freight trains full of crops and cattle.

Sometimes a traveling salesman would be sent to the town. This man would stay at Tseylingold's Inn or in a furnished room provided by Kaminer. Where he stayed was determined by the coachman who brought him to Luboml. Only on the evening of certain holidays and during the week of certain holidays was there any real use of the train in and out of Luboml. Single men from Luboml would travel to neighboring or distant towns to look for mates. Also, many bachelors came to Luboml looking for

spouses because our town was not lacking in pretty young women. Unfortunately, many of them were without a dowry.

The plain folks made their way in wagons—going on the holidays to visit the rebbe and ask for a blessing and during the summer vacation to visit their rich uncles.

I left Luboml on the train to serve in the Russian army. It never occurred to me that this would be the last time I saw my hometown and its Jewish citizens.

★

On the Ruins

It was midnight when I jumped from a freight train that had slowed down by the railroad station of Luboml. It was five years since I had last seen my hometown; five years since I was escorted by my family to the train station on my way to serve in the Red Army. This time I stood on that same platform all alone and not one person came to welcome me home.

A view of the market square on a market day, 1926.

I had not returned to celebrate my country's liberation. I had not come hoping to be greeted with hugs and kisses and pats on the back. I had returned to visit one large cemetery; my town was one big grave. I came to gather the ashes of my beloved family. I came looking for my adolescent years. I wanted to engrave in my memory all that happened in the past; to remember all those that had been tortured and consequently murdered, and whose lips were whispering the names of their loved ones.

I had come to see the ruins of my hometown, to bury my soul in the pain and heartache: to mourn those friends and relatives who perished needlessly.

That autumn morning a light drizzle wet my face as my lonely footsteps echoed down the middle of Railroad Street on my way to the town square. The time was nine in the morning. Luboml was a ghost town. There was not a live soul anywhere. A dog was not to be seen. There was not even a cat crossing the road as a sign of bad luck. The animals had disappeared along with the citizens of Luboml.

When I reached the old cemetery, the town lay before me. It had been completely flattened. It looked like an empty lot. From the far-removed corner near the cemetery, where I now stood, I could see the flour mill that had belonged to the Grimatlicht family, the Great Synagogue that was now partially destroyed, the stores on the town square, and the home of the Polish pharmacist.

Silence shrouded my town during these early morning hours, which in the past had been alive with sound from sunrise to sunset. There was only the sound of the rain falling on my backpack and the sound of my footsteps echoing in the empty space that was once my hometown.

I stopped at the central square. The old stone stores that had once housed linens, pots, clothing, materials, etc., stood with their mouths open, blackened with soot, holes in the walls, just remnants of doors and windows and empty shelves once loaded with all kinds of merchandise.

I turned toward Chelm Street, and there I came across a sign of life on that rainy morning. It was a young man standing across the street. We were both weak in body and spirit, and we stood facing each other in wonderment that we had met on this massive grave in which all our friends and family were buried. Suddenly, we both felt as if we were brothers and that fate had brought us to this place at this time. We began to run toward each other, mustering all the strength that our numb bodies allowed us, and we fell into each other's arms in total silence.

FROM DAILY LIFE

WHEN LIFE PULSATED
By Benjamin Rosenzweig

Between the two wars, a dynamic Jewish life pulsated in hundreds of towns of independent Poland. Despite the economic difficulties of the Jewish masses in Poland and the many anti-Semitic vexations both by the government and the Christian population, Jews participated in all possible phases of life. And our small Libivne was no exception.

Naturally, though their work could not be compared to the many-faceted activities of the Jewish organizations in such neighboring centers as Rovno, Kovel, and Chelm, Luboml and its Jewish inhabitants, especially the youth, were active in various domains of local Jewish life. This was reflected particularly in the work of organizations, institutions, and parties.

The municipal council bestowing the title of "Honorary Citizen" on the governor of the Luboml region. Seated at extreme right is the Jewish deputy mayor, Yakov Shtern.

One of the most important institutions was the Jewish gemine, or kehila (organized Jewish community). The kehila, in conjunction with the municipality, had a tremendous influence on the Jewish community in Libivne. It is therefore no wonder that Jewish interest in the functioning of the kehila was always great and that there were always controversies over its decisions among the various sectors of the Libivne Jews.

The fights in and about the kehila were not always about economic interests. Its concerns also encompassed local Jewish and general Jewish problems. It was for this reason that the various political parties strove so hard to have an ever stronger position in it.

Whenever the elections to the kehila were approaching, the atmosphere in town became cheerful—gatherings in the synagogues and in the shtibls; street meetings; talks and fights in private homes. The assemblies were heated affairs. Quite often they had to be interrupted; at times they grew into general free-for-alls. There were vital interests for which people fought. We must not forget that the kehila had the power to tax the Jews in order to carry out some of the purposes permitted it by the government.

The Libivne kehila was established around 1923–24. Elections were held every four years, and the following officers were elected for the 1926–30 term: chairman—Moyshe Reyzman; secretary—Shimon Shor, the former official government-appointed rabbi for the town; and his alternate—Moyshe Greenberg; Hershl Lifshitz, Yitshak Shloyme Sirtchuk, Moyshe Sfard, Meyer Landgeyer, and Shepsl Rabinovich.

In 1935, the chairman was Meyer Yitshak Veytsfrucht, who was also head of Libivne Mizrachi (Orthodox Zionist Party); the secretary was Moyshe Lifshitz. The executive board consisted of Yisroel Mekler, Hershl Lifshitz, Yehoshua Grimatlicht, Moyshe Kaufman, Aron Rusman, Yitshak Dubetsky, and Yankl Peretszon, and they served until 1939.

New elections to the kehila took place in 1939, the year of the outbreak of the war. The new council members were: chairman—Asher Tenenboym; members—Avrom Grimatlicht, Yankl Peretszon, Avrom Lichtmacher, Motl

Krayzer, Velvl Sheynvald, Nachum Shtern, and Yosl Berger.

Town Hall was the shtetl's economic nerve-center. In the first elections of the early 1920s all 12 elected members of the town council were Jewish. The position of mayor was, naturally, to be Jewish too. The Poles, however, did not like the whole business and looked for all kinds of excuses to invalidate the elections. And because they had a strong "pull," they naturally achieved their purpose.

According to a new plan, the shtetl was subdivided into regions, and neighboring villages were attached to each region. This ruse created a situation where the Jews, instead of being a majority, became a minority because of the newly added non-Jewish population of the villages. And the result was that the number of Jewish representatives in the kehila was reduced at first to eight and later to four. The municipal officers were: the mayor—a Pole; the vice-mayor—a Ukrainian; secretary—a Jew, Yankl Shtern.

During the last days before the war, Yankl Shtern served as a deputy to the city's mayor. I remember some of the names of people on the city council (at various times): Moyshe Klerer (Revisionist party), Motl Privner (Poale Tsion), Yitshak Handlsman (Artisan), Shaye Sheyntop (Bund), Shimon Shor, Moyshe Esterzon, Asher Rusman, Zhenye Afeldman.

Just as in the other Polish towns, the Poles of Libivne also appointed a committee to beautify the appearance of the shtetl. The committee had a "beautiful" name, but its hidden purpose was to weaken the economic base of the Jews.

Under the guise of beautifying the shtetl, and in the name of better sanitary conditions, the Poles introduced a motion in the city council to transfer the marketplace to an area outside the town. As in other towns, the marketplace was actually the main source of livelihood for most of the Jewish population.

Moving the marketplace would have been an economic death-knell for the Libivner Jews. The Jews therefore strongly opposed the proposed plan, and with much effort succeeded in seeing to it that the marketplace would remain where it was. The only thing that the municipality managed to enact was the transfer of the horse market out of town. This, however, was no threat to the town's Jewish economy.

Another fight loomed over the proposed removal of the public baths from the center of the shtetl: the stated motives behind it were hygienic concerns and fear of fire.

Unfortunately, it cannot be said that the Poles were entirely wrong in their claims. The Jews ultimately recognized this, and, foreseeing their probable defeat on this issue, suggested an alternative plan—that of building a new public bathhouse in another location.

Members of the municipal council: S. Royter, A. Laks, M. Fuks, Martin Alferowich, Shimon Shor.

Such a bathhouse, with all its appurtenances, would have cost around 40,000 zlotys. But before the new plan could be carried out, the Polish–German war intervened and the plan came to naught.

There were 16 shuls and other places of prayer under the jurisdiction of the shtetl's Jewish community: the Great Synagogue with its three separate little synagogues: the Stepenyer shtibl, the Psalm-sayers shilchl [small synagogue], and the tailors' shilchl; the beys-medresh, where the Radziner Chasid, Dovidl Pech, taught Mishnah; *minyan misaskim*; the Trisker shtibl; the Rizhiner shtibl; the Kotsker shtibl; the Radziner shtibl; a little shul on Chelm Street (for artisans); the Keren Kayemet [JNF] shul (leaders Motl Krayzer, Yosef Bornshteyn); Mizrachi minyan (at Yoyne Shek's); the Linat Hatsedek minyan; the Binyomen Etyes minyan (in the home of Binyomen); the minyan at the home of the Stepenyer rebbe.

Besides being devoted to keeping up the shuls and minyans, the Jews tried everything in their power to instill Jewishness in their children. The richer Jews sent their sons to yeshivas; others studied in the Talmud Torah, which in my time was headed by R. Leyb Dayan (Melamed). The chief teacher was Moyshe Kagan. The administrative board of the Talmud Torah consisted of Shloyme Samet, Avrom Sheyner, Shmuel Pregel, Yoshua Rubinshteyn (Shiye Sheyndl Ranes).

Only the Jewish religious subjects were taught in the Talmud Torah. Secular studies, which were prescribed by law, were taught in the public elementary school, housed in the same building as the Talmud Torah. Later it was transferred to another building on the street.

The public school had seven grades, and 600 Jewish children attended it. Though only Jewish children went to the school, most of its teachers were Poles. I remember some of the Jewish teachers in the public school—Yente Kessler, Gershon Tenenbaum, Korotke, Yakov Henik, Roze Elbling-Shapiro, Zhenia Goldberg from Rovno, and Hershl Greif. Yitshak Shapiro, Roze's husband, and Leybl Goldhacker taught religion. Yente Kessler was the school's principal for three or four years; Korotke was also principal for a time.

A Tarbut school was established in the early 1920s. Its teachers were Palevsky, Budman, Dubelman, and others. The Tarbut school was followed by a private Hebrew school, established by Yankl Blumen and Sholem Meltser. Both Yiddish and general secular studies were taught there. The school would put on all kinds of children's evening performances, which met with great success.

המוסר בית ספר עממי תרבות בלובלא

סהלקה _I_   № _24_ נרשם בפנקס-ההערכה

ת ע ו ד ה

שנולד ביום _____ שנת __ 19

ב _____ בקר __ במשך שנת-הלמודים 19 _23_ / _24_ את המחלקה (הראשונה)

המחצית השניה	המחצית הראשונה	שנת הלמודים 19 _23_ / _24_

Zakład: _Szkoła hebrajska prywatna "Tarbut" w l_

Klasa _I_   L. katal. klasylik. _24_

ZAWIADOMIENIE SZKOLNE.

Getman _____, urodzon ___ dnia _____ 19

w _Lubomli_ _____ uczęszczał ___ w roku szkoln. 19_23_ / 19_2_

do klasy tutejszej szkoły.

ROK SZKOLNY 19_23_ /19_24_	I. PÓŁROCZE:	II. PÓŁROCZE:
Zachowanie się:		_bardzo dobre_

End-of-term school certificate of the Hebrew Tarbut school, written in Hebrew and Polish.

החלטת המועצה הפדגוגית בסוף שנת הלמודים:

על יסוד ההתקדמות דלעיל הטועצה הפדגונית החליטה: התלמיד

19__ יום

המחנך   המנהל

בעד ההתנהגות:	בעד ההתמדה:	ההתקרמות בלמודים:	העבורות בכתב:
טובה מאד	יתרה	טובה מאד	בדיקנות יתרה
מובה	רבה	טובה	בדיקנות
הגונה	מספיקה	מספיקה	בטעוט דיקנות
בלתי הגונה	בלתי מספיקה	בלתי מספיקה	באי-דיקנות

(ציונים / הערכה)

Uchwała Rady Pedagogicznej z końcem roku szkolnego:

Na podstawie powyższych postępów Rada Ped. uchwaliła: ___

___

W Lubomli dnia 3/VII 1924

Kierowni__ szkoły: Wychowawc__ klasy: Sekretarz Rady Ped.

	zachowania się:	pilność:	postępu:	porządku zewnętrz
1	bardzo dobre	bardzo dobra	bardzo dobry	bardzo staranny
2	dobre	dobra	dobry	staranny
3	odpowiednie	dostateczna	dostateczny	mniej staranny
4	nieodpowiednie	niedostateczna	niedostateczny	niedbały

S K A L A   O C E N Y

W_____ dnia _____ 192___

Kierowni__ szkoły: Wychowawc__ klasy: Sekretarz Rady Ped.

Two final report cards for the school year, one in Hebrew, one in Polish.

THE GREAT SYNAGOGUE
By Yakov Hetman

The Great Synagogue was the glory of the city and source of its pride—though not the center of its religious life. The Jews of the city pointed from afar to the fortifications surrounding it, to the slope of its thick walls—but they did not hurry inside. It had majesty and mystery and even ceremony—but no warmth. To the non-Jews this was the representative synagogue—but to the Jews it was a minor place of worship.

During the week no one prayed there, and only on the Sabbath were its doors opened wide, though only a few minyanim [groups of ten men for prayer] came. The regular worshippers were largely the common folks, and there were very few householders (baaley batim). This was also the only place in the city where the service was conducted according to the Ashkenazic rite, whereas in the rest of the places of worship they prayed in "Sephardic" style, according to Chasidic custom.

But in spite of this, and sometimes unconsciously, the synagogue was the symbol of the greatness of the Jewish community in the town and the place for mass gatherings—in times of trouble and sadness, festivity and mourning. During holidays and festivals, and on those days when the "congregation should be called together," people instinctively came to the Great Synagogue.

The Great Synagogue was a brick structure of mammoth proportions, basically square, and there were windows about two stories high looking out of the thick walls. Above stood an encircling parapet with turrets in the middle, each one with two round holes. The whole building resembled an ancient fortress, and it was obvious to all that the round openings served as firing slots for the defenders of the fort.

The synagogue was located in the center of town, at one corner of the marketplace. Its front—the eastern side, facing the market—was separated from the market by houses belonging to the Getman-Hetman, Natanson, and Shapiro families—though the top of the synagogue looked out above these houses and could be seen from afar.

From the three other sides, there were no houses close to the building and it was possible to pass close to it except for a fenced-off section on the southern side.

The entrance to the synagogue was through the *poolish* [anteroom], with doors on the north and south. Outside, next to the southern door of the poolish, they used to set up the chuppah on Friday afternoons for young couples being married, and inside the northern gate was the genizah, where all the tattered remnants of unusable holy books, outworn tefillin [phylacteries], etc., were brought.

Within the poolish, on the synagogue's western wall, was the grand entrance in the shape of a high, broad arch resting on grand pillars—and the heavy, double wooden door, fortified with thick iron plates. The key to this door was no ordinary key, but a rather solid piece of metal, a foot long, and whoever was entrusted with it was the classic "key keeper."

And here, precisely next to the main entryway, one stopped momentarily to glance at the alms box, of which we could see only the outer metal door and the large lock that fastened it. Secondly, one looked to see whether any non-Jewish farmers and their families who had come to pray to the Jewish God in times of trouble were leaning against the walls—for it was a known fact that if a horse had been stolen or the pigs died of the plague, it was a proven panacea to come on market day to the gate of the Great Synagogue, to make a contribution and then kneel down and pray.

Now we are inside, in the front part of the synagogue, above which is the women's section, and so the ceiling is low. Here, next to the entry, are traces of heavy iron chains, and they said that these were remnants of the koneh, the place where punishment by whipping took place.

On both sides of the gate are two huge locked wooden chests. What was inside them? This was revealed on the night of Simchat Torah, when hundreds of imperfect, and therefore unusable, scrolls were taken out and used for the processions. And another large chest stood nearby, filled with sand and the foreskins of the children who had been circumcised. A huge antique chair stood there—Elijah's chair—on which it was customary for godfathers to sit when a circumcision took place in the synagogue.

Finally we are standing in the interior of the synagogue. All around, at the height of one and a half stories, are smooth stone walls, and above that, at the height of the second story, high, arched windows, in which one could see the width of the walls, about three feet thick; and above the windows, as if at the top of the third floor, the curving arches of the synagogue roof, from which chandeliers of crystal and ivory hung down until they virtually reached the levels where the people sat.

All around on the walls, under the windows, and on the retaining wall of the women's gallery on the western side, were pictures of various

A view of the Great Synagogue at the end of the 19th century. The structure to the left is the women's section.

The unique Torah ark in the Great Synagogue. (Courtesy of the Archives for the History of the Jewish People)

scenes—the primeval ox and the Leviathan, musical instruments from the Temple and emblems of the 12 tribes. Only the eastern wall was pure white, without pictures or adornments, and against this background stood the magnificent Holy Ark, with the two traditional lions on either side, as well as engravings of various tree branches.

This was no ordinary ark but a grandiose artistic creation, sculpted of stone and painted in a rainbow of colors. The lectern for the prayer leader was below, in a hollow below the floor level of the rest of the synagogue, so that the phrase "from the depths have I called you" could be carried out literally.

To the left of the prayer lectern was a high stairway that began as a framework of a decorated metal archway and brass crafted doors, continuing upwards until it reached the Holy Ark itself, where on both sides there rose a metal retaining wall, on wooden stands. The ark was sculpted of stone and reached almost to the ceiling, fashioned of carved pillars, cherubim, crossbows, flowers and plants, and other artistic forms, one atop the other until they arrived in a position of cherubic wings, spread out to each other; and all this painted in beautiful colors. . .

When I saw for the first time colored pictures of the ark in the Holy Ari Synagogue in Safed, I saw a resemblance in the figures and colors to the synagogue in Luboml. Only when I managed to actually visit the synagogue in Safed did I see that there was no comparison. Its ark is nothing more than an artistic wooden carving of the outer frame, possibly using as a model the ark in Luboml or a similar one elsewhere. But this cannot be compared to the one in Luboml, which was carved out of stone, rising more than one story high.

This ark ennobled the entire Great Synagogue, and when the priests stood on the stairs leading up to the ark, one next to the other, blessing the people "with love," it was as if wings spread out from on high and covered the people below. From these steps the fiery words of rabbis and preachers, and lectures by guests were often heard. Embittered women often ran up and down those stairs, to open the ark and to try to reverse and avert a terrible fate with their tears and wailings.

And in the middle of the synagogue stood the lectern (bima). Four thick stone pillars supported a giant dome, and in the middle, on a raised platform, reached by stairs on both sides, north and south, stood a large oak table for the reading of the Torah. This is where the shofar was blown, this is where the departed souls were recalled. And note that in the Great Synagogue the memorial services were unique, lasting a long time, for it was the custom to read aloud from the community ledger the names of all who had died, a figure reaching into the thousands. Here, too one could see and touch the two ancient Torah crowns, which according to the inscriptions were more than 400 years old.

Throughout the year it was a bit sad to come to the synagogue. The place was too large, too imposing for the sparse number of worshippers, who came as if to honor the holy place. But during two months of the year, Elul and Tishri, the synagogue wore majesty and greatness and drew many thousands. It was a custom that on the New Year all the old Torah mantles were put on the walls. Metal wire was strung beneath the windows and all the mantles were hung there on rings—mantles of many ages, sizes, and colors, shining with silver and gold, gleaming with scarlet and azure.

Suddenly the synagogue took on a new look, the glorious look given by velvet and embroidery, the gleam of letters and colors, and one never tired of this beautiful sight, looking for the remnants of the distant past.

And through the entire month of Elul, until after the High Holy Days and Sukkot, it was possible to learn the history of the synagogue and of the Jewish community in Luboml. The most attention was drawn by a huge, grayish-white Torah mantle whose permanent place was to the right of the Holy Ark (to the left of the viewer). What was special about the mantle, which was six feet long and thirteen feet high, was the fact that its decorations and letters were not embroidered but composed on layers of silver sewn directly onto the mantle. Miraculously, the letters remained on the material for hundreds of years, and it was possible to read the year it was dedicated—500 years earlier—and the name of the donor, as well.

Unfortunately no one thought of copying exactly what was on this mantle—nor did anyone think of copying down the ages of the Torahs themselves.

The special atmosphere was heightened during the High Holy Days. Nowhere else was there a shofar as curved and as large as the one in the Great Synagogue; nowhere else was there an ancient Pinkas [ledger] with the names of thousands of those who had passed away; and nowhere else was there a chest full of hundreds of defective Torah scrolls.

On the eve of Yom Kippur, when the floor of the synagogue was covered with fresh hay so people could walk without shoes, the fragrance would reach you and fill the air with a unique sort of feeling: and when the women's sections—the one at the upper exit across from the Holy Ark, and the one below in the northern, low-ceilinged section of the synagogue—were filled with the weeping and shouting of hundreds of women praying, it was an unusual experience, not an everyday occurrence; and when, on Simchat Torah evening, the synagogue filled with men, women and children, in addition to non-Jews who came to join the Jews' celebration—it was a sight never to be forgotten.

It's unlikely that this scene could have been repeated—hundreds of Jews carrying hundreds of Torahs, dancing through the hakafot (traditional processions). It was a wonderful scene when they lifted the covers of the two huge trunks and started to distribute Torahs to the whole congregation, without limit, more and more, hundreds of Torah scrolls—and the crowd came and pushed itself in and the wave kept pushing, and the hearts warmed up and faces became excited. This night of Simchat Torah was the greatest night of the Grand Synagogue.

The holidays passed and once again the synagogue stood in awesome loneliness, while still serving as a point of pride and a basis for tales about the prayers of the dead at midnight, of spirits and devils and leprechauns and other fanciful figures landing on the roof. A few boys were brave enough to try climbing up to the outdoor doorway of the roof, but they would not dare go inside. This is where imagination and legends ruled.

THE SYNAGOGUES AND CHASIDIM IN OUR TOWN
by Yisroel Garmi (Grimatlicht)

Let us remember the synagogues of our town, whose special character reflected that of the Jews of Luboml. Among these synagogues were the Great Synagogue, the large Bet Midrash (study room), the small prayer rooms, and the shtiblach of the Chasidim. We will remember and see our town with its unique spirit reflected in this world of religious life, customs, and prayers.

The Central (Great) Synagogue

The ancient Great Synagogue was like a gem that redounded to the glory and prestige of the Jewish community of Luboml. The image of this synagogue is etched deep in our hearts—everything that was dear in it was so tragically destroyed. We

are overtaken by emotional experiences that absorbed our souls during our childhood; stories about various events, secrets, and mysteries that took place within the walls of the synagogue. The beauty of the synagogue lifted our spirit, especially on the eve of the holidays, when the place was full of people, wall to wall, and filled with light.

Stories and fairytales were told by grandparents about mysterious occurrences that took place in the late hours of the night. Especially fearful and emotional were stories about dead souls that visited the shul for prayer and the reading of the Torah.

"How awesome is this place! This is the gate

View of the synagogue from the northwest, and the entrance to the *poolish* (main corridor). (Courtesy of Archiwum Dokumentacji Mechanicznej)

149

of the Lord, through which the righteous will enter." These words, written above the arched lintel of the northern entrance to the poolish of the shul, had great meaning for us.

The eternal light to remember the holy souls, lit on the wall near the entrance, and the shul sexton's custom of knocking on the gate twice before opening the door for Slichot [late-night prayer service before Rosh Hashana, the New Year] created an atmosphere of mystery and holiness about the shul. As children, we were persuaded that this was a meeting place for the dead souls of the townspeople, who from time to time visited the shul at night.

We should remember our spirit of elation when we came to shul to hear the cantor's chant, the choir singing on the evening of Slichot, the sound of *Z'chor Brit* and *Kol Nidre* on the eve of Yom Kippur. The synagogue was full of worshippers, among them many new faces—these were the Jewish families from the villages, who would come to town for the duration of the Yamim Noraim [Days of Awe] between Rosh Hashana and Yom Kippur.

The synagogue was especially impressive when it was full of men, women, and children during Simchat Torah or at times when the acquisition of a new Torah scroll was being celebrated. The Torah was carried from the home of its contributor to the synagogue, accompanied by a large crowd and the orchestra of Yakov Hersh, the klezmer.

The Torah was wrapped in a radiant new mantle and carried by the contributor, who also was wrapped in a large talit and walked under a wedding canopy. At the same time, another group of celebrants carrying Torahs was coming from the shul to join with the oncoming "groom" and accompanying crowd.

However, the highlight of the ceremony, which left a lasting impression, took place inside the shul when the Torah was placed in the Holy Ark, filled with dozens of other Torahs, very old and new, with crowns and bells, ready to receive the latest addition. For some time to come, the shul was filled with songs and dances surrounding the "groom of the Torah."

Bet HaMidrash

Next to the Great Synagogue, on the northern side, stood our town's Bet HaMidrash. Only a narrow alley that served as a passage to the market square separated the two buildings. The Bet HaMidrash was a multisided wooden building, and on its west side there was another building connected to it. This building was a synagogue belonging to the mitaskim (the Mitaskim Shtibl). An open, narrow corridor separated these two buildings.

During the week, the Bet HaMidrash was used as a place of prayer by most of our townspeople. In this building, many of the Chasidim who normally prayed in the shtibls came to pray, as did many Jews from surrounding villages. Merchants who came to our town to sell their goods also prayed at the Bet HaMidrash. The building was open to the public day and night, so individuals could keep the commandment of public prayer, and so they could say *Kaddish* or *Kedushah* whenever they needed.

From the early morning hours until the late evening, the Bet HaMidrash was full of people, with one minyan following another. A preacher who would visit the town from time to time would turn to the Bet HaMidrash, and the trustees would make sure the worshippers at all the other synagogues knew what time he would be giving a sermon, usually between Mincha and Ma'ariv prayers. Volunteers from the congregation would collect money for the sermon when people walked out the door [after services].

Since the Bet HaMidrash was relatively close to the big market as well as the small market, where fish and fruit were sold, and to the wooden stores, the place became a sort of hostel for the shopkeepers. On cold winter days after long hours standing in freezing weather, the shopkeepers would come into the Bet HaMidrash to warm up their frozen bodies or to study a book. They would warm their hands at the "fire-pot," in which glowing coals were kept. As a matter of fact, the pot was used mostly by the women, who put it between their feet and covered it with their dresses to keep the heat in.

The Bet HaMidrash also served as a public meeting place where people gathered for a variety of purposes. In that building many business meetings took place. Also, elections for representatives to local offices and to the community council were held in the Bet HaMidrash. Finally, in times of emergency, meetings were held in the Bet HaMidrash to elect individuals who would form committees to attend to urgent matters.

On the eve of the High Holy Days and other important holidays, the Bet HaMidrash was filled with people—wall to wall—due to the arrival of Jews from neighboring villages. Moyshe Avrom's Sheyner, old and frail, a Rizhin Chasid, would then spread out and display his merchandise [religious articles] to the crowds. He had taleisim, small and large, tzitzis, mezuzes, prayer books, chumashim and machzors for sale. All this was put out on a long, wide table in the right wing of the Bet HaMidrash, in the building's southeastern part.

The Bet HaMidrash also served as a temporary shelter for the town's beggars and passing travelers. The atmosphere was comfortable and inviting. All who came there found time for some light conversation with a friend to alleviate the burden of the day's worries.

The Synagogues of the Chasidim and Craftsmen

Aside from the central synagogue and the Bet HaMidrash, there were other shtiblach and synagogues in town exclusively for the groups of Chasidim and for the craftsmen of our town. Let us recall them and list them one by one in order of size.

The synagogue of the Trisk Chasidim: Due to its size and the number of congregants, this synagogue takes its place right after the Bet HaMidrash. Just by looking at its exterior, one could tell that this house of prayer was very respectable and just as pleasant on the inside. This building was made of wood and had a very high ceiling. On its south side, the synagogue had a large yard surrounded by a fence. There were two entrances, one on the north side and one on the south, accessible through a long corridor that stretched along the west side of the building. Above the corridor was a gallery

that served as the prayer area for women. Two wide entranceways led from the stairs into the synagogue.

In the center of the building stood the raised platform where the Torah was read. It was similar to the one in the Bet HaMidrash. A reader in the synagogue, who was known for the singing of psalms and admired by the Chasidim of Trisk, was Rabbi Shmuel Avrom Eltzter; also known for his prayers was Rabbi Abba Gloz. Heading the Chasidim of Trisk were Rabbi Leybl Dayan, the son-in-law of Rabbi Arye Finkelsteyn (Rabbi Leibl z"l), and also Rabbi Hersh, son of Rabbi Aron (grandfather and father of Nathan Tchelet-Blumen), whose home served as the center of learning for the shochetim [ritual slaughterers of kosher meat] of the surrounding region.

Rabbi Hersh, a wonderful man, was famous in our town, and the Chasidim of Trisk were proud of him. Most of the Chasidim of Trisk were thought of as educated and enlightened men who kept up with the times. Many took an active part in all activities that aimed at the revival of our people and the Hebrew language, and the redemption of the land of Israel.

Prayer Houses (shtiblach) of Kotsk, Rizhin, and Radzin Chasidim, and also of the "Mitaskim"

These synagogues were connected partly to the rebbe of Vlodawka and partly to the rebbe of Stepen. The synagogues were similar to each other; they were all ordinary, wooden structures that looked no different from other houses in Luboml except that they had a large number of shutterless windows.

In every one of these houses of prayer there was a place for women to pray. During the week, this space was used by students of Gemara who needed a place for intellectual concentration. The furnishings in all these synagogues consisted of long, heavy tables and benches, and cabinets full of sacred books of all kinds. These cabinets were open at all hours of the day and night to everyone who wanted to use them.

The Holy Ark was located in the center of the eastern wall, and on the right was a stand for the cantor and a mizrach inscribed with the biblical passage: "I have set the Lord always before me."

In the center of the prayer house, opposite the Holy Ark, stood a table on which the Torah was placed when it was read. Next to the western wall was a special sink for washing the hands.

Three small prayer houses were adjacent to the Great Synagogue, on the western side, as if in its shadow. The entrance to all three shtiblach was through the poolish. The first one, to the north, was the prayer home for the Stepenyer Chasidim; the second belonged to the group who recited psalms; and the third one, to the south, belonged to the tailors. Another prayer house, close to the Great Synagogue, was for the craftsmen, called the *gorndl* ["upstairs"] because it was located above a private residence.

We should also mention the Talmud Torah building, which was used as a permanent place of worship on Shabbat and holidays by a certain circle of intellectuals of the town, as well as the various minyanim that gathered on Shabbat and holidays in the clubrooms of various organizations and parties, and whose main purpose was to collect contributions from members and supporters for the honor of being called to the Torah.

There were also Chasidim from other factions, such as Gur, Karlin, and others. Those whose numbers were insufficient to put up a prayer house of their own were forced to join the shuls of others.

Basically, one could not feel a difference between the conduct of prayers and daily life in the various prayer houses and sects of Chasidim, except in the way a prayer was chanted or interpreted. The relationship between Chasidim and other prayer houses was open, and when a rebbe came to town, various Chasidim came to listen to him pray on Shabbat evening to hear his sermon on the Torah, or a new chant on the Shalosh Seudot.

In almost every Chasidic prayer house there was a group of ultra-Orthodox Jews who fought atheists and Zionists without let-up, and fought against each change from the accepted rites of previous generations. Most of these ultra-Orthodox Jews were owners of the seats near the eastern wall of the temple and were considered pillars of the worshipping community. They were strict in all matters of observance, fasting often,

Rabbi Hersh Kirsher, shochet (ritual slaughterer)

putting on a second pair of tefilin (of Rabbenu Tam), and prolonging worship, especially the *Shemona Esrey* prayer. Most of them saw it as an obligation and privilege to pray in front of the Holy Ark as representatives of the community.

They would rise early in the morning to go to the mikvah before prayer; they would come early to shul and leave later than others. Of course, they endeavored to travel to their rebbe from time to time and spend time at his court.

In each shtibl there were several men known as great scholars, outstanding in studying the Talmud and its interpretation. During the fall and winter evenings, those scholars spent long hours studying into the night and going through difficult passages of the Talmud.

I especially remember with appreciation Rabbi Yankl Moyshe Feiweles (Natanzon), my esteemed teacher at the time when I reached the age when I could study a page of Gemara and interpret it all by myself. He was an exceptional scholar with great expertise in the "sea of Talmud"; he clarified and answered all questions of the scholars in the prayer house about the intricacies of the Talmud in a joyful and peaceful manner.

The Trisk Chasidim were considered liberals and tolerant in their approach to the young people who left the straight and narrow path and abandoned God's commandments. Jews who were rejected and expelled from the Kotsk, Rizhin, and other extreme groups found refuge in the prayer house of the Trisk Chasidim, where the majority were intellectuals and enlightened Jews.

And so, for example, they did not participate in the "holy war" against eating matzot made by a machine. In the early 1920s, Itzi Meshures and his partners brought in a machine to produce matzot. The machine was set up in the home of Zecharye the builder (Zachary the miller). The machine made square, thin, crispy, and tastier matzot than the hand-made, round ones. Many of the people preferred to purchase the machine-made matzot; however, the ultra-observant Kotsk, Rizhin, and Radzin Chasidim refused to buy the machine-made matzot, and the conflict was remembered for many years to come.

Another conflict I remember, which continued for a number of years, was about who was chief rabbi. This took place after Rabbi Arye (R. Leybe) Finkelshteyn died in 1915. He was the great-grandfather of Dr. Yoseph and Arye Shtern.

The town's Jews were in no hurry to elect a new rabbi. However, at the end of World War I, hunger and epidemics brought up the controversy again.

The Kotsk Chasidim picked R. Leybish London to occupy the seat, while some of the Trisk Chasidim argued that R. Leybl Dayan, the son-in-law of R. Leybe of the Trisk Chasidim, should take the seat of his father-in-law; Rizhin Chasidim, and among them some Chasidim of Radzin and worshippers from the Bet HaMidrash, argued that both candidates were unsuitable to be chief rabbi in these modern times because the rabbi had to know Polish; so they brought to town a

View of the Great Synagogue from the east. (Courtesy of Polska Akademia Nauk, Instytut Sztuki)

new rabbi, Rabbi Pinchas Oselka, who in time received the approval of the majority of the Jewish community.

I should also mention the leaders of the Rizhin Chasidim, who performed in an unusual manner the mitzvah of *Tashlich* [casting bread or stones into a body of water during Rosh Hashana, symbolizing the casting off of sins]: after an early Mincha prayer, they walked a long way until they reached Szmeril Mordche's pond, outside the limits of the town. They did not stop, like others, at a well or water ditch near the prayer house.

They returned to the synagogue for Ma'ariv, singing all the way back through the town. We youngsters were all proud of our marchers. Along the entire route, Christian families came out to watch this strange procession.

The greatest joy came at the time of Simchat Torah, at the hakafot, when groups of chasidim of all ages sang and danced, embracing the Torah. The women would stand by, kiss the scrolls, and wish the dancers, "May you live to do the same next year." At times the groups of Chasidim used to come out into the streets—on their way to someone's home for *Kiddush* [wine and celebration]—waking up the youngsters with cries of "Holy flock"; to which they would answer in chorus by bleating "Ma-a-a-a-a."

Another occasion when the Chasidim came out in numbers was on the memorial day of their departed rebbe. Hundreds of candles lit up the shul in every corner. At midnight the Chasidim used to come to the shul and listen to the Torah and wisdom of their rebbe, because this was not only a prayer house but a meeting place of the wise as well as a social center.

THE STEPENYER SHILCHL
By Efrayim Lerner

Three other houses of worship were erected next to the Great Synagogue. The big corridor (poolish) had two entrances: a narrow, iron-covered door on the north and a strong, broad entrance on the south side, with wide iron gates and several small steps that led into the corridor. Children used the corridor as a place to play.

I want to describe one of the three added houses of worship—the Stepenyer shilchl (little shul), the place where both my grandfather and my father used to pray.

The Stepenyer shilchl was very modest. It was whitewashed and had a pair of bright lights. Benches, where those who prayed there would sit, surrounded a round table that stood against a wall near the whitewashed stove. Cut wood was piled up on the other side of the stove, ready for the winter, leaving enough room for a couple of other Jews to pray.

The rest of the wall, from the stove to the door, was occupied by a big closet of holy books. Near the door was a washstand with a copper tap and a heavy copper pot with two handles.

I will try to describe some of the worshippers whom I remember. First of all, those who sat at the eastern wall: Elye Mestsheches; Itche Yidls, the gabbai (sexton); Chayim Mestsheches; my father, Yankl Menashes; Chayim Reyzman; Shmuel Getman; Elye Stavker; and Yidl der blinder (the blind one), the gabbai's father—these were the men who prayed there during the High Holy Days.

Two brothers, Moyshe and Itshe Lerner, were important people. The older one, Moyshe, was a bit shy and did not participate in community affairs. He finished praying and headed straight for home. Itshe was a different sort of person. He did not dislike leading prayers, and leading the

Mincha service on Yom Kippur was traditionally his by right.

Another Stepenyer Chasid was Moyshe Reyzman, the gevir (rich man); but he came to pray only on the High Holy Days and on Simchat Torah eve, because he was entitled to say *Ato Horayso* (a prayer for the first eve). The *Ato Horayso* for the second night belonged to Shmuel Getman.

Nutl Melamed (Faigen), my teacher, was still another Stepenyer Chasid. He was tall and walked straight. He always wore neat clothes, sported a white shirt and a narrow black tie. He was never one to laugh, yet he was not strict and was not in the habit of becoming angry.

Another fine Jew used to pray in the Stepenyer shtibl—and I will dwell on him at greater length— Yehoshua Bibeles (that was his nickname).

He was a strong Jew, in his late fifties; he had a gray beard and always smiling good-humoredly. He always smelled of apples, for that was his trade. He kept orchards all his life, spending his summers in picking and collecting the fruit and carrying them in a basket to Chasye the marketwoman or to "Yellow Yankl."

When he was in the shtibl on a Sabbath Yehoshua could never sit still, but would run around and play tricks: he pinched the ear of one man, nudged another in his side or untied the belt of still another man and quickly turned away, looking as if he had nothing to do with it.

Yehoshua was the opposite of his wife, Freyde, who never laughed but only squinted with her short-sighted eyes. They had no children. They therefore donated a Torah scroll to the shtibl; and when their Torah scroll was read the two were the happiest of people.

View of the Great Synagogue from the northwest. The low building contains three little synagogues: from the south, the tailors; the middle, the Psalm-sayers; the north, the Stepenyer Chasidim. (Courtesy Polska Akademia Nauk, Instytut Sztuki)

It is worth mentioning one of the common Jews who prayed near the stove where the cut wood was piled up. His name was Abish the tailor, and he was very pious. Whenever Elye Mestsheches, the permanent prayer leader, was incapacitated and could not read on a Sabbath, the sexton would call on either the young man Shmuel Fuks, or on Abish.

And what can I say? The sweetness with which Abish read the Torah with the right intonation remains in my memory until today! It is still a mystery to me why such a man as Abish had to be stuck all his life behind the stove! Perhaps the fact that he was a tailor condemned him to a lower social status.

In the middle of the week, the prayers were rattled off, because the worshippers were preoccupied with worries about income and other troubles! But on Sabbath the congregation lingered over the prayers. The men would dis-cuss politics or read a sacred book. On the dawn of the Sabbath they read the Psalms; at noon they went home for a drink kept warm by hot sand on the *pekelek* (the upper part of the oven), or else by being covered with rags. And only then did the men go to Shachris (Sabbath morning prayer).

Sabbath evening, as the shul grew darker and darker, they celebrated *Shalosh Se'udos* (the third meal). They seated themselves around the long tables covered with table cloths and had a bite of challah and a piece of herring; and they sang *zmires* (Sabbath songs.).

Moyshe Tribeykish, the son-in-law of Elye Mestsheches, had a very pleasant voice. He would begin to sing and the others would join in.

Then Yoneh the shames (sexton or beadle) would come with a lighted candle, and the congregation would begin the evening prayer of Ma'ariv.

SABBATH EVE IN THE SHTETL
By Yitshak Oyvental-Kopernik

The day before the Sabbath, in May. Nature had come alive. Gardens and fields were blooming and the air was filled with an intoxicating aroma, as if bottles of perfume had been poured upon them. The Jews were preparing to greet the Sabbath.

As the day progressed, the shames, a short, thin man, began his tasks in the bet hamidrash. He picked up his thick cane and began to walk from one store to another, knocking on their doors and yelling: "Jews, Sabbath! Close the stores. You have to begin preparing for the Sabbath!" It did not take long before the storekeepers started to shut their stores and make their way home. And when the sun was just beginning to set, Jews, dressed in their silk Sabbath attire, were seen hurrying in the directions of their particular shuls.

The shtetl acquired a festive appearance. It was evident that Sabbath had come to the shtetl. People finished their prayers, returned home, and sat down to eat their festive meal. After eating, the young people poured out into the street for a walk.

The frogs were performing a concert, a beautiful symphony. The concert reminded one of the Concert of the Frogs that the famous Adam Mickiewicz had described so masterfully in his *Pan Tadeusz*. But the concert of *zmiros* [Sabbath songs] heard from the home of Abba Gluz and his sons late into the night was more pleasing to the ear.

Abba Gluz, the reader in the Trisker shtibl, a fine-looking man with a patriarchal beard and a magnificent voice, conducted his own music band, singing *zmiros* while his sons Shike and Yakov harmonized with their father with great spirit and feeling. It was truly a well-trained choir. People who were taking a walk would purposely head in that direction in order to hear the magical sounds of the *zmiros* sung by the Gluz family.

These *zmiros*, sung on Friday nights, are etched and rooted in my memory. This has remained one of the dearest memories of my beloved, never-forgotten friends (may they rest in peace). The songs ring in my ears until the present and will live on in my soul forever.

A VISIT FROM THE TRISKER REBBE
By Efrayim Lerner

When rumor spread that the Trisker rebbe was preparing to visit the shtetl on a Sabbath, the prosaic, gray, monotonous life vanished from Libivne. The Trisker Chasidim began their preparations to welcome the rebbe in a befitting manner.

The biggest commotion took place in the home of Shloyme Rayz. The rebbe usually stayed there. This was a great honor. Why had this Chasid been honored with this privilege above all the other Chasidim? There were several reasons. First of all, Shloyme was a well-to-do man, a merchant in grain, who had a spacious apartment with huge rooms. He even had a private telephone. Moreover, his house was directly across the street from the Trisker shtibl.

The preparations in Shloyme Rayz's home consisted not only of cooking many tasty dishes and all kinds of pastries, but it seemed as if the whole house was being remodeled. They painted walls, moved the furniture about, and the big parlor was changed into a dining room where the rebbe would have room enough to celebrate the traditional sharing of food with most of his Chasidim.

On Friday, the carriages arrived at Shloyme's house, bringing the rebbe, his assistant, and his Chasidic followers. They were welcomed with great fanfare.

The Trisker shtibl was packed to welcome the rebbe. Even non-Trisker Chasidim came to the shtibl to receive the blessing of the rebbe. Because of the unusual crowding inside the shtibl, a crowd stood outside in the shtibl's garden and, with great trepidation, waited for the rebbe in order to be considered worthy of his blessing.

Right after the prayer, the rebbe, with his assistant and his host, went home. In their own homes, the other Chasidim quickly ate their Sabbath meals, leaving the blessing to be said at the rebbe's table.

When everyone was gathered there, the rebbe came out of his room and made Kiddush [blessing over wine, commencing a meal]. Then the dishes were served. The rebbe tasted each of the dishes, and the Chasidim then began to grab for the *sherayim* [the rebbe's leftovers]. The rebbe ordered the Chasidim to sing *zmiros*, each time choosing a different chasid. After that, the rebbe began to expound on the Torah and the Chasidim crowded even more closely, leaning on each other's shoulders, or putting a hand behind his ear to hear better, because the rebbe spoke in a low voice.

The following were some of the Chasidim: Shmuel Avrom Eltster, Shimon Tsechshteyn, Aaron Shoychet, Shloyme Samet, and many other prominent people.

After Shacharit [morning prayer] the Chasidim came to the table again. They also came to the *Shalosh Seudot* [the traditional third meal eaten at the end of the Sabbath]. But the real celebration came at the *Melave Malke* [the ushering out of Queen Sabbath on Saturday evening]. Big lamps were lit and the Chasidim would dance. Weaving their arms around each other's shoulders, they would begin to turn, at first slowly and then faster and faster, heads and feet keeping rhythm, up and down, up and down. One could only wonder: Where did these middle-aged and older people get their energy to dance and to sing?

After the *Melave Malke*, the Chasidim would

go into the rebbe's room one by one. The assistant was sitting at the door of the room and received from each a note with his plea to the rebbe, together with a small offering of money. Each Chasid wrote a note to the rebbe, putting down his request for health, income, children, matches for his daughters, or success in business.

The gabbai gave the kvitl to the rebbe before the Chasid came into the room, the rebbe knew which request to bless. The chasid then bade the rebbe farewell and walked out with renewed faith.

The next morning the Jewish carriages came again. The rebbe got into his carriage together with his assistant and they left, ushered out by a crowd of Chasidim. The town once more became workaday, drab; Shloyme Rayz again put on his flour-covered smock and went about his business at Grimatlicht's flour mill.

"*Ma Tovu Ohalecha* . . . How good are thy tents, Jacob, thy dwellings, Israel." This sentence was engraved on the arches of the three huge windows—southern side. (Courtesy of Polska Akademia Nauk, Instytut Sztuki)

CANDID SNAPSHOTS OF OUR TOWN
By Shimon Kandelshteyn

Luboml is one of the oldest towns in Poland. This is not at all strange if we consider the structures of the synagogue and the rows of stores that are part of the district marketplace.

Such was the town: Houses were made of wood, for trees were abundant in the surrounding forests. The roofs were covered with straw or with shingles made of wood. The macadam roads were paved with basalt rocks, and the noise made by wagons rolling over them could be heard from afar.

In the center of the town was a big market square. The fair held there every Monday drew all kinds of merchants from the surrounding areas, bringing their produce to the market. Jews who made a living from trading or working lived around the marketplace.

There was a hill near the corner of the market (named for a Polish king, Jagiello), and the hill was covered with many tall, strong trees. In the summertime we would take walks and rest in the shade of the trees. And in the winter, when the hill was covered with snow and ice, little boys and young men ice-skated and went sledding.

On the other side of the market square stood the magnificent ancient Great Synagogue building with its tall, lofty stained-glass windows. The walls of the synagogue were decorated with pictures from the Holy Temple and the Zodiac. In the month of Elul, the walls were hung with splendid *parochets* (curtains that normally cover the doors of the Holy Ark), which were wonderful and beautiful.

The shul had two women's sections; one was in a gallery above the entrance, and the other was below, along the north side of the synagogue. Across from it, off of the vestibule, there were smaller synagogues attended by all kinds of societies and Chasidic sects: the Tailors' shul, the Stepenyer Chasidim shul, the shul of the Psalm-Sayers Society.

Besides the Great Synagogue, there was the Bet HaMidrash, which was attended all week long by congregants from the surrounding area. There were also Chasidic shtiblech, such as those of the Kotsker, Trisker, and Rizhiner, where on the Sabbath Chasidim came from every part of town to pray.

Sometimes the rebbe of a particular shtibl would come to "greet the Sabbath" and then huge crowds of his particular Chasidim would come to the shtibl to "sit at the rebbe's table" and hear the words of Torah and moral instruction, to sing and to take delight in the Sabbath together with their rebbe.

Younger Jewish boys went to the general school for secular studies, which they attended together with Poles and Ukrainians, but there were also private teachers in the town who taught Hebrew as a living language.

The town had many Zionist youth organizations—HeChalutz Hatsair, Beitar, HaShomer Hatsair, Mizrachi—and the young members had their souls filled with yearning for the Land of Israel, with a desire of being worthy enough to "ascend" to the Holy Land.

Luboml also had an agricultural training camp to prepare youth to be pioneers in Palestine.

Jews had been living in Luboml for many generations and were deeply rooted there, until the new Amalek arose, may his name be erased, and brought ruin and destruction to its very foundation. These were dear Jewish people, so good and so pure. May we never forget them!

MARKET DAY IN LIBIVNE
By Efrayim Lerner

Whenever I reminisce about my hometown Libivne, a day in the marketplace comes to mind. Libivne did not have a copyright on this image, for virtually every shtetl in Poland looked alike on that day, when peasants from the surrounding areas set out to the Jewish shtetls in order to trade. There were, however, several characteristics peculiar to each particular town, whether these had to do with personalities, merchandise, or other things. Well then, how did a market day look in Libivne?

The first thing a peasant did after arriving in town with his wagon was to unharness his horse,

raise the shafts of the wagon, and turn the horse around to face the wagon, where a bunch of hay was prepared for it to chew on.

Whenever the horse began to neigh it was echoed by the lowing of the calves and the mooing of the cows; and the pigs did not wait too long to add their disgusting grunts. All these sounds flowed together into one "symphony." And into this choir the cries and the yells of the people fit right in. The noise was so great that it could make one deaf.

The shtetl's merchants laid out their wares in preparation for the fair and each one of them met

General view of the market square during a fair.

the peasants (the potential buyers) with the cry: "*Panye, panye*!" [Hey, mister!].

In the midst of all the hubbub came Itshe Driker with his sack of salt from the Russmans' wholesale store. His tiny horse was harnessed to a sort of small cart of boards—three boards set on the four wheels and one board on each of the two sides. Itshe sat on top of it and bumped along the road paved with large stones, not sparing his little horse any whipping. If Itshe stopped whipping, the horse would stop in its tracks, for it was the kind of horse that would not move a step without a blow, as the many scars on its hide testified.

Chayim Kichele was negotiating a sale of his clay pots in his wooden store at the end of Chelm Street. The peasant was testing one of the pots for a possible crack by tapping on it. The rag-dealers spread their goods in the middle of the market. Big peasant boots for men could be seen on a small counter. For women there were shoes made of hard leather, with yellow gussets attached around the buttons. Peasants were standing around the counters of the tailors, measuring the length of trousers by holding them against their chests with one hand, and extending the other end with the other hand.

We could see Chayim-Wolf Olesker and his sons in the area that had been especially designated for trading horses and cattle. Several horses were tied to his wagon. The oldest son, Yankl, was leading a horse back and forth, while the second son, Leyzer, was urging it on with his whip.

Chayim-Wolf, a broad-shouldered, happy, good-humored man, with his face framed by a short beard, slapped the peasant on his extended palm while telling him the price; the peasant slapped him back, bargaining over the quoted price. Suddenly, Chayim-Wolf's youngest son showed up with a flask that he had pulled out of a box in the wagon. When the peasant saw the whiskey, his eyes began to shine and he slapped Wolf's palm as a sign that the matter was settled—the horse was sold.

The market day was over in the afternoon. The wagons of the peasants began to leave the town, making a little less noise than in the morning. It was also more quiet at the city gates; there were no more inquiries by the retailers, yelling in Ukrainian, "What do you have to sell?" Each tradesman was now sitting at home drawing up the total of cash on hand or, even more important, of profit.

The shtetl became quiet. The rough day of running around and hard work was at an end. Most inhabitants, especially the merchants, had earned a profit for the coming week, and they could now go to sleep in a much happier frame of mind.

THE PUBLIC BATHHOUSE
By Yisroel Garmi (Grimatlicht)

In describing the daily life of our town, it is worthwhile to mention the bathhouse, which played such an important part in the life of the city throughout its history. The dependence upon the mikveh [ritual bath] by a great majority of the population was tremendous, both on Mondays and Thursdays, when those ultra-Orthodox Jews who were meticulous in observance came to immerse themselves for ritual purposes, and even more so on the eves of Sabbath and festivals, when great numbers of the townspeople, young and old alike, flocked to the place to bathe themselves in hot and cold water.

Those of a delicate nature or of an aesthetic bent (among the intelligentsia) shrank from having to stand naked in the presence of the huge crowd that came on the eves of Sabbath and holidays. They preferred to come on a regular weekday, usually Thursdays, when there were fewer visitors, the place was cleaner, and they could even take a bath for a special fee paid to Itche, the attendant.

Even in summer attendance at the bathhouse did not let up, for the town was quite far from any river or lake and there were only a few shallow ponds in town that served as a laundry for the village women in summer and, in winter, as the source for ice that was put into the cold cellars and lasted until the end of summer.

With time, the importance of the bathhouse rose even more because a deep-water well was sunk in it, whose clear waters could be easily obtained with a hand pump (*der plimp*). Everyone who lived in the vicinity of the bath got their water from the well and no longer had to depend on the shallow well water that was never particularly tasty or clear and that had to be obtained

with a great deal of effort, and often a great deal of stress, if the rope broke and the bucket dropped. From early morning until late at night it was always busy around the pump and anything that broke was fixed immediately.

This well was in much better condition than a second one that was dug after some time in the center of the marketplace and whose pump broke shortly after; it was soon abandoned. On chilly autumn evenings, anyone who passed through the market would hear the sound of water, a gloomy, mysterious sound, that rose up from its spout.

The third pump, on Chelm Street (it had a wheel), worked well, but it did not have the water volume of the main well next to the bath.

Due to the bathouse's location, close to the center of town in a heavily populated area and not far from the synagogue, it served as a kind of convenient farewell point during funerals. The route of funerals usually went through the alleyways near the bathhouse, and those among the mourners who, for whatever reason, could no longer continue to the cemetery left the procession here and were able to wash their hands at the pump [done according to Jewish tradition after contact with death].

The bathhouse was in an old, large, wooden structure with two entrances: the first on the southeast side for men and the second on the west side, to the special mikveh for women.

It had a dark exterior and it appeared as one large black mass that frightened those who passed by at night. During the week it seemed deserted and devoid of life, except for the early morning hours on Mondays and Thursdays, when a few regulars came to immerse themselves in the steaming hot water—the rabbis, the dayan [judge], the shochetim [ritual slaughterers] the sofrim [scribes], and a small number of young yeshiva students who left their studies for a short while and came to fulfill this duty of immersion in the mikveh.

I still remember the great effort that my friends and I, students of R. Yankl Feiveles of the Rizhiner shtibl, made to go into the hot mikveh and try to stay there for at least 10 minutes. This was a challenge and test of our endurance, by which we wanted to prove to ourselves that we could do the same as the adults who went in "heel to toe" and came up after a while, their bodies shiny and red, their hearts beating very quickly.

Going into the hot water of the mikveh took patience; little by little, and slowly, we would dip our toes in, careful not to move the surface of the water, which would cause a painful sensation on the skin. When we managed to get in up to our necks, we stood stock still and didn't utter a sound, because of the choking sensation we felt around our necks; we listened to our heartbeats and quick pulses, which we felt all through our bodies.

Starting on Thursday afternoon, the bathhouse began to show signs of life: thick smoke would rise from the chimney, then from the windows and holes in the roof, until it looked like the whole thing would soon be engulfed in flames.

Itche, the attendant, and his non-Jewish helper, Ivanche, started stoking the boiler that heated the stones above and around it, from which on the following days steam would rise; he began heating the water in the large copper tanks and filled the round vats and other vessels, all in preparation for the following day.

The bathhouse was open to the general public on Fridays, starting at noon. The smoke and steam that arose from every corner could be seen from far away and were a signal to everyone in town, reminding them that "today is the eve of the Sabbath, and you'd best hurry to do this mitzvah and not miss the opportunity."

A unique odor—a mixture of smoke, steam, and the sulfur of the water from the pump, together with the smell from the cesspool and the

sewer that passed by on its way out of the city—carried for miles, and people living in nearby streets smelled it most!

A mixture of sounds—shouts, yells and strange sorts of howling as the result of practical jokes, could be heard coming from the bath that day; and on top of it all, "sounds of victory" that the lashers (schmeisers) made to encourage themselves while massaging and scrubbing down their "patients," who were spread out on the top stairs, surrounded by enough steam and vapor to cramp their lungs.

The masseurs would "bring them around" every few minutes by sprinkling cool water from the barrels onto their steaming bodies—and hence the shouts to Ivanche to keep up his work in bringing cool water in buckets from the pump into the bath.

Poor Ivantche, he was torn in two; on one hand he had housewives waiting to get water for their work at home, and on the other the terrible screams of the bathers, "Water, water!" accompanied by knocking on the windows that overlooked the pump. The sounds of the schmeisers pouring more water on the stones to increase the steam that rose from all corners of the building could be heard for miles.

This is how the bathhouse looked inside: in the entry way, on the southeast side, Itche the attendant took the entrance fee, the same from everyone, and for an additional fee supplied a bundle of twigs and a clean, wooden bucket. From there you came to a large space—open to the cross-winds—that divided the southern area, which served as a dressing room, from the northern section, the bath itself.

Another door on the west side of this open area led to the western section, where the women's mikveh was. There were wide benches in the dressing room along the walls, and the shelves above served as seats for those undressing and as a place for their clothes. This is where important conversations were held between those finishing their ablutions and those about to begin.

In winter, the bathers shortened their stay in this area because of the chill, hurrying through the open area, which was bitter cold and through which the winds blew from all sides. The door leading to the bath itself closed automatically because of weights and could be opened only with great strain on the arm muscles—an act the old folks and youngsters could not manage—and so they had to wait until someone strong came along.

People entering were surrounded immediately by hot air and steam, with a mixture of smoke that caused fog and some slight burning of the eyes for a short time. After a few minutes, they recovered and their eyes began to make out the dark, polluted light filtering in through the window panes covered with steam and dripping with water.

From one corner at the narrow portion of the entrance, a faint, red light flickered, the "eternal light" of R. Leyb Krazke, the faithful, long-time barber of the bathhouse. By this light he serviced his clients—cutting their hair with scissors and, together with this haircut, providing the benefits of cupping [bankes, small glass cups "attached" to the body through suction created by heat], good for all sorts of pains and backaches that accompany a cold.

In spite of his age, R. Leyb was quite agile at his job: he would speedily attach the cups, about 15 of them, up and down the back. While these were attached to his client's back, R. Leyb, with nimble, experienced hands, proceeded to cut his client's hair.

The Eastern Wall In the Bath

Just like the synagogue (not to mention them in the same breath!), the bathhouse had a kind of "Eastern Wall"—every social class had its place; the wagon drivers, horse dealers, and portly butch-

ers took the northeastern section, closer to the steam, and they actually saw to it that it came up from the circle of stones; they were the ones whose cries of surprise and pleasure filled the place while they were sweating and being massaged on the top benches surrounded by steam.

There, near the ceiling, where the air was dense with so much steam and thick vapor that it made your breath come short, that's where they enjoyed it most, splashing a bit of water on their steaming bodies every few minutes. Throughout, they let out sighs of pleasure, feeling relief almost to the point of abandon.

The shopkeepers, merchants, and others in town who crowded in on the southwestern side near the mikveh made do with the middle benches. They whiled away the time talking with their friends, barrels of lukewarm water at their feet, into which, occasionally, they dipped their red handkerchiefs and then patted their bodies—with great pleasure, accompanied by sighs of relief—all the while continuing to chat with their friends.

It's hard to exaggerate the benefit that everyone derived from the bathhouse, which not only served as a place to wash their bodies and rejuvenate their bones. It was no less a place for a bit of privacy and friendly conversation and, to a certain extent, for jokes and comic relief—if even for a brief moment—from the many worries of day-to-day existence. In the mikveh they were released from the bonds of the workaday world and prepared themselves to enter the throne-room of the "Sabbath Queen," where they would rest and enjoy themselves in her presence.

THE "RECRUITS"

The three-month period leading up to the mobilization of our town's young men into the Polish army was called the "period of torment" in local slang. During these three months our town led a double life. By day, the town belonged to adults; they traded, worked, and struggled to earn their daily bread. But when it grew dark, the control of the city passed into the hands of the future "inductees." The town became changed, filled with acts of willful mischief, which lasted till dawn.

It was then that the term "period of torment" became more than a mere figure of speech. More than once did I ask myself: From whence did the strength to endure torment come to these well-bred youths, who would do without a night's sleep and then start their day without their usual fresh rolls smeared with thick layers of butter? It felt as if these beautiful lads had been cast down; the tenor of their lives turned to ashes; and their eyes turned red from lack of sleep!

And you realized they were determined to go

A group of Jewish soldiers from Luboml who served in the Polish army in Tarnow, 1924–25. (Upper left-hand is Gershon Sojbel.)

from 150 pounds down to 100 in order to escape from serving in the Polish army.

As soon as the last lights of the city were extinguished, the recruits felt free to gather opposite the Bet HaMidrash HaGadol and beside the Great Synagogue. They would hurry to commit some mischief in the middle of the night; and afterwards they would flee and hide because the policeman Yesheniek was onto their tricks.

At break of dawn one might find on the door of Dr. Greenberg, where they had sought haven from pursuit, a sign reading: "EXPERT SHOE-MAKER, accepts all kinds of orders." And the municipality sign was hanging over a shoe store. And at the end of this period, they found, as was customary, that the wagon of Benche Druker was in a hole near his house and his nag [*shkape*] tied to the gate of the city jail.

But the main thing I forgot to tell about avoiding conscription into the Polish army: release from conscription was not necessarily won by those who had tormented themselves, but by the young men whose parents had paid off the official conscription committee's doctor.

CHARACTERS AND PERSONALITIES

ABOUT THE TOWN'S "GOOD JEWS"
By Shloyme-Boruch Rubin

The Chasidic books do not say this, but my grandfather, R. Meyer-Avrom Rubinroyt, told me for a fact that the Baal Shem Tov (the founder of Chasidism) once visited Libivne.

Wonders and miracles were attributed to a person by the name of R. Moyshe Maneles, a student of the "Seer of Lublin." He was himself a great scholar. He earned his living by teaching. After the death of his mentor, R. Moyshe began to perform miracles and people would come to him from near and far. The shtetl would be packed with so many Jews that there simply was no place for them to stay overnight.

R. Dovid Sfard, a glass store owner, lived in R. Moyshe's house. He said that R. Moyshe would often have a little drink of whiskey before beginning a lesson with his pupils. The whiskey was procured for him by one of his students from a nearby Jewish tavern. One day, when the pupil brought him the liquor, he refused to touch it. The

children looked at their "rebbe" with wonder, when suddenly the inn-keeper's little girl burst into the room, half-dead with fear and told R. Moyshe that her mother had forgotten to wash out the bottle. Everyone then realized that R. Moyshe knew this because of his prophetic vision and therefore had not drunk the liquor.

The same R. Dovid had experienced a miracle himself. He had a glass business, as noted earlier. But God did not bless him with children. When he married for the second time at the age of 68, his young wife gave him two children!

R. Moyshe Maneles' grandson R. Avrom bar-Dovid and my father R. Yeshaye had the honor of being the guardians of the eruv (a wire strung around the borders of a town, within which area objects may be carried on Sabbath, according to Jewish law). They would examine the wire and repair it when necessary. Once the eruv near the church needed some repair.

Square with Great Synagogue and the Misaskim shtibl (attached to the shul at right).

When the two men came to fix the wire, they met the priest standing near it. The priest told them that he would fix it—a symbol of good neighborliness—truly a wonder!

A Jew by the name of R. Leybish, who was a Trisker Chasid, had lived in our town in the 1890s. The children of the Trisker magid always stayed at his house when they came to Libivne. He was a *bal-madreyge* [a man of great moral rectitude], while his grand-son, Dovid, was already a *maskil* [enlightened one].

One of our interesting types was R. Aaron-Shmuel Kneler, author of the book *Minchat Marcheshet* (Lublin, 1904). His main occupation was selling the books of the Chofets Chayim (the famous Jewish scholar of Poland). R. Aaron-Shmuel was something of a kabbalist. When everyone else had finished praying, he would still be saying the *Shma*. He would always place his house keys on the prayer desk to be ready when the Messiah came. He was a fiery orator.

The other learned men in the shtetl included R. Azrilke Melamed, R. Moyshe Klingl, R. Leybish, R. Aaron Eyger, and R. Uziel Dovidls.

The gabbai of the big shul was R. Avrom-Shmuel Herts. The shul possessed unique things: old silver *poroyches* [curtains over the ark], silver Torah crowns, ancient candlesticks, and rare *yads* [pointers in shape of a hand with a pointing finger, used in reading the Torah]. My great-grandfather, R. Yitse-Shloyme, was the gabbai of that shul for 43 years!

For several years the Libivner Jews enjoyed the magnificent prayers of R. Yosele Zaslaver, a noted cantor, who officiated with a whole choir.

Sixty or 70 years ago, the Jews of Libivne led traditional Orthodox lives. It so happened that a young man came to Libivne wearing a *kapelyush* [modern hat] instead of the traditional Chasidic cap. And when he came to shul (it was on the holiday of Shavuot), his presence led to a big fight.

Luckily, the young man was the son of a synagogue trustee and the people managed to quiet down the tumult.

And if there was ever a maskil [enlightened Jew] in town, he would have to hide in order to read a [forbidden] book, or, God forbid, a newspaper!

R. AARON-SHMUEL KNELER
By D. Prister

Libivne did not have the honor of producing many authors of books, either rabbinical or secular. But we got to know one such author.

The one was R. Aaron-Shmuel Kneler. In 1907, he published the book *Minchat Marcheshet*, consisting of sermons written in the usual style of such rabbinical literature.

It was impossible to collect the exact details of his biography. The little bits that were available came from various sources, as well as from his book. As we can see from the frontispiece, illustrated here, he called himself "Aaron-Shmuel Kneler of Libomle" as he was also called by those rabbis who put their stamp of approval on his book. This name was also used by R. Yehuda-Arye Eliezer, who described him as ben iri ["son of my city"]. But the rabbi of Ustile, R. Ben Tsiyon, the son of R. Tsvi Raytsir, and the "righteous teacher" of Ustile, R. Tsvi Dovid, *z"k* [the descendant of righteous men], said in their letters of approval that Aaron-Shmuel was born in Ustile.

We read in one letter that his father was named Moyshe and that "all his life he never stirred from the tent of halacha and Torah; and the fear and awe of the Almighty shielded him all the days of his life!" There is a hint in the words of R. Tsvi Dovid, *z"k*, that Aaron-Shmuel came to Libivne not later than the beginning of the 1890s and perhaps even earlier.

R. Aaron-Shmuel was also a darshan, an itinerant preacher who traveled not only locally, through towns and cities, but also to foreign countries. In his preface the author tells us he has been doing this for more than 20 years. Therefore we can infer that he was born either in the fifites or sixties of the last century.

He also writes in his book, "Thousands of Jews have blessed me after my sermon, wishing me well for a job well done, in several of the countries where I have been."

It is not very clear why he wandered around so much. Certainly, itinerant preachers could not stay too long in one place, but even the most famous preachers did not travel to foreign lands,

Title page of *Minchat Marcheshet,* by Aaron-Shmuel Kneler from Luboml.

Approbation from R. Yehuda Arye, son of Eliezer (Finkelshteyn), for Aaron-Shmuel Kneler's book *Minchat Marcheset*.

while Aaron-Shmuel managed to visit the Land of Israel twice at a time when its roads were filled with danger to life and limb. The author describes these visits: "All kinds of mishaps from fearful enemies threatened me as I once went from the home of my father to the Holy Land, yet it was considered worthwhile being in the Land of Israel for all of the Shalosh Regolim (the three festivals)."

R. Aaron-Shmuel continues to write about "many reasons" and about troubles, but he does not describe them. He writes about his second trip to the Land of Israel:

I visited a number of righteous men and great sages on account of a certain great and terrible reason.

And he said that he told one of them,

how I was obligated to travel to Eretz Yisroel because of a vow I made during a difficult time due to various circumstances, and how I did not have enough money to cover the cost.

His wanderings and, even more, his two trips to Eretz Yisroel evidently influenced him to speak out and sermonize about Chibat Tsiyon ("Love of Zion", an early Zionist movement begun in Russia at the time). He says in his preface,

I made my heart speak out and sermonize on how terrible the corruption was and the extreme want dragging me down. Only this way can we rebuild the House of God! Only thus can we ever become a voice sounding the shofar in the midst of a desert and restore the ways of God through collective effort; by bringing back the light of learning to Jerusalem, as I enter the love of Jerusalem into my heart and into the hearts of all Israel.

There is no doubt at all that he was plagued by troubles and by poverty. Moreover, his countless trips as preacher did not improve his economic situation. Therefore, he began to earn a living by teaching. He writes in his book that he had no other income than what he earned by working in schools with his pupils. Neither did this improve his lot too much.

It seems that Aaron-Shmuel was not only a preacher, but also a *magid meyshorim* [a righteous preacher]—one who, above all, did not seek rewards. He tells in one place in his book about [Moyshe] *Alshich*, "From whose holy and faithful seas I had the privilege to drink, and to learn them in the company of community." Elsewhere he says, "I would teach 100 people every day."

Neither can it be doubted that Aaron-Shmuel was a Chasid. He injects into every sermon quotations from great Chasidim and rebbes. He also tells us about contact with many illustrious personalities, such as the Righteous Master, a holy and pure soul, a miracle performer of our generation by the name of R. Avrom, the magid of Trisk: our pure and holy rabbi (our rebbe), Yehuda Leyb Eiger from Lublin; our pure and holy master, a member of Tiferet Israel. R. Dovid Moyshe *Sh'lita* ["He should live for many more years, amen."], the rabbi from Tshortkov; the master of the Torah, the great man of light, piety and abstinence, our rebbe, the tzadik (righteous) HaCohen of Lublin.

In another place he says that he wrote another book, *Leket Hashkacha*, which remained in manuscript form.

It is worth mentioning an interesting fact about *Minchat Marcheshet.* In those days no notice about the publication of the book ever appeared in print. No mention is made of this book in the biggest bibliography of Hebrew books, by Friedberg; neither can one find it listed in any of the library catalogues of New York.

We have no idea at all as to how long Kneler lived in Libivne, nor when he died.

RABBI PINCHAS OSELKA
By Yakov Hetman

Judging him by his character, we can say that Rabbi Pinchas Oselka was an "alien plant" in the shtetl. In speech and appearance he was a true Polish Jew from Western Poland living among us Eastern Polish Volhynians. Most Jews in our town were of medium height and broad shouldered; he was tall and lanky and of a fine appearance.

He was troubled by his difference. Most Jews in our town were not too scrupulous about their appearance, whereas he always shone. He differed also in his command of Polish. In one word, we could use the word "wonder" before "Rabbi" in speaking of him! His coiffure was different too: He had unusually long peyes [sidelocks],

shaped like two tubes, which hung down his cheeks, shaking like springs.

One could not tell whether he was a Chasid (though his followers were Rizhiner Chasidim): on the other hand, most Jews in our shtetl were Chasidim. Whatever his appearance, he was most highly valued for his learning as well as for his personality. He did not feel comfortable or at ease even in his own family. His family members also were careful about their appearance—ever appearing in spotless dress.

His official wages from the kahal [local Jewish council] were not sufficient for his needs, and only the income he had from rabbinical duties on the side helped him balance his budget. This side

A traditional reception with bread and salt was extended to the Catholic archbishop by the leaders of the Jewish community. The committee was headed by R. Pinchas Oselka and the dayan, R. Leybl Melamed.

income he received for acting as a judge in rabbinical tribunals, for performing marriages, and for helping Jews sell their chometz [bread or leavened food] symbolically before Passover. But this barely helped him get by, because his followers were few in number. I remember that my father, one of the rabbi's followers, would sell his chometz to all three rabbis separately and would pay all three men, all for the sake of the holiday.

It happened once, when my father was telling the rabbi that I was studying for entrance exams to the Yeshiva Chachmey Lublin (Yeshiva of the Sages of Lublin), that the rabbi advised him to have me come and study with him, saying that perhaps his own son, Yechiel (Chilik), would also want to study (his Chilik was not one of the good students).

And so I began to come every morning, as early as possible, to the rabbi's house to study with him. We would sit and study for hours at a long table in a long room—with the rabbi at one end, Chilik at one side, and I at the opposite side. We studied Chulin (a Talmud tractate) and Tosefta (commentaries); about Mordche and the House of Joseph; as well as the ins and outs of ritual-slaughter laws, which were fluttering in the air and I was convinced that Rabbi Oselka had great knowledge and a sharp wit, for his explanations were always appropriate and fit. He gave a lot of time to an explanation.

We studied both separately and in order to encourage his son Chilik. My father used every chance to give the rabbi a gift; for example, he would send him a sack of sugar for the holidays.

The whole town knew of Rabbi Oselka's great learning, but only a few persons experienced it first hand when they carried on discussions with him about the halacha [talmudic law]. There were some men among the masses who would study the *Ein Yakov* in the Bet HaMidrash HaGadol at twilight. From time to time, he would also speak in public, for example on Shabbat HaGadol [the great Sabbath] or on Shabbat Tshuvah [the Sabbath of repentance]. Although it was to the point, his speech may have lacked the

enthusiasm of a popular speaker or the zeal of a Chasidic orator. As in his daily life, so in his relation to his fellowmen he was reserved, quiet, polite, distancing himself from them. Neither did he posses the fanatical character that some rabbis then displayed.

He was reticent even with his own family. His daughter Zelda, who was married to Lacks, and his other daughter, Broche, married to Shmuel Fuks, were considered by the town to be beauties. They were often seen in the society of young men and women who were not that pious. His son Melech, who was always particular about his boots, being careful to shine them well, kept company with freethinkers.

But it seems that the rabbi expected his son Yechiel Kive to be pious. Indeed, there was not much hope that he could ever inherit the rabbinical throne.

It is possible to say that Rabbi Oselka was, by his own choice or not, a modern rabbi—a man well learned in Torah as well as in secular knowledge; a man of fine appearance, a pleasant, able speaker, active in Jewish affairs as well as in world politics. Rabbi Oselka did not generally interfere in the petty politics of the shtetl, nor did he side with any particular party, then or later.

But people were surprised to hear suddenly that he had been chosen as a delegate to the congress of the New Zionist Organization in Vienna, held in 1935. The young generation and the misnagdim [opponents of Chasidim] began to consider Rabbi Oselka as "our rabbi"—a Zionist, an activist; a man of importance; a man who had the characteristic of perpetual motion. Even his participation in the local social services—perhaps to prevent disagreements—did not stop his going to the congress in Vienna.

It was usual to see Rabbi Oselka taking his daily walk, with a steady gait and aristocratic bearing, from his home at the corner of the market across the street from the Bet HaMidrash HaGadol to the other side of the marketplace and back. And he always walked alone.

ABOUT RABBI OSELKA
By Shmuel Fuks

The story of the rescue of Luboml's Jews from the hands of the murderous bands of pogromists, the Balechovtzes, is a tale of the courage of R. Pinchas Oselka. With the penetration of the Bolshevik army into our area in 1920, the Balechovtzes, the dispersed remnants of Petlura's Ukrainian army and their followers, joined the Polish army. The disgraceful General Balechovitz was their head. In the course of their assistance to the Polish army in its war with the Bolsheviks, they engaged in robbing and murdering the Jews.

From surrounding villages terrible news began to arrive of murder, rape, robbery, kidnappings, and the desecration of dead bodies by the murderous bands and the village bullies who joined them.

Meanwhile, news spread that part of the deadly army of Balechovtzes intended to cross the town to the front. Great fear seized the Jews of the town. R. Pinchas Oselka, as the new town rabbi, went to see the Catholic bishop, and with his fluency in the Polish language he found the proper words to present himself to the priest; both of them led a delegation of important Jews of the town that went to see the regional military commander of the Polish army, to beg him to stop the murderous Balechovtzes, who were almost at the gates of the town. A large sum of money was needed to accompany the plea, as an offering to the commandant. With the lightning speed, a collection was arranged on the spot to appease the Polish commandant.

For a long time after, the story circulated in town of how, at the fateful hour, the delegation walked through the streets of the town, headed by the Catholic priest, dressed in his black frock, and the Jewish rabbi, in his kapote [caftan] and shtrayml [Chasidic round fur hat], as the whole town followed in fear their efforts to rescue the town from a pogrom.

Rabbi Oselka, who had come from the Polish town of Mogelnitsa, was invited in 1919 by some

Rabbi Pinchas Oselka

of his followers (mainly the Chasidim of Rizhin and Radzin, who were active and prayed in Luboml's Great Shul), to come and act as rabbi together with R. London and R. Leybl Melamed (the dayan—judge).

R. Oselka was young, full of energy, and learned in secular subjects, and as rabbi he left his impression on our town. He fulfilled his function as a rabbi until 1938, when he was called back to the city of Mogelnitsa to occupy the rabbinic chair after the death of his father, R. Gavriel Oselka.

After the German occupation, all the Jews of Mogelnitsa were deported to the Warsaw Ghetto. There, R. Oselka died. The only one of his entire family to remain alive was his daughter, Broche Fuks, who went to Palestine just before World War II broke out. She lives in Tel Aviv with her family.

THE MAYOR
By Yakov Hetman

Dovid Veytsfrucht (London) was known as "the *Birgermeister*" (mayor), as he was the only Jewish mayor of Luboml during the Austrian occupation in World War I. He was the son of the Voislovitser rabbi, R. Yoshe London, and the brother of R. Leybish London, the rabbi of Luboml. He was a great scholar and had a mastery of rabbinical studies. People would say he should have been the rabbi of Luboml, rather than his brother.

Rabbi Dovid Veytsfrucht, the Birgermeister

Even though he was preoccupied as a merchant, yet he spent most of his days in studying the Torah with other people, adults or younger students in the Kotsker shtibl. Until this day I see before my eyes the image of myself, together with Alter London (later rabbi of Luboml), Asher Veytsfrucht, and Itsik Vidre as we got up at four o'clock in the morning and went to the Kotsker shtibl to listen to R. Dovid Birgermeister expounding a lesson. It was dark and freezing outside, and snow fell at times. The stove would be lit, when suddenly the door would open and in would come R. Dovid, dressed in an elegant fur coat. As he stood at the door, he would blow in and out, in and out, and stare sternly at the couple of young boys waiting for him. Without saying a word, he would go to the lectern and begin the lesson on Tosefta, Mishnah commentaries and other *meforshim* [commentaries], from time to time asking us whether we understood.

He was considered to be one of the three greatest scholars in town. The other two were R. Yankl Moyshe Feiveles (Natanzon) and R. Pinchas Oselka. Whenever there was a controversy over an interpretation of the halacha (Jewish law), people would naturally turn to R. Dovid for enlightenment.

R. Dovid was born in 1877 in Voislovits and then came to live in Luboml, where he married Gitl Sandlshteyn, the daughter of R. Moyshe-Asher, in 1898. To escape conscription into the Russian army, he went to live in Bendin, where he changed his name from London to Veytsfrucht. Then he went to live in Dombrovo-Gurnitsha.

He returned to Luboml in 1916 during the Austrian occupation and was appointed mayor by the Austrians. When the Poles replaced the Austrians, the Jews of the shtetl asked him to become the rabbi of Luboml, but he waived the honor and suggested that his brother, R. Leybish London, be rabbi instead.

His suggestion was accepted, and R. Dovid lived the rest of his life as a merchant. In 1940, during World War II, the Russians forced him to leave Luboml and forbade him to live closer than 12 miles from the border. He therefore settled in Masheve, where he was killed by the Germans in 1942.

TEACHERS (MELAMDIM) IN THE SHTETL
By Nathan Tchelet (Blumen)

A compulsory law to study Torah did not exist in our town, Luboml, until the establishment of Poland as a sovereign state. But our parents felt it their duty (a duty of the heart) to teach their children the Torah of Israel. And this duty was stronger than many laws; they were dedicated to this to the point of denying themselves food, and they performed it with a great deal of effort.

The teacher (melamed) Mendl Frechter.

When a child reached the age of three, there was great joy in the parents' home. This was celebrated as a birthday and as the first day that this little Jew would assume the responsibility of performing the mitzvah of studying Torah.

From that point on, he was no longer a child like other children but a young candidate for a great and glorious task. It often seems to me that this third birthday was more important than the thirteenth (the bar mitzvah), for on this day the fate of many young, tender children was decided for a number of years to come.

From now on there was a different scene, a different world, a different background, a different environment. We were commanded to be planted on a different earth, whose scenery was different, whose environment was different. We started with the Book of Leviticus, the Law of the Priests. There is not only study here, but also knowledge, deeds and a way of life—Torah—that is the beginning and the end. A people divided into Israelites, Levites, and Kohens (Priests) and each within their own setting, with their own destiny and fate.

When I think about the melamdim [Jewish teachers] I remember them as downtrodden in their lifestyle and only proud and tall within the bounds of the classroom [cheder]. Here they became a decisive factor, here they observed the commandment of ensuring the survival of the Jewish people, here their feet were firmly planted on the ground.

These are their names: R. Yanke Nitcheches, R. Moyshe Yoseles, R. Hersh of Koritnitza (nicknamed "the crooked hand"), R. Mendl, the son-in-law of the shochet Chayim Hersh, R. Notl Melamed (Faigen), R. Avrom der Poylisher, R. Hersh Borsht. They were all my teachers, and their memory is engraved on my heart. Each name represents another age: the first, three to six; the second, six to seven; the third, fourth, and so on. Years, seasons, responsibilities, and duties.

With the first melamed, R. Yanke Nitcheches, I became acquainted with the *kanchik*—a stick that had three leather straps at the end—a kind of homemade whip whose purpose was purely deterrent. I don't remember him actually using it. We were so little then, and R. Yanke, who even then was up in years, though strict, was good-natured, had a lot of experience with beginners, and his face radiated warmth.

His house was at the corner of Teatralna and Miesna Streets, across from that of R. Yosef Chayim Tzin the saddlemaker, and the entrance was through the porch across from Chayim Isser the furrier's house. In this house there was a matzo bakery which operated every year from Purim until Passover and there, while still a small boy, I learned to hold the roller that put the holes in the matzo so that it would not rise, God forbid.

My second teacher was R. Natan Hamnetzer. From him we learned to make sentences from words, to say the blessing *Modeh Ani* ("I give thanks . . .") after we took care of the *negl vasser* by wetting the tips of our fingers and the fingernails [essential before praying]. We also started to learn Chumash with him. As I said, this important event began with the Book of Leviticus and in honor of this occasion a little party was often held in the homes of the wealthier children.

A teacher, R. Moyshe (Yoseles) Povroznik.

The third, R. Moyshe Yoseles, was different from the other two. He was younger, closer to his pupils and their spirit, loved by them and returned that affection as well. In my memory I see him as well organized and serious in carrying out his duties, but along with that he was a quiet, smiling, understanding person. He had all the

qualities of the expert pedagogue who knows each and every one of his pupils and knows how to adapt his approach accordingly and yet to instill an atmosphere of togetherness among all students.

Every week he taught us a lesson in Mishnah. The first Mishnah was "He who places a pitcher in the public domain" (Baba Kama I) and then every week a different mishnah. When we finished Baba Kama we started Baba Matzia; we also learned the tractate Gittien with him.

He taught us penmanship and the beginning of arithmetic. He had a clear and beautiful handwriting, really calligraphic. He would write out rounded letters of the alphabet in pencil on pieces of paper, and we pupils went over the letters with pens dipped in violet ink. [When we wrote], the ink was supposed to cover the letters exactly, to neither go above or below the line; woe to the student who went outside the lines.

But his greatest point was his explanation of the weekly Torah portion, which he turned into a literary creation. A great spirit filled the classroom when he set off for that distant biblical era and brought it close to us, as if that were the essence of life and everything up to that time, everything around us really did not exist and was just a figment of the imagination.

And the last: R. Hersh from Koritnitza [*der Koritnizer Rebbe*] or, as he was called by his students, "the crooked hand," for the palm of his hand was crooked. His approach was to seek perfection in everything, whether it related to the students or to our daily prayers and the weekly Torah portion. If you missed a word or mispronounced a syllable you immediately got a crack: "You idiot! (Goy that you are!) When you get to heaven you'll get it a thousand times more, and they'll roast you on a spit of fire."

This teacher used to tell horror stories and depress the children. But with all this, he knew how to portray the biblical figures dramatically . It was forbidden to study the Prophets but you could learn the other writings. He especially liked teaching the Megillot, each one in turn.

With all his strictness and impatience, the students of those days absorbed all the variations and nuances of the chants of the several Megillot.

Particularly unusual was the tune for Ruth, which we learned the week before Shavuot.

Different feelings were felt by the young children when they studied Shir HaShirim—Song of Songs, with a special melody of the times, about King Solomon, a king and the son of a king, a tzadik [righteous person] and the son of a tzadik, etc.

We understood the love between the people of Israel and the God of Israel and were engulfed with love for Eretz Yisroel [the Land of Israel], even when sitting in the narrow choking yard on Shkolne Street. With open mouths we were in the midst of another world; we longed for the holy land as described in the wonderful words of Song of Songs.

R. MOYSHE YITSHAK KAGAN
By Shabtai Langer (z"l)

R. Moyshe Yitshak Kagan

R. Moyshe Yitshak Kagan, the director of the town's Talmud Torah, was a wonderful man and, without a doubt, is still remembered by those of his Torah students who still remain.

His influence on his students was tremendous. He was among the first to teach his students Hebrew in a modern method, speaking the language with them. He also taught his pupils the history of the Jewish people. It is therefore no wonder that most of his students later joined the various Zionist movements.

R. Moyshe was born in the village of Opalin. He came to Luboml while still a young man and sank roots there. He was a very gifted man, and his specialties were poetry and recitations. Whenever he prayed before the Holy Ark in the Great Synagogue, crowds would come to listen to him, for he had a sweet and strong voice. He was a very good reader at the altar and his pupils had learned well the cantillation used in prayer.

R. Moyshe Yitshak continued to keep in touch with his pupils even after they reached maturity. Everyone paid him great tribute as an illustrious and beloved teacher.

THE FIRST ELEMENTARY SCHOOL IN LIBIVNE
By Boruch-Mendl Frechter

In Libivne, as in the other Polish shtetlech, there was a Talmud Torah that poor children attended because their parents could not afford to pay their tuition. The shtetl had a Talmud Torah Society, which collected donations to maintain the school and to pay the salaries of its three teachers.

The trustees of this committee were R. Yakov Yeshayahu Erlich, Moyshe Afeldman, Yudl Tsvik, and Naftoli Gedalyes (Naftoli Merin). The children did not study in one place but went to the homes of their teachers and studied there.

On the initiative of Moyshe Afeldman, the society rented a large hall from Shamai Zaydl and moved the Talmud Torah there. From then on, the instruction was much better, because all of the children were in one place. It was easier to keep an eye on them and therefore to take better care of them.

Moyshe Afeldman, a cultured man, felt that the Talmud Torah alone was not enough and that there was a need for secular studies, too. He therefore began a correspondence with the famous Society for the Propagation of Culture among the Jews, which had its quarters in St. Petersburg. He asked their help in turning the Talmud Torah into a public school for both Jewish and secular subjects.

IMAGES
By Shmuel Royter (z"l)

Out of the foggy past figures appear, Jews from Luboml. The images appear and demand to be memorialized to the ages. One of these images is of a kind man with a pure soul named Motl Kreizer, who dedicated his entire life to mitzvot connected with the Jewish National Fund. This man's efforts to create a minyan for prayers so that he could contribute to JNF from those called up for aliyot to the Torah are commendable. Motl worked hard in the office that arranged for aliyot to Eretz Yisroel. The Zionist work done by this man was done with all his heart. He had no hope of gaining a thing from his labors.

Another image that stands out in my mind is that of Rav Leybl Dayan, who also dedicated his time to public service. This man had a warm Jewish heart and good values. He established institutions to help those in need. He also founded the building, Linat Hatsedek, that served as a hostel for the poor and the committee that distributed Passover aid to the needy.

Two other distinguished persons were businessmen Rav Dovid Veyner and Rav Shloyme Samet. These men were at the head of the Jewish Foundation Fund and were among those who founded the free loan fund. They were extremely dedicated and there was a strong love for Israel in their hearts. They also saw to it that when they helped others it was done modestly so that not a soul would be embarrassed by their charity.

To Rav Chayim Baran I owe personal thanks. On the Shabbat before I left for Palestine, Rav Chayim Baran came to the minyan of the Jewish National Fund and asked that I come over to his home for he wished to speak to me before my departure.

Due to the fact that I was pressed for time (because I was supposed to leave town the minute Shabbat was over) I approached him after prayers were over for a quick farewell, but he closed the door behind me and ordered me to go over to the ark and to take money for traveling expenses.

This man allowed me to break the Sabbath in order to perform the mitzvah of making aliyah to Eretz Yisroel. When I refused to take the money, he himself approached the ark, took out money in the sum of 150 guldens, forced it into my pocket and said, "This is my part, my contribution to Eretz Yisroel."

I knew that Rav Dovid Veyner and Rav Shloyme Samet had something to do with this gesture as well.

There was another group of businessmen who were my friends and worked in the People's Bank. Among them were the chairman of the board, Shmuel Getman, and board members

Activists in Keren Hayesod. *From right*, Shloyme Samet, Motl Privner, S. Rozenhak, and Dovid Veyner.

Moyshe Fuks, Yitshak Leyb Blumen, Leyzer Finkelshteyn, Shloyme Rayz and Motl Privner, the manager of the bank. Thanks to these men, many Luboml citizens were able to hold on during hard times. Many people trusted them with their secrets.

An organization that was one of a kind was the "parliament" in the Trisker Shtibl where Leybish Blumentzweig led discussions on all public matters.

These characters from my past are only a few individuals out of a long line of worthy citizens who served their community wholeheartedly and with conviction.

MECHANICAL SPECIALISTS IN LUBOML
By Velvl Royzman

The back part of Shloyme-Chayim Kiter's [Sojbel's] home, facing Miesna Street, looked like a large stable. Inside the stable was a straw-cutting machine pulled by horses. The shredded straw, called sitchke, was mixed with grain and oats and served as cattle feed. Since most Luboml homeowners had cattle, it was necessary for them to purchase daily a sack of shredded straw for their cows or horses. Therefore an investment in a shredded straw machine was a good idea.

The structure of the so-called "straw shredding stable" was primitive. In the middle of the stable stood a tall wooden pole to which a horizontal wagon pole was attached. A horse, harnessed to the pole, walked in a circle, pulling the horizontal pole which in turn moved the central, upright pole around its own axis. As the upright pole turned, it put in motion a transmission that rotated a round roller with knives attached to it on the other side of the stable; this was the actual straw shredder. As the knives rotated, they cut the straw.

The apparatus had the shape of a long box, open at the top. In order to shred straw, a bundle of straw was placed in the box where two rollers with teeth pushed and pressed the straw against the knives.

Shloyme-Chayim had five sons: Avrom, Zelig, Gershon, Meshl, and Yosl; and four daughters: Chane, Soreh, Malke, and Chaye. When the sons became older, they took over the supervision of the shredding machine.

The oldest son, Avrom, had, as they say, a pair of "golden hands" and a knack for business.

In those days, the peasants were in great need of shredding machines and other farm machines. Avrom Sojbel took advantage of this need and slowly developed a business selling such machines. He used to buy parts from factories, assemble them, and sell the machines to the peasants. Simultaneously, he perfected his skills as a locksmith and in other mechanical areas in demand. The other brothers helped out in the undertaking.

Across from the Sojbel home, behind Tratel Sheinwald's home, was an abandoned piece of land where the Sojbels constructed a building. The front of the building was occupied by the locksmith and a mechanical workshop, and the other half was designated for selling straw shredders and other farm equipment.

Here, the shredding machines were more modern. The roller had two large wheels with handles on both sides that two men could turn. There were also other shredders and farm equipment that were driven by motors. Various other mechanical jobs were performed in their enterprise. There were two large lathes, drills, motors, and other advanced machinery.

[The machine shop, named Zaklad Mechaniczby w Lubimlu—Bracia Sojbel (Mechanical Enterprise in Luboml—Brothers Sojbel), became a highly complex professional electrified enterprise, handling a variety of machine, casting and handmade parts and repairs for the entire region, including agricultural equipment, motors, bicycles, locks and keys, metalwork, etc. The founder of the enterprise, Avrom Sojbel, was a gifted inventor and responsible for a number of mechanical breakthroughs.–N. Sobel]

During the terrible time of the Nazi occupation, when the Jews were forced into the ghetto and the question of provisions became a critical

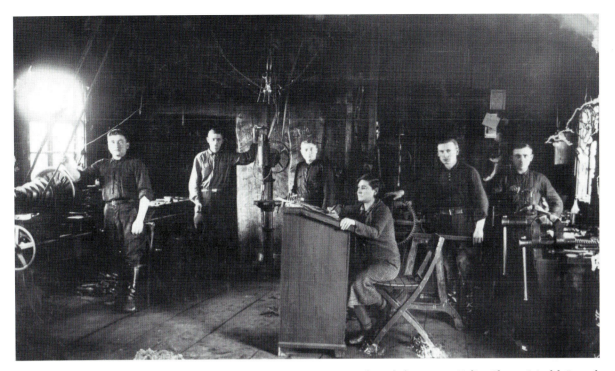

The mechanical workshop of the Sojbel brothers in 1936. *From right to left*: Avrom, Zelig, Chaye, Meshl, Joseph, and Gershon Sojbel.

issue, my older brother Motl, together with Avrom Sojbel, built a small factory for the production of oil for home consumption. This helped considerably the starving Jews of the ghetto.

The production of edible oil depends on many factors: a grinder with two rollers necessary to crush grain into powder, a motor that turns the rollers, an oven with a pot where the powder is heated to a given temperature, and a press that compresses the hot powder until the fat begins to drip out.

The factory worked in great secrecy. The machinery was so creatively constructed that it could be taken apart in a matter of minutes and hidden away in case of a sudden raid. The children of the two families involved were trained to assemble and dismantle and hide the operation quickly.

In the dark days of the ghetto, the limited production of oil, in a small measure, eased the problem of hunger.

Among the handful of talented construction masters, mechanics, and craftsmen of our town,

mainly fathers and their sons, such as the Sojbel family, Grimatlicht and others, Efrayim Royzman with his sons and his brother Meyer ("the lazy one," as he was called) who lived in the adjoining town of Masheve, stood out for their excellence.

Efrayim Royzman belonged to the group of people about whom the world says "What the eyes see, the hands can make." And so, for example, it was told that he carved out of wood two lions that supported two tablets with the Ten Commandments, located at the stairs leading to the holy ark in the big shul, and other art works for the Psalm-sayers' synagogue and other small synagogues.

The two-story rolling mill, near the road and across from Mendl Eizenberg's home, was constructed with the technical help of Efrayim, a partner in the mill. Earlier, Efrayim was the chief mechanic and machinist in the mill, which at the time belonged to Yona Ladinier and his partner Serczuk. Efrayim was exceptional in carpentry and people admired his beautiful work.

THE "COMPOSER"
By Velvl Royzman (z"l)

A young man from a neighboring town lived in the Kotsker shtibl. He was nicknamed *der Blinder* ("blind man")—he did see with both eyes, but his left eye was half-closed.

He would sleep on a bench in the shtibl. During the day he used to sit in the *tshayne* [tea house] of Elye-Yisroyel. This young man, Moyshe, had a talent for composing music. He had composed most of the marches that the Chasidim of the Kotsker shtibl used to sing while they prayed.

Whenever he completed a composition he would call together his close friends, Shimele Shliva, Simche the watchmaker, Favele the *kop* [head], and my brother Yisrolke, and he would rehearse the music with them. They would then introduce the march at prayer, and the Kotskers would adopt it as their own; and so another march was added to the rich collection of Kotsker marches.

In the years before the war, Moyshe became ill. The Chasidim put up a metal bed in another part of the shtibl where the sick Moyshe would lie. His friends did not neglect him. They brought a doctor to him, supplied him with food, and took care of him.

His friends, who did the most for him, were Yisrolke Royzman, Simche the watchmaker, and Favele "head."

THE PORTER
By Yisroel Leichter

He was raw and primitive. He had not even finished cheder. But he had a good heart and was the first to help a Jew in need.

People called him Elye Kepke. His father died when Elye was yet a child. His mother was a weak, ailing woman who did not have the strength to raise Elye as she would have liked. But Elye, despite having grown up in great poverty, developed into a tall, strong man.

Not having any occupation, he would spend time among the drivers. Since he was strong, he would help out, put his shoulder to the wheel; or help load a heavy sack or a big keg. And thus he gradually became a porter. He would carry a sack of flour as easily as one would carry a toy. Therefore he was usually hired to act as guard at weddings, so that no uninvited guest could crash the affair.

Whenever it came to blows, he was there to separate the disputants. No one dared cross him and everyone used to give in to him. And yet he, the great giant of a man, became the seeker of peace. He never raised a hand to a Jew, but if ever a gentile dared pick a quarrel with a Jew, Elye Kepke was there to teach the gentile a *parshe bolek* [give him a rough lesson], so that he would think twice before starting up with a Jew. Whenever a fire broke out, he was the first on the spot, carrying the heavy pails of water or rescuing the meager belongings from the burning Jewish home.

Humble, honest Elye Kepke, with his primitive goodness, was a well-known figure in the shtetl.

AN EPISODE
By Mordche Kandelshteyn

The mill and the electricity-producing plant of the Grimatlichts was a very important factor in the shtetl's economy. Several Jewish families made a living from that mill; they traded with the peasants who came to the mill to grind flour or to press oil out of the grain.

An episode that is etched in my memory once occurred in connection with the mill. It happened during the fair-day. A man came in with a wagon laden with flour. A horse cannot stand still but must always be chewing some-thing. The wagoner took a small bundle of hay from a peasant's cart and gave it to his horse. Some of the peasants noticed it, fell upon the Jew, and began to beat him, almost killing him. When he heard the uproar and the shouts for help, the strong Avrom Sheyner ran over, grabbed one peasant with one hand and a second peasant with the other hand, and knocked their heads together so that they fell almost unconscious upon the ground. The rest of the peasants disappeared at once.

CHAYIMKE THE WATER-CARRIER
By Basye Cohen (Zilberman)

My imagination takes me back 35 years. I see before my eyes my poverty-stricken shtetl, with its autumn mud and its summer dust. The rich men and the intelligentsia are far from my thoughts. It is the *folks-mentshn* ,the plain people who are etched in my memory. I see them clearly, as if they were standing in front of me, with their pitiful faces and their simple attire. One such folks-mentsh was Chayimke the water-carrier.

As I remember him, he must have been about 50, though he looked younger, for he was always full of humor. He never complained of his lot but was always satisfied; nor did he have envy or hatred toward anyone. Chayimke was the happiest man in the world. He asked for nothing more than warm clothing for the winter and a piece of bread to eat.

Shloyme Yucht, another water-carrier, who was a mute.

His goodness and contentment radiated from his face. When he laughed, his dimples and his yellow beard shook.

But who had the patience and the time to pay attention to Chayimke the water-carrier? He provided water for the town, carrying it from the pump in his *karamisles* [a wooden yoke carried on the shoulders, with two pails hanging from either end]. He did not know how to write and let his customers total up the cost of his labor, for not everyone paid him the same price. Sometimes he did not earn enough for the Sabbath. I would ask Chayim, "What will be?" and he would answer me, "Don't worry. When Moshiach comes, things will be much better!"

His little house stood next to the cemetery. At times I would peek into his little house and a shudder would go through my body. The walls were covered with mildew and moisture. In the winter, snow blew through the cracks in the thin walls.

I would stand and wait until Chayimke's deaf-and-dumb wife would come out. She knew exactly when I was to come. We understood each other by sign language. She had made peace with her bitter lot. It was evident that Chayimke showed her a great deal of warmth and tenderness.

I would leave their home with pain in my heart, thinking, why does God give one person everything, while another gets nothing?

There were many such Chayimkes in Libivne. Their souls were snuffed out like candles. No one ever was aware of them.

TYPES AND SCENES
By Efrayim Lerner

The whole time I was in America I always dreamt of revisiting my Libivne to see my family again; to walk again in the shtetl where I had taken my first steps as an infant.

As ill fortune would have it, the dream that I and others had cherished for so long had vanished. The cities and towns of our former homes lie in ruins together with their inhabitants, and among them all my dearest and nearest. And instead of a happy reunion with those I love, I am now writing my memoirs for a Memorial Book.

Oh, how my heart aches!

On Pesach Eve

The pre-Passover hubbub was in full swing on Kusnishtcher Street. Matzos were being baked in the home of Rochl the Black One.

Her entire apartment consisted of three tiny rooms. The beds were taken out and people slept on the floor temporarily, while the apartment was converted into a matzo bakery.

The hot air generated by the ovens could be felt outside. The perspiring *valgerins* (those who rolled out the dough) with their calloused hands were, as usual, singing as they worked.

Each time a new matzo order came in, the baker sifted the flour for this batch, then the customers would wish the mistress a happy holiday, may she live till next year. Blessings were pouring out like flour from the flour sacks. The baked matzos were tied in bedsheets and a wooden bar was inserted into the knot, so that two porters could carry it on their shoulders. The mistress walked in front of the porters, praying that nothing, God forbid, happen to the load, as it did occasionally happen, when the knot untied and plop, it all went into the mud! The porters had

to be veritable acrobats to bring their load to its destination all in one piece. And for this they were tipped handsomely!

The "koshering" of the pots and pans could be done in the public baths. For a few groshen, the bath-attendant would dip the tied-together dishes into big vats that were filled with water kept boiling by big heated rocks, and this made the pot kosher for Passover. The Jews brought to the baths only the big utensils. The small ones, like small pans and silverware, were koshered at home, in the courtyard, with neighbors working together. Big pots stood outside on huge tripods with fire under them and a thick steam from the boiling water rising from the pot. The people would tie the utensils together and dip them in the boiling water, to make them kosher for Passover.

Besides making the utensils kosher, the women also tried to hide their old, beat-up, everyday kitchen utensils, to hide their non-Passover poverty, such as boards used to make noodles, bread-baking paraphernalia, *kotsibes* (oven pokers), rolling pins, etc.—things that could not be made kosher in boiling water. They were brought into an unused room and locked up, and everything was now ready to greet the holiday with a kosher Pesach!

Moyshe Konyuch (Moyshe the Horse-Dealer)

Moyshe Konyuch lived in a small house that stood in a big courtyard near a big horse stable. The horses disturbed everyone day and night with their neighing.

They were three brothers: Moyshe, Sender, and Shaye. All three resembled each other. They even dressed alike. And when I write about Moyshe, I really mean all of them.

189

Moyshe was of middle height with a red face and a short, square-cut beard. In the winter he wore a short fur jacket belted with a piece of rope, a fur cap (*kutshme*), and a pair of winter boots made of felt called *valinkes*.

The market-fair took place in Libivne on Mondays, while on Wednesdays it was held in the neighboring town of Masheve. Of course Moyshe did most of his business during the fairs.

The trading in horses had an interesting procedure. First of all, the prospective buyer looked in the horse's mouth to see whether it had healthy teeth. Its age could be established from its teeth. Then the man would place a hand on the horse's neck, while probing with the other hand to see whether the horse had shortness of breath. Then the ceremony of making the horse walk would begin—a man led the horse by the rein, while a second man would follow with a whip, driving it. The manner in which the horse ran would often clinch the sale.

Despite all this running around at fairs and working like a horse all week long, Moyshe was a poor man; his brothers also. He could not even enjoy rest on the Sabbath. He could not sleep because his "little horses" would sing to him all Sabbath long, so that he should not, God forbid, be lonesome.

Man and Beast

Where Itche and his family got their nickname of "Driker" is a mystery. But because no one in Libivne could be without a nickname, therefore his family was called the Drikers (printers).

There were two Jews in Libivne who were real printers and who had their own printing presses. One was Yankl Sfard, and the other was Huberman. But Itche and his brothers had quite a different profession.

Itche possessed a horse and wagon. We say horse and wagon, but it only resembled a horse. Mendele's nag (Mendele Mocher Sforim, the "grandfather" of Yiddish literature, who wrote *Di Klatshe,* "The Nag") was a prince of a horse compared to Itche's "horse." He would harness it in the morning, take it to the market, and leave it in the middle of the marketplace. He did not have to tie it up—the carcass thanked God when no one disturbed it!

A horse and a small wagon.

Its true color could be seen only on its belly and on its legs, since the hide had shed its hair from the back and its sides from past whippings. The harness consisted of rags so as not to cause any sores on the neck. And the reins were made of knotted ropes tied together. The metal "hoops" on the wheels were as if pasted on with sugar-water, so that the cart would hop on the cobble-road making a noise that could be heard for miles.

Bentze "Driker," with bedding on his shoulders, on the way to jail for not having bridled his horse properly. The horse went wild.

Itche dressed in a short peasant jacket made from heavy material and pants tied with a rope-belt, wearing this outfit summer and winter. He had a short scarf around his neck, with its ends stuck into his jacket—thus he stood while waiting for a sale.

Almost every Libivner storekeeper had to use either Itche, one of his brothers, or the other carters to bring the grain, herring, or salt to their stores.

Besides the carters there were also drozhkes [horse-cabs] for passengers for hire. The drivers of the drozhkes also owned big wagons for transferring goods or taking them to the cities.

Itche Shtiner

There was a "doctor" in the shtetl whose name was Itche Shtiner, because he came from the village of Shtin, which was not far from Libivne. Young people would sometimes take a walk there after their Sabbath meal of cholent [a meat, barley, and carrot dish, kept on the stove through the night]. There was a fine harvest of small, wild pears called genilkes. When green they were not fit to eat, but when they became soft and a bit overripe, they could be enjoyed.

There were few houses in Shtin; they could be counted on the fingers of both hands. And there were only a couple of Jewish families. Shtin was on the borderline of the village of Vishnyeve.

I see Itche before my eyes as if he were alive, just as he looked many years ago.

He was of middling height, with a blond beard cut in a square shape, with blue, smiling eyes. A short, padded three-quarter coat—not long enough to be a Chasidic coat and not short enough to be heretical. And the hat matched the outfit. In winter he also wore a fur-lined coat with a black Persian collar.

I remember him mostly during the winter months, because that was the season of getting colds and headaches. The children came home from cheder [Jewish school] with sore throats from sweating and from the water that leaked into their boots. The child would start coughing and develop a fever. Malnutrition was also a contributor. The child then became a candidate for Itche Shtiner the medic.

Thursday was the main shopping day for the Sabbath. On such days during the winter, the women were vulnerable to catch colds and they too became candidates for Itche Shtiner's services.

On Fridays the men would go to the public bath. They would give the caretaker a tip, and in return he would provide them with a wooden pail and with a broom made from birch twigs to help them have a good sweat. When they left the bath and their beards were still wet as they headed out into the cold streets, the beards formed icicles on their faces. By the time they reached home, they would be sick. Their wives would cover the men with feather quilts, and if this did not help, they would call Itche Shtiner.

Itche came in with all the paraphernalia that doctors carry with them. In one box he had a dozen glass cups, a bottle of turpentine, a package of cotton, and a bottle of a certain colored fluid to swab the throat. He would check the fever and would tell the housewife to boil a pot of water.

After the examination he would wrap cotton around a wick and would dip it in turpentine, and he would light it. He would then take a cup from the basin, stick the wick in the cup, and quickly would affix the cup to the back of the patient. This procedure was repeated until all the cups were affixed on the patient's back. After about 20 minutes he would remove the cups with a loud pop. He would then rub alcohol on the patient's lumpy brown-blue back. The patient was instructed to cover up and sweat it out. Itche would then go to another patient.

If Itche felt that the sickness was serious, maybe pneumonia, he would tell the patient to call a doctor.

With children he was an expert. He would smile and be very friendly to gain their confidence. He would dip a swab of cotton in a medicine and would swirl it in the throat, after asking him to say "ah, ah."

Itche never competed with doctors. Just the opposite, he always collaborated with the doctors to help the sick. When the Jewish doctor, Meisner, left Luboml, only the Polish doctor remained in town. This doctor was drunk most of the time, day and night. He had to be assisted and sup-

ported when he climbed with his impaired foot
on the drozhke [horsedrawn coach].

He was also a big anti-Semite. In addition,
the people were not able to find a common
language with this doctor, due to their unfamil-
iarity with the Polish language. Many times the
Jews would go to one of the nearby towns of
Kovel, Chelm, or Lublin.

During the horrendous days of the German-
imposed ghetto in Libivne, Itche worked with his
last strength to save the sick, until the time of the
ultimate liquidation of the Libivner community,
in which he perished together with all the other
Jews in the town.

The melamed Reb Notl Faigen

We had many melamdim [Hebrew teachers] in
our town: R. Moyshe Yoseles (who also taught
writing), R. Nosn Hamnetser, R. Hersh Borsht, R.
Moyshe Kagan (from the Talmud Torah), R. Mendl
Frechter, R. Elye Lisnaker, R. Yakov Noytshiches,
R. Moyshe Povroznik, R. Shamay (Gemara
teacher), R. Avrom, der Poylisher, (real name,
Goldhacker), and others.

One of the most colorful of all the melamdim
was R. Notl Melamed (Faigen). He was a Stepenyer
Chasid, and he believed with perfect faith that
not the Zionists but the Messiah would bring
deliverance to the Jewish people.

Reb Notl was an excellent artist. He would
paint flowers from a model, which were then
embroidered on *tfilin-zeklach* [bags in which
phylacteries are kept], and he wrote a beautiful,
perfect Rashi script.

R. Notl also had another occupation. Every
season before Pesach he would become a matzo
baker, the best in town. At that time, his helpers
or his sons would teach the children in his
cheder.

R. Notl maintained his cheder for a very long
time, teaching about 30 children per term. This
was his manner of teaching: he taught individual
children. A child would approach his desk and he
would teach the child according to his grade level.
He would start with the alef-beys [alphabet] and
lead him through the Hebrew studies, until
Chumash and Rashi. If a child had a "good head,"
he would begin with the alef-beys and begin to
learn Chumash in one term.

The melamed Reb Notl Faigen

The students who had reached the Chumash
stage would then sit at the same table with those
who were studying Chumash and read the text
out loud, interpreting it as they went. He also
taught them to read the weekly Torah portion; the
older pupils, who were studying Rashi, were also
taught to write.

This is the traditional style with which he
began to teach a child Chumash:

"What are you learning now?"

"Chumash."

"What does 'Chumash' mean?"

"Chumash means 'five'."

"What five?"

"Our Holy Torah has five books."

"What are their names?"

"Bereshis [Genesis] is one; Shmos [Exodus] is
two; Vayikra [Leviticus] is three; Bamidbar [Num-
bers] is four; and Devarim [Deuteronomy] is five."

"And which book are you studying now?"

"Vayikra."

"What does 'Vayikra' mean?"

"It means, 'And they were called': God called
Moyshe Rabeynu [Moses our Teacher] and told
him the Law."

He was also a member of the Chevra Misaskim [Actions Society]. Thus, on the eve of Hoshana Rabba [the seventh day of Sukkot, when the fate of every Jew is supposed to be sealed in heaven], the society would meet in the shtibl at tables set with lekach [honey cake], whiskey, and fruit, and say a memorial from an old pinkas [register book] for all the past members of the Action Society for centuries back. In 1926, he took sick going to the funeral of one of the members. After a lengthy illness, he died at the age of 62.

Jews of Long Ago

Pinye der Alter (the old one) jumped out of bed like a young man, poured water over his nails (rite of washing hands), dressed quickly, washed himself from a copper jug and put on a kettle of water to boil—all while saying his morning prayers. A bowl with crumbled old challah was already set on the table. He added a spoonful of rendered goose-fat and a bit of salt, and poured hot water over it from the tea-kettle. The dry challah swelled up from the hot water, reaching the brim of the bowl.

Pinye sat down at the table and began to work on the bowl, till he reached the bottom. He then proceeded to empty the remnants of "yesterday's" cholent from the pot. He had no difficulty in chewing the dried up kugl [potato pudding] from the burned pot, for his teeth were very strong.

He was called "der alter" because he was nearly 90 years old. He would laugh at the 60-year old *tzutzikes* (little darlings) who pampered and doctored themselves constantly. Not only did he have all his teeth, but he also walked straight. In truth, his beard was half-gray, but his senses were younger than he was.

Even on the coldest days, Pinye would start out for the neighboring village on foot to repair the peasants' fur jackets—on foot, upon my word, a sack on his back, a stick in his hand, and off he went, on his way!

Pinye knew his territory very well. He had been dealing with the village gentiles for more than 50 years. They loved him for his witty tales and for his honest dealings. He had definite places where he could have a night's lodging and then continue on his itinerary. That was his way

of life, day in and day out—for all of 50 years. Friday eve and the Sabbath was the time of peace of soul and of saving up a bit of spirituality for his whole prosaic week among the gentiles.

Such were the Jews of the past generations.

Avrom Shmilyukes

A very old factory was situated in a private house on Kusnishtcher Street, across from Moyshe Konyuch's house, which stood next to Abba Klig's. This was the small factory of Avrom Shmilyukes, who manufactured handles for whips.

A person who entered the big front room would immediately see wooden handles lined up along a wall. Pliable and of different widths on the bottom, they tapered toward the top, the tip of which had a carved little head for tying a piece of rope to make it a whip. Avrom produced the handles in the second room, which had all kinds of bottles and brushes and dishes with all kinds of colors to paint these whip-handles.

The Shmilyukes' oven was so big that half of Kusnishtcher Street used to put up their pots of cholent there for the Sabbath. The long *prizbe*, a sort of seating arrangement (like a bench), extended along two walls. Sand was heaped up and enclosed by five or six wooden boards. The top was covered with sun-dried sheets of clay, forming a sort of bench. The prizbe served as a seat for the women. After their Sabbath nap, they sat there and talked about everything in the world, until it was time to say "God of Avrom" [a prayer at the departure of the Sabbath].

Avrom's clothes always reeked of paint and turpentine, and his nails were ever lacquered from working on the whip-handles.

When I left my hometown, Avrom was no more. I do not know what became of his family.

Binyomen Etyes

For a few years, the house of Binyomen Etyes was a sort of institution in our shtetl.

Theirs was a large family and many of them lived in the same house, doing together many different kinds of business. But the biggest business was the *tshechralnye*, a machine for carding sheep's wool, making yarn for spinning from the soft wool sheared from sheep. The yarn was used by peasants to weave cloth and make their own clothing.

The machine stood in the lower room. A horse was harnessed to a shaft in a stable next door. It moved around in a circle, rotating the machine. That is how the factory operated.

Next to the house a big place was reserved for the peasants' wagons. Right after the High Holy Days, this area was filled with wagons and with horses freed from their harnesses. The front room had big tables and long benches. The peasants and their wives would be seated around these tables, waiting their turn while making a meal out of slabs of black bread with lard and washing them down with vodka.

Some of the peasants would cross the street to drop in on Chayke and drink tea. Chayke the *tshaynitshke* [tea lady] would ladle out hot water from a kettle and "put out the flame" in the stomachs of the peasants, caused by eating bread and lard.

The hubbub of peasants and machines lasted from Sunday to Friday. Friday afternoon Avrom Etyes' house took on a different face. The floor was covered with yellow sand. The tables were scrubbed and covered with snow-white table-cloths. Candles were lit and the kerosene-lamps burned brightly through their clean washed glass chimneys.

Here, Binyomen held his Sabbath minyan, where most of the surrounding neighbors came to daven [pray] on the Sabbath: Sholem and Yankef Cohen with their sons, Abba Klig, Avrom Shmilyukes, Shimshen-Zalmen Yankef's, Moyshe-Notl Gortenshteyn, the Kirnesees, Pinye-Hersh, Chaye Dobes, etc.

Elye Horodler

My uncle was called Elye Horodler, because his wife Paye was originally from the shtetl Horodle, near the Bug River. He knew no other kind of life than the one in which, being through with slaving in his bakery, he would go to the Stepenyer shtibl to pray and to study the sacred books. No weather ever prevented his going there. He was a quiet man, never making a racket, never taking part in social activities.

My Aunt Paye always found time for two things: to help the poor for the Sabbath and to entertain company.

Later on their son Yankl Lerner introduced a new way of making a living. He built himself a house on the land occupied by the garden. There he built a tanning plant. Huge tanks were buried in the earth, with rims slightly above the ground. Hides were soaked in these tanks in a liquid of lime and oak-bark, and workers would stir the hides with long steel tongs. The thick skins were dyed brown, to be later formed into soles for shoes. The thinner calf skins were dyed black. The thicker hides were called *yuchtn* and were used to make boots. The still thinner pieces were used for odds and ends.

Merchants came from Lublin, Chelm and and other cities to buy the leather. Yankl and his brother Dovid (z"l) would take their wares by horse and wagon to Hrubyeshov and Ludmir. The trade would have brought in a fine income, but the Polish regime saw to it that little was left, barely enough to keep mouths filled. The rest was taken by them in taxes.

Yankef-Leyzer Chesner

Early before dawn Jews ran to pray in the first minyan. One of the earliest to arrive was Yankef-Leyzer, a haberdasher.

Like all pious Jews, Yankef-Leyzer first of all ran to render unto God his morning prayer and then he would sit down to study a page of Gemara (commentaries on the Mishnah).

All his life Yankef-Leyzer wore a long coat like the other Chasidim. It is taken for granted that he had a long beard and peyes [sidelocks], but his were somehow different from those of the other Libivner Jews.

His beard began together with the peyes so there was no distinct borderline between the beard and the peyes, only a forehead and a pair of eyes that peeped out from the forest of hair.

Sedate as he was while at prayer, in his store Yankef-Leyzer was equally as distraught, for his mind was always on his studies. He was more immersed in the passage of the Gemara he had read that day than in any item in his store. This is why he ran around in the store as if in a daze when a customer came in to buy something. His oldest son, Asher, would always come to his aid and find the merchandise.

After Asher got married he opened up a similar store. The son's store was as disordered as his father's. Boxes were in the way everywhere, and buttons lay all over the floor as he ran from one corner of the store to the other. If his wife was not in the store, customers would go to Meyertze Ludmirer or Itche Melnitzer on the other side of the marketplace.

This is a small picture of a father and son and not to laugh at, God forbid. Many Jews in other towns and in other lines of business used to be like that. Gifted merchants, brilliant minds, but preoccupied with God more than with business.

Avrom Buzis

Avrom Buzis was a *tratsh* [wood cutter]. He cut boards from round logs, hard work for a Jew. The work was done mostly in the summer. In the winter, Avrom would cut oak-bark at my father's (may he rest in peace) place.

My father dealt in wood for heating homes. He also sold oak-bark to the tanners who used it to tan leather.

It took a whole winter to cut the bark, but in the summertime the bark peeled off more easily from the oaks in the woods. The season began in the spring, between Pesach and Shavuot. The bark was dried in the sun and then stored in stables built especially for that purpose.

A big, heavy machine stood on the stable's cement floor. It had a huge wheel made of wood, which was suspended from a steel axle that rested on wooden supports. Attached to the axle were two toothed knives, like a saw. The bark was put piecemeal under the knives of the machine and the cut bark fell into a sack that hung underneath.

Avrom Buzis was a middle-aged Jew, with broad shoulders and a short blond beard. His short fur-jacket was girt with a rope. He wore quilted pants and tall boots, which were too big for him, to leave room for stuffing in more rags [*onetses*] to wrap his feet.

Avrom would get up at dawn. After praying with the first minyan, he would come to work for us.

First of all, he would snatch something to eat. He boiled a pot of water, broke into it small pieces of the Sabbath challah, which was too dry for easy cutting, and put it into a big earthenware bowl together with a piece of beef fat and a handful of salt. When steam came up from the bowl, he would sit down at the table in a relaxed manner and begin to work over the bowl, blowing and eating, eating and sweating. When the bowl was empty, he would light a bit of machorke [tobacco, a hand-rolled cigarette] and after resting, he would come into the shop to work. This was his first meal of the day.

He was a fast worker. An electric motor could not beat the speed with which he turned the handle of the wheel.

His daughter brought him his midday meal. This second meal consisted of millet with honey, a dish of sour milk, and half a loaf of bread. Another "menu" for the second meal was a pot of potatoes and red borsht made of beets. Usually after a meal, Avrom blessed the food, thanking God for giving him sustenance.

After his meal, he went back to the wheel, working until it got dark. Yes, those Jews of old were healthy Jews!

Yoneh Ladinyer

Five days a week Yoneh was busy in his flour mill. Not far from the mill there stood a big house where his whole family lived, including the sons and the daughters and their families.

He was called Yoneh Ladinyer because he came from the village of Ladinye. His real name was Mel, and mel [flour] did cover his entire face, his hands, and all his clothes.

Only on two days of the week, on the Sabbath and on Sunday, did he wear different clothes. We could then see a bit of his face, and his clothes were a bit darker than during the week.

Yoneh Ladinyer was a simple Jew. But he had picked as his sons-in-law men who were not so simple! His oldest son-in-law, Hershele Lifshitz, was a Jew who knew how to study the sacred books. I used to meet him at the home of the Stepenyer rebbe. He would talk and study the books with the rebbe's son, R. Moyshele, or with Itche Meyer Shaye Leibushes.

They called him Hershele because he was short. He had such a long beard that it did not fit his short stature: it looked as if he had stolen it from another Jew twice as tall as he. Besides being a scholar, he was also a merchant, as well as a wit.

Yoneh's second son-in-law was Moyshe Klerer. From time to time I would meet him also in the rebbe's home. Moyshe Klerer was an intelligent young man. He belonged to the Revisionist party, going to several towns as an emissary of the party. He was a fine orator who could sway his audiences.

Chaye-Beyle, Di Skiberin

She got her nickname of Skiberin from the fact that she came from Skib, a neighboring village. She had a "profession": she could cast a spell against an evil eye, foretell the future by pouring wax, or "burn" a skin inflammation. She came into our town almost every day, covering the itinerary from Skib to Libivne on foot; not going straight but passing through fields and gardens in a sort of short cut.

She was tall and lanky like a bean pole and carried a little bundle on her shoulders. The bundle had a piece of hard wax and a bunch of flax. She would invoke a "good eye" by a spell, but when someone had an inflamation, she would apply "medication."

If someone had an abscess on his face, she would take out the bunch of flax, lay it out in little rolls on a chair, cover the face of the ill person with a bed sheet, and then set fire to the flax. If the dry flax crackled loudly, it meant that there was a *royz* [vesicular skin inflamation—erisipelas]. And since flax always crackles loudly when burned, the swelling was always pronounced to be a case of *royz*. If the sick person continued to be in great pain after her ministration, then a greater doctor than Chaye-Beyle would be called in.

She followed the same procedure with pouring wax. If someone was frightened in the middle of the night when going out into the narrow alley, then Chaye-Beyle melted the wax and poured it into a pan of cold water, the wax forming various shapes. These figures told her the cause of the fright!

Chaye-Beyle had great faith in her actions, and the majority of the townspeople had faith in her ministrations.

Yoel Krutsh

Though his name was Gurtenshteyn, people called him by his nickname "Krutsh," which in Ukrainian means "a little bit crazy." He was a merchant who dealt with the peasants at the city gates. His father, Shaye Krutsh, used to travel through the villages all week long, bartering household items for rags, which he then sold either to Mendl Eizenberg or to Abba Klig. Here the rags were sorted out, packed, and sent on to paper factories. He would leave early Sunday morning and come back on Friday. A person of that profession was nicknamed in the shetl a *shmateleinik.*

We loved Yoel for his mischievous tricks and ideas; for playing a dirty trick on someone, or jesting like the proverbial Motke Chabbad. When buying eggs from a peasant, man or woman, he would count out the eggs into their laps and then go away as if to bring them money—and then they would never see him again!

If he came to buy a hen from a peasant and the bird's legs were tied, he would untie the legs and let the bird loose, using the excuse that since Jews were not allowed to eat a lame bird, he had to see that it was not lame!

Yoel's house was in a gentile neighborhood. Usually the gentiles had gardens and grass grew around their houses. When the grass began to grow in the spring, the owners expected to have a lot of hay by letting the grass grow for another month. At times, when the owner of the house was away, Yoel would hire a farmer to cut the grass. After the peasant had cut the grass, he would look for the man who had hired him to do the work and Yoel would not be found anywhere!

Such were the tricks that Yoel would play and the people would laugh.

He survived by running and hiding until January 1944, when a band of Polish Home Army "freedom fighters" killed him and 11 other Jews: the very last Jews of Luboml, the Sojbel family among them. (Only one child, Nathan Sobel, survived.)

Der Kirzhner (the Hatmaker)

He was called Shmulikl Kirzhner because of his trade. He was the shortest Jew in our town. He made sheepskin winter hats called *kutshmes* and summer caps with peaks. He himself wore a peaked kutshme, like a Don cossack!

Shmulikl usually ran. I do not remember ever having seen him walk slowly.

He always had a cane, though he did not lean on it. One end of the cane had a sculpted handle in the shape of a ladies' large button. He only used his cane when he went to the market during a fair. He would stick a kutshme on the tip of his cane and twirl it like a carousel, while yelling at the top of his voice for people to buy his kutshmes. He did this like the best actor and attracted the peasants and sold his goods.

When he was through, the market was empty. He was the last one to leave, and as he pushed his trunk of goods home, children helped him.

After a hard day of selling, he did not rest, but went at once to the synagogue to say the evening prayer or to tell a new story; and then ran to a second house of God, to do another "service," and to squeeze in a Kaddish [prayer of mourning].

When did he ever rest? At night he sewed his caps; in the daytime he was busy selling them. And at midnight he would wake up Jews to go and read the Psalms!

Efrayim Gelbord

It is impossible to talk about the tragic death of Efrayim Gelbord without first discussing the situation created for the Jews of Poland after Hitler's rise to power in Germany. As Hitler raged against the Jews in Germany, followers of the anti-Semitic National Democratic Party raised their heads in Poland, and the persecution of the Jews became more intense. There were also the little pogroms in Przytyk and elsewhere. Beatings of Jews became a daily occurrence; also picketing Jewish businesses with the slogan, "Poles, buy from Poles!" began to occur more and more often in the big cities of Poland.

Despite the fact that the Ukrainian anti-Semites were themselves oppressed by the Poles, they too found that now was the time to get even with the Jews, and rumors began to reach us about hooligans attacking defenseless Jews.

On that tragic Friday eve, a few shoemaker-hooligans, who were drunk and coming from the tavern, decided to have a little fun. At the beginning of Chelm Street, where the wooden stores stood, they began to throw boxes with goods that were on display in front of the stores; these stores were not far from the iron stores of the Lerners and Gelbords.

When Efrayim Gelbord heard the screams of the attacked storekeepers, he ran out to protect the Jews and their wares. During the fight someone stuck a knife into him, fatally wounding him, and instantly the gang vanished. With his last strength Efrayim managed to get into a store and there he fell dead on the threshold.

Thus Efrayim Gelbord fell while protecting Jewish honor. May his memory be blessed.

AVROM BLUSHTEYN
By Yisroel Garmi

Avromele Blushteyn was one of the few followers of the Jewish enlightenment among the Jews from neighboring villages who came to reside in Luboml and contributed considerably to the spread of enlightenment among the youth and to the many different cultural activities in our town.

Among these "immigrants" was Isrulik Helfant from the village of Rakovitz, who organized and directed a drama group that put on a play, *Hertsele and the Aristocrat*, which was well received by our community. Another man, Buzia Steinberg from the village of Horodno, gave private lessons in Russian on a very high level. Avrom Blushteyn, originally from the village of Pervis [on the Bug River, around 11 miles from Luboml) moved to our town in 1918 when he was in his late twenties. He lived on our street, not far from our house. After a while his neighbors got used to hearing the sweet sound of the violin that drifted out of his bedroom window.

It was not long before I became a permanent guest in his room. I would sing folk songs to him and he would catch on quickly and play them on his violin. In those days Hershl Chasid produced a play that was written by Goldfaden called *Bar Kochba*. Avrom participated in the play as the head guard of the walls of Jerusalem during Roman rule. As I remember it, Avrom sang a song in the play that was written for the occasion:

(solo by Avrom):
The righteous God
Looks from there upon us

Don't you sleep, guardsmen,
Guard the place well

(sung by the soldiers in the choir):
We hear you, we hear you
We hear you well —
Fall asleep
We will not!

After a while Avrom produced for the stage a play called *Scattered and Dispersed*, a story by Sholem Aleichem. Avrom played the part of Meyer Tchulent, the hero of the play, and performed with incredible talent.

Avrom supported himself through his photography studio, which had a good reputation in the area. Avrom was also very talented in Hebrew calligraphy. The pictures shown here are proof of that talent.

Avrom Blushteyn married a woman from our town whose name was Faya Sfard. In 1930, he moved to Montevideo, Uruguay. He had two sons, Sela Emanuel, a painter, and Saul Blushteyn, a draftsman-photographer. Both his sons moved from Uruguay to Israel and built their homes there.

In 1963, Avrom Blushteyn visited Israel in order to attend the opening of a showing of his son's paintings in Haifa. There he was reunited with many of his friends from Luboml.

Avrom Blushteyn died at a ripe old age in Montevideo. His daughter, Hannah, and his wife, Faya, continue to live there. May his memory be blessed.

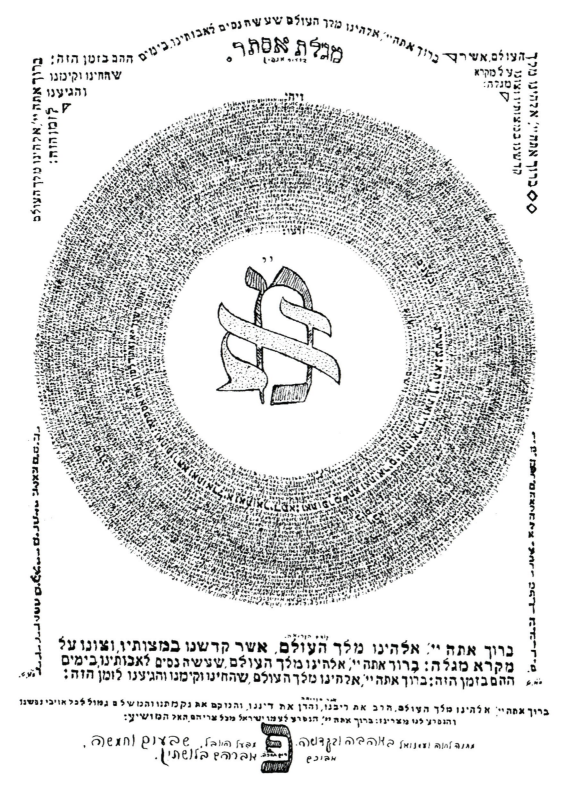

The scroll of Esther

The scroll of Esther, a variation

Various official (postal and other) cancellation stamps from Luboml.

IN MEMORY OF MY FATHER
By Victor Lichtmacher

In his young years, my father, Avrom Lichtmacher, spent most of his time studying and praying in the Radziner Synagogue. Ambitious and educated, after marrying and beginning a family he became the manager of a factory where alcohol was produced. He held the position of head engineer.

A capable man who loved people and was respected by everyone who knew him, he was elected to the town council as *ratman* [councilman] in magistrate and devoted much time to public service.

My father had a reputation in our town as a wise and good man, from whom you could get advice whether about personal or public matters. Many people came to him to solve a dispute. For example, there were heirs who were unable to divide an inheritance from their parents. He performed this service with an open mind.

Every year, my father visited the Radziner rebbe in the town of Radzin. When Rabbi Shlomele, the last Radziner rebbe, came to our town, he stayed in our home. All the Radziner Chasidim from the surrounding towns visited Rabbi Shlomele in our house.

This was often where meetings about public affairs were held—for example, the election of new members to the Jewish community (kehila) or to discuss the nomination of a candidate as the new chief rabbi.

Many events took place in our house. I remember, during one of the Radziner rebbe's visits to our home, my father, with the help of other religious Jews from our town, organized the Agudas Israel party. My father was elected president of this party.

He was also one of the organizers of Yeshiva Beth-Joseph, which I attended, and the Beth-Jacob School for Girls, where my dear sisters studied.

Although providing for a large family (of ten), he still found time to be involved in public affairs. He lived that way until World War II began.

After the Russian army entered our town, in order to make a living, my father organized a cooperative of former merchants. He was elected chairman of the cooperative and held that position until Germany occupied our town. My younger brother Reuven and I were drafted into the Russian army, therefore we survived (we both live in the United States).

Immediately after the war, I returned to Luboml in search of my family. The survivors told me that my father and 30 other leading, honorable Jews of Luboml had been taken to the Jewish cemetery and executed. My father escaped from there, although it is not known how he survived until the remaining Jews in our town were killed by the Germans and their collaborators.

My father died along with my mother Malke, my dear sisters Udis, Chaike, Soreh, Perl, and Rochl with her husband and son, my brother-in-law Leyzer with their two children, and the remainder of my relatives.

I will never forget them and always mourn their loss.

Editor's note: This article is an addition to the English translation and did not appear in the original *Yizkor Book of Luboml*.

SOCIAL, CULTURAL, AND EDUCATIONAL ACTIVITIES

OUTSIDE INFLUENCES ON LOCAL YOUTH GROUPS AND ON CULTURAL AND ZIONIST ACTIVITIES

By Yisroel Garmi

The awakening of our youth to cultural and Zionist activities must be attributed, at least in part, to the young people who came to stay from time to time in Luboml. Thanks to the influence and the activities of these young guests, the will to organize and initiate athletic, cultural and Zionist activities was awakened in the youth of Luboml.

The Group from Lutsk, Rovno and Rozhishch

The first group arrived in our town in the summer of 1916. There were about ten young men around the ages of 22 to 25. They arrived from the towns of Rovno, Lutsk and Rozhishch. At the head of the group was an adult named Binyomen Farshtey, whom I met personally several years later when I visited his home in Lutsk. Many of the young men who came to our town stayed at the home of Berl Ginzburg, which was close to the home of the Reiz family. Most of them spoke Russian; however, occasionally some German was heard.

A short time later, a small sign was posted above the entrance to the Ginzburg home. The sign read in German: "Office of the Civilian Militia." The astonishment in town grew even more when these young men attached wide armbands to their sleeves as insignia of the positions they now filled on behalf of the authorities.

From this point on we became used to seeing them every day as they patrolled the streets and enforced sanitary ordinances decreed by the occupying Austrians in the region and in our town. They insisted that a place be kept clean at all times and that order was kept. One of the rules imposed, for example, was a curfew. After nine o'clock at night, no one was allowed to travel out of town without a special permit. Also, people were fined or imprisoned for every small infrac-

tion concerning the cleanliness of our town.

Above all, what affected us most was the fact that many citizens were forced into the army against their will, or were kidnapped and forced to do menial chores for the army. For example: they were made to pave new roads, cut down trees in the forest, fix railroad tracks, and dig ditches on the front line. This civilian militia, consisting of the aforementioned young men, came under the control of the town's commissar. His name was Kosever and he was known to hate Jews.

It was a great mystery in our eyes that young, educated, Jewish men such as these would serve the conquering army and treat the citizens of our town in such a rough way. Only after a considerable amount of time, when the conqueror's rule slackened a bit and the pressure on Luboml's citizens relaxed, did the youth of our town begin to connect somewhat with the members of the militia. However, the young militia members first became close to some of the more educated young women of our town.

Very slowly the two groups began to cooperate on certain projects and activities, such as working together in the "charity [soup] kitchen" that was opened by the Joint to serve the basic needs of the poor, and collaborating in creating sports facilities for youth, which functioned several times a week.

The gym equipment was installed by the young militia members in the large lot located near the Talmud Torah. In that building lessons were given in Graetz's *History of the Jews* by Binyomen Farshtey. He presented these passages and explained them in a pleasant and most fascinating manner. The gymnastics course de-

Gymnasts from the civilian militia during the Austrian-German rule, 1916–17, under the instruction of the group from Lutsk and Rozhishch.

veloped and expanded until we, the 14- and 15-year olds, began to participate in the activities. We developed our strength and skills by climbing the tall, smooth poles, by scaling walls and different sorts of obstacles, and by doing other sorts of exercises. Our admiration for Binyomen Farshtey, our teacher and mentor (even where athletic activities were concerned), was great and immeasurable.

A number of men from the militia group married some of the more educated women of our town, and two brothers, Yechiel and Becki Rosenfeld, decided to remain in Luboml and open a pharmacy. When Austrian rule came to an end, the group of young men separated and most returned to their hometowns.

Binyomen Farshtey continued to visit our town. The day when we celebrated the Balfour Declaration, he came to Luboml and delivered a stirring speech in Hebrew, at the Great Synagogue, to the entire town. Binyomen left a strong impression upon the youth of Luboml.

The Group from Chelm and Motek Ivri

During the years 1918 and 1919, at the start of Polish rule, a group of young men arrived from Chelm. They were around the age of conscription. This group stayed in the home of R. Yeshayahu Peltz. This group consisted of about ten young men, most of whom were educated.

A member of this group was Michel'e Rubaizen. These men, who apparently belonged to the [socialist] Bund, began cultural activities in Luboml. This newfound cultural manifestation was expressed through the distribution of literature displaying the spirit of the Bund. They also organized literary and musical gatherings at which they sang songs by Y. L. Peretz, A. Reizin, D. Einhorn and others.

These young men also attempted to raise the consciousness of Luboml youth concerning the class struggle. The opportunity to do so presented itself at the funeral of Boruch Tshesner (z"l), the victim of an explosion in a spirits distillery.

At the funeral, the group carried signs of protest. They believed blue collar workers were being taken advantage of because of their status in society and that the bourgeoisie was responsible for this injustice. At the head of the group of protestors was a sign demanding that all the workers of the world unite. By the open grave of Boruch Tshesner, a few individuals delivered

A shekel from 1921 belonging to A.N. Blumen (later Tchelet).

propagandistic speeches in the same vein, and the ceremony concluded with the singing of the "International."

Apart from this group, though he too was from Chelm, was a student who resided in our town at that time by the name of Mordche (or Motek) Ivri. His student cap was from the University of Warsaw and it drew our attention. He had a pleasant demeanor and a kind face with delicate features. All our town's youth were drawn to this young man.

One day he asked me and my friend, B. Veyner (z"l), if we could organize a meeting of some of Luboml's youth. We were very excited and wanted to please him. After a few days we got a group of ten boys our age assembled in his room. He told us all about an organization called HaShomer HaTsair that had recently been founded in Congress Poland and Galicia, and that also had begun to organize in our area of Volhynia (the so-called Kressy), as well as in Latvia and Lithuania. He also told us about the goals of this new organization: to educate boys to be scouts, to teach Hebrew and to encourage immigration to Eretz Yisroel.

The young man advised us to join this organization and promised us that he was willing and ready to counsel us as long as he remained in our town. Of course, we were very excited to hear this suggestion and after a few days we called for a meeting of our town's youth. At this meeting we announced the founding of a branch of HaShomer HaTsair in Luboml.

Under the enthusiastic and spontaneous instruction of Motek Ivri, who was our teacher and mentor and who helped us take our first steps toward reaching our goal, the organization developed and earned a respectable role educating Luboml youth about Zionism and Eretz Yisroel.

Young activists of Luboml alongside members of militia from Lutsk, Rozhishch, and Rovno, celebrating event in San Remo.

THE BELLS OF REDEMPTION
By Nathan Tchelet (Blumen)

The older generation of Jews in Luboml, together with the rest of the Jews of the diaspora, looked forward to the coming of the Messiah and awaited the end of days. The Jews of the diaspora, as well as the Luboml Jews, rejoiced at the first tidings of the redemption of Jews after the end of the First World War.

The event occurred in April of 1920, when it was decided in San Remo to deliver the mandate over Palestine to Great Britain. Jews all over the world rejoiced. Newspapers from Warsaw printed special editions in order to emphasize the significance of this event.

The joy in the city was overwhelming. In the central synagogue there was a festive gathering to celebrate this great event. Children who were taught in cheders were released from their studies. Students of the Talmud Torah and all Luboml youth marched to the central synagogue, which was full from one end to the other.

For the first time, the town's youth saw the national flag waving freely in the air. Prayers of celebration were said on the occasion of the establishment of a national homeland in Eretz Yisroel. Enthusiastic speeches were given. These speeches were full of fervor and expressed an undying loyalty to the reborn Zion. The man who headed the civilian militia during the period of the Austrian conquest, Binyomen Farshtey from Lutsk (z"l), gave a speech in Hebrew. This was the first time the youth of the town heard an enthusiastic speech in the Hebrew language, and it excited the audience greatly.

Women gladly parted with their jewelry in order to contribute toward the building of Eretz Yisroel. As a matter of fact, all the citizens contributed what they could. With tears of joy in their eyes they brought all their donations to the special fund-raising committee. The happiness in our town was overwhelming.

The Zionist organizations and youth movements worked energetically. Also, a part of our town's youth began to prepare for aliyah. At the start of 1921, the first two pioneers from Luboml left for Eretz Yisroel. These two individuals were Mordche Grimatlicht and Tsvi Fuks (z"l).

In 1923, following in the footsteps of these two men, the first aliyah of pioneers from Luboml began and did not cease until World War II.

EDUCATION AND CULTURE IN LUBOML
1916–1928
By Nechome Blei (Wiener)

Obtaining a proper education in our town was a terrible problem from time immemorial. My older sister Tema fought very hard in order to obtain an education. It was especially difficult during the First World War, when the conquering forces that ruled in our town were constantly changing.

For several years the Austrian army ruled our town. This period was one of relative peace, and therefore the children were offered the opportunity to study for a while. At that time, two schools were established in Luboml by the military authorities. One school was geared only toward the gentile community of Luboml, and all classes there were taught in Ukrainian. In the other school, all the classes were taught in German.

The Ukrainian school, in which I studied for four years consecutively, was directed by two teachers of Ukrainian descent; their names were Asia and Michaska. They were young women of extremely mediocre education. Despite this, these women were pleasant, enthusiastic and very musical. They were also very patriotic toward the Ukraine and sang songs of longing for their homeland.

At the encouragement of these two teachers, we Jewish children also sang these songs with feeling. After a while, however, the Jewish students left this school because of the anti-Semitic atmosphere among the Ukrainian students and began to attend the German school, where the students were all Jews. I was the only Jew who continued my studies at the Ukrainian school, for reasons beyond my control. Only after I had finished the Ukrainian school with honors did I enter the German school in order to complete my studies.

Teachers from the Jewish-Polish public school at a reception. Among them are Jewish teachers Y. Kessler, Greif, Y. Shapiro, Elbling, and Roza Goldberg.

207

Members of Zionist Youth (HaNoar HaTsioni) and Jewish National Fund activists on a field trip,
Lag BaOmer, 1929.

The teachers in the German school were Yaina Henta Kesler and Giza. Giza got married and left town after a while, but Yaina remained and continued to teach the town's children in the Polish public school established later.

When the war was over and the Austrian army left our town, the youth of Luboml once again faced a problem. All that they had learned in the Ukrainian and German languages now had to give way to Polish. The children had to learn a strange language and a different culture. While adults suffered as a result, the change was very difficult for Luboml youth as well.

At that time, Zionist and Hebrew cultural activities got under way in town. Those among us who were especially talented soon became the leaders of the group that was forming. The ones who began these activities were, to the best of my knowledge, Israel Grimatlicht (Garmi), my brother Bebik, may he rest in peace, Zalman Fisher, Elye Frechter, and Nathan Blumen-Tchelet. It was not long before these few were joined by many others,

and all together they began public service work aimed at Eretz Yisroel.

A movement was formed that consisted of the best, most motivated and talented youth in town. On their own, these youths organized lectures and plays; they founded a library and encouraged social and cultural events in town. From time to time a representative or lecturer was sent by the central office of the movement. The cultural activities increased and the plays were received positively by the Jewish community. From the town of Chelm theatrical directors came to guide these productions.

At the same time they began to organize a vehicle for Hebrew education in town. The first teachers were brought from out of town. Among them were Asher Budman (who is also my brother-in-law), Yakov Dubelman, and Avrom Palevsky. As in the past, the Luboml youth became pioneers and made aliyah to Eretz Yisroel a process that continued until World War II.

IMPORTANT CULTURAL ACTIVITIES
By Yechezkiel Kahn

After World War I (1914–1918), Libivne, like many other towns and shtetlech, was left shaken by the bloody events through which it had passed. It also suffered from the constant clashes between the Poles and Bolsheviks after the war. These events affected not only the economic life in the town, but also Jewish cultural activities.

It was at that time that the Zionist youth organization, HaShomer HaTsair, attempted to establish a Hebrew school. With the promise of support from other Zionist activists, such as Abba Klig, Tsvi Erlich, Moyshe Sfard, the Grimatlicht brothers, Yosef Katz, Dovid Veyner, etc., the group decided to invite a Hebrew teacher, Asher Budman from Trisk (recommended to us by Tsvi Erlich). Budman was the teacher of Novgorod-Volinsk for four years, and the principal of that school was the noted pedagogue Y. Y. Wohl.

Asher Budman came to Libivne in October, 1919. The Talmud Torah of Libivne also was looking for a Hebrew teacher at the same time. And so, after he gave a sample lesson for children before a group of prominent Jews, it was decided to hire Budman for the position.

The Hebrew teacher actually made a bigger impression on the Polish school inspector than on the group of prominent Jews from our town, since he gave his Hebrew lessons in the local Polish-language public school. There were two other Jewish teachers at the local school: Yene Kessler and Gize Tchudnovsky.

It was at that same time that two Jews came to Libivne from Ludmir. They called together a meeting in the Bet HaMidrash, at which they declared that American Jews had established a relief organization, called the Joint, in order to help the Jews of East Europe, and that they had come to establish a Joint Committee in Libivne as well.

The Joint would send collected funds to this committee, which was to be responsible for all activities involving the distribution of funds to needy Jews and to institutions. Moyshe Reyzman was elected chairman of the Joint committee, which was called the Ezra committee, and Budman, secretary. Later, Shloyme Baran was elected as paid secretary of the committee, but Budman in fact continued to be the mainstay of the organization.

Children of the Hebrew school on an outing with their teachers, Palevsky, Dubelman, and Shoychat.

209

In 1919, a conference of all representatives from the Joint committees in Volhynia was called in Rovno, and Asher Budman went as a delegate from Libivne. At first, two secretaries were elected for the conference—one for Polish and one for Yiddish. But, bowing to the demands of the teachers and activists of the Rovno Tarbut school, Charkovsky, Harif, Rozenhak, and others, the conference elected Budman as secretary for Hebrew.

When Budman's Hebrew minutes proved to be the best and most correct ones, he was elected as member of the regional committee of the Joint.

The Joint Committee of Libivne cared for Jewish orphans left by pogroms. These children had remained homeless and scattered around the town and its environs. Most of them were distributed among Jewish families, with the Joint paying for their upkeep by a monthly stipend.

These Joint funds were also used to establish an ambulance corps at the beginning of 1920. It was staffed by Dr. Rosenshteyn and nurses Lize Pomerants and Nechome Friedman. The ambulance service covered emergencies not only for the Jews but also for the non-Jewish residents of the town.

In 1920, the Hebrew Tarbut school was established in Libivne. Its student body consisted of the 60–70 orphans supported by the Joint funds. The principal was Budman, who also worked with two teachers, Palevsky and Shoychat. Later, additional teachers were added to the staff: Dubelman, the brother of the Jewish journalist A. Y. Dubelman, and Levin. At first the Tarbut school was spread through several buildings. But later the four classes were housed under one roof, and it greatly improved the level of education.

In 1921, a chapter of the Tzeire Tzion party

The Orphan Committee: *top row*: M. Esterzon, Sh. Bokser, M. Grimatlicht, Z. Barnboym. M. Oselka, G. Zilberblech; *bottom row*: M. Privner, Sh. Pregel, A. Sheintop, D. Berger, A. L. Blumen, and A. Reznick.

was founded in Libivne through the initiative of Asher Budman, Meyer Natanzon, Yosef Samet, Elke Eizenberg, etc. It was started with 50 members. It became active especially in the cultural field. Warsaw would send representatives who made speeches and strengthened the party. Y. B. Malkhin, Mereminsky, Koltun, etc., were among these.

A second Yiddish library was also established, in addition to the first Yiddish and Hebrew library that had been organized by HaShomer HaTsair.

They collected Yiddish books from the homes of Jews and also bought newly published books, using funds that were raised by the library, and especially by the productions staged by the drama section.

The drama section was established by Hershl Chasid and his followers: Yisroel Helfant, Avrom Blushteyn, the Drekslers, etc. The performances based on these books had great meaning for the cultural life of the shtetl.

THE KOTSKER SHTIBL IS OURS!
By Arye Zagagi (Glazer)

The shtibl of the Kotsker Chasidim was for many years outside the purview of the Zionist functionaries and the Jewish National Fund, until it was decided once, at a meeting of the local council of the JNF, to conquer the shtibl.

They gave me the task of carrying out this decision, by dedicating the proceeds from pledges made when men are called to the Torah to the JNF. I fully agreed, perhaps because my father, may he rest in peace, was the Torah reader in the shtibl.

It must be remembered that after the death of the Kotsker rebbe, may he rest in peace, the Kotsker Chasidim were divided among his three sons. One group followed the rebbe of Sokolov, another the rebbe of Lukov and the third group the rebbe of Pulov.

The Sokolov Chasidim consisted mainly of educated and enlightened merchants; the Pulover Chasidim were the fanatics; and the Lukov Chasidim were the ordinary people. There was great diversity among all these Chasidim, even though they all prayed in the same shtibl. They even ate the third Sabbath meal (*se'udah shlishit*)

Banquet in honor of the Zagagi (Glazer) family on the occasion of their departure for Eretz Yisroel in 1926.

212

at separate tables—to the right of the ark, the table of the Sokolov Chasidim; to the left, the Pulover Chasidim; and on the far (western) end, near the entrance of the shtibl and the stove, the table of the Chasidim of Lukov. It often happened that when the Sokolov chasidim were singing *zmiros*, the Pulover Chasidim were reviewing the teachings of their rebbe.

It was under these conditions that we came, as representative of the JNF, to take over the shtibl. We were able to accomplish this with the help of the gabbai R. Zeynvel Shliva and with my father's support after the fact—though at the beginning he asked me to cancel the plan.

R. Zeynvel owned a large textile factory and was one of the most enlightened people of that shtibl. My father, R. Eliyohu Yisroel, of blessed memory, was the reader and the one who sounded the shofar in the Kotsker shtibl and in the shtibl of the Chevra Kadisha (burial society). He was well-loved in the community because he was a humble peacemaker.

One Friday evening, after the service, we spoke with R. Zeynvel, and after considerable explanations on our part he agreed that all the pledges to be made the following day during the reading of the Torah would be donated to the JNF. As for my father the Torah reader, we were certain of his consent, for his home was always a meeting place for all the emissaries from the yeshivot in the Holy Land and he always supported everything connected with Eretz Yisroel.

We were afraid that the fanatical Pulover Chasidim would cause disturbances, and so we left some of our people in the shtibl that night to listen to their conversations. And, sure enough, they learned of our plans and prepared to oppose us.

The central figure among the Pulover Chasidim was R. Dovid Veytsfrucht, of blessed memory, known as R. Dovid Birgermeister, from the time when he was mayor of the city during the Austrian occupation in World War I. He was an outstanding personality in every respect. He was learned. He was pious, forceful, and physically strong, as well. He was the one who said on that Friday evening after the worshippers left the shtibl, "This thing will never pass! Heretics will never rule in our shtibl." They decided that during the Torah reading they would stand next to the lectern and prevent the JNF people from approaching the platform.

When we learned of this, we made plans for a real conquest and we called up youth from the other synagogues. Already during the first part of the morning prayer each side was starting to move into position. The first was R. Dovid Veytsfrucht, who positioned himself by the lectern, next to the ark. Then I went up and stood on the opposite side of the table. R. Dovid actually started to push me away from the table, but he did not succeed because there was a whole group of youngsters lined up behind me.

The worshippers, who felt the conflict approaching, were moved to action. My father, who always spoke gently, this time raised his voice with these words: "What's going on here? These young people are asking for contributions to the JNF, for a holy purpose, for our Holy Land. What's all the opposition, on the Holy Sabbath, in the midst of the prayers, just before reading the Torah?"

My father's words influenced the crowd tremendously and the followers of Pulov, with R. Dovid their leader, felt they had no support among the worshippers. At least they had to leave the table and we, the young people, jumped to take over their places. Needless to say, all the contributions that Shabbat were for the JNF, and that's how we managed to penetrate the shtibl of Kotsk.

BEITAR IN LUBOML
By Yakov Hetman

Luboml was a Zionist town. Among the youth there was a general feeling and longing for Zion. The adults of the town also longed for Zion, though they did it silently. There were no anti-Zionist organizations in Luboml, and if there were signs of opposition to the movement, it was only because it was a secular movement. In this environment, which was sympathetic to the Zionist cause and in which a great interest was

Yitshak Shapira, teacher of Jewish religion in the Polish school, the first leader of Beitar in Luboml. (The picture was taken in 1929.)

expressed in what was going on in Eretz Yisroel, the anti-Jewish Arab riots that occurred in Palestine in 1929 resulted in a psychological crisis among the youth of our town. They asked if it was possible that even in Eretz Yisroel Jews would be victims of riots and pogroms. "Is it toward this end that we are rebuilding our Jewish homeland?" The answer to this question was obvious. It presented itself in the form of a new Zionist

youth movement called Beitar, "The Trumpeldor Alliance" (Brit Trumpledor) ,whose motto stood for activism and legionism.

Until it was established in Luboml, people read about this movement in the newspaper. Nevertheless, even those who were sympathizers of the movement did not do a thing. They just remained sympathizers. However, the news of the 1929 riots aroused the youth and caused a real revolution. Many of Luboml's youth—those who were organized and those who were not—joined Beitar. Overnight, Beitar became a mass youth movement.

As a young boy, I was the secretary of HeChalutz HaTsair (Young Pioneers), and I remember how all the members of the secretariat decided to join Beitar. Almost all the rest of the HeChalutz members joined us in enlisting in Beitar, with the exception of the adult counselors and a group of educated, well-bred girls. This group of girls served later as the founders of the reestablished HeChalutz HaTsair. They, among others, did not and could not subscribe to the military spirit and drastic disciplinary measures instituted by Beitar.

The founding of Beitar in Luboml began at a rally. This rally left a tremendous impression on the population of Luboml and brought out the special qualities of the new movement. The adult promoters of Beitar invited a branch of the movement, from Hrubyeshov, which was near Lublin, to visit the town. These members appeared in Luboml wearing uniforms and, most importantly, armed with rifles. A brass band marched at the front of the procession.

It is difficult to describe the strong impression that this "Jewish army" made on us. It was not just nice intelligent talk, it was Jewish youth who had military training and were carrying real weapons. These young men knew how to protect the lives of Jews in Israel. They would not allow any more bloodshed like there had been in Hebron. Here before us stood proud Jews who aroused respect even among the gentiles of our town.

At the heels of this procession in the streets of Luboml there gathered a large group of young people, which then became the local branch of Beitar. The life of our town's youth changed, and instead of the selective organization HeChalutz Hatsair there appeared in the streets a youth movement of the common people. In this movement there was a mixture of educated and well-bred youth alongside the working-class youth—including tailors, butchers and so forth, who had until now been drawn to underground leftist movements.

The first leader of Beitar in Luboml was Yitshak Shapira, a teacher of religion in the government-controlled public school. The fact that he was a teacher added prestige to the new movement. Evening classes were organized where Hebrew was taught. Cultural activities were organized and broadened.

I personally initiated and edited (along with Joseph Shtern—today Dr. Joseph Shtern who later left Beitar and returned to HeChalutz Hatsair), a magazine for youth called *Tel Chai*, which was printed using the spirograph method.

It was not long before this new movement became known in town as one that was sympathetic to the public at large. Also, it was accepted by the authorities due to its obvious nationalistic character. The leaders of Beitar were some of the most educated, enlightened youth of our town. Nevertheless, these educated youth were only a thin layer of the organization, for the rest of it consisted of common people—working-class young men.

The fact was that the educated, well-bred youth, when they joined Beitar, gave up on the social and cultural life of their natural milieu, since most well-bred young people continued to concentrate in socialist, pioneer-oriented youth movements. Nevertheless, the educated youth experienced joy and fulfillment from seeing the

Shmuel Zilberberg, second commander of Beitar.

poor youth walk with their heads high, from seeing them endowed with a newfound pride in themselves and their nation. These poor youngsters were proud of their membership in the movement. They studied Hebrew enthusiastically, and they attempted to broaden their cultural horizons.

One who contributed much to the movement was the second leader of Beitar in Luboml, Shmuel Zilberberg. He was an educated man, spoke Hebrew, and was learned not only in the Torah but in general subjects as well.

Shmuel was, for the most part, self-taught. His ungroomed appearance, however, left much to be desired. Nevertheless, although Shmuel's outward appearance was lacking, he was respected for his knowledge and education. He was thought of as a cultured man and did all he could to develop cultural and social activities in town on behalf of Beitar.

During the time in which Shmuel served as the leader of Beitar, a training group for the movement was established. Also while he was in office, arrangements were made for the inauguration of Beitar's flag. This ceremony, however, never occurred, because the flag was stolen. The theft of this flag almost led to some serious conflicts in our town. It is believed that the flag was smuggled to Eretz Yisroel, where it was apparently burned.In Luboml, another simpler flag was prepared overnight. This flag was unveiled as planned.

There was also tension and conflict in Luboml after Arlozorov [a Labor Zionist leader in Tel Aviv] was murdered, when some hotheaded men decided to attack and beat young men wearing Beitar uniforms; but in response, Beitar members only appeared more often in their official uniforms. Among the more active members of Beitar were Israel Kramer, Mendl Lifshitz, Berl Sfard, Yakov Kornfeld, Avrom Kaminer, and Noach Kroyt.

In 1934, I was nominated to be the leader of Luboml's Beitar. This nomination occurred following the visit of Menachem Begin, who was at the time the head of the Beitar leadership. At this time I had just completed my matriculation examinations, and because there were not many young men in Luboml who had a formal Polish education, I maintained good relations with the Polish authorities. Also, among the Jews I was known and respected as one of the young people who had studied at the shtibls of the Rizhin and Kotsk Chasidim.

It is for these credentials that I was chosen to lead Luboml's division of Beitar. I was the only Jew chosen as a member of a municipal organization that also trained men in the use of arms and specialized in physical education as well. As a member of the administration of the local Red Cross and as a member of the command of the civil defense, I was invited to sit on the dais at all the state ceremonies. I was also invited to attend many official receptions alongside many of Luboml's authorities.

Suddenly I found myself, an 18-year-old youth, representing as best as I could the Jewish population of Luboml as the leader of Beitar. My position in this movement led to my attending many functions. Beitar began to appear in many parades of the state, especially during the festivities of the third of May. On these occasions, a large number of young Jews in brown shirts, in front of them commanders wearing sashes on their shoulders, marched military style. The discipline was exemplary and they made a great impression on the spectators. On some of these occasions, I was offered the opportunity to deliver speeches in Polish in front of thousands of people.

On the practical side, I got members of Beitar to participate in the state's Red Cross first aid courses, as well as in civil defense exercises against poison gas, and target shooting. The ruling authorities looked upon such exercises favorably, as did Beitar, because it was an opportunity to train our men militarily and to help us achieve the goals of the movement. At the same time, some members attended national courses for instructors in Zielonka. Among these men were Nathan Eiger, Shalom Gershenberg, and Mordche Kosower.

I soon learned that Beitar had an additional purpose that would not be viewed favorably by local authorities. In those days there was much persecution and economic oppression toward Jews, whose livelihood depended on trade and commerce. The authorities encouraged the establishment of marketing cooperatives, and Polish youth who were not from the area (they were called "Poznancziks," probably because they were from Poznan) worked to organize the gentiles, especially from villages; many private businesses owned by Ukrainians also began to flourish. Also, income taxes and taxes on income growth were increased. There was a hostile atmosphere, in which Jews were being driven out of their economic positions.

The sympathy that the authorities had shown toward Beitar was based on the fact that the movement's goal was to move to Palestine and that it presented itself as a Jewish nationalist organization that looked toward a future outside the borders of Poland. What was not any less important in the opinion of the authorities was that Beitar also was nationalist in its social outlook. For this reason, the authorities were not suspicious of any local subversive activity as far as the movement was concerned. It was not long, however, before the authorities realized that pride does not have geographical boundaries and that the readiness to fight could not be confined only to the future, or to Eretz Yisroel. And so it came to be that Beitar, which had once been looked upon favorably by local authorities, suddenly became an unwanted organization because it set out to protect the lives of Jews in the area.

What occurred was that the Polish youth, the Poznancziks, began to instigate clashes with the Jews. There were a number of incidents. For example, older Jewish men were attacked and beaten on the evening of Shabbat, when the number of people returning from the shul began to thin out and they were easy victims. It became evident to the Jews that they had to reciprocate.

Once, before Shabbat, an announcement was made that all Beitar activities for that evening were cancelled and that it would be preferable for the town's youth to remain at home; actually, organized watch groups were sent out into the streets so that they could react in case of an attack on the Jews.

As they usually did, the Poznancziks attacked a number of Jews that evening. At that point our watch group reacted. Unfortunately, the response was too sharp, resulting in two of the assaulters being critically wounded. Both of them were stabbed and there was fear that they would die, so they were sent to the large hospital in Lublin. From that point on, the lives of our town's Jews became safe and tranquil once more; however, serious

damage was done to the relationship of Beitar and our town's authorities.

I argued before the civil authorities that there was no evidence that Beitar had anything to do with the incident. On the contrary, I could prove that on the account of all tensions in Luboml, I had cancelled all of Beitar's activities that night and asked all members of Beitar to remain at home that evening. Nevertheless, my evidence

A Beitar unit in Luboml in 1936. *From the right*: (not known), Sh. Gershenberg, Y. Hetman (leader of Beitar), Ch. Huberman (second in command), N. Shpira, I. Langer.

Beitar members gathering to say goodbye to M. Eizenberg, who was making aliyah to Eretz Yisroel.

and my claims were not accepted by the authorities, and all the blame was put on Beitar.

As punishment, I was informed by the mayor's office that my request for a passport so I could leave for Eretz Yisroel was denied. After several weeks, I received the passport anyway. However, the pleasant relationship with the local authorities ended while I was still leader of Beitar.

When I moved to Eretz Yisroel in 1936, Chayim Huberman, second in command, took over as leader of the unit. At present he lives in Washington. When Chayim left for the United States, my cousin (my mother's sister's son) Chayim Honig became head of the unit. This was about three years before the beginning of World War II, and the tension in the air could not be ignored.

Unfortunately, I had to learn about the activities of the last two leaders of Beitar from afar. Nevertheless, I know that the two leaders dedicated much time and effort to Zionist political activities. Also, they stressed the importance of the evacuation of the Jews from the area. Finally, as per Jabotinski's motto, these men stressed the importance of organizing a national army not only in the diaspora but in Eretz Yisroel as well, as a first step toward winning back the Holy Land.

When World War II broke out, and later under Russian rule, the activities of Beitar ceased, along with the activities of all other pioneering youth movements. The German murderers with their Ukrainian accomplices annihilated the young boys and girls of our Zionist town, Luboml.

Members of Beitar. *Standing from the right*: A. Brikman, H. Shifman, I. Raif, (not known), I. Fridlander. *Sitting from the right*: Sz. Gershenberg, M. Eizenberg, Ch. I. Povroznik, I. Shaintop, L. Erlich.

THE HEBREW HOME OF YAKOV BLUMEN
By Nathan Tchelet (Blumen)

A long time ago, long before the First World War, there was a group of people in Luboml who were extremely concerned about the spiritual and cultural future of their community. This group of people, because they were so worried about their community, invested a large amount of hard work to preserve its culture and its character. Among those who were part of this group were Dovid Veyner, Abba Klig, Moyshe Sfard, Gedalia Grimatlicht, and others who are now deceased, may God bless their souls.

The mission of these men was to bring enlightenment to the youth of Luboml. They wanted to provide the youngsters with a general education as well as with knowledge of the ways of the world. Under the supervision of these men they began to teach the children Hebrew at the Talmud Torah—not only by having morning and evening prayers but also through new instructional books like *The Hebrew Word* and *The Language of the Book*.

The first teachers were Moyshe Yitshak Kagan and Shamai Frankfurt (who was later the principal of the Tarbut high school in Kovel) at the Talmud Torah as well as the teachers Lisuk from Rozhishch and Fayvel Freed from Chelm.

When World War I broke out, a terrible fear settled on the town of Luboml, for the people had heard of harm done to Jews. They were not only

Children of Luboml public school with their teachers, near the Talmud Torah building, September 1932.

woods. Here they built bunkers in which we lived. About 2 miles away there was a village where the Germans sent me for milk, eggs, and chickens.

The German unit for which I worked was a field workshop for repairing tanks, so we were always stationed about a half mile from the front. When a damaged tank was brought in they repaired it at once and sent it back to the front.

I would wash for them and cook and serve them. Sometimes I was called to work at the front and they would bring food to me there. We reached the front by walking!

Once we were shot at by the Soviets and a Russian scouting party arrived. For some reason at that time we could not cook at our place and we had to get our food from another kitchen. No sooner did we put the food into the car, when Russian scouts appeared and threw everything out of the car, while the Germans ran into their bunkers, being afraid of being killed. But I was not afraid. I went up to the Russians and asked them to take me with them. They answered that they could not do that. "Who knows whether we ourselves will get back safely? We are only a scouting unit. You must wait until we come here officially."

In the village where I used to get food for the Germans, there lived a Pole with his two daughters. One day I asked him, "If anything should happen, could I come to you and would you hide me?" He said to me, "Anytime. My door is open to you, and I will take you in like my own child."

On Saturday evening, when the Germans were getting ready to move on, I said to Valya: "Listen to me. If you want to come with me, all well and good. If not, please let me stay behind—I do not want to go on with them. I beg you not to spoil it for me." She decided to go along with the Germans, but she told the head cook that I was staying behind. The cook came to me in anger, caught me by my collar, and pulled me into the bunker of the chief, telling him that I wanted to stay on with the Russians. The chief asked, "Why don't you want to stay with us?" And I said to him: "You can do what you want with me; I am not going on. I want to remain here." But there was no more time for further discussion, as they had received orders to

move at once. The chief's assistant gave me a candle and some bread and said to me: "Well, if you want to stay, we can't do anything about it. You have served us well. Stay here if you wish."

I went at once to the Pole and he took me in. I stayed three days with him. When the Polish army was approaching, the Pole told me to stay another couple of weeks, until he forged documents for me. I said to him, "Fine." He did not know that I was Jewish.

I somehow found out that the former prisoner of war, Pavel, was among the Pole's friends, and so I said goodbye to the Pole and left him at once.

I walked and I walked until I came to the shtetl of Ozhodov. There I met Jews for the first time. They had been liberated a half-year before. I got some bread from a bakery and continued on my way. This was in January, 1945. A blizzard was raging, carrying everything along in its big wind. Some peasants along the way refused me shelter for the night. One, however, took pity on me and let me spend the night there.

The next morning I came to Krashnik, staying on for two days. Then I left for Lublin.

In Lublin I went at once to the Jewish kehila and found many Jews there. Looking for a familiar face, I saw Shymon Kroyt from Luboml come in! He saw me too and fell into my arms, "Pesele, you are alive!" A reunion of a mother with her child could not have been more moving! Our joy was great. Saying his wife was also alive, he took me at once to his home. I stayed with them for two weeks and they treated me better than if I were their own child. They gave me food and clothing.

I found out from them that my sister and her husband had been killed, but my father had remained alive. My father had wandered in the woods for three weeks, surviving somehow until the Russians came. He had met partisans in the woods and begged them to allow him to join them, but they did not want him to (he was then 65 years of age). And so he remained in the woods. The gentiles, who gave him bread, pointed out to him the place where my sister was killed. They even told him the name of the peasant who had killed her and her husband, and described how it happened. The two were looking for me and my father after we had separated and asked the gentiles whether they had seen us. Several of the gentiles gave them food, but this murderer took an axe and cut them down! He even made my brother-in-law dig his own grave.

When I came back to my town and my brother returned from Russia, we dug up the bodies, made coffins for them, and brought their remains to the Jewish cemetery. There we dug two graves and made covers for them. Probably by now not a sign of these two graves is left.

I went from Lublin to Luboml to see my father, for by then Luboml was already in Russian hands.

The Russian border was nearby, at Dorogusk, but I had no legal documents. I traveled by freight train together with many gentiles. When the Russian border guards asked to see our papers, I made believe I was sleeping. He woke me however. "Documents!" In a sleepy voice I answered, "The same," meaning the same as the others who had been already examined. The man let me go.

We reached Yagodzin, the station before Luboml. After I left the train, I had 5 miles to walk. In the dark, I could not find the right road and struck a barbed-wire fence. The border guards caught me, put me back on the freight train, and sent me back to Poland. When I came to Chelm, I found some Luboml Jews already there and spent several days with them. They tried to get some sort of document for me to enable me to travel freely, but they did not succeed; and I decided to go to Luboml again.

This time, I went by another route—through Brisk. I got off at Podhorodno, the last station before Luboml, on the Russian side. The border patrol caught me again and took me to the militia. I told them the truth; that I had a father in Luboml and that I had no documents, because I had run away from the Germans. I said to him, "Take me to Luboml and I will get documents there." I was taken to Luboml and was brought before the militia commander, who interrogated me, keeping me there a whole day.

Meanwhile the Luboml gentiles heard about me and spread the rumor through the city that old Moshko's (my father's nickname) daughter was kept by the military authorities, who did not release her because she had no documents. When my father heard this, he grabbed his cane and ran to see me. It is hard to describe our meeting as my father opened the door and saw me sitting there.

The chief, who was in another room, heard our cries of joy. Coming into the room, he told us, "Go home. I don't want anything from you."

We came home. The windows had old sacks for curtains, sacks my father had found in the street, for the windows had no panes—they had been shattered. My father told me how he had hoped all the time that I would come back.

We waited in Libivne until my brother came from Russia. Meanwhile I was married, and in 1957 we went to live in Eretz Yisroel.

RESCUED FROM THE BIG FIRE
By Rochl Gutman (Sandlboym)

Suddenly the German-Soviet war broke out. We could not imagine that the Germans would come to us within two days, but by June 25 the murderers were already in Libivne. In two days' time we had lived through several attacks; the entire center of the town, the marketplace, and Chelm Street were burned down.

On Thursday, we began to see people in the streets. The whole town was in ruins. The following week an order was issued for all Jews to wear an armband of white cloth with a blue Star of David: and a curfew for Jews was set between 6 p.m. and 6 a.m.

On Wednesday, July 2, another order came: Jews 14 to 65 years of age were to gather in front of the movie house; anyone who hid would be shot. Several hundred Jews appeared and the murderers set them up in rows. Then the Nazis chose five Jews, Meyer Tseylingold, Shmuel Vayngarten, Yankl Gelibter, and two more, took them to the outskirts of town, and shot them there without any reason. Great fear filled the Jews.

The next day an order for forced labor was issued for all Jews, both men and women, 16–65. Those who refused to work would be punished under military laws. The Ukrainian police were appointed to guard Jews. The police had been picked from among known hooligans who were never satiated with Jewish blood. Our suffering while doing the accursed labor was indescribable.

Another decree came on Friday, July 18; men and women, 16–65, were to come to the movie house. When almost every Jew including myself came, the Germans set us up in four rows, men and women separately.

The lines stretched from Yankl Feller's store to the movie house. At 10 a.m. the Gestapo men came, with their iron helmets and leather whips, and began to count the people. At that moment a terrible storm broke out. It grew so dark that people could not see each other. Rain poured down in buckets and the Germans quickly sent the Jews to work, taking them in all directions.

Several days passed. On Tuesday, July 22, the Nazi murderers and their Ukrainian helpers came in closed trucks. They began to catch men and throw them into the trucks, taking all of them to the headquarters. There the Germans confiscated whatever they had, adding beatings and sneers to the indignities, and then took them to the city slaughterhouse, where deep graves were ready for them. They forced the Jews into these graves and machine-gunned them.

The next day no one could quite believe such a thing could have happened! Some Jews ran toward the graves. There was terrible panic among those who were left. Yet early in the morning, Jews had to report for work. They knew that their very lives were in danger and did not know whether they would come back alive.

A few days later another order came through: all Jews had to bring all their gold, silver, copper, etc. If they failed to do so, or if any of the enumerated articles were found on them, the punishment was death. The next morning, women lined up to turn in their valuables, not knowing why they deserved such a fate!

The line of Jews giving up their valuables was moving all through the day. These things had been in their families for many generations. When I reached the table to give up the little bit of jewelry I possessed, I saw other women giving up their valuable treasures, things they had inherited from their great-grandmothers: long heavy gold chains, silver cups for blessing the sacramental wine, beautiful silver Sabbath candlesticks, etc.

A month went by after the first slaughter. Early on Thursday morning of August 22, 1941, the town was surrounded by the Gestapo men and their Ukrainian helpers. The closed autos came again and Jewish men and women were again seized and taken to the headquarters. This slaughter lasted not one but all of eight days! It went on continually day and night leaving only widows and orphans alive. It was a dreadful sight—the grabbing of people and throwing them into big closed cars! There was nowhere to hide. The Ukrainian neighbors, anti-Semites, refused to let us in and stood watching and laughing and making snide remarks that we were being punished for the sins of our forefathers who had murdered Jesus.

Two of my brothers, Meyer and Shmuel (z"l), were captured, but by a miracle they succeeded in escaping from the headquarters. The other Jews were taken to the Skiber Woods, which had huge deep pits, and were exterminated. This bloody action was accomplished by the SS with the aid of the Ukrainian militia.

When things quieted down, the remaining Jews could not believe this had happened. When they began to ask peasants whether any of them had seen where the Jews had been taken, not all of them wanted to tell us the truth. But those peasants who lived near the woods told us they had heard shooting and later had seen the bodies of the murdered Jews.

This second slaughter destroyed almost the entire Jewish population of Libivne. The town lost its finest and best youth; only a few women with their children were left. There were very few Jewish men to be seen in the street after that.

After both actions ended, everything quieted down a bit. But soon a new evil decree came: The Jews were to take off the white bands and put on yellow patches, 3 inches in diameter: one in front and one in the back. Even children with no understanding of what was happening had to wear them. The first patches were put on exactly on Yom Kippur. When the holidays were over, a new decree met us—the ghetto, to which all Jews were forced to move.

The ghetto included Kusnishtcher (November 11) Street. Overcrowding made the suffering of the Jews even worse: 12 to 15 people were forced to live in one room; later came hunger and dirt! Even more tragic was the moral degradation we felt in contrast with the peasants. Those Jews who had a trade lived separately on Koleyova Street. They had red identification cards which they called "gold passes." They were led to work by the militia every day, never sure of their lives.

It was not long before a new order came to the Judenrat, telling them to provide 100 men to drive horses to Poltava. Only 11 of those men came back—the rest were butchered!

Winter came and the Germans ordered the Judenrat to provide a quota of fur coats for them. This too was fulfilled.

In January of 1942, the murderers again came with closed autos and began to catch Jews. Those they caught they beat with their leather whips so hard that the snow was covered with blood. They took the Jews to the movie house, where they were watched by the Ukrainian police. But they were released a week later. We spent the winter in dread and in pain. The Jews built bunkers in their houses as hiding places. But no matter how hard the winter was, all of us wished it to last longer, for we foresaw that worse was yet to come with the end of winter.

In fact, as the winter months of 1941–42 passed and the sun came out again in the spring, it did not shine on us Jews. No matter how harsh the winter had been and what dreadful fears we had experienced, yet we had been hoping that, with God's help, the foe would be vanquished. When the winter was over, however, we were exhausted! All our hopes had been for naught, for new actions, new decrees, and new liquidations came upon us.

For Passover, the Judenrat paid the town commandant Uhde a large bribe to allow us to bake matzos. Oh how difficult it was for us to get flour! My brother Meyer risked his life to bring flour illegally from Masheve. Someone betrayed him by reporting him to the gendarmes, and on Friday morning they came and took him away together with the flour and all our possessions. They beat my brother so mercilessly that the next day he came home all bruised.

Passover came and a new extermination action took place.

Rumor came to us that the Chelm Jews were being taken to the ovens of Sobibor. Our people were beside themselves. In Libivne, the Germans took daily loads of men to dig pits. We suspected the pits were meant for us Jews, but when we asked the Germans about them, they told us: "To get clay for clay pots."

The last months in the ghetto were horrid, for we were waiting for a violent death. As summer passed, we learned the Germans had liquidated the ghettos of Kovel, Ludmir, and Lutsk, and later on, Rovno, Trisk, and Tomashovke; Libivne remained like an island. Each morning people ran to work, not sure if they would return alive. We tried to inquire of the commissar, who reassured us that Libivne would stay quiet. The Jews began to console themselves with the hope of a miracle, because Libivne had been a blessed town a long time before!

Meanwhile the High Holy Days were approaching and Jews ran to the synagogues to pray to God for a miracle that would destroy the foe. Then Yom Kippur was upon us. With what pain in their hearts did the Jews say the Kol Nidre that night! Who can ever forget Elye Shternboym of Koleyova Street as he put on his white kitl [prayer robe] and began to pray out loud? His prayer and his cry could have moved a stone!

On that Yom Kippur day the district commissar went away, leaving an order for us to raise a large "contribution": 100 pieces of leather for boots, 100 bolts of cloth for suits and dresses, and 100 ten-ruble gold pieces.

We prepared everything and gave it to the commissar via the Judenrat when he returned before Sukkot. Upon receiving the "contribution," he again reassured us that the Jews of Libivne would be protected. There was no limit to our joy. The Stepenyer rebbe said in his sukkah that he had seen a fish in a dream and that a fish was a symbol of joy.

The first days of Sukkot were over, the pits had been dug. When the Germans and two Ukrainian helpers, Tomashtshik and Gusyev, came to take over the pits, we realized what kind of fate awaited us: The air grew tense—it was hard to breathe, Jews ran about, and gathered in circles to talk: What could they do? How could they save themselves? It was a day before Hoshana Rabba.

At 3 a.m. of October 1, 1942, Libivne was surrounded by German gendarmes and their Ukrainian helpers, who rounded up all the Jews in the marketplace.

Murdered Jews were lying in the street. Fathers and mothers were leading their own children to slaughter. How tragic it was to see how people went to their own funeral to see them undress themselves and go into the pits with their children!

October 1, at eleven in the morning, more than 2,000 Jews stood gathered together, surrounded by German and Ukrainian police. The Jews were led behind the town to the brick factory, where four huge, deep pits were awaiting the victims. The murderers lined the Jews up at the edge of the pits and shot them all to death.

During the last days before this extermination, Ukrainian acquaintances had told us that when the evil moment came, we could come to them and they would hide us. But that was, unfortunately, a lie. They tricked us into giving them our valuables and then reported us to the police for extermination. To illustrate and prove what I have said, I will go on with my painful recital about the two years between October, 1942 and July, 1944 (when the Russians liberated Libivne).

On the night of Hoshana Rabba, 1942 when Libivne was surrounded by the German murderers and their Ukrainian helpers, I, together with my brother Yidl and his two children, ran away from the shtetl. We went to a gentile who had promised to hide us. But when he saw that first day what the Germans did to the Jews, he immediately told us to leave his house.

We then went to the village of Kusnishtch and approached the headman of the village, Vasil Sulik, who had previously also promised to hide us and Meyer London. At first he welcomed us kindly and told us about the bodies of a Jewish family that had been shot near his house: they were of Moyshe Echshteyn, his wife, two children and a sister-in-law. The man kept us for two days; but when, by spying and questioning us, he found we had come to him without any money, he too told us to leave.

We were in a terrible position. Where should we go? Having no alternative, we went into a barn and hid in the straw, spending several days there without the owner's knowledge.

When the head of the village somehow found our hiding place, he went to the owner and told him he would report us to the Germans, who would arrest us. The peasant-owner, a God-fearing man, came to us and told us to run away through another door.

When the police came and did not find us, they beat up the owner because he had let us go without notifying them. It was Friday evening and we had no place to go; we were forced to ask a strange peasant for a night's lodging. And here a great miracle occurred! It was in this strange gentile's home that we lay hidden for 22 months!

Our hiding place was pitch dark—we could not see each other. On that first morning, Aniski Sulek, the owner, treated us to a loaf of bread and a bottle of water, which to us was the best food we had ever tasted!

The peasant told us the members of his house read the Bible every day, where they learned that some Jews had to be left alive as witnesses. But his wife was afraid and told us to leave, because she did not want her family to be destroyed for hiding us.

She was right, but it was very bad for us. We had simply nowhere to go. And so we stayed with them in spite of what she had said to us.

It is dreadful to describe our suffering from hunger, thirst and cold—especially that of our two children, let alone us adults, me and my brother! In addition, we were wallowing in dirt; we could not stand up, being forced to sit or to lie. And most horrible of all, we were in constant threat from the Germans.

The gentile man who kept us was also in dread of death; if we were caught, he and his whole family would have been killed. His own children did not know we were staying with him; and he had an ongoing battle with his wife over us.

Once a week the peasant would bring us a small loaf of bread and a few potatoes, enough to feed the two small children. As for us adults, we got used to fasting almost daily.

The situation was even worse in 1944, when the front line had stopped at Kovel. It was in March. The peasant, who had been coming to us every Sunday with the little loaf of bread, was taken to do work for the Germans. His wife did not want to have anything to do with us. It so happened that the Germans quartered their soldiers in the village of Kusnishtch—in the very house of our gentile! The Germans had chased the woman and her children out of their home into the stable.

Those were the days when we lay in our hole, waiting to die. We had nothing to eat for 13 days. But another miracle occurred: the peasant managed to sneak away from his work and came to see whether we were still alive. He brought some bread and a container of sour milk.

By then our children did not look human at all. The man told us the Germans were retreating from Kovel and were burning everything behind them. He advised us to leave the barn and hide in the tall fields of wheat: "It would be a pity for you to hide for 22 months and in the end be burned to death." But where could we go, we who were living skeletons? I told him we would take the risk and stay put.

We thus stayed until the end. On the last day of the German retreat the village remained deathly still. The peasants ran away into the woods, and we were the only ones left in the village. The shooting that went around our hiding place was dreadful. Many houses and the church were burned down, but our house miraculously remained untouched, as did we.

On July 25, 1944, the Russians came and liberated the village; two days later we left our hiding place. On a Sunday morning, when we came to Libivne, we did not find even one Jewish face there. Some of the houses were left intact, while most had been demolished.

The first thing I did after the liberation was to give a Jewish burial to those of my family who had been killed. I buried my husband, Yosef, z"l, who was murdered in the village of Palap by Ukrainians on Oct. 6, 1942; my sister-in-law, Tseytl, with her child Leyele; and Chavele Feygelis, who also had been killed.

A short while later, a commission came from

Moscow—a doctor, a prosecutor and two other officials of the M.G.B.—who opened the graves at the brick factory. After two years buried in the ground, the bodies lay pressed together. A woman with neatly combed hair, her braid coiled on her head like a crown, lay with a child whom she was holding close to her heart. The commission photographed everything and then covered the mass graves with earth!

May these pages remain a document of the dark days that we lived through and be a memorial to our dearest ones!

BEYOND THE BORDERS OF DEATH
By Avrom Getman

Right after the outbreak of the German-Polish war in 1939, the Germans stayed in Libivne only a few days. As we learned later, there had been a secret agreement between Berlin and Moscow partitioning Poland between the two of them. Libivne was to be in the part belonging to Soviet Russia.

During their presence in our town, the Germans behaved like normal occupying authorities. They did no ill to the Jews; they ordered all the stores to remain open; and they did not let the peasants rob us.

There was a week between the time when the Germans retreated and the Russians came in; that's when chaos broke out! The Poles and the Ukrainians then went on a rampage. The young leader, Kostetski, brought his bandits to the shtetl. There was nearly a pogrom. The Jews ran to the priest, who, together with the attorney's wife, Mrs. Myalovitska, intervened by telling the gentiles that not all Jews were Communists. The Jews of Libivne had these two to thank for avoiding a pogrom.

When the Red Army entered Libivne, the leftists in our town received them with pomp and celebration. There were many Jewish young men among them.

While the Soviets were occupying Libivne, Jewish refugees arrived from Chelm, Danzig, Bialystok, Lublin, Lodz, and elsewhere. They sneaked across the border (the Bug River), running away from the Nazi murderers. The Jews of Libivne helped the refugees as much as they could during that difficult time, by collecting money and clothing for them.

In the beginning, the Soviet authorities pretended not to notice this flood of refugees. Later, however, they arrested the newcomers and de-ported them into the depths of Russia.

Evil times were coming not only for the refugees but also for the Jews of Libivne, when Soviet leaders began to compile "black lists" of all merchants, members of various political parties, and so on. But they did not get the chance to fulfill their plans, because just then Hitler attacked Russia.

While the Russians were still in Libivne, they introduced Yiddish into the elementary school. Yankl Blumen became the Yiddish teacher. Messrs. Neyman and Frayman, refugees from Chelm, taught in that school, as did Mrs. Elbling-Shapiro, who taught algebra.

When the Germans attacked Libivne, the Russians were able to withstand the attack for four days. But during the fighting, Libivne was almost demolished by bombs and heavy artillery. Jews tried to hide in the cellars. My family, together with other Jews, hid in Zats' building which had brick walls 3 feet thick. With us were Moyshele, the son of the Stepenyer rebbe, Sime Eynbinder, and others. The Germans finally occupied Libivne.

Others have certainly already written about the German actions and the evil decrees. I want to add only one fact that is connected with an action. After all Jews were assembled in the marketplace, they were told to tell the Germans whether they were merchants or workers. Some Jews were afraid to say they were workers, lest they be classified as Communists. My brother Moyshe was standing among the workers, but when he saw our father among the merchants, he went over to his side. The Germans took all the merchants and shot them.

The Germans later denied they had shot the Jews, but said they had been taken to a labor camp. Topka, the daughter of the wealthy landowner

Kampyoni, who had a good relationship with the new assistant commissar, Uhde, told my mother that she would visit all the camps in Germany to find the captured Jews. My mother and Mrs. Gitelis began to collect money, gold, and whiskey to give to Topka in order to get information. She came back the first time, telling us that she had regards from our men. She did the same also a second time. By then the Jews became suspicious. And so I and a couple of other boys went to the pits behind the cemetery. The shtetl then learned the awful truth that the captured Jews had been shot and buried near the town's slaughterhouse.

Everyone then realized that the best way to save himself was to work for the Germans. Therefore everyone, whoever had the strength, strived to be registered for work in one of the labor camps. Through my mother's connections, I was put to work in the home of Kampyoni, the landowner, and my brother also got work there. Topka's brother, Mishko, was good to me, and whenever there was to be a round-up he would take me into his room and hide me.

Once in a while there appeared a good man among the Germans, a man who had pity on the Jews. We had such a German man, whom we nicknamed "Moyshele" because he never did us any evil and, at times, threw some morsels to the Jews. There was also another German stationed at the railroad station, whom we called Zede (grandpa) because of his not bad behavior toward us Jews.

Many Libivne Jews realized that everything we had experienced up till then only foreshadowed what was to come. This was especially in the thoughts of our youth. We felt that sooner or later the Germans were getting ready to exterminate all of us. The news we were getting from the surrounding areas left us without doubt, leading to the decision by many of our young people to flee from the ghetto into the woods. Jews also began to buy up weapons, which was a very difficult job under the circumstances. I and a friend of mine, a boy about 12–13, had earlier hidden a revolver and parts of guns that he had found, left by the retreating Poles and Russians.

One of our plans was to set fire to both ends of the shtetl during the final "action": in the confu-

sion, most of the Jews could save themselves by running away into the woods. The plan was never carried out, but many Jews did manage to escape the ghetto.

Among those who had initiated and organized the escape into the woods were my cousins Chayim Honig and Yankl Honig, and my uncle Moshke Tzukerman. The leaders represented various parties. They confided their secret to me even though I was then only a small boy, only because I had brought them the hidden revolver.

One day, Mishko, Kampyoni's son, came to my mother and told her the Germans were going to start mass killing the next day, expecting to kill every Jew in Libivne. She immediately told me to come home, where she had a package ready for my escape. Most of our group met on the outskirts of town, at the home of Moyshe Fuks. But when rumors spread that the SS men would begin at that very spot, I left to join another group which included Leybl Rusman, Shloyme Sokolovsky, Feyge Terner, and others. We were 30 persons in that group.

We managed to reach the Boris Woods, and later we were joined by Aaron Milshteyn and Dovid Pitchinkes who had escaped from the "action." They reported to us what had happened to our families and to the other Jews in Libivne. In the woods we encountered some Ukrainian Banderovtsy [terrorists and Jew killers]. Our group therefore had to split up and disperse throughout the woods. I stayed with Shloyme Sokolovsky, Feyge Terner, Yisroel Kagan, and a few other young people, among whom there were also a young girl and a young man from Warsaw who had been a Jewish policeman in the ghetto. Our entire arsenal consisted of a grenade, a revolver, and a knife.

When we came upon a peasant's home, the dogs started to bark and the peasant began to shoot. We ran into the bushes, where we lay a whole day. It was then that Sokolovsky left us.

Very soon the problem of food developed. The only means of getting food was from a peasant's house—but that was very dangerous, since we did not know what would greet us there. But we could not avoid that danger, and we thought the risk would be smaller if the girls went, openly begging for food. But this was a horrible mistake: two of the girls whom we had sent to the peasant were detained by him and we never saw them again.

After this awful misfortune, Yisroel went to the village of Yadene, where he was born, and took along the youth from Warsaw. And so I, a 12-year-old boy, was left alone, by myself with death staring me in the face.

I decided to head toward the railroad station and somehow sneak into a freight train going to Russia. To do this, I had to return to Libivne. Since I was hungry, I tried to go to the Kampyonis, but luckily a Jew noticed me as he looked out from his hiding place in a barn. It was Pinye Pleve, who called me over and told me all about the terrible slaughter in Libivne. He was planning to go to the Pulover Woods, since he knew that area well, and he suggested I go with him.

But nothing came of that plan. For while I was at the Kampyonis asking for food, a group of German soldiers came upon us and I barely managed to escape. I never saw Pinye again.

I evaded the guards, managed to sneak into the railroad station, and climbed into a slow-moving freight train that soon passed Masheve and reached Kovel. I noticed in the station many Ukrainian volunteers who wore triangular symbols on their jackets. I somehow got hold of such a symbol and pasted it on my jacket.

I continued in the train with these Ukrainian volunteers until we reached Zdolbunov. Later I boarded a train filled with German soldiers and reached Kozatin, near Kiev. I fell asleep in the big station and later begged for food in a restaurant from the German officers.

The next morning I sneaked into another freight train going to Vinnitsa. I was lucky to meet Mrs. Mialoritska, the wife of the Libivne lawyer. She told me there were no Jews left in Vinnitsa and she could not take me in because she lived there with her sisters. She did, however, barter for food some things I had been able to hide when I ran away. I slept in empty stores together with some other "comrades," who robbed me and threatened to call the police.

I was barely able to save myself from them. In the station I found a train that was going to

Zhmerinke, in Transnistria, about which I had heard earlier. While crossing the Rumanian border, I met up with new troubles: the Ukrainians guarding the border were asking for permits. I wanted to escape from them by running, but they began to shoot at me. I was lucky that it had become quite dark by then. I fell into a ditch and the guards lost sight of me.

A peasant woman who saw me told me there was a small ghetto in Zhmerinke. A Jewish woman wanted to take me in, but she first had to report me to the head of the ghetto, according to the German orders. The Judenrat questioned me and decided not to let me stay in the ghetto but sent me to Voroshilovke, which was 5 or 6 miles from Zhmerinke.

In Voroshilovke, I found 10 or 15 Jews with their families. They were truly fine people, but they said they could not help me much: The Rumanian police knew them all by sight, and if they saw a new face, it would be very bad for me and them. Having no alternative, I returned to Zhmerinke. But the chairman of the Judenrat threatened to betray me to the Germans.

I realized that things were very bad for me. And so I resumed my wanderings along roads where danger lurked at every step.

Along the way, a gentile woman saw me and told me to go to Maropa, and I started off in that direction. I also met another Jewish boy who had, like me, been chased away from the Zhmerinke ghetto.

In Maropa there lived a Jewish doctor from Tschernovits who helped me a lot. I think his name was Gutman. The president of the ghetto, Dr. Baykal from Sutcheve, also helped me greatly, giving me a place to live, food, and clothing. Some other Jews warned him not to help me, but they did not scare him.

Unfortunately, another ghetto president was soon elected in his place. This one was altogether another type of man. I could not expect any favors from him. There, too, the Germans would catch Jews and send them to work in Trichote, near Odessa. But those Jews always returned. I stayed in Maropa from the end of 1942 to 1944.

There I got to know a doctor from Lublin whose name was Diamont. I still had a couple of pieces of gold with me, and he exchanged them for me. When I caught typhoid fever and lay in the hospital, the doctor did everything he could to put me back on my feet.

When things became too hard to bear in Maropa, I sneaked out of the ghetto and went to the neighboring Nazi labor camp at Tolchin. There were about 100 Jewish inmates living in barracks.

I traded a shoe for a *laptshe* [a sort of woven shoe made from bast]. The Jews worked at hard labor from 5 a.m. to 9 p.m. digging peat—a backbreaking task that often made people ill. Food consisted of horse meat and green peas, and there was not one person who did not have the "runs."

I therefore left Tolchin and returned to Maropa. At that time the occupying forces had allowed the Red Cross to rescue some Jewish children from Rumania. The Red Cross sent me to Mohilev, where I was told that I was too old for this program (I was 16 by then) and I went back to Maropa.

This was during the time when the German lines had been broken along almost the entire front and the Russians reached our area. I began to wander back toward Poland in order to reach Libivne. Even this did not come easy. I experienced many more dangerous moments; in one place I was interrogated by the NKVD; in another place I was detained by Polish soldiers. But I managed to escape them all and somehow to reach my hometown.

It was in the middle of 1944. I met in Libivne several Jews who had saved themselves; Moyshe Blumen, Pinye Lifshits, Nathan Sobel, Binyomen Perkal, and others. Mendl Lifshits was in a hospital and died soon after. Later on, a few more Libivne Jews came: Yidl (Byegeses) Sandlboym, Beylke Shvarts, and others.

I did not stay long in my former hometown. I finally reached Eretz Yisroel through many highways and byways. There I served in the army for three years, taking part in the struggle for liberating our land, the newly created State of Israel.

IN THE CLAWS OF THE GESTAPO
By Chane Achtman (Kroyt)

During the dark days of the war and the extermination of the Jews, I stayed for a time at the home of a Polish woman in Warsaw. My forged documents listed me as a pure Aryan. One day I heard a loud knock on the door of the apartment of this woman and a loud voice ordered, "Open up!" Two fat SS men entered, told me to get dressed, and ordered me to go with them to the Gestapo office on Szuch Avenue, a place from which no Jew had ever returned. I had no reason to oppose them. I tried to explain that there had been a mistake, in view of the fact that I was a Christian, and I showed them my identity papers to prove that I was Anna Maria Zawadzka. But it was of no use. They led me away by force.

On the way to the Gestapo, the SS men suggested I go with them into a coffee house, but I answered angrily that I would not go to any

Aryan identity card under the name Anna Maria Zawadzka, used by Chane Kroyt. (Document is dated January 18, 1943.)

294

coffee house with strange men. After they failed to move me by cunning to attempt to gain my freedom by bribery or supplication, it is possible they began to believe that I was truly a Christian and had nothing to fear from the Gestapo.

At Gestapo headquarters they brought me into a cell under heavy guard. After talking to the rest of the women prisoners there, I realized there was no great hope of my ever escaping from there. I decided therefore that if I was to be lost, so be it! I must be firm in my decision and not confess that I was Jewish!

Sunk as I was in despair, after a while I heard a loud voice, which interrupted my thoughts calling: "Anna Maria Zawadzka." I calmed my emotions in order to hide my despair. The guard led me to a room where an SS man was sitting—he was a high-ranking officer and had an interpreter who spoke Polish.

He tried at first to trap me by speaking to me in German, to see whether I was a Jew who understood German. But I stood there innocently, as if I did not understand anything. Facing the interpreter who was interpreting what I said, I asked: "What does the Herr [gentleman] of the Gestapo wish from me?"

The interrogation lasted a long time. He questioned me about my Aryan identity card: perhaps I had bought it; perhaps I was not really Christian. Finally, they telephoned the concierge at 3 Novgrodska Street to ask whether there was a tenant there, a Polish Christian by the name of

Document issued in Lublin, April 20, 1942, for Chane Rappaport.

Zawadzki, and whether he had a daughter my age; and whether what I said was true, that as a court employee in Warsaw, he had fled to Russia. Luckily for me, he did not send my identification papers to the concierge for verification; had he done so, all would have been lost.

After that, they tested my knowledge of Catholicism and asked me questions concerning Christian tenets and ritual. He failed to shake me even in this, for I had been studying for a long time, and I had learned all the prayers, customs, and religious precepts as well as any pious Catholic. Nevertheless, he beat me violently, trying everything he could to make me confess I was a Jew. But I kept insisting that I was a Catholic, and with great difficulty I withstood all his punishments and torments.

The next day they brought in an anthropology expert to measure my hands, my skull, and my ears, for they were sure that members of the Jewish race had physical traits that were different from Aryans. To my luck, however, all these investigations turned out to be in my favor: the scholar reported that though my face looked somewhat Jewish, yet according to the evidence of the papers that I possessed and to my wide knowledge of the Catholic religion, plus the measurements of the organs of my body, I was definitely an Aryan.

I was therefore released. But I was told that the next day I was to bring in my documents from the regional church where I had been baptized and recorded as a Christian. To my luck, I met my acquaintances Korsutsky and Rotrubin, Jews from Lublin, as well as a relative from Luboml, all of whom were active in the Polish underground while posing as Aryans. I told them what had happened to me and that I had to obtain my baptismal papers.

"What? Go back to them? But that is sheer suicide!" they called out in wonder. "And what will you do if they don't believe you? Don't press your luck more than once!"

They gave me some money and I was forced to leave Warsaw at once. Thus I succeeded in escaping from the clutches of the Gestapo.

After much wandering, I reached Cracow and worked there as a housekeeper at the home of a Christian family in a suburb. But in the end, I ran away from the house in the middle of the night, for I had overheard a conversation between the couple that I was suspected of being a Jew. From then on I wandered around for a long time, without a roof over my head, hungry for bread and filled with fear.

Lucky for me, these were the last days of Nazi rule in Poland!

WITH AN "ARYAN" FACE
By Esther Brod Milshteyn

As soon as the Russian army left, we immediately ran away from Libivne. For as soon as the Germans appeared, we knew things would be terrible for us; And that no matter how dangerous it was to start wandering around during these dangerous times, no matter how risky, it would be much less risky than finding ourselves in the clutches of the Nazis.

We were further encouraged to flee by the fact that we had gotten hold of false Polish papers, provided to us by Yisrolik Dubelman, who was working in a Ukrainian printing shop.

Only one path was open to us: Russia. And so we decided to go toward Kharkov, since the wife of a Kharkov veterinarian had given us the address of her parents. We stayed there only two days, because the woman was afraid to keep us longer.

On the way back, I and my daughter Rivke stopped in Lemberg. I remained there the entire time till the end of the war, living on my false papers. This succeeded because of my Aryan looks.

When I returned to Libivne after the war, I found the entire Jewish community destroyed and almost all the former Jewish houses in ruins.

I met there several Jews who had been able to save themselves: Zelde Listhoyz, Chayim Listhoyz, Velvl Sheynvald, Moyshe the shoemaker's son, a woman from the village of Lubochin, Yidl Sandlboym with his children and his sister Rochl, Boruch Trachtenberg and Moyshe Geyer. Later on a few more Jews from Libivne joined us. My husband, Motl Milshteyn, was killed six months after the war began. A peasant betrayed him.

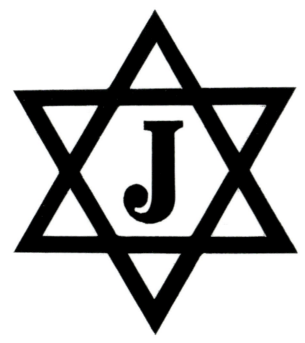

297

A MIRACULOUS RESCUE
By Sonya Shumlak

One day in the fall of 1943, I and my friend Dvoyre Lifshits, together with another Jewish youth, Mordche Meiterman (who lives now in the United States), found ourselves in the village of Zgoran. Someone there told us that in the surrounding area there were remnants of a Russian partisan group whose unit had been destroyed by the enemy. These remnants wanted to join another partisan group to continue the fight, but they did not know the area.

When we heard this, we consented to bring them to the village of Krushnits to a family of farmers that had connections with the partisans in the neighboring woods. We succeeded in reaching the desired place in the village and were forced to remain with this family for a day until we could return to Zgoran.

This farmer's son was a known Communist, and the Ukrainian nationalists, who had cooperated with the Nazis, had been planning for a long time to kill him. The son was hiding in a bunker he had dug out by himself under the barn. We went into hiding in this bunker by digging ourselves in among the sheaves of wheat. Just then they searched the barn for the son.

They found there a pot of food that had not yet had a chance to cool off, as well as three spoons. From this they surmised there must be three people hiding there and they began to search thoroughly, poking with the points of their bayonets into the sheaves.

When their search bore no fruit, they decided to set fire to the barn.

Meanwhile the farmer's wife, in fear for the lives of her son and us, ran for help into the nearby woods, where her husband was then with the partisan group. She called them to our assistance. The partisans succeeded in driving away the oppressors, and thus our lives were saved.

ON A UKRAINIAN PASSPORT
By Shmuel and Kreyndl Katz

I was a very good gardener, and during the difficult days in the ghetto I worked for Topka, in the gardens of her father, the landowner Kampyoni. I also worked for the district commissar, who was her lover.

One day I was one of 100 Jews who had gone to work at Kampyoni's garden to prune the trees. A German approached me and asked me who had given me permission to work there. When I told him it was the commissar, he hit me over the head. I fainted and lay for awhile in my own spilled blood.

When I awoke, I found the commissar and Topka standing near me. He asked me who had hit me. I was afraid to tell him, but he forced me to tell him the truth and the German received three days in prison. When he got out of prison, the German threatened me, saying I would be the first Jew that he would cut to pieces.

One day, as we were sitting in the room we rented from Veyner we heard a knock on the door. With great fear I saw before me a tall German, almost 6 feet 6 inches tall, who was drunk and asked me for whiskey. After he had some more of it, he turned to me and said he was sorry to see such good people as us suffering so much. He would have liked to help us because not every German was bad for the Jews. He also told us he came from Bendin, where Freyde, my older married sister, lived; he said he had come here to buy food and asked us to give him our Kreyndl (my ten-year old younger sister) if we wanted to keep her alive.

Without thinking, I said: "Kreyndele, go with this good man and he will take you to Freyde."

We said goodbye to each other. No one can describe the farewell scene! I have no strength to do so!

The terrible slaughter began at midnight that very same night. I was warned by Topka a couple of hours earlier and immediately told the bad news to everyone I could, including the chairman of the Judenrat, Kalman Kopelzon. I had earlier prepared a hiding place at Weiner's where I hid my father, mother, and several neighbors. As for myself and the Sankes family, I had made a hiding place for us in the new stores, and we hid there.

After several days, when we could not bear our hunger any longer, I and my brother Yitshak left our hiding place on a dark night and crawled on our bellies until we came to the Polish church. The same day our mother came. It was already the sixth day of the butchering. She told us that they had discovered the hiding place at the Weiners' and had taken everybody. Only she was able to escape. We stayed at the organist's a few days. While we were staying in the belfry, we were spotted by some children and so we had to flee very quickly.

After great difficulties, we reached the village of Pervis (Vilchi Pshevuz), where we went to the peasant Ostap, who had worked for my father for 25 years. He was very happy to see us. He told us we could stay until the war was over at his son's home in the nearby woods.

When it got dark, Ostap took us—me, my brother Yitshak, and my mother—to his son. But on the way, five soldiers suddenly jumped us.

Instinctively, I threw my coat (that I held in my

hand) at them and began to run. They shot at me, but did not hit me. Later I learned that they had killed both my mother and my brother.

While I was wandering in the woods, I came upon a peasant whom I knew and who sent me to his priest. I had nothing to lose anymore and so I went to the priest, who turned out to be a fine man. He got in touch with the organist of Libivne, who in turn recommended that I go to his friend. There I hid in a stable for a few weeks.

One morning the door of the stable was opened and I saw my peasant together with a German. I thought my end had come.

But my great dread soon turned to great joy; it was the German who had taken my sister Kreyndel to Bendin in order to save her life. He told me to hide until the next day, when he would come again.

The day before, when I had come out of the stable for awhile, I had noticed this German, who had come to see me. He kept his word. The next day he came to see me, bringing new clothes for me and a false passport in the name of Vladislav Koloshka. He also shaved me and took me along with him.

After we had been walking all day, we came to an iron bridge, where the train slowed down. We were able to jump on a freight train and arrived in Dorsk at night. There he left me at his friends' home, telling them I was a Christian. He came for me two days later and both of us went to Warsaw. There he took me to a room where I bathed and was given new underwear. From Warsaw he brought me to Chenstochov. There he took me to his other friends who, using various highways and byways, brought me into a big forest and left me there. From there I was to be on my own, at risk for my life until I reached the place of which they told me. Luckily I made it through the forest.

As I was walking, I noticed small houses not far from the station. I took a chance and went into one of them, where I found a tailor, a decent man, who was a Christian. He gave me a glass of warm

The Hotel Viktoria in Luboml, owned by the Katz family.

milk and asked me what I wanted. I told him I wanted to go to Bendin to see my sister. And the tailor answered, "I see that you are a respectable person. I will give you my passport, because the station is heavily guarded. You will later send back my passport."

Carrying the two Christian passports, I went to my sister in Bendin. We cried for joy at seeing each other and wept for the sorrow of having lost all of our family.

When I stayed at my sister's, I did not register, which was very dangerous for my sister's family. Nevertheless I stayed there for a few months. When we heard rumors that Jews were going to be taken into extermination camps (no one had spoken of it in Bendin until then), I already knew well what those camps meant! I therefore decided to go to Germany on my false Ukrainian passport under the name of Vladislav Koloshka.

I came to Opelin, Germany, where I registered at once for work in the employment office. When I told them I was a good gardener, they immediately placed me in the gardens that belonged to the city council. On the first day I was called to the Gestapo and I thought my end had come. But they only wanted my passport, to register me.

My work was not easy. I was given the dirtiest work. Three times a week I had to bury dead soldiers, take off their clothes, and put pieces of their bodies together in the coffins. The bosses gave me cognac so I would not become ill.

Even though I had my Christian passport in my pocket, the fear of death never left me for a moment. Thus, living in constant fear, I worked in the gardens for more than a year.

At times I was almost conscripted for the front, but somehow I managed to evade it each time. They wanted me to serve because they thought I was a Ukrainian.

When the Russian army came nearer, we were ordered to dig trenches. This was worst of all, for we found ourselves between two fires. I and a couple of others hid somewhere, and one night we ran away to another town, located far from the front. There I managed to get a job in a hospital garden. Six weeks later, the Russians came in. This was in 1945—and I began to make plans to escape from this accursed land.

CALAMITIES IN OUR HIDING PLACES
By Regina Alex (Rivke Gershenberg)

When we saw clearly that the liquidation of our ghetto was coming near, I and my husband Moyshe decided to run away to a gentile whom we knew.

Moyshe and I agreed to meet in the woods. But I waited and waited, and Moyshe never came. I was shaking with fear. I learned later that our gentile acquaintance, who was taking my husband and all our belongings to the tenth section in the woods, had taken out a revolver, told my husband to leave the wagon, and shot at him, luckily missing him. I heard this from my husband, whom I finally met in a forest grove.

In the morning I returned to the city to ask the Judenrat to extend Moyshe's identification papers. As I was nearing the city, I heard shots. Suddenly I heard someone call my name. I noticed from afar a young boy from Libivne, from the Pitschinkes family. He told me that the previous night the final action had taken place in the ghetto. And so I returned to the grove.

The forester introduced us to a Pole, Andzhey Armata, who lived on a farm nearby. He took us in his wagon filled with logs and brought us to a place where bushes grew in a swamp. We put branches over part of the swamp, covered them with straw, and lived there for more than six weeks. The man would bring us food once a day. We kept on begging him to take us into his barn, but he was afraid of his wife.

At the beginning of November, there was not a leaf left on the bushes. A gentile noticed us through the naked branches and demanded that we give him money (he carried an axe). We gave him all the paper money we had with us. We purposely asked him to bring us bread because we wanted to buy time while he was gone.

We knew our own gentile man was working in the fields nearby. I went to him and told him everything, and that same night he took us into his barn. Later he told us he heard shots in the bushes where men were looking for us. Instead of us, however, they had found other Jews from Libivne who were hiding near the bushes and killed all of them: Nute Fuks, Mendl Tsimerboym, and Mirl the Fisherke's granddaughter. They died on the night when our Christian took us into his barn!

In 1943, Ukrainians attacked the village where we were hiding and Vola Ostrovetska became as "free" of Poles as Libivne was "free" of Jews. The Ukrainians burned all the Poles alive, near the public school. They forced the Poles to dig their own graves before burning them.

We lay another three days without any food; Neither did we have water. Moyshe, deciding to look for another hiding place, left me and never came back.

I was sent (as a Christian woman) together with other Poles to Chelm to work in a factory. I worked there under the name of Yanina Novak until the Russians came in 1944.

302

IN THE SHADOW OF DEATH
By Chaike Koltun-Pozner

In order to save ourselves from the sudden round-ups or death in bloody actions, my family built a double wall where our whole family would hide. Because I had a small child, my mother and I went into the attic, where we hid for two days. When I had no more food for my baby, I went down to my brothers for food.

A few minutes later I heard shots in the attic. When I returned to the attic I no longer found my mother or my baby. I then went down again to join my brothers and stayed with them a few more days.

One night we left our hiding place and began to run till we came to the Zemlits Forest. My brother knew some peasants there, since he used to trade with them. In the woods we met some other Jews, so together there were 12 of us. My brother Yisoschor immediately left and came back with a loaf of bread and some water.

We lived in the woods for three months, sleeping on the ground, tortured by frost and hunger. As we sat around a fire warming ourselves, we suddenly heard shots. We started to run. It turned out to be Ukrainian police. I ran as fast as I could until I reached thickly growing trees, where I spent the night lying in the snow. Next morning I went to look for my brothers, and on the way I met three men from our group.

When we reached our former place, we found all the rest of our group lying dead; among them were my sister and brothers. We were afraid to stay there any longer and went to another part of the woods, where we spent the entire winter.

In 1943 we met in these woods some more Jews from our shtetl. Among them was my former neighbor, Dovid Tsiperbroyn, the brother-in-law of Yankl Blumen. During a sudden attack by the Ukrainian police, Dovid was shot, while I and the others were lucky enough to escape by running away to another place. I still do not know how we were able to live through all this—with no food, without clothing, and suffering from the bitter frost!

In 1944 the Russians liberated Libivne. When we came there we could not recognize our shtetl. Much of it was in ruins, burned to the ground. The old synagogue was wrecked. A Pole was living in my grandfather's house, and I told him to leave the house at once.

Later, a few more Jews from Libivne came back, but none of us stayed there, loath to live in a place soaked with the blood of our nearest and dearest ones!

RUNNING FROM DEATH
By Rochl Leichter-Weysman

When the Germans came to our shtetl, the Jewish population, including the refugees, was about 10,000 souls; but right at the beginning of the occupation, the number of Jews in the town began to diminish daily. Some died of hunger, some from hard labor, and some from being shot without any reason or cause.

The young boys and girls in the shtetl bore the same burden as the adults. I worked with them in a brigade, doing forced labor at the railroad depot. We had to carry on our shoulders 30-foot rails and to load and unload sand on the freight cars and to work fast. Moreover, if anyone tried to stop and stretch for a moment, he got a red welt on his body from a leather whip. The food they gave us consisted of small, flat rolls made of bran hull mixed with a little grass. The half-pound of bread they gave us once a day we swallowed so fast that we did not even feel it go down.

Our work began at the Bug River, the previous border before the Germans attacked Russia; and reached nearly to Kovel.

After work we were taken home surrounded by Ukrainian police with dogs. We could barely drag our feet from fatigue. In addition we would worry whether we would find everyone alive when we came home; and whether there would be any food left to keep us alive.

My family consisted of my old father, my sister and her child, and my sister-in-law with her child. If there was anything to eat, the children were the first to get the food.

At the beginning, some good men formed a committee that went to the rich people and collected donations of food, clothing, money, etc., to help the poor. But they got little for their trouble, for who was rich? And who was left who could

spare anything to share with others?

Among these committee-men was one Avrom Sheyner. When he came into a house, people would run to meet him carrying something for him! He was very wise, and the townspeople respected him and listened to him. But under the Germans, he changed so much that he could not be recognized. It was generally hard to recognize any Jew in the shtetl for the gloom that enveloped everyone; the Jews lost their lively characteristics. Only the shadows of the former people were left.

Even though my family had prepared very little food, we were very lucky in having food to eat. There was a story behind this that went back a good 20 years.

It was before World War I, when we still lived in a nearby village called Vishnyeve. There was a Christian neighbor near us whose name was Sidor Bidnyak. He was rich and very wise. My father had been in contact with him, trading with him for many years. It happened once, when my father passed through his meadow, that he found the man lying on the ground, his scythe beside him. It was 1920 or 1921, when many Polish citizens, who had run away during the war, returned home. This Pole, too, was one of those returnees and he had become very poor. My father asked him, "Why are you lying down, Sidor, in the middle of the day?" And the Pole answered him with his last strength, "You are right, my dear; but I cannot move my arms because I am swollen from hunger. I am simply dying." But my father filled him with courage and hope, gave him 10 zlotys as well as a sack of barley. The gentile became well again. A couple of days later, he said to my father: "Shmuel, as long as I live, I will never forget this; I only pray to God that He make me well and that I be strong enough to show my gratitude to you for your kind heart. You really saved me from a slow death. You gave me a gift of life!"

The man later became rich again. Whenever he met my father, he would give him a gift for the children. When the new war came, with its new troubles for Jews, again this gentile man remembered my father. Many times he risked his own life by bringing us food. That was not enough for him. He would say to my father: "If the situation is ever such that your life is in danger, all of you must run away from the ghetto and come to me. My door will forever be open for you."

For the time being, there was no need to escape from the ghetto. But our situation grew ever more dreadful and more unbearable. They had taken my old father and some other Jews to escort some horses to Russia. I will never forget our farewell with my father, I have no strength to describe the scene at his leave-taking, when we knew the meaning of his going away. But it so happened that when the policeman practically dragged my father to the Judenrat by force, because he had no strength to walk, it turned out that there were more than enough Jews to fill the quota and they let him go.

Everyone in the ghetto understood, though no one wanted to think about it, that the Jews of Libivne could not possibly escape the bitter fate that had overtaken the Jews of the surrounding towns. In order to make their lives more secure, many Jews built shelters, and we followed suit. We built two shelters because we thought if the Germans discovered one hiding place we could quickly run into the second one.

These hiding places saved us many times. But when the horrible day came to our ghetto, on the holiday of Hoshana Rabba, 1942, all of us knew that that was to be the last action. My father pushed me out by force into the street, saying to me, "Run, my child, wherever you can, my dearest daughter. Perhaps you will manage to keep alive and live to remember us and take revenge for our leaving this world in such a dreadful death! Run, my child, to Sidor in Vishnyeve. He will hide you."

I listened to my father. I disguised myself with a kind of shawl that gentile women wore and ran through side streets, till I reached a gentile whom I knew. He had a hiding place in his stable. Above that place, my cousin with his wife and children were hidden too; I knew about this. But before long, their place of hiding was discovered by the police, who shot my cousin Pinchas Chinenson, his wife and children.

As I lay hidden for three days, I would hear voices of the gentiles through the thin wall and knew that danger was coming ever nearer to me. And so I decided to run from there. No sooner said than done! In the middle of the night, when everyone was sunk in a deep sleep, and it was raining outside, I crept out of my den on all fours and left the village by side paths.

Meanwhile I collected some rain water to quench my thirst, enjoying it thoroughly, for my tongue had become hard from lack of water. I was able to snatch a few beets and carrots from gardens and I reached the hiding place of my house, which was undamaged. I lay there all of six days. Once during the night I heard a Jewish voice and I was scared. It said, "Is anyone still alive from Shmuel's family? This is Motl Grimatlicht, Motl Pinye Lipeches, who used to trade horses."

Naturally I let him into the shelter. He told me the only ones in his family to survive were his grandchildren, who were hidden with 33 others in his stable. He proposed that since both of us knew our way about, and because it was raining, we should try to lead these hidden Jews to the village of Vishnyeve. I agreed, and after much hardship, we were able to fulfill our plan.

With our last strength we were able to reach a swampy area full of bushes and sat down to catch our breath. Thick woods lay before us; they were only our friends and protectors. When we caught our breath, Motl said to me, "You, Rochl, are well known here. All the peasants also remember your father. And so I have a suggestion for you; somehow you must reach the nearest farm, get some food for all of us, and bring it here, for we must hide in the woods."

As soon as he finished his suggestion, one of the women gave me a five-ruble gold piece with which to pay for the food.

After a short walk from the group, I came upon a small hut where I saw a light. Someone was already up so early in the morning to attend to the household duties. The nearer I came to the hut, the faster my heart began to beat. When I was almost at the hut, I started to crawl on all fours. Suddenly I heard a voice and I immediately recognized it to be that of Sidor Bidnyak, who had once promised my father to help us in case of great danger. What luck! When he came nearer to where I was, I drew upon my courage and stood up, crying, "Uncle Sidor!"

After his first fright and astonishment in the dark, he said to me; "Do not be afraid, Rochele. Now that you have made it to me, you don't have to worry. Come inside."

I told him, in short, about my mission, saying that some of my people were waiting for me in the Beryozov Woods and that they were dying of hunger. Sidor himself went to bring food to these Jews and gave the woman back her five-ruble gold piece. But he kept me in his house, not letting me go back to the woods. He made me hide in a clump of buckwheat straw, which was not far from his hut. The entrance into this clump was also covered with straw, so no one could tell from outside that someone was inside. I lay there for some four weeks. Later when the time came to dig up the potatoes and store them for winter, he dug out a small hole for me and made a roof over it out of branches interwoven with straw and piled vegetables and potatoes over it. I spent another couple of weeks in this dugout.

When it became very cold and I could not remain in the potato hole any longer, Sidor came to me and told me that the members of his household knew about my presence and gave him a great deal of trouble over it. He therefore took me into his stable and hid me there, disguising my place of hiding so it would not be discovered by his family. However, they found this place of hiding too. But Sidor managed to provide me with various hiding places among other peasants whom he knew and whom he could trust.

And so my race with death began again, only with an increased tempo and with greater dread. I again took up my wandering stick, roaming from place to place; not spending the night where I spent the day!

During this time of troubles and affliction, my only joy was the thought that winter would soon be over. And so, though the Angel of Death was still plaguing my footsteps, the warm weather lifted my spirits and made the problem of getting food easier.

Easter was approaching. Since all the flour mills had been requisitioned by the Germans, the peasants were forced to use the old-fashioned trusty method of their domestic millstones found in the foyer of every home. Some of the kinder peasants, who permitted me to spend the night in a stable, hired me to turn these millstones for them. I would do the work at night, for when daylight came, I had to hide, disappear in the woods again, by hiding in the bushes. This was the happiest time of all, for I had enough to eat and sometimes even a place to sleep.

In the summertime I found the going much easier, though the dangers were the same and sometimes even greater, for shepherds and other peasant youths would wander about everywhere. Yet there was no frost to eat into my very bones, and it was much easier to find food. Many a time I would still my hunger with ripe ears of wheat in the fields where I used to hide.

In the summertime it was also easier to approach some peasant into whose house I would sneak. To pay for some food and a night's lodging, I would sew clothes and underwear for the family. The peasants told me that very few Jews had survived in the area. They also told me of a little boy, kept by a Christian family who had given him a Christian name, Bartek, and whom they passed off as one of their own. He did all kinds of work for them and tended the cows and the pigs. They also told me the daughter-in-law of Yosl Berger, the soapmaker, a beautiful and capable woman, was also hiding in the vicinity; Moyshe and Lipe Grimatlicht were also wandering around nearby, ragged and unkempt. I met them accidentally and we conversed in Yiddish, while weeping at our terrible plight.

I met by chance another townsman, a Jew who once had a tar business and lived in Libivne, on the street that led to the railroad station. I talked to him longer than with the Grimatlichts. He planned to go as far as he could from this area into the swamps of Pinsk and there join a partisan group. It would have been sheer madness for a young woman to start out on such a long and perilous journey. A few weeks later, I heard that the murderers had caught him and shot him. Later the peasants also told me that both Grimatlichts had been captured and killed.

The little Jewish boy, Bartek, who worked as a shepherd, went around freely in the open, having enough to eat, because everyone already thought of him as one of them. Everyone took care of him and watched over him like a precious thing. But one day, while he was grazing the cows in another village, he came upon some Bulbovtsy (Ukrainian Nationalists), who lied to him by saying that they were true partisans. Little Bartek believed them and told them the truth about being a Jew. They took him into the woods and shot him.

The daughter-in-law of Berger, another Libivne Jew, met a fate no different from Bartek's— or so the peasants told me.

I later heard about a Jewish woman by the name of Perl who was staying with a gentile for some time. She had some money and jewels and paid the peasant to keep her hidden. No matter how hard I tried to get in touch with her, I never succeeded.

I thus spent another winter and another summer under subhuman conditions. Another winter was closing in. From various pieces of talk that I overheard, I understood that the Germans were losing on the Russian front. Also, the partisans had stepped up their activities. But just then, when a faint ray of hope had began to show on my horizon, hope that I would somehow pull through, I almost died from a danger that arose suddenly.

I had stayed for some time in the house of an old peasant who lived alone. Since he did not know me, I had introduced myself to him as a gentile girl from the next village, whose home had been burned and whose husband had fallen on the front. The old man accepted this story and invited me to stay with him. My stay there was not too bad, for I became his housekeeper. I milked his cows, cleaned the house, cooked for him, and ate whatever I wanted.

One day two young Germans came to the house. I did not manage to run away. Instinct warned me I should not lose my nerve for a second, or else all would be lost. And so I began to play the role of a very old gentile woman, pulled my dirty shawl low over my eyes, dirtied my face with soot, and when called by the peasant, I began to set the table, walking like an old woman with a bent back, my hands shaking and listened to their conversation.

They were saying that the peasant woman was not as old as she pretended to be in her dirty outfit. I immediately realized what I had to do; I told the peasant that the cows had run into the corn and would do much damage there and I had to run and chase them out. No sooner said then done! I ran quickly outside, for the hut was near the woods and I hid there.

Later the peasant told me the Germans had wanted to hit him to make him tell them what he had done with his "daughter." Fearing the Germans would return, I had to leave my new home, the best one I had had since leaving the ghetto.

The process of wandering began anew for me. After I got to a point where I could not bear the bitter life and pangs of hunger began to torment me, I decided to go back to Sidor, who had been the first to rescue me. Even though it was quite far from where I was, I knew well all the main roads, backstreets, and small paths, so I gathered my courage and finally reached his house. I no sooner knocked on the door and called out to him my name than he opened the door and took me inside. Everyone was happy to see me, as if they were greeting a long-awaited guest. Unfortunately I could not stay long at Sidor's. A young Jewish man was hidden there too, and he shocked me so with his uncouth behavior that I had to leave the next morning. Yet I would come to Sidor from time to time to get some food.

Saving myself from great dangers and death traps, I roamed the woods like a dog without its master. Once I met a gentile girl from a village who immediately recognized me. She hugged me and kept on kissing me, she was so happy to see me! But then she began to cry, seeing how pitiful I looked in my bedraggled clothing. Her father was a fine and rich landowner named Charton Korizenes. I knew him well. During all my wanderings, I had never had such a welcome. She pleaded with me to join her, and I accepted her invitation. Her family, too, gave me a grand welcome and were happy to see me. To tell the truth, I did not know the reason for such a welcome, nor for their joy at seeing me!

I spent three weeks with them and they treated me very well. But a sudden German search, from which I miraculously escaped, made me take up my wandering-staff once again. I now began to pass myself off as a gentile. Once, when the Germans searched the house where I was staying, Sidor, who was there too, motioned to me secretly to come to his house.

When I came to him, everyone was happy to see me. Sidor told me that since it looked as if the Germans would lose the war and that the war would soon end, I should stay with him until the war was over. Naturally I agreed to this.

Meanwhile good news came to us almost daily. This was after the defeat of the Germans at Stalingrad, when they began to retreat. The gentiles in our area then began to sing another tune about the Jews and the Russians!

Soon the front approached us. It did not take long and the Germans left our area and the Russians came in.

I will never forget that day! It was a beautiful morning. Even nature adorned itself. The blue skies and the mild weather added beauty and distinction to that day. I went out into the street without fear and without apprehension. I could not believe it was not a dream. I breathed in the fresh air, feeling quietly happy just being alive. But a question disturbed my joy: "Am I the only survivor? Am I all alone. . . ?

A group of survivors at the monument for the murdered Luboml Jews, ca, 1945.

A PRISONER OF WAR WITH THE GERMANS AND THE RUSSIANS
By Velvl Royzman (z"l)

I was inducted into the Polish army on September 1, 1939. Leaving Libivne at 3 a.m. by express train, I arrived in Kovel, where the main draft center was located. The nearest members of my family came to see me off. This was the last time I saw them. Dressed in the uniform of the Polish army, I and other soldiers were taken to Upper Silesia, near the Polish-German border.

We were stationed somewhere in a small forest, ready for battle. Later the Germans crossed the Polish border, and before we knew what was happening, we were surrounded by them. Our officers suddenly disappeared, leaving us at the enemy's mercy. Each soldier ran around aimlessly, while the Germans shot at us from all sides.

A shrapnel hit the spot where I and five other soldiers were hiding. Three were killed at once, while a piece struck me in the chest and I remained lying in the field wounded.

A few hours later, when the shooting stopped, the Germans began to pick up the wounded, as well as to gather any material the Polish army had abandoned. They put me on a wagon. There must have been a great many wounded soldiers, because our echelon was a very long one. As we went along, our numbers increased, augmented by the remnants of the Polish troops, driven out of their hiding places by the Germans. When the dark of night descended, we stopped.

The human mass stretched out on the ground to get some rest, and the wagons carrying the wounded were separated and moved to the side.

All at once the Germans ordered the prisoners to dig pits. When the work was done and the people lay down to sleep, the Germans surrounded us and began shooting at us with machine guns.

Almost three-quarters of the prisoners were killed and thrown into the newly dug pits.

Those who remained alive after that night of slaughter were driven on as if nothing had happened. As time went by, the mass of people grew bigger and bigger, as both soldiers and civilians were forced to join us, having been driven together from all directions by the Germans. On the second and third nights, the Germans again committed the same slaughter as before, shooting from right and left. A horrible three days and nights they were!

After the three nights' killings, the number of wounded became great indeed. The Germans then began to sort us out, separating the lightly wounded from the seriously wounded. I fell into the second group. The lightly wounded were left at the nearest depot, while the seriously wounded were taken into hospitals. They wrote down our names and confiscated our documents, as well as everything else we possessed. They took me and four other wounded, put us on trucks, and sent us away. The four were non-Jews. We came to New Brandenburg, where the truck stopped in the courtyard of a huge hospital.

I was frightened and very fatigued from the long trip, and my chest wound was very painful. After the three sadistic nights I had witnessed, I felt nothing good awaited me. . . . A German officer came out of the hospital and, pointing to the truck, he called out, "The one who is a Jew, come right out!"

I became confused and did not know what to do! Should I answer right away, or make believe I did not understand? The other four did not understand any German. But at the moment of my indecision, something happened: Three nurses came out of the hospital and called the officer aside. From their gestures, I realized that they were discussing me; that my fate hung on their decision.

I had understood correctly. The situation was as follows: the hospital had a group of wounded Polish soldiers. Not one of these soldiers knew any German, while not one of the hospital personnel understood Polish. They therefore decided to use me as an interpreter.

I was operated on the same evening, and a few days later I was put to work, first as an interpreter and then doing other jobs at the hospital. I had enough to eat and enough clothes, and soon I felt better and grew stronger, so that I was able to bear all kinds of pain in store for me in the coming months and years.

The German Camps

After I had been in the hospital for four weeks, a policeman came for me and took me to the station. I realized I was being transferred to a camp. My pack consisted of a blanket that the nurses had permitted me to take from the hospital, and my Polish uniform.

At the station, I and other Polish captive soldiers were sitting on a bench, waiting for the train. Evidently my police escort had spread the news that I was a "*Jude*," for a line of civilian Germans began to file past me, pointing at me with their fingers: "This is the *Jude*." Some of them threw sand and rocks at me; others spat at me. If the policeman had not been there, they would have torn me to pieces! The same happened in the train the entire ride, till we reached a gathering point for all Polish prisoners of war.

While we were on our way, they made us take a bath, and the attendants used trickery to arrange it so that when we left the bath the Jews' shoes had disappeared. And so the next part of our trip we Jews had to walk barefoot and our feet became swollen, cut, and bruised.

We stopped in a field where men were working. They were building barracks. It took several weeks before they were done. They quartered us in temporary tents. The Jews had to live separately. They gave us tags with etched numbers, which we wore on a string around our necks. We had no names any more. We became just numbers!

We had to sleep in our tents on the bare earth, with only a little straw spread underneath us. We were 80 men per tent. We were not humans anymore but skeletons, naked, barefoot, swollen from hunger and cold. This was at the beginning of November, 1940. It was raining continuously. The dampness and cold penetrated into our bones!

Now we really began to struggle for our very existence. Each morning we were driven to work; digging ditches for the foundations of buildings and performing agricultural work in the fields outside the camp. At dawn before work, we were given black turbid water, which they called coffee. At noon, they gave us four little potatoes with the skins and a sour pickle. In the evening, they gave us a small loaf of bread for each four people, plus a little marmalade.

Since hunger tortured us, each one of us began to live for himself, ready to fight for every crumb of food. The worst was going barefoot, for the ground was wet, cold, and muddy from the rains; we were in danger of catching cold and becoming sick.

Each day brought us new problems, whereas the means to cope with them were minimal.

To protect my bare feet, I wove a long braid out of straw, wrapped it in the form of a sole and tied it with some wires that I stole from the builders. Thus I made *laptches* (a form of bast shoe worn by peasants). I cut a hole in the middle of my blanket and wore it as a sweater.

Every fourth day train loads with new victims arrived at the camp. One day I noticed among the newcomers Hershl Krupodelnik and Tane Kroyt from Libivne. I cannot describe my joy! A later train load brought Yisrolke Baran. From then on we, the Jews from Libivne, stuck together, shared our food, and I made laptches and "sweaters" for them too.

Very soon our camp became overcrowded and the Germans began to select men to send to other camps. Our Libivne group was among those sent to another camp, which already had finished barracks where we were to be quartered. Our Libivne group was separated: Yisrolke Baran in one barrack, Hershl Krupodelnik and Tane Kroyt in a second one, and I in a third. But in the evenings we would visit each other.

The schedule was the same as in the other camp. Days passed and the New Year of 1941 arrived. The winter was a very cold one. Many a time we discussed the fact that our fate was sealed and that we would never get out of this alive. But soon there was a change, blowing a bit of hope our way for a while and easing the pain in our hearts.

Back to Poland

The constant changes from one camp to another had robbed us of all necessities: they would snatch us at work and send us away at once, without letting us go to the barracks to pick up our things. Everything was left there: all I had was a knife, a spoon, and a can with a wire handle that served as a pot, bowl and plate. Without this I could not have gotten any food. Since I was still inexperienced in the camp lifestyle, I used to leave these items in the barracks when I went to work. When I would return from work, my personal things were gone. I finally realized that I had to take my things with me.

The first task in my new place was to get these three most important items and then attend to the business of establishing myself in new quarters.

Black market trading went on everywhere, under all kinds of conditions. You could get anything for a piece of bread or for a portion of tobacco. But it was very difficult to save a spare piece of bread. How could you spare it? We were all hungry; my whole body was swollen from hunger.

Our only consolation was that the Libivne Jews would meet once in a while. One evening I went to see Hershl Krupodelnik and Tane Kroyt in their barrack, and we were sitting and talking. Suddenly SS troops surrounded the barrack, chased everyone outside, wrote down our numbers, and drove us to the station where a freight train was waiting for us. They pushed us into the cars, locked the doors, and left us in inhumanely overcrowded conditions. We were packed together so closely that we could not move a finger.

Our Libivne group was separated again. I, Krupodelnik, and Tane Kroyt were sent away, while Yisrolke Baran was left in the camp (I later heard from his relatives that he was shot while trying to escape).

We did not know where we were going, nor what they were going to do with us. We did know one thing; no good awaited us!

We rode for 24 hours in this overcrowded train. The next day we were unloaded at a station; we were stiff from being packed so closely together, frozen from cold and tortured by hunger. After each of us ate a piece of bread with water to keep up his strength, and after having a night's sleep, we were packed again into our cars. There were thousands of us—we were not the only ones there. I searched through the mass of people in the station in hopes of finding someone I knew and I did find Yakov Melamed from Kovel. We were happy to see each other and cried like babies when we saw what had become of us.

Our group grew bigger again. Being with someone from our town made the situation a little more bearable. There was someone with whom we could share our thoughts, as if we were among our own family.

We rode for many days and nights—standing still more often than moving forward—till we reached Polish soil. We passed by Polish towns and villages. Again a spark of hope began to glow within us.

As we passed Lodz, we saw through cracks in the car walls Jews with yellow patches working at removing snow from the streets. Continuing on our way, we reached Lublin. Joy awakened within us: Thank God! We were coming closer to our hometown!

In Lublin

In Lublin we were unloaded and sent to a place with barracks that had been put up not long before. They were enclosed with barbed wire. Inside were masses of Jews sent there from all over Poland. The overcrowding and chaos were unbelievable. We were guarded by German gendarmes who gave us no food and cared very little about our condition.

From the other side of the fence the Lublin Jews threw bread and potatoes to us and looked for familiar faces. I heard someone yell, "Who is from Zgoran or from Libivne?" I announced myself and I saw a middle-aged woman, a relative of Simche Lifshits of Zgoran. She wrote down our names and promised to do what she could for us.

The next day we learned that the Germans had concentrated masses of Jews and demanded that the Lublin Judenrat provide us with food. But the Lublin Jews did not have the means to feed so many thousands of Jews. To enforce their demands, the Germans selected 600 Jews and on the way from Lublin to Partschev shot all of them. This happened on the night we arrived in Lublin; 600 Jews were taken from the barrack where we were quartered. The next morning Jews from Partschev told us about the terrible massacre.

The Jews of Lublin were shocked when they heard what had happened to the 600 Jews. The Lublin Jewish leaders made an agreement with the Germans that each Lublin Jewish family would take in two Jews from the camp, feed them, and be responsible for them. The woman whom I had mentioned earlier became guarantor for me and Yakov Melamed. Thanks to this woman, we were freed from the camp and were able to walk in freedom in the town of Lublin. Another Jewish family took on both Krupodelnik and Kroyt.

The woman who freed us (I have forgotten her name) was a poor widow who lived in a cellar; she had a true Jewish heart. We could not stay long with her, since there wasn't enough room for us. I recalled that Chane Kroyt (the sister of Noach Kroyt) lived in Lublin and I found her. She was happy to see me and received me like one of the family; I stayed with them for three weeks. Her husband, Chvetkovsky, was the only one from his entire family to remain alive. After the war he came to visit me in Lodz.

In the three weeks that I was in Lublin, I rested and regained my strength.

At the beginning of February, 1940, orders came to Lublin for all Jews to gather in a certain place, bringing their documents. Anyone who disobeyed would be shot. I knew from experience what this meant, although the Jews of Lublin did not as yet fully understand.

I immediately got together with my Libivne friends and we decided to run away to Chelm; then go from Chelm to the Bug River; run across the German-Russian border; and somehow come to Luboml. I told this to the family of Chvetkovsky (Hene Kroyt) and tried to induce them to come with us, but they did not think much of the plan. Just the opposite: they tried to dissuade us.

Chelm and Svyerzsh

We rented a horse and wagon and left Lublin at night. We managed to reach our destination without trouble, though at that time roads were filled with danger. When the Germans caught someone on the road, they would shoot him at once, especially since we, as war prisoners, had no papers and no permits to leave the town.

My cousin Miriam, who lived in Chelm, had two children, Velvele and Chayele. When the Germans had occupied Chelm, she sent Chayele to Libivne, where she stayed at our house. Therefore in Chelm we stayed with my cousin, Chayele's mother.

The Jews of Chelm were in a desperate mood. Despondent and hopeless, they sat behind closed doors and windows and were afraid to go outside, for only a week before the Nazi murderers had exterminated thousands of innocent Jews. The town looked like a living cemetery. According to a report I received from my townspeople after the war, my brother Chayim was exterminated in the Chelm camp.

It became clear to me: the sooner we got out of there, the better it would be for us.

My cousin Miriam, however, tried to talk us into staying with her and sharing with everyone whatever fate awaited us. I, on the other hand, tried to persuade her and her husband, and if not them then at least their son, Velvele, to come with us. They refused to listen.

According to information I picked up, the best way to cross the border was through Svyerzsh, a small town on the banks of the Bug (the Bug River was on the border between Russia and Germany).

We rented a horse and a sled, and at night we crossed the river to Svyerzsh.

Before I left, my cousin gave me a pair of trousers into which she had sewn a $10 bill for her Chayele in Libivne.

On our way, we decided to split into two groups, thinking it would be easier to cross the border for two people than for four; I was left with Yakov Melamed while Krupodelnik went with Tane Kroyt. Melamed and I were arrested by the Russians, while Krupodelnik and Kroyt reached Libivne safely.

That was the last time I saw them. Apparently they were later exterminated together with all the Jews of Libivne.

SIX BRAVE MEN
By Harry Bergerbest

On November 11, 1940, six brave young men left their homes and families in Luboml and were inducted into the Russian army. For Harry Bergerbest, Bebela Brief, Moishe Dubetsky, Kalman Lachter, Avrom Lichtmacher, and Yankl Melamed, family goodbyes were painful and the uncertainty of seeing their loved ones again was great.

The six friends depended on each other's companionship as they traveled to Sverdlovsk in the Ural Mountains in Russia. There they were assigned to the same unit to endure three months of basic training. The friends replaced their own families with each other. They sought comfort in retelling hometown stories and reliving childhood memories.

After training, they were stationed in Ashkhabad, Russia, near the Iranian border. In June, 1941, Germany invaded Russia. Soon after, the six friends were transported to the front lines of combat in the region of Smolensk, Russia. Five of these friends lost their lives in gallant battles against the Nazis. Harry Bergerbest lost another family.

For the first time Harry Bergerbest was without his friends. During the next eight months, Harry was transferred to several different battalions in Russia. In July, 1942, he was sent to the coal mines of Siberia.

There, he was condemned to four years of hard labor as a miner. The work was demanding, but the pride of the Polish people was strong. Both Jews and Polish nationalists banded together in the mines to form a Polish patriotic organization.

After the Nazis were defeated in 1945, Russia allowed Polish citizens to return to Poland. Harry Bergerbest left the mines of Siberia in March 1945. He arrived in Szczecin, Poland, in May 1945. By July, Harry was living in a displaced persons camp in West Germany. Here he contacted relatives in the United States who arranged for his immigration. Harry Bergerbest arrived in the United States on April 5, 1949.

Harry never forgot his five army buddies. The Nazis not only took the lives of these valiant soldiers but destroyed their families in Luboml as well. These printed words are a lasting tribute to the memories of these five dear friends and their families.

To most, they were unsung heroes doing their duty to win the war; to those who knew them, they were lasting friends who always will be remembered.

Editor's note: This article is an addition to the English translation and did not appear in the original *Yizkor Book of Luboml.*

PARTISAN HYMNS

NEVER SAY—ZOG NISHT KEINMOL!!!

Partisan Hymn of the Vilna Ghetto
By Hersh Glick (Yiddish)

Never say that this is our final way;
Though leaden skies obscure the bright of day.
T'will surely come, the day for which we pined;
Our step will crash like a whip, "Yes we are here!"
From land of palms to the distant land of snow,
We will come with our pain and with our woe!
And where'er there fell a drop of our blood,
Will sprout our spirit and our might.
Tomorrow's sun will gild our gray today.
And our yesterdays will vanish with our foe,
For if our sun and our dawn came up too late,
Our song, our watchword, will live as long as fate.
This song was written with blood and not with lead;
'Tis not the warble of a bird on the wing.
Our people wrote it among the falling walls.
Our people sang it with pistols in their hands.
Then never say that this is our final way!
Though leaden skies obscure the bright day.
It shall come, the day for which we pined.
Our step will crack, like a whip, "Yes, we are here!"

THE COMMAND OF THE ORGANIZED ARMED MEN

By Mordche Anielewich (Hebrew)

(1) Seize arms!
And he who has no gun nor a revolver,
Brandish a hatchet;
If not an axe—then
Take a knife, an iron, a rod or cane.
And strike the murderers down!
Yes, for our parents and our children!
Strike the slaughterers down!

(2) Out of the bonfire,
That etched upon our bodies
Our torture and our pain,
We will light a flame;
The torch will set our souls afire.
And light within us the flame of freedom!

UNTITLED

By Chayim Guri (translated from Hebrew by Mary Schulman)

Arise through breaches in your borders and your walls!
For our nation lives! Arise ye from your dust,
And ye shall march to sounds of blasts of shofars!
For you'll find strength from sleep and from your death;
For you'll walk firmly, heads held high,
Like sons of freedom in your own, your native land!

FIGHTERS ON THE FRONT AND IN THE FORESTS

THE UPRISING AT SOBIBOR

By Yisroel Posner

A few days before the outbreak of World War II in 1939, Poland began its mobilization. Many Jewish boys from Libivne were drafted, including me. My company was first sent to Kovel and then to Katowice. My division had six other sons of Libivne: Simche Gitelis, Velvl Royzman, Hershl Krupodelnik (Pinchas Krupodelnik's son), Fayvel Sankes, Tane Kroyt, and Leybish Kanchik (that was his nickname).

After the Poles had suffered defeat, Tane Kroyt, Leybish Kanchik, and Hershl Krupodelnik managed to return to Libivne, where they were later murdered together with all the other martyrs of the shtetl. I did not succeed in reaching Libivne. I was in Germany until April, 1940. Between 1940 and 1941 I stayed in Chelm with a Libivne family, a daughter of the Epshteyn's and Moyshe Soloveytshik, another Libivner Jew, all the time thinking of going back to our town, which was then occupied by the Soviets. My family, with whom I somehow managed to correspond, tried to dissuade me from returning because the Soviet authorities were sending returnees to prison. I therefore remained in Chelm.

When the Nazis had taken over the whole region, some of Libivne's Jews came, or were brought, to Chelm. Among them were Chayim Royzman, Avrom Reyzman, Keyle, and the shoemaker's son Avrom who lived on Pomoriska Street (where the bathhouse was). Chayim Royzman died in Chelm, and the others were killed later.

In 1942 the so-called action (liquidation) began in Chelm. It was directed against the Jews by two Gestapo men, Rashendorf and Tayman. Both excelled in a special bestiality; they would

Map showing location of Sobibor death camp. Luboml is just across the Bug River, to the southeast.

take Jewish children to the top floor of a house and hang them by the hair.

In March 1943, an SS man, Section Leader Veys, arrived at our camp. He ordered all Jewish camp inhabitants to form lines and had them driven to the station. We realized we were being taken to Sobibor, and by then we were aware that it was a death camp. On the way there, we tried to force open the doors of the railroad car and run away, but guards with rifles stood on the steps of the cars, ready to shoot anyone trying to escape. Several people still somehow managed to escape. One hundred and twenty men and 60 women arrived in Sobibor. The women and children were immediately separated from the men and were forced into "baths." The chief commandant, Officer Wagner, began to ask whether we had any trade or special skill. The Germans needed 12 carpenters and I was selected as one. I was there-fore put into the first camp, a labor camp; the rest were taken to the third camp, the death camp, selected for the crematoria. The second camp contained clothing and food.

When we arrived at the Sobibor camp, our Jewish overseer, chosen by the Germans, was Moyshe from Hrubyeshov. When the news came to us that the front was coming nearer, some of us began to plan how to escape from the death camp. Moyshe, whom I mentioned, was one of the organizers of the plot; also Leybl from Lublin, Shmuel Lerner, I and a couple of others joined the plotters.

Our first plan for a mass escape fell through when we were betrayed by a man named Ber-liner (he was really from Berlin). Moyshe and some others were shot on the spot, and Berliner became the Jewish commandant of the camp. After our plot had failed, the camp's chief officer, Frentzl, called us together and said to us: "Criminals attacked us and paid for it with their lives. You are fine men and if you work with us, we will be good to you."

About the same time another event occurred in the camp: a group of prisoners was working in the woods. A German sent two of the men to bring some water, sending along a Ukrainian guard. The Jewish prisoners killed the guard and ran away. While the German was looking for the guard, 12 more Polish Jews escaped. The Ger-mans killed some of the Jews in the woods, while the rest were returned to the camp. In the second camp, the Germans took out 10 Jews and shot them. Before they died, the 10 shouted to those of us who witnessed their deaths, "Fight the Germans and avenge our deaths!"

The Germans now feared their prisoners would escape, though the camp was well guarded. There were many watchtowers sur-rounded by three rows of barbed wire. Beneath the wires, a wide moat, 10 by 10 feet wide, was filled with water. The mine fields surrounding the camp were nearly 30 yards deep. Neverthe-less, the Germans took new safety measures. They covered the windows of the barracks with barbed wire and placed Ukrainian guards inside and outside the camp buildings.

Yet some prisoners did manage to escape. Following this, the Germans shot 20 more Jews. In 1943, a Dutch journalist managed to or-ganize the escape of 72 Jews from the camp. The Germans then massacred many people on the camp grounds.

In August, 1943, 600 prisoners-of-war were brought from Minsk to Sobibor—officers and sol-diers of the Red Army, all of them Jews. Of them, 80 men were put immediately to work. The rest were gassed and burned. Among those who re-mained alive was the commissar Sashke, a young Jewish man from Rostov. Sashke's full name was Alexander Piecharski; he was the organizer of the uprising. (After the liberation he became a lieu-tenant in the Red Army.) He decided to organize a mass escape and carefully selected those he in-tended to include in the plan, in order to avoid any betrayal. He also determined each man's role in the escape.

This was the plot: at a certain moment, de-stroy every kind of communication system, kill the Germans, and flee the camp. Those who worked in the smithy were to make hatchets and knives. In addition, they intended to use the weapons of the Germans they would kill.

The uprising was scheduled for August 14, 1943. The workers of camp #1, tailors and shoe-makers, asked their German clients to come to try on the items they had ordered at 5 p.m. At the designated time, the Jewish camp electrician, Shvarts, cut the communication lines and the lights in the camp. When the chief of the guards, Greyshut, came to the shoemaker, the latter killed him with an axe. The train-guard, Klyat, was killed in the same place. Another German, coming to the tailor, entered the building. While a boy led away his horse and the tailor was measuring his suit, a Jew killed him with an axe and hid the dead body under the bed.

The same happened in camp #2. Unterscharführer Wolf was killed in the ware-house and his body was hidden among the wares. His brother was killed in the same place. When

Yisroel Posner (Chayim Povroznik)'s story about the extermination camp Sobibor, as it was told to the famous Russian Yiddish writer Ehrenberg in 1944.

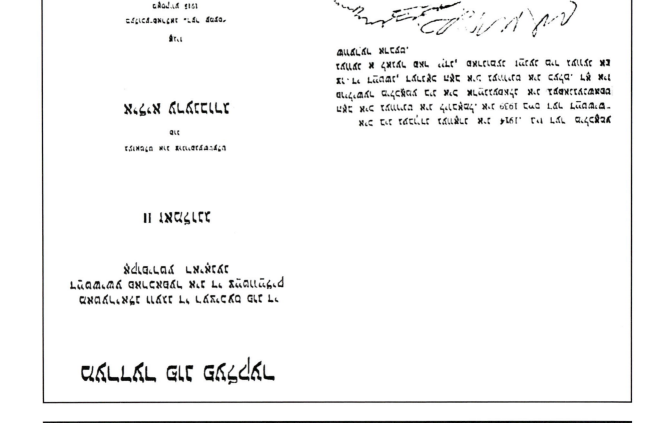

Unterscharfuhrer Beckman came into his office he reached for his weapon, but he received the same treatment. He was killed by Heinrich Engel, a young man from Lodz.

The rebels had killed 12 Germans and four Ukrainian guards altogether. During the uprising, the rebels captured arms from the Germans and used them to kill the murderers, shooting the guards in the towers. The Jews ran toward the barbed-wire fences and tore them apart with their bare hands; but many escapees were blown up on the minefields. We then got some boards and made a passage through the minefield. Altogether about 400 Jews escaped into the woods. We separated into smaller groups and ran in all directions. The Germans organized a search party; shooting at the woods from airplanes and the ground. Only about 50 of us survived. I myself managed somehow to get to Chelm, where I hid until the Red Army came. I then left Chelm and reached the American Zone in Germany.

In November, 1965, in the town of Eigen (near Koln), a trial was held against the German criminals of Sobibor; I was called as a witness and immediately recognized six of the 13 accused Nazis. One was Frenzl, the worst of the worst in the camp. He received a life sentence.

I want to conclude by adding that I recognized my father's brother's (Yank Powroznik) children in one of the transports of Jews to the crematoria. My glance took but a second, yet their little faces are etched in my memory and will remain there for my entire life!

Tobe, the daughter of Kalman Feivele's brother (Meller), was also in Sobibor. She was originally from Libivne. The Jewish electrician for the crematoria knew that I knew her well. One day he gave me a finger, the only part left of the girl's cremated body.

This token remembrance of someone I knew who was burned shall burn forever in my memory.

The Murderers of Nations

Translation from the attached text.

(An additional testimonial, written in Chelm by Yisroel Posner (Chayim Povroznik) on August 10, 1944, collected and edited by the famous Russian Jewish author, Ilya Ehrenburg).

Collected testimony concerning the murders that the Nazi occupiers committed in the occupied regions. Second collection; collected and prepared for print by Ilya Ehrenburg, for the government publishing house, Der Emes ("The Truth"), Moscow, 1945.

I was born in 1914. Until the war, I lived in Luboml. In 1939, during the German-Polish war, I was taken prisoner-of-war by the Germans. Later I escaped and lived in Chelm. There was a concentration camp there for Jews, where we were taken by the Germans to do hard labor.

In 1942, the so-called action [mass killing of Jews] began in Chelm. Dead bodies were strewn over the streets, without being removed for a long time. The Gestapo men Rashendorf and Tayman were especially bestial. They would go to the upper floors, carrying Jewish children, whom they would then hang outside by their hair.

Before the war, Chelm had 16,000 Jews. After the action, only 15–20 Jews were left. In February or March, 1943, an SS man, a section leader, came to Chelm. (I later found out his name was Veys). All the Jews of Chelm were

אין 1942 האָט זיך אין כעלם אָנגעהויבן די אזויגערו־
טענע ,אַקציע' אם יידן. מײסים האָבן זיך געוואַלגערט אין די
גאסן, און מע האָט זיי לאנג ניט צוגענומען. באזונדערס האָבן
געווילדעוועט די געסטאפאָאויצערס ראשענדאָרף און טיימאַן. זיי
פלעגן זיך אופהויבן מיט יידישע קינדער אם די איבערשטע
שטאָקן פון די הײזער און פלעגן זײ ארויסהענגען אפן גאָס,
האַלטנדיק צוגעבונדן פאר די האר. אין כעלם איז פאר דער מיל-
כאָמע געווען 16.000 יידן, איצט איז געבליבן 15—20 מענטשן.

אין פעברואל און אין מארס 1943 איז אין אין לאגער געקו-
מען צו פארן אן עסעסאָווניץ — א שארפירער (דערנאָך האָב
איך זיך דערווסט, אז זײן פאמיליע איז ווײס). אלע אײנוווי-
נער פונעם לאגער האָט מען אויסגעשטעלט אין ריעען און
אויאקנעטריבן צו דער סטאנציע. וען מע האָט אונדז אוועק-
געפירט, האָבן מיר פארשטאנען, אז דאָס איז קיין סאביבור.
מיר זײאבן שוין געווּוּסט וועגן דעם טויכ-לאגער אָדער, ווי מע
האָט אים אָנגערופן, — ,אײביקער לאגער". אין וועג האָבן מיר
געפרוווט עפענען די טיר און צו אנטלויפן. אָבער אם די טרעפ-
לעך פון די וואָגאַנג זײנען געשטאנען וואכלײט מיט קואַר-
בינען. זײ האָבן אָנגעהויבן שיסן. דאָך איז עטלעכע מענטשן
געלונגען צו אנטלויפן.

אין סאביבור זײנען אָנגעקומען 120 מענער און 60 פרויען.
די פרויען און קינדער האָט מען טיקעף אָפּגעטיילט און גלײך
אוועקגעטריבן אין ,באַד" אריין. פיל פון אונדז האָבן זום
לעצטן מאָל געזען זײערע פרויען און קינדער. דער לאגער-
קאמענדאנט דער אבערשארפירער וואגנער האָט אויסגעפענט
די מענטשן, וועד וואָס פאר א ספעציאליטעט עס האָט. דער-
נאָך האָט זיך אַרויסגעוויזן, אז די דיטשן דארפן האָבן 12
סטאליערס. צוווישן זיי בין איך אויך געווען. איך בין אַרײ-
געפאלן אין ערשטן לאגער.

די איבעריקע מענער האָט מען אוועקגעפירט אין דריטן
לאגער. עס האָט זיך ארויסגעוויזן, אז א שטיקל צײט פאר

דעם, אין פעווראל 1943, האָט אײנער א וואבמאן צוזאמען מיט
א מאנצבל און א פרוי פון די ארעסטירטע געפרווט אנטלויפן
פון לאגער.' אלס ענטפער דערום האָבן די דיטשן געשאסן אלע
150 יידן פון דריטן לאגער, וועלכע האָבן געארבעט בא די
אויוונס. אהין, אין דריטן לאגער, האָט מען עם טאקע געשיקט
די מענטשן פונ אונדזער כעלמער לאגער.

אריינגעפאלן אם אָט דער שרעקלעכער ארבעט, האָבן די
מענטשן באשלאָסן, אז זיי וועלן ניט האַרגענען זימערע ברי-
דער און שוועסטער. זיי האָבן גלײך אָנגעהויבן מאכן זיך א
וועג אונטער דער ערד. מע האָט שוין געהאט אויסגעגראבן
30 מעטער, ווען מע האָט די פארשווערער ארויסגעגעבן. דער
אונטעראפיצער נימאן האָט אלעמען געשאָסן. נײמאן איז גע-
ווען א מין ,פאליטישער ָאנפירער" אינעם לאגער. דער דאָזיקער
מערדער פלעגט גיין איבער די רײען פארורטיילטע און גע-
זען יעדן צו זאגן א ,גוט וואָרט".

איצט האָבן מיר, ארעסטירטע פונעם ערשטן לאגער, גע-
מײנט, אז אונדז וועט מען אויך האַרגענען, נאָר דער שעף פון
אונדזער לאגער דער אבערשארפירער פרענצעל האָט אונדז
פאראומאלט און געואַגט:
— פארברעכער האָבן געוואָלט אנטאלן אם אונדז און האָבן
דערפאר באצאָלט מיטן לעבן. איר, אלס לאיטישע מענטשן,
וועט ארבעטן בא אונדזן, און אײַכ וועט זײן גוט.
פרענצעל האָט איבערגעגעבן פון אונדזער לאגער 30 מענ-
טשן אם צו ארבעטן אין דריטן לאגער.

אן ערעק אין דער זעלבער צײַט איז פארגעקומען אזא
געשעעניש: א קאמאנדע ארעסטירטע האָט געארבעט אין וואלד.
א דיטש האָט צוויי ארעסטירטע אין דער באגלײטונג פון א
וואכמאן געשיקט נאך וואַסער. די ארעסטירטע האָבן דערהאר-
געט דעם וואכמאן און זײַנען אנטלאָפן. דער דיטש איז אוועק
זוכן דעם וואכמאן. אין דער צײַט זײַנען אנטלאָפן נאָך 12 טוי-
לישע יידן, א טייל ארעסטירטע, האָבן די דיטשן דערהארגעט

lined up and taken to the station.

As we were led away, we knew we were going to Sobibor. We were already aware that it was a death camp, or as we called it, the "eternal camp." On the way there, we tried to pry open the doors and jump out, but guards with carbines stood on the steps, ready to shoot. But some managed to escape.

One hundred and twenty men and 60 women were brought to Sobibor. The women and children were immediately separated and taken to the "baths"; most of us saw our wives and children for the last time. The camp commandant, Wagner, asked who had a special trade. It seemed the Germans needed 12 carpenters. I volunteered and was sent to camp #1.

אייג וואלד, און די איבעריקע האבן זיי געצוואונגען צו פויזען צו־
ריק אין לאגער. אין צווייטן לאגער האבן זיי דעם דייטשן אוועקגעשטעלט
א'ב א ל"י 10 יידן, און זיי געשאסן. פאר'ן טויט האבן זיי די אומגליק־
לעכע געשריען צו אונדז, די אידעע פון זייער דערמאָרדונג :
— קעמפט קעגן די דייטשן, נעמט געקומע פאר אונדזער
טויט !

די דייטשן האבן מורא געהאט, די ארעסטירטע זאלן
ניט אנטלויפן, האנאם דעם לאגער האט מען גוט געהיט. ארום
זיינען געווען א סאך וואך-טורעמס, אוו וועלכע עס זיינען גע-
שטאנען וואכלייט. דרוי ריינען שטעכליקן דראט האבן ארומגערינ-
גלט דעם לאגער. הינטער די דראט איז געווען א רוי-
דרויע מעטער אם דרוי מעטער — אָנגעפילט מיט וואסער. די
מינען-פעלדער ארום האבן געהאט 25 מעטער די טיף. דאָס
האָבן די דייטשן אָנגענומען ניט באואק-מיטלען. זיי האָבן
פאַרצויגען די פענצטער פון די באראקן מיט שטעכיקן דראָ
און האָבן אויעקגעשטעלט וואכקאַסטנס אויך אינעווייניק אין לא-
גער, בא די געבויידעס.

אייניקע ארעסטירטע האָט זיך דאָך איינגעגעבן צו אנטלויפן,
גט זענע צוויי קאמוניסטן, אלס ענטפער האבן די דייטשן
געשאָסן 20 מענטשן. אין 1943 האָט א העלענדישער
ארגאניזירט דעם אנטלויפן פון 72 מאַן, נאָך דעם האָבן די דייטשן
דערהאַרגעט א סאך מענטשן אין דער טעריטאָריע פון לאגער.

אין אויגוסט 1943 האָט מען אין סאָביבור געבראַכט פון
מינסק 600 קריגס-געפאנגענע אָפיצערן און שלאַכטלייט פון דער
רויטער אַרמיי — יידן. 80 מאַן פון זיי האָבן די דייטשן אָפ-
געטיילט און געלאָזט אם ארבעט, און די איבעריקע האָבן זיי
דערשטיקט און פאַרברענט, צוווישן די לעבנגעבליבענע איז גע-
ווען דער פּאַליטרוק סאַשקע [1] — א טייערער רעסטאַנדער באַקער.
דאָס האָט ער דאָס פאַרטראַכט אָרגאַניזירן א מאַסנ... אנט-

[1] סאשקע — אלעקסאנדר פעטשערסקי — אָרגאַניזאַטאָר פונעם אויפשטאַנד. —
איצט לייטענאַנט פון דער רויטער אַרמיי. — רעד.

לויפונג. סאַשקע האָט זייער פאָרזיכטיק צוגעקליבן די אַנ-
טיילנעמער פון דער פאַרשווערונג, אַז עס זאָל ניט זיין קיין
פאַראַט, ער האָט צעשטעלט די מענטשן, ער פלאַן איז בא-
שטאַנען אַט אין וואָס : אין איין מאָמענט איבערצ... אין
לאַגער די פאַרבינדונג און די סיגנאַליזאַציע, דעת... גלען
די דייטשן די העענקער און ארוסראַמען זיך פון געמען-
קענע... סאַשקע האָט געגרייט דעם אויפשטאַנד, אין דער שפּי-
דערי האָט בען גענומ... עק און מעסערס, בע האָט אויך באדרייט
געהאַט אויסניצן דאָס געווער פון די דערהאַרגעטע דייטשן.

דער אויפשטאַנד איז געווען באַשטימט אָפן 14 אָקטאָבער
1943. אינעם ערשטן לאַגער האָבן זיי האָבן סיל שנײַדער און שוסטער
אם א געוויסער שא — אם 5 אזייגער פאַרנאַכט — באַשטימט
זיערע קליענטן די דייטשן, זיי זאָלן קומען אָנמעסטן די
באַשטעלטע זאכן. אין דער דאָזיקער שאָ האָט מען דער עלעקטרי-
קער פונעם לאַגער ... יערמיסטירטער איבערגעריסן די סאַבי-

דונג-ליניע און די באַלויכטונג אין די לאַגער. ווען דער אָבערשאר-
פיורער גרישוט (דער שעף פון דער וואַך) איז געקומען צום
שוסטער, האָט אים יענער גליכאַפן שולל דערהאַרגעט מיט
א האק. דעם צוגואאכמאַכט קליאַט האָט מען דערהאַרגעט אין
דעם זעלבן שוסטער-וואַרשטאַט. איינער א דייטש איז געקומען
צו טאָרען צום שנײַדער און איז אריין אין דער זעלבע,
אין דער צײַט האָט א יונגעלע אויסגעניורט זיין פערד, דעם
דייטש האָט מען ביסן מעסטן זערלאַנגט מיט א האק אינ'ב שן
קאָפ און דעם טויטן קערפער באַהאַלטן אונטערן בעט. דאָס זעלבע
איז פאָרגעקומען אויך אין צווייטן לאַגער. דעם אונטערשאַרפירער
וואָלם האָט מען דערהאַרגעט אין קאַמאַיו און דעם מעס באַהאַלטן
אונטער די זאַכן. אין דעם זעלבן אָרט האָט מען דערהאַרגעט אויך
זײַן ברודער. און ווען דער אונטערשאַרפיורער בעקמאַן איז געקומען
אין קאַנצעלאַריע, האָט ער זיך גענומען צום געווער, נאָר ער
האָט אויך באַקומען זײַנס, אים האָט דערהאַרגעט הינריך ען-
געל, א יונגערמאַן פון לאַרו, סאַכאַל האָבן ד... אויפשטענדלער-
1285-2

דערהאַרגעט 12 דייטשן און 4 וואַכלייט. אין גאַנג פונעם אויפ-
שטאַנד, האָבן די געפאַנגענע פאַרכאַפט בא די דייטשן געווער און
האָבן דערלויב געהאַרגעט די סאַנים, געשאָסן אין די וואַכלייט
אם די טורעמס. די מענטשן זיך זיך, נאָר א סאַך האָבן זיך אויפ-
גערייסן אַף די מינען-פעלדער, דעמלט האָט מען אויסגעניורץ
בריקער און מען האָט זיך דורכגעליינט א וועג דורך די מינען-
פעלדער. אַזויארום זײַנען אין וואַלד אנטלאָפן 400 מענטשן. א
גרויסע גרויסע... שאַ האָט זיך פאַרוואַלגע... אין לאַגער, אין צענטער
איז געשטאַנען אונדזער אָנפירער, אונדזער טיַערער סאַשקע.
ער האָט א געשריי געטאָן :
— פאָר סטאַלינען, הורא !

צעטיילט זיך אם קליינע גרופעס, זײַנען מיר אוועק אין
פאַרשידענע זײַטן איבערן וואַלד. די דייטשן האָבן אָרגאַניזירט אַ
אַ: אָבלאַווע, אַעראַפלאַנען האָבן באַשאָסן דעם וואַלד. זייער
ס'יל זײַנען דערהאַרגעט געוואָרן, לעבן זײַנען געבליבן ניט מער
פון 50 מענטשן. מיר אַליין האָבן זיך איינגעגעבן צו דער-
קליבן זיך קיין כעלם, וווּ איך האָב זיך איינגעסקאַהאַלטן, ביז
ס'אין געקומען די רויטע אַרמיי. דעמלט האָט זיך צו מיר, דעם
געאַנטגעניעם פ'ן סאָביבור, אומגעקערט דאָס לעבן.

נאָכן אויפשטאַנד האָבן די דייטשן די ... אין-סאָביבור אַלע ערפ-
טרע, וואָס זײַנען געבליבן אין-סאָביבור, פאַרברענט זיי און
אומגעריסן דעם לאַגער, געבויט דעם סאָב־בורא ... לאַגער האָבן
די דייטשן גאַלצוימער — דער הויפם-אינספעקטאָר פון די טויט-
לאַגערן און דער צוויילער אינזשענער מאַזור.

פאָוראָזניק חאָים

כעלם, 10 אויגוסט 1944

The rest of the men were taken to camp #3. Somewhat earlier, in February, 1943, a Jewish guard, another man, and a woman prisoner had tried to run away. In revenge, the Germans shot all 150 Jews of camp #3 who worked in the crematoria. Our Jews from Chelm were sent to this camp #3.

Forced to do such terrible work, the Jews decided they would not kill their own sisters and brothers, and they began to dig an underground escape route. After they had managed to dig 100 feet, they were betrayed, and Unterscharfuhrer Neyman shot every one of them. Unterscharfuhrer Neyman was a sort of political leader in camp and never failed to say some "good word" to the prisoners.

Now we prisoners of the first camp feared we were to be the next ones killed. But the chief of the camp, Frentzl, called us together and said, "Criminals wanted to attack us and therefore they paid with their lives. You are decent people and if you work for us, you will be treated well." Frentzl took 30 men from our camp and put them to work in camp #3.

About the same time, another event happened. A group of Jewish prisoners were working in the woods. A German sent two Jews under a Ukrainian guard to fetch some water and the prisoners killed the guard and ran away. While the German went to look for the guard, 12 more Polish Jews ran away. The Germans shot some of the remaining Jews in the woods and sent the others back to camp. Then Germans took 10 Jews to the second camp and shot them. Before the unfortunate Jews died, they yelled to us, the witnesses to their murder, "Fight the Germans! Avenge our death!"

The Germans now feared more prisoners would run away despite the efficiency of their protective measures: The camp was surrounded by guard-towers manned by armed Ukrainian guards; the walls were protected by three rows of barbed wire; beyond the wires, there was a moat, 10 feet by 10 feet, filled with water; and minefields nearly 30 yards deep surrounded the entire camp. Yet the Germans adopted new measures, putting barbed wire on the barrack windows and posting guards in and outside the buildings.

Nevertheless, some prisoners again managed to escape. Two Jewish Communists escaped. In reprisal, the Germans shot 20 more Jews. In 1943, a Dutch journalist managed to organize the escape from the camp of 72 more Jews, and the Germans again shot down many Jews in reprisal.

On August, 1943, 600 Jewish war-prisoners from Minsk were brought to Sobibor. They were officers and soldiers of the Red Army. The Germans selected 80 of them for forced labor and the rest were gassed and burned. Among the survivors was the commissar Sashke, a dear youth from Rostov. He was the one who had masterminded and organized the mass escape, carefully selecting his collaborators in the plot in order to avoid betrayal. This was his plan: in one moment to interrupt all lines of communication and electricity, kill the German hangmen, and break out of captivity. He prepared for the revolt by having the Jews who worked in the smithy make axes and knives. They also intended to take the arms of killed Germans.

October 14, 1943, was chosen as the date for the uprising. At a set time (5 p.m.), the shoemakers and tailors of camp #1 asked their German clients to come and try on the things that they had ordered. At the same time, the electrician of the camp, also a prisoner there, cut all wires of communication and the lighting. When Greyshut, the chief of the guards, came to the shoemaker, the latter killed him with an axe as he entered. The trainmaster, Klyat, was killed in the same place. Another German came riding on a horse and went into the room of the tailors. While a young boy was holding his horse, and the German was having his measurements taken, he was hit over the head with an axe and his body hidden under a bed. The same was done in camp #2. Unterscharfuhrer Wolf was killed in the storehouse and his body was hidden among the stored things. His brother was killed in the same place.

When Unterscharfuhrer Beckman came to his office, he grabbed for a weapon, but was dealt with in the same manner—killed by Heinrich

Engel, a young Jew from Lodz. All together, the rebels killed 12 Germans and four Ukrainian guards. During the uprising, the Jews grabbed the guns of the dead Germans and continued to use them against their enemies, shooting at the guards in the towers. The prisoners threw themselves upon the barbed-wire fences, tore them apart, and escaped. Many were blown up in the mine-fields that surrounded the camp. The plotters then put boards across the minefields in order to make a path over the mines. More than 400 Jews fled to the woods! As the escaped group stood around our beloved Sashka, he shouted to us, "For Stalin! Hurrah!"

Divided into smaller groups, we ran in different directions in the woods. The Germans, however, organized a search party. As planes strafed the woods, many Jews were killed. Only 50 Jews survived of the entire group. I was lucky enough to reach Chelm, where I was hidden until the Red Army entered the town. It was only then that I, a survivor of Sobibor, felt I was alive again.

After the uprising, the Germans killed all of the remaining prisoners in Sobibor, burned them, and dynamited the camp. The Germans who had built the death camp at Sobibor were Golzeimer, the chief inspector of the death camps, and the civilian engineer, Mauser.

(Signed): Chayim Povroznik.
Chelm, August 10, 1944.

IN THE GHETTO, IN THE FOREST, AND WITH THE PARTISANS
By Wolf Sheynwald

The German-Soviet war in Libivne started on Sunday, June 22, 1941. It began in the morning as the Germans bombarded our shtetl. We believed the Russians were very strong and that they would chase out the Germans very soon. We Jews were very sure of that.

When several days passed and the situation did not change, we decided to run away. I bought a wagon and a pair of horses, took my wife, my son and daughter, packed some of our most necessary possessions, and we started out for Russia.

When we reached Kovel we could not go any further, because German troops had cut all communication along the roads to Russia. We barely made it back home.

We found most of Libivne burned down, except for the market and some houses on Golden and Kusnishtcher Streets that were still untouched.

Our troubles began very soon, as the first victims of the Germans fell.

The Germans ordered all the Jews to gather in the marketplace. Some of the Jews hid, but the majority went to the marketplace. The Germans lined up the Jews and told them someone had cut the telephone lines and it was the fault of the Jews. They began then to pick out Jews, counting off every twenty-first man. Among those chosen were Shmuel Vayngarten, Chayim Shuster, and Mayer Tseylingold. The Germans took them to the hill opposite the town market and shot them.

A few weeks later, the Germans ordered us to elect a committee that would represent the shtetl Jews to the German authorities. They appointed Kalman Kopelzon, the former head of the kehila, as chairman of the Judenrat. He called on some important Jews of the shtetl to form the Judenrat. Some did not want to be on the Judenrat but were afraid to decline membership. The members were Dovid Veyner, Nachum Baran, Motl Privner, Leyzer Finkelshteyn, etc.—12 all together. Later a Jewish police force was created consisting of 10 men. They did not generally harm their Jewish brethren.

During that time, every few days new "contributions" of huge sums of, gold, furs, and furniture were exacted from the Jews. Jews were afraid to hide these things and handed them over to the Germans.

Six weeks after the German occupation and two weeks after the formation of the Judenrat, the Gestapo entered the shtetl and began to seize Jews in the street. At that time they caught 30 Jews, took them to the new cemetery behind the town, and shot them.

Not everyone was sure they had been shot. There was a theory they had been sent to work, until R. Avrom Sheyner went at night to the pits that had been dug by the Jews earlier and extracted a coat that had been worn by one of the murdered Jews. Thus the rest of the doubting Jews were finally convinced of the awful truth.

Another extermination action took place in September of 1941. The Gestapo came again and demanded 300 Jews for forced labor. The Judenrat did not want to give them the Jews and ran to the district commissar to intervene, but it was of no avail. The Gestapo men again seized Jews in the street, supposedly for labor, and took them into the Skiber Woods, which had trenches left over from World War I. There the 300 Jews were murdered and thrown into the trenches. Before they were shot, the victims were ordered to write letters to their families telling them they were being taken to work and that they were well treated.

When these letters reached town, the optimists said joyfully, "How could we have suspected the Judenrat of sending people to their deaths?"

Still later, Jews who were artisans and craftsmen received "golden passes": this meant that because they were workers, their lives would be spared. Those Jews who did not get such passes began to build hiding places in their homes. My brother built a bunker in our stable.

My friend Chayim Laks once came to our place of hiding, bringing us golden passes. At first, I worked at piling lumber on wagons. Later I was transferred to work in a sawmill. My son and a man named Fuks worked with me in the sawmill, once owned by Chayim Kroyt. The Nazis appointed a director, a man named Shidlovsky.

Getting enough food was difficult. The district commissar allowed a ration of 3.5 ounces of bread per person a day. Workers had the opportunity to buy some food from gentiles, if they had anything with which to barter. The richer ones among us had stored up necessities, but the stored food was dwindling very rapidly.

In the houses where Jews were permitted to live, the overcrowding was beyond measure. It became still worse after the district commissar ordered all Jews from the surrounding towns and villages to settle in Libivne. After this, the Libivne population was increased with Jews from Rimatch, Berzhets, Holevne, Kremne, Podhorodno, Vishnyeve, Masheve, Chvarostov, and other villages.

The Judenrat used to allot work among the Jews, sending them to do various jobs; they had to reap wheat in the fields of the gentiles, repair roads, work in the brick factory, and even dig ditches without being aware they were digging their own graves.

One day, a group of Jews was sent to repair roads. Among them were about 50 fourteen-year-old girls. It was a day before a fair and three girls, the wealthier among them, tried to buy some bread and butter from passing peasants. Sud-

denly the superintendent of the labor battalion came upon the scene and saw them buying. He took down the names of the girls and told them to come to the district commissar together with the members of the Judenrat. The three girls were cousins, the daughters of Yitshak Melamed, Pinye Melamed, and Dovid Melamed. Another Jew, also arrested with them, was Shimon Shtraycher.

At the office of the commissar the four were sentenced to death and were shot right then and there. One of the girls, it was said, was so frightened that her hair turned white.

This happened four months after the beginning of the German occupation. The four bodies were placed on a wagon that belonged to the Judenrat, and Tratl Pomerants took them to the Jewish cemetery, while Kalman Kopelzon said Kaddish (memorial prayer) for them.

The relationship of the Judenrat to the Jews was not bad. Only those from whom the Judenrat demanded gold or money were whispering against the Judenrat, even though the committee did only what the Germans demanded. Kalman Kopelzon was a stringent man, but his job was difficult. Yet the Judenrat members were a bit better off than the rest of the Jews, for they got more food.

The hospital was situated outside the ghetto. It was run by Jews, with Dr. Edward Amshchibovsky as the head. He lived in the town, outside the ghetto, and his brother-in-law, the dentist Martin Glasman, also lived in the town.

One day the two families ran away. Though the district commissar threatened all kinds of fines and sent a search party after them, they never were found.

The escapees had used forged Aryan passports. Several hundred Jews from Libivne were able to get false Aryan papers, but not all were able to save themselves.

Those Jews not assigned to labor would be taken on Saturdays and Sundays to work for the Kampyonis, pruning the fruit trees in their gardens. Incidentally, old Kampyoni's daughter, Topka, worked in the office of the district commissar and later married him. The Judenrat provided the commissar and Kampyoni's daughter with Jewish laborers and even with gardening tools. It was very hard work. The Germans guarding the Jewish workers would beat them. Some were so badly hurt that they required hospitalization.

I continued to work at the sawmill and did all kinds of unskilled labor. Whenever there was a rumor that an action was expected, on that day we did not go out to work but would stay in Chayim Kroyt's sawmill and hide in the attic. One day, the Gestapo came to the sawmill and found no one there except for the young boy, Buzi Kroyt, manager of the sawmill; they killed him on the spot.

The terrible actions the Nazis would organize finally convinced the Jews that the Nazis were preparing a final extermination of all the Jews. More and more people in Libivne began to plan a means of escape. Finally we found out that three long and deep pits were being dug near the brick factory, ditches 165 feet long and 30 feet wide.

Kopelzon reported that the Germans had told him big machines would be installed in these holes to increase production of bricks: Since the town had been destroyed by fire, these bricks would be used to rebuild the houses; and since bricks were needed for this project, the factory had to have increased production. Not too many Jews were left to believe the German lies.

In 1942 we heard rumors that partisans lived in the Shatsk Woods. One day, they blew up the bridge between Shatsk and Luboml, an act that gave hope and encouragement to those planning to escape.

Soon rumors began to circulate in town that the Germans were going to surround the ghetto. The rumors were spread by the Ukrainian police. Kopelzon, who had brought over his son-in-law, Meyer Yitshak Veytsfrucht, from the liquidated community in Rovno and made him a member of the Judenrat, again reassured everyone that the district commissar had promised there was no danger. Once again that was an outright lie.

Two days before Hoshana Rabba of 1942, Lithuanian, Ukrainian, and German police came into our ghetto. They were accompanied by the Gestapo, who surrounded the ghetto. Most of us had prepared hiding places. I had as well, digging a hole 60 feet long and 3 feet wide. Because I

could not carry out the earth lest I betray myself, I decided to cover the pile with wooden boards. The entrance was off to one side, so I could sneak into it and close the door behind me.

When I felt the time of liquidation was near, I told my son Meyer to run away, so he, at least, would be able to save himself. My son took a rifle and together with 30 other young people ran into the woods. Some of his companions were Leibele Russman, Yosl Fuks, Yidl Katz, etc. Though Ukrainians were shooting at them, the Jews succeeded in reaching the woods unharmed.

I and my dear ones hid in the hiding place, which had enough room for eight or ten people. But when my neighbors heard about the shelter, they came, too, so that there were now 20 of us in the shelter. We stayed there a day and then heard someone enter the house. After a long search, the police said no one was there and left. After we had been there two days, on the eve of Hoshana Rabba, an older man with us, Yisroel Leyb Mesh, began to scream that we should let him go to the synagogue.

We realized we could do nothing with him, since he had become confused and we had to let him out. He went into the house, recited psalms, and lay down to sleep. We heard him again reading psalms and then came two shots.

On the third day I said to my wife: "We have to leave our shelter to get food and water. We will die anyway. Let us try to save ourselves. Whoever wants to come with us is welcome!"

The night was dark and the police were standing 60 feet apart. Ten of us left the hiding place: I, my wife, my daughter, and seven others. The rest did not want to leave. We had already reached the mill and only had to cross the road toward the fields when a policeman turned toward us as we began to run—he evidently heard our running steps—and began to shoot. A bullet hit my sister-in-law, who fell dead.

Only one street was left for us to cross. We had to pass a house of a gentile. As soon as I moved I was caught by another policeman, while my wife, my daughter, and my other sister-in-law with two children were waiting for me. When my sister-in-law saw I was detained, she ran away.

The policeman was an acquaintance of mine

who had worked with me in the woods. I begged him to let me go and he asked me for money. I gave him everything I had in my pockets and told him my wife and my children were with me. When he told them to come nearer, they approached and he demanded money from them too. My wife was so frightened she gave him everything she had. He let us go and we started to cross the fields.

But a second policeman heard us walking and began to shoot. My acquaintance, the policeman, also began to shoot, but he shot into the air, so we managed to escape. The others, hearing the shots, thought that we had been killed and ran from the area.

We reached the woods and I was familiar with all paths in it because I had been working there. When we reached a village 7 miles from our shtetl, we drank our fill of water and continued on our way. As we came to another small forest and lay down to rest, a group of shepherds appeared, but ran when they saw us. They posed the greatest danger to us, as the Germans had spread the lie that Jews were cutting the throats of gentiles and that the shepherds should, therefore, betray any Jews they met and they would be rewarded.

We immediately ran from there. Later we came near the house of a peasant whom I knew—his name was Boyar. When Boyar came out in the morning and saw footprints on the ground, he understood someone was there. He looked until he found us in the woods, but promised not to betray us. He also asked us not to tell anyone he had seen us and later sent his daughter to us with some sour milk and bread to still our hunger. We stayed there two days.

During that time we were joined by our brother-in-law, Hersh Laychter. He told us our Libivne hiding place had been discovered and the Germans had shot his wife and the children, while he had been able to escape. He was despondent and wanted to give himself up to the Germans. It took me a long time to persuade him not to do this.

We stayed there eight more days, until shepherds learned of our whereabouts and we were forced to flee again. On the way we met a gentile known as a thief, who told us to stay near him. His name was Tichon Martilets. Though we feared he would betray us, we decided to stay with him.

We built a little shed of bent twigs, where we lived for four weeks. He would bring us potatoes. After four weeks, he brought more Jews to us, who did not stay long but went deeper into the woods because they were afraid. One Sunday they built a fire and the police surrounded them, shot one of them, and took the others alive. Later I learned the police had shot Miriam Getman and her daughter.

After this misfortune, it became dangerous to stay in the woods much longer, and so we left for another spot, where we stayed six months. At this new place, another Jew joined us. His name was Avrom Lubochiner. Our gentile thief had told him there were other Jews in the forest and brought him to us. There were thus five of us.

Our toughest problem was getting food. At first I would beg food from peasants whom I knew, and who, I felt, would not betray us. Later we began to steal from peasants. We would go into a village, sneak into a stable, and take whatever we could. Some peasants owed me money, and they paid their debts to me with corn. A poor peasant woman who lived in the woods allowed us to stay in her attic and even baked bread for us from the corn I had received. We stayed with her for four weeks. When Passover was near she told us she knew we had to eat special food then and gave us some honey and eggs; and we left for the woods again.

One peasant whom I knew told me there were partisans in the woods and promised to arrange for us to see them. When he told the partisans about us, they came for us with a cart and took us to their camp.

We rode about 6 miles until we reached their position. The partisan detachment was very large. It had three companies and its main mission was to sabotage trains. I, my wife, and my daughter were attached to the third squad, while the other two men joined another squad. They asked us whether we knew the side lanes that led to the railroad. We told them we were familiar with all roads and paths in the woods, since we were locals. They made us rest and let us shave and bathe.

The squad of 35 had 12 rifles and one machine gun. When the leader asked me whether I could shoot, I said yes, though I never had held a gun in my hand. When he noticed how badly I handled the gun, he understood that I could not shoot. But he was a fine man and taught me how to handle a gun. When I finally learned the art of shooting, I was put on guard duty, four hours at a stretch. The password was "thirteen." When one said "six," the answer was to be "seven" (which added up to thirteen).

My wife had duties in the health department. The doctor of this group was a Russian Jew who took my wife and my daughter to work with him, caring for the wounded.

My brother-in-law took part in the operation of blowing up the railroad line between Libivne and Masheve. The partisans hung the explosives under the belly of a horse and led the horse by its bridle. When they came near the railroad, they waited in the woods until night fell, when they could manage to lay the mine unseen.

When it grew dark, one partisan crawled near the rails to lay the mine. We had to wait until the explosion went off. We were also ordered to take prisoners, to obtain information from them. We also had to bring our wounded back to camp. Our group had a strong gentile youth who crawled near the guard, covered his mouth, and dragged him to us. We tied him up and brought him into the woods—we called such a prisoner a "tongue." We tied him to a tree and told him if he gave us information we would let him live with us in the woods; if not, we would shoot him.

A month later we received orders to retreat to our base at Gorodskovole; but before pulling out, we settled a "debt" with a peasant who was betraying war captives, among them many Jews. A group of partisans, among them a Jew named Trachtenberg, took the peasant into the woods. There was a trial, and the death sentence was pronounced and carried out on the spot.

While supplying ourselves with food before leaving the area, we fell into a bit of trouble with Germans. They caught us as we were grinding

wheat with a handmill. But our leader ordered a fast retreat in order to avoid casualties.

We walked for 5 *versts* (about 3.3 miles) over fields before we reached the woods, where we spent a whole day. When we heard that some other partisans were in those woods, I knew my son must be among that group. When we met up with them, however, I did not find him. One man I knew told me that my son had been shot while fighting Ukrainians and that my brother-in-law, who was in the group, had also fallen as a victim.

I told the bitter news to my wife, who fainted and then could not stop weeping. The leader spoke to her, saying they were heroes who fell in battle; that if she would not stop crying, we—I, she, and my daughter—would be ousted from the partisan camp. And so we had to bite our lips and stifle our terrible pain!

During that time our ranks were increased by other partisans and several escaped prisoners of war, five Jews among them. I remember two: Mordche and Leybl Karger.

We did not stay long in any one place but wandered about the woods until we reached the shtetl of Kamien-Koshirsk. There was not a soul left in that shtetl. For the first time in a long while we began to live like human beings—in a house. Naturally, we posted guards, for the Germans were not far away.

We could not remain long in the shtetl, for fear we would be surrounded by Germans. And so we went into the woods again. Meanwhile, winter was approaching and we had to provide winter quarters in the forest, dugouts we called *zemlyankes*. We dug out huge holes in the ground, 10 feet wide, 3 feet deep and 100 feet long; we then put boards over the holes (hewn from trees in those woods) and made three zemlyankes for the three detachments in our camp.

We did not lack food in the forest, but there was a scarcity of clothing. We received an order to join a group that was assigned to the task of bringing clothing and 20 cows. Trachtenberg was with me. We had to cross a small stream. The peasants had some boats but hid them, and we had to ford the river on foot. It was already so cold that our wet things froze to our bodies.

When we reached the village, I was told to go to the village *Soltis* (head) and tell him the partisans were demanding 20 cows. He told me he did not have any cows.

While searching at the home of another peasant, we (I and Trachtenberg) found a hidden cache of clothes, including two fur coats, which we requisitioned. The other partisans, who managed to get drunk and came back with empty hands, were punished.

Many times men who had been sent out to look for things never came back; a few were Jews. My company had three Jews; another company had 12–15. The partisans of that group had shot a Jew whom the leaders had sent out on a foray with them. Most Jewish partisans were so afraid to go that they would refuse an assignment.

On the other hand, some Jews would be anxious to go out and fight. One in my troop, whose name was Karlgan, had the title *geroy* ("the hero") and he became our leader. His father is now in Israel.

We received orders to take a small shtetl near Kovel, where we would make contact with the Red Army coming toward Kovel from the opposite side. My daughter was supposed to go with the fighters.

But the plan to unite with the Red Army fell through, since the Russians had failed to take Kovel and therefore could not come to meet us. We had to retreat. While in retreat, our partisan group met a big group of armed Germans and engaged them in battle. We brought our 74 wounded people back to the base in the woods.

There was an airfield not far from our camp, and Russian airplanes took our wounded to a hospital.

After eight days, we again received orders to meet up with the Red Army, which was near Kovel. By then we had received some reinforcements from Russian soldiers from other parts of the country. The Russians took the young partisans into their army and made them regular soldiers. The older partisans, as well as women and children, stayed on in the village of Kochotska-Vola. I remained in this village with my wife and daughter.

The village had an outbreak of typhoid fever; my wife succumbed to this sickness and died after 14 days of suffering. I gave her a Jewish burial in the town of Sotshi.

My daughter caught the disease from her mother and became sick. Having lost my wife and son, I feared losing the only dear person I had left. I fed her, giving her fresh milk and watching over her like the apple of my eye. But as she grew steadily weaker, I hired a horse and wagon and took her to the village of Rafalovke, which had a pharmacist by the name of Bass. He took my daughter into his home, gave her medicine, and saved her. He is now in Israel.

Meanwhile, the Soviets began to draft all men up to the age of 50 into the Red Army. I, too, received an order to appear before the army authorities. Since my daughter was still very weak after her serious illness, I could not leave her alone. Even in this matter Mr. Bass was able to help me, and I escaped the draft, remaining in Rafalovke.

When Kovel was liberated, I decided to travel through Kovel back to my hometown. When I and my daughter came to Libivne, we hardly found a single house undamaged. My brother's house was one that had remained intact, but there was hardly a soul left in town besides Moyshe Lifshitz, his wife, Chane, and a brother, Pinie, and four boys who had saved themselves by running into the woods [Nathan Sobel, Avrom Getman, Moyshe Blumen and Binyomen Perkal]. There were about 20 Jews left altogether.

Moyshe Lifshitz had been in Libivne for two weeks, working as a bookkeeper. He helped me get a job, for the *rayispolkom* (government office) needed a man to buy and sell animal skins. I was hired and soon became a director. I then hired three gentiles who had saved Jews. One was the gentile who had hidden Yidl Byeges, who is now in Israel. I also gave work to the gentile who had saved Moyshe Lifshitz and his wife, Chane.

My staff consisted of ten people—three gentiles and seven Jews—and we usually held meetings that stretched well into the night. I, as a director, had to participate in these meetings. Those gentiles who had been German collaborators were sent to work in Donbas. They never came back.

Life went on for four months until the arrival of Denisyuk from Gor-Soviet. He was a truly evil person. One day he called over the four Jewish children who had survived and told them he would send them to work in Donbas. Thereupon I and my daughter went to him, saying, "Isn't it enough that these children have gone through such terrible experiences during the war? But instead of sending them to school, you are sending them away to work together with murderers and traitors in Donbas? The four children were Nathan Sobel, Avrom Getman, Moyshe Blumen, and Binyomen Perkal.

The gentile was insulted and told me he would send my daughter there, too. But higher authorities intervened and his evil plan failed.

Rochl Leichter lived with us. When the Ukrainian leader of the shtetl's work force wanted to send her to Donbas too, I went to the Ukrainian and begged him not to do this to her; when the Ukrainian did not listen to me, I approached the first secretary of the Party and told them this Ukrainian man had been in my Fyodorov partisan group and when sent out on a mission he had run away.

The man was called before an investigation committee and was asked whether it was true that

Yitshak Orbuch with his wife, Sonya, and Shmuel Melamed (z"l) at the gate to the UNRRA assembly center in Zeilsheim, Germany, 1946.

he was a deserter. He answered that he had not deserted, but had run to another partisan camp. But he could not convince the examiners and was removed from his post. Rochl was saved.

I worked thus for six months, until the Soviets decided to form a commission to decide who had the right to be repatriated to Poland.

When we received permission to go, we said goodbye to the Jews of Libivne. Before we left, we learned that two Jewish girls had been saved by hiding in the homes of peasants in a nearby village: the children did not know they were Jewish. We took them to sleep over in our house on the eve of our return to Poland. But in the morning we discovered the two girls had run back to the village.

We crossed the Soviet border on our way to Chelm, stayed in Chelm for a short time, and then continued on our journey through Lodz, Szczecin, and finally Berlin. From the American Zone in Berlin we went to Zeilsheim, where we stayed for three years. We then emigrated to America.

I finally wish to add a few words about my exterminated family. My brother Abraham was killed in 1943 in the vicinity of the town of Matzev. The date and place of his death are unknown. The place where my brother Chayim died is likewise unknown. My brother Simche Sheynwald was killed in a village during the winter of 1944. His wife and four children died there, too. I do not know where and how my brother Tratl died.

My sister Henye Lentschitsky (Sheynwald) was exterminated together with her whole family. The same is true of my sister Freydele Vishnits (Sheynwald).

My son fell in a fight with the Germans in 1943. I do not know when and where my son Shneyer fell.

Yitshak Orbuch accompanies Eleanor Roosevelt (*center*) during her visit to the Zeilsheim camp in Germany, 1947.

Jewish survivors from Luboml at commemoration for Holocaust victims, in Zeilsheim,
Germany in 1947.

AS A POLE WITH THE PARTISANS
By Joseph Karpus (Veytsfrucht)

On June 22, 1941, at 4 o'clock in the morning, I was awakened by my wife: "Just listen to what is happening in the street!" The air was filled with a piercing noise from passing airplanes. The noise continued for another 20 minutes, together with explosions from shells falling in the city.

I immediately went to my military unit, where I was employed as a quartermaster. When I reached the area, I was met by the commander, who told me to distribute warehouse goods to the Red Army soldiers only as he instructed. When I approached the warehouses, I found 8–10 military wagons and supply agents waiting with orders from my superior officer for a variety of goods.

Exercising caution, I tried to ascertain the situation at the border. However, all I could learn was that the regimental commissar had told his men to fight to the last drop of blood.

Throughout the day, German airplanes flew sorties over the town, unchallenged by anyone because the Russians lacked the means. Periodically, shells from the German artillery exploded around the town. Besides the shellings, we did not have any specific news.

On Wlodzimierska Street, the former post office was now the mobilization office. Young and middle-aged men stood in line waiting for orders. With time, the line grew shorter. Many men who left the line were Ukrainians who refused to serve on the front lines and men who had grudges against the Russian government.

The night from Sunday to Monday passed peacefully. The following morning, the town was without government and one could feel approaching chaos and confusion in the air. Young, single men free from family responsibili-

ties ran toward what had been the Polish-Russian border.

On Tuesday, the situation deteriorated. The peasants used force and burglarized the warehouses where I was employed. The robberies were a clear indication that no one was in charge of the town. We came together, friends and acquaintances, to discuss whether we should proceed toward the old Polish-Russian border. Some were of the opinion that we should not leave. First of all, on the run we would be threatened with hunger. Second of all, reports were reaching us about Ukrainians waiting on roads and killing those who were going east. Furthermore, there were reports of Germans approaching the town of Kovel in an attempt to cut off the Russian army. As a result of these developments we decided to stay put.

The same evening we heard machine-gun fire. It was obvious to me that the enemy was very close. When I approached the police station everything became clear. There was no one inside the building. Doors and windows were open. They had all left, abandoning the local population.

The same night, the Germans entered our town and already on Wednesday morning were conducting door-to-door searches demanding a wide range of items. The day after the Germans entered our town, they established a local government under the control of a German commandant, a Gestapo man. In the beginning of September, an assistant to the commander, a Gestapo man named Uhde, came to our town and began to administer it.

The newly formed police and city council, consisting exclusively of Ukrainians, were under the control of the German commandant. For every minor favor extended to the Jews, these people demanded payment in gold. Knowing full well what was awaiting the Jews of Luboml, they kept quiet so they could squeeze from the Jews everything they owned. And at a later date they looked on with joy and actively participated in the great Jewish Holocaust.

A Judenrat was formed and a force of 10 to 20 Jewish policemen was approved. They all wore special armbands.

The first decree required all Jews to wear a Star of David sewn on a white armband. The Jews were ordered to report every day for forced labor or face a death penalty. Utensils made of copper and silver had to be turned in at a prearranged location. Every day, a few hundred Jews went to work in various places, including the train station, a sawmill, etc. From the first day of forced labor, the Jews were severely beaten by German and Ukrainian overseers.

The marketplace for Jewish labor took place every day, beginning at 6 a.m., near the Judenrat office. All Jews called to work had to appear at the marketplace. Later came the Ukrainian customers with slips, and a Jewish policeman led the Jews away to the assigned workplace. At the end of the workday, he brought them back.

The Judenrat was assigned one bakery exclusively for baking bread for the Jews. Every working individual was apportioned 7 ounces of bread and a child or a nonworking person 3.5 ounces of bread per day. The bread was bad, but no one dared decline it. Outside the stores where bread was distributed, hundreds of inhabitants, men and women, waited in long lines to receive their allotted portion.

Together with all decrees came an order requiring all peasants to sell their foodstuffs to the cooperative and forbidding the sale of any merchandise to Jews.

The decree brought about an instant, general state of anxiety. Everybody began to worry about ways of procuring food reserves. Peasants brought products but bartered them for shoes, clothing and other items. The prices of goods were continuously climbing, and people who had nothing to barter could not receive anything

from the peasants. They had to be satisfied with the measly ration of bread.

Tuesday, July 1, the town commandant issued a decree ordering all men to appear the following morning in the town square with a pail and broom and be ready to sweep the streets. A considerable number of people came out.

Then the town commandant appeared, in the company of gendarmes and police. Five young men were selected from among those gathered. They were: Meyer Tseylingold, Shmuel Vayngarten, Moyshe Zilberman, Jacob Gelibter, and Shmuel Shuster. The commandant stated that the day before, on the road between Luboml and Borki, the telephone lines had been cut. Furthermore, he said, it is certain that Jews had carried out this act of sabotage. The five Jews were therefore sentenced to death.

The men were taken directly to the hill near the area where the Jewish men were assembled. A few minutes later, we heard gunfire. Jews were sent to remove the remains and take them to the Jewish cemetery.

The following morning, 50 young men, including myself, were taken to work repairing the road leading from town to Masheve. The road near Marmorkow was very sandy and the German trucks could not go through it. Twenty-five Jews brought used bricks in carts from buildings, and 25 other men laid the bricks into the sand. At 11 a.m., we were given 15 minutes to eat and they distributed black ersatz coffee.

We had not started to eat when an SS man exclaimed: "Why are the filthy Jews stuffing themselves?" Chayim-Wolf, Aliesker's son, went over to the SS man and explained that we had been working since 7 a.m. and a German supervisor had given us a 15-minute break. The SS man pulled out a rubber stick and began hitting the Jew over the head until the poor man fell to the ground in a pool of blood. The same German beat up three other Jews.

One day, a rumor spread through town, in the name of someone in the Judenrat. It was said that anybody who worked at a steady job would receive an identification card from the labor office and would not be harmed. However, nonworking individuals or those who could not find steady employment would be sent to labor camps.

The news caused a panic among the Jews. Whoever had a peasant acquaintance or a Ukrainian employee tried, with a variety of presents such as leather, fabrics, antiques, and gold, to secure a steady place of work.

I and some friends found jobs at the train station, sorting and loading the goods left by Russians.

After working for a few weeks, on July 22, 1941, our overseer, who happened to be our neighbor, came and told us to hide. He informed us about the arrival of many trucks full of German Gestapo who were conducting door-to-door searches, rounding up young men and taking them to the Bug River. The Germans said they were taking the Jews to work on the railroad line in Chelm. On this particular day, more than 300 Jewish men were rounded up.

The truth was, as we learned at a later date, that all the rounded-up inhabitants were taken to the other side of the Jewish cemetery, where large, open pits were prepared, with machine guns set up over them. The Jews were brought in trucks, gathered around the perimeter of the pits. As they were shot by machine-gun fire, their corpses fell into the ditches. Many of the murdered were still alive as they fell into the pit. They were buried alive.

As it was later reported, the ground did not rest for a long time. One could see the earth moving up and down.

Some of the massacred people, in the last moments before execution, exclaimed, "*Shma Yisroel*! [Hear, O Israel!] German outlaws! One day you will pay dearly for the innocent Jewish victims."

Those who remained alive continued to seek a place to work and food for their families. At the same time, people began to build hideouts. Many good craftsmen offered a variety of plans. Hideouts consisted of hollow spaces dug under the floor, with openings that could not be seen, or double walls in a given place in the house such as the attic, basement, etc. Every time there was a knock on the door, the men went into hiding and the women opened the door. The Germans searched the homes, and if they did not find anybody, they often beat the women with rubber sticks. At that point, the Germans were not rounding up women.

Exactly a month later, the Judenrat received an order to deliver enough wool fabric for 50 suits, to be delivered within two days. The fabric had to be blue and of high quality. In addition, the Jews had to submit 300 gold five-ruble pieces. In response, the Judenrat was called into session and it was decided to ask all Jews who were believed to be rich for voluntary contributions of gold pieces. Former fabric merchants were asked to bring fabric.

The first rows then took place. The selected wealthy individuals announced that they owned neither gold nor fabric. Many did bring gold to the Judenrat voluntarily, but much less than what had been requested. As a result, the first 24 hours were not very successful.

The less wealthy people stood around the Judenrat building saying that because of the wealthy everyone would perish. They demanded that the Judenrat employ more stringent measures to come up with the demanded items, or allow the people to search the homes of the rich.

In the end, the community succeeded in blocking the searches and scandals. All German demands were met. Two men from the Judenrat, the president and the members of the quartermaster unit, delivered the items to the Germans. The members of the community stood around the Judenrat building, awaiting news about what the town commandant said and how he received the Judenrat representatives.

After three hours, the representatives returned and reported that the commandant was very pleased, so much so that he had even smiled when he stated that everything would be all right and no harm would come to anyone as long as the Jews continued to work.

The next few days were quiet. People could breathe with ease. However, the peace did not last long. The better the Germans were doing at the front, the worse they treated the Jews. Increasingly, hunger became an issue, and many families, experiencing hunger, came to the Judenrat to ask for food supplies. The Judenrat established a relief fund for poor families, providing mainly bread.

On August 22, 1941, the Germans rounded up 500 men and women, among them my wife, and detained them in Kampyoni's sheds. Meyer London's daughter, Andzia, who succeeded in hiding out in Pavel Kurnos' orchard adjacent to his house, was turned over to the Germans by Pavel's son-in-law—Sidoruk the bricklayer.

From the 500 arrested, only 11 women remained alive—among them my wife. The following day, the remaining detainees in the sheds were executed 4 miles from Luboml, in the small forest of Horodno.

The town's atmosphere was unbearable. The crying and wailing were indescribable. In addition, many people did not report, as usual, to work at the Judenrat. Some had been caught, others were in hiding and afraid to come out. The Judenrat became fearful that a new edict would result from its inability to supply the necessary number of workers.

It was decided to give money to the representatives who came to get workers. Furthermore, they also were promised that the work missed on that day would be made up the next day.

The scheme, however, did not succeed. The following morning, the labor supervisor visited the sawmill and noted that many workers were missing. He demanded to see the president of the Judenrat. The president then was badly beaten and was ordered to deliver, the following morning, double the number of workers and 500 rubles in gold no later than three in the afternoon.

The Jews were frightened, trying to persuade each other that they must report to work lest the situation become much worse. The gold was gathered as requested. In the morning, about 400 men and women were lined up in rows. They were sent to various workplaces.

While the blood of the murdered Jews in the Horodno forest was still warm, the peasants from the nearby village of Borki began searching the dead bodies for valuables and Ukrainian police and officials became drunk with the loot.

Autumn came to town. It was raining and the streets were muddy. The souls of the people were sad. Even those who had some food reserves began to suffer want. The number of Jews who could work began to dwindle.

In January, 1942, yet another roundup of Jews took place, but this time they escaped with only a scare. Five hundred Jews were detained in the Radio cinema. They remained there for a week and were then released.

At the end of January, 1942, the Jews were burdened with yet another mandatory contribution: 100 men's fur coats, 50 women's fur coats, two lamb and sealskin coats, and 500 rubles in gold. The Judenrat treasury had then enough money to purchase expensive coats and gold coins. The difficulty was in securing the furs. This was an article for which the peasants would give anything, but the merchants insisted that they didn't have any furs.

The Judenrat contacted a few local peasants who used to prepare furs and prepared to pay them the highest price. However, 50 furs were too many to locate. It became necessary to contact city merchants and send the Jewish police to search Jewish homes.

Everybody was genuinely surprised when in one of the Jewish homes 170 furs were found. The Jew in whose home the furs were found began to beg that no one should find out about the furs and donated the 50 needed furs. In this manner, within five days, the entire contribution was collected.

When the president of the Judenrat delivered the contribution, he asked the commandant for some heating materials for families living in cold homes. The commandant replied favorably to the request.

Beginning in May, 1942, the Judenrat received an order to supply 300 Jews to drive horses. It was a very difficult to prepare a list of 300 people, because these people almost certainly would not return home.

Yet the list of 300 Jews was put together and I was on that list. Foreseeing the peril awaiting us, on the day preceding the deadline, namely May 5, I took off my yellow [Star of David] patch and began walking out of town toward the village of Horodno to a peasant acquaintance, Yefim Jaszczuk, who used to work for my father, may his memory be blessed, with the intention of hiding out in his place until the Jews selected for driving horses had left town.

I stayed at the peasant's home for two nights. On May 7, I started walking back to town. On the way, I met my wife, who was coming to tell me everything was back to normal in town and I could return home. On May 8, I returned to my former place of work.

Eight days before Passover, as I was approaching the warehouse where I worked, I found someone had broken in and, as I suspected, pilfered honey and wax. When the proprietor came, I reported the theft. He, in turn, reported the theft to the police. At midday, I was detained and arrested as the guilty party.

My incarceration in a cell where the walls were smeared with Jewish blood, as well as the entire frame-up about my robbing the warehouse, had a frightening impact on me. My only comfort was in the fact that the town commandant was a close acquaintance of ours and I hoped we'd be able to negotiate with him about my release.

The next morning, during the interrogation by the commandant, I asked if he would permit my wife to bring me food and in doing so hinted that my wife "will take care of everything." After the interrogation, upon returning to my cell, I saw through the window my wife and older brother strolling near the prison. A few hours later, I was given food from home and I understood that my family was negotiating with the commandant for my release.

And finally, after Passover, I was released from prison.

I was afraid to return to my place of work, and I didn't want to work at the job in town arranged by the Judenrat, so I decided to seek employment outside the town's limits. Moyshe Gershenberg (Avrom Reise's son), may he rest in peace, a good acquaintance of mine, helped me in my search for a job. With his help, I found a position in Kokurubisht Forest, near the village of Palap, where I and 21 other Jews were employed. Twelve men worked at loading long and short logs, three worked as forest inspectors, and seven cut trees and prepared firewood.

I remember the names of the following for-est workers: inspectors—Gershon Grinshpan, Mendl Meshkis, Moyshe Gurbratch. Workers—Moyshe Gershenberg (deceased), Dovid Meshkis (deceased), Motek Handelsman (deceased), Yakov Ginzburg (deceased), Eliyohu Goldbursten (deceased), Nute Bialer (deceased), Yakov Verbla (deceased), his son Verbla, 14 years old, Mendl Tsimerboym (deceased), Zalman Mulfeld (deceased), Yehoshua Grimatlicht (deceased), and I—Joseph Karpus.

Moyshe Gershenberg (deceased) and I befriended the forest ranger Nowakowski. He informed us that in the forest where we were presently located there were Russian troops dropped by Russian airplanes.

We conveyed the information to the rest of the Jews in our group. We then decided to seek out the Russian troops. To gain this objective, two of our men ventured every morning into the forest to reconnoiter the situation. So that the overseer would not notice that two men were missing every day, the remaining men had to make up the assigned workload, something not easy to accomplish.

We did not succeed in establishing contact with the Russian troops. Consequently, as a precautionary measure, we built a hideout in case Gestapo men came to search the area. We also agreed on a meeting place in the forest.

Mordche Handelsman and Yakov Ginzburg took it upon themselves to secure weapons. In two weeks, we had one rifle and two revolvers.

At the end of May, on a Monday, we were ordered to load 12 platforms. On this particular day it rained very hard. It was very difficult to load because the logs were slipping from under the ropes. When the overseer noticed that by midday we had loaded only five wagons, he notified Luboml.

At 3 p.m., four Germans arrived with two dogs and asked who was responsible for the workload. Yakov Verbla was pointed out. The Germans started to beat him, together with his son. When the two fell to the ground, the Germans set the dogs on them. The dogs tore their clothes and bit Yakov's son's leg. Then they beat Eliyohu Goldburten and Motl Handelsman. They ordered us to load all the wagons or we would all be shot. We all came out to load the logs. With our last strength we completed the work at 2 a.m. The miracle was the well-lit night.

It was July. The work in the forest became harder. We were growing weaker yet we still had to fulfill the quota. We stumbled on an idea: we did not split all the logs, instead loading about 50 percent as they were—round. To ensure the overseer would say nothing about it, from time to time we brought him a present.

On July 15, the hideout was completed. It could accommodate 25–30 people. The rifle was hidden in the hideout, while the revolvers we kept in our room by night and, during the day, with us at work.

At the end of July, Nowakowski informed Moyshe Gershenberg that there were partisans in the forests 20–25 miles from Kamien-Koshirsk, in the vicinity of Wielka-Glusha and Lubashev. Moyshe and I decided to procure a map and venture in that direction. On Shabbat, Moyshe and I went to town, to Shmuel-Leyb Huberman, where we found a map of the region.

During the German occupation, the son-in-law of Shmuel-Leyb, Chayim Klewartowski, as well as his son, Isaac Huberman and a print-worker Melnik, all worked in a print shop. As Klewartowski was looking at the map, he said: "If you want, I can make you passports using any name you want."

For this, he asked a certain fee. Of course, we accepted the offer. The same week, we had our photographs taken to have four passports made—for us and for our wives. For the time being, we decided not to fill in the name, religion, or nationality.

Once we had the passports, we needed permits to leave town and papers indicating our destination, as well as confirmation that we had worked and been discharged from work.

Binyomen Eizenberg, who before the war lived in Danzig, worked as an interpreter for the district commissar. I trusted Binyomen Eizenberg, so one day I told him the whole story and asked him to help me with the above-mentioned matters. He told me outright that he could get me permits to leave town, but as for work permits, he had no access to them. They were

under the control of a Ukrainian named Bulavka.

He asked me about my plan. I told him about it, as well as about the passport I had already made. Then he asked me to arrange passports for him and Feyge Ginzburg, the daughter of Berl Ginzburg, who was about to become his bride.

A few days later, Benjamin brought me the departure permit from the district commissar. I arranged the passports for him.

It was already the beginning of September. Moyshe and I continued working in the forest and made plans for our risky trip.

Moyshe began to look for a peasant who would agree to take us and whom we could trust. On Shabbat we once again went to Libivne. There the situation was very bad. The demands by the German could not be met anymore, neither with money nor work. Many families were starving. They did not have anything more to give the peasants.

However, the worst was the atmosphere in town, because it was hinted that there was only one more month to live. Everybody was giving away items, even furniture, to peasant acquaintances. In my home, the mood was desperate. A Ukrainian acquaintance told my mother-in-law the Jews had only a few days to live.

When I was at home, Moyshe came and told me he had made arrangements with a peasant who agreed to take us. The peasant's name was Panas from the village of Pervis. I told Moyshe I knew this peasant to be a big swindler. Moyshe in turn told me no decent peasants were ready to go. In addition, there were four of us and we were not afraid of him. We agreed to travel on September 30, 1942.

When the peasant came to pick us up, my wife, who was seven months pregnant, refused to go. The peasant suggested we should not travel together. Moyshe and his wife should go first. Once Moyshe reached the destination and saw that it was possible to stay there, he would let us know. I accepted the suggestion and decided with Moyshe that once he reached the destination he would write me a few words on Panas' belt.

We said goodbye to Moyshe and went to the Judenrat to get an extension on our permits. We waited a few hours, but the Judenrat representative did not return from the district commissar. At 4:30, the Judenrat representative returned and informed us our permits had not been extended. He also confirmed the news that Gestapo and police from other towns had arrived in town. It became clear to us the end was near.

On the way home we stopped by to see our friend Simche Kramer (the watchmaker). He told us that a few hours earlier the Germans had taken back all the watches they had brought in for repairs, even those he could not fix. Later, we met Yosef Melamed (Yosl Kerpeles) the tailor. He also told us the Germans had taken back everything they had given him to sew, even unready garments that had just been cut. This was done not only by the Germans but Ukrainians as well. All these signs were indication of a new action.

The time was a few minutes after five. We came home and began to prepare a small package for everyone—underwear and bread. We decided to go to an acquaintance of ours, a peasant who lived 3 miles out of town, on the way to Masheve.

We locked our home and went to the meadows behind Yosef Amerikaner's home. There we lay until midnight. Suddenly, I noticed the old Christian, Abramowicz, leaving his house to feed the horses.

I crawled over to the stable, identified myself, and asked him to help us reconnoiter the road so we could cross. At 2 o'clock in the morning, the man's son, Nikolai, not only helped us cross the road but the railroad tracks as well. At this point, we were about a mile or two from our destination. After a long search in the dark of night for the right place, toward morning we finally arrived at the home of our peasant acquaintance.

The moment we approached Ivan's house, a dog began to bark. The peasant came out and ordered us to remain quiet because he did not want his son to know we were there. In addition, his neighbor's son was a policeman. He gave us a place in the barn.

The peasant brought us news from town that all the Jews had been murdered and that Jews found in hideouts were being shot everyday. The Ukrainians participated in searching for and handing over Jews to the Germans because for every Jew the Germans paid in sugar and salt.

Among the Jews handed over to the Germans was Chayim Kroyt, the proprietor of the sawmill. The peasant told us Chayim Kroyt had hid in the

Photocopy of an identification card under the name Wanda Karpus, used by Rivke Shliwa during the Nazi occupation.

pits of the Wishniewo brick factory. However, the owner of the brick factory, Terebucha, had taken Chayim out of a pit, tied his hands, and handed him over to the Germans in town.

This is how the first week passed. My wife began to complain about pains and that she couldn't stay the whole time lying down. We returned to our old plan of traveling as Christians. Yet we did not know what had happened to Moyshe Gershenberg and if we could proceed. I told our peasant the whole story and asked him to visit the village of Pervis, locate the peasant Panas, and ask about Moyshe. Ivan went and returned with bitter news that Panas knew nothing and had not taken any Moyshe. I was of the opinion that Panas had murdered Moyshe. Still, we decided to travel there as Christians.

After we pleaded with him and paid him well, Ivan agreed to take us in the direction of Glusha. On October 15, 2:30 in the morning, we came down from the attic, organized ourselves, filled out the documents, and began our journey. The peasant knew the roads well, and at dawn we arrived at the police post in Masheve. The German guard told us to stop. He checked our documents and told us to proceed.

Three miles along the way, the road was sandy and it became difficult for the horses to pull the load. They refused to budge. Having no alternative, we said goodbye to the peasant and thanked him for his good deed. We continued on our way, hitching rides on passing carriages, until we reached the village of Buczen (Bicin).

Near the village we met a local peasant and I attempted to hire him to take us toward Glusha. He agreed and asked us, in the meantime, to come into his home and wait until his return. After waiting a long time, I decided to try to get a means of transportation from the local village committee. The representative promised he would take care of it, and in the meantime I returned to the home of the peasant.

Suddenly, four Ukrainian policemen arrived on the scene and demanded to see documents. The senior officer took all the documents and said: "What kind of Pole are you, you are a Jew with whom I worked together before the war." I pretended not to hear, but he continued to ask: "You

don't remember me?" and started to recall our working together.

I saw that further denials were out of the question, so I decided to admit who I was and at the same time told him: "Nikolai, you remember how well we got along. And if I succeeded in escaping from the ghetto, do you have to be the one to kill us?" He replied that he had made a mistake saying what he did in front of his friends. Now he could not help me because they could report him to the Germans.

He ordered us to come with him and the other policemen. We walked about a mile from the village, and when we came to a cluster of bushes, Nikolai ordered us to enter it. My wife understood we were about to be shot and she began to shout, "Shma Yisroel." My heart turned to stone. I could not utter a word.

Nikolai ordered me to open the packages. He divided the items among his friends. He told me to give him my watch and I gave it to him. He saw two rings on my hand and told me to give them to him. I also gave him the money as he ordered. Luckily, they were satisfied with this. They left us with 10 yards of white linen and a thousand rubles.

As we walked out to the road, a peasant passed by and Nikolai told him to take us to the village of Wilemcza, where the peasant was going. There we found a peasant who agreed to take us to the village of Buzaki. In return, we gave him a dress.

In Buzaki I continued to seek transportation. However, I was informed that all questions relating to transport had to be addressed to the elder of the village. I came before him and introduced myself as the designated forester in Wielka-Glusha. I asked him to arrange a carriage to take me to Glusha.

The elder replied that in order to do this, he needed permission from the police in a village 3 miles away. However, he agreed to wait until peasants on the way to Kamien-Koshirsk passed by, at which time he would order them to take us to Glusha.

It was getting dark and no carriages were passing through town. We began to walk in the direction of Mala-Glusha. On the way, we stopped in the home of peasant, a "Shtundist," and he gave us food. When I told him we were going to Glusha, he dissuaded us from going there, because partisans came there and murdered foresters, especially Poles. He proposed that I accept a position as a gamekeeper 2 miles from his house because the previous gamekeeper wanted to leave. The gamekeeper sent me to the forest commissar in Kamien-Koshirsk, who in turn gave me a letter to his brother-in-law, Milash Dart, who would go with me to the commissar.

When I came to the brother-in-law of the gamekeeper in Kamien-Koshirsk, it was Sunday morning. He was dressed and ready to go to church. He told me to join him in church, where he would introduce me to Commissar Ofke. My wife and I had no idea how to behave in a church, but we had no choice. We entered the church and lowered ourselves to our knees with everybody else. We watched the behavior of the Poles and followed suit.

Upon leaving the church, Milash introduced me to the commissar. He promised to receive us in his residence at 3 o'clock in the afternoon. In our conversation, I told the commissar we were Poles, that we had done forced labor for the Germans in uniting the rivers Bug and Switerz. However, we said, the work was too hard so we ran away. I further told him I was by profession a forest inspector and was asking his help.

He told me to come to his office the following morning and he would give me a position as forester in Wielka-Glusha (exactly where I had intended to travel before).

In the office of the forest commissar, I had to fill out a questionnaire consisting of 37 questions and only then did I receive the job as forester in Wielka-Glusha. I was provided with official transportation to the place of work, and the chief forester found us a large furnished room in town, in the home of a widow.

On October 21, I began my job; however, in light of the fact that I had no idea about my work, I used to take the papers home in the evening and try to make head and tails of them. I also made an effort to keep my distance from the Poles in town. However, they tried hard to get close to me. The reason was that their wood allotment

depended on my decision and winter was around the corner.

We had no radio or newspapers, but we heard that Jews in cities and towns were being murdered. The peasants would catch the hiding Jews and bring them to the police so they could get the reward of kerosene or salt.

On November 7, I received a circular stating that in connection with the demand by the Reich's commissar, all foresters must submit within seven days the following documents: a statement from the last workplace; a statement as to one's education as a forester. The following morning I informed my supervisor that I couldn't produce the required documents on such short notice because they were with my parents, and I asked him to extend the deadline for about two months or release me from the job.

He replied that it was impossible to extend the deadline. However, he proposed that I go to the police and speak with Commissar Ofke, who had given me the job. We did so, but Ofke's reply was negative.

I barely finished my conversation when my landlady came and informed me that my wife had labor pains. I went directly home, bringing a midwife. The next morning a baby was born. The doctor ordered my wife to stay in bed for the next 20 days.

On November 10, in the morning, I submitted my papers from the office, and by doing so I received a statement that I had worked as a forest ranger and quit of my own free will. I said goodbye to my coworkers and went home.

Once I was home, my wife and I began to review our bad situation. First, people in town would begin to wonder why I quit my job; second, we couldn't leave because of my wife's health; third, we had no place to go or person to help us.

That day, we were visited by Majewski, director of a dairy, who brought us a package of fresh butter in honor of the new baby. He noticed we were very sad, and when I told him what had happened, he offered me a job in his place. For appearance's sake, I scowled a little at the offer because this was not my profession, but in the end I agreed and the director left satisfied.

On November 11, in the morning, I started

working in the new place. I was supposed to visit the region, which was big, and every day I went to another village.

Once, I was returning home on foot from the village of Gorki where the family of Majewski was residing. When I approached the river, suddenly I heard a cry: "Keep still!"

I saw a partisan on a horse. He asked who I was and what I was doing there, and I told him everything. He took my address and promised to visit us at night. Later I learned he was the commander in this region.

With the Partisans

During November we were visited a few times by the partisans, who received from me all kinds of information. We lived through terrible days because we watched how the police would often bring in Jews from their hideouts, order them to dig ditches, and shoot them in front of our windows.

On the morning of December 14, the partisans attacked the police post, killed the policemen, and burned down the building. At the same time, they broke all the machines in the dairy and removed from the basement the butter designated for delivery to the Germans. At 6:30 in the morning, the mission was completed. At 7 a.m., I left home for work. At the entrance to the building, I met Jurek Pietrowski, the accountant, and together we entered the factory and saw the destruction. Coming out of the basement, Jurek nearly tripped over a large piece of paper, which he picked up. It was a map of partisan bases. I took the map and hid it well.

On December 18, I had a visit from two partisans. During our conversation, I asked the partisans to ask their commander to come and see me because I had something important to discuss with him. When I handed the commander the map, he shuddered and then thanked me repeatedly. He told me that Commissar Boris Nikolayavitch had lost the map during the mission. As he was saying goodbye to me, he promised to arrange a meeting between me and the chief commander.

On the 22nd, in a village apartment near the Pripet River, I met with the chief commander,

Ivan Grigoriewicz Shubitidze, a very tall, well-built Georgian, dressed in a military uniform taken from a German officer. He was very interested in my past. I gave him the agreed-upon version: that I was an escapee from a work camp that had the task of uniting Lake Smitiani with the Bug River; that I was a Pole and a forester by profession.

I received assignments from the commander. Among the orders was one demanding that I visit, more than once, the town of Kamien-Koshirsk to receive certain materials, because the partisan brigade was preparing to attack the headquarters of the district commissar of Kamien-Koshirsk, 3 miles from the town of Kamien-Koshirsk, in the village of Ulble.

In my conversation with the commander, I asked about the possibility of moving my family into a partisan camp. His answer was that I was already on the list of partisans, but it was more important that I carry out my assignments outside of the forest.

At the beginning of 1943, I went to our meeting place in Nievir. There the chief commander awaited me, and together we traveled to a few Polish villages to talk with peasants about organizing into partisan units. Going to the airport, on the way to Sworin, we met a young Jewish man in the forest. He was a doctor from Glusha, Lipe Ovinovicki, deceased, who greeted us warmly. The commander told me headquarters did not want to accept him into the partisan unit.

We arrived in Sworin at the onset of darkness. At that time, a large partisan unit of Sergei Ivanowicz Sikorski, the commander of the Brisk organization, was stationed in town. Over a glass of vodka, we discussed the idea of organizing the surrounding population into fighters against the Germans. The next morning, we returned to Nievir.

Ivanka Khurda, a Ukrainian commander, was stationed there. He received us nicely with refreshments. He had received an order from the commander to offer help if I asked him for it. Other partisan units in the region received similar orders. My commander left for the camp and I returned home in Glusha. My wife told me that while I was away, many Poles had asked about me, among them one named Konopacki.

A few days after my return, a Pole named Makowiec came to see me and announced that a Polish parachutist known under the pseudonym of Korczak had arrived in the Polish colony of Kundzielicha and would like very much to meet us. For security reasons, I did not agree to the meeting. A few days later, when Korczak met with partisans at the colony, Konopacki brought the Germans, who surrounded the house, killed the partisan Vasili Maliewski and my former co-worker Jan Pitko, and burned down the two homes where the meeting was taking place. Korczak managed to escape. In connection with this, I had to leave right away for Nievir, send a report to the commander and wait there for a reply.

In the Nievir camp I saw in one of the last rooms a young, handsome man, a tailor, Sirozha (Shloyme) Sokol, and a young beautiful seamstress Natasha [Hinde], both from Kamien-Koshirsk. I had an interesting conversation with them on a variety of subjects.

Sirozha asked me to convey regards to his parents and brother, Aron, who were working in construction at a peasant's farm in the village of Zarogorzne. I also secured him a permit to visit his parents for one day. Sirozha Sokol was killed while discharging mines. His parents and brother are living in America. At present, Natasha also is in America.

In Krimna, on the road between Kamien-Koshirsk and Lubieshow, the Germans established a security point consisting of 37 Poles with military training. The post was located next to the main road, and everyone who traveled from Kamien to Lubieshow had to pass this police point. The Poles received light arms from the Germans and said they were there to protect Polish families from Ukrainian bands.

In the Polish colony of Dubrowo, I had a confidant in charge of Polish questions, H. Gajewski, through whom I made contact with the police post in Krimna. In a short period of time, Gajewski managed to organize a meeting between myself and the commandant of the post, Worchucki, a former officer in the Polish army.

The first meeting was set to take place in the Polish colony of Koszowice, in the home of a Pole, Cweklinski, on December 2, 1943. Worchucki was advised to come alone and to inform no one should about the meeting. Worchucki came with a member of his staff, Dombrowski. He excused himself for not coming alone by saying that coming alone would seem suspicious to people of the post because he never traveled without an escort. I informed them about the seriousness of the situation and the Polish material we had received from Moscow. I asked if there was any possibility that the entire post could go over to the partisans. The reply was they had to consider the proposal and discuss it with the police of the post.

Because of growing rumors about movements of large Ukrainian partisan units 45–50 miles from our home, I moved my family to the colony of Borszina, near Gorki-Mukuszin, located within the partisan zone of activity. This took place in March, 1943. Toward the end of the same month, the Poles in Dombrowe received information about Ukrainian partisans approaching their villages.

Gajewski came running to me for advice. He proposed that we ask our commandant for forces to fight the Ukrainians. I understood that now was the time to liquidate the post and integrate its soldiers into the partisan unit. Following a discussion between myself, Gajewski, and the commandant of the Polish police post, I left with the Ordzonikidze Detachment for Krimna, where we carried out the liquidation of the post.

We took 34 soldiers and 37 guns. Three soldiers did not want to come with us. Of the 70 Polish families, 55 came with us and the rest remained in place. Those who remained were elderly people who did not have children.

On April 6, we arrived in Nevir. I took over an eight-room synagogue building, where I established the headquarters as well as quarters for 34 soldiers, together with a kitchen.

On the way to the village, I saw a small Jewish boy, Jacob Shuster, with very long hair, dressed in light clothes. I called him over and asked his name and what he was doing there. He told me he had escaped from the Kamien-Koshirsk ghetto and was staying there with his aunt Basye. I asked if he would like to join my partisan unit and guard my horses, and he immediately agreed.

Shuster brought in an adult Jew, Joseph Stepak. He became the unit's butcher. Jacob Shuster's aunt lives at present in Moshav Ein-Vered, and he lives somewhere in Israel. Joseph Stepak brought to me two young Jewish men: Avrom Ber from Kamien-Koshirsk and Dersewicz, a lawyer from Lodz. When I learned from them that they were former officers of the Polish army, I immediately inducted them into the unit and provided them with the two extra guns in the headquarters.

Warchucki found out about this. With an angry expression on his face, he asked why I had given the two guns to the Jews. I answered that I didn't make any distinction between Jews and Poles, that we took in with open arms anyone who wanted to fight the Germans. Especially since the two Jews were former officers of the Polish army, they definitely deserved the weapons. He walked away from me not fully satisfied; however, I appeased him and added that I was not any less a Polish patriot than he.

They started recruiting soldiers, and in one month our unit grew to 73 armed soldiers. The Molotov Brigade was divided into two units. From it was created the Pinsk Brigade, to which belonged the following units: Ordzonikidze, Stalino, Nemitovo, Czapajewo, and our unit, Kosciuszko.

I received an order to go to Posluwskie Forest and, near the village of Seminowicze, locate a suitable place where I should start building dugouts for 200 men.

In a house in the village of Kulieno, on my way to select the place for the camp, I met a Jew from Ratne, Dovid Grabov, with two women and a child. The family was in great need and we were very helpful to them. Dovid was killed in March, 1944, by a mine explosion. The women and the girl, who at present is also a mother, all live in Argentina.

On July 20, the earth huts were ready. At the time, our unit consisted of 115 men.

I sent Ber and Dersewicz to the brigade com-

mander to bring weapons for a few soldiers. The following day, they were supposed to return, but we did not see or hear from them. An extra 8–10 hours passed beyond the expected time, and they were still not back. I was very disturbed and went out looking for them.

When I arrived at the Suvorovo unit's outskirts, I was told by the commander, Waska Zarzicki, that the previous day they had heard shooting from the nearby small forest: the two men who came for the weapons were practicing shooting because for some time they had not used firearms. This is why the weapons were taken from them, they were arrested, and at the moment were awaiting trial.

I began to beg Waska to release them, but he was not ready to listen to me because the commander, the infamous murderer Saszka Kozicki, already had been informed about the incident. I realized the situation was serious and we might lose two Jewish souls. I departed for the headquarters to see Ivan Grigoriewicz to ask him to release the two arrested Jews.

The brigade commander and I traveled directly to the headquarters of the Suvorovo unit, where we received an order to release the two soldiers and get back the two guns. At the outskirts of the unit, I took the two men with me. I began to prepare the unit to relocate to the newly organized camp in the Posluwskie Forest. On the way to our destination, at the partisan outpost in Wietla, we were greeted by Brigadier Szubitidze, Commissar Prutwesnia, and staff member, Darasz. I and five other partisans traveled ahead.

Near the village of Mokuszin, next to the big cross, stood a Jewish woman wearing a large, black beret, carrying a Red Cross medical knapsack. Introducing herself, she told us her name was Fania Salomon. When she heard we were on our way to the new camp, she said she wanted to be our nurse, which she was by profession. With our commander's approval, we took her to our camp, where she worked as a nurse until the end, when we left. Today, Fania Salomon-Lac lives in Israel.

WITH THE RED ARMY
By Dovid Melamed

The Germans entered Libivne in 1939, but left it soon after. The town was defenseless. There was great fear among the Jews. From time to time, Ukrainian gangs came to town, carrying big sacks in which to put the loot they took from the Jewish homes and businesses. Both Jews and gentiles then formed a defense militia that managed to chase away the unwanted guests. This was during the Ten Days of Penitence between Rosh Hashana and Yom Kippur.

Also, the remnants of the destroyed Polish army, men hiding from the Germans in the woods between Chelm and Libivne, would shoot at any Jew, yelling, "You Jews, Communists!"

For two whole days, the bandits went on a rampage in our shtetl. There were victims of their bullets; one was R. Yidl Raychers, who was shot on Chelm Street, and another was R. Dovid Palaper, shot on Masheve Street as he tried to close the shutters of his house.

On the same night that the Germans disappeared toward the nearby Bug River, the Red Army entered the town. This was on the eve of Yom Kippur.

The next morning, the people went out into the street as life appeared to become more normal; but it could not be said that all Jews were too pleased with the new rulers.

In our home, for instance, there was great joy, for we hoped our brother Leybl now would be able to visit us. But our hopes soon vanished when we received word that he had been killed by the Soviets.

In the Red Army

Some time passed, after which I was drafted into the Red Army. This was in 1940, when I was sent to the Far East.

On June 22, 1941, we heard over the radio that the Germans had crossed the Soviet border. The commissars and political officers harangued us about the necessity of protecting the fatherland. The Germans were already at the gates of Leningrad, and in 1942 my division, which had an excellent war record, was ordered to the front in that city.

I took part in the fighting and was wounded. I was sent to a hospital in Sverdlovsk (in the Ural Mountains), where I spent four months. After that I was discharged and was certified unfit for duty for a whole year.

I and other wounded soldiers were sent to a labor camp. If I still labored then under the illusion that I was in a labor battalion, which is what they called it, I see now that the great forest, with its filthy barracks, could only really have been a prison camp.

Back to the Front

After resting a while and regaining my health, I was sent to another place. In this *voyenkomat* [military recruiting office] they gave me a military uniform and ordered me to join the artillery unit. We engaged in various war exercises.

After six weeks of basic training, we were sent to the front again. It was February, 1944, when we reached the White Russian front, near Lutsk–

343

Kovel. My division stopped at Kovel's defense line [a town near Luboml].

We took part in a strong offensive action on March 25, when I was wounded again—in my leg. I was given first aid and sent to a division hospital. When I was examined, I realized I was seriously wounded. A few days later the surgeon came to me and told me if I wanted to stay alive, I should consent to having my leg amputated.

After the amputation, I was sent deep into Russia, somewhere in the Caucasus, where I remained until the end of the war. On April 15, 1945, I left the hospital, after its commissar awarded me two medals, one for victory over the Germans and one for bravery in action.

In Libivne After the War

After a period of time, during which I got married, I and my wife decided to go to Libivne, the town where I was born. The first Jew I met upon leaving the railroad station and reaching Chayim Reyzman's house was Moyshe Rakovestser. He remembered me and we began to tell each other stories! Tears filled his eyes as he described his experiences during the German occupation. As we said goodbye, I wept out loud at the destruction of my hometown and its inhabitants.

As I continued on my way, I did not recognize any of the streets. Near the house of the Gelmans I found the skeleton of our synagogue: a huge desolate place amid ruins of walls, on which huge letters spelled out, *Ma tovu oyholecho, Yakov, mishk'no'secho Yirsroel* [How goodly are thy tents, O Jacob; thy dwellings, O Israel!].

Not far from the house of Kalman Faveles, a young man approached me. He recognized me at once and even remembered my name, but I did not recognize him. He told me he was the son of Avrom Sojbel and his name was Nathan. He also told me he lived on the same street and that if I wanted, he would take me in to stay with him.

I stayed with him and found a real home there. The next day I met more Libivne Jews who had saved themselves by hiding with gentiles.

At first I found it very difficult to stay where so much Jewish blood had been spilled. Some gentiles, on meeting me, would ask me, "And how did you manage to stay alive?" They were surprised a Jew had managed to escape death!

I tried to make a home there and create a new life for myself together with the small remnant of our former Jewish community; but I found it almost impossible to live where the very air breathed of the fresh deaths of all those who were near and dear to me. We therefore left our once-dear Libivne and emigrated to Israel.

ON A DANGEROUS MISSION
By Mendl Zilberman

Mendl Zilberman as a Polish soldier.

In 1941, when the terrible war between the Russians and the Nazis began, I and my wife lived in Kovel. After three days of war, we left for Kiev. Ten days later, both of us were drafted into the Red Army.

I had to fight on many fronts—in Kiev, Rostov, and Stalingrad. Later, when Russia began to win the war, my comrades and I found ourselves near Kovel, Masheve, and at last, in Libivne. I met the Ukrainian Fedos, whom I knew from Masheve Street. When he saw me, he became so frightened that for a moment he lost his voice. He must have had many Jewish deaths on his conscience!

The first Jew I met was the sister of Yidl Sandlboym. At her home I met Yidl's two children, a little girl of 8–10 and a boy of 6–7. The little girl could not walk by herself but had to hold on to the walls. The little boy could not speak normally, he spoke in a very low, hoarse voice. When I asked why he spoke this way, Yidl told me he got that way because when he was hidden in a pit he was not allowed to speak loudly. This became a habit with him and now he could speak in no other way.

In that house I also met Moyshe Elfant (Rackovester), Yakov Reiz, and several other Jews of Libivne, but I did not see anyone from my household. Yidl told me a Ukrainian had taken our house in its entirety and had it reconstructed in his village of Borki (Boris). I wanted to go to the village of Boris together with a few soldiers and burn down the house, but Yidl held me back, saying the same Ukrainian could come back to town and take revenge on him.

From Luboml we proceeded to the town of Chelm and from there to Praga, on the outskirts of Warsaw. Our unit took up positions at the town of Korchev near Otvotsk, and the Germans were on the other side of the Vistula River.

On a certain morning I was called to the headquarters of the battalion. They informed me that a few of us had been selected for a mission to bring in a live German from the other side of the river for questioning, for they needed information about the German army positions in Warsaw. A few weeks earlier, some Polish soldiers had been sent on a similar mission, but they gave themselves up to the Germans.

Besides me, my group consisted of my captain and two other soldiers. After we were quickly taught some secret passwords, we were to be taken across the river by a peasant, a long-time resident of that district.

When we reached our destination, the peasant was already there waiting for us. We were dressed in peasant clothing and I carried a machine-gun (as seen in my photograph). I had also two cartridge belts, each with 12 bullets, four hand grenades, and a flare gun.

We managed the first half of our mission successfully, crossing the Vistula in ten minutes. When we came to a high bank, we scattered and began to crawl, edging along on our bellies.

When we reached the top of the earthworks,

we found a dugout shelter very close to us and heard Germans talking inside. We were given orders not to enter this dugout unless there was only one German there, and so we lay outside for about an hour.

Suddenly, the door of the dugout opened and a man came out, closing the door behind him. He was coming straight toward where I lay. As he turned with his back toward me, I hit him over the head with the flat part of my automatic gun. He let out a wild roar and fell. At once, the captain and one soldier began to pull him toward the boat, while the two of us stayed behind. The door suddenly opened again and two figures appeared, certainly having heard the cry. When they came closer, we opened fire and shot them and ran toward the boat.

At that moment, the Germans fired a white flare, so that the whole area became lit up. In reply, I shot off a red flare, the agreed-upon signal for our artillery to open fire at the German position.

A terrible barrage of bullets now flew from both sides, while we managed to scramble into the boat, with bullets flying over our heads. Fortunately, none of us were hit.

We had successfully accomplished our mission. Important information was forced out of the captured German, and all of us were thanked most profusely by the whole staff.

CHAYIM ROZENBLIT: PARTISAN AND SOLDIER IN THE WAR OF LIBERATION
By Nathan Tchelet (Blumen)

Chayim Rozenblit fell during the Israeli War of Liberation in the Tzemach region of the Emek-Hayarden, on the 9th of Iyar, 1948. He was buried in the military cemetery at Degania, on the shores of Lake Kinneret, and his tomb was engraved with his name and serial number as a member of the Israel Defense Forces—#173320.

Chayim, the son of Avrom and Pesye, was born in 1918 in the village of Masheve, near Luboml. His father was a pious and a God-fearing Jew, who brought up his son Chayim in the ways of the Holy Torah. At first, Chayim studied in a public school and later continued to study on his own. In 1935, he joined the

Chayim Rozenblit (z"l) in Kibbutz Kinneret.

hachshara kibbutz (Hechalutz training farm) to prepare himself to emigrate to Palestine as a pioneer. But fate was cruel to him and it was doubtful whether he would ever make aliyah, for World War II intervened in 1939. He saw with his own eyes the horrible terror the Germans perpetrated against the Jews of Luboml. His personal diary of the era is an authentic witness to Jewish life in Luboml and in the villages in the days of the Nazi occupation and of the liquidation of the Jews in the pits of the brick factory.

Chayim got weapons from a Polish acquaintance and fled Luboml into a forest. But he returned. The Jews had been concentrated in a ghetto there, and Chayim wanted to rescue his family. His mother was able to escape from the ghetto, and for a long time they went together from town to town in the surrounding areas, until his mother was murdered.

Chayim joined the partisans, helping them wreak vengeance. And at last he joined the Red Army and fought until victory came. After the war he went to Germany, where he joined the partisan kvutza, Negev. After various hardships and wanderings, he finally came to Palestine in 1946, on the ship *Tel Chai*. Together with his friends from his kvutsa, he became a member of Kvutzat Kinneret, where he lived until he fell in the War of Liberation.

347

THE SURVIVORS AND THE RETURN TO LIFE

ARISE, THEN, ALL YE SLAIN

Arise then, all ye slain and all ye persecuted!
Arise ye from your graves and from your cellars!
Arise through beaches in your borders and your walls!
For our nation lives! You could not wipe us off the face of the earth!
For our nation lives! Arise ye from your dust,
And ye shall march to sounds of blasts of shofars!

For you'll find strength from sleep and from your death;
For you'll walk firmly, heads held high,
Like sons of freedom in your own, your native land!

By Chayim Nuri
(translated from the Hebrew by Mary Schulman)

THROUGH THE FIRE
By Simche Gitelis

Like all other Jewish shtetls, Libivne was not made of rich Jews. Neither was there a lack of poor people. Yet the Jews of Libivne, either individually or as a group, helped their poorer brethren in need.

On Fridays some Jews would go by horse and wagon to collect challes [Sabbath bread] for the poor, who would use it on the Sabbath as prescribed by tradition.

Timosh Gershimyuk, a righteous gentile, with his wife, from Koshary village. They saved Chane Melamed-Gitelis, Esther Melamed-Fisher, Motl Fisher, Mrs. Bronshteyn and her two children, for more than two years, 1942–45, until the Liberation.

Poor strangers in our midst were taken care of by the Hachnoses Orchim [charity to strangers] society. The head of this group was my in-law, Leybish Melamed, who had inherited the job from his father, Eliyohu (Lesnakes) Melamed. The old pinkas [community record book], more than 100 years old, had the names of all members of that society.

Our young people were anxious to leave the town forever, but where would they go? Palestine and other countries were closed to them. And when the war with Germany broke out, the fate of almost all of us was sealed.

I, as a draftee in the Polish army, immediately was taken as a war prisoner by the Germans. In addition, I was wounded in one eye and spent four weeks in a Lodz hospital, from which, miraculously, I was discharged. After long suffering, I was able to come back home. Since my eye became better, I was able to get work from the Russians.

Even under the Soviets, our situation was bitter enough. We were all low in spirit, dejected. Some of our people were deported to Siberia. But that was like paradise in comparison to the murderous deeds perpetrated by the Germans on Jews in the areas under their control.

After the Soviet-German war broke out, I was able to reach Kharkov through various highways and byways. There I found my brother, Shimshon, who had been there since 1918. I could not stay long, however, since the Germans were coming nearer and nearer to that city. Therefore I, my brother, and his family left Kharkov for Central Asia, settling in Frunze. A few months later, my brother was drafted into the Red Army and he fell in battle near Moscow.

In 1945, Moyshe Lifshitz wrote to me that my bride-to-be, Chane Melamed, her sister Esther, and Motl Fisher were alive. I went through indescribable torments before I finally was able to reach Libivne.

When I came there, they told me the gruesome details of the violent deaths of my family, of the destruction of the shtetl and of how the few survivors had managed to stay alive. For 24 months they lived hidden in the house of a peasant in the village of Koshary, lying in an attic over a stable, where horses and pigs were kept. They were constantly hungry. The peasant, Timosh Gershimyuk, would bring them food three times a week to keep them from dying from hunger. Often danger came very close, imperiling also the peasant and his family. They were saved only by miracles. When they were finally able to leave the small attic, they had to learn how to walk again.

After spending a few days in Libivne, we went on to Chelm. How could any of us even think of remaining there, on earth once so near and dear to us, but which now was cursed for all eternity?

THE FIGHT FOR A CHILD
By Shmuel and Kreyndl Katz

My sister Freyde, the daughter of Leyzer Katz, owner of the Victoria Hotel in Libivne, went to live in Bendin after her marriage. A few months after World War II began, I learned that my sister, her husband, and their older son had been killed by the Nazi murderers, but that her little girl, Shula, had been saved by a gentile, to whom my sister had entrusted the child.

I did not have the address of the gentile, nor did I know his name. I therefore spent a lot of time traveling through the Bendin area asking questions, but I could not get any clues. One day, after I had been searching for many months, I learned where my little niece was hidden. Entirely by accident did the news come to me.

I took along my younger sister, Kreyndl and we went to that place. When we reached it, we discovered the little girl was kept by Germans. On the one hand, our joy at seeing her alive was boundless; but on the other hand it broke our hearts to see how she looked: she wore a torn dress, she was barefoot, and she was eating a dry piece of bread.

We brought her some sweets and told her who we were, and we gave proof to the people that we were her real aunt and uncle. We also showed them the girl's photographs and promised to give them whatever money they asked if they would give us back our niece. This would have been in addition to the diamonds and fur coats my sister had given them at the time. Their answer was that they would give the child only to the real mother. If not, they would keep the child.

I made up my mind to take the child away from the gentiles no matter what. My heart was aching even without this new problem. It was enough that my oldest sister and her loving husband and child had been killed; why should this little five-year-old child be left with gentiles when she was born a Jew?

For a long time I would go to that village almost daily trying all kinds of ways to get the child away from them. But they had baptized the child and threatened to kill me if I bothered them again.

I saw that I could not get the child back amicably so I decided to take the case to court. I had no money for a trial, but I got hold of a lawyer who was kind enough to take the case without charge.

Many people attended the trial. The gentiles who had the child insisted they would not give her up, since her parents were not there. Moreover, the child was already a converted Christian. Difficult as it was to believe, I lost the case. I made an appeal—and I lost again.

By then we had given up all hope of getting the child. Suddenly one of our acquaintances told us the chief prosecutor of the Warsaw court was a Jew. We got a letter of introduction to him and went to Warsaw to see him, inducing him to investigate the case. He went with us to Katowice, where the first trials had taken place, and subpoenaed all the documents.

A new trial was ordered at his insistence, and this time two of the presiding judges were from Warsaw. The prosecutor was also from Warsaw, though no one knew he was a Jew. At this trial, the little girl was weeping and crying that the gentiles were her real parents and that she did not want to go to anyone else. The gentiles who had hidden her again repeated their position that they would not give up the child if the real mother could not be found.

The prosecutor gave a long speech. He argued that though the little girl was baptized, she had remained the same Jewish child; that almost 95 percent of the Jews had been destroyed by the Nazi murderers, including her parents. In such an extraordinary situation of genocide, a brother or a sister also had the right to bring up the child of a murdered mother, for the child was their flesh and blood, after all. The child, therefore, had to be given over to the sister and brother of the dead mother.

This time the court ruled that the child should be placed in an orphanage for three months and then the little girl must be given to me as her guardian.

Even after the court decision we went through a great deal of trouble. First of all, the little girl kept crying that she wanted to go back to her "parents"; secondly, the gentiles threatened me with death if I would not give up to them the "soul they had saved." To avoid danger, we brought the child to our other sister Chaye, a survivor, who lived quite far from us. Later the little girl moved with Chaye and her family to Israel, where they are living now.

ACTIVIST NACHMAN WEISSMAN
By Israel Leichter

Nachman Weissman (z"l) as a soldier in the Israeli Army.

Nachtsche Weissman was an activist, for such was his nature. When he did something, he did it with his full heart and soul—in both his private life and in his communal activities.

Nachman was not one to delve into spiritual things, but he did accomplish much in practical affairs, first in his own shtetl and later on a much broader scale. Libivne had a hachshara kibbutz of the Hechalutz movement, and Nachman played a very important part in this kibbutz, especially in raising funds for its upkeep, not such an easy accomplishment in a small town.

The members of the hachshara earned a great part of their upkeep by doing lumber work. Nachman helped them get such work and at times even put his own shoulder to the wheel. When the chalutzim (pioneers, being prepared for Palestine at the kibbutz) were given an amount of work they could not possibly handle by themselves, he would organize young sympathizers from the shtetl to help saw and chop the 220 or so yards of wood.

Nachman's energy helped Jews after the Holocaust. He himself was lucky to have spent the entire time of the great Jewish catastrophe in the Soviet Union, where he did suffer, though not as bitterly. Right after the war, he returned to Poland to become active in the Bricha (an organization that took Jews illegally across the borders), helping them in their torturous trek to Palestine.

Nachman was sent to one of the most important areas of the Bricha activities, on the border between Poland and Czechoslovakia, where he became a leading comrade of the Ichud party, which consisted of General Zionists responsible for maintaining the area and helping Jews cross the border in safety.

During the day, Nachman was occupied with keeping order in the big house, where the survivors would sometimes be given lodging; at night, he and his comrades would be busy loading trucks with Jews, helping them cross the border in secret. I do not know where he got all the energy to do this hard, exacting work.

When the Bricha center had to be closed after it became impossible to keep its activities secret any longer, Nachman went to Warsaw to work for the Joint [American Jewish Joint Distribution Committee]. He was in charge of distributing food and clothing, an activity of special importance to survivors in Poland, as well as to those Jewish repatriates streaming into Poland from Soviet Russia. In addition to food, spiritual nourishment also was needed to give hope to the despondent and Nachumtsche performed this mitzvah [good deed] with a full heart; he worked for the Joint for about two years.

But the most important and most difficult work Nachman did after the Holocaust was finding and rescuing Jewish children from the hands of gentiles who had hidden them during the time of the great misfortune. Some gentiles brought the children back to their Jewish families; but others were stubborn and insisted on converting the children to the Christian faith.

Nachman was one of a small group of Jews who used to ride around in various villages, seeking out children who had been hidden by Christians. As soon as they heard of a case, they went at once to that place. It was not only difficult but dangerous, for their very lives were threatened by the peasants.

Sometimes they were able to get the child by peaceful means; but sometimes they had to use force against peasants who refused to give up the children willingly.

Horrible scenes would then take place. One of these cases was that of a 15-year-old boy, whom Nachman took from a gentile and brought to Warsaw. The boy told him his mother had also brought his little sister to another peasant. Having traced the man, the Jews gave him a large sum of money for the girl (10 years old by then) and took the child away. But the girl tried to run away several times. When they tried to keep her back, she would scream, "What do you want from me, you *zhides* [Jews]?"

Nachum told me of a case where a Jewish child had to be removed by force from a Polish family because they refused to give up the child.

Nachum and a bunch of youths went to the peasant's house at night, dressed as Polish police. They told the family to lie face down on the floor, using the pretext that they had come to search for hidden weapons. They warned the peasant that if he cried for help, they would burn down his house with the whole family in it. They quickly grabbed the Jewish child and rode away in an auto. About half a year later, after the child was safely in Israel, the group sent the peasant a handsome sum of money for having kept and hidden the child.

When in 1948 the Arab-Jewish war broke out in Israel and the Arab nations united against the newly formed State of Israel in order to destroy it, Nachman Weissman left Poland and went to Israel, where he enlisted in the Jewish army to fight the enemy.

Nachman remained in Israel, where he gradually built his own family nest. His horror-filled experiences in the ghetto, in Soviet Russia, and his wanderings and hardships had damaged his health. It was not his fate to feel free for very long and enjoy the Jewish state and his wife and children, for he died in 1963.

FROM VILLAGE TO VILLAGE
By Yisroel Shicht

I was born in the village of Shtin, 3.5 miles from Luboml. Until I was seven I and my brother (z"l) lived in the village and my grandfather taught us. More than once I would run away from home to help my Ukrainian friends with their cattle in the pasture.

When my father found out I was not studying, he feared that this might be the fate of the other children as well, and he decided to move us all to town. In Luboml I studied with children a year or two younger than I. From the age of Bar Mitzvah I studied in a yeshiva till the age of 18 and then I left to go to hachshara [training] for HaPoel HaMizrachi.

In the meantime, World War II broke out. I came home and was mobilized into the Russian army just before the war between Russia and Germany broke out.

I found out later that when Luboml was conquered, the Germans gathered men and told them they were needed for labor. My father was among them, and my 17-year-old brother decided to go also to help father. The Germans took the men to the Jewish cemetery and shot all of them. My mother remained with my three sisters and one brother.

When the Germans liquidated the Luboml ghetto, my 14-year-old sister and 11-year-old brother succeeded in escaping the ghetto. Since our house was outside the ghetto, a Polish family named Lapotinski resided there.

After the war I returned to our town and visited the Polish family in our house. They told me that they had fed my brother and sister but could not let them hide because they feared the Germans. Apparently they headed to the forests and their fate was the same as the rest of the Jewish population—they were found frozen in the forest.

Text of a letter published in *Davar* in 1945, written by Avrom Getman to Yehuda Kreyn. Title: "From the Killing Pits . . . Tell them what happened . . ." Avrom Getman asked Mr. Kreyn to write to his brother, Yakov Hetman, in Eretz Yisroel. Avrom relates his horrible survival experience in Luboml and thereafter, in a very depressing and painful manner.

The town was totally demolished—only the houses in the outskirts remained standing. The entire center of the town was destroyed. I was not able to see the ruins and I understood the emotions of the few survivors. How could they remain on this cursed land soaked with the blood of their loved ones? I understood I had no future there, and as a member of the hachshara in the past I started my long journey to Eretz Yisroel.

My journey was not easy. I was in refugee camps in Germany, like all other Jewish refugees, and from there I arrived in Israel in an illegal refugee ship.

Today I own a farm in a moshav [cooperative agricultural settlement]. The villager has returned to the village, but this time as a true farmer in the State of Israel.

THE PARENTS WHO DID NOT MAKE IT
By Arye Oron (Shtern)

For as long as I can remember, I've known Jews—a Jewish community, a town that was for the most part Jewish. During my childhood, I did not differentiate between the community and the town. Everything was Jewish: the courtyard, the school, business, trade and work.

However, gradually a wide, astonishing gap between present and future was revealed to me. In the present we saw everything as if it were ours. In the future, nothing belonged to us. At a young age we began to sense this truth. As time went on we were told of this by way of subtle hints, and finally it became evident that we, the youth of Luboml, had no future. Although it seemed we ruled the town, socially and economically all our resources really were blocked and our destiny was predetermined and within sight.

When you seem to have no future in your country of birth, you begin looking for a future elsewhere. To us, the Zionist youth of Luboml, two things were clear: that the diaspora was undesirable, and that the place for which we longed was Eretz Yisroel. We, the youth, lived with a dual certainty: that we had no future where we were born and grew up, and that in another part of the world, in Eretz Yisroel, we had hope of a real life.

This was our destiny. It was both positive and negative. We found ourselves living and working in a country we could not identify with; it was a country not created for us, a country that oppressed us. On the horizon we saw a different country, a country in which all our dreams for the future lay waiting for us.

Considering this background it is easy to understand the extreme reactions of the young men of our town. Many recruits inflicted injury on themselves to obtain a release from the Polish army, and then these men, who previously had done everything in their power to avoid hard work, volunteered upon arriving in Eretz Yisroel to participate in dangerous activities on behalf of the Haganah.

The war between the sons and their fathers was not over ultimate ends. It was an inner struggle among the parents concerning their children's departure to the world at large, the timing of the matter, their children's professions and continuing education. There was also the matter of the separation of parents from children and their chances of reuniting in the future in their new home.

Nevertheless, both generations took the same approach to life. The development of Eretz Yisroel was at the core of most people's spiritual existence, as were the Tarbut school, the youth groups, the study of Hebrew and Hebrew literature, activism in the Jewish National Fund and in the Jewish Foundation Fund, and the holding of elections for the Zionist Congress (which affected us more than any Polish election). The youth of our town, young and old, all were involved in these activities and important events.

Another deep impression from my childhood and youth is connected with the gap between generations—grandparents, parents, and youth. Our grandparents worked diligently to preserve religion, while the youth already were protesting against it and therefore were seen as skeptics, even as agnostics.

However, what was common to both sides was that they met in the synagogue. The older generation came to pray there, and the youth came to demonstrate their beliefs and their agnosticism. They managed to do this in discussions held freely within the walls of the synagogue, and in gatherings outside. In those days, when I was still in the Trisker shtibl, I was impressed by the deep and honest faith of the older generation. On the other hand, I strained my ears to hear heresies concerning God and his Messiah spoken by Eliezer Finkelshteyn, himself a descendant of R. Leybe, may he rest in peace.

From time to time in the Trisker shtibl arguments broke out between the conservative elders and the insolent youth. I do not remember what the arguments were about or why they occurred. However, when the eve of Yom Kippur was upon us, every youngster showed up at the synagogue for fear that those who did not attend would embarrass their families by staying home. When Nathan Blumen's grandfather, the shoychet [ritual slaughterer] R. Chayim, may he rest in peace, who had a majestic appearance, announced on the eve of the *Kol Nidre* prayer that "we permit ourselves to pray alongside transgressors," I shuddered out of respect and politeness and also because of the feeling that R. Chayim's words were directed at Eliezer Finkelshteyn and his friends.

Thousands of Luboml Jews, hundreds of young men and women, the best of our youth who lived the life of Eretz Yisroel while still in our town, were destroyed, murdered. They did not make it to Palestine; they lived and died on the cursed soil of Poland.

Those of us, the handful of us, who did make it to Eretz Yisroel and built our homes there were embittered by fate, by the fact that we could not save our parents and fulfill their dreams of living in the land of the Jews and spending the rest of their life with us, their children.

Memories of the home of our mothers and fathers follow us everywhere. I myself felt these memories most strongly during occasions that themselves possessed much external splendor.

At these times I was shrouded by a cloud of memories and my heart grieved that my mother and father were not privileged, and I was not privileged, to be together at those occasions.

Before the establishment of the State of Israel, I dedicated years of my life, in Italy, to helping survivors. When the state finally was established, I was nominated to be the first official consul for Israel in Rome. I conducted an official visit to a survivors' camp in the south of Italy. An Italian general, commander of the district, and his wife escorted me and my wife, and a convoy of motorcycles served as escorts of honor. The Jews of the camp decorated the gates with Hebrew writing, and at the entrance we were greeted, according to the Jewish tradition, with bread and salt on a silver tray. During all the excitement surrounding me, memories of my father and mother came to me, and I was sad they were not with me in the convoy, that they were not even in the audience, that they were not even alive.

More than a dozen years passed and here I was presenting a treaty as Israeli ambassador to the president of Venezuela in Caracas. This time there was a royal march in the streets and a military parade in the palace yard. *HaTikvah* [Israel's anthem] was played by a military band, and the treaty was given to the president in a fancy hall in the presidential palace.

On the way back, near the Pantheon, my wife was waiting for me with our two children, Sophia and Nechemia, and this time I was leading an honorary convoy of children from the Jewish school, and as an honored guest I placed flowers on the grave of the national hero of Venezuela, Bolivar. Finally, in the presidential palace, among thousands of Jews and filled with incredible excitement, I nevertheless felt alone and lonely, remembering that my parents were not with me and that they were not able to see, hear, or know anything of what was going on.

THE ACTIVITIES OF THE BENEVOLENT SOCIETY OF LUBOML AND THE SURROUNDING AREAS
By Shmuel Fuks

The Second World War severed all existing ties between the citizens of Eretz Yisroel [then Palestine] and their relatives in Luboml. During the Russian rule in Luboml there was still some news from time to time. However, when the Nazis took over, what was once worry turned into fear for the lives of our dear ones.

Newspapers did not bring any hope into our lives; rather, what we knew of the Nazis' cruelty toward our brothers brought trepidation into our hearts. We waited anxiously for someone to come from the town who perhaps would bear the message that it was not all true and as real as the newspapers made it seem.

The first to come from across the sea was Eliezer Wolk, who arrived as a soldier with the Anders Army, a Polish unit organized in Russia to fight the Nazis.

This man went to the central synagogue in Tel Aviv upon his arrival and asked the worshippers there if they knew Shmuel Fuks. As it turned out, he found someone there who knew me and who brought the man to my home on Wolfson Street.

We were happy that he had come and we related to him as if he was a member of the family. To our despair, however, he did not know much about what was going on in Luboml because when he escaped from the town on his way to Russia everyone still was alive.

On the list of "Teheran Children" who reached Palestine, I found a youth from Luboml around 15 years old whose name was Isaiah Goldenson. I invited him to my home as well. Nevertheless, even he could not tell me much about the fate of our relatives in Luboml. This boy

was with us for nearly two years. He then left for America, where his uncle lived.

The third youth to arrive, in February of 1946, was Nathan Sobel, who came with the first Youth Aliyah group of 43 orphaned children from Europe, arriving from Berlin via France. From him we learned about the total destruction of Luboml Jewry that occurred during World War II. He was the first to tell in detail what had occurred.

The fourth individual from Luboml to arrive in Israel was Avrom Getman. From him we learned more about the extermination of our families and about the atrocities of the Nazis. He also lived with us in our home until his brother Yakov Hetman was released from a detention camp in Kenya where he was sent by the British for participating in terrorist attacks staged by Etzel [the Irgun] and Lechi [the Stern Gang].

In the meantime, letters began to arrive from other survivors. We found out which of them had been in camps and who had been in the forests. We began to feel that we must organize so that we could lend a helping hand to our brothers in need. Some of our landsleit [fellow townspeople] gathered. Among them were Yechezkiel Kornfeld, Shloyme Veytsfrucht, Tsvi Fuks, Dvoyre Gitklig, and Basye Zilberger-Cohen. This group organized a committee to help our brothers in Europe and elsewhere.

Our plan was to collect money to pay for packages to be sent to the survivors, as well as to provide for new immigrants, giving them some encouragement. We managed to collect a small amount of money and sent some packages abroad. We also helped those few who managed to reach

Israel as best we could with our meager means.

We all gathered at the synagogue in which I worshipped and in the home of Tsvi Fuks (z"l). We also turned to our brothers in America for help, but we received no response at the time.

The activities of the committee to help survivors were still going on when Nathan Blumen [Tchelet] returned to Tel Aviv. I invited him to participate in our committee's activities, and he obliged willingly. In this manner I handed over to him the responsibilities of the committee and he began to take over as its leader.

Committee Functions

When Nathan Blumen joined our efforts, the committee gained impetus. From that moment on, Nathan and his wife, Malke, became completely dedicated to the matter of the immigrants from Luboml. All their time and effort went to help them.

All immigrants who set foot in Israel learned the Blumens' address, on 31 Aliyah Street. Malke and Nathan's home was where all immigrants

met; still maintaining all their ties from the old country, this was where they became acclimated and acquainted with their new homeland. In the Blumen's home, the old-timers from Luboml met with the new immigrants and talked over tea and cookies.

In this same home, many listened in silence to horror stories concerning the fate of the citizens of Luboml, and they were not ashamed when the tears rolled down their faces as they mourned the deaths of loved ones who had been murdered.

In the Blumens' home, American citizens who had emigrated from Luboml met with Israeli relatives, also from Luboml, as well as with new immigrants from the town. Finally, in the Blumens' home all the committee members dedicated to help the new immigrants met and discussed ways to raise or lend money in order to help care for the newcomers.

The first activity organized by the committee was the setting up of a free-loan fund. From 1949 to 1950 there was a period of considerable poverty. Considering the fact that many new im-

Welcome party for former residents of Luboml residing in the United States, 1960.

migrants arrived during this time, the loan afforded them in the sum of 50 or 100 lira, without interest and for an unlimited time, proved a very big help. In certain cases money was given as a gift rather than a loan.

The free-loan fund was established through the contributions of former residents of Luboml. When Nute Eiger was in Israel in 1949, he promised to send a large sum of money upon his return to the United States—and he was true to his word.

Also, 400 lira [125 British pounds] were sent from Argentina. The rest of the money consisted of donations collected in Israel from emigres from Luboml. At the time of the first large memorial gathering in 1948, committee members raised money and gave all their funds to the free-loan fund.

From then on, these yearly memorial gatherings became a time for the collection of contributions. From year to year, around the time of Hoshana Rabba–Shmini Atzeret, the anniversary of the day the Luboml Jewish extermination began, there occur memorial services for the victims of the Holocaust, as well as for those who died in Israel. These take place at both informal get-togethers and general gatherings of the townspeople.

Many meetings between natives of Luboml visiting as tourists and former Luboml residents living in Israel were arranged by the aforementioned committee. These meetings took place in a large auditorium where refreshments were served. These gatherings were an opportunity for a meeting of the masses—that is, of all Luboml emigres, many who had not seen each other for years.

Many smaller gatherings took place at the home of Blumen-Tchelet. All this allowed for the opportunity to have Luboml natives from Israel and the diaspora strengthen their ties.

The organizing committee also established ties with Yad Vashem [Holocaust memorial in Jerusalem]. There, on the lower level, a plaque was erected as a memorial to the citizens of Luboml who perished in the Holocaust.

With the start of the drive for contributions to build the Heichal Volyn, again Nathan Blumen

(Tchelet) took on the task and succeeded in raising thousands of lirot registered as a contribution from the committee of the Organization of Immigrants from Luboml. When the Heichal was completed, a memorial to Luboml citizens was held there in 1969.

From that year on, all the memorial services took place in the Heichal Volyn. The Heichal gave the Organization of Immigrants from Luboml a room for memorial services and meet-

Commemorative plaque in the Chamber of the Holocaust in Jerusalem, in memory of the destroyed community of Luboml.

Postcard and placard designed by Luboml survivor Nathan Sobel, 1949. It reads: "Seven years since the destruction of the Luboml Jewish community." *Second line:* "Luboml community and vicinity," superimposed on "European Jewry." *Third line*: "10,000" superimposed on "6,000,000." *Fourth line*: "Hoshana Rabba, 5703, October 1, 1942."

ings. This room was also shared with the community of Masheve.

We have no specific information as to who held which offices in the organization committee. For this reason we will list here the members of the committee who worked hard and dedicated their time and effort to the citizens of Luboml.

The following are their family names in alphabetical order: Blumen-Tchelet, Nathan, chairman; Lifshitz, Moyshe, treasurer; Gitklig, Dvoyre; Fuks, Shmuel; Hetman, Yakov; Feintuch, Efrayim; Veytsfrucht, Shloyme; Fuks, Tsvi (z"l); Zohar, Hannah; Firsht, Zipporah; Cohen, Basye; Kornfeld, Yechezkiel; audit committee: Achtman, Hannah; Bar-Giorah, Menachem; Fuks, Shmuel.

והסביבה בישראל	ארגון יוצאי לובומל
הזמנה	איינלאדונג

הנך מוזמן(ת) בזה למסיבת	איר ווערט דערמיט איינגעלאדן אויף דעם באנקעט

ח"י לעצמאות ישראל   **18 יאר מדינת ישראל**

ע"י שולחנות ערוכים   ביי געדעקטע טישן

בהשתתפות אורחים בני עירנו   מיטן אנטייל לאנדסלייט געסט פון

מארה"ב וארגנטינה   אמעריקע און ארגעלטינע

אייגר נתן ורעיתו דורותי   בלושטין יובבד

ברגמן צירל לבית גינזבורג ובעלה פנחס   גרשנגגורן אביגדור ורעיתו חנה לבית פרידמן

הולץ אברהם ורעיתו לאה   הלפרין יהודית לבית צורף

פפר חנה לבית גינזבורג ובעלה נחמן   קנדלשטין מנדל

שיינוולד וולול ורעיתו חוה   שמס לובה לבית וישניץ

שמס קלרה

המסיבה תתקיים ביום חמישי א' אייר תשכ"ו   דער באנקעט וועט פארקומען דעם

(21.4.1966) בשעה 7 בערב באולם .קרשניק"   21.4.66 7 א זייגער אווגט, אין זאל .קראשניק"

רח' יונה הנביא 4, תל-אביב ע"י קולנוע .ירון"   תל-אביב, רח' יונה הנביא 4

אוטובוסים וג 17, 4.   בכבוד רב   אוטובוסן וג 17, 4.   מיט אכטונג

הוועד   דער קאמיטעע

Official invitation to a formal banquet, from Lubomlers in Israel to Lubomlers in the United States and Argentina. It took place on April 21, 1966 in Tel Aviv. It was also the 18th anniversary of Israel's independence. Sixteen guests attended.

LIBIVNER JEWS IN ARGENTINA
By Zelik Faigen

At the beginning of the 1880s, during the wave of raging pogroms in tsarist Russia, Jews, haunted and tormented by hunger, need, rightlessness, and other troubles, began the great mass immigration to America and to a lesser degree to other countries. Divine providence dictated that much of European Jewry would save itself and form many Jewish communities all over the Americas, where Jews received rights and protection as free citizens.

At that time, Argentina did not lie in the direct path of the Jewish migrations. No information about "hot, faraway" Argentina reached the Russian Pale of Jewish Settlement. It was only with the beginning of the 1890s that a small trickle of Jewish immigrants began to flow toward Argentina, thanks to the ICA (Jewish Colonization Association), established by Baron Maurice de Hersh, who bought great tracts of land for Jewish colonization. There were Jews in Argentina before that time, but they were few and far between.

At the same time, when Jewish colonists arrived in Argentina to work the land, another segment of the Jewish community came to Buenos Aires, where they worked as carpenters, tailors, weavers, peddlers, and *quente* [sellers of goods on credit].

Most Libivner Jews who went to Argentina arrived in the 1920s. Some had gone earlier but the majority arrived in the late 1920s and early 1930s.

The East European shtetl was crowded and the youth were idle. And so they began to dream of faraway places, where they sought for a way out of the despondent "desert" in which they found themselves.

America did not let them in because of restrictive quotas. Neither could they reach Palestine because of the small number of certificates for entry there. This situation drove them to Argentina. Not only young people, but also the middle-aged went there with their entire families, looking for an escape from their difficult economic situation.

In the 1920s it was a very easy matter to go to Argentina. It was enough to register in one's foreign passport that one was either a farmer or a wage-worker in order to get a visa for Argentina immediately. Later, in the 1930s, Jews also had to have immigration papers to be able to go to Argentina.

The wave of immigration continuously flowed toward the West until the outbreak of World War II.

The relationship between the Libivne Jews in Argentina was loose. There was little contact between them. Each person was busy with his own problems. Occasionally, a landsman [fellow townsperson] would invite a Jew from Libivne to a celebration. There was no Libivne organization or society as in other countries. This could be explained by the fact that few immigrant families were from Libivne proper. Most people were from surrounding villages: Opalin, Lubochin, Nodizh, Rimatch, etc.

At this point, it must be pointed out that there was an exception—a man who, though young, did not think only of himself but helped newly arrived landsleit both materially and with brotherly warmth. He was our landsman, Aaron Prusman (z"l), son of Boruch Hersh and Chaye the Fisherke. He had arrived in 1927, so it was only two years since his own arrival, yet he already had helped many of the newly arrived Jews from Libivne get settled.

It is also important to mention a second landsman, one of the veterans, Meyer-Chayim Shostak. He came from Opalin but had married a Libivne girl. He was one of the first founders of the Society of Nature, an easygoing guy beloved by us all. He was the so-called "ambassador of the Jews from Opalin."

It was only in 1945 that the Libivne Society was organized in Argentina. In June of that year a group of former Libivne Jews met in the house of the eldest Luboml Jew in town, R. Nachum Tzimerboym (may he rest in peace) in order to found the Libivne society.

The bloody war had just ended and we still did not know whether anyone was left alive in our old hometown. There might be some survivors who had escaped death, and it was necessary to organize at once to give them help.

A temporary committee was appointed immediately to organize such a society. Many attended the first meeting, in August, 1945, where officers of the new society were elected. The chairman-elect was Nachum Tzimerboym; vice chairman, Yochanan Bargrum; secretary, Zelig Faigen; other members of the committee, as well as an audit committee also were elected.

At the first meeting of the executive committee and after a long debate, it was agreed to name the group the Society of Landsleit of Libivne, Opalin and Environs. Opalin was added because of the great number of Opalin Jews who joined as members of the society.

On October 7 we had the first memorial meeting for our holy martyrs. The same evening we announced the relief campaign for 1946. The sum of 3,000 pesos was raised from the attending members. During the year, the contribution rose to 5,000 pesos (four pesos to an American dollar).

During the first year, the society arranged several family gatherings and a movie evening, which raised our funds substantially. Much money for relief of survivors also was raised at every happy occasion of the landsleit. Neither did we stint in our efforts to contact our shtetl compatriots, be they in Israel, New York, or other areas. Little by

little, news of our surviving friends began to trickle in to us, first individually, then in the tens, and finally we had quite a lot of names of Libivners who had escaped with their lives.

The first long list of 170 who had survived was mailed to us from Israel by Nathan Sobel. He accompanied his roster with a long letter of lamentation, in which he described in detail each survivor's story of the gruesome massacres committed by the Nazi, Ukrainian, and Polish murderers against our dear ones from our hometown. The dense letter, filled with minute details, was 30 pages long. Yet we still did not know the addresses of the rescued Jews, nor could we send them any direct aid as yet.

In August, 1946, we sent 125 British pounds to the landsleit society in Israel, so it could directly help the survivors coming to Israel.

Meanwhile, we did not neglect to give aid to the poor landsleit in Argentina, or to help with funds needed for documents for their relatives across the ocean, whom they wanted to bring over to America. By 1947 we had established a correspondence with 40 Libivne survivors in Poland, Italy, Israel and Germany, as well as sent them packages and money gifts.

A ladies' auxiliary was formed as part of the society. Its members were Mine Stier, Rochl Shildergemeyn, Sofie Gershentzwayg, Dora Boter, and others. These women helped run the meetings and raised money for our relief work.

At first, we joined the federation of landsmanshaftn, but we later left it because of a difference of opinions on various national questions.

When the creation of the State of Israel by the United Nations was announced in November, 1947, our society arranged a big celebration, attended by 300 landsleit.

The following notice in the Buenos Aires daily newspaper *Di prese* described the festive mood of this celebration of the friends of the Libivne Society and the relief work it did:

> On December 14, 1947, we celebrated the second birthday of our society at a gathering in a packed hall. The president, G. Tzimerboym, opened the meeting and spoke about the gala, which coincided with the great occasion of the founding of the Jewish state—a very historic occasion. Sponta-

neously the people sang HaTikvah (Israel's national anthem) and the Partisan Hymn. The secretary, Zelig Faigen, reminded the audience that all those who had been fortunate enough to escape the Nazi clutches and had been found worthy enough to see the creation of the Jewish state must feel a dual obligation to add their energies to the realization of the Jewish state.

The president then read a report about the successful work of the past two years for relief for the survivors. He pointed out that during that time, the society had sent 54 packages and 6,000 pesos to survivors outside Argentina and over 1,500 pesos to local Argentine landsleit. 1,000 pesos were contributed to the seven million campaign; 100 pesos for the Jewish hospital; 100 pesos for the Peretz Book Fund; 100 pesos for the Paris orphan home; 200 pesos for the Jewish Committee of Cremona; and smaller donations to other worthwhile institutions. The report was applauded most heartily.

The society's relief work continued for many years. The officers had remained almost the same during this time, except for the treasurer, who from the second year on was a man from Opalin, Bernard Gershentzweig. The chairman of the society, Yochanan Bargrum (z"l), had the post for several years. When the writer of these lines was chairman, his secretary was Leon Furman. The work of relief continued for many years under the old staff of officers.

Recently, the work of relief has become weaker for several reasons. The economic condition of the survivors has gradually normalized. Each one has established himself in his new homeland—Israel, Argentina, and America—and no longer needs our help. We, the activists, have grown older, and it seems to us that our obligations have been fulfilled.

The work of the Libivne Society took a new direction—it established a cooperative credit union. The new credit-cooperative received a license from the Argentina government and assumed the name "La Liberal."

A group of Luboml landsleit in Argentina at a banquet in honor of the State of Israel.

The cooperative's task was to make loans to members so they could start a business in order to make a living, improve an established business, or deal with a bad financial situation.

Those active in raising and administering the fund were volunteer workers, giving their time and energy to this undertaking.

It is worthwhile emphasizing the devotion of the president of the cooperative, Yochanan Bargrum, and the bookkeeper, Dovid Sher, who put the cooperative on a sound financial basis and guarded its interests.

At present, the head of the cooperative and of its work is Yosef Shicht, who follows the tradition with the same devotion as the former officers to make the cooperative able to help those members in need of a loan for some purpose.

During the historic days of 1967, the cooperative contributed a much greater sum than usual to the State of Israel.

THE FORMATION AND ACTIVITIES OF THE LIBIVNER SOCIETY IN NEW YORK
By Velvl Royzman (z"l)

The Libivne Benevolent (Relief) Society of New York was founded in 1906. The date is recorded in the bylaws, published when Benny Sheingarten took over the chairmanship. The date appears also in the signed contract between the society and the United Hebrew Cemetery in Staten Island.

This is the only document left from that time. The contract specifies the purchase of a piece of land in Richmond, Staten Island, for the purpose of a cemetery, from the United Hebrew Cemetery. They paid $1,000 for the land, in monthly installments of $100. The contract was signed by the president of that time, T. Shnaydmil, and by the secretary, Yone Byalish.

At that time, the society went by the name of Libivne-Volhynia Relief Society. We do not know how many members it had then, since no minutes were saved and all the original members have long since gone to their eternal rest. After a short time, a group of members separated from the original society—the more pious, Orthodox group of the members. They formed their own group and called themselves the Shomrey Shabos (guardians of the Sabbath). They still exist and have their own synagogue.

A second group separated to "make Sabbath for themselves" (to do their own thing). They adopted the name Libivne Young Men, and became a branch of the Workmen's Circle. They have their own meeting rooms, and they too are still active.

In 1911, Favl Verber became president, and Yakov Vishnits, secretary.

There are some older members of the society who remember the days of World War I. It is a fact that the society functioned from 1914 to 1918.

It is important to mention one important piece of activity by the society during that time. After the war ended and before life had become reestablished, organized gangs of Ukrainian bandits went on a rampage and perpetrated pogroms on Jewish communities in Eastern Europe.

The Balechovtzes were the perpetrators of pogroms in Volhynia. They would attack towns and villages where Jews lived, slaughter the Jewish inhabitants mercilessly, and rob their possessions. Many Jews managed to save themselves by hiding in Libivne. But even Libivne was subject to the danger.

In 1919, Abie (Avrom) Kahn went to Libivne as a tourist; the society gave him $1,200 to help victims of the pogroms who needed help desperately. Libivne already had formed a relief committee of its own, headed by Rabbi Oselka, with two other rabbis as members: R. Leybish London and R. Leybl Melamed. Under the aegis of the Roman Catholic priest, the committee contacted the leader of the Balechovtzes and paid him $400 (a big sum at that time) as protection money not to touch Libivne. Thus Libivne proper escaped pogroms because of money sent them by the New York Libivne Society.

In 1918, Yose Bubish became president, and Yakov Lerner became secretary.

The society used to send Passover aid to Libivne every year. It would also support the Talmud Torah in Libivne, nor would it forget plain poor Jews who needed help.

Benny Sheingarten took over leadership of the society in the 1930s. Leybish Peritszon became vice-president, and Kalman Kramer, secretary.

They wrote a constitution which was printed in a booklet and changed the society's name to

Libovner-Voliner Benevolent Society. The constitution consisted of 13 articles and many paragraphs.

The procedure for becoming a member was very strict. Upon joining the society, each member had to take an oath and also was obligated to carry out the duties as set forth in the constitution.

There were 185 members at the time, calling themselves brothers and sisters. Parents enrolled their children, and the children enrolled their children. The membership consisted of almost all activists among the landsleit in New York.

Meetings were held twice a month, while general meetings were called four times a year. Children's benefit funds were collected at the general meetings, a tradition carried on till the present. The members enjoyed all of the benefits that the society offered, such as: 1) the right to be buried in the society cemetery (after "120 years") with all expenses paid in full; 2) the family of the deceased received a lump sum at the time of death ($1 for each member).

The society had several subcommittees: a committee to visit sick members; a finance committee; and a Chevra Kadisha (burial committee). An ill member had access to the society's doctor. The loan committee was ready at all times to lend money to those in need. The society also had funds put aside for helping other landsleit in New York who were not members, when, for example they could not pay their rent, or if they were unable to make a wedding for a child.

The society was then located at 96 Clinton Street. This building was used as a synagogue on the Sabbath and holidays; the rest of the time it served as a meeting place for the societies.

In 1935 a new executive committee was elected, and Benny Sheingarten was reelected as president, Israel Friedman as vice-president, and Kalman Kramer, secretary.

When World War II broke out in 1939, all contact between the society and the Jews of Libivne was cut off. Our shtetl Libivne was in ruins, together with all the other Jewish communities in Europe.

Our parents, sisters, and brothers had been slaughtered, and everything Jewish had been torn out by the roots. The only ones that miraculously remained alive, a small remnant, were living in the DP camps and finally emigrated to Israel.

In 1948, with the birth of the Jewish state, young Israel could not give very much to the new immigrants who had to build new lives for themselves with empty hands.

Therefore, after the proclamation of the State of Israel, the society formed a committee whose purpose it was to send help in the form of packages to Israel for the newly arrived landsleit. The elected committee consisted of Noach Tzimerberg, Moyshe Krishtal, Nathan Eiger, and Hershl Gershengorn.

In 1956 the society rented a little shul from the Tschechanover Society at 74 Norfolk Street, in New York City. The shul was used as a synagogue on Saturdays, while at other times it was used as a meeting place for gatherings.

In 1961, the society again sent $800 with Nathan Eiger to the Israel Luboml loan fund. Later it sent another $800 with Reuven Shneider (z"l); and still later, with Velvl Sheynvald (z"l), to the same group. Also, in 1967, the society sent $1,000 with Nathan Eiger and Avigdor Gershengorn for the Israel loan fund.

In 1962, Benny Sheingarten died and the society lost a most capable man. Benny Sheingarten had served the society loyally, with his whole heart and soul! He had served for over 30 years. The next president was Israel Friedman, and Dorogusker, vice-president.

At the elections of 1964, Israel Friedman was reelected as president, Nathan Eiger and Shapiro as vice-presidents, and Avigdor Gershengorn, treasurer. At new elections in 1965, Eiger was elected president, Efrayim Lerner, vice-president, and Avigdor Gershengorn, treasurer.

The same year, the society acquired land from Beth-El Cemetery in Cedar Park, New Jersey; the new cemetery was needed because the Staten Island cemetery was almost full. The land cost $20,000.

A year later, in 1966, the society moved from Norfolk Street to the Forward Building at 175 East Broadway. They had to move, for the older members who had lived near the Norfolk Street location had died and the younger ones moved to better areas. The little shul stood empty, and its Torah scrolls were not used any more!

There were nine Torah scrolls altogether; two of the nine were sent to Israel, brought there by Rabbi Eliyohu Friedman, who is now living in Jerusalem; the other seven presented a problem. A meeting of the society was called to solve this problem and the seven scrolls were bought for $2,100 by the president, Nathan Eiger, who sent them to Israel too.

New officers were elected in 1969: Nathan Eiger, president; Israel Friedman, vice-president; Avigdor Gershengorn, treasurer; Velvl Royzman, recording secretary; Isaac Shechter, secretary. These officers are in power at present. We have a membership list of 200.[1]

Velvl Royzman (z"l)

[1]While preparing the article written by Velvl Royzman for print, news came to us that he had died suddenly.

Velvl Royzman (z"l) was a devoted member, giving his whole heart and soul to the project of issuing this *Yizkor Buch* (Memorial Book) in memory of our holy martyrs. He was a member of the editorial board in America. His articles written for the *Yizkor Buch* are an important part of the monument for our annihilated former home, Luboml.

Together with his brother, family, and friends both here and in other countries, we grieve for him, saddened by his untimely death. May his memory be blessed! May his soul be bound in the bonds of life.

OUR DEAR YAKOV HETMAN (Z"L)
By Yisroel Garmi

Yakov was born in Luboml in the year 1916 to Shmuel Tsvi and Miriam (z"l). He was born into a Chasidic home, and his parents were well-to-do. Yakov had five siblings: four brothers and a sister. During the Holocaust the entire family was wiped out, with the exception of one brother, Avrom, who presently resides in the United States.

Yakov began his religious studies in cheder, the traditional Jewish elementary school. Later, he continued his studies in the Bet Midrash. He was instructed there by the greatest Torah scholars in the town of Luboml: Rav Pinchas Oselka and Rav Dovid Veytsfrucht. Finally, he studied at the yeshiva. Furthermore, while Yakov attended all these schools he also studied secular subjects at the Tarbut school and later with private tutors.

In 1931, Yakov took an entrance examination to get into the Yeshiva Chachmey Lublin. At the same time he took an entrance examination to get into the sixth grade of the high school of the Jewish community in Chelm, which was under the management of Dr. Michael Handel. After changing his mind several times, Yakov decided to continue his studies at the high school rather than the yeshiva. Later, he moved on to the high school of Clara Erlich in Kovel, where he finished his studies with honors.

After Yakov received his matriculation certificate he remained in Kovel for another two years. There he was appointed to the local leadership of Beitar.

In the year 1936, Yakov made aliyah to Eretz Yisroel and began studying in the department of arts and humanities at the Hebrew University in Jerusalem. In 1940 he completed his studies successfully.

During the period in which he studied in Jerusalem, Yakov was nominated again to be a leader in Beitar, and from 1939 he served as a member of the religious committee of the student union. He was director of the loan and mutual-aid fund of the student union as well. Furthermore, he served as chairman of the Revisionist students' organizations, Yavneh and Yodefet. Yakov participated in the editing of a periodical called *Masuot* and published many of his own articles in it.

Yakov Hetman (z"l)

370

He also took an active role in the under-ground activities of Irgun Tzvai Leumi (Etzel), a nationalist military organization that fought the British and Arabs in Palestine. He led a student unit belonging to Etzel and a youth group. Also, Yakov was a secretary of the headquarters in Jerusalem. In 1942, on the night of the Battle of El-Alamain, when there was fear of a German invasion, Yakov was nominated to lead an anti-Nazi espionage unit belonging to Etzel. He also organized the organization's branch in Jerusalem.

In July of 1944, at the beginning of the Etzel revolt against the British, Yakov was arrested and sent to a camp in Latrun. Later, he was sent by the British along with the first exiles to Eritrea, the Sudan, and Kenya.

Yakov was held there for more than four years, until August of 1948. During his imprisonment, he edited a daily paper called *Exile in Kenya*. He also established and edited, along with his exiled friends, a periodical dealing with literature and matters of nationalism. This periodical was called *Badad* ("Loneliness"). He also wrote a book, *Imprisonment and Exile.*

When Yakov returned to Israel after having been exiled in Kenya, he was nominated to be editor of the weekly newspaper *Herut* ("Freedom"). When this paper started coming out as a daily, Yakov began serving as editor for the Saturday edition of the paper and then was assigned to be chief night editor.

In 1951, Yakov married Aviva Shenhav-Sheinbein. She had a master's degree in biochemistry from the Hebrew University. In 1952, a daughter was born to the couple; her name is Miriam. From 1949 to 1950, Yakov taught history and Hebrew in Rishon LeTzion at a secondary school with a specialization in natural science. From 1952 to 1954, he taught at Gimnasia Herzliah, Tel Aviv. Not satisfied with teaching alone, Yakov continued his work as chief night editor of *Herut*.

During this same period, Yakov took a final examination in his major subject, which was Jewish history. As a result, he acquired a master's degree in arts and humanities.

At the beginning of 1956, Yakov obtained a position as head of the Dvir publishing house and resigned from his position as night editor. In this same year, Yakov's second child was born and was named Shmuel.

Toward the end of 1957, Yakov returned to the newspaper business. This time he held the position of chief night editor of the paper *HaBoker.* He remained at this position until January of 1965.

In October of 1959, Yakov began an additional part-time job during his free daytime hours. He joined the department of education of Tel Aviv-Yafo and served as a pedagogical assistant to high schools.

As time went on, Yakov was nominated to the position of director of the high school department. From 1969, he was director of the department of post-primary education in Tel Aviv-Yafo. Yakov continued publishing articles in daily papers and periodicals. He was also an editor at the periodical *Culture and Education*.

At the same time, he was working toward his doctorate in history. The topic of his work was "The Holy Rabbi Yeshaya Horowitz: "His Personality, His Work and His Influence." [Rabbi Yeshaya Horowitz was a 17th-century rabbi often called the *Shenei Luchot HaBerit* after his book by that name.]

When it was decided to publish a memorial book of Luboml, Yakov worked with dedication on this project for several years. He took upon himself the position of assistant editor of the Hebrew section of the book. He established the outline and the framework of the book concerning the major sections. Yakov was on good terms with the editor-in-chief, Mr. B. Kagan, who now resides in New York, and with the rest of the committee members from Luboml, who reside in the United States.

In the month of May, 1973, Yakov went along with a group of professional educators on a tour of schools in London for the purpose of advanced study in the field of education.

Only a few days had passed since Yakov left Israel for London when the bitter, astonishing news of his death reached home. He was killed in an automobile accident in London on the morning of Tuesday, May 15. Still in shock and plagued with grief, Yakov's friends and family escorted him on his last journey to the cemetery in Nachalat Yitshak, his final resting place.

All Yakov's family, friends and acquaintances, many from Luboml, were touched by his death in the worst way. Who would have thought that Yakov, who had put forth so much effort in producing a memorial book to his fellow citizens in Luboml, would himself wind up in the book? Fate was cruel and uncaring.

You meant so much to us, dearest Yakov. You were endowed with so many wondrous qualities of a good upright Jew. You were a lover of freedom and sought to free your nation and to this end you put forth so much conviction, so much effort and self-sacrifice. In all that you did you were a man of action, working to fulfill your dreams. You approached every task with such fervor and conviction. Your life was comparable to a multicolored, embroidered work that was strange yet wonderful, weaving together daring, courageous acts along with the learning of Torah and culture. You were a man of grace, beauty, and charm, a modest, humble, noble-minded man. How were you taken from the land of the living?

It is a shame, a shame that we must mourn you so, and that you are no longer with us. We do not forget you. May your soul be bound up in the bond of everlasting life, and may you rest in peace.

MEMORIAL PRAYER
IN MEMORY OF THE HOLOCAUST MARTYRS

The following prayer is read at the completion of a chapter or a tractate of the Talmud, or during a memorial meeting for those who died in the Holocaust.

Hear, O Lord, who art full of mercy, who hast given a soul to every living thing with Thy Hand, and who put the breath of life into the body of man. May it be Thy will, for the sake of our Torah and our prayer, to look down upon the souls of Thy people Israel, myriads of them! the old and the young; men, women, and children who were slaughtered for the sanctification of Thy name; who were butchered, strangled, and burned to ashes by the German murderers (may their memory be wiped off the face of this earth). The victims were like the cedars of Lebanon, the mighty in the Torah; they were pure and holy, the heads of yeshivas and their congregations in the holy communities; they delivered their souls for the sanctification of Thy name. For the sake of our dear ones who died before their time, may

Thou remember them for good, O God, the remnant of the righteous of the world, and avenge Thou the blood of Thy servants that was spilled. As it is written in the Torah of Moses, the man of God: "Hear ye, gentile nations, that the blood of My servants shall arise and will avenge the enemy, and that He shall forgive His people and His land." As Thy servants, the prophets, wrote, "And I shall avenge their blood and I shall dwell in Zion!" And it is written in the Holy Books, "Why did the gentiles ask, 'Where is their God?' And it is known by the gentiles, as witnessed by our eyes, that vengeance comes for the spilled blood of My servants."

May their souls be bound in the bonds of eternal life; and may they rest in peace together with all the other dead people of Israel. And do so in Thy memory; and send us the Messiah, the Righteous One, to deliver us from exile; and gather us from the four corners of the earth into our land; and may we be found worthy of the final redemption in a very short time, Amen!

תְּפִלָּה

לְזֵכֶר קְדוֹשֵׁי הַשּׁוֹאָה

הַנֶּאֱמֶרֶת בְּסִיּוּם פֶּרֶק אוֹ מַסֶּכְתָּא וּבְאַזְכָּרוֹת

אָנָּא ד' מָלֵא רַחֲמִים

אֲשֶׁר בְּיָדְךָ נֶפֶשׁ כָּל חַי וְרוּחַ כָּל בְּשַׂר אִישׁ, יְהִי נָא לְרָצוֹן לְפָנֶיךָ תּוֹרָתֵנוּ וּתְפִלָּתֵנוּ בַּעֲבוּר נִשְׁמוֹתֵיהֶם שֶׁל מֵאוֹת רִבּוֹא מִיִּשְׂרָאֵל, זָקֵן וָנַעַר, אֲנָשִׁים וְנָשִׁים וָטַף שֶׁנֶּהֶרְגוּ עַל קִדּוּשׁ הַשֵּׁם, נִשְׁחֲטוּ וְנֶחְנְקוּ וְנִשְׂרְפוּ לְאֵפֶר עַל-יְדֵי הַצּוֹרְרִים הַגֶּרְמָנִים יִמַּ"שׁ, בֵּינֵיהֶם אַרְזֵי הַלְּבָנוֹן, אַדִּירֵי הַתּוֹרָה, קְדוֹשִׁים וּטְהוֹרִים, רָאשֵׁי יְשִׁיבוֹת וְתַלְמִידֵיהֶן, תִּינוֹקוֹת יִשְׂרָאֵל שֶׁלֹּא טָעֲמוּ טַעַם חֵטְא וְצַדִּיקֵי עוֹלָם – רַבָּנֵי יִשְׂרָאֵל עִם קְהִלָּתָם קְהִלּוֹת הַקֹּדֶשׁ, שֶׁמָּסְרוּ נַפְשָׁם עַל קְדֻשַּׁת הַשֵּׁם וְכֵן בְּעַד קְרוֹבֵינוּ שֶׁנִּסְפּוּ בְּתוֹכָם –

יִזְכְּרֵם אֱלֹהֵינוּ לְטוֹבָה

עִם שְׁאָר צַדִּיקֵי עוֹלָם וְיִנְקֹם נִקְמַת דַּם עֲבָדָיו הַשָּׁפוּךְ. כַּכָּתוּב בְּתוֹרַת מֹשֶׁה אִישׁ הָאֱלֹהִים: הַרְנִינוּ גוֹיִים עַמּוֹ כִּי דַם עֲבָדָיו יִקּוֹם וְנָקָם יָשִׁיב לְצָרָיו וְכִפֶּר אַדְמָתוֹ עַמּוֹ. וְעַל-יְדֵי עֲבָדֶיךָ הַנְּבִיאִים כָּתוּב לֵאמֹר: וְנִקֵּיתִי דָמָם לֹא נִקֵּיתִי וַד' שֹׁכֵן בְּצִיּוֹן. וּבְכִתְבֵי הַקֹּדֶשׁ נֶאֱמַר: לָמָּה יֹאמְרוּ הַגּוֹיִים אַיֵּה אֱלֹהֵיהֶם, יִוָּדַע בַּגּוֹיִים לְעֵינֵינוּ נִקְמַת דַּם עֲבָדֶיךָ הַשָּׁפוּךְ.

תְּהִי נַפְשָׁם צְרוּרָה בִּצְרוֹר הַחַיִּים

לְהַחֲיוֹתָם בִּתְחִיַּת הַמֵּתִים עִם כָּל מֵתֵי עַמְּךָ יִשְׂרָאֵל בְּרַחֲמִים, וּשְׁלַח לָנוּ אֶת מְשִׁיחַ צִדְקֵנוּ לִפְדוֹת אוֹתָנוּ מִגָּלוּתֵנוּ וְקַבְּצֵנוּ יַחַד מֵאַרְבַּע כַּנְפוֹת הָאָרֶץ לְאַרְצֵנוּ וְנִזְכֶּה לִגְאֻלָּה שְׁלֵמָה בִּמְהֵרָה, אָמֵן,

THESE ARE THE NAMES
OF ALL THE HOLY MARTYRS
FROM LUBOML AND ENVIRONS
WHO PERISHED IN THE HOLOCAUST

A

Achtelberg

Zelig; wife, Chaye (from Podhorodno); children, Feyge, Motl, Yankl, Dobe, Tsipoyre

Achtshteyn

Liptsye; children

Moyshe; wife Biltse; son and daughter

Yosef; wife; children

Afeldman

Zhenya

Akerman

Manye; wife; children

Alter

Boruch; wife; children

Motl (from Dorsk); wife; children

Armarnik

Fayvel; wife; children, Roze, Yisroel, Yankef, Gitl, Leybl, Yoyne, Soreh

Asher

(the tinsmith); wife; children

Axelrod

Aron Yechiel; wife Tobe Chane; children; Libe and husband Vaynus, Dobrish Malke, Henye Reyzl

Sheftel (and wife and children)

B

Babad

Moyshe; wife; children, Zlate and four more children

Baler

Yitshak; wife; children

Baran

Chayim; son, Shloyme

Yisroel; wife; family

Shmuel; wife, Chane

Shloyme; wife; children, Hershl and Tobe

Manes; family

Esther; family

Barg

Shmuel; wife, Sheyndl; daughter, Yehudis

Nute; wife, Tove; children, Dvoyre, Yosef

Liber; wife; children

Yosef; wife; children

Avrom-Yitshak; wife; children

Bargrum

Hershl; wife Yite-Leye; children, Rivke, Yechiel

Chayim; wife, Rosye; children, Freyde, Yoel, Malke

Shmuel; wife Babtshe; two children

Gultsye (née Koltun); two children

Meshl; wife, Manye; son, Sgure

Barnboym

Hershl; family

Chayim-Mordche; family

Barshtat

Shmuel; wife, Beyle; children

Baum

Tsine (née Kroyt)

Berger

Yosef; wife; son, Leybl

Yisroel; wife Leye (née Techor)

Shmuel; wife

Bergerbest

Yisroel; wife; children

Nute; wife; children

Chayim

Ayzik; children, Motl, Margolis, Nute, Tsirl

Beylinson

Moyshe; wife; children

Bialer

Nute; wife, Brayne; daughter, Esther

Yakov

Avrom

Yoel; wife, Soreh

Libe

Mechl; wife; children

Kalman; wife, Esther; children

Biber

Mayer-Chayim; wife; children

Yakov-Sholem; wife, children

Blecher

Moyshe; wife, Rivke; children

Hershl; wife; children

Blumen

Aron; wife, Sheyndl

Yitshak-Leyb; wife , Beyle; children, Mordche, Pesye, Chaye

Yakov; wife, Tsipoyre; children, Yitshak, Miriam-Leye, Chayim-Tsvi, Gershon

Blumensayg

Leybish; wife, Soreh; children, Rochl, Yite, Dvoyre

Blushteyn

Eliyohu; children, Sheyeve, Yeshaye, Velvel, Moyshe, Basye, Royze, Rochl, Genye

Aron; wife; children, Fradl, Yakov, Chaye

Mordche; wife; children, Gitl, Roze, Nisn, Chane, Elke, Moyshe, Malke, Menachem

Yechiel; wife, Chave; children

Bokser

Moyshe; wife, Broche

Shmuel; wife, Mashe; children, Motl and Soreh

Bornshteyn

Yosef; wife; children

Brandman

Aron-Yoyne; wife; children

Brayer

Meyer; wife, Etl; children, Tsirl, Rochl, Chaye, Pesye, Rivke

Brikman

Yakov; wife; children, Aron, Azriel, Yitshak

Tevl; wife; children

Briv

Yisroel; wife, Rivke; children, Yankl, Bebe and four more children

Bronfeld

Reytse

Shmuel

Yakov

Bronshteyn

Fishl; wife; children

Buchleyzer

Pinye; wife; children

Bukovsky

Leyb-Hersh; wife, Freyde (née Katz); son

Byaloglovsky

Elye (Kepke)

Yidl

C

Chinenzon

Getsl; wife; children

Yitshak; wife; children

Yakov; wife; children

Chosid

Chayim; wife; children

Moyshe; wife; children, Hershl and Gitl

Chvetkovsky

Henye (née Kroyt)

D

Danziger

Shimon; wife, Freye

Dendechis

Yakov; wife, Freyde; children, Fishl, Roze, Binyomen

Dimetshteyn

Avrom; wife; children

Dobrovodki

Dovid; wife; children

Donyevits

Volf; wife, Brayndl; children, Nachum, Rivke

Dornboym

Yosef; wife, Maye; children, Sholem, Mordche, Mashe

Yosef; wife

Dorogusker

Fayvel-Dovid; children, Yente, Leye, Chayim

Leybish; children, Chaye, Yankl, Zecharye, Fayvel, Sime, Leye, Shaye

Dubetsky

Binyomen; wife, Tobe

Nachum; wife, Henye; daughter, Tobe and more children

Itsl; wife, Chasye; son, Nachum

Yitshak; wife, Chane; children, Moyshe, Motl and more children

Yehudis; children, Freydl, Yakov, Moyshe

Abish; wife, Chayse; sons, Nachum, Moyshe and more children

Dubelman

Yisroel; wife; two children

Dunyets

Moyshe-Yidl

Yitshak

Eliyohu; wife, Feyge; daughters, Beyle-Rivke, Teme, Golde

E

Ehrlich

Leybl; wife

Soreh

Avrom Yitshak; wife; children

Soreh; daughter

Yakov; wife, Feyge

Gershon-Henech; wife, Matl; children, Hershl, Zlate and another daughter

Hershl; wife, Esther-Reyzl; children, Fradl, Pesl, Golde

Eichenboym

Leybish; wife; children

Eichorn

Avrom-Leybish; wife, Libe; children

Eidelberg

Berish; wife, Chane; daughter Menuche

Eidelman

Dovid; wife, Yocheved (née Shifman); children, Moyshe, Zlatke, Zalman, Golde

Eidelshteyn

Moyshe; wife, Freyde; daughter Brayndl

Eiger

Chave

Einbinder

Moyshe; wife, Sime; daughter Chiske

Einhorn

Yitshak; wife; children

Moyshe; wife, Broche; children, Soreh, Mordche; one more son

Dvoyre

Eizenberg

Moyshe; wife, Freyde; daughter Brayoll

Mendl; wife, Soreh; son, Binyomen

Eizenman

Chayim, (chimney-sweep)

Elbirt

Yoyne; wife Beyle (di Shvartze); children, Feyge, Basye, Mordche, Chenye, Avrom, Moyshe

Yitshak; wife Beyle (di Vayse); children

Manes; wife, Chane; children Boruch, Chave, Chaye

Shloyme; wife; children

Elfant

Chaye

Shloyme; wife Chane Sheyndl; children

Eltster

Shmuel-Avrom; wife Esther-Reyzl; children

Yoynasan; wife, Beyle; children, Chane, Aron

Moyshe; wife, Zlate; children

Yitshak; wife; children

Feyge Rochl; husband; children

Englender

Leybl; wife Rivke; children

Epshteyn

Rivke; children, Leybl, Dvoyre, Chave

Esterzon

Chaye; children, Hershl, Feyge

Moyshe; wife Broche; children, Soreh, Mordche,
    and another son

Dvoyre

F

Falk

Moyshe-Ruven; wife, Zelde; children, Shmuel,
    Chane, Hinde, Pinchas, Chaye, Leye, Hilde

Fayferman

Royze; daughter, Freydke

Avrom; wife; children

Shmuel; wife, Freye

Faygnbaum

Binyomen

Fayner

Moyshe; wife, Dvoyre; sons, Yidl, Buzye, Lipe

Feldmaus

Menachem; wife, Chaye (née Rayf); sons, Avrom,
    Tsvi-Zecharye, Yisroel, Boruch

Feller

Yakov; wife, Dobrish; son, Chayim

Yisroel-Hersh; wife; children

Feygelis

Meyer; wife; children

Moyshe; wife; children

Bentsi; wife; children

Asher; wife; daughters, Malke and two others

Fidl

Yitshak; wife; children

Fidlman

Yakov; wife, Freydke; children, Dvoyre, Bubi

Finkelshteyn

Aron; wife, Etl (née Klig); child

Eliezer; wife, Reytse; children, Dovid, Rivke

Fisher

Chave-Leye

Simche; wife

Avrom; wife; children

Utschi; family

Mume; wife Chasye (née Krammer)

Fishman

Beti

Lusi

Flantsboym

Feyge; mother; sister

Flaysher

Zalman; wife, Etye; children

Flechtman

Yitshak; wife, Sheyndl; children

Folkovitsch

Chayim-Hersh; wife, Soreh; children

Foygl

Chaye-Keyle

Frechter

Mendl; wife, Rochl.

Berish; wife; children, Moyshe, Sime, Yakov,
    Shifre, Gershon

Mordche; wife

Moyshe; wife, Gitl (née Shicht); children

Yakov; family

Freyzinger

Yakov (Pekelik); wife; children

Fried

Shmuel; wife; children

Fayvel; wife; children

Friedland

Betsalel; wife; children

Yosef; wife, Frume

Friedman

Mordche; wife; children

Yakov; wife; children

Shloyme; wife; children

Akiva; wife; children

Yakov; wife, Zhenya; children

Heynach; wife

Shmuel; wife, Chavtze; children

Frimerman

Moyshe; wife, Sosl; children, Ayzik, Tobe, Dovid

Zalman; wife; children

Fuks

Nute; wife, Dvoyre; daughter, Shifre

Moyshe; wife; children, Yosef, Yite, Shmuel, Leybl

Pinchas; wife, Neche; children

Zeynvel; wife, Shifre

Shmuel; wife, Malke; children

Furshifer

Yosef; wife, Rivke; three children

G

Gelbord

Hershl; wife; sons, Efrayim, Shaye

Yoyne; wife, Perl; children

Etke (née Rayf)

Geler

Chaye

Yakov; wife; children

Motl; wife; children

Chaye (from Shatsk)

Gelibter

Yitshak-Dovid; wife, Dobe

Yakov; wife, Etl; children

Gelman

Moyshe; sons, Binyomen, Ayzik

Shmuel-Avrom; wife, Chiltse; sons

Gershenberg

Avrom; wife

Shmuel; wife; daughters, Mashe, Chave

Aron; wife; children

Moyshe

Gershengorn

Gitl (née Shuster); husband; five children

Tsivye (née Shmuckler); husband; two children

Elye; wife, Itke; children, Feyge, Kalman, Chane, Libe

Gershteyn

Nute; wife, Chaye

Shmuel-Leyb; wife; children

Gershtnblit

Shloyme; wife

Gershtnbroyt

Leybl; wife, Royze; children, Rivke-Beyle, Chane, Yechiel, Pinye, and three more children

Getman (see also Hetman)

Soreh

Chane; six children (from Nadizh)

Geyerwald

Dovid; children, Dobe, Shmuel, Ben-Tsiyon, Gitl, Yerachmiel

Geyshis

Ruven; wife, Sime; children

Ginzburg

Yosef; wife, Rochl

Feyge; husband; children

Berl; wife, Tobe; children Shmuel, Feyge

Avrom; wife, Elke (née Eizenberg); daughter

Falik; wife, Malke; children, Yoel, Esther, Blume

Kalman; wife; children

Yakov; wife, Etl; children

Gitelis

Zlate-Rochl

Yeshaye; wife, Golde; four children

Chamke; husband

Yosef; wife; children

Zalman

Gitklig

Shmuel; wife, Pesl; children, Avrom, Shimon, Sosl, Mordche

Leye

Leybl; wife; children

Shmuel; wife

Yoel; wife, Peye

Yehoshua; wife, Tobe; children, Yoel, Munish, Esther

Givant

Fayvele; wife; children

Avrom; wife; children

Gleizer

Vovi; wife; children

Asher; wife; children

Hinde

Liptsye; wife; children

Gloz
Abba; wife; sons, Binem, Yankef

Goldberg
Yakov; wife, Sosl
Nute; children, Tobe, Yisroel, Mordche, Soreh, Dovid, Malke
Shimon; wife; children
Chayim-Wolf; wife, Rane; children
Miriam; children
Yakov; wife; children
Tsipe (née Gershengorn); children, Feyge, Kalman
Feyge; son, Hershl
Yosef; wife, Blume; children, Yitshak, Hershl, Rivke, Ite, Chaye, Yakov

Goldburtn
Simche; wife; children
Sheyndl; sons, Moyshe, Fayvel
Elye; wife

Goldenzon
Leyzer; wife; children

Goldfun
Yechiel; wife; children
Yeshaye; wife; children
Yitshak; wife, Feyge

Goldhaber
Dovid; wife, Rochl; children
Rivke (née Klinglechis); husband, Leyzer Volf
Michal; wife; children

Goldhacker
Avrom; wife, Etl; children, Chaye, Meyer-Chayim, Tsvi, Moyshe

Goldman
Dovid (Urkes); wife; children

Granatshteyn
Pinchas; wife, Chaye; daughters, Esther, Yide

Grebelkis
Yoel; children, Dvoyre, Perets, Malke

Greenshpan
Gershon; wife, Rivke; children

Greenvaks
Yankl; children, Chane, Mendl, Chaye-Soreh
Avrom; father; sisters

Grimatlicht
Avrom; wife, Rochl; daughters, Mindl, Rivke, Feyge
Mendl-Chaye
Yehoshua; wife, Feyge; children
Pinye; wife; children
Yitshak-Meyer; wife, Rivke
Mordche
Gedalia; wife, Soreh; son, Gershon
Abba; wife, Gitl; children
Soreh (Lipe's wife); children Gedalia, Yitshak, Dvoyre
Shimon; wife, Chane; son Pinchas
Bela; children
Eliyohu; wife, Rivke

Grosman
Hinde; (née Blushteyn); husband

Gruber
Leybish; wife; children

Guntsher
Aron; wife; children
Eliyohu; wife; children

Gurbatsch
Moyshe; wife; children

Gurevich
Zalman; wife, Rivke; children

Gurtenshteyn
Moyshe-Nutl; wife; children
Shimon; wife; children
Pinye; wife; children
Yente; daughter, Chasye
Hershl
Yoel; wife, Chaye (née Vaks)

Gurtenshwarts
Moyshe-Meyer; wife, Chave
Yakov; wife, Feyge; children

Guter
Avrom; wife; children
Yeshaye; wife; children

H

Hak

Binyomen; wife; children
Ben-Tsiyon; wife; children
Chayim-Yosef; wife; children
Yitsi; wife; children

Handlsman

Nisn; wife
Yitshak; wife; children, Chaye, Yankef, Chiske, Maye
Mordche; wife, Leye

Has

Sani; wife

Hastik

Berish; wife, Blume; children, Chayim-Leyb, Yakov, Nachum, Miriam, Leybish, Berl
Mordche; wife; children

Helfman

(Attorney) wife, Lusye (née Afeldman)

Hersh

Tratsh (gravedigger); wife; children

Hetman (see also Getman)

Shmuel-Tsvi; wife, Miriam; children, Feyge, Moyshe, Chayim-Zev, Arye-Leyb (or is this two people?

Heybish

Leye (from Dubenko)

Hirshnhorn

Boruch; wife, Frume; children

Honig

Yisroel-Yosef; wife, Feyge; children, Chaye, Yankef, Chiske, Mayke, Leye, Binyomen
Yitshak; wife; children
Fishl; wife, Mashe; children
Meyer;wife; children

Hornshteyn

Dine; daughters, Chane and Rochl
Pinchas; wife, Feyge; children, Teltse, Yitshak

Huberman

Shmuel-Leyb; wife, Gitl; children, Ayzik, Rayle; sister
Yeshaye; wife ; daughter, Pesl

Huz

Yakov; wife
Moyshe
Shloyme; wife, Teme; children

K

Kagan

Ben-Tsiyon; wife, Soreh (née Sojbel); children, Moyshe and another boy
Dovid; wife, Tsine; children, Reyzl, Tcharne, Hershl, Lube
Pesl; family
Rivke; family
Gitl; daughter, Chaye
Moyshe-Yitshak

Kalmisis

Yoyne;children,Sheyndl,Yente,Soreh,Menashe

Kaltracht

Yisroel; wife, Dvoyre
Moyshe; wife; children

Kaminer

Hinde; daughters, Sosl, Perl; son-in-law, Alter
Avrom; family
Yisroel

Kandelshteyn

Mendl; wife, Maye; children, Shoshana, Efrayim
Yisroel; wife, Rochl
Arye; wife; children
Chane; husband; children
Rivke; husband; children
Simche; wife; children
Yakov
Shmuel; wife; children
Eliezer; wife; children

Kaner

Leybl; children, Reyzl, Noach, Dvoyre, Dovid, Aron, Rochl, Chane-Rivke, Soreh
Avrom; wife; children
Etye; daughters, Frume, Chaye

Karger

Moyshe; wife, Elke

Katz

Eliezer; wife, Frume; son, Yitshak

Avrom; wife, Tobe; children, Yankef, Munish, Leye, Fishl

Moyshe; wife; children

Moyshe; son, Fishl

Berl; wife, Keyle; daughter, Tobe

Katzenelenboygn (see Twersky)

Katzenelboym

Moyshe; wife; children

Katzman

Noach (Yeshiva President); wife; children Moyshe-Yitshak

Keylis

Yidl; children, Chane, Shloyme, Soreh, Avrom, Yitshak, Keyle, Hinde, Chaye, Pesye

Klerer

Moyshe; wife, Yocheved; son, Maytshik

Klig

Abba; wife, Dache; children, Meyer, Esther, Pinchas, Ethel

Koltun

Yisoschor; wife; children

Buzye; wife; children

Shloyme; wife; children

Yehoshua; wife; children

Kontchitsky

Yakir; wife, Chaye-Feyge; children, Shayke, Leye, Perl

Moyshe; wife, Rochl; children, Yakov, Chane, Leybl

Volf; wife; children, Basye, Fayvel, Ruven, Chane-Gitl, more

Kopelzon

Kalman (Judenrat head); wife, Soreh

Korb

Chaymke (watercarrier); children, Reyzl, Yosef, Shimshon, Gitl, Tsipoyre

Kornfeld

Mordche; children, Broche, Shmuel-Hersh

Yitshak; children, Chane, Yakov

Michael; wife, Miriam

Yehuda

Avrom

Yitshak

Chaye

Binyomen

Zalman

Rivke,

Motl

Yisroel

Tsvi

Moyshe

Beyle

Aron

Arye

Elke; husband, Binyomen and daughter

Korotke

Shmuel; wife; children

Kovertovsky

Chayim; wife, Rivke (née Huberman); children

Koyfman

Menashe; wife, Lana; children, Feyge, Chayim

Leyzer; wife, Zlate; children

Krammer

Hersh; wife, Yocheved; son, Maytshik

Avrom; wife, Soreh; children, Rivke, Yakov, Yosef, Leye, Basye

Reyzl; daughters, Leye-Fradl, Chasye

Yisroel; wife; children

Shuster, Leye; husband; children

Yisroel; wife, Chaye

Simche; wife, Perl; children

Hersh; wife, Gitl; daughter, Rivke; children

Krayn

Broche

Krayzer

Mordche; wife, Feyge; daughters, Eydl, Esther, Miriam

Shmuel

Avrom

Maye

Krelin

Meyer-Chayim; wife; children

Krepl

Yechiel; wife, Mintsche; children, Pesye, Fishl

Kreymer

Leybish; wife, Beiltsche; children

Dovid; wife, Chaye; children

Kroyt

Pinchas; wife, Esther; sons, Yakov, Shmuel, Munish

Chayim; wife, Serl; son, Buzie

Moyshe; wife, Reyzl; sons, Noach, Betsalel

Yisroel; wife, Feyge; children

Chayim; wife; children

Krupodelnik

Dovid; wife; children

Chayim; wife, Soreh; children, Shimon, Dovid, Shoshana, Hinde

Pinchas; wife; children

Kunifas

Meyer-Chayim; wife; children

Elye-Boruch; wife; children

Shimon; wife; children

Kupershteyn

Nachman; wife, Soreh; children

L

Laks

Shmuel-Zelig

Avrom; wife, Zelde; sons, Moyshe, Shaul

Yitshak; wife, Feyge; two daughters

Chayim; wife, Bine; two sons

Langer

Shimon; wife; children, Yisroel and one more

Zev; children, Sheyndl, Chane, Chayim, Aron

Landgeyer

Avrom; wife; children

Yakov; wife; children

Meyer; wife, Feyge; children

Asher; wife

Moyshe; wife, Sosl; children

Landsberg

Max Hersh; wife, Paula; son

Lantsman

Avrom-Yitshak; wife, Zlate-Rochl; children, Zisl, Moyshe, Shiye, Motl, Pesl

Rivke-Leye; children, Aron, Nisn, Esther, Chane, Moyshe

Efrayim

Laychter

Leybl; children, Shayve, Yehoshua, Avrom, Nechome, Kalman, Naftoli

Lechtschevsky

Motl; wife, Chaye (née Hornshteyn)

Leder

Noach; wife; children

Yisroel; wife, Pesye; children

Lederman

Tobe

Lempert

Moyshe; wife; children

Lentsinsky

Yitshak; wife; children

Eliyohu; wife; Henye; children, Rochl, Fride, Mashe, Miriam, Tcharne, Feyge

Avrom; wife; children

Shmuel; wife; children

Lerner

Yitshak; wife; children, Sime, Yankef

Frume; sons, Aron, Dovid; daughter

Leybish; wife, Rochl; son, Shmuel; daughter

Yakov; wife, Dvoyre; children, Hinde, Roze, Eliyohu, Peye, Serl, Chaye-Mirl, Blume, Sheyne

Levi

Tsivye; children, Chave, Srulik

Ruven; wife; children, Perl, Shmuel, Yakov, Pinchas

Chise; children

Lichtenshteyn

Chaye-Soreh

Avrom; wife; children

Yisroel; wife Beyle; children

Lichter

Yechezkiel; wife, Pesye; son, Leybl

Lichtmacher

Aron-Leybish; wife; two children

Avrom; wife, Malke; daughters, Hadasa, Soreh,
Chayke, Perl, Rochl, Rechl

Motl; wife; children

Lifshitz

Velvel; wife, Etl

Hershl-Binyomen; wife, Feyge-Blume; daughters,
Soreh, Roze, Beyle, Tcharne

Shmerl; wife, Soreh; daughter, Tcharne

Mendl; wife

Leyzer; wife; children

Simche; wife, Rivke; children

Hershle; wife, Chane; daughters, Elke, Matl, Soreh,
Royze

Yeshaye; wife; children

Lindenboym

Motl; wife; children

Yisroel; wife, (née Kroyt); children

Lis

Yehoshua; wife, Rochl; children

Listhoys

Leye (née Kroyt)

London

Golde-Rivke (Rebetsin)

Alter Ben-Tsiyon (Rabbi); wife, Soreh; children

Dovid; wife; children

Meyer; wife, Feyge; children, Hentse, Yitshak-
Boruch

Mechl; wife, Perl; children

Luksenburg

Motl; wife; children, Chave, Yente, Esther, Tevl,
Sonye

Yitshak; wife; children

Lubochiner

Leybl; wife, Esther-Beyle; children, Moyshe, Aron,
Fani

Eliezer; wife

Binem; wife; children

Aron; wife; children,

M

Margolin

Nachum; wife; sons, Moyshe, Nusi, Yakov

Mayderdrot

Yitshak; wife; children

Bentsi; wife; children

Mayzls

Dovid; wife; children

Yoyne; wife, Chane

Leybl; wife; children

Dovid; wife; children, Dvoyre, Tsodik

Mekler

Yisroel; wife, Chane; sons, Chayim, Leybish,
Shmuel

Dovid; wife; children

Rantsche; husband

Shmuel; wife, Maye; sons Motl, Hershl, Yosef

Leybish; wife; children

Moyshe; wife; children

Mel

Soreh

Moyshe; wife; children

Henech; wife; children

Mordche; wife; children

Mendl; wife, Chaye; child

Melamed

Moyshe; wife, Basye; children, Soreh, Chaye-
Tsirl, Boruch, Arye

Leybish (Leshniaker); wife, Elke; children,
Shmuel, Hinde, Esther (née Fisher)

Yisroel; wife, Tsivye; children, Hershl, Chane,
Rochl

Asher; wife; children

Yosef; wife; children

Ruven; wife; children

Yakov; wife; five children

Eliezer; wife; children

Avrom (son of Eliezer); wife; children

Moyshe; wife; children

Hershl; wife, Feyge

Binyomen; wife

Dovid; wife; children

Yitshak; wife; children

Chayim-Wolf; wife; children

Hershl; wife; children

Avrom; wife; children
Pinye (Tchodes); wife; children
Meyer (Tchodes); wife; children
Feyge (from Nadizh)
Leybl (Rabbi) (the judge); wife, Frume; daughters,
    Gitl, Beyle
Shamai; wife; children
Moyshe; wife, Chane-Libe; daughters

Meler

Hersh; wife
Malke; husband
Fayvel; wife; children, Tsvi, Tobe, Moyshe
Kalman; wife, Machle; daughter, Gitl

Melnik

Berl
Boruch
Itsl

Melnitser

Matityahu; wife, Dine; children

Meltser

Dine (née Pregal); husband, Simche; children

Menaker

Avrom-Yehoshua; sons, Motl, Yisroel
Motl; wife; children

Mendelson

Alkona (Kunye)
Chayim; wife; children

Mesh

Shaye; wife, Soreh
Hinde
Shaul
Leyb
Malke
Boruch
Moyshe
Alter
Mordche
Shloyme
Hershl
Dovid
Srul
Bentsi
Avrom; wife, Rochl; children, Yitshak, Yocheved,
    Sime
Dovid; wife, Sosi (née Fisher); daughter

Meshkis

Mendl; wife; children
Dovid; wife; children
Shmuel; wife; children
Asher; wife; children

Meshures

Yitsi; wife; children
Chave
Yosef; wife; children
Yakov; wife; children
Dan

Milshteyn

Sender; wife; children
Motl; son
Dovid; wife; children
Chayim; wife; children
Elye; wife; children

Munik

Noach; wife; children
Gultsye; son, Binyomen

Murfeld

Zalman; wife; children

Murin

Dovid; wife, Rochl-Gitl; daughters, Sheyndl,
    Chayke, Tobe
Berl; wife, Rochl; children

N

Natanzon

Yakov; wife, Basye
Yosl
Yoel
Libe
Motl; wife, Meri; children
Meyer; wife; children
Golde

Nisnboym

Yasha; wife, Tcharne (née Lifshitz); daughter,
    Chane

Noyman

Moyshe-Mechl (Sexton, Kotsker Shtibl); wife;
    children
Avrom; wife, Blume

Noymark

Pesach; wife, Lube

Nyeizvestny

Aron-Yosi; wife; children

Noach; wife; children

O

Okoska

Yosef; wife, Perl (née Kopelzon); children

Oksman

Moyshe; wife, Soreh (née Gitlig); children, Munish, Shmuel

Opaliner

Rafael; wife, Soreh

Oselka

Pinchas (Rabbi); wife, Freyde; children, Melech, Yechiel, Gitl, Rivke

Oyventhal

Esther; son, Chanan

Boruch; wife, Basye

Rashke; children

Israel

P

Paluch

Leybish; wife; children, Betsalel

Motl; wife; children

Pech

Dovid; wife, Chane-Gitl

Pelts

Avrom; wife, Elke (née Eiger); children, Aron, Broche-Leye

Chaye; children, Beyle, Roze, Oyzer, Chane, Feyge

Perets

Shimshon; wife, Chane; sons, Ben-Tsiyon, Mendl

Peretszon

Perets; wife, Leye; children

Perkal

Pinchas; wife; children

Perlmuter

Zishe (newspaper distributor)

Petrushka

Shike; wife; children

Pilman

Malke; children, Yankl, Suri, Freyde, Leye

Shmuel-Avrom; wife, Tobe (née, Ginzburg); sons, Yakov, Moyshe

Pitschinkes

Yitshak

Shmuel; wife; children

Moyshe; wife; children

Note; wife; children

Poleturk

Gitl

Yocheved

Sime

Pomerants

Meyer-Chayim; wife, Rochl

Chaye

Tanchum

Moyshe

Tcharne

Gitl; husband; children

Etye

Zeynvel

Yisroel-Boruch

Mishke

Yisroel-Mordche; wife, Frume

Sheyndl-Teme

Tratl; wife, Chasye

Avrom-Yankl; sons, Boruch, Yosef, Shmuel-Velvel, Fishl

Povroznik

Moyshe; wife

Yehoshua; wife; children

Chantshe-Reyzl

Pregal

Shmuel; wife

Leybish

Moyshe; wife, Henye,; children, Yehuda, Chasye, Rivke, Pines, Moyshe

Privner

Motl; wife, Chaye; son, Eliezer; daughter

Prusman

Boruch-Hersh; wife, Chave

R

Rabchuk

Moyshe; wife, Fradl; mother; children, Menuche (another one)

Rabinovitsch

Shloyme; children, Chaye, Avrom, Michael, Esther, Hinde, Shabse

Raychshtul

Chayim-Wolf; sons, Eliezer, Leybl, Kopl

Rayder

Avrom-Sani; wife, Leye
Dovid; wife, Pesye; children
Eliezer; wife

Rayf

Binyomen; wife, Rochl; children
Aron; wife; children
Shmuel; wife, Leye; children
Meyer; wife, Taybl; two children
Zishe; wife, Sheyve; daughter, Chaye Tcharne

Rayz

Shloyme; wife, Chayke
Hershl; wife, Yite; children
Pinchas; wife; children

Regnboygn

Chane-Rochl
Soreh-Leye; husband; child
Chayim; wife, Golde; children, Yoel-Tsvi, Esther
Avrom-Hersh; wife; children

Reyzman

Miriam-Leye
Mendl; wife, Taybl (née Mekler); children
Leye; sons, Yitshak, Avrom
Hershl; wife; children

Reznik

Avrom; wife, Leye; son, Yosef

Royter

Shepe; children, Esther, Yakov, Rivke, Avrom, Chane
Hersh; wife; children

Royzman

Motl; wife, Malke; children, Yakov, Leybl, Chane, Froyke
Yisroel; wife, Gitl; daughters, Pesl, Chayke
Chayim; wife, Miriam; sons, Froyke, Yoyne Sheyndl

Rozenblit

Yisroel
Chayim-Wolf (from Masheve); wife; children
Avrom; wife; children
Tanya (née Metropolska); daughter, Lube

Rozenboym

Elye; wife, Esther (née Kroyt); daughter

Rozenshtrauch

Sani; wife, Rochl-Leye
Yite; children, Chane, Yehoshua
Yitshak; wife; children

Rozenzweig

Hershl; wife, Feyge
Rivke; husband, Shloyme; children, Menuche, Avrom-Yankl, Moyshe
(née Goldberg), Blume; husband, Yosl; children, Yitshak, Hershl, Rivke, Ite, Chaike, Yakov

Rubinshteyn

Yehoshua; wife, Dvoyre
Zalman
Moyshe; children, Pinchas, Herts, Berish
Soreh; children

Rusman

Aron; wife, Sheyndl; son, Leybl
Asher; wife, Dvoyre; children
Yosef; wife, Malke; children
Shmuel; wife; children

S

Samet

Shloyme; wife, Libe
Yosef; wife, Sheyndl; children
Yitshak; wife, Gitl (née Dubetsky)
Shimon; wife, Soreh (née Katz)

Sandlboym

Yosef; wife, Soreh

Hertske; wife, Perl (née Lichtnberg)

Shmuel; wife; children

Frume

Meyer; wife, Tseytl

Sandlshteyn

Avrom; wife; children

Meyer; wife, Feyge; sons, Motl, Asher, Moyshe

Saninzon

Boruch; wife; children

Leybl; wife; children

Yitshak; children, Rane, Dovid, Srul

Leyb; wife; children

Segal

Mordche; wife; children

Sertsuk

Yitshak-Shloyme; wife; sons, Dovid, Avrom

Hershl; wife, Rivke

Yosl; wife; children

Chayim; wife; children

Sfard

Moyshe; wife, Feyge; sons, Dovid, Aron

Berko; wife; children

Yakov; wife, Tobe; children, Pesye, Dovid, Yosef

Shames

Pesye-Tobe

Mordche; wife, Gnendl; daughters, Beyle, Soreh

Asher; wife, Maye; sons, Shmaye, Chayim

Itshe (Sexton, Trisker Shtibl)

Shantsfracht

Velvel; wife; children Sheyndl, Soreh, Meyer

Zeynvel

Shapiro

Mendl

Leyzer; wife; children

Munish; wife; children, Nachum, Broche, Meyer-
  Shaye

Shmuel; wife; children

Yitshak; wife, Roze (née Elbling); children

Shechtman

Liptsye; children

Hersh Leybe; wife; children

Shek

Hersh

Yoyne; wife; children

Yisroel; brother and sister

Shenker

Avrom; wife; children

Nute

Shmuel-Leyb

Sher

Velvel; wife; children

Moyshe; wife; Zlate; children

Sheynblat

Yakov; wife, Chaye; children, Esther, Yoel,
  Munish

Sheyner

Yehuda

Avrom; wife; children

Sheyngarten

Hersh Ber; wife; children

Fayvish; wife; children

Sheyntop

Yeshaye; wife

Sheynwald

Avrom; wife; children

Chayim; wife; children

Simche; wife, Malke; children

Tratl; wife, Mindl; daughter, Reyzl

Beyle; sons, Shneyer, Meyer

Shmuel

Yeshaye; wife

Shich

Shmuel; wife, Yente; children

Naftoli; wife; children, Sheyndl, Liptsye, Esther,
  Daniel, Leye

Shildergemeyn

Henye

Moyshe-Dovid; wife, Sheyndl

Zalman

Moyshe

Rochl

Chaye

Mordche

Nachum

Yehuda
Moyshe-Yoyne; wife, Roze; sons, Binyomen, Zalman

Shliva
Shmuel-Zeynvel
Berl; wife, Tobe; children, Yakov, Menuche, Soreh
Shimon; wife, Libe; daughter, Chane
(Rozenzweig) Feyge

Shmuel
Velvel (gravedigger); wife; children

Shneyer
Avrom; wife Chane; children

Shochet
Meyer; wife, Perl; children

Shor
Shimon; wife, Balbina; children, Halina, Gutek

Shraga
Simche; wife
Efrayim; wife; son, Chayim
Yankef; wife, Esther
Shloyme; wife; children
Hertske (from Berzhets); children, Miriam, Leye, Yehuda

Shrayer
Motl; wife; children

Shtadler
Elye; wife; children
Chaye

Shteynmarder
Dan; children, Yakov, Mindl, Tsipoyre, Motl, Chave, Leye

Shtern
Nachum; wife, Poytsye; daughter, Pitsye
Hershl; wife, Broche
Munish; wife; son
Yakov; wife, Pesye; children, Yehuda, Avrom-Yitshak, Melech, Leybl, Soreh-Malke

Shternboym
Motl; children, Zlate, Boruch, Brayndl, Moyshe
Berish; children, Tsirl, Avrom, Feyge, Gitl
Elye; wife; children
Tsvi; wife; children
Yitshak; wife; children
Nute; wife; children

Shteynberg
Vovi; wife
Dovid; wife, Bronye; children
Sholem; wife, Rochl; children, Mordche, Roze
Buzye (Boruch)
Noach; wife; children
Yakov; wife, Pesye; children, Yehuda, Avrom-Yitshak, Melech, Leybl, Soreh-Malke

Shtilerman
Matityahu; wife; children
Falik; wife; sons, Mendl, Matis, Dovid

Shtracher
Shmuel; wife; children
Nachman; wife; children
Naftoli; wife; Libe (née Kontchitsky); child
Yosef; wife; children
Leyzer; children, Rivke, Yankef, Shimon, Yosef, Zeynvel, Avrom-Hersh, Shmulyek

Shtrom
Yosef; children, Malke, Moyshe, and Meyer

Shuster
Yakov-Yisroel; wife
Aron; wife; children
Avrom
Yoyzi; wife, Chaye-Soreh; daughter, Blume
Yitsche; wife; children
Shmuel; wife, Pesl (née Samet); children
Yosef; wife, Tobe-Malke; sons, Mordche, Moyshe, Yitshak
Nachum; wife, Perl; children
Moyshe; wife, Zlate
Asher; wife, Perl; children, Dvoyre, Efrayim, Leybish
Leyzer; wife, Roze; three children
Falik; wife; sons, Mendl, Matis, Dovid
Leye (née Shuster); husband; children

Shvarts
Chayim-Meyer; wife, Pesye
Avrom; wife, Soreh-Gitl; daughters, Hinde, Roze
Zelig; wife; children
Dovidl; wife; children
Shiye (from Dubenko)

Shvartsblat
Pinchas; wife, Feyge (née, Ginzburg)

Sojbel (Soybel)

Shloyme-Chayim (Kiter); wife, Beyle;
Avrom-Leybish; wife, Basye-Rochl (née Faigen); children, Aron-Tsvi, Soreh-Tove, Ben-Tsiyon
Gershon; wife, Dvoyre; children, Sorele and a boy
Wife of Zelig (in Kovel); two children
Meshl
Chaye
Yosl

Sokolvsky

Chayim; wife; children

Soloveytshik

Shmuel; wife, Mindl (née Helfand)
Betsalel; sons, Moyshe, Getsl, Shimshon, Boruch
Gitl

Somen

Binyomen; wife; children
Golde; two children
Motl; two children, Malke, Gershon

Sposub

Asher; wife; children
Yakov; wife; children

Stenzheritser

Yehuda; wife
Fishl; wife; children
Leybish; wife; children
Berish; wife; children
Pesl; husband
Sime; husband, Shmuel; children

Stepenyer

Rebbe (see Twersky)

Stolyar

Yehoshua; wife; children
Tratl; wife; children

Stompel

Itsi; wife, Perl; children, Feyge, Miriam, Reyzl, Yehuda
Yosef; wife; children

Sukatscher

Mechl; wife; four children
Meyer; wife; children

T

Tchesner

Yakov-Leyzer; wife, Soreh
Asher; wife; children
Ben-Tsiyon; wife, Sosl; children, Munish, Esther
Shloyme-Chayim; wife, Perl; children
Motl; wife; children
Nute; wife
Avigdor
Moyshe; wife; children
Chayim; wife; children

Techor

Meyer; wife, Soreh; children, Chane, Rivke, Avrom, Leye

Tenenboym

Asher; wife; children

Terner

Noach; wife, Chane; children
Motl; wife
Yisroel; wife; children
Yitshak; wife
Nachum; wife; children
Berl; wife; children
Gedalia; wife; children
Feyge; mother

Test

Liptsye; wife; children
Boruch; wife; son Yakov and other children
Moyshe; wife, Feyge (née Shuster); children

Teytlboym

Yoyne; wife
Hinde
Meyer; wife; children
Yakov; wife; children
Yitshak; wife; children
Meyer-Leybe; wife, Esther; children, Beyle-Gitl, Dvoyre, Frump, Yakov, Abish, Perets

Toyzman

Ruven; wife, Soreh; children

Tseylingold

Chayim-Hersh; wife
Meyer; wife; children

Tsvirn

Chayim; wife, Malke; son, Shloyme

Twersky

(Katzenelenboygn), R. Boruch (the Stepenyer Rebbe); wife, Hende (née Horovitz)

(Katzenelenboygn), R. Moyshele, (son of Stepenyer Rebbe); wife; three children

Tzechshteyn

Shimshon; wife, Tcharne; daughters, Etl, Malke

Dovid; wife, Feyge; children, Tobe, Zalman-Aron

Moyshe; wife; children

Tzimerberg

Avrom; wife, Dvosi; children, Chane, Soreh, Dovid, Leye, Moyshe

Binyomen; wife; children, Chane Zelig, Yoyne, Mordche

Tzimerboym

Mirl; son, Yosef

Mendl; wife, Tsipoyre; children, Chayim-Hersh, Miriam-Zisl, Basye

Moyshe; wife; child

Rive (from Shatsk); child

Tzin

Yosef-Chayim; wife

Leybish; wife; children

Soreh-Gitl; husband; children

Yakov; wife; children

Leye

Tziperbron

Dovid; wife, Frume (née Ehrlich); children, Leye, Yitshak, Fride

Tove

Tzitznovitsh

Soreh

Tzizhes

Avrom-Chayim; wife, Reyzl; children, Mendl, Avigdor, Efrayim, Sheyndl, Yehuda, Zalman, Miriam

Tzukerman

Moyshe; wife, Beyle-Soreh (née Vaynshteyn); children

Fayvel; children, Chane, Yente, Rivke, Avrom

Yosef; wife; children

Dovid b'Rab Uziyel; wife; children

Avrom (from Pishtsh); wife

Yitshak; wife; children

Avrom-Chayim; wife, Reyzl

V

Vaks

Esther (née Frechter)

Valdgeyer

Yisroel; wife, Chane (née Sojbel); children, Gitl, Yosl, Leybish, Moyshe Varshniter

Henech; wife, Yente; daughters, Rivtse, Pola, Leye; families

Veksler

Leybe; wife, Miriam; children, Avrom, Fishl, Rochl, Freyde

Yeshaye; wife, Yente; daughters, Roze, Teme, Chane

Soreh Verber

Shmerl; wife, Henye; children, Groynem, Machle

Yoyne; wife; children

Verbla

Yakov; wife, Lifshe (née Bronshteyn); children

Veykus

Shmuel; wife (née Marin); children

Veyn

Fishl Veyner

Dovid; wife; children

Veyngarten

Shmuel; wife, Elke; children, Moyshe, Sheyndl

Veynrib

Motl; wife; children

Veynshlboym

Aron; wife, Esther

Alter; wife; children

Zecharye; wife; children

Zlate; children

Gitl; children

Yakov; wife; children

Veynshteyn

Moyshe; wife, Yehudis

Shmuel; wife, Mashe; daughter, Chinye

Yankef; wife; children

Zalman; wife; children

Asher; wife; children

Avrom; wife; children

Veysberg

Sholem; wife, Nechome

Veysman

Nachman

Mordche; wife; children

Hersh; wife; children

Liptsye; wife; children

Moyshe; wife; children

Veytzman

Yitshak; wife, Chaye-Soreh; children, Leybe, Tobe, Dvoyre

Yitshak; wife, Esther (from Berzhets); children, Ben-Tsiyon, Shmuel, Sime, Sheyndl

Veytsfrucht

Dovid; wife, Nechome

Meyer-Yitshak; wife, Chaye; children, Yakov, Rochl

Vidra

Michael; wife; children

Zalman; wife; children

Nachum; wife

Munish; wife; children

Eliyohu; wife; children

Vishnits

Chayim-Heshl; wife, Freyde; children, Yitshak, Miriam

Volk

Yakov; wife, Soreh; daughter, Malke

Volvushes

Elye; wife, Rikl; daughters, Sosi, Yente

Shepe; wife, Maye; daughters, Reyzl, Yente

Avrom-Yitshak; wife, Miriam; children, Moyshe, Dobe

Ben-Tsiyon; wife, Chave; daughters, Leye, Freyde, Elke, Esther

Eliyohu; children, Ruven, Leye, Leybe, Moyshe, Perl

Leybe; wife, Chasye Keyle; daughters, Leye, Soreh

Moyshe; wife; children

Y

Yadinow

Chave-Reyzl; daughter, Malke

Yarinksboym

Emanuel; wife, Soreh; children, Pinchas, Golde

Yoyne

Shamesh (Sexton of the Great Shul); wife, Tsipe; sons, Dovid, Shloyme

Yucht

Yitshak; wife, Yente; children

Uri; wife, Miriam; children, Elye, Menuche

Avrom; wife; children

Yung

Broche; son, Yitshak

Feyge

Z

Zagelboym

Avrom; wife; children

Leybl; wife; children

Zats

Yosef; wife, Yite; sons, Asher-Leyb, Yakov, Yisroel, Efrayim, Shimon

Zayd

Brayndl; daughter, Zhenya

Yakov; wife; children

Dovid; wife; children

Zaydl

Yakov; wife, Esther

Zeltser

Chane; daughter, Sosl

Yosi; wife; children

Zeyfer

Chayim-Boruch; wife; children

Zeygermayster

Brayndl (née Shternboym)

Zhelaznik

Beyle (from Dubenko)

Ziegelman

Sime

Yosef; wife, Sheyndl; children, Chaye-Libe, Tove

Zigelboym

Reyzl

Yosef; son, two daughters

Zilber

Sheyndl; husband; children

Zilberblech

Gedalia; wife, Hentse; children, Fayvel, Roze and another two children

Shaye-Dovid; wife, Soreh; children, Bronye, Chane, her husband and child

Zilberberg

Yankl-Hershl; wife; children

Munish; wife; children

Shmuel; wife; children

Yosef; wife; children

Zilberman

Malke; daughters, Soreh, Henye

Chayim-Rafayel; wife, Sheyndl; children, Rochl, Tsvi, Pesach

Moyshe; wife, Chane; sons, Michael, Yakov

Dovid; children, Leye, Michael, Chane, Rivke

Zilbershteyn

Chayim; wife; children

Zimmerberg

Itke

Aron; wife; children

Binyomen; wife, Simke; children, Chane, Pinchas, Zelig, Chayim

Eliyohu; wife, Soreh; two daughters, Chane and one more

Pesach; wife; daughter, Chane

Avrom; wife, Dvosi

Chave-Reyzl; daughter, Malke

Zishe

(the Baker); wife, Chasye; daughter, Bunye (and husband Buzie)

Zumerfeld

Esther-Beyle; daughters, Chaye, Broche, Soreh, Reyzl, Edyl

THE FALLEN SOLDIERS OF OUR TOWN AND ITS ENVIRONS, WHO FOUGHT IN THE YOM KIPPUR WAR

Son of Bat-Sheva and Menachem Bar-Giora (Munish Ginsburg)

Lieutenant Chayim Bar-Giora (z"l)[1]

Chayim was born in Tel Aviv on August 4, 1944. He enlisted in the Israel Defense Forces, joining their armored division. By the time he was through with his service, he had reached the rank of lieutenant.

Upon discharge from the army, Chayim joined the merchant navy. After finishing all his studies in the naval school and passing the examinations, he received the rank of officer third rank.

After receiving his appointment, he served in the merchant navy for three and a half years, spending his leisure time in the pursuit of two favorite hobbies—photography and music. The Six-Day War found Chayim in the middle of the Pacific Ocean, on his way to Hong Kong. Chayim expended much effort to reach his unit in the Israel Defense Forces, and arrived at the end of the war.

After his discharge from the merchant navy, Chayim continued to study electronics in the school of engineering, of the Tel Aviv University. There he met his future mate, Soreh Goldfried. They were married, and after a year and a half, their daughter, Yael, was born. Chayim was a devoted husband and father, and both of them built their warm nest. It was a home filled with happiness and hope for the future. But the Yom Kippur War broke the thread of his life, when he was only 29! On the 4th day of Tishri, 1974, while on a dangerous patrol duty at the northern bank of the Suez canal, he was mortally wounded by a direct missile hit that penetrated his armored vehicle. He was killed, leaving a wife and a one-and-a-half-year-old daughter, his grieving parents, and a sister.

Chayim fell on the field of battle in enemy territory, and his place of burial is unknown to this day.

His memory shall not depart from our hearts for all eternity. May his memory be blessed!

[1]From the eulogy in his memory.

Regimental Sergeant Yoav Blumen (z"l)[2]

I met Yoav on the fourth day of the war at Camp Yarden in the Golan Heights. I came there to repair my tank, which had been hit earlier. Yoav had come there with the remnants of his division, in order to equip tanks that were now being taken out of emergency supplies. The camp was a station repairing tanks that had been damaged in battle or which were confiscated from enemy storehouses.

Our meeting was filled with emotion! In the midst of the battles during which many of our comrades had already fallen, in which our divisions alternately advanced or were repelled, in which everything was hazy and unclear. Imagine meeting under such conditions an old friend from home. Indeed, it was a great moment!

Yoav was smiling at me, his old happy self. He was telling jokes or pulling someone's leg, to the entertainment of the others. He soon told me that the tank in which he was riding had been hit twice and that the second time he was forced

should know that for no one would I have been ready to be a gunner, but for Yoav. I trusted him absolutely. I must say of him that Yoav was a real professional, an expert in everything that had to do with tanks!"

[2]From the eulogy in his memory at Kibbutz Reshafim.

Son of Moyshe and Hadasa, grandson of the Hebrew teacher Yakov Blumen.

Son of Chane (Tanchum Veynshteyn's daughter) and Yehoshua Zoar.

to repair the tread of the tank while under heavy artillery fire and air attacks:

"Twice fortune smiled on me," he said, as he paused for a moment. "Who knows whether the third time my luck will hold too . . . I have a foreboding, which is not a good one, about what is awaiting me."

After it became clear to me that it was impossible to repair my tank, I offered to change places with him.

"Forget it," he said to me with a smile. "These are the men of my company, and I cannot abandon them this way, without any supervision. Besides, I have two officers now in command of the men and someone has to look after them, too.

At the end of the day, Yoav left with a column of tanks from the base. I waved goodbye to him and he returned my wave.

I did not know then that it was the last time that he waved goodbye.

Later, after the battles, when I asked one of the officers about Yoav, he answered me, "You

Azriel (Uzi) Zohar (z"l)

Azriel was born on May 27, 1943 (Iyar 23). He attended the officer's school of the navy, studying marine mechanics and later served in the Israel Defense Forces as a naval mechanic.

When he was released, he enrolled in the mechanical engineering school at the Technion. At his graduation in 1968, he earned great praise as a student of distinction. He received his M.Sc. degree in 1973 from the University of Tel Aviv, where he also won distinction.

Everybody predicted for him a brilliant future in the field of science. During his work in military industrial production, he made a most important contribution to the country's security. He also took part in fighting in the Yom Kippur War, serving on the southern front.

Azriel was taken from us before his time. On April 3, 1974, he died before he reached his 31st birthday! He left a wife and two daughters.

May his soul be bound in the bond of eternal life!

APPENDIXES

- Encyclopedia articles reproduced in the original
  Yizkor Book of Luboml

- Recent newspaper and magazine articles about Luboml
  which do not appear in the original.

לובאמל (ליבעוונע)

א שטעטל, וואָס לויט די סטאַטוטן פון די „ארבע־הארצות", האָט געהערט צו דער „מדינה" פון בעלז־כעלם. אזוי האָט גע־ וואָלט די אדמיניסטראַטיע פון די יידישע קהילות פון יענער עפאָ־ כע. ר' יואל סירקעס, דער ב"ח, וואָס איז געווען רב אין לובאמל (ווי אויך אין בריסק און קראָקע), האָט אין זיין בארימטן „בית־ חדש" זייער פיל באַשריבן (אין יאר 1600) די לאגע פון די יידן פון לובאמל (וואָס האָט זיך גערעכנט פאר איינע פון די עלטסטע יידישע קהילות אין פוילן). די שול אין לובאמל איז געווען בא־ קאַנט אין דער וועלט מיט איר פראכטפולן גלאַנץ. אין יאר 1729 איז געווען אין לובאמל א גרויסע שרפה און ס'איז פארבליבן גאַנץ די שוהל, דער קאשציאל און די פראַוואָסלאַוונע קירך. ס'איז פאראַן א רשימה פון די „נשרפים" (בן־ציון כ"ץ, אלעקסאנדער הַרקאַווי און מאיר באַלאַבאַן האָבן זייער פיל געשריבן וועגן די יידן אין לובאמל). לויט וועלכער מען קאן זיך באַקענען מיט די פראָפעסיעס פון די לובאמלער יידן מיט א 250 יאר צוריק: שניי־ דער, צירולניקער, יוועעלירן, גלעזער, א חוץ קרעמער. אין יאר 1765 זיינען אין לובאמל געווען 1200 יידן, וואָס פלעגן צאָלן פאָ־ דאטקעס, אין יאר 1947 — 2000, אין 1897, אויף 4.470, איינוואוי־ נער, אין לובאמל זיינען געווען פאַדאַטקעס־צאָלער 3.297 יידן. זייער צאָל פאר דער לעצטער מלחמה איז געווען דאָפּלט.

אין 1913 בין איך געווען אין לובאמל, אויף דער איינלאַדונג פון אונדזער כעלעמער פייוול פריד (וואָס איז דאָרט געווען א לערער). ס'איז געווען „כ' תמוז" און אין אן אנגעפילטער, אן אָנגעפאַקטער שוהל — אין דער אלטער היסטאָרישער שוהל — האָב איך גערעדט צו די יידן. למחרת, האָט מען מיך אויסגע־ וויילט אלס דעלעגאט פון לובאמל צום 11־טן ציוניסטישן קאָנ־ גרעס. אזוי אז ס'זיינען פאראן פעדעם, וואָס פארבינדן מיך צו דער אלטער קהילה פון דער „כעלעמער־מדינה" !...

אונדזער יידישע געשיכטע פארמעגט אויך אירע קאפריזן. א לובאמלער יד טאַרלאָ האָט זיך באזעצט, נאָך פאר דער ערש־ טער וועלט־מלחמה, אין פארטוגאַל. ער איז געוואָרן א וויכטיקער וויין־סוחר פון פאָרטאָ, פארקניפט גרויסע באַקאנטשאפטן מיט פאָרטוגעזער רעגירונג־קרייזן און ער האָט זיי געמאַכט א פאָר־ שלאָג: פאָרטוגאַל זאָל זיך רעהאביליטירן פאר דער אינקוויזיציע, נישט מער און נישט ווינציקער! און אזוי ווי פאַרטוגאַל פארמאָגט אין אפריקע א קאָלאָניע, אנגאָלא, זאָל מען עפענען אירע טויערן און אריינלאָזן דאָרט יידן. אבער ניט סתם עמיגרירן, נאָר דאָרט זאָל ווערן געשאפן א יידישע טעריטאָריע. אין אנגאָלא, האָט ער געשריבן איז דער יידישער פרעסע, זיינען פאראן דיאַמאַנטן און קאָפּע, און אנדערע פראָדוקטן, בקיצור — דאָס איז אן „ארץ זבת חלב ודבש". די גאנצע יידישע פרעסע, אין אלע לענדער און אין אלע שפראכן, האָבן וועגן דעם געשריבן און דער נאמען פון דעם לובאמלער יידן טאַרלאָ איז געוואָרן באַוואוסט אין אלע תפו־ צות.

Y. Milner, *Notitzen un Zichroynos. Yizkorbukh Khelm.* Johannesburg, 1954, pp. 416-417.

לובומל (Люболь), עיר נפתית במחוז וולין (ע"ע)

שבבריה"מ, 15 ק"מ מהנהר בוג. עד 1939 בתחום פולניה. — הישוב היהודי בל', תחילתו עם יסוד העיר במאה ה־14, ויהודים נזכרים שם לראשונה בשנים 1372— 1380. במאה ה־16 שיגשגה הקהילה; ב־1557 העניק לה המלך זיגמונט־אוגוסט (ע"ע) את הזכות להישפט אצל הווייווה, עם זכות־עירעור בפני המלך, בלא להיזקק למוסדות השי־ פוט העירוני. ביהכ"נ בל' הוא מן המאה ה־16 או ה־17, והוא מסוג בתהכ"נ הבצורים (ע"ע בית־כנסת, עמ' 649—650). מרבני ל' החשובים באותה תקופה: ר' שמעון וולף אורבך, ר' אברהם ב"ר יעקב פולק (ע"ע), ר' משה מת (ע"ע) ור' גדליה ב"ר מאיר (מהר"ם) מלובלין. בגזירות ת"ח נהרגו בל' יהודים רבים. בתחילת המאה ה־18 היתה ל' הקהילה המבוססת ביותר בגליל חלם־בלז.

ב־1847 היו בל' 2,130 יהודים, ב־1897 — 3,297 (כ־75% מכלל התוש'), וב־1931 — 3,807 (כ־93%). אחרי הכיבוש הגרמני (יוני 1941) התרכזו בל' פליטים יהודים רבים, ובספ־ טמבר 1942 הגיע מספרם ל־10,000. מהטבח, שהתחיל ב־2 באוקטובר 1942 ונמשך שבעה ימים, נמלטו רק כ־150 איש.

א. פעלדמאן, די עלטסטע ידיעות וועגן יידן אין פוילישע שטעט אין xvi–xvii יארה' (בלעטער פאר געשיכטע, i): 1934 ; י. הילפרין, פנקס ועד ארבע ארצות, מפתח, בערכו, תש"ה ; ב. איינהשטיין־קשב, די יידן אין וואלין, 1939–1944 (פון נאָענטן עבר, v), 1959.

א. ל. ק.

→

לרשימה זו מעיר מר ישראל גרמי את הדברים הבאים. מר טערלא לא היה יליד לובומל, מוצאו לפי ידיעתי מאודיסה. ידוע כי למד חקלאות בארץ־ישראל בבית הספר החקלאי „מקוה ישראל" במחזור אחד עם מאיר דיזנגוף וא. קראוזה (לאחר מכן מנהל בית הספר במשך שנים רבות). מר טערלא נשא לאשה את ג'ניה אפעלדמאן, בתו היחידה של מר משה אפעלדמאן (משה לייזרס) מנכבדי העיר שלנו. לזוג טערלא נולדה בת ושמה היה לוסיה, שהתגוררה עם אמה וסבתה בעיירה. לאחר שמר שמר טערלא נפרד מאשתו יצא לפורטוגאל ושם התגורר עד יום מותו. הבת לוסיה למדה משפטים באוניברסיטת ויינה, ואח"כ חזרה לעיירה, והיתה פעילה מאד בתנועה הציונית ומוסדותיה. נספתה עם בעלה בעיר לוצק.

LUBOML : Town in the government of Volhynia, Russia. Jews lived there as early as the sixteenth century, though the attitude of the Christian inhabitants toward them was distinctly hostile. In 1557 the Jewish community resolved that none of its members should buy property within the city, for there was danger of its being attacked or set on fire by the Christian inhabitants. In 1576 this decision was reaffirmed by the leaders of the community with the indorsement of R. Abraham Polyak. Those who had violated this rule were warned to sell their property to Christians, under penalty of a fine or of some other punishment. Outside the town the Jews owned eight parcels of land; some of them leased grist-mills, and others leased three lakes, paying for their leases in money, pepper, saffron, and salt fish to the total value of about 400 gold ducats. The population of Luboml in 1897 was 4,600, of whom 3,300 were Jews. It has 349 Jewish artisans and 52 Jewish day-laborers. The seventeen ḥadarim give instruction to 370 pupils, and 60 are instructed in the Talmud Torah (1898).

BIBLIOGRAPHY: Katz, *Le-Ḳorot ha-Yehudim*, p. 7, Berlin, 1899; *Regesty i Nadpisi*, i. 241, St. Petersburg, 1899.
H. R.   S. J.

The Jewish Encyclopedia, vol. VII p. 203, New-York and London, Funk and Wagnalls Company, 1904.

Encyclopedia Judaica, Berlin: Eshkol, vol. X, cols. 1171-1173.

LUBOML, Bezirksstadt in der Woiwodschaft Wolhynien in Polen. Juden lebten hier schon im J. 1516. Unter König Sigismund August erlangten sie im J. 1557 ein Privileg, das sie von jeder anderen Gerichtsbarkeit außer der woiwodischen befreite und ihnen zugleich das Appellationsrecht beim König sicherte. Im J. 1564 entrichteten die Juden 40 Gulden an Abgaben. König Michael Wiśniowiecki bestätigte im J. 1671 alle Privilegien der L.er Judenschaft. Anfang des 18. Jhts. betrugen die Schulden des Kahals an den Chelmer Pijarenorden 11 000 Gulden. Die Kopfsteuer machte im Jahre 1721 833 Gulden aus. Infolge der Feuersbrunst im J. 1729 wurde die Kopfsteuer auf 544 Gulden herabgesetzt. Während des Stempelns jüd. Bücher im J. 1776 legten 105 Personen in der Stadt 1200 Bücher vor. In den 80-er Jahren des 19. Jhts. zählte L. 2064 Einwohner, darunter 66 % Juden. 1921 lebten hier 3141 Juden (3328 Einwohner); im Bezirk waren 5604 Juden (Gesamtbevölkerung: 56 264). Die gemauerte, noch heute (1933) bestehende Synagoge aus dem 16. Jht. gehört zum Typus der Festungssynagogen, die in den östlichen Gebieten Polens zu Verteidigungszwecken dienten (Abb., Bd. III, Sp. 231/32).

Akty Wilenskoj komisji XXVI; *Bersohn*, Dyplomatarjusz, Nr. 291, 93, 67; *Wierzbowski*, Matricularum etc. V, Nr. 2313, 3223; *Lustrationen*, Abt. 46, Nr. 114, 127; *Memoriale an die Finanzkommission* (Warsch. Finanzarch.); *Statystyka Polski* XXIII; *Dispartimenten d jüd. Kopfsteuer* (Warsch. Hauptarch.); *Skorowidz*, s. v. W.   E. R.

Rabbiner. Der erste bekannte Rabbiner in L. war R. Zebi Hirsch, der um 1575 dort wirkte. Seine Nachfolger waren: R. Abraham b. Jakob Pollak (um 1587), Schwiegersohn des R. Isaak b. Bezalel aus Wladimir; R. Mose b. Abraham Mat (seit 1597), später in Przemyśl und Opatow; R. Simeon Wolf b. David Tewel Auerbach (später in Lublin, Przemyśl, Posen, Wien und Prag); R. Joel Serkes (s. d.); R. Mose (gest. 1617); R. Gedalja b. Meir, Lublin (1618 bis 1647); R. Mose b. Isaak, Schwiegersohn des R. Samuel Edels (bis 1653; später in Lublin); R. Elieser b. Menachem Margulies (um 1667); R. Jakob b. Mordechai (1674—1680); R. Jona b. Hillel ha-Levi; R. Elieser Leser (um 1710), angeführt in „Mezudat Dawid" von seinem Enkel R. David b. Mose (Altona 1736); R. Issachar Bär b. Meir aus Lublin (seit 1722); R. Josef b. Israel (ca. 1741-1757); R. Israel Jona Landau (um 1800); R. Mose Chajim (gest. 1868); R. Jehuda Arje Finkelstein (Ende des 19. und Anfang des 20. Jhts.).

Gans, Zemach David (J. 5333); *Fünn*, Kirja Neemana 171; *Friedberg*, Luchot Sikkaron 9; *idem*, Bene Landau le-Mischpechotam; *J. Kohen*

Luboml, *Lubomla*, mko rząd., pow. włodzimierski, okr. polic. i gm. L., odl. od Warszawy 268 wiorst. R. 1870 miał 425 dm., 2064 mk., w tem 66 proc. izr., 2 cerkwie, kościół, kaplicę, browar, młyn, 4 garbarnie, 62 sklepy, 25 rzemieślników, 6 jarmarków. R. 1881 nawiedzone silnym pożarem. Paraf. kościół katol. ś. Trójcy, z muru wzniesiony 1412 r. Parafia katol. dek. kowelskiego: dusz 3562. Filia: Bendiuha, kaplice w Ziemlicy i w Horodnie. Stacya L. drogi żel. nadwiśl. leży o 2 w. od stacyi poczt. L., o 20 w. od Maciejowa. Jerzy Narymuntowicz ks. belski otrzymał to mko na dzierżawę lenną skutkiem traktatu między Olgierdem a Kazimierzem W. w 1366 r.; w roku jednak 1377, za panowania króla Ludwika węgierskiego, stracił je razem z całą ziemią chełmską, losy której zawsze L. dzielił, a która też wówczas do korony została przyłączoną. W r. 1392 przebywał w L. Władysław Jagiełło czas pewien i tak sobie go upodobał, że na pamiątkę tego wystawił tu kościół, istniejący dotychczas, chociaż kilkakrotnie w ciągu tylu wieków się palił. Jest cerkiew w L. pod wez. ś. Jerzego, fundacya której sięga ogromnej starożytności, a podanie ludu glosi, że wyszła tuż z pod zamkowej góry, gdyż podle niej stoi. Za czasów rzeczypospolitej było to miasto starościńskie i miało zamek na górze. Lustracya ststwa lubomlskiego z 1569 r. przytacza dość ciekawych szczegółów, z których jawnie się pokazuje, że owczesny L. świetniejszym był od dzisiejszego. Dość wspomnieć, że podówczas samych piekarzy było 27; mko dawało dochodu zamkowi 109 złp. 3 gr. Konstytucyą za Zygmunta III zaliczono L. do dóbr królewskich, na których suma posagowa królewny oparta była. Gdy królewna wyszła za mąż, L. w 1659 r., wraz z całem ststwem darowano dożywociem, przez stany rzpltej, Wychowskiemu wojewodzie kijowskiemu i hetmanowi kozaków, za zasługi okazane państwu. Świetne czasy nastają dla L. z przejściem takowego w końcu XVIII w. na dziedzictwo Branickich. Wówczas przynosiło miasto dochodu, mianowicie w 1782 r., tylko 26470 złp. Braniccy założyli tu swoją rezydencyą, ogromny pałac z ogrodem. Miasto się zabudowało po większej części i do połowy XIX w. było niezmiernie ożywione, skutkiem rezydowania w pałacu Branickich, którzy starali się wszelkiemi sposobami je podnieść i zaprowadzać dla mieszkańców udogodnienia — ponieważ zaś były to niezmier-

кн. Могилевской губ.

Любомль — м. Волынской губ., Владимірскаго у. Жит. 4030, двор. 57. 2 православныхъ церкви, католическій костелъ. Костеобжигательный заводъ (на 4800 р.) и дегтярносмолевой (на 2230 р.). Пять ярмарокъ, еженедѣльные базары. Въ 1289 г. Л. упоминается въ числѣ городовъ, принадлежавшихъ кн. владимірскому Іоанну Васильковичу. 17-го сентября 1812 г. близъ него происходило дѣло между русскими войсками Чичагова и Тормасова и австро-саксонскими корпусами, предводимыми Шварценбергомъ и Реньe и занявшими выгодную позицію за широкимъ каналомъ, на болотистой мѣстности. Когда попытка фронтальной атаки на эту позицію не удалась, Чичаговъ рѣшился обойти противника съ обоихъ фланговъ, но въ ночь на 18-ое австросаксонцы снялись съ позиціи и отступили къ Влодавѣ.

Любопытный (Павелъ Онуфріевичъ,

Encyclopedia Slovar (Russian). Petersburg: Brockhaus-Efron, 1896, vol. XVIII, col. 218.

nie rozległe dobra, obejmujące masę okolicznych wsi, więc ruch i ożywienie od głównego punktu rozchodziły się po okolicy. W połowie obecnego wieku dobra lubomlskie przechodzą do rąk rządu. Około 1870 r. wszystkie dobra lubomelskie jako „fermy" rząd rozdał na własność rozmaitym urzędnikom, którzy położyli zasługi na polu administracyi. Mko, tak dawniej ruchliwe, zagłuchło zupełnie i letargicznym snem spało, dopóki w tym kierunku biegnąca kolej nadwiślańska nie urządziła tu swojej stacyi. Od tego czasu ruch się znowu obudził, jakkolwiek nigdy taki, jak dawniej. Wiele też na zubożenie miasta wpłynął cały szereg pożarów. Wedle taryfy pogłównego, do ststwa lubomelskiego zaliczały się następujące wsie i dobra: Lubomla, Lawale, Skiby, Zapole, Rymacze, Jahodyn, Hołowno, Bereźce, Lubochinie, Nudysz, Wiśniów, Kośniszcze, Krymno, Rejowiszcze, Mostór, Olesko, Komorów, Szacko, Szczodrohost, Zabrodzie, Powiecie, Tur, Kortylesy, Samorowiec i Radosław. W r. 1771 posiadała je Antonina Rzewuska, wojewodzina wołyńska; spłacając zeń kwarty złp. 26,470 gr. 27, a hyberny zł. 6808 gr. 16. Okr. polic. L. obejmuje gminy: L., Olesko, Rymacze, Huszcza, Zahorany, Hołowno, Krymno, Szack, Pulma. W mieście L. urodził się słynny kaznodzieja dominikański z czasów Zygmunta III, Seweryn Lubomlczyk.   *F. S.*

מתוך *Słownik Geograficzny Królewstwa Polskiego*, tom V p. 444—445. nakładem Władysława Walewskiego, Warszawa 1884, druk „Wieku".

Любомль (Luboml) — въ эпоху Рѣчи Посполитой городъ Холмской земли, въ евр. административномъ отношеніи центръ бѣласко-холмской области (בלז). Еврейская община въ Л. одна изъ старѣйшихъ въ Польшѣ. Въ 1557 г. мѣстный кагалъ принялъ важное рѣшеніе, приведенное въ «בית יוסף» Іоеля Сиркеса, гласящее: никто не долженъ пріобрѣтать домъ или землю не-еврея въ предѣлахъ городской стѣны, потому что, если христіане не будутъ жить среди евреевъ, то грозитъ опасность, что они положутъ евр. дома или будутъ настаивать на изгнаніи евреевъ. 19 лѣтъ спустя это постановленіе было повторено. Повидимому, постановленіе сохранило силу до 1600 г., когда Іоель Сиркесъ записалъ его. Объ исторіи общины сохранилось мало данныхъ. Школьникъ Моисей б. Самуилъ погибъ въ Тульчинѣ во время нападенія казаковъ (1648). Неизвѣстно, когда была построена старая синагога, грандіозное зданіе; отъ пожара, истребившаго въ 1729 году весь городъ, остались въ цѣлости синагога, костелъ и церковь. Списокъ пострадавшихъ домохозяевъ даетъ понятіе о занятіяхъ мѣстныхъ евреевъ Л.; кромѣ лавочниковъ, встрѣчаются ремесленники (портные, ювелиры, стекольщики и цирульники). Въ 1765 г. числилось въ кагальномъ округѣ Л. 1226 плательщиковъ подушной подати. — Ср.: Каz, Lе-Korot ha-Jehudim be-Russia, s. v.; Регесты, II; Liczba, 1765; Балабанъ, Правовой строй евреевъ въ Польшѣ, Евр. Стар., 1910, 189; Гаркави въ Chadaschim gam-Jeschanim, дополн. къ VII т. Грена въ евр. перев.; J. E. VIII, 203.   *Г. 5.*

— Нынѣ мѣст. Волынск. губ., Влад.-Вол. у. По ревизіи 1847 г. «Любомльск. евр. общество» состояло изъ 2.130 душъ. По переписи 1897 г. въ Л. жит. 4.470, среди коихъ 3.297 евр.—Въ 1910 г. въ Л.—одна талмудъ-тора.   *8.*

Любоничи—мѣст. Минск., Бобр. у. По переписи

Yevreskie Encyclopedia (Russian). Petersburg: Brockhaus-Efron, 1896, vol. X, col. 440.

1556. XCIX, 281

Tenże król, na wstawienie się swej rady, a z uwagi na biegłość w prawie mojżeszowem mieszkańca miasta Lubomli, żyda Hirsz, zwanego Jeleń, wynosi go na stopień doktora prawa i pozwala mu sprawować ten urząd, według przywiązanych doń atrybucyj w gminie Lubomlskiej.

Jeleń Judaei Lubomliensis in Doctoratum erectio.

Sigismundus Augustus etc., significamus etc. Quia nos intercessioni certorum consiliariorum nostrorum pro Hirsz dicto Jeleń iudaeo Lubomliensi: Nobis benigne factis annuentes, simulque commendatam habentes honestam conversationem illius in lege mosaica peritiam, quo nomine superioribus annis iudaei Lubomlienses cum officio doctoratus legis mosaicae in civitate illa praefecerant, eandem authoritate nostra Regia officio doctoratus totius communitatis iudaeorum Lubomliensium: administrando, designandum et praeficiedum duximus designamus et praeficimus hisce literis nostris, idque ut ad extrema vitae iusdem tempora. Dantes et concedentes ei plenam et omnimodam potestatem officium doctoratus communitatis iudaeorum Lubomliensium, gerendi, poenas excommunicationis contra inobedientes more iudaico promulgandi atque ad debitum effectum deducendi, officio doctoratus de more et antiqua consuetudine proventus debitos exigendi, et officium doctoratus pertinentia exercendi et peragendi. Ita quod vivente Hirsz iudaeo neque conventus iudaeorum Lubomliensium; neque privatae ex communitate personae eum ab administratione doctoratus alienare aut privare poterint. Idque sub poena sexagentorum aureorum ungaricalium, quatenus communitas eum a functionibus alienare doctoratus contenderit. Privatae vero ex communitate personae mulctam ducentorum aureorum hungaricalium incurrent. Cuius medietas fisco nostro, altera vero medietas capitaneo nostro Lubomliensi, irremissibiliter luenda et persolvenda erit, et nihilominus poena et mulcta per eos luita eum in officio doctoratus reservare debuerit. Quam concessionem nostram administrandi doctoratus iudaerum Lubomliensium Hirz iudaeo a nobis factam, generoso Joanni Dembinski, capitaneo nostro Lubomliensi ad noticiam deducentes mandamus, ut iudaeum Hirz in hac concessione nostra et praerogativa doctoratus conventus iudaeorum Lubomliensium conservet, idque communitati iudaeorum Lubomliensium serio iniungant, ut iudaeum Hirz pro vero et legitimo doctore suo legis mosaicae agnosceant, eique de proventibus ad officium illud pertinentibus respondeant, non obstantibus quibuscumque literis nostris, si quas in contrariam emanare contigerit pro debito suo et gratia nostra facturi tua factura: In cuius rei fidem sigillum nostrum est appensum. Datum Lublini in conventu regni generali, sabbato ante festum ascensionis domini proximo. Anno domini millesimo quingentesimo sexagesimo sexto, regni vero nostri anno trigesimo septimo.

Velentinus Dembinski, regni Poloniae cancellarius subscripserat.	Relatio magnifici domini Valentini Dembinski de Piotrowicze regni Poloniae cancellarii Lubomliensisque capitanei.

Document for 1556 in the name of King Zygmunt August on the appointment of "the Jew Hersh, known as Yellin" as head of the town of Luboml.

Warm, Vibrant Shtetl Life on the Brink of Doom
By Aaron Ziegelman

When I think of my town in Poland, Libivne, I think of my childhood dream—to return there as a rich American. That was our dream in those days of emigration—to come back rich, powerful, and bearing gifts that we would apportion in royal fashion to all the friends we left behind.

When I think of Libivne, I see the streets, the market, my mother working in her restaurant—a place that drew me like a magnet as only the place that holds your mother can draw you, when you are a child growing up without a father.

I remember the little grocery store next door, run by my aunt. The school, the cheder. I remember the food we ate. It was meager, but I didn't know it then—a fact that has always amazed me since. For dinner, noodles and milk; for lunch, a roll with tomato. Yet, I never felt poor. Perhaps, as long as you have enough to eat, you really have to be told you are poor to feel poor.

I suppose I began to suspect how poor we had been only when we got on the ship, the S.S. *Pilsudski*, which took us to America.

The ship took us through a roaring storm that had every passenger green in the face, retired to his bed, with barely the strength to keep his heaving stomach in place. As a consequence, the ship's dining room was empty all but for one passenger—me. Having had a taste of the food, whose variety and splendor I had never dreamed existed until I set foot in that ship's dining room, I was going to allow nothing, not storms, not heaving stomachs, nor any other force of nature, to keep me from missing even one of those meals.

But of Libivne, I remember more. I remember loving faces, among them the face of Srulik, our roving photographer, who would walk the streets taking pictures of people as they strolled on the Sabbath. I remember the market days when the peasants would go to Srulik's studio, in the building where my mother had her restaurant, to have their pictures taken. I can still see the curling irons that the women used to fix their hair before the photographs were taken, still see the explosion of powder from Srulik's photography equipment that lit up the room.

I remember the soccer games and the young men of the town. Especially, I remember their heroic efforts to avoid being conscripted into the army—the 72-hour marches they took to exhaust themselves before taking a physical, the thousands of eggs they consumed to raise the level of albumen in their blood.

I can still taste the ice cream made by hand, superior to any ice cream I have tasted since. And I can see the local ice house itself, a place of endless mystery to me, with its sawdust covered floors. I remember the adventure of taking chickens for slaughter, the grisly fascination with which I watched this process.

I remember the scenes in my mother's restaurant, especially at mealtimes. It was an impressive sight to me to see the peasants who were her customers consume an entire quart of vodka at one meal. And I see before me a more delicate image: the memory of the small blond girl, Meinke, who stirred my earliest tender feelings, and my two girl cousins, whom I loved.

I do not find it easy to think of what became them.

I remember the long trips, by horse and buggy, to Holevne, excursions where, entranced, I watched the workings of our relatives' windmill. I recall the special sense of occasion that would come over me when the local matchmaker would bring prospective bridegrooms to our neighbors—to single women of marriageable age.

I always managed to be there to observe this drama, which allowed me to test my youthful analytic skills as to whether a particular meeting would be successful. At some point during these meetings, I would always say to myself— since no one else was interested in soliciting my opinion in these matters, "This is going to click," or "This one won't work."

The serving of the tea was my infallible clue to the success or failure of the match. I was informed early on by an uncle of mine that if the prospective groom's parents said, "That's very good tea," or "The cookies are delicious," then things were going well. The absence of any flattering comments about the refreshments was a sure sign, on the other hand,that things were not going to work out.

Above all these thoughts, the image that stays in my mind's eye is the scene at the station, the day of our departure for America, with the whole town turned out to wish us farewell. My friends, with whom I had played soccer, who gave me gifts as I gave gifts in return, along with all the rest of the Jews in our town, young and old, walked the several miles to the station with us. I remember my uncle's last admonition to me, to recite the Kaddish for my father.

They left us with cries of goodbye and good wishes—the last image I have of the Jews of Libivne. And it is in that moment of life that they are held fast for me, in my mind's eye, frozen in memory from which no evil can take them.

Aaron Ziegelman, a New York businessman, is vice-chairman of the Reconstructionist Rabbinical College's board of governors. He, his mother and sister immigrated to America in 1938 from Libivne, most of whose 8,000 Jews were shot by the Germans Oct. 1, 1942. This article was first published in 1985 in the Reconstructionist *magazine, and was subsequently reprinted in the* Hartford Courant *and New York's* Jewish Week.

Farewell portrait of friends and family at the Luboml railroad station, taken on the occasion of the Zygielman family's departure for America, 1938.

A Return to Luboml—And Dark, Distant Memories
By Jane Ziegelman

November 22, 1991

It seems an impossible travel destination—you can't visit an abstraction. I have trouble believing that Poland is a concrete place, a geographical location. To me it is a mental attitude, a condition. When a Jewish person gets depressed, that's Poland.

But, after several months of planning, Poland is to become real for our family. Arrangements have been made so we can spend a few days in Luboml—Libivne in Yiddish—the town where my father was born.

This area is in the Ukraine and only recently has been opened to foreigners. The region is sensitive because it is so close to the Soviet-Polish border, where there are supposedly military installations. Luboml is also fairly close to Chernobyl—about 200 miles.

My father, Aaron Ziegelman, left Luboml in November 1938 with his mother and sister. Most of the family had stayed behind and was caught in the ghetto—his two grandmothers, his cousins. His father had died some six years earlier, from an infection the local doctor didn't know how to treat. In June 1941 the area fell under Nazi occupation, and in October 1942 the Jewish population was wiped out.

Now, 49 years later, eight people are making this trip, all connected to Luboml. Bernie Meller runs a sporting goods company with his wife, Dolores, and their two sons. He escaped from Luboml the morning after the German army took the town from the Soviets.

Bernie survived the war fighting in the Polish army. Later, as we drive through towns around Luboml, he asks the driver to pull over so he can take pictures of a landmark—the sign at a crossroads, a train platform. His memories are sharp-edged. Victor Gershengorn, now 82, is more reticent about his past and more sentimental. His family in Luboml was large and well-off. They were grain merchants. Victor lost three sisters, a brother and their children to the war. Victor himself left Poland as a young man in 1930. His wife, Anne, also was born in Luboml. They married in New York in 1935.

Goldie Samet, who married a Lubomler, had come from Europe to America as a baby. Her husband died two years ago, and she's making the trip on his behalf.

For this group, the return to Luboml is a confusing trip—like going home when you thought it would never be possible, and like spending time in a cemetery—a living, working cemetery.

We arrive in the Warsaw airport. My father says he remembers Warsaw as the place where he first ate a hot dog. It's also where he first "experienced" a telephone.

My family's driver, Zbignew, is 33 years old but looks like 43. The others are traveling by van. Their driver's name is Tom, "Like Tom Jones," he says, "the singer-player."

We drive for several hours before reaching the Soviet border. At first we think there's been an accident, because cars are stopped and people are milling around on the shoulder. This is the beginning—or end—of a 4-mile line of cars, most with Soviet license plates, all waiting to cross.

Zbignew says they've been waiting for a minimum of three days, and that most were in Poland to get hard currency for Soviet goods—

soccer balls, transistor batteries, caviar, kitchen utensils. It's hard to imagine how the money from these odds and ends justifies the wait.

Flashing our U.S. passports, we skirt the line, driving on the wrong side of the road. Finally, we come to the main checkpoint. One final question-and-answer session on the Soviet side of the border, and we're ushered through.

Here, the line of cars waiting to cross into Poland is twice as long.

A few miles out of Brisk, the border city, the landscape quickly turns rural. It's flat like the Midwest, but it doesn't look like the Midwest. The light is different for one thing, more diffuse, and the shadows are softer.

Even the air is different. The road is lined on both sides by an arcade of trees. We pass fields of mown hay and corn, and fields where cows are grazing.

There is an occasional cluster of small wooden houses painted ocher on top and red on the bottom, with bright blue window trim. The picket fences along the road are also painted blue and white, which I think are the colors of the Ukrainian flag. We drive past a man in a motorcycle helmet collecting flowers on a slope, a woman lying on her side next to a couple of grazing cows, some men fishing in an irrigation ditch.

We arrive in Lutsk around sunset and pull up to the Hotel Ukraine, just off the main square. The decor inside is grand—in a desolate way. The ceiling in the lobby is encrusted with sugary pink-and-white plaster molding, but otherwise the lobby is bare—no furniture except for a wood-paneled filing cabinet with locked drawers.

Joining us for dinner in the hotel restaurant is an 80-year-old Ukrainian Jewish man and his son, who traveled a day and half to get here. The father is a heavy-set man with white hair and a vaguely wedge-shaped head. His handkerchief is out all through the meal as he mops the sweat from his face.

We learn he had three sisters and three brothers, all killed during the war. He tried to convince them to run when the Germans came, but they refused, chiding him for being a panic-monger. People at nearby tables are looking at us. Our conversation is in Yiddish, so everyone must know we're Jewish.

The next day, after a couple of hours on the road, Zbignew turns off onto a dirt driveway. Galena, our official Intourist guide, rides with us in the front seat. My father asks where we are now. "This is Luboml," she says in a casual way.

"This is it? This is it?" He sits up straighter. We drive along a cobblestoned street that turns to dirt. The houses give way to a hilly field sparsely dotted with low, spindly trees. We turn off the dirt road and start driving slowly across the grass, the minivan leading the way.

There's a mysterious car behind us now, a beat-up old Lada with a few people inside. We can't figure out who these people could be. The van ahead of us stops in the middle of nowhere. Three small Ukrainian kids are sitting in the grass a few yards away watching us.

Over a small rise in the field is the site of a mass grave where Luboml's Jewish population was massacred and buried in October 1942. A rusting fence marks off an area about the size of a large living room. There's a monument inside the fence made of black stone with an inscription in Ukrainian.

Bernie Meller reads it aloud but doesn't translate. I know it says something like "Here lie 5,000 Ukrainian citizens murdered by the fascists."

The people in that car behind us are the town's three remaining Jews. Hannah, her grown daughter, and an old man, neatly dressed, with patent leather shoes on his feet.

Bernie has taken memorial candles out of his travel bag. He and Victor try to light them, but the wind is too strong. Another man from Luboml who lives in New York, Nat Sobel, has nightmares about the ground here, that it starts heaving. That's why he couldn't come with us. Dolores Meller says a lot of people have that same dream.

Standing over the grave, one feels sure that terrible things have happened here. The ground still looks freshly tamped, it looks uncomfortable. I am standing on the very spot where the war happened, where history exploded, and it's my history. To dream that the ground was heaving doesn't seem far-fetched.

We drive to the center of town, where the market square used to be and where my grandmother used to have her restaurant. The streets along the way are dirt or cobblestone, the houses made of timber that juts out at the corners to form a crisscross pattern. They're painted white with brown shutters.

They have TV antennas but no indoor plumbing. Geese walk in the streets, single file. Men and women ride their bicycles through mud and puddles.

The streets in the center of town are paved. Most of the old shops are gone, replaced by dour Soviet buildings. The market also is gone, but while a shady green park has taken its place the basic outline is the same.

More people have joined the group. When we sit down for lunch the table has 18 place settings. The check comes to $2.

After lunch, Bernie leaves the table abruptly, toting his video camera, heading for the square. My father follows with Victor.

The men identify familiar buildings—the Catholic church just beyond the park and a barn-like structure made of narrow wooden slats that used to be a drugstore and still is, it turns out.

An elaborate war memorial with a grand staircase crowned by an obelisk stretches along one edge of the square.

Victor Gershengorn finds his old home, a boxy cement structure once considered luxurious by Luboml standards. Now it's been divided into four apartments, and a couple who lives in one of them comes out to meet us. The woman's front teeth are a solid row of gold.

My father's house is gone. The street names have been changed along with the house numbers, so it's hard to know for certain. We take a picture of the spot where he thinks it stood.

The old Jewish cemetery is now completely overgrown with trees and brambles. There must be thousands of graves here, but only three or four headstones are standing. The rest were stolen by Ukrainians, says our guide, rubbed clean and reused.

The men tramp further into the woods, past a garbage dump, to the spot where the first batch of Jews was shot by the Germans. It was a group of men who were told they were needed for work duty. After the men were shot, the Ukrainians went to their wives and told them not to worry, everything was all right, but their husbands needed a fresh change of clothes. Then they sold the clothes for pocket money.

Nothing is the same, not a thing, not one percent, people keep saying. Anne Gershengorn can barely stand to lay eyes on the place. It's like someone took a map, she says, and then they took a crayon, and went like this! She makes a wild gesture with her fist. Then they took the map and ripped it to shreds!

She continues with her eyes fixed straight ahead. You know what they say—any city without Jews is a dead city.

Only my father seems to feel just the opposite is true. The way he sees it, nothing has changed. Even the horsedrawn carts are the same, the same bow-shaped wooden carts.

It is business as usual in the streets of Luboml. Women sell tomatoes off the back of a truck, kids walk on the main street eating sweet rolls from the bakery. The place seems light-years away from Moscow.

The Jews in Luboml felt roughly the same way in the 1930s. Their lack of concern seems mindboggling today. Anti-Semitism was nothing new to them. People had time to get out before war was declared, but it's still a mystery to my father why his relatives never emigrated when they had the chance.

The next morning, my father decides we should pack up now, take our things to Luboml, and drive from there to Warsaw at the end of the day.

Day two in Luboml and Hannah has cooked a tremendous lunch. She's standing in the kitchen when we arrive, a pile of potatoes on the floor next to her feet, a pot of soup cooking on the stove, and a sponge cake baking in a sort of tin box near the door.

My father can't get over how similar her house is to the way his house used to be. "This is it! This is it exactly, how it was!"

We rush through lunch to keep an appointment with the mayor. Apparently Hannah is involved. To make herself presentable for the mayor she ties a babushka under her chin. As usual it's the men, accompanied by Hannah, who take part in this meeting, while the women sit in the car.

The men look excited when they come out of the government building an hour later. One objective behind the meeting is to arrange for the town to fix up the gravesite. My father Victor, and Bernie donate some money for repairing the fence, building some steps and adding an inscription in Yiddish to the monument already there.

The mayor has arranged for a police escort to take us to a nearby border crossing only 10 miles away where tourists aren't usually allowed to go. But hours later, after much trouble, we wind up at the regular crossing.

By nightfall we are on the Polish side of the crossing. Sitting in the car, we open a beer-sized bottle of Russian cognac from Hannah and take a few swigs with the sponge cake she gave us. Delicious.

Jane Ziegelman, a freelance writer living in New York, recently returned from a family trip to Luboml in the Ukraine, the birthplace of her father, Aaron. This is her account of the trip, reprinted with permission from the Jewish Week.

The Sheltering Sky
How One Sukkah Holds within It Many Memories
By Toby Axelrod

Oct. 1, 1993

All our huts are temporary, I guess. Right now the home of my grandfather, Jacob, my Zede, in Great Barrington, Mass., is unoccupied, slowly decaying, letting in almost as much starlight and rain as his sukkah was designed to do.

That sukkah is one-of-a-kind. Every year, after Yom Kippur, Zede—a rabbi who emigrated from Poland in 1925—would enlist the help of a neighbor to open his sukkah. Not a traditional, transient structure, Zede's sukkah was a shed separated from the house by a narrow alley crammed with a hoe, rakes and other garden tools.

The shed's peaked roof opened at the top, via ropes and rusty pulleys attached to high posts on either side of the structure. Zede, a little man, his head covered with a black yarmulke and pants held up with two belts, would stand at the foot of a post and pull hard on the rope. With a creak the pulley would start to turn. Slowly the roof would open, revealing the latticework ceiling, a Star of David at its center and last year's *s'chach*—corn husks—poking through.

Inside were a wooden table and several folding chairs, obscured in later years by a jumble of rags, boxes of old belongings, furniture and a mirror. These would be shoved aside so we could sit at the table and eat in the sukkah's moldy interior.

Though the building now is falling to ruin, damaged by vandals and New England winters, my memories are untouched. Like the temporary dwellings of our Jewish ancestors in the desert, my Zede's sukkah stands again through the telling.

I learned from him about telling. In his heavy accent, he would speak of life in Luboml, Poland (now Ukraine), at every opportunity. He didn't need to close his eyes to remember—he only pointed his finger and the shtetl streets would assemble, its inhabitants come to life.

"It was right in our town. I'll never forget it," began many stories, including my favorite one of Sukkot in Luboml.

"I remember his name: Kalman Farvele. He lived over here, and we lived over there," he would say, pointing his finger. Farvele and his wife, whose name never came up, lived near Luboml's train station and operated an inn where travelers "could get a bite to eat."

But the inn "was small, and he wanted to enlarge it," said Zede. "So every year Farvele would build a sukkah—with a foundation— maybe 15 feet closer to the road." After the holiday, the new sukkah would become part of the restaurant. Soon, on a road where "maybe two horses and wagons could pass, now there was room for only one to go."

The townspeople complained, but Zede guessed the police had been bribed to overlook the problem. The people persisted, declaring that "Farvele could keep the sukkah for one week, but when it came time for Simchat Torah it had to go."

And now my Zede would begin to chuckle.

"I'll never forget it," he would continue. "A man named Avrom Rachel Brandel—he was strong like an ox—he picked another fella, a strong guy, and they tied two ropes onto the sukkah and they took the ropes on their shoulders." The two pulled the whole sukkah into the middle of the road.

408

Now, Zede could not contain his laughter. "And Kalman Farvele was sitting inside with his wife, and they were hollerin' murder."

Finally the police noticed. The townspeople explained to the police, and the police chief said to Farvele: "Look at this map. Your house is there, not here. This road is for two horses and buggies, and now only one can go. What business do you have building your sukkah out like this? You deserve what you got."

The police told the Farveles to get out of the sukkah, "and they took the whole sukkah apart, and then after this they never did it again."

"So that's what happened," Zede would conclude. "They learned a lesson from that."

It took me a while, though, to learn my lessons. Vivid as the stories were, I struggled to believe the Farveles had existed, let alone that their sukkah was pulled into the street with them screaming bloody murder inside.

Only after Zede was gone—he died in January 1986—did I find another wall for my sukkah. It happened when I attended a meeting of the Luboml Society, a group of emigres and Holocaust survivors from my Zede's hometown.

For the first time since his death, I heard the Luboml accent again. I heard Lubomlers reminisce and plan to visit their birthplace, something impossible before glasnost.

I had one question on my mind, though. "Does anyone remember Kalman Farvele?"

Sure, said one man. "He had a little place where you can eat a meal. He had a business where he made seltzer water. He was a Kotsker Chasid, a very religious Jew and a nice yid . . . and his second wife was Machle.

"Kalman Farvele had a brother who was a cripple, blind and very poor, and he made a living by every night going around to look around the town to see that nobody is killed. He had a bed with a pillow in the Kotsker shtiebel."

No one remembered the sukkah story. But that they had known Farvele himself was enough for me. The sukkah stood again, and I could see Avrom Rachel Brandel again and hear my Zede's laughter again.

Later I volunteered as an editor for the Luboml Society's major project, the translation into English of their entire *Yizkor Buch*, the memorial book about Luboml to which emigres and survivors contributed after the Holocaust.

Not knowing Yiddish, I had my first chance to read about the world my Zede had inhabited and that had lived in him. And though the stories deal with all aspects of shtetl life, the theme of wandering emerges above all: the insecurity and transience of life and the courageous journeys of emigres.

Surrounding all is the sukkah, that mutable structure, barely protecting, barely connected to the ground but always open to the sky.

Reprinted with permission from the Jewish Week.

Finding Libivne
By Fred Wasserman

April 14, 1995

In 1938 Esther Ziegelman, a widow, and her two children Luba and Aaron, left Luboml, Poland for America. Recording the moment—in fact, fixing it for all time—is a photograph taken of the three just before their departure, surrounded by dozens of family and friends. The Ziegelmans were going to join Esther's brothers who had already settled in New York City. The family, the friends, the world they knew, were completely destroyed just four years later when the Jews of Luboml (Libivne in Yiddish) were massacred by the Germans.

Now, some 56 years later, Aaron Ziegelman, a successful New York businessman, has initiated and is sponsoring the Luboml Exhibition Project to help preserve the history and memory of the *shtetl* . The Project is developing an exhibition for venues in New York, Israel, and possibly other locales. Here on a grand scale is the private searching for roots—trying to portray a whole town, an entire way of life. Libivne has been dispersed. The pieces—scattered people, photographs, objects and memories—must be gathered together to recreate the town, even if only metaphorically.

Remembering What Came Before

The exhibition's goal of portraying the people and the life of Luboml (and not just the story of the *shtetl's* liquidation), is emblematic of a significant shift or broadening in the way people are approaching the Holocaust. Increasingly attention is extending outward from the events of the Shoah *per se* to an interest in the world which existed before. For example, A Living Memorial to the Holocaust—Museum of Jew-

ish Heritage, currently under construction, has taken as its mission collecting and exhibiting not only the Holocaust, but also the world before, the aftermath and the history of Jewish immigration to the United States over the last three centuries; and the museum at Yad Vashem is planning to give significantly more attention to life before the Holocaust. By learning about the richness of Eastern European Jewish culture, and on a more personal level looking for their own ancestral *shtetlekh* , people are seeing the Holocaust as part of a much larger Jewish historical picture and deepening their understanding of the full import of the Shoah.

One Town's Story

Luboml had one of the oldest Jewish communities in Poland, dating back to the 14th century. In the 1930s, the town had a vibrant community of 3,500-4,000 Jews (around 90% of the town's population) with another 6,000 Jews in the surrounding area. The community supported a Great Synagogue, many *shtiblekh*, Zionist organizations, *khadorim* (traditional Jewish elementary schools), a Talmud Torah, a drama group, a bank and a library.

The town's Jews were killed in a series of "actions" which culminated in the final executions which began on Hoshana Raba 5703 (October 1, 1942). Only 51 Luboml Jews (excluding those who emigrated before the Holocaust) are believed to have survived the war, variously by hiding, joining the partisans, adopting false identities, or serving in the Soviet army. In 1974, many of the survivors and other Libivners published a comprehensive *yisker-bukh* (memorial book); an English translation, to be published

410

shortly after many years of preparation, will be one of very few *yisker-bikher* entirely translated into English.

Survivors rarely have tangible mementos; it is the families who emigrated in the 1910s, 20s, and 30s who are more likely to have had the luxury of carrying things with them. As Project Director, I have personally spoken with many Libivners. Typically people don't think they have anything, maybe a few photographs. They often think I'm crazy when I ask for documents and three-dimensional objects—household and religious articles, clothing, children's toys.

But with a little persistence, it's surprising how many people start to think of things which they or their parents or their in-laws carried with them when they emigrated. And they always have another cousin I should call who might have something. They all seem to know each other—after all this was a small town and everyone seems to be interconnected through blood and marriage. Sometimes it feels as if I'm at the center of this great *mishpokhe*, acting as a go-between for people who have lost touch with each other over the years.

Tangible Memories

The outreach effort has been quite successful. To date, the Project has made copies of almost 800 photographs from over 50 sources in the United States, Israel, Canada, Argentina, Brazil, and Poland.

The Project has also located a number of artifacts for potential use in the exhibition, generally humble objects which carry poignant family stories. Notable finds include phylacteries in a velvet pouch embroidered with the words "Luboml, Poland" sent to a bar mitzvah boy in New York in the 1930s; a wedding invitation for Sore Lichtmacher and Leyzer Kershenboym, married in Luboml in 1932; a pair of silver wine cups which were buried in Luboml and retrieved by Rivka Shlivo Karpus following the war; a U.S. non-quota immigration visa for Icek Moszek Axelrod, 1927; a series of documents which show the emigration of Zelig Faigen from Luboml to Buenos Aires in 1928, including a passport, medical certificates, and poems given to him

when he departed; Moshe Shalev's identification card from Palestine, 1936; a fork and spoon given to Bracha Fuks by her mother when she made *aliyah* to Palestine, ca. 1935; Shabbat candlesticks and a matzoh cover brought to New York in 1920 by the Bokser family; a towel Miriam Hetman embroidered as a going-away present for her son Yakov when he made *aliyah* to Palestine in 1936; Rosh Hashana cards; an unusual Passover card; and fourteen minutes of rare (and extraordinary!) film footage shot by American tourist Ethel Zim during her visit to Luboml in 1933.

In the course of this research it has become clear that the amount of visual documentation in public repositories is fairly minimal. Luboml is located in northwestern Volhynia, a border area which has gone back and forth between Poland and Russia /Soviet Union (it is now officially in Ukraine) and often been the site of warfare. This region experienced an extraordinary amount of destruction and apparently only limited documentation has survived. This makes the work of the Luboml Exhibition Project that much more significant. As a result of our exhibition research we are developing a significant photographic collection which ultimately will be donated to a museum or archive, preserving Luboml for generations to come.

Why, people often ask, Luboml? Even Lubomlers themselves say the place "isn't unusual, it's just like every other town." But therein lies its significance, for Libivne is in some sense "every-*shtetl*." With its Great Synagogue and many small *shtiblach*, its myriad Zionist organizations, its marketplace and many small shops, with the Hasidim and the secular, the traditional and the modern, Luboml reflects the life of many Eastern European Jews. In the specificity of Luboml, visitors to our exhibition will find the universal, and hopefully sense a little of what life was like in their own ancestral *shtetlekh*.

Fred Wasserman is the Director of the Luboml Exhibition Project. He curated the exhibits at the Ellis Island Immigration Museum and co-authored Ellis Island: An Illustrated History of the Immigrant Experience. *Mr. Wasserman also served as a Guest Curator for "Becoming Visible: The Legacy of Stonewall" at The New York Public Library.*

This article originally appeared in *Sh'ma*, volume 25, issue 492 (April 14, 1995) and is reprinted with permission from *Sh'ma*.

A Still-Life Shtetl
Rebuilding the Life and Times of Luboml, One Faded Photo at a Time
By Toby Axelrod

Sept. 1, 1995

It is a silent reunion. In shades of brown and ivory they sit, stiff and proper, before romantic painted backdrops. Others lounge on the grass with friends gathered around. Formally, a couple stands with two young children, staring straight at me.

I look at them one by one—and hundreds more like them: family photos in folders, filling two drawers in the tiny office of the Luboml Exhibition Project in Midtown Manhattan. It's the largest gathering of Luboml's souls since the shtetl—my father's birthplace—was destroyed 53 years ago.

For several months the photos have been arriving from Canada, Israel, Arizona, Argentina, and Brooklyn in response to notices in the *Jewish Week* and elsewhere. A few of the many envelopes came to my desk, and I would open each with reverence, as if entrusted with something holy. I understood afresh the superstitions some have against being caught on film. The photos are all that remains. And those eyes, those expressive hands touched a world I knew only through the stories of my grandfather, Rabbi Yakov Axelrod.

"I'll never forget it," was how he usually began. I can hear his voice any time because I recorded hours and hours of his storytelling and have spent years transcribing the tapes.

But I never thought my personal obsession would converge with the dreams of so many other people, to create a museum exhibit about Jewish life in that obscure little Polish-Ukrainian town. The photos, documents, and objects gathered in that midtown office today are waiting to be seen, and they will be seen, thanks to the sponsorship of Aaron Ziegelman, who left Luboml as a boy in 1938.

It's hard to believe I will set foot in that town myself—the goal is to find more material for our collection. But first, I will put down the last corrections on our toughest project: the translation of our entire *Yizkor Buch* from Yiddish into English.

Hundreds of such books about the life and demise of European Jewish towns were written after the war by survivors, but most of these rich volumes are gathering dust on bookshelves, inaccessible to all but those who can read Yiddish. Two have been translated into English.

Several years ago I volunteered to help edit Luboml's tome, for selfish reasons—I wanted to read more about the town I knew through my grandfather's stories. Now, as I check the spelling of names of those killed by the Nazis, a list that closes the 400-page book, I marvel that a window is to open for others on a world lost forever.

The book translation was begun years ago by members of the Libovner Voliner Benevolent Society, with survivor Nathan Sobel and his wife, Eleanor, at the helm.

Recently, Aaron Ziegelman started the exhibition project. For him, the journey began several years ago as an effort to unerase his past. He managed to find relatives around the world, reconstructing a family tree and orchestrating a reunion.

Eventually, he decided to sponsor the creation of an exhibition chronicling life in the shtetl. Since last summer, hundreds of photos and items have been gathered for display at museums in New York, Israel and other venues.

Luboml's embrace is expansive. From the day I met Nathan Sobel, my first Lubomler outside my immediate family, I have felt drawn into a widening circle of people touched directly and indirectly by this history—emigres like Aaron, Abe Getman, Victor Gershengorn, Benjamin Rozenzweig, and others.

Now that family includes Fred Wasserman, who directed the Ellis Island museum and has been brought in by Aaron to gather material and develop the shtetl exhibition.

What is it about Luboml that catches up even a non-landsman? When I visited Fred's little office one recent afternoon, he gingerly took out a carefully wrapped item that had arrived in the mail from Arizona—a black silk embroidered shawl once worn by a Jewish woman in Luboml.

Fred's expression as he held it toward me told me that for both of us, the shawl is more than a beautiful piece of work. The shawl, neatly folded; the silver Kiddush cup, dry as a bone; the empty tallit bag embroidered with the name "Luboml"; labels from Luboml's kosher winery—each tells a story.

Luboml, I have learned, not only was the town where my great-grandmother ran an inn and liquor store. It was where my grandfather bribed the police chief to look the other way when Jewish shops opened on Sunday, where little boys played tricks on their cheder teachers, where potential couples were introduced in a pear orchard.

For 700 years there have been Jews in Luboml. The community grew and was cut down and grew again, surviving wars and pogroms over the centuries like so many hundreds of small towns in Eastern Europe. The people came back again and again. By the time of their final destruction, in October 1942, Luboml's Jews numbered some 5,000.

In the book, survivors describe the killings that went on throughout the yearlong German occupation, culminating in the mass murder of thousands on that one day, Hoshana Rabba, Oct. 1, 1942.

But the book is as much a celebration of the life that came before. One recent Sabbath, I read aloud to friends about how after the Sabbath meal families would take a walk by a certain home just to hear the father and his sons singing *zmiros*. On Passover, I shared with my family the description of the kashering of pots, dishes and utensils in giant pots of boiling water set up outside. I read aloud about the local folk doctor, who used glass cups to draw poisons from the body. And the horse dealer, who would examine a nag's teeth before clinching a sale.

I relished the descriptions of men enjoying the steamy communal bath on a cold winter day, of women rushing into the synagogue to wail and pray for relief from an epidemic, of fights between chasidim, debates between rabbis, and pranks by youth.

Often the descriptions end with words such as these: "I do not know what became of these people."

I know that for some of them, these stories and photos are all that's left. It is both astonishing and gratifying that Luboml's Jews should come to symbolize all the lost Jews of shtetls near and far, whose names are preserved at Yad Vashem and stories told in dusty volumes.

At present, we are exploring possible venues for the exhibition and seeking a publisher for the book. But for me and so many others, that these elements have come together at all is an enormous pleasure and represents an important step on our journey.

It's a journey that began for me with my Zede's stories. His memory was excellent, perhaps because he washed his face in the first snowfall every year. He said it kept his "braims" fresh.

Now I do that every year, too, ice melting against my face. Today, I think of this as I look at these photos and they, silently, look back at me.

Reprinted with permission from the Jewish Week.

Rosh Hashanah card portrait of Mendel and Rochl Frechter, 1929.

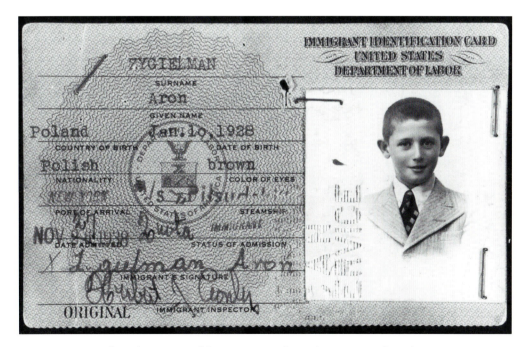

U.S. immigrant identification card for Aron Zygielman (Aaron Ziegelman), 1938.

The Road to Luboml

A Writer Retraces the Footsteps of Her Grandfather in the Ukrainian Countryside and Finds Strength and Sorrow
By Toby Axelrod

Oct. 13, 1995

A few months before he died, my Zede told me something was bothering him. His home-care nurse had taken him for a drive in town, Great Barrington, Mass. She drove around and around. And suddenly, he said, they came to a town exactly like his own.

"And we drove, and we came to a house exactly like mine. And I went in, and it was just the same as this." My Zede rubbed his forehead. His waking dream confused both of us. But today I understand his vision anew.

I see it as a premonition: of finding oneself on a half-familiar road, feet crossing old pathways, coming to rest in the empty space once filled by the lives of parents and brothers and sisters.

Last month, nearly ten years after my Zede, Rabbi Yakov (Yankl) Axelrod, rejoined the Almighty, I returned to a place I had never seen but that was familiar: Luboml, the Polish-Ukrainian town where my Zede began life. He left alone for America in 1925. Two years later, his wife and their child, my father, joined him in Great Barrington, where my Zede was rabbi of Congregation Ohav Shalom for nearly 60 years.

My return is the rewinding of my grandfather's exodus. I am traveling with Aaron Ziegelman, who left Luboml as a young boy in 1938, and Fred Wasserman, director of the Luboml Exhibition Project (see accompanying story). Our journey has been mapped out by genealogist Miriam Weiner of "Routes to Roots" and her local representative, Vitaly Chumak of Moldova, our interpreter and guide. As we drive north from Lvov, Slava Rimar at the wheel, the past becomes present; I have the dizzying feeling of traveling backward.

We pass through Vladimir Volinsk, where my Zede went to yeshiva, and Kovel, where he had relatives; through flat farmland studded with pine forest, along roads lined with tall topol trees, reflective white belts painted round their wide torsos.

At 35 miles per hour on broken roads, we go back. An aproned woman sits on the grass, selling apples from a basket. A man holding a stick stands by the roadside near two cows and a goat. A little girl wearing a white ribbon as big as her head crosses the road with her mother.

We stop. Cows in a small herd dance across the road like delicate ladies, their mincing legs pressed together. Behind them are the stick-wielding shepherds: she in babushka, he in cap, each flashing a silver-toothed grin.

A horse-drawn wagon lazily approaches carrying hay, sacks of potatoes and an entire family sitting on top, their legs dangling off the sides, feet bouncing to the horses' steady clop.

Only the rubber tires are new, says Vitaly.

Life seems as I had imagined it to be 70 years ago. But there are no Jews.

In cement letters taller than me, Luboml announces itself. Mayor Pyotra Mochnuk—accompanied by two girls in Ukrainian costume—presents a huge, round bread topped with a tiny dish of salt.

"Welcome to our town and your town," he tells us. "We have the same good people today as many years ago." He kisses my hand.

Many years ago, Luboml was a Jewish town. Jews were here since the 14th century. In the late

1930s, there were about 5,000. Luboml was almost entirely Jewish. Today, there are about 9,000 people in Luboml, including one Jewish woman who was not born there.

I trace my ancestors at least to the early 19th century there and in Masheve, a nearby village. "Aaron Masheve" was the nickname of my Zede's father, a rabbi; Zede's mother was Tauba. They had six children: Leibe, Malke, Henia, Sheftl, Yisroel and my Zede, Yankl, who was sent off to yeshiva for rabbinic training.

In 1921, he married Bela Lichtenshteyn of Luboml. Her mother, Chaye Sura, had asked Zede's father, "You want a nice girl or you want gelt?"

The couple made a living from one of four shops owned by Bela's mother. Chaye Sura gave a shop to each of her children as a wedding gift.

In 1923, my father, Itzie, was born. "And they made a party, oh boy. If we didn't have 1,000 people we didn't had one," my Zede told me in his heavily accented English. "They said when you come to a pidyon haben, God forgives the sins what you done for years. So everybody came."

Zede's mother, Tauba, "was a wonderful person. You are the name of her," he often reminded me. "They was 100 percent Jewish," he said. "If you will be 10 percent what she was, I will be happy.

"I remember when I had to go to America, they came to say goodbye to me. Huh. That was rough. Mama was crying terrible. She said, 'God know if I'll ever see you again.' Those words still hang on me."

When Germany attacked Soviet-occupied Poland in June 1941, Luboml immediately was taken. As in virtually all shtetls and cities they overran, the Nazis established a guarded Jewish ghetto. Fourteen months later, after Simchat Torah in October 1942, the Jews were killed. They were forced to strip and walk down Matseyuska Street, surrounded by German and Ukrainian police and dogs, 20 minutes to a brick factory outside town, where large pits had been dug. Most were shot at the edge of these ravines, falling in on top of each other. People say blood rose from the earth for days, maybe weeks.

We found the yellowed letter, written in Russian and dated April 8, 1945, in Zede's dresser drawer after he died.

"Dear and beloved and only brother to survive the war," it begins. Yisroel had fled to the Soviet Union. He described the fate of the family.

Our beloved mother . . . stubbornly didn't want to go out to the pit, to avoid getting undressed. So the Germans murdered our most beloved Mama near the mill.

Our dear sister Henia hid [for a year] with her little son . . . but a woman from the village turned her in (the name of the woman who turned in our sister is Domka Stoyanovich) . . . and as a consequence the last of our family was also murdered.

This is the result, my dear brother, for our parents, family, and all the Jewish people during the occupation of the German bandits. I cannot be at peace or be calm, and I will not be at peace for as long as I live . . .

I have two goals in Luboml: to help "Frrredah" and "Meester Zeegelmun" gather testimony for the project and to find my own roots (I am "Tawbya"). The tasks braid together: As older citizens tell what they remember, Aaron Ziegelman and I see faces of our own families. Most of these people are just old enough to remember the very end of Jewish life here.

While recollections have endured, most Jewish structures did not. Years after the Germans killed the people, the Soviets destroyed the 17th-century synagogue and old cemeteries, reusing their stones.

Anatoly Vasilovitch Drosdovitch grew up in Luboml. As a boy, he had a favorite teacher, Rosa Friedman, who taught German in the Polish school. She was Jewish. "I loved her very much," he told us. The last time he saw her was on the day of her death, under Nazi guard. She was with her daughter, Janka, and called out to him and another Ukrainian student: "Come and kiss me." They ran to her.

She was killed by one of her former students, he tells us. He talks while sitting with three women in a building that was a Jewish school.

A local official listens, refusing a lunch invitation.

At his dining room table, Peter S. opens his diary to a page from October 1942. In the entry he described finding bodies by the road, covered with birds. He does not want us to see the part that reads, "Jews are easier to kill than flies, because flies move very quickly and are small, but Jews are large and move slowly." Before we leave, his wife gives us pears from their tree.

A little dog yips at us as Raya Skarshevska opens the door to her home. We sit around her table and listen.

When she was 5, she says, she saw a Jewish girl in a fine black dress and a beautiful red ribbon in her hair. The girl removed these things and dropped them on the road. She walked on naked, looking straight ahead.

Little Raya wanted the ribbon. Her mother, Vera, warned her not to touch it: "Today they are killing Jews, tomorrow they will kill us," she said.

Around that time, a woman pushed her wounded daughter toward's Raya's house. Raya's mother hid the girl under the kitchen floor. That girl now lives in Israel and has a family of her own. Vera was honored as a righteous person by Yad Vashem.

The red-ribbon girl did not return.

The Honig girls of Luboml were well-dressed, my Zede recalled. Their father, Froim, had worked in America and come back to Luboml with money. The daughters "spent right and left on good clothes. And he saw the money goes like water." Froim returned to America.

"I thought he goes in the street and he picks up the money. Yeah. He never told us what he was doing." A few years later, my Zede went to America and bumped into Froim on the Lower East Side.

"He was driving a pushcart. It was already dark and the weather was not so good. . . . I felt embarrassed, but I came over and I said, 'Mr. Honig?'

" 'Oh, Yankl' you here?

"'Yes,' I says. 'I came not long ago.'" My Zede bought all his bananas and oranges. "You can go home now, you don't have to stay in that weather," he said.

It turned out Froim Honig was borrowing money to buy his fruit. Every week he paid back some and sent the rest of his earnings to Europe.

"So I wrote a letter to the family there," my Zede told me, "and this is what I wrote: 'You think that your father is a rich man. If you would see him the way he stays on a pushcart, then you wouldn't spend the money right and left.' "

"After this, they wrote him that they shall not.

"In a short time he died anyway. That kind of a person, he caught a cold, he got pneumonia and he went."

Luboml's little houses are surrounded by vegetable gardens. A chicken steps between the wooden slats of a fence, followed by her brood, all talking to themselves as they scan their circle of dirt. White ducks sit reflected in a puddle on the road. A pig shrieks in its barn; a goat is led to a grassy spot in the park and tied to a post; a tiny kitten mews by the lowlit entrance to a bar.

"It's our zoo," laughs Mira Gusyeva, 20, who acts as an interpreter. She says even chickens find their way back home at night. Then, streets are quiet except for the occasional drunkard. During an evening walk, I hear a chorus of voices singing a Ukrainian folk melody. The night is cool and lit by a big moon.

When my Zede, Yankl, was a newlywed here, his mother-in-law became gravely ill. He took a train on the Sabbath to fetch a doctor in Lublin. But his rabbi told him, "When you come back to Luboml you put the doctor on a [horsedrawn] taxi and you shall walk home."

"So I did," my Zede told me. "But I walked so fast that time, I was young, like a deer. And I came home before the taxi, because I made a zigzag."

Today, I do the same. From place to place, my hosts lead me through back yards and alleys and parks, along muddy paths between muddy streets.

As in many towns and cities in newly independent Ukraine, street names here have been changed. In Luboml, Lenin Street now is Independence Street. It seems every town now has one.

And no more rubles: the currency is coupons. I change $20 and get nearly two million. A vodka and orange water at the bar costs 15,000.

Luboml has four bars; one is on the balcony of the town's notorious hotel, which is frequented by smugglers crossing the nearby Polish border to Chelm. The one operating restaurant opens only when Mr. Ziegelman has a reservation. There are no other customers. The department store is nearly empty; a local grocery store has shelves stacked with vodka bottles.

I want to stay in the local hotel, but Mira Gusyeva grimaces when she hears this. "You are invited to stay with us," she says. Her father, Misha, heats up water for my bath. They have an outhouse, but their indoor bathroom has a toilet—the first I have seen. Not even the mayor's office and museum have a bathroom. One must go out back across a muddy courtyard to a little wooden closet. Inside is a bench with hole in it.

The Gusyeva home is comfortable. Lena, Mira's mother, prepares delicious blini with sour cream. In the morning, I drink fresh goat's milk.

On Sunday, I set off with Pyotr Yuschuk on the road the Jews were forced to walk. When we reach Borki, we will have a memorial ceremony with Aaron Ziegelman and Fred Wasserman, as well as Boris Karp and Leybl Tzimerboym, two Jews who at one time lived in Luboml. A hunched woman in a babushka greets Pyotr, a 25-year-old school teacher; when we say where we are going, her face drops.

She tells us: she saw a Nazi grab a child by the feet and swing him against a post. She takes us to the home of Maria Lutsak, who also remembers. She saw a child crying. Pyotr translates, drawing his fingers across his eyes and face. A German took his gun and shot the child and mother and dragged them away by the hair. Maria covers her face with her hands.

The road winds uphill between trees and fields. Ducks sit in brown puddles; scraps of clothing and trash lie in the ditches. It is quiet.

"I think about this often," Pete says, looking across a green and brown field, "that this is the last sight of nature, of life, the last breath. They know that they are going to die." Around us move Jews on legs not their own, a will not theirs. The world is turned over: Heaven is at their feet.

Tzimerboym lives today in Lutsk, a city near Luboml. He lived in Luboml before the war. He tells me my great-grandfather used to buy fish in his mother's shop. "Wrap up a nice piece of fish for me," Aaron Masheve would say; and then he would walk back to Masheve.

On Chelm Street, we come to Tzimerboym's former home. A new house stands there. A woman waves us into the yard and points to the old foundation running through the garden. "She tried to get it out, but it was stubborn," Tzimerboym explains.

That tenacious root takes on added significance in light of local superstitions. It is bad luck to build over a cemetery or to use old tombstones in a foundation. In Luboml, there are several such buildings around the former Jewish cemetery.

The tombstones in the Christian cemetery bear etched images of the faces of the deceased. Trees wind upward between the stones. Because we go in the evening, we must retrace our path exactly when we leave.

Mystery follows every step; I worry I may do something wrong. It's important, says Mira: "You must finish the champagne in your glass; whatever is left are your tears."

I hire a car to take me on a day-trip: to Vladimir Volinsk, where my Zede went to yeshiva; to Kovel, where we had family; and to Masheve. Pyotr and Mira come with me. Valya drives.

In Vladimir Volinsk, I find a school that might have been the yeshiva. I meet Rosa, a Jewish woman who still lives in the town where all her family was killed—by one of her former schoolmates, she tells us. She sings a Yiddish song for me.

We see a sidewalk made of Jewish tombstones. As we rub the dirt from the Hebrew letters, a little woman comes out of a tiny house and shrieks: "Don't take away my sidewalk! I need it!"

In Kovel, the Jewish cemetery was destroyed 10 years ago, its stones used in the foundations of government buildings. The former synagogue now is a sewing factory.

Sima Schichman, a Jew from Kovel, takes us to the place where 20,000 Jews were killed. A monument is being created at the highest spot on this swollen, grassy expanse.

Sima worries: Her family is moving to Israel. Who will care for this holy place when they are gone? After every heavy rainfall, she returns with a small box and picks up bones. Today, she kneels and feels the earth: she picks up the leg bone of a child; then, part of a pelvic bone. Valya, eyes to the ground, picks up part of a skull.

Nearby, a middle-aged man is harvesting mushrooms. He is bent over, scouring the scrubby earth with his eyes.

"Why do you do this, don't you know what is here?" Sima asks him.

"Of course, but this is an excellent place for mushrooms," he says. "I have been coming here since I was a child."

By early evening, we are in Masheve, nearly back to Luboml. A late-summer sun slants across the wide fields in this tiny village, setting haystacks afire.

Pyotr asks the first older man he sees: "Do you remember the Axelrod family?"

"Axelrod? . . . Axelruth!" the man says, cap low over his eyes, his face reflecting the orange sunset. He thinks and talks. "Ah-ron," he says. "Ah-ron Axelruth."

A family passes on their wagon, parents, grandparents and children, staring at us. A brown colt races down the road to catch up with them.

"Henia," he says. "Malke. Yisroel."

He remembers Henia's wedding day. It was just like a Ukrainian wedding, he says: She wore a white dress, and they had music. A fiddle, a clarinet—"Jewish music," he says.

Do you know Domka Stoyanovich, Pyotr asks.

Yes, the man says. She has been dead for 20 years.

Do you remember where the Axelrods lived?

Near the little church: He points across fields and fences.

We get back in Valya's red car and bounce across the rutted roads until we can't drive farther. Pyotr's aunt lives here. He asks her: Do you know where the Jewish family lived? Yes. She leads us down the road toward the west; the puddles and sky are silver and orange.

A woman greets us. We ask her, and yes, the Jewish family lived next door. Her gold teeth shine.

We walk with her to the door of her house. Her 93-year-old father is sitting on a wooden bench, back to the sun. His eyes are clear.

"Tatu," she yells into his ear. "Yah?"

"Do you remember the Jewish family that lived next to us?"

"Axelrod."

He looks at me.

Does he remember the names, I ask.

Mira translates. And the daughter yells in his ear again.

"Tatu . . . do you remember the names?"

"Ah-ron; Liebe; Malke; Henia; Sheftl . . . and Yankl went to America."

The air and ground are shaking.

What happened to them, Mira asks. "They were all killed," he says.

I move toward the fence. Go ahead, they tell me. I walk out on the upturned earth of this little field; both sky and ground are gray-purple. "Maybe they saw the same trees," says Mira, standing with me and Pyotr.

Before I left for my journey, my father blessed me and had me recite the prayer for safe travel, asking God to guide me toward "life, gladness and peace" and protect me from "all manner of punishments that assemble to come to earth . . . Blessed are you, HaShem, Who hears prayer."

I am sure my Zede recited the same prayer 70 years ago, before leaving his mother at the train station for a long life filled with gladness and peace. His words echo in the empty space once filled by the lives of parents and brothers and sisters.

Reprinted with permission from the Jewish Week.

Building An Exhibition
Luboml's Best of Times and Worst of Times, in Photographs
By Toby Axelrod

Oct. 13, 1995

When he came to America in 1938 at the age of 9, Aaron Ziegelman vowed to return to his shtetl, Luboml, as a rich man bearing gifts for his family.

The dream came true in part: When Ziegelman went back to Ukraine from New York last month, local reporters described him as "Americanski meel-yon-aire bees-nees-man." But Ziegelman did not come to lavish gifts on his kin. His 100 cousins, aunts, uncles and grandparents were killed by the Nazis in October 1942, along with some 4,000 remaining Jews of Luboml.

Ziegelman's purpose was to gather material and testimony for the Luboml Exhibition Project, which he inaugurated last year. For his Luboml hosts, he brought presents. For his lost family, he brought the *El Maleh Rachamim,* a mourner's prayer.

"The only gift I can give them now is an exhibition dedicated to their lives, so they won't be forgotten," said Ziegelman, general chairman of the Reconstructionist Rabbinical College, who made the trip with exhibit curator Fred Wasserman and this reporter, the daughter of a Lubomler.

Again, Ziegelman stood where his family's home had been on Listopada Street. He asked Lubomlers if he could draw water from their wells, to relive a childhood sensation. "It hasn't changed. It's just the same," he repeated, though the absence of Jews was as real as the rush of water from the tipped bucket.

Before we arrived, local elders had talked mostly to each other about the past. Now, a well of memories poured forth for new listeners: stories about Jewish friends, teachers, neighbors,

shopkeepers; and destruction, torture, terror, death. Those memories proved more durable than the synagogue and cemeteries knocked down after the war by the Soviets, their stones used in new foundations.

Though most Jewish buildings were destroyed, local historian Mikola Dzei led us to them as if their ghosts still stood. He and museum director Alexander Ostapuk spent hours with Wasserman and Ziegelman, poring over documents and photographs.

They and other citizens added hundreds of items to a collection already 1,200 strong, consisting mostly of family photos. Now, says Wasserman, "We have photographs showing Jews and Poles and Ukrainians interacting, working together: the fire department with a few Jewish members; a birthday party with a few Jewish and Polish and Ukrainian kids. It shows a whole side of life that wasn't suggested by the material we had."

Some of the photographs will debut Nov. 7 at the annual dinner of the Living Memorial to the Holocaust–Museum of Jewish Heritage.

Other items collected include survey maps from the 1930s, with names of inhabitants; a fragment Some of the photographs will debut Nov. 7 at the annual dinner of the Living Memorial to the Holocaust-Museum of Jewish Heritage.

Other items collected include survey maps from the 1930s, with names of inhabitants; a fragment of a silver menorah discovered by workers digging a new foundation; a glass bottle from the kosher distillery; receipts from Jewish businesses, with signatures.

And a gift from Olga Satyuk.

Olga had invited Wasserman and Dzei into

her home to see her icons. "She was very proud of them," says Wasserman. "She wanted us to stay for tea and shots of brandy even though it was 11 in the morning.

"And then she pulls out a fragment of a candlestick, bronze, all crummy and old and patinaed. She had dug this up in her garden the year before when she was planting flowers and she made a presentation: 'I want you to have it for your exhibit.' "

Until Olga had held it in her hand, turning it over and shaking off the earth, the candlestick last was grasped by the Jew who buried it. Surely he expected to come home again—like Aaron Ziegelman—and set it on his Sabbath table.

Reprinted with permission from the Jewish Week.

Letter from Ukraine
Documenting Luboml
By Aaron Ziegelman

Dec. 15, 1995

Luboml is wedged into the northwestern corner of Ukraine, ten miles or so from the Polish border. It's most accessible, however, from Lvov, now a Ukrainian city a couple hundred miles due south, and the point of departure for a recent return to the town of my childhood.

As we neared the outskirts of town, my memory of the local geography was reactivated: This road, which turns into the town's main street, leads directly to the old market square, the former site of my mother's restaurant. When I was a boy in Luboml, the restaurant was a favorite haunt of mine, especially on market day when hundreds of farmers would converge on the town, crowding the market square with their horsedrawn carts.

Our car pulled up to a policeman posted in a booth by the side of the road. Vitaly, our interpreter, told him of our arrival. The policeman made a phone call and we were told to wait. About ten minutes had passed when I noticed two cars had stopped. We were approached by five men in business suits and two women in Ukrainian folk custom, one holding a large, round bread, the other a cup of salt. Vitaly introduced one of the men as the mayor of Luboml. The women offered each of us bread and salt, a ritualized greeting traditional to Eastern Europe. The warmth of their reception made me feel like one of their own, not necessarily a Jew, just a returning townsman.

We drove into town and meet with the chief of the Luboml region. We were joined by a TV crew from Lutsk, and a local newspaper reporter. The mayor asked me to address a meeting of the town deputies. I told them about the project and explained the mission of our visit: to locate historical information and materials which relevant to the exhibition we are organizing about life in Luboml between the wars. When I opened the floor to questions, they were mostly curious about my life in America. What I did for a living? How I had "made it" in America?

In the afternoon we were summoned to the mayor's office where a gathering of town officials has been assembled. The mayor presented me with the key to the city. I graciously accepted the honor, saying that I am proud to be a "Lubomler," but in truth, I was ambivalent. Key to the city? This is not my city anymore. My city is a cemetery. To extend this show of respect to a Jew would have been unthinkable in the Luboml that I knew.

★

In addition to the Luboml Region Museum, Luboml had its own resident historian, Mikola Dzei, who had taken it upon himself to document, in painstaking detail, the past life of his town. Mr. Dzei led us through the streets of Luboml, pointing out the sites of former Jewish landmarks, the old mivka, the synagogue, the little shuls where the Chasidim used to pray. I asked if he could take me to my old house, so he led us down 11 Listopada Street, the central artery of the old Jewish community. The house was no longer there, but I stood on the ground where it had once been.

Mr. Dzei has amassed a formidable stockpile of historical documents including old maps, census reports, newspapers and scores of photographs. He has pictures of street scenes showing what the town looked like, and shots of Jews in daily interaction with their Polish and Ukrainian neighbors-Jews in the volunteer fire department, in classes at the Polish school and in the workplace. Most astonishing is a photograph of the marketplace in 1926, full of cows, horses and people. In the distance is a building where my family's restaurant was located. He also has all sorts of ephemera, including dozens of little worn scraps of paper—receipts from many of the Jewish businesses which prospered in Luboml in the 1930s.

Mr. Dzei had arranged an interview for us with three elderly women. I asked the women questions which might jog their memories of daily Jewish existence seen from the Ukrainian perspective. Were their families friendly with the Jews? Did they do business together, Jews and Ukrainians?

One woman, Lida, said her children used to play with Jewish children; she produced an old photograph taken on her daughter's birthday many years ago. The picture shows a group of children dancing together, Jews with Ukrainians posing arm in arm.

We began to discuss the German occupation. Lida told about the arrival of the German army. Her family had lived on Listopada —even though they were gentiles—and one day a German soldier told her father they had to evacuate the house because they were making the street into a ghetto for the Jews. The family would be given another house, the soldier said, but the father refused to comply and the family stayed put. At this point, Lida began to cry. She said she could remember the day the Jews were marched to the edge of town. "It was about ten o'clock in the morning, I went outside and I saw this group of Jewish people in the street. Big dogs were guarding them. The people were very quiet. They didn't speak or scream."

★

I taped an interview in Yiddish with a man named Tzimerboym, one of few Luboml Jews who has lived in the area, more or less continuously, since the 1920s. Born in Luboml, he married a girl from the neighboring town of Shatsk, where the couple settled and had five children.

On the day the Germans invaded eastern Poland, Tzimerboym happened to be in Luboml visiting his parents. When he realized what was happening he tried to return to Shatsk, but the countryside was crawling with soldiers. So he turned east toward Russia, and once he had crossed the border, he asked a gentile woman to deliver a message to his wife and children. I imagine they were supposed to meet up with him in Russia, but the message was never delivered. Tzimerboym survived the war as a soldier in the Russian army. He returned to Shatsk after the war and learned, of course, that his family had been killed.

I asked him why he never left. "Who will take care of the Jewish cemeteries?," he replied. Tzimerboym has made himself into a guardian of cemeteries, familiar with the location of every overgrown Jewish graveyard and mass burial in the surrounding countryside. He obsesses with the idea of building a major monument to the Jews of Shatsk.

After the interview, Tzimerboym led us through the hilly fields just beyond Luboml to the memorial on the site of the killing fields where the Jews of Luboml were slaughtered. In this mass grave my grandmothers, my aunts and uncle and my two little cousins are buried. We put on taleisim and recited prayers for the dead.

Later, we went to visit the so-called new cemetery. Graves had been desecrated, a few destroyed as recently as last year. Tzimerboym took me to the spot, now an empty field of weeds, where his parents' graves were located. We bowed our heads and it is the first time that I have ever said Kaddish for my father (who died in 1933) at—or at least near—the site where he was buried.

★

Looking back on the visit to Luboml, I am reminded of a childhood dream that I would return to Luboml one day with presents for all of my friends and relatives. The impossiblity of realizing that dream has left me with a sense of incompletion. This trip wasn't the triumphant return I had imagined, but my promise to document the life of Luboml's Jews is the only gift I can offer them now.

Reprinted with permission from the Forward.

Esther Ziegelman (seated, center), daughter Luba (with braids) and son Aaron (with cap) in a family photo, ca. 1938.

An Effort to Restore Jewish Memory
By Gustav Niebuhr

March 30, 1996

If the Holocaust is understood as not just an attack on Europe's Jews but on their history as well, then Aaron Ziegelman's project is an effort to restore a portion of Jewish memory and reverse some of the Nazis' destruction.

Mr. Ziegelman, is best known as a New York businessman who has converted more than 100 apartment buildings to co-ops since the 1970s. He also serves as general chairman of the Reconstructionist Rabbinical College in Wyncote, Pa.

Less well known is his work of the last two years, assiduously gathering documentary evidence on the pre-World War II life of Jews in Luboml, a village a couple of hundred miles southeast of Warsaw.

For Mr. Ziegelman, 68, this is an intensely personal project.

He was born in the village, but immigrated to the United States in 1938 as a 10-year-old with his older sister and their widowed mother. They left behind a community of about 5,000 Jews, who called the town by its Yiddish name, Libivne. By the time the Soviet Army liberated the village from the Germans in 1945, only 51 of the Jewish residents remained, and they were scattered.

The history that Mr. Ziegelman is recovering extends well beyond his own family.

"It's Aaron's personal search," said Fred Wasserman, an independent curator who is director of the Luboml Exhibition Project "But it's gotten a lot bigger," he added, becoming "a search for a town."

Mr. Wasserman developed exhibits for the Ellis Island Immigration Museum and served as a guest curator for the New York Public Library's exhibition on gay and lesbian history, "Becoming Visible: The Legacy of Stonewall."

The Luboml project includes more than 1,500 photographs and about 300 personal objects that belonged to residents of the town. Some items are to be displayed at Yad Vashem, the Holocaust museum in Jerusalem, in October.

For now, a tiny portion of the collection— 38 photographs and a videotape in which elderly people describe life in the village—is on display weekday and Sunday afternoons through April 15 at the West End Synagogue, at Amsterdam Avenue and 69th Street. (The exhibit is closed during Passover, April 3-5.) The remainder of the collection is in fireproof cabinets at the project's offices on Broadway.

One recent morning, Mr. Ziegelman and Mr. Wasserman showed a visitor around, talking about the photographs. Some have the quality of professional work, like the ones that show Luboml's synagogue, a fortress-like building. Other photographs have the feel of the snapshots that they were, taken by friends of friends. In one, a smiling woman, about to immigrate to Palestine, bids goodbye to a friend. In another, a beaming young mother holds her infant son aloft.

Mr. Ziegelman paused before a photograph of a crowd at Luboml's railway station. It records his family's departure. Of the more than 40 people gathered around his mother, sister and him, only one survived the Nazis.

At one point, Mr. Ziegelman choked up and stepped away to compose himself. He said he felt

Unidentified girl, Riwka Milstein and Roza Szwarc, 1937.

guilty about having been secure in the United States while his birthplace was destroyed. "So I want to do something," he said.

Referring to the six million Jews killed by the Nazis, he said, "If you can memorialize these people, show how they lived, it's no longer a statistic."

Michael Berenbaum, director of the United States Holocaust Research Institute, said Mr. Ziegelman's project was not unique. Yaffa Eliach, a professor of Judaic studies at Brooklyn College, has spent years researching a Lithuanian Jewish community whose Yiddish name was Eishishok; those photographs are displayed in a tower at the United States Holocaust Memorial Museum in Washington.

Such projects as Professor Eliach's and Mr. Ziegelman's convey a power beyond that of memorial books, Mr. Berenbaum said. "You see how much richer the physicality is, when it's recorded this way," he said.

Mr. Ziegelman said he got the idea for the project after seeing the movie "Schindler's List." He said he felt that another story needed to be told, about the prewar lives of European Jews.

"Fortunately, I had a lot of material at home," he said. "My mother was a great saver."

To broaden the collection, Mr. Ziegelman and Mr. Wasserman sought out relatives of people who emigrated from Luboml before the war, ran notices in Jewish magazines and even put an appeal on the Internet. "We have material at this point from over 100 families in the United States, Israel, Brazil, Argentina, Poland, Ukraine and France," Mr. Wasserman said.

Last year, the two men traveled to Luboml, now in Ukraine, to do research in the museum there and interview residents about their recollections of the Jewish community. Luboml's Mayor gave Mr. Ziegelman the key to the city.

The full collection which Mr. Ziegelman hopes to display in New York, is a multimedia assemblage, with personal objects like a silver tray and kiddush cup, a girl's colorful frock and immigration documents.

Mr. Ziegelman prizes a short home movie of Luboml, made by a visiting American in the 1930s.

Lately, he has begun to think that his collection serves as a point of orientation for American Jews wondering about their own long-lost roots In Eastern Europe.

He gave a talk in the synagogue a few days ago and encountered a woman who had driven up from Philadelphia to hear him.

"When people see this," Mr. Wasserman said, "It reminds them of where they're from, the stories they heard from their grandmother. It's reclaiming history, and it's passing it on."

Reprinted with permission of the New York Times.

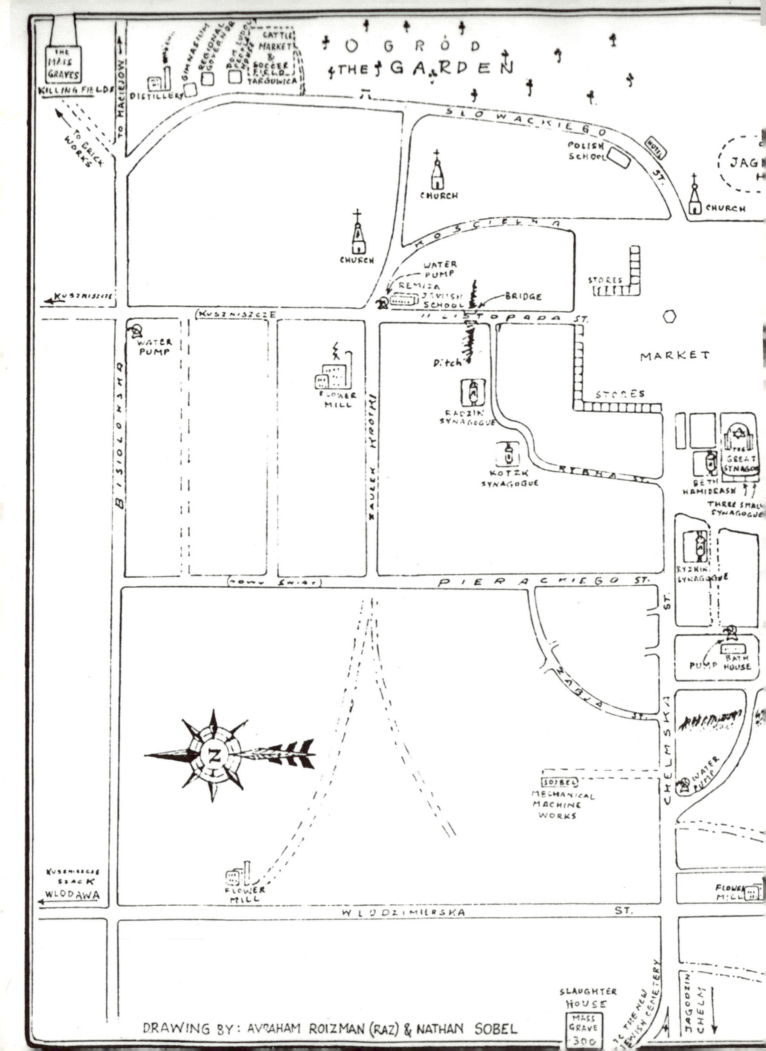

DRAWING BY: AVRAHAM ROIZMAN (RAZ) & NATHAN SOBEL